I0814344

GUDERIAN'S PANZERS

From Triumph to Defeat on the Eastern Front (1941)

CRAIG W. H. LUTHER

STACKPOLE
BOOKS
Essex, Connecticut

STACKPOLE BOOKS
The Globe Pequot Publishing Group, Inc.
64 South Main Street
Essex, CT 06426
www.globepequot.com

Copyright © 2025 by Craig W. H. Luther

All rights reserved. No part of this book may be reproduced in any form or by any electronic or mechanical means, including information storage and retrieval systems, without written permission from the publisher, except by a reviewer who may quote passages in a review.

British Library Cataloguing in Publication Information Available

Library of Congress Cataloging-in-Publication Data

Names: Luther, Craig W. H. author
Title: Guderian's Panzers : from triumph to defeat on the Eastern Front (1941) / Craig W.H. Luther.
Description: Essex, Connecticut : Stackpole Books, 2025. | Includes bibliographical references. | Summary: "Military historian Craig W. H. Luther draws on new material, from letters to diaries, to tell the story of General Heinz Guderian's armored force during Operation Barbarossa and fleshes out the story with vivid firsthand accounts from the soldiers who slugged it out with the Red Army on the eastern front"—Provided by publisher.
Identifiers: LCCN 2025005325 (print) | LCCN 2025005326 (ebook) | ISBN 9780811777476 cloth | ISBN 9780811777483 epub
Subjects: LCSH: World War, 1939–1945—Campaigns—Eastern Front | World War, 1939-1945—Campaigns—Soviet Union | World War, 1939–1945—Tank warfare | Guderian, Heinz, 1888–1954
Classification: LCC D764 .L8766 2025 (print) | LCC D764 (ebook) | DDC 940.54/217—dc23/eng/20250401
LC record available at https://lccn.loc.gov/2025005325
LC ebook record available at https://lccn.loc.gov/2025005326

∞™ The paper used in this publication meets the minimum requirements of American National Standard for Information Sciences—Permanence of Paper for Printed Library Materials, ANSI/NISO Z39.48-1992.

In memory of my dear friend and colleague Christoph Nehring (son of General Walther K. Nehring).[1] *Thank you, Christoph. I am forever grateful to you for your enthusiasm and support of my work on the eastern front.*

If ever there was a savage war, this was it.

—MARTIN VAN CREVELD

The relative tactical and operational superiority of the panzers over their opponents was never greater than in the first half of July 1941, on the high road to Moscow. Guderian spoke of attacks going in like training exercises.

—DENNIS SHOWALTER

Two days ago, I reported about my great worries. Unfortunately, they get worse with each passing day. . . . The enemy, the size of his country, and the treacherous nature of the climate were considerably underestimated, and that's now taking its toll.

—HEINZ GUDERIAN TO HIS WIFE, MARGARETE, 10 DECEMBER 1941

It is an honor and a duty to remember the troops and those who have given their blood and their lives.
(*Es ist eine Ehrenpflicht, der Truppe und derer, die Ihr Blut und Leben gegeben haben, zu gedenken.*)

—KURT FREIHERR VON LIEBENSTEIN

Contents

List of Maps

BLACK-AND-WHITE MAPS

COLOR GERMAN GENERAL STAFF MAPS (IN PHOTOSPREAD)

Abbreviations

(German, English, Russian)

abds.	evening
AA	*Aufklärungsabteilung:* reconnaissance battalion
AA	anti-aircraft
Abt.	*Abteilung:* branch (administrative), battalion, or unit, depending on the context employed
AFV	armored fighting vehicle
AK	*Armeekorps:* army corps
AOK	*Armeeoberkommando:* army headquarters staff
APC	armored personnel carrier
AR	*Artillerie-Regiment*
Arko	*Artilleriekommandeur:* artillery commander
AT	anti-tank
BA-MA	*Bundesarchiv-Militärarchiv* (the German Federal Military Archives in Freiburg, Germany)
Bd.	*Band:* volume (of book or journal)
Bf	*Bayerische Flugzeugwerke*
Btl.	battalion
CAS	close air support
C-in-C	commander-in-chief
CP	command post
d.G.	*des Generalstabes:* of the General Staff
FHO	*Fremde Heere Ost:* Foreign Armies East
Fla	*Fliegerabwehr:* air defense (anti-aircraft)
Flak	*Fliegerabwehrkanone:* anti-aircraft artillery
FMS	Foreign Military Study
GAF	German Air Force

GD	*Grossdeutschland*: Greater Germany
Gen.d.Art.	*General der Artillerie*
Gen.d.Inf.	*General der Infanterie*
Gen.d.Kav.	*General der Kavallerie*
Gen.d.Pi.	*General der Pioniere*
Gen.d.Pz.Tr.	*General der Panzertruppe*
GenQu	*Generalquartiermeister:* chief supply officer of German Army General Staff
GenLt	*Generalleutnant* (see appendix A, "Equivalent Military Ranks")
GenMaj	*Generalmajor*
GenSt	*Generalstab:* German Army General Staff
GenStdH	*Generalstab des Heeres:* German Army General Staff
GFM	*Generalfeldmarschall*
GHQ	general headquarters
g.K.	*Geheime Kommandosache:* secret document
GKO	State Defense Committee (Stalin's war cabinet)
GPU	State Political Directorate (Soviet Union)
GRU	Soviet Main Intelligence Directorate
HE	high explosive
HGr	*Heeresgruppe:* army group
HKL	*Hauptkampflinie:* main battle line
Hptm	*Hauptmann*
HQ	headquarters
HQu	*Hauptquartier:* headquarters
HVP	*Hauptverbandplatz:* main dressing station
Ia	*Erster Generalstabsoffizier:* an officer responsible for operational issues at the division, army corps, army, and army group levels
Ib	*Zweiter Generalstabsoffizier:* supply officer responsible for supply at the division level
Ic	*Dritter Generalstabsoffizier:* an intelligence officer responsible for enemy intelligence and counterintelligence (*Abwehr*)
ID	*Infanterie-Division*
ID (mot.)	*Infanterie-Division* (motorized)
IfZ	*Institut für Zeitgeschichte:* Institute of Contemporary History (Munich and Berlin)
IG	*Infanterie-Geschütz:* infantry gun
i.G.	*im Generalstab:* a member of the German General Staff
IR	*Infanterie-Regiment*
IRGD	*Infanterie-Regiment "Grossdeutschland"*
JG	*Jagdgeschwader:* fighter wing
K	*Kradschützen:* motorcycle riflemen

Kdr	*Kommandeur*
Kfz	*Kraftfahrzeug:* motor vehicle
KG	*Kampfgeschwader:* bomber wing
KGr	*Kampfgruppe:* battlegroup
KIA	killed in action
Kom.Gen.	*Kommandierender General:* commanding general (army corps level)
Korück	*Kommandant des rückwärtigen Armeegebietes:* commandant of rear army area
Kp	*Kompanie*
KTB	*Kriegstagebuch:* war diary
KV	*Klementi Voroshilov:* for KV-1 and KV-2 tanks (Soviet)
le.FH	*leichte Feldhaubitze:* light field howitzer (105mm)
le.GrW	*leichter Granatwerfer:* light mortar (50mm)
le.IG	*leichtes Infanterie-Geschütz:* light infantry gun (75mm)
le.MG	*leichtes Maschinengewehr:* light machine gun
le.Pak	*leichte Panzerabwehrkanone* (37mm AT gun)
Lkw	*Lastkraftwagen:* truck or transport vehicle
Lt.	*Leutnant:* second lieutenant
Lt.-Gen.	lieutenant general
Maj.-Gen.	major general
m.Pak	*Mittlere Panzerabwehrkanone* (50mm AT gun or French 47mm AT gun)
MG	*Maschinengewehr:* machine gun
MGFA	*Militärgeschichtliches Forschungsamt:* Military History Research Center (Germany)
MIA	missing in action
mot.	motorized
N	*Nachlass:* personal papers
NCO	noncommissioned officer
NKGB	People's Commissariat of State Security (Soviet Union)
NKO	People's Commissariat of Defense (Soviet Union)
NKVD	People's Commissariat of Internal Affairs (Soviet Secret Police)
OB	*Oberbefehlshaber:* commander-in-chief
ObdH	*Oberbefehlshaber des Heeres:* commander-in-chief of the Army
ObLt.	*Oberleutnant:* first lieutenant
ObstLt.	*Oberstleutnant:* lieutenant colonel
Offz.	*Offizier:* officer
OKH	*Oberkommando des Heeres:* High Command of the Army
OKL	*Oberkommando der Luftwaffe:* High Command of the Air Force
OKW	*Oberkommando der Wehrmacht:* High Command of the Armed Forces

OpAbt	*Operationsabteilung:* Operations Branch of the Army High Command
OQu	*Oberquartiermeister:* deputy chief of the Army General Staff
OQu I	*Oberquartiermeister I:* deputy chief of staff for Operations in the Army High Command
OT	*Organisation Todt*
Pak	*Panzerabwehrkanone:* anti-tank gun
PD	*Panzer Division*
Pi.	*Pionier:* combat engineer
POL	petroleum, oil, lubricants
PR	*Panzer Regiment*
Pz	*Panzer*
Pz I	Panzer I (tank)
Pz II	Panzer II (tank)
Pz III	Panzer III (tank)
Pz IV	Panzer IV (tank)
Pz 35(t)	Panzer 35(t) (tank of Czech origin)
Pz 38(t)	Panzer 38(t) (tank of Czech origin)
PzJg(Jäg)	*Panzerjäger* (anti-tank troops)
Pz.B.	*Panzerbüchse* (light AT rifle)
PzG	*Panzergruppe:* panzer group
PzK	*Panzerkorps:* panzer corps
Pz.Rgt.	*Panzer Regiment*
R	*Reich*
RAD	*Reichsarbeitsdienst:* German Labor Service
RD	rifle division (Soviet)
Rgt.	*Regiment*
RH	*Reichsheer* (denotes German Army records at BA-MA)
RL	*Reichsluftwaffe* (denotes *Luftwaffe* records at BA-MA)
RVGK	High Command Reserve (Soviet)
SD	*Sicherheitsdienst:* Security Service (branch of the SS)
s.FH	*schwere Feldhaubitze:* medium field howitzer (150mm)
s.GrW	*schwerer Granatwerfer:* medium mortar (81mm)
s.IG	*schweres Infanterie-Geschütz:* medium infantry gun (150mm)
s.MG	*schweres Machinengewehr:* heavy machine gun
SP	self-propelled
SPW	*Schützenpanzerwagen:* armored personnel carrier
SR	*Schützen-Regiment:* rifle regiment (in motorized infantry and panzer divisions)
SS	*Schutzstaffel:* elite guard of the Nazi Party
SS Reich	SS Motorized Infantry Division *Reich*

STAVKA	Soviet Supreme Command
StG	*Sturzkampfgeschwader:* dive-bomber wing
StuG	*Sturmgeschütz:* assault gun
Stuka	*Sturzkampfflugzeug:* dive-bomber
(t)	*tschechisch:* Czech (origin)
TD	tank division (Soviet)
TOE	table of equipment
Uffz	*Unteroffizier:* noncommissioned officer
USSR	Union of Soviet Socialist Republics (Soviet Union)
VA	*Vorausabteilung:* forward (or advance) detachment
VB	*Vorgeschobener Beobachter:* forward observer (artillery)
VVS	*Voenno-vozdushnikh sil:* Soviet Air Force
z.V.Pz.Gr.	placed at the disposal of the panzer group

Foreword

It is almost as hard to imagine histories of Operation Barbarossa becoming unpopular as it is to imagine another single moment in human history, like sunrise on Sunday, 22 June 1941—three million men, thousands, or tens of thousands, of horses, artillery pieces, armored fighting vehicles, and aircraft on each side facing off along an 1,800-kilometer front. Führer Adolf Hitler's massive campaign against the Soviet Union initiated a war that defies comparison. Along with the Battle of the Atlantic—without its Allied victory there would have been little material support for Soviet Russia, no D-Day, no strategic bombing campaign—the existential struggle between the Nazi and Soviet regimes was decisive to the European Theater in World War II. Further, Operation Barbarossa is the point where the two main geopolitical trajectories of the Third Reich intersect: military expansionism and eliminationist racism. Or as Craig Luther describes Barbarossa in the present volume, "a colonial-style genocidal war of conquest."

Like a shark that must keep moving forward through the water to survive, Hitler's Third Reich needed to advance from victory to victory. After defeating the Second Anti-Hitler Coalition in the spring of 1940, the dictator could not rest on his laurels. Germany's principal strength lay in its army. Even if Hitler had had the inclination or patience to pursue sea or air campaigns against the United Kingdom (and, later, the United States), he did not have the navy or air force with which to do so. Therefore, invading the USSR had three benefits from his point of view: (1) here was an enemy his army could fight, (2) the Soviet Union was close at hand, and (3) according to Nazi thinking, food, oil, and other raw materials in the south of the USSR would provide essential resources with which to confront the United Kingdom and United States. Two Nazi political and cultural realities must also be factored in: Germany would also theoretically destroy the world's only communist state, while most of Europe's Jews lived in the former Pale of Settlement, ready for extermination.

Following its paradigm-shattering victory in northwest Europe the summer before, the German Army had no peer. Nevertheless, many *Wehrmacht* leaders knew war against the Soviet Union would be a very tough proposition. A generation earlier, many of these same men had been subalterns when, for three years, the czar's bungling army fought Imperial Germany to a standstill. They understood firsthand "the tyranny of distance," the tenaciousness of the Russian soldier, and the primitive conditions and infrastructure. But now, after victories in Poland, Scandinavia, northwest Europe, and the Balkans, the *Wehrmacht* had a keen new weapon that carried all before it: the "blitzkrieg." By June 1941, this skillful combination of loose command and control, the internal combustion engine, aircraft, radios, and other features constituted a combined-arms team that no other army could counter (yet!). For at least another year the *Wehrmacht* would use the blitzkrieg (not a proper German doctrinal term) to humiliate opponent after opponent from Leningrad to Libya.

Having proved their decisive value in the west in 1940 and in the Balkans just weeks before Barbarossa, panzer groups would again be put to the test in the vastness of Soviet Russia. In large part, the fortunes of Hitler's eastern army depended on its four panzer groups. Thoroughbreds of the battlefield, these formations did Barbarossa's heavy lifting. On the offense, they gobbled up terrain in daily chunks of up to 50 to 100 kilometers, while in the defense they held exposed spearheads against desperate and determined 360-degree attacks. They had first priority on close air support assets, and the best roads were dedicated to their use. Despite the fact that mechanized divisions (panzer and motorized) made up but a small percentage of the German Army, they grabbed both contemporary headlines and the postwar imagination.

Enter Craig Luther and *Guderian's Panzers*. He knows his way around the Barbarossa campaign as well as any military historian, and here he marries two winning themes during the campaign's opening six months: the fiery and largely self-anointed godfather of the panzer branch, General Heinz Guderian and his 2 Panzer Group.

Prior to September 1939, there was nothing preordained about German panzers or the blitzkrieg technique. Both could have ended up as the costly on-again, off-again doctrinal confusion of the Red Army, or as the misunderstood and misused branch of the British and French armies, or ignored and neglected like in the US Army. However, both hardware and software had two powerful and influential patrons in Hitler and Guderian (although there were certainly many others). At an interwar panzer demonstration the dictator famously said, "That's what I need, that's what I want to have!" With a lot of help, ambitious self-promoter Guderian took over from there.

While there is no denying that Guderian had battlefield skills and even occasional flashes of brilliance, his reputation was largely made on the backs of his hard-fighting and long-suffering soldiers. Luther gives voice to them here. During World War II German generals enjoyed celebrity status not unlike the later Beatles or Michael Jordan, complete with Hollywood-like glamour portraits on cigarette cards. Guderian exploited this as he did his politically well-connected wife (with her ties to Heinrich Himmler). At numerous points during Barbarossa, he combined all these features to simultaneously demonstrate the up- and downsides of the *Wehrmacht's* *Auftragstaktik*, which pushed responsibility for critical decision making down to the lower ranks. After the war, Guderian proved equally adept at manipulating relationships (e.g., with B. H. Liddell Hart) to both enhance his highly varnished reputation and minimize his criminality.

As Luther did earlier with *First Day on the Eastern Front*, his investigation of the campaign's first day, here he focuses on one formation that summer and fall: Guderian's 2 Panzer Group. *Guderian's Panzers* begins with some useful introductory material but then becomes a straightforward chronological treatment of the campaign from the eyes of Guderian and his men. One strength of Luther's books is the many excerpts from soldiers' diaries, letters home, and other personal papers. Of particular interest is his coverage of the mid-July to mid-August 1941 "meltdown" of the German High Command over the question of Moscow versus Kiev. In this telling episode, the pragmatic Guderian springs a last-minute 180-degree flip-flop in the Führer's favor, torpedoing Franz Halder. Did this knavery help guarantee him the future army chief of staff position?

Robert Kirchubel[1]
Tampa, Florida
July 2024

Acknowledgments

This book grew out of a manuscript I published in May 2023 with *Strategy & Tactics Quarterly* ("Guderian's Panzers," *S&TQ* #22). While I have significantly expanded the narrative, I have used the same (simple and straightforward) organizational template as required by the quarterly magazine in the original publication. The *S&TQ* template thus provided a framework for a much more meaningful study of Guderian and his panzer troops.

So let me begin by thanking Dr. Christopher (Doc) Cummings, the owner of Decision Games and publisher of *Strategy & Tactics Quarterly*—firstly, for engaging me to write for the quarterly and, secondly, for enabling me to purchase back the rights to my manuscript at a fair price. I am also grateful to Chris Perello, an associate editor at S&T Press, for carefully walking me through the process of writing for the quarterly (very different than working for a book publisher!) and, thus, helping me to prepare a manuscript that furnished the foundation for this book. For the four black-and-white maps, I am again grateful to Joe Youst, a talented cartographer who not only created the color maps in *S&TQ* #22 but prepared the maps for my last two major publications: *Moscow Tram Stop: A Doctor's Experiences with the German Spearhead in Russia*, by Dr. Heinrich Haape (edited/annotated by Craig W. H. Luther), and *Soldiers of Barbarossa: Combat, Genocide and Everyday Experiences on the Eastern Front, June–December 1941* (edited by Craig W. H. Luther and David Stahel). Both of these titles were released by Stackpole Books in 2020.

I am, of course, deeply indebted to the senior history editor at Stackpole Books, David Reisch, who shepherded this project seamlessly through Stackpole's exacting editorial process. *Guderian's Panzers* is the fourth title we have released together over the better part of a decade, and David's experience and professional acumen have once again proved invaluable. I have come to view David not simply as a colleague, but also as a friend, as someone I can, and do, trust implicitly, because he's always been true to his word. Among the "support staff" at Stackpole Books I must also acknowledge assistant editor Justine Connelly, senior production editor Nicole Myers; and copyeditor Jen Kelland for their patience, expertise, and support. Of course, there were many other folks at Stackpole who played a role in the preparation of this book, and I'm grateful to all of them for their invaluable assistance.

As a military historian of the eastern front from 1941 to 1945, I am only too aware that I stand on the shoulders of my many colleagues, for without their years of research, writing, publishing, and sharing, my own efforts in this important field of study would have been rather more precarious. In this context, I think first and foremost of David M. Glantz (Col., U.S. Army, ret.). Colonel Glantz is the acknowledged "dean" of eastern front historians, having published more than fifty works on the 1941/45 Russo-German War. Following the collapse of the Soviet Union, David (one of the few among us who has mastered the Russian language) was the first to systematically draw upon the Russian military archives—his many books based on this archival material greatly expanding our awareness of the conflict from the Soviet perspective. To show our debt to Colonel Glantz, Dr. David Stahel and I dedicated our book *Soldiers of Barbarossa* to him; moreover, this new book of mine on Heinz Guderian and his panzer group in Operation Barbarossa benefited immensely from Colonel Glantz's decades of pioneering research and writing.

Dr. Stahel is an associate professor of European history at the University of New South Wales; he also teaches at the Australian Defence Force Academy. Collaborating with David on *Soldiers of Barbarossa* was a remarkably productive experience, enabling us to make a unique contribution to the historical literature on the eastern front in World War II. Over the past fifteen years, David has published five books on the Barbarossa campaign, and I have plumbed the depths of his fine narratives for my own recent publications. For this book, I found David's study of the Battle of Kiev (*Kiev 1941: Hitler's Battle for Supremacy in the East*, 2012) of particular significance.

For once again being part of my "team," I owe a debt of gratitude to Mrs. Lara Steinke for editing the manuscript; as always, she did a wonderful job, giving me confidence in my work that I would not have had otherwise. For help with photographs, I am indebted to Jon Davidson, Frederick Cotterell, and Jason D. Mark. Jon, a collector of World War II photographs, provided me with several (never before published) pictures I have used in this book. Frederick is a friend and creator of the terrific YouTube site, Military1945.com, which produces excellent short videos with rare film footage primarily addressing the eastern front. (One can also find many of Frederick's great videos on my website, barbarossa1941.com.) Jason is also an eastern front author, having recently published *Guderian's Foxes: Aufklärungs-Abteilung 29 in Photos from Barbarossa to*

Typhoon, one of the finest works on the eastern front I have had the pleasure to read. In addition to hundreds of hitherto unpublished photographs, Jason's book also includes an informative narrative and detailed maps. I am most grateful to Jason for graciously allowing me to publish more than a few of the photographs in *Guderian's Foxes* in this book.

I must also thank prolific eastern front historian and colleague Robert Kirchubel (Lt. Col., U.S. Army, ret.) for his constructive engagement with my manuscript and for his fine foreword, which he eagerly prepared at my request. To my friend and colleague of almost forty-five years, Dr. Jürgen Förster (we first met on a wonderful cruise down the Rhine River while I was a Fulbright Scholar in Bonn, West Germany, in 1979/80), I once again extend my gratitude for his invaluable support and help with securing some terrific photographs from the German Federal Military Archives (*Bundesarchiv*). For actually ferreting out the photographs from the German archives, many thanks to Benjamin Haas and his excellent research service; the photographs that Benjamin provided have significantly enriched this volume. Dr. Roman Töppel, one of Germany's leading eastern front historians, volunteered to read the manuscript and provided a most useful critique. Indeed, I cannot thank Roman enough for his contribution; he spent many hours diligently (and, I admit, quite critically at times!) evaluating my manuscript and making useful suggestions. This book is a demonstrably better book for all of his hard work on my behalf.

To my friend of many years and brilliant computer specialist, Alexander Kunstmann (who had an uncle who fought with a panzer division in Russia): I'd simply be lost without your expertise, and we both know that, don't we!

To my "wing man," Dr. David Day—thank you for always standing at my side and offering the encouragement I needed to bring this book-writing journey to a gratifying conclusion. And to anyone I've forgotten, please forgive my unforgivable oversight.

To my wife, Marie Therese Luther, how comforting it was for me to know that, after a long day of research and writing, you, Anthony (our dog), and the cats would be waiting for me to join you all by crawling wearily into bed.

Introduction

This book examines the generalship of Heinz Guderian and the operations of his panzer forces during Operation Barbarossa, Adolf Hitler's surprise attack on Soviet Russia that began on 22 June 1941; it concludes with the panzer general's dismissal from frontline service on the eastern front the day after Christmas 1941. The foundation of this study is my twenty-five years of research and writing on the initial months of the war in the east[1]—a war that caused some 70 percent of the casualties sustained by Germany's armed forces from 1941 to 1945. Hence, it is hardly hyperbole to posit that it was the Red Army that broke the back of the *Wehrmacht* (German Armed Forces), despite incurring some fourteen million fatal losses in the process. (Demographers put the aggregate human toll—military *and* civilian—at about twenty-seven million for the Soviet Union during its "Great Fatherland War." By way of comparison, the United States military suffered a total of 406,000 fatal losses in both the European and Pacific theaters during World War II.)

Because this is a work of military history (on both the operational and tactical levels), I do not address in any detail Guderian's attitude toward Hitler's regime, its criminal objectives, or National Socialism in general. Nor do I explore his putative complicity in crimes committed by the *Wehrmacht* in its conduct of Hitler's war of extermination (*Vernichtungskrieg*) against Soviet Russia and its people. There is no shortage of books on the German Army's criminal behavior inside the Soviet Union during World War II, so I've left that sorrowful topic to others.[2]

In his postwar memoir—certainly in the chapters on the eastern campaign of 1941—Guderian largely ignored the thorny issue of war crimes, instead focusing on his singular role as "Hitler's most prominent panzer leader."[3] Readers interested in a primer on Guderian and the topic of war crimes are urged to get hold of Russell A. Hart's excellent revisionist biography (2006), which offers a disturbing yet sensibly argued examination of Guderian and his connection to criminal acts, including the notorious *Kommissarbefehl* (Commissar Order)[4] and the operations of the *Einsatzgruppen* (death squads) inside Soviet Russia. In his short yet provocative study of the panzer general, Hart argues, inter alia, that Guderian fully supported Hitler's justification for waging war against Soviet Russia as a preemptive strike and noble undertaking to save Germany (and all Western civilization) from the horrors of Bolshevism. I should point out, however, that even if Guderian had come, by 1941, to at least outwardly adopt the core tenets of National Socialism (as Hart posits in his biography), he can in no way be associated with radical general officers like Walter von Reichenau, an Army commander in the east notorious for his order of October 1941 that supported Nazi genocidal policies against Jewish "subhumanity." In fact, I recall no recorded cases of Guderian himself issuing anti-Jewish or criminal orders of any kind, although it seems he did (arbitrarily) slightly alter the "Decree on Military Justice" to ensure the discipline of his troops.[5]

In the preparation of this book, I drew upon my publications on Operation Barbarossa over the past decade or so. With that as a starting point, I added a large measure of additional material pertaining to Guderian and his panzer operations in the east; this included letters to his wife, Margarete; diary entries and/or letters of major German field commanders in the east; and graphic personal accounts of German officers, NCOs, and simple soldiers slugging it out with the Red Army along the forward edge of battle. Of course, I also perused Guderian's war memoir, *Panzer Leader*—to be sure, a significant contribution to our understanding of the war in the east, yet one that, until relatively recently, has been accepted much too uncritically by many historians. This study also includes two very useful appendixes: (1) an insightful examination of the nature of German panzer operations on the eastern front (appendix F), and (2) a detailed look at the organization and major weapons systems of the German Army in June 1941 (appendix G).

As a professional military historian, however, I find most compelling the raw, unvarnished perspective of the soldier at the front—what historians call the view from below (*von unten*). In pursuit of this universal story of men at war, I have, over the decades, collected—from archives, from published and unpublished sources, and from veterans themselves—thousands of field post letters (*Feldpostbriefe*) and diary entries written by ordinary German soldiers. And yet, it would be unjust to characterize their letters and personal diaries as "ordinary," given the remarkable subject matter and the fact that many of these personal accounts are not only informative (on so many levels) but surprisingly well written (after all, Germany had one of the finest educational systems in the world at that time; thus the German people were, as a rule, quite literate). In any case, this amazing material fills the pages of this book and provides you, the reader, with extraordinary insights into the operations of Guderian's panzer forces on the eastern front.

Augmenting and adding context to the many personal stories is my explicit narrative covering the operational and tactical events as they unfold along the front of Guderian's panzer group, on the right wing of the central army group of the *Ostheer* (eastern army). Indeed, this book should provide the reader (buff and military historian alike) with a superior grasp of German maneuver warfare during the early stages of the war in the east and what made it so effective. "The relative tactical and operational superiority of the panzers over their opponents," averred the late Dennis Showalter, "was never greater than in the first half of July 1941, on the high road to Moscow. Guderian spoke of attacks going in like training exercises."

In chapter 2, which addresses the "frontier battles" from 22 June to 9 July 1941, I devote an inordinate number of pages to the first day of Operation Barbarossa. While doing so was, admittedly, self-indulgent, I had my reasons. First, the fighting that went on during the first twenty-one hours (Guderian launched his attack at 0315 hours) was spectacular in nature and mirrored in microcosm the almost preternaturally bloody and brutal conflict that would continue for the next three and a half years. Second, a few years back, I published a big book (about 175,000 words, excluding more than sixty pages of endnotes) about the first day of the war on the eastern front that, oddly enough, is titled *The First Day on the Eastern Front: Germany Invades the Soviet Union, June 22, 1941*. (The book, which addresses that "appalling moment in time"[6] in granular detail, was recognized by a longtime aggregator/reviewer of books on World War II as one of the best half dozen books on World War II released in 2018.[7] But enough of that.)

The longest chapter in the book is chapter 3, and there are reasons for that too. This chapter covers the cauldron battle at Smolensk from about 15 July through 5 August 1941, which culminated in another remarkable German victory but also brought an end to the German war of maneuver and witnessed the beginning of costly positional warfare. During this fateful three-week period, the blitzkrieg along the vital central axis toward Moscow was stopped in its tracks, and with that the prospect of a rapid German victory in Operation Barbarossa forever faded away. Indeed, it is not an overstatement to posit that, by early August 1941, Germany had lost the war.

For reasons adumbrated above, *Guderian's Panzers* is weighted—albeit not too heavily—toward the initial six or seven weeks of the Barbarossa campaign, during the high summer of 1941. The book is also weighted—rather heavily in this case—toward the German side of things, which, while understandable (given the topic), is an injustice of sorts to those courageous combatants on "the Other Side of the Hill." Once again, I had my reasons—most significantly pressures of time, resources, and logistics. That duly noted, I have "ghosted" neither the Soviet leadership nor the Red Army—both show up often in the narrative.

At this point, I should briefly address an issue that is the bane of every military historian: the eternal struggle with numbers—to wit, personnel strength/losses; figures for tank strength/losses; numbers of trucks, trains, artillery, aircraft, and so forth. While these figures change from day to day in combat situations, they are often frustratingly at variance in the source materials. I bring this up with regard to figures for the aggregate tank strength of Guderian's panzer group at any given time, as well as for the tank strength of its constituent panzer units. I have gleaned these data from many sources, ranging from secondary works to official records of the *Wehrmacht*. However, for the period from October through early December 1941, I have often relied on an excellent (and overlooked) study prepared shortly after the war by Guderian's highly capable chief of staff during the Barbarossa campaign, Kurt Freiherr von Liebenstein. His study is exquisitely detailed and, inter alia, provides very precise tank strength reports for Guderian's panzer forces; his source materials include the war diary of 2 Panzer Group (Second Panzer Army), war diaries of constituent corps, situation maps, and even his own diary notes (*Tagebuchnotizen*). Thus I found his study to be of great value.

Not to be overlooked, of course, is my discussion of Guderian's performance as a panzer leader. And here I believe I manage to at least scratch the surface of his strengths and weaknesses—not only as a soldier and a leader of men but as a man whose personal attributes ranged from undeniably remarkable to self-serving, even shameful (e.g., his acceptance of large, secret financial gifts—in more common parlance, "bribes"—from Hitler).[8] Like most men who emerge as titans in their times, Guderian was both a great man and a flawed man. Having asserted that, a clarifying comment: By "great man" I do not mean to imply a moral judgment, only to recognize his significant achievements on the world stage—from his integral contribution to the creation of Germany's panzer corps in the 1930s through his towering role in Hitler's wartime *Wehrmacht*.

While the subsequent narrative probes only a fraction of Heinz Guderian's life and military career, his six months as a high-ranking field general on the eastern front were, without doubt, the most momentous of his life—a period in which he harnessed all his professional acumen, as well as his mental and physical strength (not to mention his courage on the field of battle), and laid it all on the line in service of his country. While he can be criticized for many things, he cannot be criticized for that. In the final analysis the tragedy of Guderian's life is that, like so many Germans in Hitler's Third Reich writ large, he placed his honor, his trust, and, in his specific case, his exceptional abilities as a soldier in the service of a genocidal totalitarian regime whose monstrous scope of evil he either never fully grasped or simply refused to acknowledge.

Prologue

Adolf Hitler unleashed his surprise attack on Soviet Russia (code-named Operation Barbarossa) at dawn on Sunday, 22 June 1941. Calculated to crush the hated (and feared) "Bolshevik-Jewish" enemy in a mere matter of weeks, Germany's assault on Russia launched a war—no matter how you measure it, the greatest military confrontation in recorded history—that would rage for 1,418 days, culminating in the destruction of Hitler's Third Reich and his suicide in the bunker below the Reich Chancellery in Berlin on 30 April 1945.

Biographers of Hitler and historians of Nazi Germany have sought for decades to determine just why he took the fatal decision to strike at Soviet Russia in 1941. Some have focused on the calculus of the strategic-military situation that developed between July 1940—following the *Wehrmacht*'s spectacular six-week victory over France—and June 1941; others have emphasized the continuity of the racial and ideological convictions embraced by the German dictator since the 1920s; still others have sought a synthesis of the two perspectives. Moreover, recent scholarship has stressed that Hitler waged war upon Russia because *this* was the war he had most wanted from the very moment he came to power. To invoke the words of the late Manfred Messerschmidt in his introduction to volume four of the quasi-official German history of World War II, Operation Barbarossa was "Hitler's real war" (*eigentlicher Krieg*).[1] In the final analysis, Hitler viewed war between Germany and Russia as an ineluctable confrontation—an apocalyptic struggle between two mutually exclusive *Weltanschauungen* (worldviews) culminating in a racial war of extermination.[2]

A central role in Hitler's ill-fated eastern adventure was played by *Generaloberst* Heinz Guderian and the tankers and motorized infantry of his 2 Panzer Group (*Panzergruppe* 2). In the summer and early fall of 1941, they swept relentlessly across the wretched roadways and through the primeval forests of central European Russia, and despite stiffening enemy resistance, unsustainable losses in men and materiel, and increasingly tenuous lines of supply, Guderian's panzer group—leveraging its superior training, tactics, and experience—registered remarkable territorial gains while achieving victories of unprecedented scope in the "cauldron battles" (*Kesselschlachten*) of Belostok-Minsk, Smolensk, and Kiev.

Yet, despite the great victories, by late November 1941, Guderian's Second Panzer Army (redesignated as such in early October 1941) found itself largely immobilized—its forward progress now limited to a few kilometers a day in sharp contrast to the rapid advances of the summer campaign. In fact, after five months of brutal attritional warfare, his panzer army had been reduced to a mere shell of its former self—its panzer regiments left with but a handful of tanks, its motorized infantry battalions reduced to company strength. Bereft of their combat power, facing a tenacious and reinvigorated opponent, Guderian's ragged divisions failed to achieve their final Barbarossa objectives and, by early December, were lurching back in defeat.

Operation Barbarossa, which had begun with so much promise for Guderian's command, and for the *Ostheer* as a whole, had collapsed in catastrophic failure. But why was this so? How was it that, with each splendid victory, *final* victory seemed to move further beyond Germany's grasp? A vexing paradox to be sure, but one that can be illuminated by an examination of Guderian's role in the first half year of the Russian campaign, in the process providing insight into the failure of Barbarossa writ large.

AT THE REICH CHANCELLERY IN BERLIN (14.6.1941)

A mere eight days before the attack on Russia, Hitler secretly assembled the commanders of his eastern army groups (North, Center, and South), armies, *Panzergruppen*, and air fleets at the Reich Chancellery for a final series of conferences on the impending campaign. The participating general officers (also among them were: C-in-C of the Army, *Generalfeldmarschall* Walther von Brauchitsch; Chief of the Army General Staff, *Generaloberst* Franz Halder; and Chief of the OKH Operations Branch, *Oberst i.G.* Adolf Heusinger) had been assigned a strict agenda of arrival routes and times, as well as different street entrances by which to reach the sprawling Chancellery complex—prophylactic measures to conceal from overly curious Berliners that something *very* big was about to be set in motion.

Behind the Chancellery's tall granite walls, the conferences began at 1100 that morning. Following a few words of welcome to his assembled lieutenants, Hitler invited them to report on their intentions for the opening phase of operations in their respective sectors of the front. The field commanders of Army Group South went first, followed by those of Army Groups North and Center. According to Hitler's *Luftwaffe* adjutant, Nicolaus von Below, Hitler, for once, rarely interrupted, but rather listened attentively to the reports being made.[3] The generals' tone was optimistic; the overall picture they presented was of an enemy who, while admittedly superior in numbers, was markedly inferior in the quality of both men and materiel.

In the midst of the generals' recitations, at 2:00 p.m., Hitler broke for lunch with more than two dozen of his top commanders. About an hour later, the Führer called for silence and began to lecture his distinguished audience on the reasons behind his decision to attack the Soviet Union. If months before he had informed his generals that war against Russia would be a merciless nineteenth-century colonial-style war of annihilation (*Vernichtungskrieg*),[4] he now stressed the preventive character of the impending conflict, convinced as he said he was of the requirement to eliminate the "grave threat" Russia posed to Germany's back.[5] He also predicted that, while the battle would be difficult, the enemy tenacious, the worst would be over in about six weeks.

That afternoon, Hitler continued his discussions with the commanders of Army Group South. The mass of the Red Army, he averred, was anticipated on the front of Army Group Center; once it had been annihilated, Army Group South could expect to be reinforced from the *Ostheer*'s central army group. Brauchitsch and Halder both listened but were careful to say nothing (see chapter 4). At some point, Hitler also emphasized the operational objective that had become an idée fixe of sorts—the capture of Leningrad, which he called the "cradle of Bolshevism" and which held a particular fascination for him as the former Saint Petersburg of the czars and symbol of Russia's claim to great power status.[6]

In his memoir, Guderian recalled—no doubt disingenuously—that "[Hitler's] detailed exposition of the reasons that led him to fight a preventive war against the Russians was unconvincing."[7] During the military conference that afternoon, he was asked—he does not say by whom—how much time his tanks would need to reach the ancient city of Minsk, the capital of Belorussia some 300 kilometers (linear distance) from Guderian's start line in occupied Poland. To this question—remarkably the only one he was asked—he replied, "Five to six days."[8] As matters turned out, the panzer general was almost right on the mark, for his spearhead would reach the outskirts of the city on 28 June, the seventh day of the war. Unfortunately for the German invaders, Hitler's prognostication of just six weeks of hard fighting was rather short of the mark.

Part I

FROM THE FRONTIER TO SMOLENSK

Following the spectacular six-week victory over France in June 1940, Adolf Hitler and his generals turned their attention to planning what they envisaged as a short blitzkrieg campaign against Soviet Russia. By December 1940, the basic strategic/operational framework for Operation Barbarossa was in place;[1] the details had been hammered out in a matter of mere weeks by the German Army General Staff. By spring 1941, the force buildup for the impending campaign was in full swing, the men, tanks, vehicles, trucks, and munitions traversing the borders of the German Reich and flowing east in a steady stream of troop trains numbering as many as 200 per day. Meanwhile, *Wehrmacht* field generals in the east trained and deployed their troops and prepared their attack orders; prominent among them, fresh off his celebrated victories in France, was Panzer General Heinz Guderian, destined to lead his tanks to even greater success in Russia in the summer of 1941.

Forming the right wing of the *Ostheer*'s central army group, Guderian's *Panzergruppe* 2 broke through Red Army frontier defenses in the initial hours of the eastern campaign. In the days and weeks that followed—Guderian pushing himself and his men to the limits of human endurance—the panzer group plunged hundreds of kilometers into Soviet territory; in doing so, it succeeded in breaching the vital Soviet defensive barrier at the Dnepr River in the second week of July and, by early August, had contributed decisively to two historic victories for Hitler's eastern army: the cauldron battles of Minsk and Smolensk.

The stunning successes of Guderian's panzer forces (as well as those of the other three panzer groups in the Barbarossa order of battle) aroused a certain awe, even incredulity, at Hitler's *Wolfsschanze* (Wolf's Lair) headquarters—tucked away in the dense forests of East Prussia, not far from the town of Rastenburg (and built specifically to function as the nerve center for the Russian campaign). Yet, however dazzling, these early victories in many respects were not quite what they seemed. Simply put, the farther the German spearheads pushed into Russia along all axes of advance, the weaker they inevitably became. For Guderian, as early as mid-July, attrition due to combat and the breakdown of vehicles and equipment on the primitive Russian road net had become a serious concern. Moreover, the deeper his tanks drove into Russia, the greater became the logistical challenges (e.g., shortages of spare parts, replacement engines, and fuel and oil for tanks and vehicles), relentlessly reducing his numbers of operational panzers. And most noteworthy of all, Red Army resistance, far from abating, was becoming even more vigorous and effective despite the Russians' enormous losses, slowing and weakening Guderian's forces.

By 5 August 1941, the Battle of Smolensk was over, leaving the ancient city of 170,000[2] in ruins, dozens of Soviet divisions smashed, and several hundred thousand *Rotarmisten* destined for the POW pens. However, the vexing paradox of Operation Barbarossa remained: Despite the seemingly singular results of the first six weeks of the campaign, for Guderian and his panzer group—now marooned deep inside Soviet Russia—final victory remained as elusive as ever.

Yet, for Guderian—and, indeed, for Hitler and most of his generals—sobriety would only come with hindsight. Flushed with victory, on or about 5 August, the panzer general ordered his staff to prepare for an advance on Moscow. Still, he was now feeling the strain of a brutal campaign that had already run on as long as that much easier affair in France of the previous summer, yet whose end seemed nowhere in sight. In a private letter home (6 August) he remarked, "How long the heart and nerves can stand this I do not know." In a second missive (12 August) he was equally blunt: "Have I not become old? These few weeks have imprinted their marks. The physical exertions and battles of the will make themselves felt."[3]

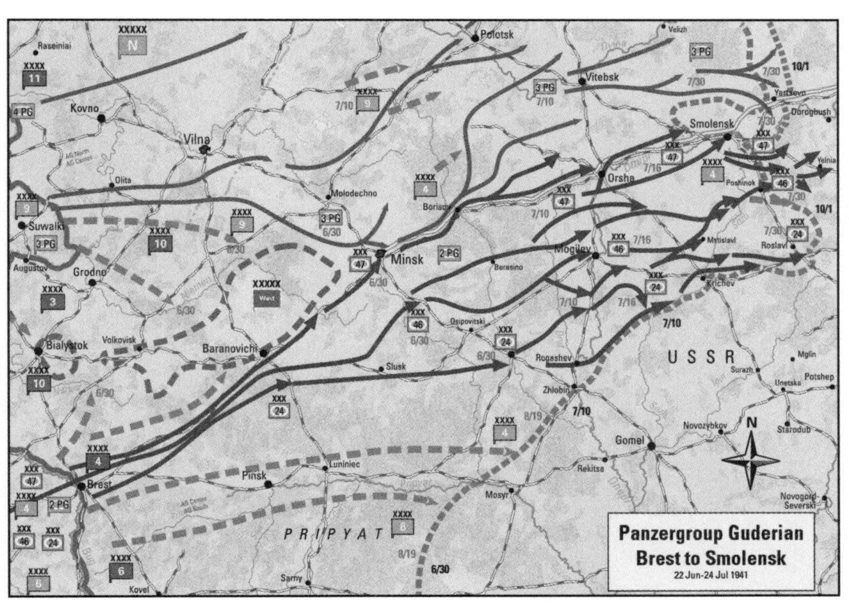

Operations of 2 Panzer Group: 22.6.1941–24.7.1941

1

Preparations for the Eastern Campaign

By June 1941, the fifty-three-year-old Heinz Guderian could look back on a uniquely distinguished military career that had begun in the Imperial German Army in 1907. He had served ably on the western front in the Great War, initially as a *Leutnant* in command of a wireless detachment during the Battle of the Marne in the summer of 1914. A gifted soldier of keen intellect,[1] Guderian rose in rank to *Oberleutnant* (November 1914) and then to *Hauptmann* (December 1915), his subsequent wartime postings including the Flanders front, the Ypres front, and Verdun during the brutal *Materialschlacht* (war of materiel) of 1916.[2] Serving as a staff officer he largely avoided the abattoir of the trenches, while also developing his own aggressive command style of leading from the front lines. By February 1918, he had risen to a position in the elite Greater German General Staff. After the war, Guderian served in the 100,000-man *Reichswehr*, and by the late-1930s he was playing an integral part in crafting the concept of blitzkrieg warfare, based on the combined operations of tanks, motorized infantry, and aircraft, linked together by modern (radio) communications. His contribution to the creation of Adolf Hitler's tank corps is well known, although Guderian most certainly used his memoir to (successfully) inflate his role in this arena:

> Heinz Guderian has been lionized by many as the legendary father of the German armored force and brilliant practitioner of "blitzkrieg" maneuver warfare. Guderian created this legend with his own highly-influential, yet self-serving and distorted memoir, which remains one of the most widely read accounts of the Second Word War. Unfortunately, too many of Guderian's biographers have accepted Guderian's view of his accomplishments without sufficient critical scrutiny. The result has been an undeserved hagiography of Guderian. While undoubtedly a great military figure, Guderian was a man of appreciable ego and ambition—a volatile, impetuous, and difficult personality determined to achieve

> his vision of a war-winning armored force, irrespective of the consequences. . . . In the end, he proved to be a man prepared to distort the truth in order to establish his place in history. In doing so, he denigrated the myriad important contributions of other Germans as he took personal credit for what were, in reality, collective accomplishments. He succeeded in creating a legend that has endured long after his death.[3]

In the opening stages of World War II, Guderian led 19 Panzer Corps with great distinction in Poland (1939), then Belgium and France (1940); during the second (and final) phase of the French campaign, his command was enlarged to embrace three corps and redesignated as Panzer Group Guderian. In recognition of his singular achievements, he was promoted to full general rank (*Generaloberst*) on 19 July 1940. A bold and fearless leader of men—in combat he often exposed himself to great personal risk, convinced that destiny protected him from injury or death—he would drive himself and his men to extremes of endurance in the summer of 1941.

HITLER TURNS EAST (DIRECTIVE NO. 21)

It was sometime in November 1940 that Guderian first became privy to Hitler's intent to attack Soviet Russia. "I made no attempt to conceal my disappointment and disgust," he put down in his memoir. "As one of the uninitiated, I could only now hope that Hitler was not seriously planning an attack on the Soviet Union, and that all these preparations were a bluff."[4] He claimed to be disturbed by the looming specter of a two-front war, and that may well have been so. Yet the panzer general's pronounced anticommunism—de rigueur among the higher-ranking officers in Hitler's *Wehrmacht*—left him only too willing to be selected for a significant role in "Hitler's War" against the Bolshevik behemoth in the east. (Guderian had observed after World War I, while in Mitau on the Baltic, "The Bolsheviks . . . cavort like beasts.") The truth of the matter then is that Guderian came to fully embrace the impending Russian campaign—despite its uniquely thuggish underpinnings as a colonial-style genocidal war of conquest.[5]

On 18 December 1940, Hitler signed Führer Directive No. 21, "Case Barbarossa." Only nine copies were made of the top secret eleven-page document, which laid out in broad strokes how the Soviet Union was to be crushed in a rapid campaign (*Sowjetrussland in einem schnellen Feldzug niederzuwerfen*) even before the conclusion of the war with England. In theory, at least, the directive was elegant in its clarity and simplicity of purpose: The mass of the Red Army was to be encircled by the German armored spearheads west of the two great river barriers, the Dnepr and the Western Dvina, and then eliminated in a spectacular battle of annihilation (*Vernichtungsschlacht*)—a super "Cannae," whose doctrinal antecedents reached back to the theories of the great nineteenth-century military philosopher Carl von Clausewitz, the elder Moltke, and Schlieffen. The final objective was to erect a barrier against Asiatic Russia on the general line Volga-Archangel. If necessary, surviving industrial areas in the Urals could be eliminated by the *Luftwaffe*. All preparations for the coming campaign were to be completed by 15 May 1941.[6]

After Soviet forces west of the Dnepr-Dvina line had been destroyed, the war, it was believed, would essentially be over; all that would remain would be mopping-up operations and pursuit into the interior to destroy those enemy elements that had escaped destruction and to reach the final geographical objectives. In other words, German planners anticipated only weak and desultory enemy resistance after the initial frontier battles had been fought to a successful conclusion. Their intelligence—derived in the main from top secret high-level reconnaissance flights over Soviet territory and the monitoring of Red Army wireless traffic in the border regions—had provided them with a reasonably accurate assessment of Soviet dispositions up to a depth of several hundred kilometers from the German-Soviet demarcation line;[7] yet, beyond that, remarkably little was known about potential Soviet strength and dispositions. The Germans, however, simply assumed that the mass of the Red Army was deployed at or near the border and that, once these forces were disposed of, only remnants would remain. It was a fatal assumption.

It should also be emphasized that, unlike Poland (1939) and France (1940), the Russian campaign was envisaged by Hitler and his generals as a true blitzkrieg, the outcome to be determined in a matter of weeks by means of a single, devastating blow—the 1941 equivalent of a nuclear first strike. Placing Barbarossa in a historical context, Hitler and his General Staff wanted to operate like Moltke on the strategic level, by isolating and defeating each opponent singly, and like Schlieffen at the operational and tactical level, by destroying the enemy in a short war through a massive battle of annihilation. In this manner, they could overcome the traditional dilemmas posed by Germany's central European position and its modest human and material resources.

THE OKH DEPLOYMENT DIRECTIVE

In response to Hitler's directive, General Staff planners in the Army High Command (OKH) crafted a detailed deployment directive (*Aufmarschanweisung*) and submitted it to the Army leadership at the end of January 1941. The document, signed by GFM Walther von Brauchitsch, Commander-in-Chief of the Army, began by again emphasizing the requirement to smash the bulk of the Red Army in the western border regions through daring operations of armored forces driving deep behind the front and preventing the organized withdrawal of enemy forces into the interior of the Soviet Union. The deployment directive laid out in some detail the individual tasks of the three army groups assigned to the Russian campaign—North, Center, and South—and of their armies and panzer groups. The mission of the *Luftwaffe* was briefly addressed: "eliminate as much as possible the influence of the Russian air force while supporting the Army's conduct of operations at its points of main effort [*Schwerpunkten*], in particular by Army Group Center and on the main wing of Army Group South."[8] The directive admonished the troops to be prepared for the Russians to make use of chemical weapons, even dropping them from the air.[9] Thus, the OKH was braced for the Soviets to respond to the German attack with a harshness and brutality far in excess of earlier campaigns—a foreboding not without basis in fact.

The OKH deployment directive also embraced an intricate timetable for assembly and concentration of German forces in the east. While the initial German advance beyond the frontier was to rely on truck transport for logistical support (due in part to the serious shortcomings of the Soviet Union's rail infrastructure), the buildup of forces for the offensive was to be managed mainly by rail—a challenge so colossal in scope it required thousands of trains to move about three-quarters of the German armed forces to their new theater of operations. In fact, from February through mid-July 1941, well over 10,000 trainloads were unloaded in the east. The deployment plan called for this vast migration of men and materiel to take place in five phases (the fifth and final phase beginning after the outbreak of hostilities and comprising the majority of the OKH reserves); most of the foot (marching) infantry divisions were to be transported in the initial phases, while the rail movement of the panzer and motorized formations was not—for reasons of security—to commence until the final few weeks before the invasion.

Dr. Rudolf Gschöpf, a forty-year-old Catholic priest (*Divisionspfarrer*) in 45 Infantry Division, recalled the mighty procession of men, tanks, vehicles, and artillery as the formations of Army Group Center advanced inexorably toward their Barbarossa start lines. The tinge of excitement his account betrays must have been universal among the *Landser* (German term for GI)—the sense of the power and invincibility of German arms overwhelming.

> At the end of April 1941, the transport of the division from the area around St. Quentin to the east began. . . . Our route cut straight across Germany. After three days, we halted in the environs of Warsaw. . . . During this transfer to the east, the division suffered a heavy blow: The division commander, *GenMaj.* Körner, wanted to use the journey through Germany to pay his family a brief visit, but had a fatal accident en route in his automobile. . . . He was succeeded by [*GenMaj.*] Schlieper.
>
> There now followed a couple of weeks' rest, even if a certain amount of training still had to continue. So we were back in Poland! A lot had changed here in this country since we had left it in November 1939! . . .
>
> At the end of May the division began to advance further east via Siedlce up into the area around Biała-Podlaska. The former Polish barracks in the town itself

> offered accommodation for a portion of the troops; the greater part took up quarters in the surrounding villages. . . . The concentrations of troops became ever more evident. Heavy movements could be observed, especially at night. Tanks, heavy artillery, anti-aircraft guns, engineering equipment, and much else besides trundled eastward toward the Russian border. A conspicuous number of discussions in the headquarters staffs; intense activity in the orderly rooms; visits from unknown and high-level commanders—all of this meant even the simplest men could clearly see that great things were imminent [*dass grosse Dinge bevorstünden*].[10]

Although Hitler and his generals were in agreement on the basic strategic objective of the coming campaign—to wit, the destruction of the mass of Soviet forces west of the Dnepr and Dvina Rivers—their perspectives on how to achieve this objective skewed in quite different directions. Despite the fact that the initial operational priority for Army Group Center was the city of Smolensk, Hitler and the Army High Command wanted the first encirclement battle to take place no farther east than Minsk (about half the distance to Smolensk). GFM von Bock, Commander, Army Group Center, as well as his two panzer group commanders, Guderian and *Generaloberst* Hermann Hoth (3 Panzer Group), had a much bolder concept in mind: They wanted the initial encirclement to reach as far east as Smolensk, more than 600 kilometers from the Barbarossa start line. Such an approach, they averred, would enable their panzer forces to push beyond the Dnepr and Western Dvina river lines, whereas closing the armored pincers at Minsk would disrupt their advance and force them to fight a more difficult battle for these vital river crossings later on. Yet, for the Führer and his Army General Staff, such a bold operational démarche was a bridge too far; they decided to hold to the shorter encirclement at Minsk, thereby eliciting more than a little bitterness and frustration on the part of Bock, Guderian, and Hoth after the start of the eastern campaign.

Yet an even more serious dispute emerged during German planning for Barbarossa—although this time the OKH and key field commanders were in agreement. The OKH, and field generals, which included Bock and Guderian, were convinced that only the capture of Moscow would bring about the complete collapse of Soviet Russia. As far as Guderian was concerned—although he fully understood the need to destroy the Red Army in the frontier regions—the seizure of the Soviet capital signified an objective of such decisive psychological and political importance that it became for him an end in itself. ("Nowhere," avouched Guderian biographer Russell A. Hart, "did Guderian more clearly reveal his strategic myopia than in his stubborn belief that the capture of Moscow would collapse communist rule and end the war in the east."[11]) Hitler, however, while conceding Moscow's strategic value, considered it a secondary (even tertiary) priority, only to be sought after the destruction of Soviet forces in the Baltic region, a linkup with Finnish forces, and the eradication of the Red Army in the western Ukraine; moreover, these objectives were to be strongly supported by armored units of Bock's army group. While this strategic dissonance at the highest levels of command would be largely glossed over during the planning phase, it would reemerge with a vengeance only weeks after the start of Barbarossa (see chapter 4).

THE BARBAROSSA FORCE STRUCTURE[12]

Army Group North, commanded by the sixty-four-year-old GFM Wilhelm Ritter von Leeb and the smallest of the three army groups, was composed of twenty-nine divisions (twenty infantry, three panzer, three motorized infantry, and three security divisions) organized into two infantry armies (Sixteenth and Eighteenth Armies) and one panzer group (4 PzG); total personnel was roughly 640,000 men, with the panzer group possessing about 600 tanks.

Army Group Center, commanded by the sixty-year-old GFM Fedor von Bock and the largest of the three army groups, consisted of more than 1.3 million men assembled in 50.5 divisions (31 infantry, 9 panzer, 6.5 motorized infantry, 3 security divisions, and 1 cavalry division) organized into two infantry armies (Fourth and Ninth Armies) and two panzer groups (*Panzergruppen* 2 and 3). Between them, the two panzer groups boasted a total of about 1,900 tanks (considerably more than the other two army groups combined).

Army Group South, commanded by the sixty-five-year-old GFM Gerd von Rundstedt, comprised forty-one divisions (twenty-five infantry, four light, five panzer, three motorized, one mountain, and three security divisions) arranged in three infantry armies (Sixth, Eleventh, and Seventeenth Armies) and a single panzer group (1 PzG). Total personnel amounted to 972,000 men, while the panzer group was outfitted with some 715 tanks.

In addition to the first-echelon forces of the three army groups, twenty-eight divisions were held in reserve by the OKH; several others were stationed in northern Finland. All told, on 22 June 1941, the Barbarossa force structure amounted to more than 3 million men, 3,350 tanks, 250 assault guns, 7,146 artillery pieces,[13] 600,000 vehicles, and 625,000 horses organized into 151 divisions (among them 19 panzer and 15 motorized divisions.)[14] The ground forces of the *Ostheer* were supported by nearly 3,000 bombers, dive-bombers, fighters, fighter-bombers, transport aircraft, and reconnaissance planes of the *Luftwaffe*; of these, 2,250 were operational on *Barbarossatag*.

THE OTHER SIDE OF THE HILL

Facing the *Wehrmacht*'s invasion force in the Soviet western frontier zone were some 2.9 million men (171 divisions, including 40 tank and 20 mechanized divisions) arranged in five special military districts (Leningrad, Baltic, Western, Kiev, and Odessa), which, following the advent of Barbarossa, were at once redesignated as the Northern, Northwestern, Western, Southwestern, and Southern fronts (a front being roughly equivalent to a German army group).

Buttressing these forces was a second strategic echelon of five armies (fifty-seven divisions) of the STAVKA (Soviet Supreme Command) reserve. This powerful force—unlike Red Army formations along the frontier—was virtually unknown to German intelligence and was still in the process of deploying along the Western Dvina–Dnepr river lines when Barbarossa began; in fact, on 22 June 1941, neither the forward military districts nor the STAVKA reserve armies had completed their deployment in accordance with official Soviet mobilization and deployment plans. In the aggregate, the Red Army in June 1941 was composed of over five million men arranged in twenty-seven armies (303 divisions, among them 61 tank and 31 mechanized divisions), with some 20,000 tanks and 20,000 aircraft. While the vast majority of these tanks and aircraft were obsolete, Soviet Russia's massive military establishment embraced more of both than any other nation in the world.[15]

Challenging GFM von Bock's formidable assemblage and defending along the Minsk-Smolensk axis was Army-General D. G. Pavlov's Western Special Military District (Western Front as of 22 June 1941). Pavlov's command comprised 670,000 men, 2,200 operational tanks (largely obsolete models, but several hundred were the new heavy KV and medium T-34 tanks), 14,000 guns and mortars, and 1,600 combat-ready aircraft (figures rounded). These forces were organized into four armies (3, 4, 10, and 13) and included six mechanized corps. However, when the invasion began, only a small number of Western Front's rifle divisions were actually manning border defenses, and most of these divisions were deployed with one regiment forward and two in garrison. Moreover, much of Pavlov's armor was still quartered in its peacetime garrisons and, perforce, hardly prepared to make a rapid transition to mobile wartime operations. Adding to the virtually insurmountable challenges facing Soviet Western Front was that the border fortifications in its sector were far from complete (as was the case across the entire frontier for the Red Army).[16]

GUDERIAN GETS TO WORK

Disappointed by their soldiers' performance in the Polish campaign of 1939—after-action reports from field commanders had complained that the infantry was not aggressive enough in the attack, while Guderian had observed several occasions when his motorized infantry and panzer units exhibited nervousness before going into action—the Army High Command had set about to sharpen training and combat capability between the Polish and French campaigns. Beginning in the fall of 1939, the German Army spent seventeen hours a day, six or seven days a week, implementing "with precision and enthusiasm" the OKH training syllabus—a "ruthless and relentless" training program that stood in stark contrast to the generally "lackadaisical practice" of most French formations during the "Phony War" of late 1939 and early 1940.[17]

After the French campaign, the Army High Command promulgated directives for even more intensive training, this time in preparation for a very different kind of war—that against the Soviet Union. Panzer divisions were to undergo extensive training in combined-arms tactics; they were also to be prepared to defend alone against close-in attacks (*Nahangriffe*). Motorized infantry units were to train to fight unsupported and to clear forests and villages rapidly. Foot (marching) infantry were to execute long, strenuous marches to prepare for the rigors of traversing vast, inhospitable distances.[18] Troops were also to be trained to dig narrow, deep foxholes (*Schützenlöcher*) to provide protection against enemy tanks.[19]

In mid-November 1940, *Panzergruppe Guderian* (as noted, the designation of his command during the latter phase of the battle for France) was redesignated as *Panzergruppe* 2. Destined to lead the largest of the four panzer groups earmarked for Barbarossa (with just under 1,000 tanks), *Generaloberst* Guderian immersed himself in the myriad details of the approaching campaign with his usual vigor and thoroughness. He was drawn into its preparations relatively early and was acutely aware that war with Russia would pose the greatest challenge of his life. And despite the strict requirement for secrecy, he acknowledged to his men that the next campaign would be much more difficult than those in Poland and in the west.

Along with the always strenuous and unremitting staff work, the panzer general sought to promote the realistic training of his troops—for instance, by schooling them in overcoming difficult terrain (e.g., swamps or marshland) and building corduroy roads. Training in the German Army, even in peacetime, had always been tough—"long, arduous, realistic," as one author has characterized it.[20] German training programs aimed to replicate combat conditions as closely as possible. Troops were trained in all types of weather and around the clock, day and night. Exercises with live ammunition—a practice employed by the pre-1914 Imperial Army during its annual summer maneuvers—were routine,[21] exposing men to serious injury or death. (German military authorities accepted the 1 percent fatality rate sustained during such training as the necessary price for saving soldiers' lives in combat.) Training was also forward-looking, with each soldier learning to perform his immediate superior's mission as well as his own, in case he had to take command.

Every effort was also made by Guderian and his staff to incorporate the "lessons learned" from the six-week French campaign. At the end of August 1940, they had summarized their experiences in France as follows:

> In combat between tank formations, our tanks proved to be superior after only short firefights. Reasons: 1) [the] great accuracy [*grosse Treffsicherheit*] of our

> own weapons; 2) [the] high rate of fire, which partly made up for the lack of penetrating power [of our weapons]; 3) hits by Panzer IIIs and IVs on enemy tanks, even when they didn't penetrate, had such an impact on morale, that the shaken enemy tank crews frequently set out the white flag; 4) [the] great speed and maneuverability of our own tanks; 5) superior leadership, training, and combat morale; 6) radio contact, and, with that, good possibilities of leadership and greater flexibility.[22]

Yet training in the German Army for combat under Russian conditions was by no means "uniform or systematic." Indeed, a truly specialized program was impossible for several reasons. For example, there were no suitable training grounds—no regions in France, the Netherlands, or central Europe—where the Army could train for combat in deep forests, extensive swampland, or sandy areas. Obstacles to realistic training—particularly for tank units and motorized infantry—also resulted from shortages of fuel and vehicles. In one respect, however, the German Army took special measures for coping with the problems of Russian terrain: The combat forces were equipped with light vehicles, and impedimenta were reduced to a minimum. German-issue transportation included large numbers of Polish *panje* carts drawn by native horses—Russia's conventional means of conveyance. All unnecessary baggage and every bit of nonessential ballast that soldiers are wont to carry was to be left behind at large collecting depots.[23]

Despite the many challenges—commanders and troops would also have to cope with inaccurate and/or out-of-date Russian maps—German field commanders (Guderian among them, of course) did all they could to prepare their charges for war. Instructive in this context are the training manuals issued by GFM Günther von Kluge (C-in-C Fourth Army), for they embrace typical concerns of the *Ostheer*'s senior leadership while also reflecting the healthy respect the German Army officer corps—many of whom had fought in the east in the Great War—had for the Russian Army. As Kluge understood (albeit not from personal experience),[24] any fight with the Red Army was going to be a serious affair. On 20 March 1941, he ordered his subordinate commanders to step up their training activities. The training, he ordered, should emphasize a toughening of the troops, since in Russia the soldiers would often be without even the simplest "creature comforts." The men were to train to march great distances, while efforts were to be made to protect the troops from chemical or biological weapons. (Note: Only days before Barbarossa began, GFM von Brauchitsch visited his army field commanders in the east. What he told them was sobering: The Russians could be expected to use flamethrowers and gas; they would contaminate wells and stocks of supplies, while seriously threatening rear lines of communication. As he told the staff of Fourth Army on 12 June 1941, one had to be prepared for *der Russe* to wage "war by all possible means.")[25]

Kluge warned his men that the enemy (still unnamed) was likely to attack in several thick waves, with strong support from tanks and artillery; as combatants, they would be tough and disdainful of their losses. He stressed that his infantry would have to effectively coordinate all of its firepower to repel such attacks. In addition, the infantry was to train for greater toughness in close combat (a specialty of the Russian fighting man) and to overcome its aversion to fighting at night. Because they could also expect to be assaulted by tanks, the infantry should be instructed to emulate Finnish and Spanish infantry by aggressively attacking enemy tanks with explosive charges. The field marshal also foresaw special problems arising from the enormous scope of the Russian theater of operations, where his units would frequently be left with unguarded flanks. To address this concern, he recommended that units become accustomed to providing for adequate reconnaissance and security, paying particular attention to large forests, where Russian cavalry might lurk. Security, he admonished, must also be made more robust for German staffs; hence, all headquarters personnel were to be familiar with and expect to use their side arms.[26]

Prior to the start of Barbarossa, several initiatives were also undertaken by the Army High Command to upgrade the weaponry of the German Army. These included the introduction of new—or improvements to existing—weapons systems to boost the firepower of both infantry (e.g., introduction of the *StuG* III assault gun) and armor. Between June 1940 and June 1941, the entire German panzer arm was not only upgraded with better tanks but reorganized and expanded from ten to twenty panzer divisions; however, due to the low rate of tank production, the doubling of these divisions could only be achieved by greatly reducing the number of tanks in each division—the contraction in the number of tanks being partially offset by allotting each panzer division a second motorized infantry regiment and through upgrades to artillery, signal, combat engineer, and supply units. The re-equipping of Guderian's panzer battalions included phaseout of outmoded Panzer I and Panzer II tanks (almost all of the former, a majority of the latter) and their replacement with better-armored and up-gunned Panzer III and Panzer IV tanks.[27] Only after 22 June, however, would the Germans realize that efforts to improve the panzer forces had fallen far short of the mark. This was because little to nothing was known about the Red Army's new, heavier, more powerfully armed KV-1 and T-34 tanks, which were now making their way into the Soviet force structure and would come as a profound shock to the *Ostheer.* In fact, "the qualitative advantage of these Soviet tanks was enormous. In practical terms it meant that none of the German tanks regardless of armament could penetrate the armor on the T-34 at ranges above 500 meters. . . . The KV-1 was simply impervious to all tank-mounted German firepower as well as the standard 37mm anti-tank guns issued to infantry divisions."[28] (Note: For a detailed discussion of the upgrading of German tank forces, see appendix G.)

As an essential part of their own schooling for the Russian campaign, Guderian and his staff carefully studied the wars of Charles XII and Napoleon in Russia. On 26/27 February 1941, Guderian led a major operational-level war game (*Kriegsspiel*) in Posen (in German-occupied Poland) based on the Barbarossa directive. The basic objective of the war game was to ascertain just how well the directive would function at the operational level (*auf operativer Stufe*) of command. A key result was that the Dnepr River, some 500 kilometers from the Russo-German frontier, could be reached by D+11. (An advance detachment of one of 2 Panzer Group's panzer divisions would, in fact, reach the Dnepr on 2 July 1941, precisely eleven days after the start of the campaign.) On 28 February, Chief of the Army General Staff Halder recorded in his diary, "*Gen.Lt.* [Friedrich] Paulus: . . . Report on the results of the *Kriegsspiel Guderian*. Very pleased."[29]

While Guderian promulgated his orders, conferred with subordinate (and superordinate) commanders, visited the troops, and held discussions with the *Luftwaffe*, his staff put together an exquisitely detailed dossier with the necessarily obfuscatory title of "Counterattack in the Case of an Enemy Attack" (*Gegenangriff im Falle eines feindlichen Angriffs*). The dossier, dated 14 March 1941, was ten centimeters thick and filled with vital particulars on the upcoming campaign, among them maps showing friendly/enemy positions, logistical data, and even precise details about the fords in the Bug River at the Russo-German border.[30]

In an order to his assigned divisions, the formidable panzer general let it be known just how much he expected of his men:

> Our panzer group, on the right wing of [Fourth Army] and advancing ahead of it, is to break through the frontier positions on both sides of Brest-Litovsk and strike out along *Panzerrollbahn*[31] 1 and 2 toward Slutsk and Minsk, and then into the area of Smolensk, in order to destroy the cohesion of the enemy army. After breaking through, it is of decisive importance to advance as far as the gasoline will take us, at full throttle, without pause or rest, marching day and night, without consideration for any threat to the flanks. . . . The main thing is to advance far, and to shoot little. [*Es kommt darauf an, viel zu fahren, wenig zu schiessen.*][32]

After being briefed by Guderian about the "very difficult mission" (*sehr schwere Aufgabe*) that lay ahead, *Generalmajor* Walther K. Nehring, C-in-C, 18 Panzer Division (47 PzK, 2 PzG), briefed his divisional staff on 17 April. He informed them that the impending operation would make "enormous" demands on the men (*enorme Leistungsanforderungen*). Until they were clear of the forests and in open terrain, good for tanks, there was to be "no rest" and "no sleep." Rations, he told them, would be meagre (*dürftig*); getting munitions to the front a challenge. Due to the difficult terrain and primitive roadways, vehicles were to be handled carefully (*nicht überlasten*). The primary weapon (*Hauptwaffe*) was the tank, while the mobile infantry were to operate in such a manner as to exploit the success of the panzers.[33]

Yet, if Guderian was prepared to ruthlessly push and drive his panzer troops to their limits, he expected no less of himself. Despite the far greater expanses of the eastern theater of operations—and the unprecedented challenge this posed for command and control—he would continue to lead from the front, just as he had done in Poland and France (indeed, as he had rapidly learned to do during World War I). "His solution to the problem of distance was simply to drive himself, his chauffeurs, and his staff twice as hard. Repeatedly, he came under direct enemy fire and on a number of occasions he had narrow escapes."[34]

As Guderian explained in his memoir, on the first day of the offensive, the task of his panzer group was "to cross the Bug on either side of Brest-Litovsk [and] to break through the Russian defensive positions, then [in the days and weeks that followed] . . . quickly to exploit the success gained and advance to the area Roslavl-El'nia-Smolensk. The intention was to prevent the enemy from regrouping and forming a new front, and thus to lay the groundwork for a decisive victory during the 1941 campaign. My panzer group was to receive further instructions when its objective[s] had been reached."[35] However, with the start of the campaign barely weeks away, the panzer general (so he claimed in his memoir) had received at his headquarters "only bare indications" of the High Command's intentions for the second phase of the Russian campaign after his—and the entire *Ostheer*'s—initial objectives had been achieved, a situation that, if indeed true, must have aroused a certain unease.[36]

The deployment directive of the Army High Command provides additional details on the mission of Guderian's panzer forces:

> 2 Panzer Group, in cooperation with Fourth Army, is to break through the enemy forces along the border at and north of Kobrin and, through a rapid advance on Slutsk and Minsk in cooperation with 3 Panzer Group, which is advancing into the area north of Minsk, create the conditions for the destruction of all enemy forces in the area between Belostok and Minsk. Operating closely with 3 Panzer Group, it will then rapidly gain the area at and south of Smolensk, preventing the concentration of enemy forces in the region of the upper Dnepr and thereby securing freedom of action [*Handlungsfreiheit*] for the army group for its further tasks.[37]

To accomplish his assigned tasks, Guderian elected to deploy his three panzer corps with two forward in the initial attack echelon and one in reserve. Because his two attacking panzer corps were massed along a narrow front of just 70 kilometers on the right wing of Army Group Center, they would be able to concentrate overwhelming force at decisive points against defending Soviet forces. Aligning his operations closely with those of *Generaloberst* Hermann

Hoth's *Panzergruppe* 3 (on the left wing of Bock's army group and attacking from the Suwalki triangle, a terrain feature that projected deep into Soviet territory), Guderian (as noted) was to direct his initial thrust via the town of Slutsk toward the Belorussian capital of Minsk, where the two panzer groups were to link up in a deep double envelopment some 250 to 300 kilometers from the frontier, resulting in the encirclement and liquidation of opposing Soviet forces.

Following the planned cauldron battle (*Kesselschlacht*) in the Belostok-Minsk sector, the armor and motorized infantry of *Panzergruppen* 2 and 3 were to press on rapidly to the east—preventing the Red Army from rebuilding a solid front along the Dvina-Dnepr river lines, fording both river lines, and linking up again behind surviving enemy forces near the city of Smolensk—over 600 kilometers (linear distance) from the start line and for GFM von Bock's Army Group Center the first operational objective of the campaign.

For Guderian's 2 Panzer Group—and all of Army Group Center for that matter—the long road east lay through Belorussia, a poor and relatively primitive region in 1941[38] with its profusion of dilapidated farmsteads and hamlets. The terrain was dissected by numerous rivers and streams, permeated by lakes, bogs, and marshes, and covered with immense tracks of dense, primeval forest of spruce, oak, pine, and birch—terrain features that, together with the paucity of metaled roads and rail lines, would disrupt the rate of advance and pose immense operational and logistical challenges for the German invaders. Indeed, beginning on 22 June, Guderian's panzer divisions would have to navigate the deep belts of forest along the frontier, which, in some cases, stretched for nearly 100 kilometers before yielding to open country.

Yet, as *X-Tag* moved ineluctably closer, Guderian had more immediate concerns on his mind. As described, his panzer group was to cross the Bug River (out of the German-controlled *General-Gouvernement* of Poland) on either side of the town of Brest-Litovsk; however, adjacent to the town was the citadel of Brest-Litovsk, an imposing fortress that dominated one of the panzer group's vital lines of communication (Panzer Route 1) and, thus, needed to be neutralized immediately. Yet, how to accomplish the task? In Guderian's view, it was hardly a mission for his tanks, for the waterways that intersected the fortress, along with its deep, water-filled ditches, rendered the place "immune to tank attack."[39]

The solution was to assign an infantry corps to Guderian's group with the task of assaulting the fortress and protecting the inner flanks of the panzer corps as they traversed the frontier. To this purpose, he turned to his superior, GFM Günther von Kluge, whose Fourth Army abutted *Panzergruppe* 2 on the left and occupied an attack frontage along the meandering Bug River northwest of Brest-Litovsk. Yet the two strong-willed commanders—for personal or professional reasons, or, more likely, both—had developed a rocky relationship. They had clashed first during the Polish campaign and again in France; during the Russian campaign, Guderian's dislike of Kluge would soon burgeon into outright hatred, despite the fact that Kluge would try on several occasions to patch things up, only to be repeatedly rebuffed. In this instance, however, Kluge conceded the logic in furnishing the infantry corps to Guderian, who, in turn, offered to subordinate his panzer group to Fourth Army to ensure unity of command for the initial assault; the offer was accepted.[40]

Thus, for *Barbarossatag*, 2 Panzer Group—again the largest of the four Barbarossa panzer groups—encompassed three panzer and one infantry corps, consisting of about 240,000 men organized in 15.5 divisions (5 panzer divisions, 3 motorized divisions, 6 infantry divisions, 1 cavalry division, and 1 motorized infantry regiment). The three panzer corps were 24 Panzer Corps, commanded by *General der Panzertruppe* Leo Freiherr Geyr von Schweppenburg; 46 Panzer Corps, commanded by *Gen.d.Pz.Tr.* Heinrich von Vietinghoff; and 47 Panzer Corps, led by *Gen.d.Pz.Tr.* Joachim Lemelsen. Collectively, they boasted an aggregate of 994 tanks (among them 57 command tanks) distributed over thirteen tank battalions.[41] The group's 12 Army Corps—assigned the critical mission against the citadel of Brest-Litovsk—was commanded by *General der Infanterie* Walter Schroth. GFM von Bock was generous in assigning general headquarters (GHQ) troops to Guderian's group; these included the following formations, which were distributed among the four corps (for a more detailed breakdown of these GHQ troops, see appendix B).

- Assault Gun Battalions 192 and 201
- 4 105mm cannon battalions
- 1 mixed artillery battalion
- 4 150mm medium howitzer battalions
- 4 210mm heavy howitzer battalions
- 1 210mm heavy howitzer battalion (limited mobility)
- 1 150mm cannon battalion
- 2 *Nebelwerfer* rocket-projector battalions
- 1 *Nebelwerfer* rocket-projector regiment
- Machine Gun Battalion 5
- 3 anti-tank battalions
- 2 flak (*Fla*) battalions
- Flamethrower Tank Battalion 100[42]

Several light and mixed *Luftwaffe* flak battalions were also assigned to the panzer group. Rounding out the GHQ units was a large contingent of engineer troops, including bridge-building, construction, and road-repair battalions. As one of Guderian's biographers observed, "It must have taken considerable effort, as well as all his power of persuasion to acquire [so many GHQ units for his panzer group]."[43]

Providing air support for Guderian's powerful arsenal of men and machines was the *Luftwaffe*'s 2 Air Corps (*II Fliegerkorps*), which included 115 Ju 87B Stuka dive-bombers and a complement of Bf 110 fighter-bombers. *II Fliegerkorps*, commanded by Air General (*General der Flieger*) Bruno Loerzer, was one of the two air corps—the other being 8 Air Corps (*VIII Fliegerkorps*), led by Air General Wolfram Freiherr von Richthofen and assigned to Hoth's *Panzergruppe* 3—that made up GFM Albert Kesselring's 2 Air Fleet (*Luftflotte* 2), responsible for air support to Bock's army group.

COUNTDOWN TO INVASION

By early June 1941, the pressures on German field commanders like Guderian must have been beyond intense as they sought to complete preparations for the enormous undertaking now bearing down on them like a runaway freight train. On 10 June, with the launch of Barbarossa less than two weeks hence, a rattled General Lemelsen (47 PzK) registered the following observations—insightful on so many levels—in his personal diary:

> 10.6.41:
>
> The past days have been very full with work and many worries and troubles. The closer the appointed time approaches, the more nervous everybody becomes. Now, all of a sudden, by order of the Commander-in-Chief of the Army, in our sector the infantry of a 7th wave division is to attack instead of our riflemen! Overturning everything again, now, so close before the appointed time? Impossible!
>
> Very heated exchange with Guderian yesterday in Warsaw. I wish it had already started, this period of suspense is terrible.
>
> The day before yesterday, I was at the front of the sector in extreme heat, a lot of dust, and even more mosquitoes. The Bug is still carrying a lot of water, long stretches are still flooded. The Russian is feverishly fortifying his position; new wire obstacles, anti-tank ditches, and bunkers. It is going to be a very difficult attack. The main thing is that the Bug continues to fall to its normal water level; then we'll do it alright!
>
> The population here is shocking, only Polaks and Jews, and so dirty, miserable, and inferior, it would make you shudder; they now get only 65 grams of bread per person each day, which is, however, enough to starve; it is truly astonishing that people live on that, or better put, can decay on that.

Several days later (15 June), Lemelsen's unbearable suspense came to an abrupt end: "Today the die is cast [*die Würfel sind gefallen*]. That is, the [*X-Tag*] was made known, so now, praise God, there's clarity that it's about to go off. And now we'll all wait feverishly on the day. Hopefully, the dear Lord will send us good weather, nothing as bleak and cold as now."

Two days after that, Lemelsen, on whom so much depended for the success of Guderian's operations, opened up about his turbulent commander:

> 17.6.41:
>
> Yesterday I was at the front of our sector again. The Russian is working feverishly on constructing anti-tank ditches, and if he now has another five days' time, he'll prepare all sorts of other lousy tricks. The Bug, thank God, has fallen further, so that this concern is now eliminated.
>
> Today, the command post of the corps headquarters is being moved forward; I will drive on with the chief of staff and Ia [operations officer] in the early morning, there is still too much to do here. *Generaloberst* Guderian just came by, it's his birthday today and so I had the opportunity of giving him my best wishes; he can, when he is in a good mood, be dreadfully nice and good, but if he gets a rush of blood to the head, then it's all over! [*wenn ihm aber das Blut in den Kopf schießt, ist's aus!*] You have to know him. I admire him a lot even so, because he is a total soldier.[44]

One can only wonder what Guderian must have thought, knowing that, despite the size of his panzer group, he possessed fewer tanks than he had in France in May 1940. Given the seemingly endless spaces of European Russia, he was also acutely aware that his modest forces would have to operate on much larger attack frontages than during the French campaign—attack frontages that would expand dramatically as his tanks drove deeper inside Russia due to the country's pronounced funnel-shaped geography.

On 15 June, following the final Barbarossa conference between Hitler and his eastern generals at the Reich Chancellery, Guderian flew to Warsaw, where his staff was quartered. As he recalled, "The days until the opening of the attack . . . I spent visiting the troops and their jumping-off places and also the neighboring units in order to ensure full cooperation. The march to the assembly areas and the final preparations for the attack passed smoothly enough. On 17 June I examined the course of the River Bug, which was our front line."[45]

For reasons of secrecy, only in the final days before the start of the campaign (18–21 June) did the panzer and motorized divisions of the *Ostheer* lurch into their jump-off positions along or close behind the demarcation line with Soviet Russia. One of these units was 17 Panzer Division, a key component of Guderian's panzer group—a fact apparent from the white "G" emblazoned on the stern of all its tanks and vehicles as a tactical identification sign—which reached its final assembly area in a dense pine forest nearly adjacent to the frontier.

> For two days they had been lying in the dark pinewoods with their tanks and vehicles. They had arrived, driving with masked headlights, during the night of 19/20 June. During the day they lay silent. They must not make a sound. At the mere rattle of a hatch-cover the troop commanders would have fits. Only when

> dusk fell were they allowed to go to the stream in the clearing to wash themselves, a troop at a time. . . . [They] had been moved first to Central Poland and then brought here into the woods of Pratulin. Here they were, [a few kilometers] from the Bug River, which formed the frontier, almost exactly opposite the huge old fortress of Brest-Litovsk, occupied by the Russians since the partition of Poland in the autumn of 1939.
>
> The [panzer] regiment was bivouacking in the forest in full battle order [*kriegsmässig*]. Each tank, moreover, carried 10 jerricans of petrol strapped to its turret and had a trailer in tow with a further three drums. These were the preparations for a long journey, not for swift battle.[46] [As Guderian had assured his panzer troops, "the main thing is to advance far, and to shoot little."]

After months of tireless activity, Guderian could breathe a sigh of relief knowing that the movements of his panzer group up to the Russo-German frontier—movements made mostly at night during this four-day period—had gone off without a hitch. The strategic concentration for Operation Barbarossa was complete.

Also giving Guderian reason for optimism were his final observations about his Russian adversary across the Bug River:

> On the 20th and 21st I visited the forward units of my corps to make sure that all preparations for the attack were satisfactorily completed. Detailed study of the behavior of the Russians convinced me that they knew nothing of our intentions. We had observation of the courtyard of Brest-Litovsk citadel and could see them drilling by platoons to the music of a military band. The strongpoints along their bank of the Bug were unoccupied. They had made scarcely any noticeable progress in strengthening their fortified positions during the past few weeks. So the prospects of our attack achieving surprise were good.[47]

That things were shaping up well for Guderian and his panzer group is also apparent from his final letter home before the invasion to his beloved wife, Margarete (16 June). Gone were the grave doubts about the Russian campaign he had alleged in his memoir, and after noting a "general fear of the mosquito plague" in the east, he wrote, "Aside from that, however, the mood is good everywhere and full of hope, and I think that we'll make it."[48]

Shortly before dawn, 22 June 1941, as the final minutes before the attack slipped away, senior German commanders and staff officers assembled at observation posts across the eastern front. Guderian, having shortly after midnight received the code word *Kyffhäuser* from all his corps, signifying they were ready for action, set out at 0210 hours on that "fateful" (*schicksalschwer*) morning for his forward command post at Hill 158, south of the town of Bohukaly. It was still dark when he arrived there at 0310. Atop the hill, overlooking a bend in the Bug River, was a wooden observation tower—from there, he could make out the lights of the city of Brest-Litovsk, 15 kilometers to the southeast. The formidable citadel just outside the city—its forts and casemates seemingly directed at his front line like an "anchored battleship"—lay in darkness.[49]

In *Hitler Moves East*, the late Paul Carell offers a gripping portrait of *Generaloberst* Guderian's command post on the cusp of war:

> At the foot of Hill 158, in a patch of wood, was the advanced command post of 2 Panzer Group, the brain of Guderian's tank force. . . .
>
> During the preceding night, the night of 20/21 June, the staff officers had arrived in greatest secrecy. They were now sitting in their tents or office buses, bending over maps and written orders. No signals came from the aerials: strict radio silence had been ordered, lest the monitoring posts of the Russians became suspicious. Use of the telephone was permitted only if strictly necessary. Guderian's personal command transport [*Befehlsstaffel*]—two radio vans, some jeeps, and several motorcycles—stood parked behind the tents and buses, well camouflaged. The command tank approached. Guderian jumped out. "Morning gentlemen."
>
> The time was exactly 0310. A few words, then Guderian drove up the hill with his command transport to the observation tower. The luminous minute-hands of their wrist-watches crept round the dials.
>
> 0311 hours. In the tent of the operations staff the telephone jangled. *Oberstleutnant* Bayerlein, the Ia, or chief of operations, picked up the receiver. *Oberstleutnant* Brücker, the chief of operations of 24 Panzer Corps . . . was on the line. Without greetings or formality he said, "Bayerlein, the Koden bridge was all right."
>
> Bayerlein glanced across to Freiherr von Liebenstein, the chief of staff, and nodded. Then he said, "That's fine, Brücker. So long. Good luck." He replaced the receiver.
>
> The bridge at Koden was the kingpin in the rapid tank thrust across the Bug at Brest. An assault troop of 3 Panzer Division had orders to capture it by surprise a few minutes before the start of the operation, to eliminate the Russian bridge guard on the far side, and to remove the explosive charges. The coup had succeeded.[50]

Gen.d.Pz.Tr. Lemelsen had driven down to the Bug River with his escort officer to observe his riflemen and combat engineers in their final assembly areas. GFM von Kluge, C-in-C, Fourth Army, and his staff were in the sector of 31 Infantry Division, also close to Brest-Litovsk and just a few kilometers from the Bug. As Kluge's Chief of Staff, *Oberst* Günther Blumentritt, later recalled, "We watched the German fighter planes take off and soon only their taillights were visible in the east. . . . As [zero hour approached], the sky began to lighten, turning to a curious yellow color. And still all was quiet."[51]

Only hours before, Lemelsen had jotted in his journal, "It is profoundly peaceful everywhere, the cows and horses are in the field, and the *panje*-horses are raking the potatoes, and what will it look like tomorrow morning? The bombs and shells will explode everywhere, and the houses will burn, the residents flee. The contrast is too unreal."[52]

2

The Frontier Battles[1]

The soldiers of the *Ostheer* marked the final days of peace with weapons and equipment checks and routine maintenance; in their few spare moments some played soccer games or took part in equestrian competitions. Panzer and motorized units reconnoitered their approach routes and final assembly areas, which, as much as possible, were sheltered away in wooded areas. Once in their assembly areas, designated assault formations made ready for combat—for instance, by clearing barriers and obstacles, such as barbed wire entanglements, along their respective attack frontages. Radio silence was strictly enforced by all units; ammunition was quietly brought forward, and extra containers of fuel were hung on tanks and vehicles. Artillery and other heavy weapons were shepherded into their firing positions. Telephone wire was laid between the gun batteries and the forward observation posts. Dr. Alfred Opitz, then a thirty-year-old *Obergefreiter* in 18 Panzer Division (47 PzK), recalled after the war, "On 21 June, the noise of motors and vehicles began to roar and drone in the broad extent of forest to our rear. Tanks and heavy artillery seemed to be moving up from there. Now and then, a reconnaissance aircraft circled over the river terrain. The air was thick enough to stifle; it smelled of something horrendous."[2]

Last-minute reconnaissance of terrain and enemy forces beyond the frontier was carried out, some of the reconnaissance teams furtively inspecting border regions disguised as local hunters and farmers, even carrying farm implements to complete the deception. Liaison was established with supporting combat and combat-support units; frontline commanders were briefed on their missions. In the final hours, chocolate and cigarettes were distributed to troops, some of whom were fortunate enough to receive an allotment of schnapps, one bottle per four men.

It was not until these final hours of peace that most of the three million men poised along the frontier from the Baltic to the Black Sea learned what their mission was to be—a surprise attack on the Soviet Union. Their commanders, by the "dim illumination of shielded flashlights,"[3] read out to them Hitler's historic proclamation, ending weeks and months of agonizing uncertainty—and more than a few outlandish rumors—about what the future held in store. The proclamation began and ended with the following passages:

> *Soldaten der Ostfront!*
>
> Troubled by deep concerns, condemned to months of silence, the hour has finally arrived in which I may speak to you, my soldiers, openly. . . .
>
> At this very moment, Soldiers of the Eastern Front, a concentration of forces is underway which, in its extent and scope, is the largest the world has ever seen. . . . When this greatest front of world history now advances, then it will not only be to secure the conditions for the final conclusion of this great war in general, or to protect those countries affected at this moment, but rather to save the entire European civilization and culture.
>
> German soldiers! You are thus entering into a struggle that is both difficult and laden with responsibility. For:
>
> The fate of Europe, the future of the German Reich, the existence of our *Volk* now lie in your hands alone.
>
> May the Lord God aid us all in this struggle!
>
> Adolf Hitler
>
> Führer and Supreme Commander of the *Wehrmacht*[4]

The night of 21/22 June was dark, with only a "faint crescent of the waning moon."[5] Concealed in forests, farmsteads, and fields along the frontier, the *Soldaten der Ostfront* waited. Heavily armed and equipped, their weapons ready to fire (*schussbereit*), their hand grenades armed, taking their last, slow draws on their cigarettes, they waited—waited in growing and almost unbearable tension as the final hours, minutes, seconds ticked irretrievably away. Last-minute preparations kept many of the men busy, and few but the most seasoned veterans were able to snatch a few hours of sleep before the "big show" began. What, they wondered, would they encounter beyond the border? Were the Russians waiting for them? Or were they still largely in the dark about the firestorm about to break over them—about the hecatombs of Red Army dead (and their own, had only they known it) that were to follow in its wake?

THE WAR BEGINS

Shortly after 0300 hours, thousands of German guns, ranging from super-heavy rail-borne artillery to light and medium howitzers and infantry mortars, unleashed a storm of steel shattering the morning calm along the 1,800-kilometer front. As the first slivers of light peeked tentatively over the horizon, the initial wave of more than three million German soldiers swept across the Russo-German frontier from Memel' on the Baltic coast south to the Hungarian border. Overhead, squadrons of *Luftwaffe* bombers struck towns and cities as far afield as Sevastopol', Kiev, Minsk, Kronstadt, and the Baltic ports of Tallin and Riga, while dive-bomber, ground-attack, and fighter aircraft obliterated dozens of forward Soviet airfields and destroyed hundreds of Red Army planes on the ground. The *Luftwaffe* also targeted ammunition and fuel depots, fortifications, barracks, bunkers, artillery positions, and Red Army headquarters.

All three German army groups achieved tactical surprise along their respective attack frontages. Within hours, German assault detachments had captured intact every bridge across all the border rivers. "Everything began according to plan [*Alles tritt planmässig zum Angriff an*]," noted GFM von Bock in his personal diary. "Strangely [*Merkwürdigerweise*] the Russians didn't blow a single one of the existing Bug bridges. . . . It is striking that nowhere have they shown noteworthy artillery, apart from northwest of Grodno against 8 Army Corps. Our *Luftwaffe* is apparently far superior [*turmhoch überlegen*] to the Russian's."[6]

Dazed and disoriented, many Red Army troops were caught unprepared in their camps and barracks. Yet, if Soviet resistance was at first surprisingly light, the German *Ostheer*, despite achieving massively superior force ratios at the key points of attack, on more than a few occasions encountered effective, even fanatical Red Army resistance on this first day of the war; in fact, some NKVD border units and troops assigned to local fortified regions fought to the last man—a harbinger of what was to come in the days and months ahead.

For Guderian's 2 Panzer Group, the war began at 0315 hours with an artillery barrage of thirty minutes duration.[7] Along the front of Lemelsen's 47 Panzer Corps, northwest of Brest-Litovsk, 18 Panzer Division (fifty batteries, all calibers) blasted enemy positions and put down a protective smoke screen. "At exactly 0310," wrote Heinz Döll, an officer in the division, "we were ready to fire. Somewhat restively I followed the minute and second hands of my watch until the firing order came. At 0315 a lightning bolt of gigantic dimensions tore through the night. Thousands of artillery pieces shattered the silence. I will never forget those seconds. But just what they signified for the world, for Germany—that was beyond comprehension."[8] To 18 PD's immediate left, 17 Panzer Division opened fire with 240 guns, striking known Soviet field positions, bunkers, and observation towers. The 10 Panzer Division (46 PzK), held in reserve, did not take part in the opening assault; its artillery batteries, however, were posted to 18 Panzer for the opening barrage. A history of 10 PD, published by its veterans' organization (*Traditionsgemeinschaft*) in 1993, offers insight into the complex preparations for the artillery barrage, before describing the barrage itself:

> In the late afternoon of 21.6.[41], the observation posts are manned, the computing units [*Rechentrupps*] move into the firing positions. When evening falls, the

Führer's proclamation is read out, which begins with the words: "Soldaten der Ostfront!" And suddenly all the guessing games that had been going on are at an end, everybody knows that the weapons will be doing the talking once again. . . .

Weather reports, known as "Barbara Reports" by the artillerymen, have been coming in every two hours since evening at the batteries' computing section posts. The trajectory of the shells is, of course, influenced by various factors, such as temperature, air pressure, humidity, wind direction, and wind force. When firing blind, these variables have to be taken into account, and so every two hours the computing units calculate all the firing commands for the planned barrage [*Feuerschlag*] anew. And then the X-hour is announced: 22.6., 0315 hours!

At 0300 hours, the firing commands are adjusted for the last time, there is nothing more for the computing units to do. The guns are aimed and loaded, the battery officers have the handset of a field telephone to their ear; they look at their watches. The artillery commander has reserved for himself the order to open fire. Over on the horizon, a pale light, just a narrow sliver, is very weakly discernable. A quiet shiver, more like a thrill, takes hold of the soldiers standing in the night. The battery officer repeats the words that are coming out of the telephone: "10 minutes more."—"5 minutes more."—"1 more minute."—"30 seconds more."—"15 seconds more,—and 10 seconds,—8, 7, 6, 5, 4—battery . . ." He raises his arm and thrusts it down, the command "Fire!" erupts from his mouth like thunder and lightning—a single bolt of lightning flashes across the whole sky, a deafening crash tears through the silence. And then shell after shell speeds across the Bug, rising to a drumfire [*Trommelfeuer*] due to the sheer numbers of batteries standing to the left and right.

Over there, a wall of dense smoke and dust rises sluggishly, blotting out the pale slivers on the horizon. Then suddenly German rocket projector batteries [*Werferbatterien*] join the fray: howling and whining, whole series of rockets with long trails of fire and smoke sweep across into the inferno. The first rays of sun light up the edges of the clouds and the wall of smoke in a bloody red. And with the first light come the Stukas, seeking out their targets, positioning themselves in a row, circling and plunging earthward, dropping their bombs and pulling up again. And behind them, black smoke pours up into the sky again. . . .

When day has come and the rolling barrage [*Feuerwalze*] has ended at the limit of the artillery's range, as the gunners from 90 Artillery Regiment collect the empty cartridges and the ammunition boxes and the sounds of combat across the advancing front rumble like a receding storm, suddenly Russian bombers appear above the German positions, approaching in strict formation, as if on maneuvers.[9]

German fighters, Messerschmitt Bf 109s from the airfield at Biala Podlaska, rose to intercept the enemy bombers. Pouncing on their prey from behind, the nimble Bf 109s fired short bursts from their 20mm cannon. One of the intruders was soon hit and plunged earthward, trailing thick plumes of smoke in its wake; then, a second bomber went into a spin and broke apart in midair. None of the Russian bombers made it to their objective.[10]

At no point on the eastern front was the initial bombardment more intense than against the citadel of Brest-Litovsk, where the Germans unleashed a veritable whirlwind of fire—the progressive stages of the intricate fire plan incongruously named after flowers ("Anemone," "Crocus," "Narcissus," etc.).[11] Rudolf Gschöpf, a chaplain in 45 Infantry Division, likened the shelling of the fortress to a "hurricane," which "broke loose and roared over our heads, the likes of which we had never experienced before and never would again."[12] To *Leutnant* Erich Bunke (31 ID), it was as if the "jaws of hell" had opened, while the thousands of shells arcing across the dawn sky made the "air vibrate."[13] War correspondent Gerd Habedanck noted the "strong [drafts] of air [that] blew into our faces" and that "young willows were bent over as if in a storm."[14] Walther Loos (45 ID) recalled the "thunder and howling of wailing shells," ranging from the smallest to the largest caliber, as they passed overhead and streaked toward their targets on the opposite bank of the river: "Involuntarily ducking our heads, we were almost forgetting to breathe. However, a second later the artillery fire of a different heavy gun gathered such a deafening and breath-taking strength like I never experienced later. Even those participants in the First World War among us later acknowledged that at that time, they had never experienced fire of such concentrated power. The sky turned red, and even though it was night, it became as light as day."[15]

The immense artillery fire unleashed by 2 Panzer Group across its front—supported by Kesselring's air fleet—crippled Red Army command and control, adversely affecting Soviet response times even if they managed to emerge from their shelters and dugouts unscathed. After pummeling its initial targets with sustained fire, the German artillery shifted its fire farther downrange, while continuing to lay down a protective screen for the advancing assault troops.

Eschewing tactical intricacies, Guderian's attack simply slammed headlong into the center of Lt.-Gen. A. A. Korobkov's 4 Army. In the sector of the panzer group, where the frontier meandered along the Bug, assault formations of infantry and combat engineers plunged into the river in rubber dinghies or assault boats (*Sturmbooten*). Echeloned in depth, the spearheads of 24 and 47 Panzer Corps crossed the river barrier on both sides of Brest-Litovsk, while in the center of Guderian's line, 12 Army Corps launched a furious assault on the Brest fortress. Contrary to expectations, the initial attack met only minor resistance, and, in some cases, there was no resistance at all—"something to which officers like [the] Fourth Army Ic (Intelligence Officer) at Miedzyrzec, *Major* Erich Helmdach, could attest having been briefed on recent Army Group Center listening reports (*Horchmeldungen*) from monitored enemy communications."[16]

The tanks and mobile infantry of 2 Panzer Group were soon rolling across the captured Bug bridges. At other points along the river (there were no bridges in the sector of Lemelsen's 47 PzK) combat engineers labored furiously to build additional bridges to shepherd troops, weapons, vehicles, and equipment to the far bank. In some instances, weapons and equipment were ferried across the Bug, while in the sector of 18 Panzer Division a battalion of amphibious tanks (*Tauchpanzer*) plunged right through the four-meter-deep river and crawled up the eastern bank. The special tanks, originally intended for Operation Sealion (the canceled invasion of Britain), had all openings sealed and were outfitted with air intakes and exhaust snorkel pipes.[17]

24 PANZER CORPS (22.6.1941)

South of Brest-Litovsk, Geyr's 24 Panzer Corps put in its main assault with 3 and 4 Panzer Divisions, holding its 10 Motorized Infantry Division in reserve. Led by *Generalleutnant* Walter Model, 3 PD possessed a total of 215 tanks (110 Pz IIIs and 32 Pz IVs), while *Generalmajor* Willibald Freiherr von Langermann-Erlencamp's 4 PD boasted a complement of 177 tanks (105 Pz IIIs and 20 Pz IVs). Both divisions would rapidly slip past the enemy border defenses from the area about Koden and begin to drive on Minsk, several hundred kilometers to the east—4 PD on the route designated as Panzer Route 1 (*Panzerstrasse* 1), which led via Kobrin and Slutsk to Bobruisk; 3 PD (initially at least) along a parallel track to the north. For 22 June—*Barbarossatag*—Geyr urged his panzer troops on with the slogan "Through and forward" (*Durch und vorwärts*).[18]

In the sector of 4 Panzer Division, on the far right wing of Guderian's panzer group, the first wave of the division's rifle brigade (*Schützenbrigade*) crossed the Bug at 0330 hours on pneumatic boats, meeting no enemy resistance; they were quickly followed by the forward observers of the division's artillery regiment, while pneumatic ferries shepherded the first heavy weapons (including a light artillery battery) and a handful of motor vehicles across the river. The weather was clear and fine and the terrain (on the northern edge of the Pripiat' Marshes) mostly flat, though covered with wooded areas and heavy undergrowth and crossed by watercourses and swamplands; the few villages in the region were poor and dilapidated. Recalled Hans Schäufler, a signal officer in 4 PD, "The first assault detachments crossed in assault boats and rafts. At 0400 hours, we moved to a staging area in a patch of woods right on the river [Bug]. The resistance across the way was slight. At 1200 hours, we crossed the river on pontoon ferries with our radio vehicles. . . . Our vehicles wormed their way through the knee-deep sand of the Bug lowlands. The civilians, former Poles, were very friendly. They cooked eggs and milk for us."[19]

The war also began well for Model's 3 Panzer Division. Meeting only desultory defensive fire, after just a few hours the division's assault teams had cleared the east bank of the Bug, and after neutralizing a series of enemy bunkers, infantry of 3 PD's two rifle regiments secured their first objective—the border village of Stradecz, defended to the last man by a badly overmatched Soviet rifle division.[20]

By 1000 hours, the situation was well enough in hand that the main body of the division's tanks could begin to cross the Koden bridge (captured, it will be recalled, in a coup de main just minutes before the start of Barbarossa).

At 0935 hours, the divisional war diary noted that enemy resistance was still "very weak." (*Feindeindruck: Bisher sehr schwacher Feind.*)[21] Within an hour, however, the division had run into serious difficulties—not as a result of enemy action but due to the massive vehicle congestion caused by "catastrophic road conditions" along the division's route of advance (*Vormarschweg*). Simply put, vehicles were becoming stuck in a swamp, making it impossible to continue on the planned road route. Model hastened to the site of the stoppage, only to have his vehicle get stuck as well. After conferring with Geyr, he ordered his troops (1500 hours) "to turn to the right" and use Panzer Route 1 for its further advance; in doing so, 3 PD managed to reach the *Panzerstrasse* before the spearheads of 4 PD. In any case, both panzer divisions were, by mid-afternoon, prepared to follow each other on the same route.

By now, the *Kampfgruppen* of 3 Panzer Division had begun to engage the Red Army forces in their path. These included "disorganized bits and pieces" of 6 and 42 Rifle Divisions of Maj.-Gen. V. S. Popov's 28 Rifle Corps. Popov's men struggled to organize a defense under the worst possible conditions:

> Poorly trained to begin with, both divisions had been maintained at reduced manning levels and had recently been deprived of much of their field artillery. These men had not been at a high level of alert when the German bombardment started, and the efforts of their commanders to turn them out of their barracks into prepared defensive positions were hindered not only by enemy artillery but also by swarms of *Luftwaffe* fighter-bombers appearing with the dawn. When the main bodies of the divisions of the 24 and 47 Panzer Corps hit them, "the Russian defenses might have been a row of glass houses," observed one German lieutenant.[22]

Having dispensed with Soviet border defenses along its attack frontage, the vanguard of Model's 3 Panzer Division pressed on for the town of Kobrin. In a matter of hours, Model's division, along with 4 Panzer Division on its right and Lemelsen's (47 PzK) two panzer divisions on its left, had ripped a 50-kilometer gap in the front of Korobkov's 4 Army. In a desperate attempt to push back the rampaging panzers, the two tank divisions of Soviet 14 Mechanized Corps (22 and 30 Tank Divisions) began to strike at the spearheads of Guderian's armor. Commanded by Maj.-Gen. S. I. Oborin, the recently formed 14 Mechanized Corps was badly understrength, having begun the day with less than 500 tanks, virtually all of them obsolete T-26 light tanks;[23] moreover, some of the tanks were armed with no more than a machine gun and, in general, suffered from a paucity of armor-piercing ammunition and spare parts.[24] Seriously complicating matters was the fact that Oborin's command post had been bombed by the *Luftwaffe* at 0500, knocking out communication links, while the opening German artillery barrage and aerial assault had produced 20 percent casualties in 22 Tank Division and demolished much of the division's ammunition, fuel stockpiles, and artillery.

When the Soviet 22 TD finally collided with Model's panzers, the results were thus foreordained. In the ensuing encounters—in some cases, Soviet tanks simply tried to slip past their tormentors and escape to the east[25]—the armor of Maj.-Gen. V. P. Puganov's 22 Tank Division was systematically dismantled by Model's superbly trained and experienced tank crews supported by waves of Stuka dive-bombers, transfiguring the division's unwieldy march columns (which had no anti-aircraft protection) into "long strings of blazing wrecks" along the few roads to the east of Brest. By day's end, 22 TD had lost almost half its tanks and was low on ammunition and fuel; the next day, its commander would be killed trying to launch a counterattack.

Despite being slowed by traffic congestion and road conditions—which, it seems, were not much better on Panzer Route 1—by late afternoon, advance elements of 3 PD had motored well beyond the Bug and were closing on Kobrin. In its evening report to 24 Panzer Corps HQ, 3 PD observed that the challenges of navigating the swampy, sandy terrain had posed a greater hardship than had opposition from the enemy.[26]

47 PANZER CORPS (22.6.1941)

Forming the left wing of Guderian's panzer group, Lemelsen's 47 Panzer Corps put in its attack astride the town of Pratulin (northwest of Brest-Litovsk)—its 18 Panzer Division advancing on the right and 17 Panzer Division on the left (29 Motorized Division was in reserve). The 18 PD was well equipped with 218 tanks (114 Pz IIIs, 36 Pz IVs)—its commander, *Generalmajor* Walther K. Nehring, an international expert on armored warfare who had collaborated closely with Guderian and others in the 1930s to develop tactical blitzkrieg theory and create the German panzer arm. *Generalleutnant* Hans-Jürgen von Arnim's 17 PD began operations with a complement of 202 tanks (106 Pz IIIs, 30 Pz IVs). As noted, along the front of 47 Panzer Corps there were no Bug bridges; corps engineers would have to build them. That meant that Lemelsen's two panzer divisions would need to rapidly develop a deep bridgehead—one robust enough to repel any Soviet attempt to crush it before the bulk of the corps' armor had been committed to the drive east. The main axis of advance was to be along Panzer Route 2 (*Panzerstrasse* 2), "an arbitrary link between the towns of Pruzhany, Slonim, and Minsk. Guderian's main effort was here."[27]

At 0315 hours, in the "last shadows of the night," the first waves of assault troops, beneath a protective umbrella of artillery fire and smoke screens, shot across the Bug River in rubber rafts and assault boats. Less than thirty minutes later, the first Ju 87B Stukas appeared above the battlefield, their sirens howling as they plunged at steep angles toward their targets below. Before Barbarossa was an hour old, lead elements of 17 and 18 PDs were firmly lodged on the eastern bank, armed with weapons that included light anti-tank guns and heavy machine guns. Some Russian pickets opened up with automatic rifles and light machine guns but were soon silenced. Hitherto, the German assault parties had come upon no enemy artillery fire. While the Germans dug in, "everything that could be pumped into the bridgehead was ferried across. The sappers at once got down to building a pontoon bridge."[28] In his personal diary, Erich Hager, a tank radio operator in 17 Panzer Division, recorded his initial observations as the attack got underway:

> [0315] our artillery fire begins. A mighty display of firepower. We are standing ready for attack. However, the Russians skedaddle. At midday we come to the Bug, stand for an hour at the bridge, which has been built. See my first air battle. 8 bombers were shot down by our aircraft. Awful to watch. Crossed the Bug. We come to the first of our dead. Snipers were the culprits? Wounded Russians are still lying here. Password is drive and keep driving. All through the day and night.[29]

At 0443 hours,[30] the first of the eighty amphibious tanks (Pz IIIs and IVs) of Nehring's 18 PD dipped into the Bug and disappeared underwater, betrayed only by a trail of bubbles and a snorkel air intake. The specter of "swimming tanks" created a sensation of sorts and, in one instance at least, more than a modicum of skepticism: "The artillerymen told me about an unbelievable experience," marveled an officer in 18 Panzer. "At our crossing point, they said, tanks dived into the Bug like U-boats and then reappeared on the east bank. Must be pretty strong tobacco that they're smoking, I thought to myself, but it was true."[31]

> Tank after tank—the whole of 1st Battalion, 18 Panzer Regiment, under the battalion commander, Manfred Graf Strachwitz—dived into the river. And now the first ones were crawling up the far bank like mysterious amphibians. A soft plop and the rubber caps were blown off the gun muzzles. The gun-loaders let the air out of the bicycle inner tubes round the turrets. Turret hatches were flung open and the skippers wriggled out. An arm thrust into the air three times: the signal "Tanks forward."
>
> Eighty tanks had crossed the frontier river underwater. Eighty tanks were moving into action.[32]

Oberstleutnant Strachwitz's panzers reached the far bank just in time to chase off a clutch of Soviet armored cars, knocking out several. Wasting no time, General Nehring mounted one of the assault boats of his combat engineers and crossed the river. After the vehicles of his tactical headquarters—the general's

APC command vehicle, two Pz III command tanks, two self-propelled flak guns, some thirty motorcycles, and so forth[33]—had been shepherded across on pontoon ferries, Nehring, accompanied by several of his staff and Graf Strachwitz, joined his tanks as they began their advance. Commencing their "panzer raid" into Russia, they headed northeast toward Pruzhany, far outpacing the wheeled components of the division.

At 0650 hours, Guderian crossed the Bug in an assault boat in the vicinity of Kolodno; as soon as his command car and two armored wireless trucks had been ferried into the bridgehead, he struck out for Nehring's vanguard: "I began by following the tank tracks of 18 Panzer Division and soon reached the bridge over the Lesna, whose capture was important for the advance of 47 Panzer Corps; there I found nobody except some Russian pickets. The Russians took to their heels when they saw my vehicles. Two of my orderly officers set off after them, against my wishes; unfortunately they both lost their lives as a result."[34]

As recorded in the *Kriegstagebuch* (war diary) of 2 Panzer Group at 0800, both 17 and 18 PDs were making good progress. At 1025, the leading tank company of 18 PD reached the Lesna River 10 kilometers north of Brest-Litovsk and crossed on the still intact bridge. With Guderian in tow, Nehring's tanks rolled on down Panzer Route 2 and, without regard for their flanks—and ignoring the fact that the mass of the division's armor was still well to the rear—continued their pursuit of the badly shaken enemy. It was a textbook case of blitzkrieg in action.

Across the front of 2 Panzer Group, nine bridges were in use by midday, three of them newly constructed by engineers, which enabled the tanks of 47 Panzer Corps to achieve significant gains on this first day of the war. In his diary, Lemelsen recorded his satisfaction with the opening act of the campaign:

> It was certainly a pretty grand experience, that start to the attack. . . . At 0315 hours precisely . . . the hellish concert of the artillery let rip and, at the same time, the riflemen plunged into the water with pneumatic boats and made the crossing with those and assault boats. Contrary to expectations, the reaction of the enemy was extremely limited, which meant that construction of the bridge could start very quickly; astonishingly, neither did enemy artillery open up nor did their planes drop bombs. All the bunkers that had been located through weeks of observation were incomplete and unmanned. The greatest difficulties were caused by the very wet terrain on the other side of the Bug before you could get to a solid pathway. I soon crossed over the river in my command tank and accompanied the forward elements of 18 Panzer Division. Then we went inexorably onward along the Bug, at first straight to the east—the enemy had not thought of that—and then to the northeast across the Lesna. All the bridges were intact—our greatest concern—a sign that the Russians had been taken completely by surprise.[35]

If *Gen.d.Pz.Tr.* Lemelsen was delighted by the results of the first few hours of the campaign, the same can hardly be said of Col. L. M. Sandalov, Chief of Staff to Soviet 4 Army. Like his commanding officer, Lt.-Gen. Korobkov, he had spent the days and weeks before 22 June refusing to believe that his country was about to go to war. Even after the bombs began to fall, he clung to the conceit that war could somehow still be avoided: "Yes, until the last moment you and I didn't believe it. Until we saw with our own eyes the ruins of the building that housed the army's headquarters, until we heard about the death of people close to us, everyone continued to hope that this still isn't war. We readily believed that some kind of hostile forces had cooked up an unheard of provocation and that if we didn't give in to it, then we could avoid war."[36]

At some point during the day, Colonel Sandalov drove out to the front and observed with his own eyes the debacle unfolding at the frontier:

> The railroad tracks at Zhabinka station were clogged with rail cars smashed and burned by the enemy's aviation and the station was destroyed. An artillery cannonade could be heard from the direction of Brest. Enemy planes unceasingly strafing the troops who were hurriedly outfitting a new defensive line around Zhabinka [on the Muchaviec River]. Lines of civilian population moving to the rear stretched along all the roads and paths. From time to time uncoordinated groups of military personnel and even small subunits would appear on the roads. Blocking detachments would stop them and send them to the nearest units of the 28 Rifle Corps. . . .
>
> Having set out on the Warsaw highway, I was constantly forced to pass individual cars and columns of trucks with belongings being evacuated from Brest. . . . From time to time we came across groups of freshly mobilized citizens, accompanied by representatives of the military commissariats. But there were a lot more refugees—men, women, and children. They all had bundles, knapsacks and bags. Deathly tired, with sorrowfully sunken faces, they silently moved toward Kobrin, hiding under the trees and in the bushes from the enemy air force.[37]

The tanks and motorcycle riflemen at the forefront of Nehring's assault had soon seized their next geographical objective—the village of Vidoml'. It was now that the tank regiments of Soviet 30 Tank Division (14 Mechanized Corps) debouched from the woods southwest of Pruzhany and moved out to attack. Once again, the hapless Soviet armor was no match for the German tank crews and the dogged and repeated sorties of Kesselring's bombers; by late afternoon (1730 hours), the war diary of 18 PD had registered the destruction of thirty-six Red Army tanks.[38] After several hours of fighting, Maj.-Gen. S. I. Oborin, Commander, Soviet 14 Mechanized Corps, decided to break off the uneven contest, issuing orders for the attack to be resumed early the next morning with all three divisions of his badly battered corps.

FORTRESS OF BREST-LITOVSK (22.6.1941)

While Guderian's two forward panzer corps raced across the frontier on either flank (46 Panzer Corps began the campaign in reserve), in the center of his front *Gen.d.Inf.* Walter Schroth's 12 Army Corps (31, 34, 45 IDs) was engaged in a merciless struggle for the fortress of Brest-Litovsk. The Germans had hoped to seize the fortress in a coup de main but would be bitterly disappointed by the outcome of the day's fighting.

The task of taking the fortress was assigned to Schroth's mostly Austrian 45 Infantry Division, commanded by *Generalmajor* Fritz Schlieper. In addition, 45 ID was to capture the four-span railway bridge over the Bug (and directly northwest of the citadel) and the five bridges spanning the Muchaviec south of the town of Brest while securing the high ground just beyond the town. If successful, this would clear the way for the advance of Guderian's tanks along *Panzerstrasse* 1, the route assigned to his 24 Panzer Corps.

With German *Wochenschau* newsreel cameramen on hand to film the spectacle, the attack commenced at precisely 0315 hours. Opening up on the citadel in a short preparatory barrage were the nine light and three medium batteries of 45 ID, along with nine 210mm heavy howitzers, two mighty 600mm "Karl" siege guns, and the 4 Rocket Projector Regiment, whose nine *Nebelwerfer* batteries dropped 2,880 missiles on the fortress in rapid succession. Artillery of the neighboring 34 and 31 Infantry Divisions (12 Army Corps) also contributed to the fire plan.

Following the initial *Feuerschlag*, swarms of Stuka dive-bombers appeared above the fortress, plunging earthward and disgorging their bombs. German combat engineers and infantry emerged from the thickets lining the Bug, crossed the river in rubber dinghies and assault boats, and began their assault on the citadel. The combat teams of 45 ID methodically bit their way into the fortress, which sat at the confluence of the Bug and Muchaviec Rivers, whose waters had been used to form four partly natural and partly artificial islands studded with strongpoints of all kinds (hundreds of casemate and cellar positions, armored cupolas, dug-in tanks, bastions or old casement forts complete with towers, etc.), all deftly concealed in thick undergrowth and clumps of tall trees. Even the barracks were reinforced with walls 1.5 meters thick that could withstand fire from all but the heaviest-caliber artillery.[39]

Despite such challenges, the initial German attack brought encouraging results. On the northern axis, assault parties secured the vital railway bridge in less than fifteen minutes. German armored cars began to roll across immediately and, by 0415 hours, assault guns of the neighboring 31 ID were also crossing the bridge. Progress against the citadel itself also appeared to be good, with the attacking battalions forcing their way deep into the fortress in some locations. Both 12 AK and 45 ID were encouraged by the early results, with the latter reporting at 0625 hours that "the division believes it will soon have the citadel firmly in hand."[40]

Then the "worm began to turn." By 0730 hours, Schlieper's 45 ID was reporting that strong elements of the garrison were now firing from behind on the forwardmost German units. The assault detachments, scattered among the bushes, trees, buildings, and ruins of the fortress, had become so enmeshed among its defenders that artillery support was no longer possible. Soviet sharpshooters concealed in trees or firing from rooftop outlets began to take a heavy toll, particularly on German officers and NCOs. Others fired at the Germans from buildings, cellars, or sewers, even while hidden in garbage cans or behind piles of rags. Among the officers of 45 ID to perish this day were three battalion commanders.[41]

Faced with furious Russian resistance, by midday Schlieper decided to withdraw his battered assault units from the fortress under cover of darkness; the Russian garrison was to be tightly encircled and reduced by artillery fire. Early that evening, GFM von Kluge (Fourth Army) arrived at the CP of 45 ID. He confirmed Schlieper's decision, pointing out that the fighting for the fortress was now of only local significance, for the key bridges had all been captured, and traffic across the railway and along Panzer Route 1 was now possible. Unnecessary losses were to be avoided; the enemy, Kluge ordered, starved into submission. The bitter and bloody fighting had cost 45 ID 311 dead—21 officers and 290 NCOs and enlisted men—perhaps greater losses than those sustained by any other division of the *Ostheer* on 22 June 1941.[42]

In a publication released by the German Armed Forces High Command (OKW) in 1943, a participant in the fighting for the fortress of Brest-Litovsk on 22 June 1941 recorded his initial impressions of the Red Army soldier:

> The battles on the islands extremely difficult. Complex terrain: groups of houses, clusters of trees, bushes, narrow strips of water, plus the ruins, and the enemy is everywhere. His snipers are excellently camouflaged in the trees. Camouflage suits made of gauze with leaves attached to them. Superb snipers! Shooting from hatches in the ground, basement windows, sewage pipes. . . .
>
> First impression: the Bolshevist fights to his very last breath. Perhaps because of the threat of the commissars: those who fall into German captivity are shot. (According to statements by the first prisoners.) At any rate: no slackening of fighting power, even though resistance futile since citadel is surrounded.
>
> Silent night. We dig the first graves.[43]

Organized resistance from surviving Soviet soldiers inside the citadel would not be broken until the end of the month.

BARBAROSSATAG: A BRIEF ASSESSMENT

We recall that Guderian had crossed the Bug River early in the morning and, along with his command staff, had begun his fateful odyssey into Soviet Russia. Upon making contact with Nehring, Guderian accompanied his trusted subordinate and lead elements of 18 Panzer Division until mid-afternoon. At 1630, "I returned to the bridgehead at Kolodno and from there I went at 1830 hours to my command post. We had managed to take the enemy by surprise all along the entire panzer group front. . . . The enemy, however, soon recovered from his initial surprise and put up a tough defense in his prepared positions. The important citadel of Brest-Litovsk held out with remarkable stubbornness for several days."[44]

By day's end, as darkness enveloped the battlefield, Guderian could look back with satisfaction on the day's results. Despite failure to seize the Brest fortress, the spearheads of his panzer group, supported by the Bf 109 fighters and Stuka dive-bombers of 2 Air Corps, had shattered Soviet 4 Army and were well beyond the frontier. The lead tanks of 3 Panzer Division (24 PzK) were approaching Kobrin, more than 30 kilometers beyond the border; on Guderian's left wing, 18 Panzer Division (47 PzK), chasing down *Panzerstrasse* 2, was only 20 kilometers southwest of Pruzhany, which would be seized the next day.[45]

On the left wing of Army Group Center, Hermann Hoth's *Panzergruppe* 3 had also torn a gaping hole in the Soviet defenses; together, Hoth and Guderian had inaugurated the envelopment of Soviet Western Front in eastern Poland and Belorussia. Moreover, with 2 Air Fleet destroying more than 900 Red Army aircraft (most of them on their airfields), the *Luftwaffe* had gained air superiority in the sector of Bock's army group.

Generaloberst Franz Halder, Chief of the German Army General Staff—and, like Bock and Guderian, no doubt pleased by the outcome of *Barbarossatag*—noted in his private diary that the enemy had been surprised by the German attack:

> His forces were not in tactical disposition for defense. The troops in the border zone were widely scattered in their quarters. The frontier itself was for the most part weakly guarded. As a result of this tactical surprise, enemy resistance directly on the border was weak and disorganized, and we succeeded everywhere in seizing the bridges across the border rivers and in piercing the defense positions (field fortifications) near the frontier. . . . Our divisions on the entire offensive front have forced back the enemy on an average of 10 to 12 km. This has opened a path for the armor.[46]

Halder went on to point out (quite correctly), "After the first shock, the enemy has turned to fight. There have been instances of tactical withdrawals and no doubt also disorderly retreats, but there are no indications of an attempted operational disengagement. Such a possibility," he insisted, "can moreover be discounted. . . . The [Soviet] command organization is too ponderous to effect swift operational regrouping in reaction to our attack, and so the Russians will have to accept battle in the dispositions in which they were deployed."[47]

Finally, while noting that Guderian's right wing (Geyr) "was for a time held up in difficult wooded terrain"—a situation that Halder believed "could have been avoided"—he also concluded from this first day's action that Guderian's left wing (Lemelsen) "has pierced the opposing enemy forces and has gained operational freedom of movement." The two coming days, he submitted, "will show in what way Guderian can dispose of the enemy motorized forces around Minsk. Once they are beaten, the operational success of this armored group is assured."[48] And beaten they would be, in an encirclement battle of historic dimensions.

THE MINSK CAULDRON BATTLE (THROUGH 9.7.1941)

Following the breakthroughs along the frontier, the pace of Guderian's and Hoth's operations was so rapid, the chaos and disruption visited upon Army-Gen. D. G. Pavlov's Western Front so great, that command and control of his armies collapsed from the outset. Unable to function on a level even approaching the lightning tempo of the *Panzergruppen*, Soviet field commanders reacted sluggishly and ineffectively along the key axes of the German advance.[49] To make matters worse, little in the way of support could be expected from the Soviet dictator, Joseph Stalin, or the Soviet High Command, for with communications badly disrupted by the *Luftwaffe* and sabotaged by German special forces (Regiment 800, the so-called *Brandenburgers*), they were dangerously uninformed about the situation at the front (and would remain so for several days).

Ignoring Soviet units on their flanks, Guderian's tanks struck out, rapier-like, along two axes—to the northeast toward Minsk (47 PzK) and due east toward the Berezina (24 PzK). The detailed situation maps, prepared daily by the Operations Branch of the German Army General Staff, show his panzer divisions—represented by blue ellipses—rapidly slipping around the southern flank of Soviet Western Front and beginning to forge one arm of the larger outer encirclement ring (a second, smaller pocket would be formed farther west, between Belostok and Mosty, by the infantry of Kluge's Fourth and Adolf Strauss's Ninth Armies).

On 23 June, Lemelsen's 47 Panzer Corps, brushing aside the remnants of Soviet 14 Mechanized Corps, advanced on Baranovichi, nearly 200 kilometers beyond the frontier (linear distance). Farther south, Geyr's 24 Panzer Corps shattered Red Army resistance west of Kobrin and drove the defending Soviet task force from the city. The already badly mauled 14 Mechanized Corps, the armored reserve of Soviet 4 Army, struggled desperately to defend against Guderian's juggernaut, but by day's end, what remained of the corps was forced to beat a hasty retreat eastward. The corps, which had entered the battlespace with 478 tanks, had been reduced in strength to just 250; two days later, it had barely 30 combat-ready tanks at its disposal. As noted by eminent eastern front historian David M. Glantz, such a catastrophic attrition rate was typical for Soviet mechanized units during the initial engagements near the frontier.[50]

The singularly successful tank-on-tank battles with Soviet 14 Mechanized Corps during the first forty-eight hours of Operation Barbarossa not only buoyed the confidence of the tank crews of 18 Panzer Division but, as this entry in the divisional war diary reveals, strongly reinforced their feelings of superiority vis-à-vis their Russian opponent:

> 23.6.41:
>
> 0630: The operations group is ordered to decamp from the assembly area to the Bug crossing. . . . A staff officer is sent ahead to report the reason for the long absence of Operations Group I to the division commander.
>
> On his arrival, the report reaches the division commander that III./Pz.Rgt. 18 reached the Jasiolda sector at 0730 hours without any particularly heavy enemy action and that they have created a small bridgehead there. Many tanks were destroyed by II. and III./Pz.Rgt. 18 during their advance to the Jasiolda—once more demonstrating the superiority of the German over the Red tank force. Despite the fierce battles, 18 Panzer Regiment has suffered hardly any losses from enemy fire. Renewed evidence for the absolute superiority of German panzers. . . .
>
> The morale in the panzer brigade is particularly strong thanks to the kill rate that it has achieved, since nobody reckoned with such great success and such clear superiority right from the first days of the campaign. The Bolshevist as an individual fighter [*Einzelkämpfer*] is extraordinarily tenacious and dogged. Since he has been incited against the Germans, he expects the worst if he is taken prisoner. On many occasions he tenaciously defends himself to the last round [*sich bis zum letzten Schuss zäh verteidigt*] to avoid capture at all costs.[51]

The swift destruction of 14 Mechanized Corps by Guderian's panzers, however, was due in part to the fact that the corps had no T-34s or KVs in its inventory, only older-model tanks; as the following entry in the journal of German Fourth Army illustrates, these tanks failed to impress its commander, GFM von Kluge: "At 1915 hours [Kluge] tells the chief of staff from Pruzhany that he has been with *Generaloberst* Guderian. . . . The C-in-C also reports that around 100 shot up Russian tanks are lying on the road leading from the south to Pruzhany; a 'tank fright' [*Panzerschreck*] is really unnecessary, because these were 'virtually ridiculous things' [*beinahe lächerliche Dinger*]. On the other hand, the Russians have to a certain extent put up a brave fight: they had leapt onto the German panzers and shot into the hatches with pistols."[52]

The most spectacular advance on this second day of the war was achieved by *Generalleutnant* Walter Model's battle-hardened 3 Panzer Division, the *Berliner Bärendivision* (Berlin Bear Division). Model, the monocled fifty-year-old Prussian general and future field marshal, who would soon acquire a "solid reputation as an energetic commander and brilliant tactician,"[53] had, in less than forty-eight hours, pushed more than 150 kilometers beyond the frontier, his vanguard racing for the Berezina. The lightning thrust of 3 PD along Panzer Route 1 on 23 June 1941 is vividly recounted in a postwar history by the division's veterans' organization; it brings into bold relief the superior training and experience of the German tank crews at the start of the campaign:

> 6 Panzer Regiment rises at 0430 hours because the supply train with the precious fuel has arrived. Immediately after refueling, the tanks rattle on ahead. III./PzRgt 6 drives at the head of the column. The road is heavily choked with sand and the tanks can only get through slowly. In spite of this, the lighter vehicles of the advance detachment make progress and are soon in front of Kobrin, which the Russian is defending.
>
> III./PzRgt 6 arrives shortly after 1100 hours and resolutely comes to grips with the nests of enemy resistance at the western edge of the town, destroying them. While pushing into the town, light Russian tanks turn up and are destroyed without exception. High-explosive shells also crash into the houses from which Russian machine gun fire flares up. After a quarter of an hour the detachment has extinguished all resistance. . . .
>
> Soon the regiment has got through the town and all elements have reached the road heading east. . . . A journey begins which will be significant for this day, 23 June 1941.
>
> The tanks of 3 Panzer Division push ahead unrelentingly along the wide road. Movement off the road is impossible because impassable marshland stretches out to the left and right. The Russians have been driven from the road; only the abandoned vehicles, guns, discarded weapons and equipment are a reminder that the enemy is hastily withdrawing. Sometimes our panzers find it difficult to maneuver past the enemy vehicles which often lie across the roadway. The Soviet infantry have fled into the high cornfields and from there are shooting at the German columns following in their open all-terrain vehicles. The troops have to disembark from their vehicles and repulse the Russians at bayonet-point [*mit der blanken Waffe*].
>
> I./PzRgt 6 unexpectedly happens upon Russian tanks at Buchowiecze at 1540 hours. The enemy tanks have suddenly broken out of the nearby forest and taken the German columns under fire. *Major* Schmidt-Ott immediately put all his companies into action and, in an envelopment maneuver, destroys 36 Russian tanks, type "T-26"; 2./PzRgt 6 (*Oberleutnant* Buchterkirch) alone manages to dispose of 12 tanks in only a few minutes. Polish farmers direct the attention of passing German panzer crews to hidden Russian defensive positions. The light platoon from 6 Panzer Regiment (*Leutnant* Jacobs) is directed toward the small village of Podberje, away from the march route. Here, the tanks come across 6 heavy guns and tractors. The Russian gunners are so surprised by the appearance of the Germans that they give themselves up. Reinforced by medium tanks, 7./PzRgt 6 is ordered forward to join III./PzRgt 6 to support the battalion in its fairly sizeable skirmish with fleeing Soviet columns.
>
> The advance detachment has reached the main district town, Bereza-Kartuska, along the rail line to Minsk, and broken initial resistance with its own forces prior to arrival of 6 Panzer Regiment. . . . The advance detachment and the panzer

regiment are far ahead. The rifle brigade can only follow slowly, as the only road is more than a little jammed. . . .

The division command post has been transferred to Kobrin via Zabinka on this day. The operations group moves into the church to the east of the bridge. The population is predominantly friendly to the Germans and caters to the soldiers in the rear baggage train and supply columns. A lot of valuable material from the Soviet 4 Army, which had its headquarters in Kobrin, falls into the hands of intelligence staff (Ic) here. . . .

Despite this success, *Generalleutnant* Model does not grant his soldiers any rest. He himself has arrived in Bereza-Kartuska[54] and orders that the fleeing enemy be pursued without respite. *Major* Beigel, Commander, Combat Engineer Battalion 39, quickly regroups the advance detachment and immediately continues the advance. The tanks and motorcycles push unrelentingly along the road without regard for withdrawing enemy groups. They drive through villages and forests, cross bridges over the many small river courses, and quickly quell resistance that flares up at their flank. At the railway crossing southwest of Byten the Russian resistance increases. The light scout vehicles [*Spähwagen*] fire from all barrels. Soon the wooden freight station goes up in flames. Then the first panzers arrive.

Suddenly well-aimed artillery fire strikes the road. But there is no way of eluding it. So the tanks, followed by the motorcycle riflemen, clatter onward. The journey goes on for 3 km through the night, through the dark forest and the Soviet artillery fire. At 2200 hours the lead platoon of 7./PzRgt 6 (*Leutnant* Ruehl) arrives at the bridge across the initial sector of the Shchara River. The tanks roll unmolested across the wooden bridge and advance a few kilometers beyond it. The motorcycle riflemen and combat engineers take over the defense of the small bridgehead. The tanks then return in the darkness to rest.[55]

By nightfall, 3 Panzer had rendered 107 Soviet tanks hors de combat (bringing its total of destroyed Soviet tanks for the first two days of Barbarossa to 197) and destroyed or captured several hundred Soviet artillery pieces.[56] For his accomplishments on this day, *Major* Beigel, who led the advance detachment (*Vorausabteilung*), became the first officer of the division to be awarded the coveted Knight's Cross (*Ritterkreuz*). His official award document read in part, "The capture of a vital bridge over the Shchara succeeded through lightning-quick action [*blitzschnelles Zugreifen*], creating the conditions for the rapid advance of a *Panzerkorps*."[57] At the moment, however, elements of Model's division, rear services mostly, were strung out all the way back to occupied Poland and did not begin to cross the border until the following day (24 June). As for the mercurial Model, he barely escaped death on 24 June, when a direct hit by Soviet artillery demolished an eight-wheeled armored car moments after he dismounted the vehicle; the four-man crew did not survive.[58]

Once again, Guderian's operations had benefited from the effective cooperation of Bruno Loerzer's 2 Air Corps. On 23 June, Bf 109Fs of 51 Fighter Wing, led by the twenty-eight-year-old fighter ace *Oberstleutnant* Werner Mölders and operating from a cluster of airfields east of Warsaw, used their 20mm cannon to knock out at least twenty-five Soviet tanks near Pruzhany. By day's end, 2 Air Corps had run its total of Russian aircraft destroyed (in the air and on the ground) to the improbable figure of 716, while losing just 12 planes itself.[59]

As was their wont, German panzer generals led from the front, and setting the standard was Guderian himself. Such a command style was fraught with great personal risk—all the more so during the early days and weeks of the eastern campaign, as the panzer units often pushed perilously deep into Soviet territory without regard for their flanks or what was going on in the often still unpacified regions behind them.

Thus, it was on 24 June, barely three days into the campaign—and the same day as Model's harrowing brush with eternity—that Guderian experienced the first of several narrow escapes he would have in the east. At 0825 that morning, he drove toward the front at Slonim (northeast of Pruzhany) where fighting was still in progress. On the way, he encountered Russian infantry that were sweeping the road with fire. An artillery battery of 17 Panzer Division and dismounted motorcycle troops returned the enemy fire, albeit to no discernable effect. Guderian then joined in the action, firing the machine gun from his armored command vehicle. This succeeded in dislodging the enemy, and he was able to drive on. At 1130 hours, Guderian reached the CP of 17 Panzer Division on the western outskirts of Slonim. Here he found not only the division commander, *Generalleutnant* von Arnim, but also the corps commander, *Gen.d.Pz.Tr.* Lemelsen:

> While we were discussing the situation there was a sudden burst of lively rifle and machine gun fire in our rear; our view of the road from Belostok was blocked by a burning lorry, so that we were in ignorance of what was going on until two Russian tanks appeared from out of the smoke. They were attempting to force their way into Slonim, with cannons and machine guns blazing, and were pursued by German Panzer IV's that were also firing heavily. The Russian tanks noticed the group of officers, of which I was one, and we were immediately subjected to a rain of shells, which, fired at such extremely close range, both deafened and blinded us for a few moments. Being old soldiers we had immediately thrown ourselves to the ground; only poor *Oberstleutnant* Feller, who had come to us on a mission from the Commander of the Training Army, and who was unaccustomed to active service, was too slow and suffered a very painful wound as a consequence. Also, the commander of an anti-tank battalion, *Oberstleutnant* Dallmer-Zerbe, received a severe wound from which, I regret to say, he died a few days later. The Russian tanks succeeded in forcing their way into the town where they were eventually put out of action.[60]

Having survived the encounter, Guderian visited the front line at Slonim, then took a Panzer IV straight through no-man's-land to Nehring's 18 Panzer

Division. By mid-afternoon, he was back in Slonim, from where he soon struck out for his panzer group CP at Pruzhany—a drive that took him directly across the path of a clutch of Russian infantry, who were dismounting from their vehicles on the outskirts of Slonim: "I ordered my driver, who was next to me, to go full-speed ahead and we drove straight through the Russians; they were so surprised by this unexpected encounter that they did not even have time to fire their guns. All the same they must have recognized me, because the Russian press later announced my death; I felt bound to inform them of their mistake by means of the German wireless."[61]

By the end of 24 June, organized Soviet resistance east of Brest-Litovsk, along the axis of 2 Panzer Group, had largely ceased to exist. While remnants of Red Army units conducted slow delaying actions as they fell back to the east, the entire southern flank of Soviet Western Front had begun to crumble. By 25 June, 47 Panzer Corps had cleared Slonim, where 17 Panzer Division, running the gauntlet between Soviet formations desperately seeking to escape encirclement and fresh Soviet forces assembling around Baranovichi, had been temporarily cut off the night before; at the same time, lead elements of the corps' 18 Panzer Division had reached Baranovichi, less than 150 kilometers from Minsk. Directly to the south, Model's 3 Panzer Division (24 PzK) was bearing down on Slutsk, nearly 300 kilometers beyond the frontier. Guderian now dispatched his 29 ID (mot.) (47 PzK) to the northwest, toward Volkovysk, into the rear of Soviet 10 and 3 Armies. Volkovysk was a "particularly important target, for its road network controlled all Soviet lateral and forward movement, as well as resupply between Belostok and Minsk."[62] Meanwhile, remnants of Soviet units from southeast of Belostok to Pruzhany had sought refuge in the forests; the German infantry were in rapid pursuit.

While the advance (*Vormarsch*) progressed at a rapid pace, the Soviet Air Force (VVS) demonstrated that, despite its enormous losses, it still remained surprisingly active, at least along the most dangerous axes of 2 Panzer Group's advance, as underscored by two accounts involving 3 Panzer Division on 24 and 25 June, respectively:

> 24.6.41:
>
> All at once the Soviet Air Force is there! Nobody had reckoned on their still being active, since no Russian planes had been observed in the first couple of days. From 1345 hours the enemy fighter and bomber aircraft strike the road in rolling attacks, bringing the advance to a halt. The operations group of 3 Panzer Division, which is following the panzer brigade to Niedzwiedziewa, is also attacked several times.[63]
>
> 25.6.41:
>
> On [this day], due to lively enemy air activity, the main body of 6 Panzer Regiment took cover in a few forested areas at either side of the route of advance

> [*Vormarschstrasse*]. Only the 2nd Battalion with the 5th Company, under *Oberleutnant* Jarosch von Schweder at the vanguard of the division, pushed further on across the initial sector of the Shchara River. In the meantime, the Soviets sought to halt the German advance with intense bombing attacks, which affected the regimental staff in particular. There were several dead and wounded, while four wheeled vehicles were completely destroyed and two flak guns suffered direct hits.[64]

Yet neither Soviet air attacks nor Red Army engineers blowing the bridges along the routes of advance were able to significantly disrupt Guderian's tanks and motorized infantry, which continued to tighten the noose around Soviet Western Front from the south. On 26 June, Model's 3 Panzer Division, continuing its furious drive, captured Slutsk, about 110 kilometers from Bobruisk and the Berezina, the last major river barrier before the Dnepr. The next morning (27 June), 47 Panzer Corps captured Stolpce, less than 75 kilometers from Minsk, despite coming under incessant attack from Red Army units migrating southeast from the Belostok-Novogrodek sectors in an effort to escape encirclement and annihilation.[65]

On 28 June, 0000 hours, Guderian's subordination under GFM von Kluge's Fourth Army was finally lifted, and *Panzergruppe* 2 was placed once again under direct control of Army Group Center—this in recognition of the fact that Guderian had finally achieved complete operational freedom.[66] (In the sector of *Panzergruppe* 3, Hoth had achieved this feat on the very first day of the war.) The panzer general was no doubt relieved to no longer be under Kluge's nominal control—at least for the time being. As noted in chapter 1, relations between the two men had long been strained and continued to deteriorate during the Barbarossa campaign; on one occasion, Kluge would become so frustrated with Guderian's penchant for disregarding orders—a character flaw manifest in both the Polish and French campaigns—that he threatened the panzer general with a court-martial. In late June, both men wrangled for control of a sorely limited number of divisions—proof, if not recognized at the time, that the Germans were attempting to do too much with too little—and clashed over their radically different approaches to fighting the war. Kluge, fixated on sealing the pocket (for which purpose he had "poached" several of Guderian's units, among them 29 ID [mot.]),[67] was clearly not interested in taking more ground to the east at the cost of imperiling his impending success at Minsk. Guderian, however, was convinced of the need to keep moving—to maintain momentum to the east, to keep the enemy off-balance, to seize distant objectives. (In frustration, he wrote to his wife, Margarete, singling out Kluge for having "distinguished himself to good effect as a brake on progress."[68]) Simply put, the opposing strategic conceptions of these two leading eastern generals were irreconcilable and illustrative of the split within the German command. Both men turned to higher authorities (i.e., Halder and Bock) to win support, only to find their superiors sympathetic to both alternatives but fully supporting neither. Moreover, Hitler, suspicious in principle of his panzer generals and increasingly alarmed by the breakneck pace of their advance (fearing a dangerous overextension of his precious panzer units), was, like Kluge, inclined to act as a brake on progress.

In line with his operational imperatives, Guderian's immediate priority was thus not the destruction of Soviet forces caught in the cauldron taking shape between Belostok and Minsk; rather, it was to breach Soviet defenses along the Dnepr River, and he was determined to do so even if it meant violating his orders. On 26 June, with the spearheads of Hoth's *Panzergruppe* 3 barely 30 kilometers from Minsk, GFM von Bock had directed Guderian to wheel northward with the mass of his armor and to close the outer pocket by linking up with Hoth at Minsk; by 30 June, however, only two of Guderian's divisions (17 Panzer and 29 Motorized) were in position along the southern shoulder of the pocket, while seven of his divisions were continuing to push on toward the Dnepr far to the east. In Guderian's defense, he had been granted permission to advance toward the Berezina (and the Dnepr); yet, by leaving only the thinnest of screens to hold his sector of the pocket, he was, at a minimum, violating the spirit of his orders.[69]

On 27 June, he wrote to his wife for the first time since the start of the campaign—the incipient strain (both mental and physical) of the brutal contest in the east apparent in his words: "Today, after six days of battle, a first short greeting with news that I am well. We are deep in enemy territory and, I believe, have had a very considerable success. . . . The battle started early on the 22nd where I left off in 1939. The first blow achieved surprise and had a devastating effect. A few strenuous days followed with little time for eating and sleeping and no time for writing." He expressed regret for the losses among his men, including several officers with whom he had been close. He went on: "All this is very sad. The enemy resists bravely and bitterly. The fighting, therefore, is very hard. One just has to put up with it. . . . Troops and equipment again in good order, everything else is ship-shape too. Heat, gnats, dust [and] I am missing my bath."[70]

On 28 June, 3 Panzer Division took Bobruisk. Model then ordered his exhausted infantry to seize a bridgehead over the Berezina—the "River of Birches"—without regard to losses. This they dutifully did, despite heavy casualties; only artillery support and Bf 109Fs of Mölders's 51 Fighter Wing (*Jagdgeschwader*) saved them from being crushed by Soviet counterattacks. An entry in the war diary of 3 PD (2100 hours, 29 June) described the bitter fighting:

> The Russians have attacked our right flank—in cases "in droves," penetrating our forwardmost elements amid cries of "Urrah"—but were driven back and have withdrawn under cover of suddenly descending ground fog, hiding in fox-

> holes from which they only occasionally rattle off well-targeted rifle and machine gun fire at [our] riflemen. The result of this is a number of losses (fatalities and wounded). In the main, they have established their position on either side of the railway embankment and at the tip of the forest, 3 km southeast of Bobruisk. An arc of disruptive fire comes from 75 AR on a level with Titovka. Enemy artillery fire is only very isolated and untargeted. As soon as darkness falls, the fire suddenly picks up again; the Russian also begins to attack again from the left of the road and after firing flares. But this attack also slackens once more and the regiment manages to hold the small bridgehead, while a platoon of anti-tank guns is deployed for reinforcement.[71]

Despite the serious losses, Model's reconnaissance teams were soon probing east from their modest bridgehead toward the Dnepr.[72] In just seven days, his division had dashed some 400 kilometers beyond the Russo-German frontier.

By now, both flanks of Soviet Western Front were in a state of collapse. On 27 June, 3 Panzer Group reached the high ground above Minsk (Hoth would seize the flaming city the next day), while Guderian's 17 Panzer Division approached its southern outskirts. With some 250,000 inhabitants, Minsk had been badly disfigured by a series of savage *Luftwaffe* raids. Those Red Army forces who had managed to retire eastward through the city saw not a city but a funeral pyre. Even the parks were awash in flames. The landscape was shrouded in smoke, and blasts shook the air. Wave upon wave of *Luftwaffe* bombers visited death and destruction while thousands of refugees fled east, only to become victims of German fighter pilots.[73]

With Guderian more intent on pushing eastward than on sealing the pocket, the Soviets were given at least a twenty-four-hour reprieve, enabling large numbers of *Rotarmisten* to slip through the trap. It was a problem that the panzer general largely ignored, and in his postwar memoir he simply glossed over the incomplete nature of the encirclement, content instead to portray his achievements in the opening days of the campaign as a signal success. Not until 29 June did the tanks of Nehring's 18 PD, racing up to Minsk from the south, finally make contact with *Panzergruppe* 3. The outer encirclement ring was now ostensibly closed, although the southeastern shoulder remained far from hermetically sealed. Trapped inside several pockets stretching from Belostok through Novogrodek to Minsk were the remnants of four Soviet armies (3, 4, 10, and 13). Western Front had practically ceased to exist as an organized force.

On 29 June, Guderian sent a brief "battle report" to his wife, his optimism clearly manifest: "Our undertaking has measured up to the high expectations. . . . The first hostilities were so successful and our superiority was so apparent that the enemy has shown signs of exhaustion and moral despondency since yesterday." On 1 July, he wrote, "We're approaching the last major section of the [Soviet] front. If we succeed in passing it, then the route to the interior of the empire is open and the campaign, in my view, can no longer be lost."[74]

As Guderian's panzers rumbled eastward toward—so it seemed—almost certain victory, the death squads (*Einsatzgruppen*) of the SS behind the front were seeking out and systematically murdering Jews, Communist Party officials, intellectuals, and other putative enemies of the Reich's new European order. "Several German generals," mused Guderian biographer Kenneth Macksey, "were aware of the pogrom—though few, if any, [of] its enormity. Nearly all, especially the engrossed operational commanders, ignored it."[75] As for Guderian, he was not in the habit of visiting the rear areas of his forces, the so-called *Etappe*, or zone of communications, which was where the death squads were doing their work. However, as noted by Russell A. Hart, the *Einsatzgruppen* had standing orders to report to local Army commanders, from whom they drew their supplies; thus, it is "inconceivable that Guderian was not at least partially aware of their activities within his zone of command. In fact, the SS and police commander responsible for *Einsatzgruppe B* that operated alongside Army Group Center reported 'no difficulties' with any of the Army commanders, which implies direct and willing cooperation from Guderian."[76] Yet complicating this picture is the panzer general's propaganda officer, Paul Dierichs, who recalled his commander's fury when two Soviet civilians were murdered by the SS early in the campaign; moreover, Guderian wrote to his wife, "The people look on us as liberators. It is to be hoped they will not be disappointed."[77]

On 30 June 1941, Guderian flew in a bomber to the CP of 3 Panzer Group to meet with *Generaloberst* Hoth to discuss "the future coordination of our activities."[78] Both panzer generals chafed under the restrictions placed on their movements by Hitler and the Army High Command (OKH); both were also convinced that the mobile units tied down along the *Kesselfront* needed to be replaced by marching infantry, so the panzer groups could strike out in force for the Western Dvina and Dnepr river lines and prevent the Soviets from rebuilding a cohesive defensive front behind these formidable topographical barriers. Officially, however, a resumption of the advance toward the rivers and Smolensk was for the time being prohibited, as sealing off and clearing the cauldron of the enemy were the clear priorities of Hitler's headquarters. Hitler, in fact, was again rattled by the potential overextension of the panzer troops—this time fingering Geyr's 24 Panzer Corps at the Berezina and forbidding its further advance to the east. Indeed, as GFM von Bock noted in his memoir, only "reconnaissance forces" were to be sent east across the Berezina and toward the Dnepr, while the panzer groups maintained the containment of the eastern pocket (i.e., west of Minsk).[79]

Deus ex machina, an order arrived that very day from Halder, Chief of the Army General Staff, instructing Hoth and Guderian to prepare to advance against both rivers along the line Rogachev–Mogilev–Orsha (Dnepr)–Vitebsk–Polotsk (Dvina). The new operation, which Halder deemed of decisive importance, was to begin as soon as possible; its successful execution would establish favorable conditions for the capture of the area around Smolensk, including the strategic land bridge west of the city, which stretched from Orsha to Vitebsk, along the watershed between the two rivers. As Halder, Bock, and the panzer generals knew all too well, possession of this area was a vital prerequisite for the capture of Moscow.

Both Hoth and Guderian would press for an early start to the new operation; Halder, however, "given the need to reorganize forces for the renewed attack [and perhaps to mollify Hitler's growing anxiousness] . . . was not prepared to release the panzer divisions until 5 July. Subsequent pressure finally brought this forward to 3 July, although even this represented more of a delay than the panzer commanders would have liked. Agreeing on an exact starting date was in many respects aimed purely at placating higher command, as in practice there were already much more than just reconnaissance forces striking out to the east." Indeed, it was "well within the character of [both Hoth and Guderian] to 'interpret' their orders in terms of the wider strategic goals of the campaign and therefore implement actions as they saw fit, conveniently excusing themselves from any meticulous definition of insubordination."[80]

RACE TO THE DNEPR RIVER

No sooner had Nehring's 18 Panzer Division reached the outskirts of Minsk than Guderian ordered it to move at once (without support) on Borisov, on the Berezina (17 PD was left in position along the southeastern shoulder of the encirclement ring). In response, at daybreak on 30 June, Nehring's tanks bolted east over surprisingly good roads, striking out for the Minsk-Smolensk-Moscow *Autobahn*. After days of struggling along wretched roadways, the tank commanders "were beaming";[81] they began a brilliant "Panzer raid" that would take them over 100 kilometers into the rear of Soviet forces and culminate (1 July) in the capture of the town and a bridgehead over the river. (After the war, Nehring would characterize the bold operation as a *Himmelfahrtskommando*, in other words, as a "suicide mission.")[82] Observing the progress of 18 PD's advance detachment from high overhead was *Gen.d.Pz.Tr.* Lemelsen, C-in-C, 47 Panzer Corps:

> 1.7.41:
>
> We are still located in Stolpce with the staff, because the threat to our flanks continues to be considerable. But 18 Panzer Division has already begun advancing to Borisov today and at midday had already reached the Berezina River. Hopefully they will pull off the historic crossing as successfully as did Napoleon. I flew in the *Storch* this morning to the division in Sinoleviza, approximately 130 km (the distances here are enormous), and could observe the entire advance of the division from the air. March discipline is, thank God, improving from day to day.[83]

Once again, the Russian defenders were caught off-balance by the speed and daring of the German advance. Yet, once again, they fought tenaciously, counterattacking with tanks that almost reached the divisional CP and pounding the attacking units of 18 Panzer Division with artillery, inflicting serious losses. But the operationally valuable bridgehead was held. Through 18 Panzer's spectacular coup de main and the singular success of Model's 3 Panzer Division, the prerequisites for an advance to the Dnepr were rapidly falling into place. Clearly impressed by the latter's achievements in the initial days of the campaign, Guderian gushed in a letter to his wife (1 July), "Model is coming along splendidly, both in terms of his leadership and his personal bearing."[84]

By the beginning of July 1941, *Gen.d.Pz.Tr.* Heinrich von Vietinghoff's 46 Panzer Corps (10 PD, SS ID [mot.] *Reich*, IR [mot.] *Grossdeutschland*), which had begun the campaign in reserve, was reaching the front of Guderian's panzer group, where it was inserted between 24 Panzer Corps (on its right) and 47 Panzer Corps (on its left). Much to Guderian's displeasure, still tied down along the southern and southeastern shoulder of the Minsk cauldron on 2 July were his 17 Panzer Division, 29 ID (mot.), IRGD (committed several days before), and Machine Gun Battalion 5. Two divisions of Hoth's group, one panzer and one motorized division, were still holding the sector of the pocket directly west and northwest of Minsk.[85] In his personal diary, Lemelsen marveled at the extraordinary martial qualities of the *Rotarmisten* trapped inside the pocket, while also noting just how thin was the German picket line around it: "All along the roads there are shot up trucks, anti-tank guns and artillery pieces as well as many dead. Again and again one is struck by the pluck and doggedness [*Schneid und Zähigkeit*] with which the Russian soldier fights and by the cunning combat methods he employs. The sack around the Russian 10 Army is closed. Guderian and Hoth have linked up at Minsk, but the net [around the Soviet forces] is damned weak and has many holes."[86]

On 2 July, Halder forbade Guderian from withdrawing any of the units of his panzer group away from the encirclement ring without orders.[87] The order was due to the fact that the panzer general had been siphoning off forces from the ring to buttress his upcoming attack, "a circumstance that produced the first open clash between Kluge and Guderian and plainly illustrated the difficulties commanders were having balancing operational demands with available forces."[88] The day before, Guderian had been specifically ordered by Army Group Center not to jeopardize the encirclement of Soviet forces west of Minsk by "drafting" more forces for the impending offensive. The panzer general attributed these instructions to "another bout of Hitler's over-anxious trepidation." Writing to his wife, he said, "Everybody is scared of the Führer and nobody dares say anything. Regrettably, this is what causes a useless waste of blood."[89]

Defiant and willful as always, on 1 July Guderian ordered 17 Panzer Division away from its position on the pocket front and toward Borisov, only to have his order swiftly countermanded by Kluge. The next day (2 July), the panzer general paid a visit to 17 PD, and while no record exists of what transpired there, the division subsequently set off for Borisov. Returning to his headquarters, Guderian dispatched a communiqué to Kluge at Fourth Army, insisting that a "mishap had occurred in the transmission of orders to 17 PD," as a result of which the division had failed to receive the order to remain on the encirclement front, and part of it had departed for Borisov. Thus, as Guderian put in his memoir, "it was too late to do anything about it." On the same day, however, a similar "mishap" took place on Hoth's front, "causing Kluge to seethe with fury that, on the eve of his ascension to the new command of Fourth Panzer Army, which [would control both] Hoth's and Guderian's panzer groups, he was being confronted by a generals' conspiracy." The irate field marshal summoned Guderian to appear the next morning at 0800 hours at his headquarters in Minsk, with the intention of having *both* panzer generals court-martialed for insubordination. Appearing before Kluge, Guderian was "strongly taken to task" for what he described as an "accident." In the end, Guderian succeeded in convincing the field marshal that it was all just a misunderstanding and that the prudent course was to simply put the matter to rest.[90]

On 3 July, in accordance with the instructions of OKH,[91] both 2 and 3 Panzer Groups officially resumed their advance toward the Dnepr and Western Dvina, respectively.[92] Of course, knowing the priorities of both Hoth and Guderian, one can reasonably posit that their furious push toward the two river barriers had never really stopped since the moment their tanks rolled across the Russo-German frontier, even if delayed at times by the frustrating requirement of having to divert precious resources to the task of closing and holding the Belostok-Minsk pocket (a requirement that Guderian, as we have seen, often simply ignored). Be that as it may, the panzer groups were now operating across an extended front of more than 300 kilometers with virtually nothing in reserve—their movements impeded by heavy summer rains, which transformed the sandy roads and tracks into a bottomless sludge. Meanwhile, German aerial reconnaissance had revealed that the Soviets were assembling fresh armies behind both river lines; these were the armies of their second strategic echelon, about which German military intelligence had no knowledge prior to the start of the campaign. Hoth and Guderian would have to hurry!

To manage the new operations, the OKH and Army Group Center converted GFM von Kluge's Fourth Army into Fourth Panzer Army and gave him control over 2 and 3 Panzer Groups. Conversely, Kluge turned over most of his infantry divisions to the newly activated headquarters of Second Army (*Generaloberst* Maximilian Freiherr von Weichs), which assumed responsibility for the encirclement ring. The purpose of the reorganization, which went into effect at 0000 hours on 3 July,[93] was to better coordinate the operations of—and no doubt to gain more control over—the impetuous panzer generals by placing them under an intermediate headquarters; no doubt it was also an attempt to assuage Hitler's anxiety about the tanks pushing ahead too far too fast. The new command arrangement, which lasted throughout most of July, worked out poorly, leading to more personality clashes between Guderian and Kluge; in fact, Guderian, when he first got wind of the plan, threatened to resign. As for Kluge—a gifted field commander but uncomfortable with the slashing and chaotic operations of a blitzkrieg—he was hardly suited to lead a large armored force. Even the OKH and Bock soon grew frustrated with Kluge's less aggressive style of leadership, and Bock, concerned that the panzer units were being scattered across too broad a front, urged the field marshal on 6 July to concentrate his forces: "Make a fist somewhere."[94]

On 3 July, Model's 3 Panzer Division was the first of Guderian's divisions to reach the Dnepr—at Rogachev, on the far right wing of Geyr's 24 Panzer Corps. His men had enjoyed little rest or sleep for days; his French- and Czech-manufactured trucks were beginning to break down from the pounding they had taken on the wretched roads, while tank strength was declining, more due to the fine, ubiquitous dust, which cut the life expectancy of tank engines in half, than to enemy action. Yet the dynamic division commander pushed his men onward without respite—success now, he reasoned, would save lives later. Thus, the battle to forge a bridgehead continued unabated despite sustained and savage Russian resistance.

Spearheading the advance of 3 PD was a battalion of submersible tanks (originally intended for Operation "Sealion," the invasion of Great Britain) of 6 Panzer Regiment. Crossing the Drut River, they rumbled eastward another eight kilometers, reaching the Dnepr northeast of the burning city of Rogachev by nightfall. While this action was in progress, infantry and combat engineers of the division burst into the city, only to be met by murderous fire from the Russians defending in the houses and buildings. German anti-tank crews struggled to manhandle their guns into position, taking the enemy strongpoints under direct fire. Slowly, deliberately, infantry and combat engineers of 3 PD's two rifle regiments "chewed" their way into the city. At several points, the infantry reached the Dnepr, evoking intense machine-gun and artillery fire from the far bank, forcing them to seek cover. Yet, just outside Rogachev, several small infantry *Kampfgruppen* of 3 Rifle Regiment were able to build a tiny bridgehead on the far (eastern) bank of the river. The Russians, however, had demolished all bridges over the Dnepr.[95]

Throughout the night, a hurricane of fire—from thirty-six batteries (up to 150mm) in position along the far bank, southeast of Rogachev—was loosed on the tenuous German positions. Savage street fighting went on as well, with German losses mounting by the hour, among them several of Model's key combat officers: *Oberleutnant* Spillman (6./SR 394)—KIA, along with many of his men; *Major* Zimmermann (II./SR 3)—wounded (for the third time); *Oberleutnant* von Becker (8./SR 3)—badly wounded, his unit suffering serious losses; *Leutnant* Fritze—KIA; *Leutnant* Gleitz, leader of the combat engineer assault team—KIA along with three of his men.[96]

The next day (4 July), Model continued his efforts to get across the Dnepr—this time, after a swarm of Stukas sought (without success) to silence the heavy Russian artillery fire, launching a set-piece assault. A battalion of infantry (II./SR 3), debouching directly from Rogachev, soon faltered in the withering enemy fire (in two days, one of the battalion's companies was wiped out, while the remaining four sustained 146 casualties). To the north, however, another *Kampfgruppe* (which included elements of 6 Pz.Rgt.) was more successful. Here, three submersible Panzer IVs plunged into the Dnepr, barely 100 meters wide at this point, and crawled up the other side. While one of the tanks was dismembered by Russian fire, killing its five-man crew; the remaining two furnished supporting fires long enough to enable the infantry to get across as well. Thus had a second small bridgehead been established; it was, however, soon sealed off from the rest of 3 PD by a storm of Russian artillery fire and fighting for its life against waves of Russian infantry.[97]

Fifty kilometers upstream, at Stary Bychov, *Generalmajor* von Langermann-Erlencamp's 4 Panzer Division (24 PzK) also crossed the Dnepr on 4 July. And here, too, the fighting was severe. As part of the "Stalin Line" (a robust system of fortifications along and behind the Soviet Union's 1939 frontier), the garrison town was well defended and protected by a stout anti-tank ditch. In its assault on Stary Bychov, 4 PD's panzer regiment suffered its greatest single day's losses since the beginning of the war in September 1939: eighteen dead, ten wounded, and six missing. In one engagement, the regiment lost several tanks in swift succession, knocked out at point-blank range after being ambushed by a dense Russian screen of well-concealed anti-tank and anti-aircraft guns and artillery firing over open sights. Forty-eight hours later, the panzer crews, given up for dead, had made their way back to the regiment, having swum across the Dnepr.[98]

By now, it was becoming apparent that Guderian, at least on his right wing, might have "pushed too far too fast."[99] While lead elements of 3 Panzer Division struggled to cross the Dnepr, the rest of Model's division was strung out across muddy roads as far back as the Berezina; elements of 4 Panzer Division were struggling along the road from Slutsk to Mogilev; 10 ID (mot.) was dangerously dispersed over many kilometers near Zhlobin; and 1 Cavalry Division was still tramping across the outer fringes of the Pripiat' Marshes. The closest supporting units, those of 46 Panzer Corps, were astride the Berezina, far to the northwest.

Put another way, Guderian's spearheads "stood poised on the brink of victory and disaster at the same moment, and not a few German officers began to realize viscerally just how large the Soviet Union was."[100]

Perhaps aware of the exposed position of Guderian's right wing, on 6 July, the Russians went over to the offensive. Lt.-Gen. V. F. Gerasimenko's 21 Army began a series of counterstrokes that precipitated 24 Panzer Corps' first major crisis of the campaign. Two Soviet rifle corps struck positions of 3 Panzer Division at Rogachev and *Generalleutnant* Wilhelm von Loeper's 10 Motorized Division near Zhlobin (just west of the Dnepr), and while the Soviet assaults were poorly coordinated, Geyr's panzer corps was deployed for pursuit and lacked so much as a small tactical reserve. Penetrating rapidly and with tactical surprise into Pobolovo, the Soviets wiped out elements of Loeper's division. After two days of fierce, costly combat, the Germans finally succeeded in driving back the attackers. Yet it was now apparent that Soviet strength around Rogachev was simply too strong; thus, on 7 July, Model elected to evacuate his Dnepr bridgeheads, his infantry and supporting elements retiring across the river on pneumatic boats under cover of darkness.[101] That same day, the Red Army registered another notable tactical success when 46 Panzer Corps was unable to capture the bridges around Mogilev, while farther south, 4 Panzer Division had yet to move beyond Stary Bychov. Moreover, attrition was beginning to take a serious toll on the panzer divisions; by 9 July, 3 PD's tank strength had fallen to 153 (from 215 on 22 June).

"Small as it was," concluded Model biographer Steven H. Newton, "Gerasimenko's counterattack had delivered the first check to Guderian's impetuous plunge toward Moscow."[102] Indeed, being forced onto the defensive for the first time since the start of the campaign had administered a severe shock to Model and the men of his 3 Panzer Division. As recorded in the division's postwar history, "After the intoxicating victories of the first days of the war, no one had counted on the Russians gathering the strength to put up such strong resistance on the Dnepr, even though the so-called Stalin Line was at the river."[103]

Meanwhile, on Guderian's left wing, Nehring's 18 Panzer Division had made slow but steady progress toward Orsha after resuming its advance on 3 July, while 17 Panzer Division (both 47 PzK), having finally extricated itself from the encirclement ring at Minsk, was soon moving up on 18 Panzer's left, toward Senno. Here, too, German forces closing on the Dnepr were challenged by bad weather and troublesome terrain. An unexpected challenge arose for Lemelsen's panzer corps when 18 PD had its first encounter with Soviet T-34 and KV tanks. After the war, Nehring looked back on the harrowing experience:

> The aerial reconnaissance of the division's flying squadron, which had always served us excellently, had, on 2 July, reported the approach of 100 tanks, including very large ones. So the division was prepared for new developments when the

advance, in accordance with orders, was continued on 3 July along and to both sides of the highway toward Smolensk-Moscow. . . .

The two tank spearheads collided at Lipki, east of Borisov. It was a tough battle, in which both T-34 and 52-ton tanks[104] appeared for the first time, and whose armored plating our "little tank guns" [*Panzerkanönchen*] were not able to penetrate—and certainly not the anti-tank guns we had then, of 37mm caliber, and not even the few available 50mm guns. Despite this, the Russians withdrew from the battlefield, leaving many heavy tanks behind—whether because of their poor leadership, or because of the fortitude of our own [tank and AT] crews, or because of our flexible tactical leadership, or thanks to our excellent gunnery. Our shells may not have penetrated—but they hit home! [I] saw immobilized 52-ton tanks with our 50mm shells buried up to the guiding ring in their armor plating, causing the crews to bail out. . . . In order to engage the heavy Russian tanks with some hope of success, 88mm flak or 100mm long-barrel cannon of the divisional artillery were [thereafter] always brought right up front—a measure that really proved its worth on 7 July in the area of Tolochino (the former quarters of Napoleon I).[105]

The troubling ineffectiveness of their anti-tank guns against these well-armored behemoths also forced the *Landser* (German term for GI) to turn to more radical measures in an effort to neutralize them, such as bundling several hand grenades into a concentrated charge, which an intrepid soldier then had to place near—or on—the enemy tank. As for Guderian, he at once recognized the superiority of these new Russian tanks over existing German models, and it disturbed him; however, it would take a seminal tank battle in early fall for the dire implications of these superior Russian tanks to become fully apparent.

For the German *Landser*, however, the tank scare (*Panzerschreck*)[106] provoked by the new Russian tanks was but one in a series of shocks they would experience early in the Barbarossa campaign. Others included (1) the introduction of Soviet rocket artillery (the famous *Stalinorgel*); (2) mass wave attacks of often poorly trained and equipped Soviet troops, who were butchered in droves by the German machine gunners (many of whom were disturbed by the death they inflicted on such an industrial scale); (3) the Red Army's effective and ubiquitous use of snipers (*Heckenschützen*), who took the lives of so many German soldiers, both at and behind the front; (4) the repeated violations of the laws of war, among them the mutilation and murder of German POWs and attacks on doctors and other Red Cross personnel; and (5) the Soviet use of women in combat roles, which, as revealed in personal diaries or field post letters, seriously offended the bourgeois mentality of the typical German soldier. Such was the eastern front, a theater of war whose (reciprocal) barbarism and atavistic cruelty were its defining features.

Like Guderian, *Gen.d.Pz.Tr.* Lemelsen (47 PzK) was beginning to feel the strain of a campaign fraught with unparalleled—and increasingly unmanageable—

challenges. In his personal diary on 6 July, he covered a range of issues of serious concern to the panzer generals of Army Group Center as they struggled to maintain the momentum of their operations despite the ongoing resistance of higher headquarters:

> It is raining; this is seriously impeding all movements, because the roads immediately dissolve; in any case, they usually go through marshes and are only just traversable during the dry season. So we are currently struggling step by step through the most difficult terrain and are so eager to cross the Dnepr at Orsha, but our forces available for this have been considerably weakened, because 29 ID (mot.) was held back at Minsk. The Führer wants to clean out the cauldron at Belostok first and only continue onward after that. So he has ordered all forces to be left at Minsk. But if we want to advance farther east at all, then we will have to be quick about it, before the Russian brings more strong forces to the Dnepr line, or else it will cost us a lot of blood. That is why we had permission from the *Panzergruppe* to punch our way ahead east to the Dnepr with both panzer divisions, but we will gradually run out of steam if 29 ID (mot.) doesn't rejoin us from behind.[107]
>
> The advance of 17 Panzer Division from Minsk has had serious consequences after all. I had Guderian with me yesterday evening, and he was very depressed. He has thus been accused of disobeying an order and there was a heated exchange between him and von Kluge, in which the latter threatened him with court-martial [*Kriegsgericht*]. Very, very unfortunate if the forces, in their urge to advance, are encumbered by a leaden weight at their back. That will be debilitating. As a result, the mood today has sunk to absolute zero [*Die Stimmung ist daher heute unter den Nullpunkt gesunken*], exacerbated, of course, by our not really advancing in the way we want, and by the cold and wet weather, which is really putting the brakes on us. Well, after rain comes sunshine. Let's hope so, anyway![108]

By 7 July, 18 Panzer Division, moving east along the highway from Minsk to Smolensk and having reached Tolochino (less than 50 kilometers from Orsha), was bearing down on the Dnepr. 17 Panzer Division, now commanded by *Generalmajor* Karl Ritter von Weber (the division's third commander since the start of the campaign),[109] stood at Senno (50 kilometers northwest of Orsha), where it suddenly faced a serious crisis when struck by Soviet armor. "The last few days have again been most difficult," Lemelsen wrote on 10 July:

> The sunshine may have returned, but despite the roads drying off, intense enemy resistance meant any advance was difficult. The 18 PD is just too battle-weary now, it lacks the right fighting spirit, which in any case can't be expected of the Saxons. There were tough battles around Tolochino for 18 PD and very severe crises for 17 PD at Senno. The 17 PD . . . was very heavily attacked the day before yesterday at Senno by at least one Russian armored division. I flew in a *Storch* to them at Tolpino and found a critical situation there. Tolpino was under heavy

> enemy artillery fire, the houses were burning, and the Russian was attacking from the north and south in massive waves with countless tanks. Our riflemen fell back, batteries were overrun by the Russians—things looked bleak.
>
> I flew back at once to my command post . . . and directed Stukas to attack this strengthening enemy, who was continually drawing reinforcements from Orsha. This provided relief and by the evening, 17 PD was again in control of the situation. It could have gone very badly. And Russians with tanks are still swarming between the individual groups of this division.
>
> Over 100 [enemy] tanks were destroyed on this day during the battles of both divisions, burning tanks could be seen everywhere. The 17 PD needed a very long time to reorganize itself, to rearm, and refuel, especially since the supply columns were cut off from the division at Tscheriza and had to be rescued by tanks first.[110]

Despite such bitter enemy resistance, all three of Guderian's tank corps (24, 46, and 47 PzK) were closing on the Dnepr. Guderian, however, having failed in his initial attempts to puncture the river barrier at Rogachev, Stary Bychov, and Mogilev, decided to regroup his forces and shift his assault to more promising sectors. Yet he now faced a critical decision: "Was I to continue my advance as rapidly as heretofore, to cross the Dnepr with panzer forces only, and attempt to reach my primary objective [i.e., the Roslavl-El'nia-Smolensk area] as quickly as possible according to the original plan of campaign? Or should I, in view of the measures that the Russians were taking to construct a defensive front along the line of the river, break off my advance and await the arrival of the infantry armies before launching the battle for the river?"[111]

These questions, posed by Guderian in his memoir, were crucial, for during the Belostok-Minsk cauldron battles the infantry of Fourth (later Second) and Ninth Armies had fallen as much as 250 kilometers behind the surging panzer divisions. On 7 July, the infantry of a half dozen army corps were still bunched up between Baranovichi and Minsk, 200 kilometers and more from the Dnepr, with other infantry units even farther to the rear. To await their arrival at the front, which would take days despite forced marches of 30, 40, even 50 kilometers a day, would enable Soviet forces along the Dnepr to grow considerably stronger. "Whether the infantry," Guderian recalled, "would then be able to smash a well-organized river defensive line so that mobile warfare might once again be possible seemed doubtful. . . . [Thus] I ordered an immediate attack across the Dnepr and a continuation of the advance toward Smolensk."[112]

Guderian's decision, we are told by the panzer general, once again brought him into conflict with his more conservative superior, GFM von Kluge. On the morning of 9 July, Kluge appeared at Guderian's CP in Borisov, where, according to the latter, an "exceptionally heated conversation" ensued. Perhaps influenced by Guderian's initial failed attempts to breach the Dnepr, Kluge believed that the panzer units (alone) would not be sufficient to push through the defenses of the Stalin Line along the Dnepr without robust infantry support; hence, the crossings should not be attempted until such support became available. Guderian defended his contrarian views "with obstinacy," informing Kluge that his (Guderian's) preparations for the assault "had already gone too far to be cancelled" (confronting superiors with faits accomplis was one of his typical stratagems). Moreover, Guderian was confident his renewed attack would not only succeed but prove decisive (a telling perspective that reveals just how much he tended to exaggerate his own self-importance): "I expected that this operation would decide the Russian campaign this very year, if such a decision were at all possible." Confronted with Guderian's arguments, Kluge relented. The operation would begin the next day, 10 July. Still, the unhappy Kluge got in the final word, saying, "Your operations always hang by a silk thread!" (*Ihre Operationen hängen immer an einem seidenen Faden!*).[113]

(Note: According to eastern front historian David M. Glantz [Col., US Army, ret.], this encounter with Kluge, laid out so vividly by Guderian, never in fact took place. As Glantz noted—and GFM von Bock's diary confirms—Kluge was sick in bed on 9 July. According to Glantz, it was not Kluge but his chief of staff, *Oberst* Günther Blumentritt, who visited Guderian's headquarters on that day, speaking with Guderian's chief of staff, *Oberst* von Liebenstein, while Guderian was off at the front. Whether or not the event so dramatically recounted by Guderian actually took place, its tenor reflects the two men's very different operational outlooks and, certainly, their growing antipathy toward each other.)[114]

MINSK CAULDRON BATTLE: RESULTS

By 9 July 1941, Soviet resistance inside the Belostok-Minsk pocket had collapsed. In his diary on 8 July, GFM von Bock estimated that his armies and panzer corps had destroyed 22 rifle divisions, seven tank divisions, six motorized brigades, and three cavalry divisions; as of 7 July, Bock noted that 287,704 prisoners had been taken (among them several corps and division commanders)—a figure that, according to German estimates, was to rise to 324,000 over the next few days. The material booty was also tremendous, amounting to more than 3,300 tanks and 1,800 guns destroyed or captured, along with immense quantities of fuel, ammunition, and rations. All told, according to official Soviet figures, Soviet Western Front had sustained 417,729 casualties, including 341,012 "irrecoverable losses" (dead, captured, and missing), out of a total force of just over 670,000 men during the eighteen days of battle in the western frontier regions.[115] Western Front also lost 4,799 tanks (many having simply run out of fuel), 9,427 guns and mortars, and 1,777 combat planes (most of which were destroyed on the ground) during the fighting from 22 June to 9 July 1941.[116]

As for the hapless General Pavlov, he had been replaced as commander of Western Front by Marshal Semen Timoshenko on 1 July. Pavlov was then ordered back to Moscow, where, on Stalin's orders, he was tried and shot.

While German figures for Soviet prisoners are probably inflated (through inadvertent inclusion of civilians), Belostok-Minsk was, by any measure, an unprecedented victory—one that, in the west, would have yielded decisive results. In the east, however, it was a quite different matter, as the Soviets simply continued to commit fresh forces to the fight despite their dreadful losses. And while these new armies were not as well trained or equipped as the armies they were replacing, they were there, and although most of them were eventually destroyed, they would still manage to inflict irreplaceable losses of men and materiel on the increasingly attenuated *Ostheer.*

In general, the remarkable resilience and regenerative powers of the Red Army were beginning to leave an indelible impression on the German soldier, giving rise to a restive trepidation. The uncommon fighting prowess of Soviet forces had even caught the attention of Dr. Joseph Goebbels, Hitler's propaganda minister; from his office in Berlin, he noted in his diary (28 June), "The first big pocket is beginning to close. . . . But [the Russians] are fighting well and have learned a great deal even since Sunday."

Also cause for concern was the fact that Guderian's tank strength was declining far more rapidly than it had in France in 1940. The immense distances, the poor roads, the endless dust and mud—all were factors that, along with increasing Red Army resistance, added to the rate of attrition. By 11 July, 18 Panzer Division had been reduced to eighty-three mission-capable tanks (39 percent of its initial strength), while sustaining well over 2,000 personnel losses. *Generalmajor* Walther K. Nehring warned that the high loss rates of his division should not be allowed to continue "if we do not intend to victor ourselves to death" (*wenn wir uns nicht totsiegen wollen*).[117] Yet, in the second week of July 1941, such concerns were far removed from the euphoria that reigned at Hitler's Wolf's Lair headquarters in East Prussia, where the Führer and his General Staff alike were convinced they were on the verge of a historic victory.

3

The Smolensk Cauldron Battle

For Adolf Hitler and the German High Command, Operation Barbarossa had begun with decidedly sensational results. By the second week of July 1941, the *Ostheer*, its powerful panzer forces forging ahead, had pushed hundreds of kilometers beyond the Russo-German frontier. Army Group South, fending off fierce counterstrokes by strong Soviet mechanized corps, had penetrated to a depth of 350 kilometers—*Generaloberst* Ewald von Kleist's 1 Panzer Group punching through the Stalin Line on the pre-1939 Soviet border and, by 12 July, standing with two panzer divisions on the Irpen River, on the approaches to Kiev. Advancing even more rapidly, Army Group North had covered about 500 kilometers, seizing Lithuania, Latvia, and most of Estonia; on 10 July, *Generaloberst* Erich Hoepner's 4 Panzer Group began what was hoped to be the final drive on Leningrad; within days his spearheads had forged bridgeheads across the lower Luga River, barely 100 kilometers from the outskirts of the city. In the center of the expanding front, Army Group Center had made the most spectacular gains, its two panzer groups lunging more than 500 kilometers into Soviet Russia, swallowing up most of Belorussia, and reaching the Western Dvina and Dnepr Rivers.

Over the next several days, along the central axis, the armor and mobile infantry of 2 and 3 Panzer Groups shattered Soviet defenses along both river lines; racing east as far as 180 kilometers, they rapidly seized Smolensk and vital ground just beyond the ancient city, trapping large Soviet forces in pockets north and west of Smolensk. This second major encirclement battle—which, the Germans hoped, would be decisive—had, by early August 1941, culminated in the destruction of several more Soviet armies.

Once more elated by their unprecedented triumphs in the east, Hitler and his military advisors began to prepare for the next phase of the war to follow the (seemingly) imminent destruction of Bolshevik Russia. Among the projects contemplated by German military planners in the first flush of (impending) victory over Soviet Russia were (1) a vast pincer movement through the Caucasus and via Libya and Egypt into the Middle East as far as Iran and Iraq, followed by the establishment of a base of operations in Afghanistan, from which to threaten India; (2) an advance through Spain and Gibraltar into Northwest Africa (Dakar), to build a bastion against America; and (3) the capture of the Azores in the North Atlantic, for use as an airbase from which to launch long-range bombers against America's eastern coastline. The objective of these and other initiatives, however fantastical, was to transform Hitler's continental European conflict into a *Weltblitzkrieg* against the Anglo-American bloc, resulting in final victory (*Endsieg*) and Germany's attainment of unchallenged global hegemony. On the Führer's orders, armament production was to be shifted away from the Army to the *Luftwaffe* and the *Kriegsmarine* to prepare the Reich for this final showdown with the United States and Great Britain.[1]

So confident were Hitler and his High Command of victory over Russia that, on 15 July 1941, the OKH Operations Branch produced a memorandum that called for pulling most of the infantry divisions out of Russia beginning in early August 1941, followed by the return of the first mobile units in September. Only fifty-six divisions (thirty-four infantry, twelve panzer, six motorized, three mountain, and one cavalry) were to stay behind in the Soviet Union, to hold a line stretching from Astrakhan to Archangel and to conduct punitive raids into the Urals, including a potential panzer raid aimed at eliminating Soviet industry in the region.[2]

Yet, just as Hitler and his advisors were turning away from Russia to ponder the conquest of the world, in the second half of July, the pace of the German *Vormarsch* was slowing abruptly along most of the eastern front, the result of stiffening Soviet resistance, concomitant German attrition, and growing logistical failures.

By late July, Bock's army group, its forward progress now stymied by mounting Soviet pressure across its entire front, was still struggling to eliminate the pocket at Smolensk while beset by burgeoning logistical problems and mounting casualties. As a result, the OKH ordered a halt to Army Group Center's advance on 30 July to allow it to rest and refit. (The month of July 1941 had cost the Germans 63,000 dead in the east, more than any month in the Russian campaign until Stalingrad in December 1942 and January 1943.)[3]

Throughout this period, *Generaloberst* Guderian continued to command his troops from the front lines—the forward edge of battle—despite the fact that his aggressive style of leadership was slowly taking a mental and physical toll. On the final day of July, the panzer general confided in Margarete, "The battle is harder than anything before. . . . It will take some time yet."[4]

CROSSING THE DNEPR (10/11.7.1941)

As noted above, the initial failure of Guderian's *Panzergruppe* 2 to breach the Dnepr at several points in early July—in particular, the failure of 24 Panzer Corps at Rogachev—had convinced him of the need to regroup his forces and shift his assaults to other points along the river line. By the evening of 9 July, with his three panzer corps settling into their assembly areas, he was poised to begin a second attempt. Moreover, he was prepared to launch this "decisive" operation without waiting for the arrival of the infantry corps of *Generaloberst* von Weichs's Second Army, still far behind the front lines despite exhausting forced marches.

Guderian's planned river crossing was part of a larger operational scheme devised by *Generaloberst* Halder, Chief of the Army General Staff, and approved by Hitler on 8 July. In an ambitious double envelopment, *Panzergruppen* 2 and 3—with Hoth forming the left and Guderian the right wing—were to capture the strategically vital Vitebsk-Orsha-Smolensk triangle (the so-called Smolensk gate, a roughly 80-kilometer gap between the two rivers and a natural weak spot in the Russian defenses), in the process encircling and annihilating the bulk of the remaining Soviet forces west of Moscow. With the enemy around Smolensk thus finished off, Hitler, and presumably Halder, assumed German forces would be able to occupy the region up to the upper Volga without serious fighting. Yet, although Halder foresaw a difficult struggle with strong Red Army reserves, he remained blissfully unaware that the STAVKA (Soviet Supreme Command) was hastening to assemble the five fresh armies of its second strategic echelon behind the Dvina and Dnepr river barriers to defend around Smolensk. As noted in chapter 2, the appearance of these armies would come as a most unpleasant surprise to the German High Command.

Guderian's operational plan was to conduct his assault against whatever remained of Marshal Semen Timoshenko's Western Front in a staggered fashion on 10/11 July. Justifiably concerned about the condition of his panzer group, which had marched and fought without surcease, he "deliberately sacrificed the principle of concentration" by deciding to attack on two successive days without a specific *Schwerpunkt* (center of gravity).[5] His ultimate objective was the narrow land bridge between El'nia on the Desna River and Dorogobuzh on the Dnepr, which offered the most direct route to Moscow by way of Viaz'ma and Mozhaisk. Resources available to Guderian included about 450 operational panzers[6] (less than half the number available to him on 22 June) and the concentrated airpower of GFM Albert Kesselring's 2 Air Fleet (*Luftflotte* 2).

Having shepherded the heavy howitzers and long-range artillery into position, 2 Panzer Group's thrust across the Dnepr got underway at dawn on 10 July. The assault groups of 4 Panzer Division and 10 ID (mot.) (24 PzK) punched across the river at and north of Stary Bychov,[7] supported by Stukas and fighters of

Werner Mölders's *Jagdgeschwader* 51. An officer in 4 PD described the beginning of the attack that morning:

> 10 July—0500 Hours: The artillery was firing with everything it had. A unique hissing emerged from the woods behind us. We threw ourselves flat on the ground. A howling—growing first stronger and then receding—went on for several minutes and deafened out all of the other sounds of war. Bundled tails of flame and smoke headed across the river. For the first time, we experienced the employment of a new weapon, the *Nebelwerfer*, which we also referred to as the *Do* gun. The rockets detonated on the far side among the enemy positions with a dull crash. Black mushroom clouds climbed skyward from the earth.
>
> One wave of bombers after the other headed eastward. The Russian anti-aircraft guns bellowed in response. Bands of Stukas split apart above our heads and tipped over individually. They worked over the enemy field positions and the enemy batteries. The engineers ran at double time down to the riverbanks and threw their assault boats and pontoons into the tepid waters of the Dnepr. It was probably about 100 meters wide in this area.[8] The motors were turned on; the rudders heaved into position. Up to that point, not a rifle round had been fired.[9]

Working feverishly, the German combat engineers soon had a footbridge in place, which the first riflemen used to feel their way across. They were followed by anti-tank and infantry guns ferried to the far bank on large pontoons. Before the Russian artillery had registered on the crossing point, the first assault detachments were already slipping into the forests beyond the Dnepr. After several hours of fighting, Langermann-Erlencamp's 4 PD and Loeper's 10 ID (mot.) had taken possession of a sizeable bridgehead. The operation had come off without a hitch. By evening, the lead elements of Geyr's 24 Panzer Corps had pushed several kilometers beyond the Dnepr and cut the road leading from Mogilev to Gomel.

The next day (11 July), Guderian's panzer troops breached the Soviet Dnepr defenses at two more points, this time between Orsha and Mogilev: At Kopys (47 PzK) and at Shklov (46 PzK).[10] At 0610 hours, in "beautiful sunshine," Guderian departed his command post—now at Tolochino, less than 50 kilometers west of Orsha and the site of Napoleon's headquarters in 1812—and struck out for Kopys to observe the crossing by *Generalmajor* Walter von Boltenstern's 29 ID (mot.); accompanying him was General Efisio Marras, the Italian military attaché, who had arrived at Guderian's CP the night before:

> In view of the dense clouds of dust put up by our advancing columns the drive along the river bank was most unpleasant. This dust, endured now for weeks on end, was equally hard on men, weapons, and engines. In particular the cylinders of the tanks became so clogged that their efficiency was considerably affected. At the headquarters of the 29 Motorized Infantry Division, near Kopys, I found both the corps and divisional commanders and was briefed on the situation. Regiments

> 15 and 71 were already over the river and had reached the edge of the woods east of Kopys; we watched them advance against two enemy divisions (the Russian 66 Army Corps, consisting of the 18 and 54 Rifle Divisions). The enemy was laying down weak harassing fire on the area around the divisional headquarters, which was also mined. We had good observation of the advance of our infantry and of the bridge-building that was being carried on immediately beneath where we were standing.[11]

Following the departure of the Italian attaché, Guderian was ferried across the river in an assault boat to follow the progress of his forces. By mid-afternoon, Boltenstern's infantry, supported by a battalion of assault guns, a flak battery, Pak, and pioneer units, had their bridgehead firmly in hand. Meanwhile, attempts by Weber's 17 Panzer Division to get across the Dnepr directly south of Orsha soon ran into serious trouble. Weber's assault troops had managed to carve out a fragile foothold on the eastern bank despite withering enemy fire; seriously outgunned, the commander on the spot, *Oberst* Licht, elected to withdraw from the bridgehead and pull back across the river—an action strongly supported by Guderian.

In the sector of Vietinghoff's 46 Panzer Corps (immediately to the right of Lemelsen's 47 PzK), successful river crossings were also made. *Generalleutnant* Ferdinand Schaal's 10 Panzer Division, supported by the elite *Grossdeutschland* Regiment,[12] crossed the Dnepr at a point south of Shklov (about 20 kilometers north of Mogilev), despite heavy Russian artillery fire and repeated attack from the air. The activities of the IRGD on the morning of 11 July are vividly outlined in the following account:

> The night of 10./11.7.[41] is very cold. As it turns to day, the Infantry Regiment *Grossdeutschland* stands ready at its jump-off positions; pneumatic boats and ferries are brought forward, the division's artillery is ready to fire, but enemy artillery fire is also falling on the assembly areas.
>
> At 0500 hours, the Stukas appear over the Dnepr and toss their bombs on the identified targets. The artillery uses the Stuka attack to home in on its targets—ammunition already has to be rationed!—and begins its barrage punctually at 0515 hours. At 0520, the men from Infantry Regiment *Grossdeutschland* push their assault boats and pneumatic floats into the water. Despite the Russian defensive fire, the first wave is across to the other bank by 0535 hours, and 20 minutes later the message comes that the infantry has already pushed ahead around a kilometer.
>
> 1st Battalion, Infantry Regiment *Grossdeutschland*, has as its opponent the "Stalin Students," who fight fanatically. There are heavy losses on both sides, but the "Grossdeutschen" fight ahead with élan. By 0620 hours they have expanded their bridgehead to a depth of 2 km.[13]

Although heavy Russian artillery fire delayed the construction of pontoon ferries and initially made it impossible to bring up bridging materials, the men of

Grossdeutschland continued to widen their bridgehead. To buttress the German counterbattery fire, corps artillery assets (cannon and heavy howitzer batteries) added their weight to the artillery duel. Under cover of these protective fires, the regiment's heavy infantry weapons were ferried across the river.

Directly to the north of IRGD and 10 Panzer Division, SS-*Gruppenführer* Paul Hausser's SS Motorized Infantry Division *Reich* launched its attack from the immediate vicinity of Shklov. However, before the SS grenadiers could commence their crossing, they first had to clear the Russians from strongly fortified positions atop Hill 215, on the west bank of the Dnepr.[14] Not until midday, 11 July, was the division able to fight its way through and assemble for the river crossing. Despite such challenges, and although the bridges in its sector had been damaged by air attack, the division successfully established its bridgehead. By day's end, the spearheads of 46 Panzer Corps were already 12 kilometers east of Shklov.[15]

Through his successful operations on 10/11 July 1941, Guderian had established a string of bridgeheads across the Dnepr River between Orsha and Rogachev; in doing so, he had punctured the Stalin Line and split the seam between Soviet 13 and 20 Armies. In fact, Guderian's river assault had rendered Timoshenko's defenses along the Dnepr, from Kopys southward to Mogilev and Stary Bychov, utterly untenable. Simply put, Timoshenko was losing control of the battle—a situation Guderian would be quick to exploit.

Among the officers on Guderian's staff who had closely observed the frenzied but purposeful activities of their revered commander during the Dnepr River crossing was *Oberstleutnant* Karl-Henning von Barsewisch, the panzer general's *Luftwaffe* liaison. To him, Guderian was a "superman, a ball of energy and brainy too." In his diary, Barsewisch gushed, "When Guderian makes decisions it is as if the War God himself rides above Walstatt. When his eyes flash Wotan seems to hurl lightning or Thor swings his hammer."[16]

THE DASH TO SMOLENSK

Having punched his way through the Dnepr river line, Guderian was optimistic that organized Soviet resistance would soon collapse. The panzer general was convinced—quite erroneously—that the river barrier had been the enemy's last line of defense and that his forces were now facing the remnants of a shattered Red Army. "I hope to defeat them in the coming days," he wrote home to Margarete, "and achieve in the process a success that will decide the campaign in our favor."[17] As historian David Stahel observed, "There was no ambiguity about how Guderian saw the campaign continuing. Not only was the war being won, but he was the one winning it."[18]

Guderian's tanks rolled rapidly eastward toward the open country south of Smolensk. On 13 July, 17 Panzer Division seized Orsha, a major rail junction on the Dnepr about 100 kilometers southwest of Smolensk; by day's end, 29

Motorized, bursting out of its bridgehead at Kopys, was halfway to the city. Farther south, 10 Panzer Division (46 PzK) captured Gorki and rumbled southeast toward the Sozh River, while 4 Panzer and 10 Motorized Division (24 PzK) debouched from Stary Bychov—the advance of the two panzer corps trapping major components of Soviet 13 Army in and about Mogilev. The Soviets, who had transformed the town into an impregnable fortress, resisted defiantly. Guderian wasted little time trying to subdue it—that task was better left to the infantry of Weichs's Second Army, which had reached the Berezina and was rapidly pushing east in forced marches. "Gallant Mogilev" would hold out until 27 July 1941.[19]

While these operations were underway, *Generaloberst* Hoth's *Panzergruppe* 3 had also been making steady progress on the northern wing of Army Group Center. Thus, by nightfall, 13 July, the spearheads of the two panzer groups—7 Panzer Division (Hoth) and 29 Motorized (Guderian)—were only about 55 kilometers apart and rapidly converging on Smolensk. Marshal Timoshenko's Western Front was now fighting for its very survival, threatened as it was with encirclement by the headlong advance of the German armor.[20]

In its daily report for 13 July, the Operations Branch of the German Army General Staff noted "furious counterattacks" (*heftige Gegenangriffe*) against GFM von Kluge's Fourth Panzer Army,[21] which, it will be recalled, had maintained uneasy control of both Hoth's and Guderian's panzer groups since 3 July. The reference is to what Guderian would later call the "Timoshenko offensive," which began on this day and continued until 16 July. The Soviet marshal's intent was to cut off and destroy both of Army Group Center's panzer groups while restoring Western Front defenses along the Dnepr. Yet, given the realities at the front, Timoshenko's plan was not remotely feasible. Of the handful of armies taking part in the offensive, only 21 Army succeeded in carrying out its orders with any success at all by pushing across the Dnepr and briefly threatening German communications at Bobruisk, on the Berezina. Moreover, by provoking some confusion in German ranks, elements of Soviet 13 Army were able to extricate themselves from impending encirclement east of Mogilev. Despite these modest gains and the unrelenting pressure applied by the STAVKA, Timoshenko was unable to arrest the drive of the German armor on Smolensk.

Guderian, meanwhile, now enjoying complete operational freedom, pressed on at a torrid pace, pushing men and machines ruthlessly, without concern for the open flanks of his panzer corps. By nightfall, 14 July, Boltenstern's 29 Motorized Division (47 PzK) was approaching Smolensk from the southwest, followed by the few operational tanks of Nehring's 18 Panzer Division. In addition, 10 Panzer Division (46 PzK) had almost reached the Sozh, its ultimate objective the strategically important town of El'nia, on the Desna southeast of Smolensk. On the far right flank, Geyr's 24 Panzer Corps screened the 2 Panzer Group advance. German air activity was robust, with Bruno Loerzer's 2 Air Corps flying 885 sorties against Soviet 21 Army on 14 July;[22] the rail link between Smolensk and Moscow was also struck for the first time that day.[23]

Guderian's dynamic and demanding style of leadership—understandable as the stakes could not have been higher—sometimes put his troops in perilous positions, as the following account by *Generalmajor* Nehring (C-in-C 18 PD) illustrates:

> On 12 July, the crossing of the "wheeled elements" [*Radteile*] of [18 Panzer] Division began on a poorly constructed military bridge, while the panzer units had to cross on ferries. As a result of this and of enemy action, there were delays.
>
> The division's next objective was Krasnyi. The roads there were only sketchy, the terrain sandy, wet in the Rossosenka sector, the bridges not capable of heavy loads. Although 17 Panzer Division did not succeed, as our lefthand neighbor, in crossing the Dnepr between Kopys and Orsha, and although ground and air reconnaissance reported a stronger enemy with tanks on what was thus our vulnerable flank, the corps ordered that no covering forces could be diverted. The principle of the rapid thrust into the depth [of the enemy front] went too far in this case and was carried out at the cost of tactical necessity. The consequence was that enemy tanks succeeded in destroying the majority of the division's supply services on 14 July near Dobryn, capturing the division's files, and coming close to capturing the divisional staff without the *Generalsstaffel*, which was located much further forward.
>
> Nevertheless, the area around Krasnyi-Gusino is reached on 14 July, as ordered. The division's task here is to act as flank cover for the attack of 29 Motorized [Infantry] Division on Smolensk, which results in heavy, strength-sapping forest battles. . . . Although the envisaged objectives are achieved, the troops are rather battle-weary [*recht abgekämpft*]. Panzer and motorized vehicles have suffered a great deal on the poor roads and are in need of technical overhaul, for which the spare parts required for the multiplicity of vehicle types to be found in the division are lacking. On the whole, supplies across the great distance from the homeland to Smolensk have not yet been secured.[24]

By late 15 July, advance elements of the "magnificently led" (Guderian's words) 29 ID (mot.)—the "Falcon" division—despite the dreadful condition of the roads, stubborn Russian resistance on the ground, and attacks by waves of Soviet Air Force (VVS) bombers that resulted in serious losses, reached the southern outskirts of Smolensk,[25] while Hoth's 3 Panzer Group had seized Iartsevo, 50 kilometers northeast of Smolensk (and just 300 kilometers from Moscow), severing the main road and rail links with the city. Twenty Soviet divisions—among them the remnants of two mechanized corps—now faced potential annihilation inside the incipient pocket, which extended westward from Smolensk toward Orsha. Another spectacular German cauldron battle was taking shape. However, with Guderian's panzer group still a good distance from Hoth's 7 Panzer Division at Iartsevo, the Smolensk pocket was far from hermetically sealed.

On the morning of 16 July 1941, Boltenstern's 29 ID (mot.) attacked into Smolensk, seizing the golden-domed Uspenski Cathedral and the railroad bridge over the Dnepr. Bock was elated by the news. Yet, while the southern end of the city was rapidly secured, the northern bank was more bitterly contested. Boltenstern's panzer grenadiers, supported by tanks of 18 Panzer Division, would require several days of costly street fighting to pry loose the rest of the city from its defenders—129 and 152 Rifle Divisions of Lt.-Gen. Mikhail F. Lukin's 16 Army.[26] As *Generaloberst* Lemelsen (47 PzK) noted in his diary, the fighting was often house to house, at close quarters, with bayonets and hand grenades.[27] By 18 July—that is, after less than a month in action—18 Panzer was in a "wretched state," having lost more than three-quarters of its tanks (it began the campaign with 218) and nearly half of its anti-tank guns, a reflection not only of the ferocity of the fighting but of its crippling impact on German tank forces when left without support from the foot infantry.[28]

Acutely cognizant of the extreme pressures facing its mobile units, Army Group Center ordered the infantry divisions of Second and Ninth Armies to advance with utmost speed to their relief. Forced marches (*Gewaltmärsche*) of 30, 40, even 50 kilometers per day through the "vast oppressiveness of Belorussia" were not uncommon. Simply put, the German infantry did two things in the summer of 1941: they marched, and they fought. After the initial frontier battles, however, they mostly marched, from dawn to dusk, as they sought to catch up with the tank and motorized formations ranging far to the east. The brutal pace of the advance (*Vormarsch*), coupled with the unholy trinity of heat, dust, and thirst, forced the German *Landser*, particularly the marching infantry, into a "daily existence that they often found difficult if not impossible to accept" (*zwangen den Landsern ein Leben auf, in das sie sich nur schwer und oftmals gar nicht hineinfinden konnten*).[29] Werner Heinemann, an officer in 23 Infantry Division (Second Army), in a field post letter to his wife, dramatically portrayed the rigors of the forced marches:

> 17.7.41:
>
> How can those back home even begin to fathom how many countless sacrifices and how much sweat and deathly exhaustion of the infantry soldier make up such pursuit marches as these? The apathy of man and horse is often so great, that not even a kind word helps. War is the toughest thing there is in life, and it is in the breathtaking tempo of our operations that the key to our rapid final victory lies. You have to have the courage to be tough, or else you can only conclude that you "can't go on!" Everything has to go on, and as fast as possible, but it's frequently bitterly difficult to have to demand everything and more, over and over again. (Emphasis in the original)[30]

By mid-July, the infantry of *Generaloberst* von Weichs's Second Army were only beginning to reach the Dnepr. The map of the Operations Branch of the

German Army General Staff for 15 July shows advance detachments of two of Weichs's divisions (137 and 292 IDs) straddling Orsha (where the Dnepr bends sharply east toward Smolensk), while farther south advance elements of 31 ID were at Bychov.[31] However, another ten days would pass before the German infantry would finally succeed in relieving all of Guderian's forces from the *Kesselfront*.

By reaching Smolensk, Guderian's panzer group had covered roughly 600 kilometers in twenty-five days since the start of the campaign, an average daily advance of 24 kilometers.[32] It was a truly remarkable accomplishment, a testimony to the stamina, willpower, and professional acumen of the fifty-three-year-old panzer general. On 17 July 1941, Guderian was awarded the Oak Leaves to the Knight's Cross, becoming only the fifth man in the Army, and the twenty-fourth in the entire *Wehrmacht*, to receive the coveted award.[33]

Yet, despite Guderian's brilliant achievement—or perhaps because of it—the losses of his panzer group were mounting ominously. On 11 July 1941, an *Oberst* Ochsner, following a visit to both Hoth's and Guderian's panzer groups, reported back to Chief of the Army General Staff Halder, stating that the panzer troops had suffered serious losses in both men and materiel and that the blistering operational tempo had made all the men tired (Ochsner also noted that the Red Army was well led and fought with great determination). By 12 July 1941, 3 Panzer Division (24 PzK) was so exhausted that its chief of staff asked for support from the corps reserve; on 13 July, Geyr's other panzer division (4 PD) was down to just twenty-five operational tanks[34] (although its situation would improve in the days ahead, with the arrival of spare parts and replacement vehicles). As a rule, however, despite heavy losses in troops and equipment, few replacements were reaching the front. About this time, the divisional Catholic priest in 18 PD wrote,

> Ambulances [*Sankas*] come and go, unload their sad cargo, and disappear again in the direction of the front. I go from room to room. All words fail here. Quiet whispering and groaning, usually silence, large, wide-open eyes. Only here and there a tired smile. Behind the building, in a shady corner, the dead: officers and men. The numbers ever increasing. They are young people, barely come of age, for the division is, of course, comprised almost exclusively of active troops.[35]

More generally, with Operation Barbarossa less than a month old, Bock's Army Group Center—like the *Ostheer* writ large—was beginning to suffer from a "debilitating lack of military resources," which, in the days and weeks ahead, would force "the juggling of units between crisis points and [give] rise to increasingly bitter disputes among commanders. There were simply not enough resources to meet the mushrooming demands of the war."[36]

THE SMOLENSK CAULDRON (THROUGH 28.7.1941)

Soviet forces in the Smolensk pocket embraced the bulk of 16, 19, and 20 Armies. Because the German infantry had yet to reach the forward edge of battle, the panzer and motorized divisions of Army Group Center assembled a cordon of tanks, half-tracks, and dismounted truck-borne infantry around the trapped Soviet armies. In the north, *Gen.d.Pz.Tr.* Rudolf Schmidt's reinforced 39 Panzer Corps (3 Panzer Group) was able to forge a fairly solid front along the northern shoulder of the pocket; along its southern perimeter, however, Lemelsen's 47 Panzer Corps, locked in heavy combat and holding a frontage of about 100 kilometers with just ten battalions,[37] was unable to cover the final few kilometers to link up with *Generalmajor* Hans Freiherr von Funck's 7 Panzer Division (39 PzK) near Iartsevo. This left a narrow corridor along the swampy banks of the Dnepr, stretching eastward from the cauldron to the village of Solovevo (some 15 kilometers south of Iartsevo), and through this corridor a stream of Red Army forces exited the pocket to safety. Once again, the underlying dilemma for the *Ostheer* was all too evident: It was simply incapable of addressing the growing challenges of terrain, time, and resources.

In its war diary on 15 July, 3 Panzer Group registered its frustration: "Unfortunately, the linkup with 2 Panzer Group is lacking, just as at Minsk."[38] The days ahead would bring even greater frustration, reaching all the way to Hitler's headquarters at Rastenburg, as Guderian, instead of wheeling northeast—as he clearly could have done—with his 46 Panzer Corps to seal the gap, elected to continue its drive toward the high ground at El'nia, fixated as he was on maintaining momentum toward Moscow. The stubborn panzer leader's determination to downgrade the encirclement front to a secondary priority for his panzer group signified that, in the Smolensk cauldron battle, tens of thousands of Soviet soldiers would avoid death or capture and escape to fight another day. Guderian's willful action—taken in flagrant disregard of the operational imperatives of GFM von Bock, GFM von Kluge (Guderian's immediate superior), and *Generaloberst* Hoth—would render the Smolensk *Kesselschlacht* (cauldron battle) an incomplete victory at best.

By 18 July, infantry of *Gen.d.Inf.* Hermann Geyer's 9 Army Corps finally began to reach the southwestern shoulder of the encirclement ring. This enabled 17 Panzer Division to be pulled off the *Kesselfront* (northeast of Orsha) and shifted to an area south of Smolensk, where it was committed against Soviet forces attacking northward toward the city; in the course of this action, *Generalmajor* Ritter von Weber (C-in-C 17 PD) was mortally wounded on 19 July and died the next day in a field hospital at Krasnyi.[39] Command of 17 PD was given to *Generalmajor* Wilhelm Ritter von Thoma, one of the *Wehrmacht*'s most senior and experienced panzer officers.

While Weber was being mortally wounded, the command post of Lemelsen's 47 Panzer Corps was suddenly attacked by Soviet forces advancing on Smolensk. Lemelsen described the harrowing event in his diary:

> Sunday, 20.7.[41]
>
> 4 weeks' battle!
>
> It was a very black day yesterday, which will remain unforgettable. . . . The enemy was attacking Smolensk from the south with one division and heavy artillery, and came upon our command post first. He exerted pressure on us from the south and, as it went on, also from the east. We were only very weakly protected by our security platoon and one flak MG company, and thus I ordered 29 [ID (mot.)] in Smolensk to provide support with one company of motorcycle riflemen. Despite this, the enemy approached ever closer and his Urrah! could be plainly heard. A *Kampfgruppe* of our corps' signal battalion, radio company, was ambushed by the Russians and butchered in an utterly bestial manner. 18 men were later found, among them the magnificent *Leutnant* Partschefeld, all murdered in the cruelest manner, most of them by shots to the back of the head.[40]

Meanwhile, Soviet forces inside the pocket sought desperately to break through the fragile German picket lines, the daily report of the OKH Operations Branch on 18 July reporting "desperate breakout attempts."[41] The panzer divisions, perennially short of infantry, had never been intended to perform in such static defensive roles—a panzer operations manual, published just six months before the Russian campaign, devoted twenty-six pages to the "Attack," while the topic of "Defense" was essentially dismissed in two paragraphs—and they lacked not only time when it came to organizing their defensive pickets but also the expertise required to establish the coordinated defense in depth discussed in infantry training manuals. In France and Poland, mobile units had tended to superimpose a hasty, ad hoc screen of security pickets around an encircled enemy force, but in Russia this often proved ineffective.[42]

Pressure was now mounting on Guderian to slam the pocket shut; yet he was not about to do so at the expense of suspending his drive on El'nia and the crossings over the Desna River. GFM von Bock stressed to GFM von Kluge the urgency of closing the trap near Iartsevo; the next morning (19 July), he telephoned Fourth Panzer Army headquarters and spoke to Kluge's chief of staff, *Oberst* Günther Blumentritt, directing him to ask Guderian "whether or not he is in a position to carry out the order of three days ago to link up with 3 Panzer Group near Iartsevo. If not, I have to commit other forces to do so."[43] The conversation then took an uncomfortable turn. "[Bock] asked: 'Is everything alright with the command there? Why, for example, is the Infantry Regiment *Grossdeutschland* still milling about far behind the front?' At this point Kluge jumped in and said that he had overheard the conversation and had to defend the panzer group against my accusation of poor command—which resulted in a brief argument."[44]

In fact, Guderian had been making an effort (of sorts) to close the pocket by marshaling forces for a drive toward Dorogobuzh, southeast of Iartsevo. On 18 July, he ordered Nehring's badly depleted 18 Panzer Division toward Dorogobuzh, but the division (as noted) had already lost most of its tanks and almost half its anti-tank guns (personnel losses had also been high). When Kluge got wind of Guderian's intent—to move 18 PD from the southern rim of the cauldron before the foot infantry had arrived ("in essence . . . attempting to close one hole by opening another")[45]—he immediately reversed the order. And he did so without even informing Guderian, so strong had the antipathy between the two men become.

Guderian made a second attempt on 20/21 July, this time dispatching elements of Hausser's SS Motorized Division *Reich* northward toward Dorogobuzh; yet the attack faltered due to difficult terrain and Soviet aerial bombing. On 23 July, Guderian visited the forwardmost units of SS *Reich* to assess the situation, the visit convincing him of the need to postpone the attack. "All attempts to advance toward Dorogobuzh," he later acknowledged, "were a complete failure" (*Die Versuche, in Richtung Dorogobush vorwärtszukommen, scheiterten allerdings völlig*).[46] In any case, despite Guderian's rather disingenuous postwar assertion that he had been "very anxious" to help Hoth close the pocket, his actions proved otherwise, in particular his decision to continue to direct Schaal's 10 Panzer Division to El'nia.

By now, sealing and eliminating the Smolensk pocket—in the face of mounting enemy pressure—had become an obsession of sorts for the commander of Army Group Center. His patience wearing thin, Bock confided in his diary on 20 July 1941, "At the moment, there is only one pocket on the army group's front! And it has a hole! For so far we have unfortunately been unable to achieve the union of the inner wings of the two armored groups at and east of Smolensk that we have been striving for for many days."[47] Once again, Bock was critical of Kluge and his Fourth Panzer Army command, which he characterized as useless for failing to take a stronger stand with Guderian to ensure closure of the pocket. When 2 Panzer Group hailed the capture of El'nia as a great success, "which has to be exploited!," Bock was dismissive. The only thing that mattered, he replied, was the "hermetic sealing of the Smolensk pocket while screening to the east."[48] To reinforce his point, he dispatched a General Staff officer directly to 2 Panzer Group, bypassing Kluge's headquarters entirely, while also having *Generalmajor* Hans von Greiffenberg, his chief of staff, speak to Guderian by telephone to further underscore the urgency of the army group's instructions.

With the increasingly exhausted mobile units unable to seal the pocket, the *Luftwaffe* tried to do so from the air, striking Soviet troop positions and lines of communication and also flying close-support missions. Yet, while the fighters, fighter-bombers, and bombers of the *Luftwaffe* could strike by day with great destructive power, precise target identification was virtually impossible at night due to the paucity of distinctive terrain features; simply put, the *Luftwaffe* lacked the all-weather, round-the-clock capability required for such a demanding mission. In his postwar memoir, Kesselring admitted that his 2 Air Fleet could only do so much:

> These battles led to the cauldron battle around Smolensk (from mid-July to the beginning of August), which was a great success (over 300,000 prisoners), but on the other hand provided nothing decisive, in other words just a "common victory" [*ordinären Sieg*]. It could have been decisive, if a gap located at the east of Smolensk could have been closed. My own requests for urgency and those of the Commander-in-Chief of the *Luftwaffe* failed in the execution. A narrow gap, a few kilometers wide, through the middle of which ran a small river valley with camouflaging ground cover, allowed a considerable number of the [Soviet] forces to leak out in the course of a few days, above all during the nights. While the close-support planes were able to reduce much of this leakage during the day through unrelenting attacks, the Russians could still make use of the twilight and nighttime all the more successfully. The Russian soldiers who escaped to their rear in this way—I estimated this at over 100,000 men—became the skeleton of new Russian units.[49]

The fact that neither Guderian's nor Hoth's panzer groups could cover the final patch of ground to plug the corridor near Iartsevo and seal the pocket speaks volumes about just how worn out the mobile forces had become. The strain on the men was palpable, the result of physical exhaustion, inexorably mounting casualties, declining panzer support, and growing concerns about shortages of artillery shells and other munitions desperately needed to hold the main battle line (*Hauptkampflinie*) against the ferocious Soviet counterattacks.

By 19 July, attrition since the start of the campaign had cost Guderian's group 830 officer casualties, while overall losses of 2 Panzer Group amounted to at least 15,228 men (dead, wounded, missing).[50] Moreover, losses of armored fighting vehicles had reached staggering proportions. For example, 4 PD had just forty-four operational tanks on 21 July (actually a slight increase in combat-capable tanks from the week before);[51] 10 PD possessed just nine fully combat-capable tanks, with an additional sixty-six—many with minor engine damage due to a lack of oil—able to perform limited defensive tasks; and, of course, Nehring's 18 PD had also lost the bulk of its armor. (On 22 July, 18 PD received an allotment of thirty new Pz III and Pz IV tanks, which managed to bring Nehring's division up to 20 percent of its authorized strength; however, by 24 July, ongoing heavy combat had reduced divisional strength to just twelve operational panzers.) Greatly inhibiting the rehabilitation of Guderian's tank forces was the fact that barely a trickle of new tanks and engines was reaching his panzer group, Hitler and OKH opting instead to allocate the great majority of new production to the new divisions being raised for post-Barbarossa tasks; indeed, as of late July 1941, only forty-five replacement tank engines were being provided on a monthly basis across the entire eastern front.[52]

Along with combat attrition, the supply situation also evinced a dangerous trend. On 22 July, the quartermaster general's war diary of 2 Panzer Group stated that the munitions situation had become "critical," especially for Geyr's 24 Panzer Corps; two days later (24 July), the stocks of shells available to Vietinghoff's 46 Panzer Corps were also considered "critical," while the situation of Lemelsen's 47 Panzer Corps was merely viewed as "tight." What this meant for the troops at the front is perhaps best illustrated by Schaal's 10 PD at El'nia, for which ammunition had to be hauled by truck from supply depots over 400 kilometers to the rear. On 21 July, the division's war diary noted that the munitions situation had become "strained" and that artillery shells could only be used sparingly.[53] As a result, drastic measures were taken, such as allowing only sighted firing with artillery, which, in the face of incessant enemy attacks, only placed an additional psychological burden on the panzer troops.

Despite the burgeoning crises created by ongoing attrition of men and materiel, serious supply shortages, and the deepening physical and psychological strains on tank crews and panzer grenadiers, the combat continued with unabated fury across the front of Guderian's panzer group. Still without adequate infantry support (by 21 July, the marching infantry was only beginning to reach the panzer group), the positions of Guderian's forces—along the southern rim of the Smolensk cauldron (47 PzK, less 17 PD), at El'nia (46 PzK), and in the south from Krichev to Propoisk (24 PzK)—remained for the most part extremely porous. Without the attached *Luftwaffe* flak batteries using their high-velocity 88mm guns in a ground support role, the predicament of his panzer corps would have been even more precarious.[54]

Finally, over the next few days, several infantry corps (5, 8, and 9 AKs) reached the Smolensk battlefield, enabling Guderian's (and most of Hoth's) armored and motorized units to be pulled off the encirclement ring by 25 July;[55] henceforth, the task of compressing and breaking up the Smolensk pocket fell largely to the foot infantry.

Despite Bock's growing frustration—and Hitler's close attention to the problem[56]—it was not until three days later that the narrow corridor east of Smolensk was finally closed. At 2015 hours on 28 July, Lemelsen's 47 Panzer Corps reported to Guderian's headquarters that elements of its 17 Panzer Division and 3 Panzer Group's 20 ID (mot.)—advancing from the south and north, respectively—had made contact at the village of Ratchino, on the Dnepr River 11 kilometers south of Solovevo, finally sealing the pocket.[57] That was the good news; the bad news was that this vital operational success would be short-lived, for the desperately fighting Russians would again pry open the corridor several days later, much to the supreme disgust of GFM von Bock.

That same day (28 July), an elated panzer soldier in 17 PD, no doubt reflecting the pride of his comrades, boasted about his division's success: "You will have heard about the fighting around Smolensk on the radio. Those were my proud soldiers who achieved the breakthrough, the flag raised in victory. We are standing just outside Moscow, all units welded together into an iron chain, the like of which the world has never before seen. Only a short while still, and then that great event of world history will take place."[58]

THE BATTLE OF ROSLAVL (1.–5.8.1941)

It will be remembered that Roslavl, about 100 kilometers southeast of Smolensk, was one of Guderian's original Barbarossa objectives. On 23 July, the Soviets began to strongly counterattack from an area near the town, precipitating a crisis for the badly depleted 18 Panzer Division (which had just been withdrawn from the encirclement ring) and putting extreme pressure on the southern flank of *Panzergruppe* 2. The enemy pressure across 18 Panzer's front grew so intense that even Guderian feared the division's complete collapse. On 25 July, the war diarist of 18 PD made a troubling observation: "Everywhere new enemy columns with artillery." The next day (26 July), he recorded, "Constant heaviest artillery fire, of a kind the troops have seldom experienced" (emphasis in the original).[59] The divisional diary went on to question the morale of the men, which the report of a battalion doctor diagnosed as collective battle fatigue:

> A state of absolute exhaustion is noticeable among all men of the battalion. The reason is a far too great mental and nervous strain. The troops were under a powerful barrage of heavy artillery. The enemy charged them . . . penetrated their positions and was repulsed in hand-to-hand fighting. . . . The men could not shut their eyes day and night. Food could be supplied only during the few hours of darkness. A large number of men, still serving with the troops at present, were buried alive by artillery fire. That the men were promised a few days of rest but instead found themselves in an even worse situation had a particularly grave effect. The men are indifferent and apathetic, are partly suffering from crying fits, and are not to be cheered up by this or that phrase. Food is being taken only in disproportionately small quantities.[60]

Despite the doctor's devastating diagnosis, Nehring's panzer grenadiers—ably supported by the *Luftwaffe*—stood their ground until the arrival of the infantry brought welcome relief. That they managed to do so despite such demonstrably adverse conditions was testimony to the discipline and professionalism of the German Army of 1941.

The violent assaults on 18 Panzer Division—and also against the elite IRGD,[61] now subordinated to Nehring's division—were part of the Red Army's first major counteroffensive in the Smolensk region. Planned by General G. K. Zhukov, Chief of the Red Army General Staff, it called for Marshal Timoshenko's strongly reinforced Western Front to "encircle and destroy the enemy's Smolensk grouping"[62] and recapture the city. In response, Timoshenko assembled several large "operational groups" (each based on an army) in a wide arc extending from Toropets in the north to Roslavl in the south with the goal of striking several powerful blows toward Smolensk along converging axes. Although the Soviet marshal directed the bulk of his forces against Hoth's 3 Panzer Group, considered the most immediate threat to Moscow, "Group Kachalov," the strongest of the operational groups (based on Lt.-Gen. V. I. Kachalov's 28 Army, with 145 RD, 149 RD, and 104 TD, supported by two air regiments), struck out northwest from Roslavl toward Rudnia, Pochinok, and Smolensk on the morning of 23 July.[63]

Although Kachalov's group was composed of poorly trained formations, lacking adequate artillery and tank support, its offensive threatened to envelop both flanks of Nehring's 18 Panzer Division, as well as the forward positions of Vietinghoff's 46 Panzer Corps in the El'nia salient. In response, Bock reinforced the threatened sector with two infantry divisions from Geyer's 9 Army Corps (263 and 292 IDs). While Kachalov pressed his attacks furiously for several days, his forces performed poorly, the general and his chief of staff reduced to trying to teach basic combined-arms tactics to subordinate commanders while the battle was ongoing; after registering minor gains, the Soviet assault collapsed in the face of determined German resistance. The German forces, however, lacked the strength to push Group Kachalov back to Roslavl. By 28 July, 18 Panzer Division had withdrawn into the forests southeast of Smolensk, where it would remain to refit until mid-August 1941; *Grossdeutschland* was dispatched to El'nia.[64]

After consultations with the OKH, Bock's solution to the "Kachalov problem" was an all-out assault with Guderian's southernmost panzer corps (24 PzK) against the base of the attacking Soviet group at Roslavl, a major road junction and communications node. Kachalov's group would be encircled and annihilated; the threat to Guderian's southern flank removed.

On 27 July, Guderian, accompanied by his chief of staff, *Oberst* von Liebenstein, flew via Orsha to the headquarters of Army Group Center in Borisov; there, in the presence of Bock and Brauchitsch (Army C-in-C), Guderian briefed his plan of attack, and Bock approved it. Guderian requested, and was provided with, additional infantry for the offensive: 7 Army Corps with four infantry divisions (9 AK had already been placed under Guderian's command). The enlarged panzer group was elevated in status to an army group (*Armeegruppe Guderian*), while Kluge's Fourth Panzer Army headquarters, active since 3 July, was unceremoniously dissolved. Once again, to his immense relief, Guderian would report directly to the commander of Army Group Center.[65]

Guderian and his staff hammered out the details of the impending attack. His infantry divisions, however, would have to do with limited tank support for, by 29 July, his panzer divisions were down to just 286 operational tanks, 128 of them obsolete Panzer IIs. Subtracting the 19 command tanks left Guderian with just 97 Pz IIIs and 38 Pz IVs in his order of battle. In its war diary, 2 Panzer Group noted that these figures for operational tanks were "utterly negligible" (*äusserst gering*; emphasis in the original), as they represented the entire available inventory of four panzer divisions (3, 4, 17, and 18 PDs). As Guderian surely understood, these were shockingly low figures given his command's burgeoning tasks.[66]

On the evening of 31 July, Guderian took a moment to present the Knight's Cross (*Ritterkreuz*) to generals Lemelsen (47 PzK) and Nehring (18 PD) and to *Oberstleutnant* Franz, the chief operations officer of 29 ID (mot.). Two days before (29 July), Guderian received his Oak Leaves to the Knight's Cross (awarded 17 July), personally delivered to the panzer general by *Oberst* Rudolf Schmundt, Hitler's chief *Wehrmacht* adjutant.

The next morning (1 August), Guderian put in his attack. Before he did so, however, the commander of 3 Panzer Division also presented Knight's Crosses to several battle-hardened soldiers of his command, among them *Oberfeldwebel* Albert Blaich, a young tank commander in the division's 6 Panzer Regiment:

> On the morning of 1 August, the division commander, *Generalleutnant* Model, came to the front. Almost the entire 6 Panzer Regiment had fallen in. A short while later, the commander of the 3rd Panzer Battalion, *Hauptmann* Schneider-Kostalski, *Feldwebel* Reinicke of the 2nd Company, to whom the Knight's Cross had been awarded on 9 July, and *Oberfeldwebel* Blaich stood before the division commander, who personally presented the three Knight's Crosses. . . .
>
> After Model had presented the Knight's Crosses to Schneider-Kostalski and Reinicke, the slim general with the monocle approached the *Oberfeldwebel* at a brisk step, waited for him to make his report, and then stretched out his hand in greeting.
>
> "*Oberfeldwebel* Blaich," said Model, "it is a joy and an honor for me to present the Knight's Cross awarded to you on 24 July."
>
> General Model had his adjutant hand him a small box, removed from this the Knight's Cross with its broad black-white-red ribbon, and hung it round Blaich's neck, who was visibly both proud and nervous in equal measure. "I congratulate you. You are the 10th member of the Division permitted to wear this prestigious award."
>
> Then Model drove back to the division command post. This time there was no celebration. Together with the 4 Panzer Division, the division was to win the Krichev-Roslavl road beyond the Ostyor River and capture Roslavl.[67]

The tanks of Geyr's 24 Panzer Corps (3 and 4 PDs) debouched from their bridgeheads over the Sozh River at Krichev while the infantry of *Gen.d.Art.* Wilhelm Fahrmbacher's 7 Army Corps advanced on the panzer corps' left flank. The initial assault was supported by Stukas and other assets of Loerzer's 2 Air Corps,[68] but these were greeted with such savage anti-aircraft fire over Roslavl that none of them (about thirty-five aircraft) returned to base without battle damage. Model's armor and mobile infantry soon ripped a gaping hole in the front of Soviet 13 Army (on Kachalov's left flank), the panzers pouring through in a "veritable flood." They then wheeled northeast along the Roslavl road, 3 Panzer taking up blocking positions there while 4 Panzer raced on for Roslavl. In concert with these lightning moves, Fahrmbacher's infantry advanced on the city from the northwest, an advance detachment severing the railroad line from Roslavl to Rudnia.

The next day (2 August), 9 Army Corps—with its 292 ID in the van—strongly supported by artillery and 150mm *Nebelwerfer* rocket projectors, began to move south toward Roslavl from the area around Rudnia. By day's end, the foot infantry of both army corps were bearing down on the city from the north and west, while the tanks and panzer grenadiers of Langermann-Erlencamp's 4 Panzer Division were within striking distance, barely eight kilometers southwest of Roslavl, despite tenacious Russian aerial bombing (an attack by recently introduced and heavily armored Soviet Il-2 *Sturmovik* ground-attack aircraft struck the divisional command post on this day, resulting in heavy casualties).[69]

In what had been a textbook operation, both Kachalov's right and left flanks were now turned, his group facing imminent disaster. Encouraged by the rapid progress, Bock observed, "The attack on Roslavl is going well. The enemy troops there are poor, our losses are slight. It is a pity that we are at the end of our tether just now, and also that a thorough replenishing of the panzer divisions can no longer be postponed."[70]

The next morning (August 3), the battle reached its climax. From their positions just outside Roslavl, the *Landser* of 23 Infantry Division (7 AK) watched in awe as Loerzer's Stuka squadrons smashed the city in repeated attacking waves. Brushing aside heavy anti-tank, anti-aircraft, and artillery fire, 4 Panzer Division's *Gruppe Eberbach* (led by *Oberst* Heinrich Eberbach, Commander, 35 Pz.Rgt.), having enveloped Roslavl from the south, stormed the city and captured it by 1045 hours.[71] Due to the bold nature of the advance, the Germans also secured "a portion" of the bridges in the city (although the big bridge across the Ostyor River was destroyed).

Capitalizing on its success, *Gruppe Eberbach* pushed on to the northeast, linking up with advance elements of 292 Infantry Division (9 AK)—which had struggled southward along muddy roads, the result of a sudden downpour[72]—at a destroyed bridge across the Ostrik River, east of the village of Kosaki and 17 kilometers beyond Roslavl; in doing so, they closed the trap around Kachalov's dazed and overmatched forces.

One of the participants in the attack on Roslavl was Fritz Koehler, who described the memorable day in his diary:

> The start of the attack has been set for 0630 hours, and thus we go forward at that time. We advance along a broad front, a multitude of heavy weapons follows us. After about an hour, we receive the first rifle fire, and a Russian artillery piece has already taken us under direct fire. Our artillery responds, and once our heavy infantry weapons have also joined in, the Russian gun is soon reduced to silence. But one of our panzers also comes to grief and is shot up in flames. We push further forward and take around 150 Russians prisoner. In addition, we capture 12 to 15 modern flak guns (probably of American manufacture). . . . In the meantime, we have reached the edge of Roslavl. White Very signal lights are flaring up to the right and left. Panzers and motorcycle riflemen have most likely already pushed into the enemy's flanks. We do not even experience any resistance and clean out the town. We find only isolated, scattered Russians. However, the Russians have set fire to the oil and gasoline supplies before they fled. Unfortunately, there is almost nothing to "organize" in this town. That sort of thing was better in France.[73]

Throughout the battle, Guderian had shuttled to and fro between the spearheads of his attacking corps—on the final, decisive day of the attack, even advancing on foot with the leading rifle company of 507 Infantry Regiment (292 ID). Over the next two days, the Germans systematically sealed off and liquidated the pocket; when they tallied up Red Army losses, they counted 38,561 prisoners of war, along with 250 tanks and other armored vehicles, 613 guns of all types, and some 1,800 trucks, vehicles, and prime movers (even an armored train) captured or destroyed—figures equal to well over 80 percent of Group Kachalov's original force.[74] Lt. Gen. Kachalov perished in the fighting near the village of Starinka, 16 kilometers north of Roslavl. It was, recalled Guderian, "a considerable and highly satisfactory victory."[75]

Although clearly another brilliant feat of German arms, the actual outcome of the Roslavl battle left much to be desired (Guderian's postwar pronouncement notwithstanding). Once again, a German cauldron victory had resulted in but a partial success. While the pocket was closed on 3 August, it was not yet hermetically sealed, meaning that large numbers of *Rotmarmisten* would manage their escape. Several days later (6 August), Halder, clearly frustrated—but perhaps also begrudgingly envious—put down in his diary, "Enemy elements thought to be trapped at Roslavl have escaped. The Russians have an uncanny ability for moving on roads impassable for our troops and build concealed river crossings."[76] And while the operation culminated in another "painful Soviet defeat, the fact that it was the only offensive action Army Group Center could manage—and a small one at that—to redress the many trouble spots on its front says much about Bock's strategic paralysis. Indeed, given the degree of pressure on Bock's extensive front and the absence of any substantive reserves, Halder judged Bock's decision to attack toward Roslavl as 'downright careless.' The operation was also instructive for its cost. Just two days after the start of the offensive 4 Panzer Division had lost almost a quarter of its tanks."[77] In the final analysis, the battle of Roslavl remains an undisputed German success at the operational level of war; however, it is also "instructive of the limitations of the German Army in the east and a warning against the enduring optimism for a large-scale offensive solution to the still elusive German victory."[78]

In the wake of his victory at Roslavl, Guderian wrote to Margarete, "I fought a battle at Roslavl, conquered the town, took 30,000 prisoners, 250 guns and much other material including tanks. . . . A pretty success. But still somebody [i.e., GFM von Bock] interferes as before and endeavors to deploy the tanks in dribs and drabs, ruining them by useless journeys. One despairs! How I can overcome this stupidity I do not know."[79] On 12 August, he again confided in his wife, perhaps betraying a dark premonition of what the future held in store: "I would not wish to be in this area [Roslavl] in the autumn: it is not very pretty. . . . Waiting always brings the dangers of immobility and static warfare: that would be terrible."[80] Guderian, of course, wanted to keep moving, because movement (*Bewegung*) was the sine qua non of blitzkrieg warfare. Yet with Barbarossa now nearly two months old and movement toward the east, toward Moscow, having ground to a halt (see chapter 4), it was not only Guderian among Hitler's generals who was beginning to despair.

THE KILLING FIELDS OF THE EL'NIA SALIENT (46 PzK; 19.7–8.8.1941)

As we have seen, in mid-July, Guderian made a fateful decision. After defeating the Soviet Dnepr line defenses, instead of dispatching his 46 Panzer Corps northeast to join with the spearheads of Hoth's 3 Panzer Group beyond Smolensk—thus forging a solid ring around the Soviet armies trapped north and west of the city—he had ordered Vietinghoff's tanks and motorized infantry to seize a bridgehead over the Desna River at El'nia, 300 kilometers west of Moscow. This was achieved by *Generalleutnant* Schaal's 10 Panzer Division on 19/20 July after bitter house-to-house fighting resulting in heavy losses to both sides.[81]

Over the next two days, 10 Panzer, despite the fact that most of its surviving tanks were now immobilized due to the lack of oil, spare parts, or replacement engines, sought to widen its bridgehead at El'nia despite furious enemy resistance. In one Soviet attack on the morning of 20 July, the Germans destroyed eighteen tanks, ten of them knocked out by a single *Unteroffizier* in the division's *Panzerjäger* battalion. Soviet prisoners divulged that their superiors were bringing up any forces they could lay hands on to retake the town. As if to amplify their point, at midday, heavy Russian artillery fire, up to 210mm caliber, began to rip and tear at the German lines, the shelling by mid-afternoon swelling to an enormous barrage (*Trommelfeuer*). This was followed by another Soviet attack strongly supported by armor, which was again repulsed, this time with the destruction of twenty-five Red Army tanks. Undeterred, the Russians continued to press their assaults, only to be thrown back again by the beleaguered panzer grenadiers bolstered by 7 Panzer Regiment's handful of operational tanks. All told, the Germans destroyed fifty Russian tanks and took 700 prisoners on this day.[82] Yet these defensive victories were but a foretaste of what was to come in the killing fields of El'nia.

Located 82 kilometers southeast of Smolensk, near the headwaters of the Desna River, El'nia was a typical small town of western Russia. Typical it may have been, but it embraced several conspicuous features that fired Guderian's imagination: a bridge over the Desna River, a rail station on a main east-west rail line, and, most significantly, high ground (due east of the town) that dominated the outermost approaches to Moscow. In other words, El'nia offered a vital foothold from which to continue the all-important drive on the Soviet capital; thus, for both Germans and Russians alike, El'nia and its environs signified what Sun Tzu had characterized as "desperate ground"—terrain that had to be defended or captured.

Yet, as soon became apparent, the German bridgehead at El'nia manifested serious tactical liabilities. For example, the salient was surrounded on three sides by powerful (and perpetually reinforcing) Soviet forces, while the confining and difficult terrain within the salient—much of it what the Germans called *Kusselgelände* (scrubland), covered with low trees and brush that seriously hampered visibility—tended to nullify mobility and shock effect.[83] Moreover, the mobile units of 46 Panzer Corps that fought at El'nia in late July and early August 1941—first 10 PD, later joined by SS *Reich* and IRGD—did so at a distinct disadvantage, for both Schaal's 10 Panzer and "Papa" Hausser's SS *Reich* were fatigued and below strength, while ammunition (particularly artillery shells) and fuel were in chronic short supply. (Because stocks at the "advanced" supply depots more than 400 kilometers to the rear were so low, German motorized convoys often had to travel back to the nearest working railhead, a distance of 750 kilometers from the El'nia salient.)[84] Like all German tank units, 10 Panzer also suffered from a paucity of combat infantry and, perforce, was poorly postured for the role of positional defense to which it was now consigned.

Despite such challenges, 46 Panzer Corps would have to hold the salient against relentless Soviet counterattacks, supported by armor, artillery, and airpower (until finally relieved by foot infantry moving up from the rear); as a result, the corps found itself in an almost perpetual state of crisis while suffering unsustainable losses of both men and materiel. In a serious miscalculation, the Germans had assumed that their positions around El'nia were temporary and that their eastward drive would resume as soon as the infantry had "tidied up" the Smolensk pocket and become available for other duties. However, as was so often the case during the summer campaign of 1941, this assumption was soon overtaken by events outside the Germans' control. At El'nia, Army Group Center became ensnared in a remarkably savage eight-week bloodbath that would ultimately engulf some ten of its divisions in a battle of attrition—"a cauldron of fire and steel"—unlike any the German Army had experienced since the Great War of 1914/18.[85] For, although Soviet forces opposite the salient consisted mostly of recently mobilized, poorly trained, and often poorly equipped rifle divisions, they were lavishly equipped with artillery (including many heavy-caliber guns), providing them with a combat arm of tremendous lethality.

Under the conditions of positional (static) warfare now taking shape—and not just within the El'nia salient but, by the close of July, across the front of Army Group Center writ large—the excellent Soviet artillery arm began to make itself increasingly felt. During the first phase of the war, Soviet artillery had played a relatively minor role; indeed, as one German report noted, "During the days of the war of movement [*Bewegungskrieg*] the Soviet artillery had a negligible impact [*geringe Wirkung*]"; as a result, "sizeable losses did not occur."[86] In their foxholes and bunkers, however, the *Landser* were now frequently outgunned by longer-range Soviet artillery with seemingly inexhaustible stockpiles of shells, leading the report to conclude, "The powerful impact of artillery fire on our own troops is now becoming clear. . . . As a final judgment and consideration of the relative advantages and disadvantages [of German and Soviet artillery], it is clear that the German artillery is far superior [in every respect]. That said, with regard to the enemy's artillery, the German troops 'have also met their toughest opponent.'"[87]

But even if the Germans' artillery arm was better led and technically more proficient, that hardly mattered if their guns couldn't shoot. For it was at this juncture in the Barbarossa campaign that the flow of munitions to the front, over the increasingly overstretched arteries of supply, often slowed to a trickle, denying German artillery units the capability of responding with effective counterbattery fire. As one German corps commander recalled, his 263 ID was, in late July, receiving at most 1,000 shells per day for its thirty-six light field howitzers (and for other caliber weapons even fewer); collectively, this allowed for barely five minutes of fire each day at the guns' most rapid rate of fire, or for each gun to fire one shot a minute for thirty minutes a day. "We soon learned," Geyer wrote, "that in the defense it was not barrage fire or artillery duels . . . but digging in quick and deep that was decisive and saved lives."[88]

On 1 August, 46 Panzer Corps reported to Army Group Center that, in the average area of a company, as many as 200 shells landed in five minutes as the

German infantry huddled helplessly in their foxholes. On 2 August, 268 Infantry Division reported 300 to 400 shells striking the sector of a battalion in one hour. On 3 August, Vietinghoff's corps was pounded by 1,550 shells, the majority coming from heavy-caliber 152mm guns. Barrages such as these soon transfigured the 60-kilometer-wide salient into a cratered wasteland. Made privy to such reports, Halder characterized the Russian artillery fire as "insufferable" and anxiously observed that "the holding of this 'bridgehead' costs us much blood."[89] That the Germans held out at all was at least in part due to effective support from the always reliable Stukas of Bruno Loerzer's 2 Air Corps.[90]

In his memoir, Helmut Günther, a veteran of the motorcycle battalion in the elite SS Division *Reich*, recalled the almost unbearable strain of the violence and death within the salient:

> In the days that followed, we were to get no rest. Ivan made our lives miserable with tanks, infantry, and artillery fire. . . . El'nia demanded its victims. The companies grew ever weaker. The fate of Forster's squad hit us all like a blow [*war es allen wie ein Schlag*]. Now it was clear to every one of us that this Russia would be a very hard nut to crack. If some of us had not already lost it, then here in the El'nia bend we lost the fragile innocence of youth. That day, very little was said in the entire battalion. The deaths of Forster's squad affected us to the marrow.[91]

Shortly after the elimination of Forster's squad, *Gen.d.Pz.Tr.* Vietinghoff issued a special proclamation to the troops of his panzer corps.

> Headquarters
> 46 Panzer Corps 10 August 1941
>
> Corps Order of the Day (*Korps-Tagesbefehl*)[92]
>
> After one of the intense defensive engagements on the northeast front of El'nia, *Gruppe Forster* of the 1./SS-*Kradschützen-Battalion*, which had the mission of screening the left flank of the company, was found as follows:
>
> The squad leader, SS-*Unterscharführer* Forster, with his hand on the arming wire of the last hand grenade—shot in the head—
>
> Number 1 Machine Gunner, SS-*Rottenführer* Klaiber, his shoulder still firmly against the machine gun and one round in the barrel—shot in the head—
>
> Number 2 Machine Gunner, SS-*Sturmmann* Buschner and
>
> Number 3 Machine Gunner, SS-*Sturmmann* Schyma—both dead in the foxholes, rifles in firing position.
>
> Dispatch rider, SS-*Sturmmann* Oldeboerhuis—kneeling, dead at his machine, his hand on the handlebar so as to carry the last report.
>
> The rider, SS-*Sturmmann* Schwenk, dead in his foxhole.
>
> As for the enemy, all that one saw were the dead, lying at hand-grenade hurling range in a semicircle around the squad's position.
>
> An example for the term "Defense" [*Verteidigung*].

We stand in honor of such heroism.

I have requested that these names be published in the Roll of Honor of the German Army [*Ehrenblatt des deutschen Heeres*].

The Commanding General
signed/von Vietinghoff-Scheel
General der Panzertruppen[93]

The fighting within the El'nia salient is described in fulsome detail in the *Kriegstagebuch* (war diary) of 2 Panzer Group (entries from the diary are provided below).[94]

22.7.41:

1040 ours: The supply situation for 46 Pz.K. has worsened due to the poor condition of the roads and fierce enemy attacks at El'nia, which are resulting in high consumption of ammunition. The corps reports:

1. A severe shortage of 100mm and 210mm howitzer [*Mörser*] ammunition.
2. A 100 cbm oil shortage.

1700 hours: 46 Pz.K.—Command post moving forward to Strigino. 10 Pz.-Div. and SS-Div. *Reich* are attacking to extend the positions around El'nia. Details unknown.

2230 hours: 10 Pz.-Div.—The enemy attacked at El'nia from southeast and northeast in the morning hours in dense columns with heavy artillery fire. The attacks were repelled with bloody losses for the enemy.

23.7.41:

1100 hours: Report of 46 Pz.K.:

The enemy is attacking from the east in divisional strength near El'nia. Our lack of artillery ammunition is becoming painfully acute.

1300 hours: 10 Pz.-Div. and SS-Div. *Reich* extended their positions around El'nia. The enemy is attacking especially fiercely from the south and southwest. Enemy assembly areas in the north are identified. The reconnaissance battalion of SS-Div. *Reich*, which was at Kaskova, had to be withdrawn via Garavitsa in the face of superior enemy forces to the railway station at Glinka (20 km northwest of El'nia).

24.7.41:

1200 hours: 46 Pz.K. reports:

The situation at El'nia is extremely tense, repeated enemy attacks on 3 sides, heavy enemy tanks from the southeast. Now the enemy is also attacking us from the direction of Dorogobuzh. The corps is urgently requesting the release of I.R.G.D. [Infantry Regiment *Grossdeutschland*]. If possible, at least 1 battalion [of the regiment] is to be supplied immediately.

To resolve the ammunition shortage, artillery ammunition is being requested from 17 Pz.-Div.

[End 46 Pz.K. report.]

1450 hours: Report of 46 Pz.K.:

The situation on the left flank at El'nia is critical. The enemy is pressing hard on Ushakova from the north. To stabilize the situation, the corps requests that either a battalion of I.R.G.D. is immediately made available, or that 17 Pz.-Div. takes over the sector Ushakova-Glinka railway station.

1700 hours: 46 Pz.K.—Command post 4 km west of El'nia. 10 Pz.-Div. and SS-Div. *Reich* in battle with strong enemy, who is attacking from southeast, east, and now also from north. The enemy attacks are supported by heavy artillery and tanks. The situation in this sector is critical. The left flank has to be moved back into the line south of Ushakova-Glinka railway station.

25.7.41:

0600 hours: 46 Pz.K. SS-Div. *Reich*—Throughout the entire night heavy artillery fire on the division's sector. According to prisoner statements, the enemy is planning a large-scale attack today at 1100 hours.

[2 Panzer Group], however, cannot provide the corps with any reserves, since I.R.G.D. is still tied down [in another sector].

0825 hours: Report of 46 Pz.K.:

Since the delivery of artillery ammunition has been delayed by a day, and the last ammunition reserves have nearly all been used up in the course of the night and in the early morning, and as a result of the failure to deliver urgently required elements of I.R.G.D. and the lack of artillery ammunition, the situation can only be considered extremely tense [*äusserst gespannt*].

2300 hours: 46 Pz.K. Renewed fierce enemy attack from the direction of Bogoroditskoe (12 km northeast of El'nia) and Ushakova on the sector around El'nia. Counterattack is underway.

In the battles around El'nia on 25.7., the corps destroyed 78 enemy tanks, including 8 heavy tanks, and 8 aircraft.

26.7.41:

1350 hours: After the *Luftwaffe* reported an hour ago that enemy tanks were already gathering at Dadischtcheva (13 km northeast of El'nia), the *Flivo* [*Luftwaffe* liaison officer] is now reporting 40 enemy tanks at Kaskova advancing on El'nia.

1355 hours: To reinforce 46 Pz.K. against these enemy tanks, Pz.Jg.Abt. 611 (hitherto by 47 Pz.K.) is being subordinated to it. . . .

1535 hours: The situation in sector of 46 Pz.K. is becoming more critical. The enemy has succeeded in breaching the front of the rifle brigade of 10 Pz.-Div. south of El'nia. There are no reserves left to restore the situation. . . .

1730 hours: . . . 46 Pz.K.—Corps command post unchanged.

The situation is especially critical in the battle around El'nia. The corps is attacked all day long by strongly superior forces with tanks and artillery.

At Lipnia, the enemy managed a penetration, which could not yet be sealed off. During the enemy attacks south of the railway, 11 enemy batteries were identified.

Extremely heavy artillery fire is inflicting constant heavy losses on the troops. In addition, there is the constant impact of enemy bombers. Due to the artillery fire, evacuation of the many wounded is not possible at the moment. The attacks from the direction of Dorogobuzh resulted in a localized withdrawal of the front in the north.

Absolutely no reserves are available to the corps. The artillery ammunition is so depleted that no more shells can be used to contest the enemy's artillery [*Art.-Bekämpfung*].

10 Pz.-Div.'s panzer brigade has been immobilized for several days by lack of oil and fuel.

The corps might just succeed in holding its positions, but only amid severe bloody sacrifices.

Due to the delay in relieving I.R.G.D., no reserves can be delivered to the corps at this time.

27.7.41:

0600 hours: . . . 46 Pz.K.—In sectors of 10 Pz.-Div. and SS-Div. *Reich* the night was quiet. . . . The situation of the corps has somewhat eased, as during the night the first transports with ammunition and oil arrived, as did Pz.Jg.Abt. 611 and elements of I.R.G.D. . . .

1700 hours: . . . 46 Pz.K. . . . Thanks to repeated attacks by the combined forces of *Nakafü* II [Close Air Support Leader II], delivery of artillery ammunition, and the bulk of I.R.G.D., the corps' situation at El'nia has eased.

The enemy attacks continue, but with somewhat decreased intensity. The enemy artillery fire is, as before, very uncomfortable [*sehr unangenehm*] and inflicts losses.

29.7.41:

1035 hours: 46 Pz.K. inquires whether the supply of additional forces can be expected, since the corps had incurred considerable losses during the defensive battles.

A reinforcement of the corps, except with the 268 Inf.-Div., is not possible at the moment for *Armeegruppe* [*Guderian*], but a request has been lodged with [Army Group Center]. . . .

1745 hours: . . . 46 Pz.K. . . . Lively patrol activity in the area around El'nia in sectors of 10 Pz.-Div., SS-Div. *Reich*, and I.R.G.D. The enemy was no longer attacking at this time, but resurgent artillery activity was detected to the north of El'nia.

268 ID—partly brought up to El'nia in trucks—in the evening hours begins with relief of 10 Pz.-Div.

30.7.41:

0600 hours: . . . 46 Pz.K. 10 Pz.-Div.—IR 499 of 268 ID relieved elements of the division on its left flank. . . .

I.R.G.D. has been fully deployed.

Since 0230 hours, along the entire corps sector, enemy attacks with tanks, artillery, and aircraft, some of which are still in progress. . . .

1035 hours: Ic–*Armeegruppe* [*Guderian*] reports that a captured Russian flyer, an *Oberleutnant*, has stated the following:

By order of a higher Russian staff, El'nia is to be taken today. He himself was transferred with 170 bombers to Viaz'ma for this purpose.

Close Air Support Leader is being informed about this. The facts—attacks from 0230 hours on 46 Pz.K.—confirm the veracity of this statement. . . .

1745 hours: . . . 46 Pz.K. . . . Several enemy attacks with artillery and tanks were repelled in the El'nia sector. Localized incursions were cleared up. Today the corps reports 13 enemy attacks and an increase in the number of batteries identified so far.

In the coming days, further attacks will have to be reckoned with, especially at the flanks of the El'nia salient.

31.7.41:

0600 hours: . . . 46 Pz.K.—With the exception of localized artillery fire, the night was quiet by 268 ID, 10 Pz.-Div., and SS-Div. *Reich*. . . .

1745 hours: . . . 46 Pz.K. . . . The enemy attacks again in the El'nia salient from the southeast and north with strong artillery and tanks. Enemy air attacks on headquarters staffs and the forward line. . . .

2300 hours: . . . 46 Pz.K.—Corps command post 4 km west of El'nia. Since 0300 hours uninterrupted enemy attacks, which continue even now (2100 hours) in the south, southeast, northeast, north, in part with tanks amid heavy artillery fire. Our own artillery is severely handicapped by lack of ammunition.

Due to enemy artillery fire, there are continual losses of materiel and personnel. I.R.G.D. alone had 92 casualties from 28.–30.7. IR 499 of 268 ID had 82 casualties in the first 24 hours, among them 30 dead.

The relief [of 10 Pz.-Div.] by 268 ID comes to an end during the night of 31.7./1.8.[95]

(Note: On 30 July, the Soviet offensive at El'nia became the responsibility of General G. K. Zhukov following his appointment as commander of the Red Army's Reserve Front.[96] His primary asset was Maj.-Gen. K. I. Rakutin's 24 Army, consisting of nine rifle, three mobile, and two militia divisions—the latter comprised largely of workers' militiamen from Moscow. Upon assuming the front command, Zhukov "sharply criticized" Rakutin's previous offensive operations and began to prepare a fresh assault against the German bridgehead.)[97]

Between 22 July and 3 August 1941, 46 Panzer Corps recorded 3,615 casualties defending the El'nia salient, most of them, no doubt, from the unremitting Soviet artillery fire.[98] Casualties of close to 300 men per day were, of course, unsustainable in the long term. Still, the German High Command remained reluctant to pull out of the salient, still hoping to use it as a springboard for future operations; in any case, Hitler was in principle opposed to withdrawals of any sort, even if they were tactically expedient.

Not until 8 August did the bloodshed at El'nia come to an end for the surviving *Landser* of 46 Panzer Corps. By that day, the infantry divisions of *Gen.d.Inf.* Friedrich Materna's 20 Army Corps (15, 268, and 292 IDs), now temporarily assigned to *Armeegruppe Guderian*, had finished replacing all of Vietinghoff's battered formations within the El'nia salient proper.[99] In addition, flak batteries of the *Luftwaffe*'s I Flak Corps, with their devastating "88s," were brought up to bolster the defenses. Following their "relief," SS *Reich* and IRGD were inserted right back into the main battle line (*Haupfkampflinie*), this time in positions northwest of El'nia and covering the northern flank of the salient, replacing 17 Panzer Division and elements of 29 ID (mot.), both of Lemelsen's 47 Panzer Corps. Just prior to its relief, on 9 August 17 PD (since late July led by *Generalmajor* Wilhelm Ritter von Thoma) was struck repeatedly by robust Russian forces, provoking a slaughter clinically recorded by Lemelsen in his journal the next day:

> Yesterday *der Russe* attacked 17 Panzer Division the whole day with 2 divisions and strong artillery, powerful mass attacks in several waves one after another, which were scythed down by our machine guns and artillery fire. Mountains of corpses piled up. Naturally, incursions along the division's 35 km long front could not be avoided, but they were all ironed out by the counterattacks of our panzers, and the old line was entirely back in our hands yesterday evening.[100]

On 18/19 August, SS *Reich* and *Grossdeutschland* were finally relieved by infantry units of Geyer's 9 Army Corps and withdrawn for rest and refitting. Over the previous four weeks (through 15 August), the grenadiers of SS *Reich* had repelled eighty-three separate Soviet attacks while conducting twenty-seven counterattacks of their own.[101] By 23 August, *Generalmajor* Fischer's 10 Panzer Division had turned over its positions along the Striana River, southwest of El'nia,[102] to 268 ID and withdrawn behind the front (into a partially wooded area west of Pochinok, 40 to 50 kilometers south of Smolensk) for rest and refurbishment.[103] (By the end of the month, 10 PD would be back in action—this time to clear up an enemy breakthrough across the Desna River southeast of Pochinok in the sector of GFM von Kluge's Fourth Army.)

Meanwhile, with the threat of collapse still hanging over the German front at El'nia (20 Army Corps had a single battalion in reserve and was suffering from shortages of artillery shells),[104] Guderian ordered both Vietinghoff and Materna to a meeting on 14 August. The evening before, the panzer general had discussed the prospect of abandoning the salient—thus shortening the German line—with the Army Group Center chief of staff, *Generalmajor* von Greiffenberg. Guderian, however, was reluctant to do so: A withdrawal would hand the Soviets their first major victory of the war, which they would put to good use as propaganda.[105]

The emergency meeting on 14 August "was intended to decide the fate of the El'nia salient and sharply divergent opinions were exchanged."[106] General Materna (20 AK) was convinced that the position had to be abandoned; the evening before, he had "complained bitterly" to Vietinghoff that his 15 Infantry Division was particularly threatened, having lost thirty-five officers over the past two days alone, and that holding on to the current position was "pure insanity." On 14 August, Materna pleaded for withdrawal, arguing that his badly attenuated infantry divisions could no longer hold against a determined enemy attack. Vietinghoff (46 PzK), however, opposed giving up the salient, pointing out that a withdrawal would simply encourage the enemy and enable him to step up his attacks. While Guderian was inclined to take Vietinghoff's position, in the absence of clear operational priorities (i.e., Hitler and his High Command were still at loggerheads over the future course of the campaign; see chapter 4), he found it difficult to make a decision.[107]

When Bock asked Guderian what was needed to hold the position there, the panzer general's conditions included a sizeable increase in the flow of munitions and the recommitment of "strong *Luftwaffe* forces" at El'nia. While the field marshal could not promise a major improvement in the delivery of munitions ("the utmost was already being done in that regard"), he did speak to Brauchitsch about shifting Kesselring's 2 Air Corps—which *Reichsmarschall* Hermann Göring, without consulting Bock, had abruptly assembled farther south in the sector of Second Army to protect the southern flank of the army group—back to the El'nia front. In this, however, Bock was not successful; the bulk of 2 Air Corps remained where it was.[108]

As for the commander of Army Group Center, he too was unsure what course of action to take. On 15 August he put in his journal,

> Another inquiry to Guderian on account of the El'nia salient; his reply: he hoped to be able to hold it if two divisions from 9 AK relieve the motorized divisions still deployed there[109] and a further division is positioned behind the El'nia salient as a reserve. That is possible and is being considered. It is difficult to decide whether holding the salient is right or wrong. If the Russians continue to attack, then holding is wrong; if they cease their attacks in the foreseeable future it is right, for El'nia is a springboard for a further advance [on Moscow!] and also offers a certain protection for the road and rail junction of Smolensk.[110]

Although Bock had appealed the matter to GFM von Brauchitsch at OKH the day before (14 August), ultimate responsibility for making a decision was returned to him.[111] A victim of his High Command's (and Hitler's) enduring indecision, the army group commander would have to decide on his own whether to hold or abandon the El'nia salient. Most likely influenced by Halder, who warned Bock's chief of staff against abandoning the salient,[112] Bock eventually resolved to hold at El'nia; and this despite Guderian's sudden volte-face and proposal that the salient be given up! In his memoir, the panzer leader justified his change of heart:

> Up to this point, all the steps taken by the Panzer Group had been based on the belief that both the Army Group and the OKH regarded the operations toward Moscow as the decisive move. Despite the [Borisov] conference of 4 August [see chapter 4], I had not given up hope that Hitler would agree with this point of view which—to me at least—seemed the natural and obvious one. On 11 August I was disillusioned on this score. My plan of attack, with point of main effort through Roslavl toward Viaz'ma, was turned down by the OKH and described as "unsatisfactory."

With his plan rejected, Guderian soon concluded that the salient at El'nia no longer had any purpose and had simply become "a continual source of casualties." Yet, here too, Guderian was overruled: El'nia was not to be abandoned.[113]

The above remarks by Guderian deserve additional scrutiny: While it is of course true that both OKH and Army Group Center viewed Moscow as the decisive objective, Hitler, in fact, did not. Beginning in early December 1940 (and consistently thereafter), the German dictator had made clear that the Soviet capital was, at best, a secondary objective of the Barbarossa campaign, and after the capture of Smolensk, the armored units of Bock's army group were to swing north, toward Leningrad, and south, into the Ukraine (see chapter 4). Guderian surely knew this—that his fixation on Moscow (and thus El'nia) was totally at odds with Hitler's strategic ideas. Perhaps, like Halder, he had hoped that the spectacular successes along the Minsk-Smolensk axis during the initial phase of the campaign would simply sweep Hitler along toward Moscow. By late July to early August, however—given the dramatic slowdown in the pace of Army Group Center's advance—any such wishful thinking had been overtaken by events.[114]

Be that as it may, the decision to hold the El'nia salient meant that the fighting and dying there would go on for several more weeks. The *Landser*, of course, in their trenches and dugouts along the perimeter of the salient—the deepest eastward penetration made by the *Ostheer* on the entire eastern front—were hardly privy to the ongoing debates of their field commanders or to the concerns and anxieties at the highest levels of command in Rastenburg and Berlin. Yet, if the fighting had grown more savage—the enemy tougher and more determined—the morale of the *Ostheer* remained high, its faith in ultimate victory unshaken.

On 15 August 1941, "Hans Otto," a soldier in 268 Infantry Division—since 1 August fully committed to the abattoir that was the El'nia salient—penned a field post letter (*Feldpostbrief*) to an unknown recipient:

Our group can claim to have been the forwardmost boot of the German *Wehrmacht* for approximately 14 days. Since the end of last month we have been an irritating thorn in the pelt of the Russian bear, which he has been trying to attack with all his might. Despite all of his artillery, he does not succeed in removing this thorn, and his bloody infantry losses are unimaginable. The town I.,[115] which we surround, will one day be an important name in the history of this campaign.

Yes, these battles are tough, and in our ranks, too, death tears a hole in the ranks of our best every day. But in these battles, the soldier has now learned to become tough, too, and shown that he is also equal to "storms of steel," just like his fathers in the World War. The grandeur of many an expression from that time now becomes clear. The incessant metallic hammering of the artillery, the crashing explosions of the shells, and the zipping and humming of shrapnel makes its own music. And when that can be heard constantly from morning til night in any sector of the front, unending, without any indication that they are having to pause for breath over there, then you can put yourself in the position of the fighter in the World War.

But our guys have become tough in all this and have an admirable level of self-confidence, and if the Russian comes with infantry and tanks, then a bloody reception awaits him. And it matters not at all if one or two tanks break through the lines because one of our Paks was destroyed and no other weapon can stop it. For then the infantryman leaps from his foxhole with hand grenade, Molotov cocktail, and a concentrated charge, and finishes it off as matter-of-factly as if he were conducting a peacetime demonstration.

Our *Ostmarkers* have particularly proved themselves here, defending a commanding elevation (125.6), which the Russian attacks again and again. And here is laid bare the spirit of the fighter in the current war, he who knows for what he fights and, if necessary, dies, in contrast to the stupid cannon fodder that is only whipped forward over and again by the Reds' pack of lies and a pistol or a machine gun.[116]

THE SMOLENSK CAULDRON BATTLE: THE OUTCOME

By 1 August 1941, the dimensions of the cauldron—which had slowly "wandered" to the region due east of Smolensk—had been compressed by encircling German forces to just 20 kilometers from east to west and 28 kilometers from north to south. (After being pulled off the pocket, in late July both 17 Panzer Division and 29 ID [mot.] [47 PzK] found themselves back on the southern shoulder of the encirclement ring.) Still fighting desperately to escape—and running short of fuel and ammunition—were the remnants of fifteen to twenty Soviet divisions,[117] comprising fewer than 100,000 men. From outside the cauldron, the Soviet operational group under Lt.-Gen. Konstantin Rokossovksy (Group Iartsevo) had sought repeatedly to break through the front of 39 Panzer Corps (3 PzG) and reopen a corridor to the trapped Russian forces; late on 1 August, it finally succeeded in doing so, pushing aside the fragile German picket lines on the eastern periphery of the pocket and recapturing the crossing over the Dnepr at Ratchino. Thus, only four days after the Germans had closed the pocket, the Soviets had once more opened a small breach (just six kilometers wide) through which they sought to escape to the east as reported by *Luftwaffe* aerial reconnaissance.[118]

GFM von Bock, thoroughly aghast that the pocket again had a hole in it, ordered 17 Panzer Division to extend its defensive screen and close the gap by linking up with 20 ID (mot.) (3 PzG) near Ratchino. Meanwhile, Soviet forces inside the shrinking cauldron finally received formal authority to breakout en masse to the east, the breakout attempt beginning in earnest on the night of 2/3 August. Some of the fleeing *Rotarmisten* tried to overwhelm the company-size strongpoints of 20 ID (mot.); others sought to escape by slipping through the defensive screen of 17 PD and "running a gauntlet" eastward past the German positions before seeking to ford the Dnepr in places where it was quite shallow. As they did so, the Germans endeavored to smash the fleeing enemy columns with repeated air strikes and massed artillery fire.

Because neither Thoma's 17 PD nor *Generalmajor* Hans Zorn's 20 ID (mot.) was able to push through to Ratchino[119]—illustrating just how dramatically their offensive power had declined—thousands of Soviet troops succeeded in exploiting the narrow opening between the two divisions and withdrawing to safety across the Dnepr. Of course, tens of thousands of trapped Red Army soldiers were not so fortunate, as this diary entry of an unknown German soldier in an artillery battalion of an infantry division on the perimeter of the *Kessel* illustrates:

> 2.8.41:
>
> I do not want to describe in any more detail the images to be seen here on the battlefields and on the roads, because it is neither believable nor imaginable for somebody who has not seen or experienced it for themselves. Only now have we seen what a human being signifies. They lie around, in countless numbers. Body parts are torn away; some were only wounded, but then bled out as they dragged themselves forward a few meters in pools of their own blood. Others in turn are burned and charred. Horses are mutilated and full of holes, motor vehicles and tanks are burned down to their iron shells. With time, you get used to all these scenes; but the smell is unbearable and has such a powerful effect that one often has to put off meals.[120]

It is no exaggeration to posit that the three-week Smolensk *Kesselschlacht* had bordered on the apocalyptic. Another German artillery soldier, who fought in several theaters of war throughout World War II, recalled, "The fighting around Smolensk in July and August [1941] was the heaviest and deadliest I saw during the war."[121] When *Gen.d.Pz.Tr.* Lemelsen inspected the city shortly after its capture he described it as a "smoking pile of ruins" dominated by the "wretched remains of burned-out houses."[122] An aerial photograph of Smolensk, snapped by a German soldier in the spring of 1942, revealed a grotesque scene of unimaginable destruction, bearing witness to the savage nature of the fighting there.

Facing fierce opposition to the end, German forces did not complete the destruction of Soviet units trapped inside the pocket until 5 August 1941. On this very day, however, Guderian experienced a moment of crisis as he raced from place to place in an effort to prevent a large body of Russians from escaping encirclement. After Guderian became aware that a threat had developed against a tactically important bridge at Ostrik, according to his *Luftwaffe* liaison, *Oberstleutnant* von Barsewisch, "he rushed immediately to the point . . . full of rage, and closed the gap with a battery of anti-aircraft artillery that he led personally into battle. There was this fantastic man, standing by a machine gun in action against the Russians, drinking mineral water from a cup and saying, 'Anger gives you a thirst!'" Barsewisch continued, "Guderian is well known by his 300,000 men. It is amazing the respect with which he is greeted everywhere he goes."[123]

The daily report of the OKH Operations Branch (5 August) stated laconically, "The Battle of Smolensk has ended. Enemy attacks have slackened along the entire eastern front of [Army Group Center] due to the exhaustion of the enemy."[124] The OKW lauded the victory in rather more flowery prose, declaring that the unprecedented spaces involved, the severity of the fighting, and the "relentless series of annihilating blows against the Bolshevik armed forces, give to the great Battle of Smolensk its historically unique character [*geschichtlich einzigartige Gepräge*]."[125] That evening, Bock released an order of the day commemorating the glorious German *Sieg*:

> With the destruction of the Russian divisions cut off at Smolensk, the three-week "Battle at the Dnepr and Dvina and of Smolensk" has concluded in another brilliant victory [*glänzenden Sieg*] for German arms and German fulfillment of duty. Taken as booty were: 309,110 prisoners, 3,205 captured or destroyed tanks, 3,000 guns, 341 aircraft. The numbers are not yet complete. This deed of yours, too, has become part of history! It is with gratitude and pride that I look upon a force that is capable of such an accomplishment.
>
> Long live the Führer!
> Signed: v. Bock
> *Generalfeldmarschall*[126]

While it is unknown just how many thousands of Soviet troops succeeded in escaping from the Smolensk cauldron, documentary evidence reveals that, of the three Soviet armies (16, 19, and 20) trapped inside, as many as 170,000 men were killed or captured; since the pocket most likely had contained more than 220,000 men in mid-July 1941, this means that some 50,000 of them were able to escape over the three-week period of the Battle of Smolensk.[127] Yet the Red

Army divisions that managed to evade total annihilation had been reduced to 1,000 or 2,000 men and, in some cases, even fewer. Also devastating were the losses of tanks and artillery; in fact, by early August, the Soviets suffered from a serious shortfall of tanks, artillery, and other heavy weapons across the entire eastern front, having lost close to 6,000 tanks (destroyed or captured) on the central front alone since the start of the campaign.[128]

In light of the *Ostheer*'s splendid victories along the central axis of advance from 15 July to 5 August 1941 (including Guderian's at Roslavl), Bock, at his CP in Borisov, was now convinced that his army group had emerged from the fighting with a decisive victory; he had, he believed, completed the destruction of most of Soviet Western Front, and after his mobile units were given a brief respite to rest and refit, he could resume his relentless march on Moscow, now beckoning barely 300 kilometers to the east.

Less enamored with the outcome at Smolensk was *Generalmajor* Hoffmann von Waldau, Chief of the *Luftwaffe* Operations Staff, who observed in his diary on 14 August, "The 'encirclement battle' of Smolensk has not led to the destruction of [Soviet] forces to the extent expected." Waldau attributed this failure primarily to the "exceptional toughness of the Russian opponent, his tactically skillful leadership, and knowledge of the terrain," which enabled large numbers of Russian troops to escape from the pocket.[129]

On "the Other Side of the Hill," the results of the three weeks of battle along the Smolensk axis left behind a distinctly different impression compared to that of Bock and the OKH. While Soviet forces had sustained horrific losses in men and materiel, they had succeeded in salvaging parts of their encircled armies and rebuilding a coherent defensive line along the entire 700-kilometer front of Bock's army group, from Velikie Luki in the north, past Smolensk, to the Dnepr River west of Gomel. The Red Army had also inflicted serious losses on Army Group Center, particularly upon the motorized infantry component of the panzer and motorized divisions. And if the Battle of Smolensk did not culminate in the victory heralded by Soviet propaganda, the Red Army had, for the first time, seriously blunted the momentum of the German blitzkrieg, temporarily denying Bock, Guderian, and Hoth the operational freedom they so coveted in the direction of Moscow.[130] As a result, the STAVKA was convinced that its strategy of active defense, of mounting more and more powerful counteroffensives, was paying off. Indeed, after barely six weeks of war and a series of historically unprecedented defeats, neither the Red Army nor the Soviet state was showing signs of collapse, rendering the prospect of an ultimate German victory that much more elusive, if, in fact, such a victory was still even possible.

To return to Guderian's candid observations to his wife on 31 July: "The battle is harder than anything before. . . . It will take some time yet."[131]

Portrait of *Generaloberst* Heinz Guderian. He is wearing the Knight's Cross (27 October 1939) with Oak Leaves (*Eichenlaub*), the latter distinction awarded on 17 July 1941. He became only the fifth man in the Army and the twenty-fourth in the *Wehrmacht* to receive the Oak Leaves to the Knight's Cross. (Public domain, via Wikimedia Commons)

General Guderian aboard his armored radio command vehicle (*Funkpanzerwagen*, Sd.Kfz. 251/3) during the French campaign of 1940. (Bundesarchiv, Bild 101I-769-0229-15A/Borchert, Erich (Eric)/CC-BY-SA 3.0, via Wikimedia Commons)

Column of Panzer IVs of *Generalleutnant* Hans-Jürgen von Arnim's 17 Panzer Division motoring east on the German *Autobahn* (6 June 1941). The division began Operation Barbarossa with a complement of 202 tanks, including 30 Pz IVs. (D. Garden and K. Andrew)

Just hours before the start of Hitler's surprise attack on Soviet Russia, officers across the eastern front read the Führer's proclamation to the *Soldaten der Ostfront*. (Bundesarchiv, Bild 183-L25085, Foto: o.Ang., 21 June 1941)

German troops cross the Bug River at the Russian fortress of Brest-Litovsk at 0315 hours on 22 June 1941. The 45 Infantry Division (attached to Guderian's panzer group for the initial assault) would sustain more than 300 KIA on this day. (Museum Berlin-Karlshorst)

Guderian's half-track command vehicle (Sd.Kfz 251/3) being ferried across the Bug River on 22 June 1941. Outfitted with extra radio gear, the 251/3 was one of many versions of this armored personnel carrier used by the Germans in World War II. (Bundesarchiv N 802/30)

Soviet combat planes destroyed on the ground by the *Luftwaffe* in the first hours of the German attack; by midnight, the Soviet Air Force (VVS), according to official German sources, had lost some 1,800 aircraft, more than 900 of them attributed to GFM Albert Kesselring's 2 Air Fleet.

A German light mortar crew (50mm *leichter Granatwerfer* 36) in action at the fortress of Brest-Litovsk (22 June 1941). Despite the furious German barrage that struck the fortress at 0315 hours, *Generalmajor* Fritz Schlieper, C-in-C of the attacking 45 ID, considered it to be much less of material and largely of psychological significance. (Pen & Sword)

In an iconic shot taken on 1 July, *Generaloberst* Guderian poses for the camera as his tanks and motorcycle infantry drive off into the distance. The panzer general began Operation Barbarossa with fewer tanks than he had at the start of the French campaign in 1940, and this despite the fact that he would operate on frontages much wider than in France. (bpk Bildagentur/Heinrich Hoffmann Archive/Bayerische Staatsbibliothek/Munich, Germany)

A pensive Guderian early in the Russian campaign. The panzer general is wearing his Knight's Cross but as yet without the Oak Leaves (awarded on 17 July 1941). The other medals include a World War I Iron Cross First Class (above that is a World War II clasp to the Iron Cross that was awarded to those who had already earned the distinction in the Great War). On the right is the Panzer Assault Badge in Silver. (Bundesarchiv N 802/125)

German motorcycle infantry (*Kraftradschützen*) advance alongside a column of transport vehicles kicking up a storm of dust. The vehicle on the far right is a half-track; the soldier sitting low in the first motorcycle is holding a machine gun (MG 34). The tactical sign of the motorcycle infantry is plainly visible in two spots on the rear of the motorcycle. (Bundesarchiv, Bild 101I-265-0003-13A, Foto: Mossdorf)

A group of Panzer IIIs in an assembly area (late June)—most likely in the Ukraine (all the tanks of *Generaloberst* Ewald von Kleist's 1 Panzer Group were of German manufacture) or perhaps on the central front. The Pz III was the German Army's main battle tank, and although up-gunned with a 50mm L/42 main armament (which become standard in the "G" series), it was no match for the more heavily armored Soviet T-34s or KV-1s. (Bundesarchiv, Bild, 101I-186-0199-08A, Foto: Springmann)

Tanks and motorized infantry of Guderian's 2 Panzer Group enter the town of Pruzhany (most likely 23 June 41). The light tank on the right is a Panzer II. The "G" for Guderian's group is visible on the fenders of the front three vehicles. These vehicles and men almost certainly belonged to *Generalmajor* Walther K. Nehring's 18 Panzer Division, as Pruzhany was along the division's route of march (*Panzerstrasse* 2). (Unknown, PD, via Wikimedia Commons)

German tanks on the move. On the Panzer IV in front one can see the extra bogie wheels. Farther back, on the right, is another Pz IV, while a couple of Pz IIs make their way down the hill. (Bundesarchiv, Bild 101I-265-0040A-22A/Vorpahl/CC-BY-SA 3.0, via Wikimedia Commons)

In late June, *Generalmajor* Walter von Boltenstern's 29 ID (mot.) was holding part of the Belostok-Minsk encirclement ring west and north of Slonim. This 50mm anti-tank gun has been brought into position to engage approaching Soviet tanks desperately seeking their escape from the cauldron. The crew is prepared to fire. The leader monitors the situation with his field glasses. The gunner has positioned the barrel to best strike an approaching tank. Behind the gun crew, the soldiers are ready for close combat—armed with rifles and stick grenades. (Jason Mark/Leaping Horseman Books)

Encircled and increasingly desperate, the trapped Soviets attempt another breakout on 30 June. They attacked at 0300 with tanks, cavalry, infantry, and artillery support. Yet the soldiers of Boltenstern's excellent 29 ID (mot.) are well prepared, come what may. The Pak front shown in the photograph consists of two 37mm anti-tank guns and one 50mm AT gun (in front). (Jason Mark/Leaping Horseman Books)

A destroyed Soviet T-34/76 tank (late June or early July). Some Soviet commanders put wives and children inside their tanks before trying to escape from the Belostok pocket. However, they largely perished and were buried in mass graves. Postwar exhumations of the unmarked graves revealed items that identified the tankers as members of a particular unit. (Jason Mark/Leaping Horseman Books)

Soviet T-34s abandoned in marshy terrain. Early in the Russian campaign Soviet tanks often fled from the roads to avoid *Luftwaffe* fighters, fighter-bombers, and Stukas, only to become immobilized, as these tanks are. (Bundesarchiv N 802/125)

Panzer IV of *Gefreiter* Erich Hager (17 PD) at the gravesite of *Unteroffizier* Wedde, near Minsk. Wedde, the driver in Hager's tank, was killed on 28 June, when three shells struck their tank from a distance of just twenty to thirty meters. In his journal Hager wrote, "Shells struck the driver and just missed me. I can only speak of luck that I didn't get hurt. I'm so sorry about Wedde. He didn't make a sound. He must have been killed outright." (D. Garden and K. Andrew)

Assembly area of a large number of German armored vehicles in Belorussia near the town of Slutsk. Nearly 300 kilometers beyond the frontier, Slutsk was secured by Model's 3 Panzer Division on 26 June. No division of Guderian's panzer group drove farther or faster than Model's in the heady initial days of the Barbarossa campaign. (In the foreground, the Sd.Kfz. 253, a light observation vehicle used by artillery forward observers in panzer and motorized infantry units; in the background Pz II and Pz III tanks.) (National Digital Archives, public domain, via Wikimedia Commons)

German tanks in the "fog of war" not far from Minsk. Since there are no markings on the tanks, there's no way of telling if they belong to Guderian's or Hermann Hoth's panzer group. The tank on the left is a Panzer IV. (U.S. National Archives)

Landser belonging to 2 Panzer Group's 17 Panzer Division are taking a short break; supply trucks are in the background (late June 1941). (Jon Davidson)

upply trucks of Guderian's 2 Panzer Group driving through the devastated town of Minsk (ca. July 941). The column includes Krupp *Protze* six-wheeled 6 × 4 lorries. The farther east Guderian's forces dvanced, stretching supply lines, the greater became the logistical challenges; indeed, such were the emands made upon the truck transport units—given the appalling Russian roadways—that after just few weeks of war, Army Group Center had lost one-third or more of its truck fleet. (National Digital rchives, public domain, via Wikimedia Commons)

uderian meeting with *Generalleutnant* Model (date/location unknown). Model's 3 PD began the cam-aign with 215 tanks, including 110 Pz IIIs and 32 Pz IVs. On 24 June, Model barely escaped death hen a direct hit by Soviet artillery blew apart an eight-wheeled armored car (killing the four-man crew) oments after he dismounted the vehicle. (Unknown German Army photographer, public domain, via Vikimedia Commons)

Guderian and *Generaloberst* Hermann Hoth, C-in-C 3 Panzer Group, share a jocular moment. Photograph may have been taken when the two generals met on 30 June 1941 at Hoth's command post to discuss "the future coordination of our activities." Both panzer generals chafed under the restrictions placed on their movements by Hitler and the Army High Command. (Bundesarchiv, Bild 101I-265-0024-21A/Vorpahl/CC-BY-SA 3.0, via Wikimedia Commons)

Autobahn Smolensk-Moscow—a sign that must have quickened the pulse of every *Landser* who saw i along the march to Moscow. The Soviet capital was approximately 1,000 kilometers from the start lin of Guderian's panzer group. (Jon Davidson)

Guderian and Kluge engaged in a serious discussion (standing between them is Walther von Axthelm, C-in-C of I Flak Corps) (August 1941). The German advance had slowed dramatically by this time, and doubts were beginning to surface about the *Wehrmacht*'s ability to bring Barbarossa to a successful con-lusion. The two men had never gotten along, and their relationship continued to sour during the summer nd fall of 1941. Shortly after becoming commander of Army Group Center in December, Kluge would send Guderian packing. (National Digital Archives, public domain, via Wikimedia Commons)

GFM von Bock (pointing at map) in a conference with *Generaloberst* Hoth (middle) and Air General Wolfram Freiherr von Richthofen (C-in-C 8 Air Corps). The photograph was taken on 8 July 1941, as he cauldron battle of Belostok-Minsk was coming to a close. (Bundesarchiv, Bild 101I-265-0048A-03/Mossdorf/CC-BY-SA 3.0, via Wikimedia Commons)

A Panzer IV of 17 Panzer Division knocked out near Smolensk (summer 1941). Although the Smolens *Kesselschlacht* ended in another remarkable German victory, it also significantly slowed the pace of th German advance. By August, the initial blitzkrieg campaign had come to an end, and most of the front c Army Group Center had congealed into positional warfare. (D. Garden and K. Andrew)

A self-propelled German tank destroyer (*Panzerjäger Sfl.*), armed with a Czech Skoda 47mm anti-tan gun and belonging to Pz.Jäg.Abt. 529 (ca. 25 July 1941). Behind the turret, on the engine deck, are crate of ammunition, bedrolls, and pots and pans. This unit was fighting with Boltenstern's 29 ID (mot.) at th time. (Jason Mark/Leaping Horseman Books)

errific photograph of a German assault gun (*Sturmgeschütz* III) belonging to *Sturmgeschütz Abteilung* 203 uly 1941). When this photograph was taken, the StuG III battalion was fighting with the advance detachnent (*Vorausabteilung*) of 29 ID (mot.). The StuG III witnessed its first major combat during Operation arbarossa, providing the infantry with a notable increase in firepower. However, only 250 of these assault uns—outfitted with a 75mm L/24 main armament—were committed to the eastern campaign in June 941, organized in eleven battalions and five separate batteries. (Jason Mark/Leaping Horseman Books)

ne of the collection points of weapons/equipment captured by the Germans during the Smolensk cauldron battle. The caption on photograph reads *"grosse Vernichtungsschlacht von Smolensk"* ("great battle f annihilation of Smolensk"). In this pile of weapons one can make out Red Army artillery of many caliers. Once again, at Smolensk, the Germans achieved a great operational victory; and, yet, once again, was far from decisive. (U.S. National Archives)

Women among the ruins of the ancient Russian city of Smolensk (photograph taken in August 1941) In his journal, *General der Panzertruppen* Joachim Lemelsen (C-in-C 47 PzK), wrote on 21 July tha Smolensk "is a smoking pile of ruins [*ein rauchender Trümmerhaufen*]; there is not a single house un damaged—the majority simply pitiful remains of houses that have been burned down. A sad spectacle. (National Digital Archives, public domain, via Wikimedia Commons)

A terrific photograph—another taken by *Propaganda Kompanie* 693—of Guderian leading from the fror in his armored command vehicle (August 1941). The back of the photograph reads, "Guderian accompa nies the attack of his tanks in his command vehicle." (*In seinem Befehlswagen fährt Gen.Ob. Guderia den Angriff seiner Panzer mit.*) (Bundesarchiv 802/48)

estroyed Soviet equipment near Roslavl. Supported by two infantry corps temporarily attached to his anzer group, Guderian's forces encircled and destroyed a large Soviet grouping around Roslavl at the eginning of August 1941, taking almost 40,000 prisoners. In a letter to his wife, Guderian called his ictory there "a pretty success." (Bundesarchiv N 802/30)

massive explosion (cause unknown) somewhere along the road to Moscow. The vehicle is most likely uderian's command car. Guderian himself appears to be standing near the passenger door, holding hat looks like a map. Throughout the Barbarossa campaign, the panzer general experienced many rushes with death. (Bundesarchiv N 802/19)

Part II

INTO THE UKRAINE

THE KIEV CAULDRON BATTLE

German historian Dr. Jürgen Förster astutely summarizes the impact of the initial weeks of the Russian campaign on Adolf Hitler and his General Staff:

> The great operational successes after 22 June 1941 satisfied German expectations. They increased the *Wehrmacht*'s high level of self-esteem [*Selbstwertgefühl*] at all levels. After only two weeks, the Army and Hitler viewed the campaign in the east as already won. But only a few days later it became apparent that it had not been possible to destroy the "mass of the Russian army" west of the Dnepr-Dvina line, that the Bolshevist system continued to function, and that the Soviet adversary had been underestimated. Even the "intellectual elite" of the German General Staff had not been guided solely by "sober professionalism" in their operational planning. It was not just in Hitler, but also in this institution, "then highly respected throughout the world," that elements of "the unpredictable, even irrational," had been in evidence. The actual situation at the front in July/August 1941 forced the abandonment of outdated assumptions, which were in part the result of an ideological view of the enemy. This process was—particularly after the euphoria of the first two weeks—painful [*schmerzhaft*] for *all* involved, even if blame for the failure of the blitzkrieg was later placed solely at Hitler's door.[1]

As it became apparent to Hitler and his generals that their eastern blitzkrieg had failed to take down the Russian colossus, they were suddenly confronted by the need to recalibrate their strategy for the next phase of the campaign. The fundamental issue was whether to continue Army Group Center's drive toward Moscow with the consolidated (albeit now seriously compromised) strength of its two panzer groups or to divert GFM von Bock's tanks and mobile infantry to objectives on the wings—toward Leningrad and a linkup with the Finns in the north, and/or into the Ukraine, the industrial region of the Donbas, and the Caucasus in the south. The ensuing debate between Hitler, his Army High Command (OKH), and his field generals would drag on for weeks and signify the first serious strategic crisis of the eastern campaign. To continue with Dr. Förster's analysis:

> The severity of the argument over the *arcanum* of victory already reflected the growing recognition among the German leadership that their planning principles were flawed, that the blitzkrieg was not going to be won in 1941, and that the *Wehrmacht* would, in 1942, be "forced into an offensive against new Red forces that would cost more blood and time."[2] Yet still there was hope that it would be possible to bring the operations to a satisfactory end state before the winter broke. The newly available private sources—as well as those sources already long known—from the Operations Branch of the General Staff of the Army, make manifest that it was not just Hitler who was really "very nervous" [*sehr nervös*] or appeared "extremely impatient" in view of the developments along the eastern front, [while] repeatedly intervening in the on-going individual operations, and "all too arbitrarily" [*allzu selbstherrlich*] altering the *Schwerpunkt* [point of main effort] of the entire operation. Yet [these sources] also substantiate that "no one within the Führer's immediate circle—and certainly not the C-in-C of the Army"—offered any serious resistance to Hitler. The Army leadership was without resolve [*entschlusslos*] . . . and thus avoided "prompt and tough" decisions, which were left to Hitler to make.[3]

Meanwhile, *Armeegruppe Guderian*, following its victory at Roslavl, continued operations well into August designed to secure its deep right (southern) flank, a basic prerequisite for renewing an advance on the Soviet capital. At Krichev, General Geyr's 24 Panzer Corps succeeded in destroying several Soviet divisions in short order; this was followed by joint operations along the Gomel axis between *Generaloberst* von Weichs's Second Army and Guderian's army group, resulting in the destruction of a Soviet army and the capture of tens of thousands of prisoners. For Guderian, the road to Moscow finally lay open.

On 21 August, five weeks of open conflict between Hitler and his generals and uncertainty about the future course of the campaign would come to an abrupt end; on this day, the German dictator issued new orders charting a clear course for the next phase of operations: the capture of Moscow would have to wait; rather, the final decision of the Barbarossa campaign was to be sought on the flanks—with Army Group North (GFM von Leeb) and Army Group South (GFM von Rundstedt). To this end, several divisions of Hoth's *Panzergruppe* 3—along with an entire air corps of Kesselring's 2 Air Fleet—were to head north to support Leeb's final drive on Leningrad (in fact, these transfers were already well underway), while *Armeegruppe Guderian* was to drive south into the Ukraine, where the highly exposed position of Soviet Southwestern Front, opposite Army Group South, had created a unique opportunity for another dramatic German *Kesselschlacht*—an opportunity Hitler was now quick to seize.

Bock and Guderian, while deeply disappointed by Hitler's new orders (Guderian even put in a dramatic appearance at the *Wolfsschanze* in a last-ditch effort to change the Führer's mind), made every effort to make the Ukraine operation a success. Guderian drove his men mercilessly—his goal being to complete the diversion into the Ukraine as rapidly as possible and to resume the advance on Moscow. As was his wont, he again ignored orders from superiors, preferring to conduct his operations as he saw fit. He also complained—bitterly and repeatedly—that he needed additional forces to accomplish his mission; so exasperated did Bock become that, in early September, he went so far as to request the dismissal of the mercurial panzer general. Brauchitsch, however, asked Bock to think it over, and although he relented, he jotted in his diary, "I cannot hide my worries about new difficulties with this outstanding and brave commander."[4]

In mid-September 1941, the spearheads of Guderian's badly mauled forces, despite incessant rains (turning roads into quagmires) and desperate Red Army resistance, would link up with advance elements of *Generaloberst* von Kleist's 1 Panzer Group east of Kiev, initiating the most spectacular cauldron battle of the summer campaign. Once again, it appeared that the German invaders might be on the cusp of final victory.

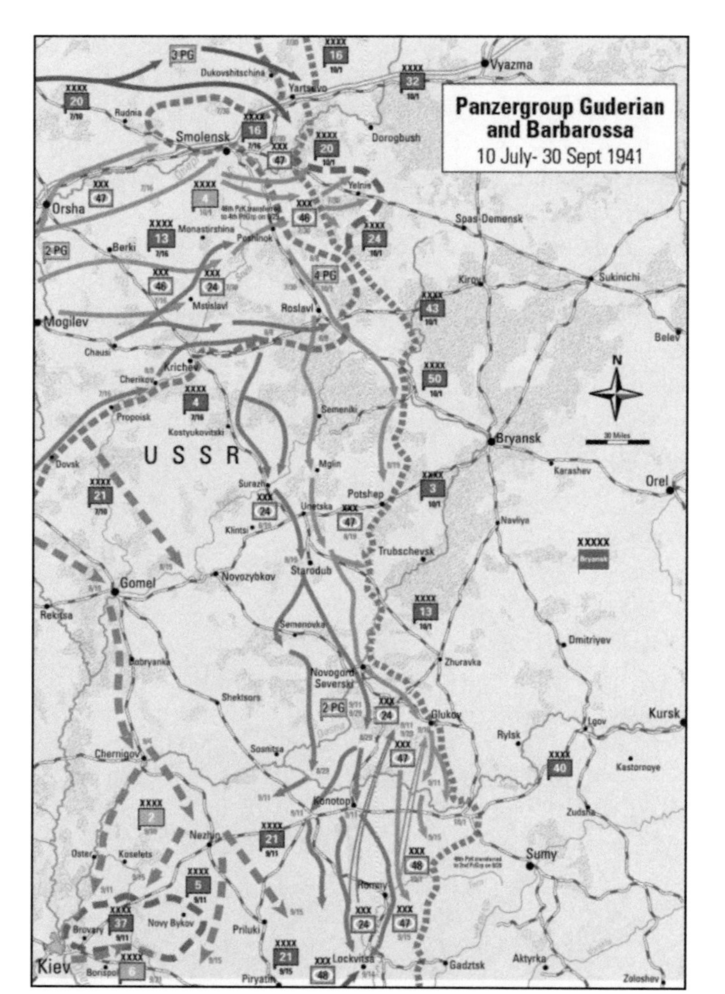

Operations of 2 Panzer Group: 10.7.1941–30.9.1941

4

Indecision and Delay

With the successful outcome of the Smolensk cauldron battle in early August 1941, Hitler, his Armed Forces High Command (OKW), Army High Command (OKH), and GFM von Bock could look back with genuine satisfaction on the staggering successes of Army Group Center during the first six weeks of the Russian campaign. In this astonishingly short period, Bock's army group had smashed the Soviet frontier defenses; crushed the Soviet High Command's second strategic echelon along the Western Dvina and Dnepr Rivers; seized Smolensk, the historic gateway to Moscow; and killed, wounded, or captured hundreds of thousands of Red Army troops, most of them at the expense of Soviet Western Front.

Yet, in spite of such historic victories, Hitler, his General Staff, and his eastern generals were soon faced with the fact that the war they had unleashed on Soviet Russia was not going to plan. The first of their facile assumptions to fall by the wayside was that not only the Red Army but the Soviet state too would collapse if the *Wehrmacht* destroyed the bulk of their forces west of the Dvina-Dnepr river barriers; and yet, by 10 July, it was apparent that this assumption was patently false. While Bock's forces had destroyed several Soviet armies in the Belostok-Minsk cauldron, they had then encountered five more Soviet armies along the two river lines, and despite encircling and destroying three of these second echelon armies in the Smolensk region (by 5 August), they were attacked by yet a *third* echelon of fresh Russian armies (Marshal Semen Timoshenko's operational groups) in late July and early August. As noted, the overarching objective of Operation Barbarossa had been to eliminate Soviet Russia—as characterized by this author—with the 1941 equivalent of a nuclear first strike: a single blow so powerful, so devastating, that it would suffice to crush the Bolshevik state in a blitzkrieg-style campaign of just two to three months' duration. Yet not only did this now appear to be less and less likely, but, as we have seen, the Soviets had continued to drive fresh forces into the field, much to the bafflement of the Führer and his generals.

Also apparent to senior (and lower-level) German commanders was the growing (and disquieting) realization that the war against Soviet Russia signified something quite distinct from the campaigns against Poland and in the west. For example, as demonstrated by the experiences of Guderian's panzer group, it quickly became apparent that a kilometer on the eastern front was something much different from a kilometer in the west. Indeed, the primitive road system had seriously hampered movement of both mobile and horse-drawn units from the moment they crossed the frontier, while the rail infrastructure—also sorely inadequate and using a different gauge (one that had to be laboriously converted to the narrower European standard gauge by German railroad troops at the rate of some 10 to 12 kilometers per day)[1]—placed a palpable strain on German logistics. Making matters worse was that the tank and motorized formations—the elite, rapier-like tip of the *Ostheer*—suffered the most from these problems, for they invariably operated far ahead of the foot infantry. Thus, shortages of fuel and ammunition severely impaired the ability of Guderian's and Hoth's panzer groups to operate effectively in the depths of the battlefield.

Posing perhaps the greatest challenge to the German invaders was the complete collapse of their assumptions about the attitudes, morale, and combat capabilities of the Russian officer corps and common Soviet soldiers. Based on the Red Army's less-than-sterling performance in Poland (1939) and Finland (1939/40), the Germans had assumed that neither Soviet officers nor rank-and-file soldiers would be able to withstand the magisterial blows administered by the panzers, Stukas, and well-trained and experienced *Landser*. If predicated in part on objective analyses, such perspectives were deeply rooted in National Socialist ideology and long-standing racial biases, which posited that inherently inferior Slavic officers and soldiers could not—or would not—fight on a par with their superior German adversaries. By August, however, such assumptions had long since faded away, the German *Landser* having grown to respect (and fear) the remarkable fighting qualities of the Soviet soldier.

Yet what did this all mean for Hitler, his military leadership, and the millions of German soldiers now deep inside Soviet Russia? In a few words, it meant that, given the unexpected failure of the *Ostheer* to decisively triumph over the Red Army in a short blitzkrieg campaign—and this despite the dramatic initial victories of Army Group Center—a new strategic pathway to victory would have to be forged. Efforts to do so—in effect, to improvise a second Barbarossa campaign—would result in weeks of indecision and delay as Hitler, the OKH, and senior field commanders (Bock, Guderian, and Hoth, in particular) endlessly debated the way forward. And yet, as the weeks went by, doubts began to emerge about whether victory was still even achievable.

EUPHORIA GIVES WAY TO ANGST

As the blistering summer days of July 1941 rolled by and the German casualties mounted (by the end of month the *Wehrmacht* had sustained the astounding figure of 88,000 fatal losses on the eastern front),[2] the more perceptive officers in the OKH began to realize that victory over Russia was still far from certain. Even *Generalleutnant* Friedrich Paulus, Deputy Chief of Staff for Operations (OQu1) in the OKH, and Halder's righthand man, was beset by a "creeping disquiet" that tempered his initial optimism about the eventual outcome of the campaign. Paulus, it will be recalled, was one of the primary architects of Operation Barbarossa; on 22 June 1941, after reviewing the first optimistic reports from across the eastern front, he had predicted the blitzkrieg offensive would take just six to eight weeks to crush Russian resistance.[3] To be sure, he had anticipated tenacious combat in the campaign's opening phase but that the Red Army would then rapidly come apart due to the *Wehrmacht*'s overpowering blows. But now Paulus was plagued by doubt. Meeting with his son Ernst, a *Leutnant* in the Army, outside Smolensk in July,[4] the father intimated that he was "deeply concerned" (*sehr besorgt*) by the strength of the Red Army in both numbers and equipment. Observed Paulus's biographer Torsten Diedrich,

> [Paulus] had known about the problems that were still to come—the lengthening supply routes, the securing of sufficient technical and human replacements for ever increasing 'combat wear and tear' [*Kriegsverschleiss*]. At the same time, however, he had been cautious about his fears, had not placed great emphasis on his concerns, but, as was his nature, had kept a low profile and upheld the general tone of the blitzkrieg prognosis, not least to avoid casting doubt on his own plans.[5]

At the Army High Command's compound in the Mauerwald, 20 kilometers from Hitler's *Wolfsschanze* headquarters, Paulus, Heusinger (Chief of the OKH Operations Branch), Halder, and their military staffs worked tirelessly in an effort to meet the escalating and often unexpected challenges posed by the war against Soviet Russia:

> Barely a day went by on which the staff got to bed before midnight. A permanent high level of stress developed, which wore down the nerves and energy of the General Staff officers. During these days Paulus was more than the usual extremely industrious and pedantic worker. He sat at his desk, so his adjutant recalls, from 0830 hours until late into the night, surrounded by his adjutant and the special-duties staff officer, neither of whom felt they were working to full capacity, because Paulus preferred to do everything himself. He wrote out plans in pencil in highly legible writing, methodically, weighing up every word; he frequently corrected himself, not, as he did later, by crossing something out, but rather by erasing and rewriting.

> In such stressful phases this caused problems for Paulus's strained health. His delicate stomach forced him to eat a special diet. He had his meals prepared in his own kitchen by a cook. If this was not possible, then he kept to the strictest possible diet. As a result, his tall figure always appeared gaunt and haggard. The condition of his health, but also his own character, made him seem serious and reflective. In his calm temperament stress would manifest itself in greater absent-mindedness and, in times of greater psychological strain, in uncontrollable tics on one side of his face.[6]

As for Chief of the Army General Staff Franz Halder, he was busy recalibrating his assessment of the Russian "colossus." On 8 July, he had reported to Hitler that only 46 of the 164 Russian rifle divisions identified by German intelligence were still active on the main fronts (89 of them "were totally or largely eliminated"), while only 9 of 29 identified armored divisions were still combat capable.[7] On 23 July, however, he dramatically revised the Red Army's order of battle to show 93 divisions still capable of combat. The enemy, Halder concluded, while "decisively weakened," was by no means "finally smashed." Because Soviet manpower reserves were thought to be inexhaustible, Halder argued "even more forcefully that the aim of further operations had to be the destruction of the areas of armaments production around Moscow."[8] Three days later (26 July), in a scene repeated all too often in the summer of 1941, Halder again revised his estimate upward: "*Overall picture*: Enemy defense is becoming more aggressive; more tanks, more planes. In addition to 10 new divisions previously listed, 15 more new divisions have been reported."[9]

Although a much more sobering picture was beginning to emerge of the formidable task facing the *Wehrmacht* in the east, the military leadership clung to its increasingly untenable position that defeat of the Soviet Union remained imminent. At the military conference on 23 July, Halder went so far as to assure Hitler that Moscow and Leningrad could be reached by late August, the Don and the Volga Rivers by the beginning of October, and Baku and Batum in the Caucasus oil region by 1 November 1941. There is some question, however, as to how sincere Halder's projections were, given that he was still pulling out all stops to convince his Führer to maintain the *Schwerpunkt* of the German assault along the road to Moscow.

As for Hitler, he was fretting over the predicament of his eastern armies now trapped deep inside the depressing vastness of European Russia. Contributing to his anxiety was the catastrophic failure of his military intelligence agencies to accurately assess the size and strength of the Red Army. Following a visit to the *Wolfsschanze* (ca. 20 July), Admiral Wilhelm Canaris, chief of the military intelligence and counterintelligence department of the OKW, described the mood there as "very jittery," as it was increasingly apparent that the Russian campaign was not "going by the book."[10] On the evening of 17 July, Canaris had visited Bock at his headquarters in Borisov, about which Bock commented, "He fears the worst" (*er sieht schwarz in schwarz*).[11]

In his personal diary on 25 July, *Hauptmann* Karl-Wilhelm Thilo, OKH Operations Branch, noted that unexpected delays in military operations were making Hitler "very nervous."[12] On 28 July, during a short walk with his Army adjutant, *Major* Gerhard Engel, and his chief *Wehrmacht* adjutant, *Oberst* Rudolf Schmundt, Hitler confided that the situation in the east was causing him sleepless nights as he wrestled with what course of action to take next. The German dictator also fell ill as later chronicled by his *Luftwaffe* adjutant Nicolaus von Below:

> He failed to appear for meals and the daily situation conferences: It was quite obvious from his appearance how miserable he felt. Dr. Morell said it was probably a slight apoplexy. Hitler's heart and circulation were not in good order, but within a short while he would return the Führer to his former self. After a few days there was a noticeable improvement. We were ordered to observe the strictest silence about Hitler's condition. This was a health crisis with potentially serious consequences, however, and it worried me sufficiently to confide it to my brother on 30 July.[13]

The change in mood within the *Führerhauptquartier*, in contrast to late June and early July, was captured in the diary of Propaganda Minister Joseph Goebbels. On 1 August, he wrote, "One concedes openly, that the estimation of Soviet military strength was somewhat mistaken. The Bolsheviks are displaying stronger resistance than we expected and, above all, the material means available to them are greater than we had assumed."[14] (Three weeks before, on 9 July, Hitler had assured Goebbels, "The war in the east is essentially won. We will still have to fight a series of difficult battles, but the armed forces of Bolshevism will not be able to recover from defeats they've already suffered."[15]) Ten days later (10 August) Goebbels wrote, "It will still require very hard and bloody blows until the Soviet Union lies shattered [*zerschmettert*] on the ground."[16]

In early August, *Hauptmann* Georg Heino Freiherr von Münchhausen, adjutant to *Oberst* Heusinger, summarized in his journal the new thinking rapidly taking hold inside the Army High Command, as the pressures of space and time began to inexorably intrude:

> It is often possible to doubt that we will manage to beat the Russians decisively and take possession of their main industrial regions in the very brief period up to the fall. Even at best, we won't make it to the Volga, and it is still highly probable that, with the aid of the industries in the Urals and in Siberia, new armies will emerge next spring! If these are dangerous, which may well be assumed, given the general nature of the Russians in this campaign, the resulting war on two fronts

> will have the worst consequences for the overall course of the war! Hopefully things will turn out differently!!![17]

Oberstleutnant Hellmuth Stieff also served in the OKH Operations Branch in the summer of 1941. An intelligent and insightful officer who grasped the broader strategic picture, Stieff—later to be executed for his role in the anti-Nazi resistance—had become increasingly bitter over the direction of the war and what he perceived as the growing corruption of the German General Staff. On 2 August, from the OKH compound in the Mauerwald, he poured out his thoughts in a long missive to his wife; because of the many insights it offers, the letter is cited at length:

> My dear little Ling!
>
> . . . Of overall developments it can be said in general that not all expectations have been met to the fullest extent hoped for—expectations, which, in my opinion, were unreasonably high in some areas. My opinion that this time we would be dealing with a struggle between two world views and new ideas, in which the severity of the struggle would acquire a completely different dimension, has been fully confirmed. Moreover, we have not only deceived ourselves about the military strength of our opponent, but also underestimated the abilities of his leadership. The forces that this life-and-death struggle has unleashed in this regard in our opponent are, in any case, quite considerable. With the exception of the double battle of Belostok-Minsk—where, using the element of surprise, the encirclement and destruction of considerable numbers of Russian forces led to the full achievement of our goal—the other battles, aside from localized successes, have only led to further frontal wrestling [*frontalen Abringen*]. We may have maintained the upper hand everywhere in this, and the enemy has suffered considerable losses in the process, but the big operational impact [*grosse operative Auswirkung*], which has been the objective, has not been forthcoming—there should be no illusions about this. . . .
>
> Our operation has stalled in the center, less perhaps due to enemy counter actions than to the natural attrition of our mobile units, which, after all, have been in combat and advancing for 4 weeks without cessation, and are now in desperate need of a rest period to accomplish repairs on their vehicles and to replace personnel losses they have sustained of up to 30 percent. For this, they need to be relieved from the enemy, whose constant counterattacks do not let up, by the infantry divisions. This has already been implemented in part, but in part is only possible after clearing the Smolensk cauldron, where the enemy is holding on so tenaciously that he practically has to be killed one by one, because their fear of their commissars is still greater than their fear of us. For when commissars are no longer present, then our propaganda leaflets have a strong effect, and the people and their officers come over to us in their masses. Unfortunately, though, that is always an exception. . . .

> You can imagine the nervousness at the highest level [i.e., Hitler]. If it were not so sad, you would laugh out loud about the strange effects that causes! . . . [Whether], however, the ambitious goals can be reached this year may well remain anyone's guess. I fear that it will not be the case and we will have to advance once again with some elements of the Army in the coming year. Naturally, our situation is decisively worse as a result, and that gives the USA, despite all their concerns about the Japanese, the impetus either to enter into the war or to pull the kinds of dirty tricks [*Schweinereien*] like the one they did with Iceland,[18] which is already proving fateful [*verhängnisvoll*] for our conduct of the war in the Atlantic.
>
> For the first time in this war, I have doubts as to whether we will be equal to the task. If our second strike in the east[19] does not positively galvanize developments there—and on this there is still some hope, since the Russian seems to still want to seek a decision with his last remaining forces, whereby we would be relieved of the concern of what effectively would be a war on two fronts—if, then, this hope is not fulfilled, then we will lose so much of our advantage in the other theaters of war that the outcome of this war really will be in doubt. . . .
>
> One product of this nervousness at the highest level is the manner in which we report. In my view, it is bad. The *Wehrmacht* reports are no longer anything more than a medium of political propaganda, are drawn up only by him [i.e., Hitler] personally with no concern for the impact, impressed on him often enough, on the mood and expectations of the combat forces, for whom they are the only means of briefing on the overall progress of the battles. What is more, they exaggerate purported successes in such an abhorrent way and are anything but sober reports of the facts. Their truth content can justifiably be doubted. It is a shame that now even the last bastion of decency in this state is being sacrificed on the altar of a system led by corrupt or lunatic persons. I am bitter [*sehr verbittert*] like never before during this war and certainly like never before in the course of a campaign.[20]

The first formal "cracks in the High Command's confident façade"[21] appeared on 6 August 1941, when *Generalmajor* Walter Warlimont, Chief of the OKW's National Defense Branch (*Amt Landesverteidigung*) and General Alfred Jodl's deputy, produced a "Brief Strategic Overview on the Continuation of the War after the Campaign in the East." In the document, Warlimont stated that the military leadership must consider the fact that its armies in the east were not going to reach their operational objectives—a line from the Caucasus oil region in the south, to the Volga, and northward to Archangel and Murmansk—in 1941; perforce, an open front would remain in existence during the coming year.[22]

By 11 August 1941, the transformation in the Army High Command's analysis of the Russian campaign was complete. As Halder confided in his journal that day,

> What we are now doing is the last desperate attempt to prevent our front line from becoming frozen in position warfare. . . . Our last reserves have been committed.

> . . . The whole situation makes it increasingly plain that we have underestimated the Russian colossus, who consistently prepared for war with that utterly ruthless determination so characteristic of totalitarian states. . . . At the outset of the war we reckoned with about 200 enemy divisions. Now we have already counted 360. These divisions indeed are not armed and equipped according to our standards, and their tactical leadership is often poor. But they are there, and if we smash a dozen of them, the Russians simply put up another dozen.[23]

Hitler, meanwhile, having sufficiently recovered from his brief illness, had visited the CP of Army Group Center at Borisov on 4 August to confer with his battlefield commanders (see below). Back at the Wolf's Lair the next day, he told Brauchitsch that (like Halder) he feared the front was in danger of congealing into static warfare, just as it had in 1914.

By 7 August, Hitler was ill again, this time seriously so with dysentery. For three weeks, he suffered from diarrhea, stomach cramps, fever, and other attendant maladies. No doubt the somber and oppressive atmosphere of his East Prussian compound, the daily situation conferences that dragged on for hours, sapping the strength of Hitler and his generals alike, and, most of all, the creeping doubts about the outcome of the war with Russia had all conspired to produce the downturn in his health; and this at a critical juncture in the campaign as Hitler debated his generals over operational alternatives for the next phase of Operation Barbarossa.

MOSCOW, LENINGRAD, OR THE UKRAINE?

By mid-July 1941, following the start of a second series of encirclement battles north and west of Smolensk, Hitler had become aware that his Army General Staff was setting a clear course toward Moscow. The Führer, however, abiding by his own strategic vision—as laid out in the original Barbarossa directive of December 1940—still considered the Soviet capital an objective of secondary (even tertiary) significance; as a result, and much to the dismay of Brauchitsch, Halder, and the rest of the staff at the OKH, the German dictator and warlord began to intervene energetically in the military planning process.

On 19 July, Hitler promulgated Führer Directive No. 33, laying out his vision of future operations along the eastern front. The directive stipulated that the *Schwerpunkt* of the *Ostheer*'s efforts was to shift from the center to the wings; specifically, Hoth's panzers—following the destruction of Soviet forces at Smolensk—were to be sent north to support Leeb's drive on Leningrad, while strong elements of Guderian's panzer group were to wheel southeast into the Ukraine and cooperate with Rundstedt's army group. These points were rammed home in a supplement to Directive No. 33 issued several days later. Moscow would have to wait.[24]

Hitler's new directives sent shock waves through the OKH, as the latent discord between the Führer and his Army General Staff over core operational concepts of the Russian campaign—reaching all the way back to late 1940—suddenly burst out into the open. The crux of the conflict between Hitler and his generals was this: While Hitler sought to inform his decision making via a synthesis of political, economic, and military factors—leading him to conclude that a decisive outcome could only be achieved by switching the weight of the German assault to the north (Leningrad and the Baltic) and the south (the Ukraine, Donbas, and Caucasus)—Moscow remained the idée fixe of his chief military advisors, who were convinced that the main Soviet forces were assembling along the approaches to the capital in an all-out effort to prevent its capture, thus exposing them to destruction in a final great battle of annihilation. In a report for the western Allies prepared by Halder after the war, the former *Chef des Generalstabs des Heeres* stated,

> The center of gravity [*Schwerpunkt*] of Russian strength was therefore in front of Army Group Center. . . . The General Staff had been brought up with the idea that it must be the aim of an operation to defeat the military power of the enemy, and it therefore considered the next and most pressing task to be to defeat the forces of Timoshenko by concentrating all available forces at Army Group Center, to advance on Moscow, to take this nerve center of enemy resistance and to destroy the new enemy formations. The assembly for this attack had to be carried out as soon as possible because the season was advanced.[25]

When Hitler's directives were passed down to the field commands, the impact was equally electrifying. Of course, it was Bock's army group that was most directly affected by the new orders, and he responded with outright indignation, going so far as to suggest the abolition of his command (most likely, a veiled threat of resignation). After all, if his army group was to be "carved up into three parts" as he put it in his journal, "there will be no need for [my] headquarters."[26]

The Führer's flurry of purposeful activity culminated in Directive No. 34 on 30 July. Influenced by the fierce and wide-ranging Soviet counterattacks then ongoing against Bock's army group, Hitler decreed that it was to suspend its eastward drive—which, in any event, had already slowed to a crawl—and "go over to the defensive, taking advantage of suitable terrain." Moreover, before beginning new operations, both Hoth's and Guderian's panzer groups were to be pulled from the line for "quick rehabilitation as soon as the situation allows."[27] While no one could have predicted it at the time, Army Group Center would not renew its drive on Moscow for two full months.

HITLER VISITS ARMY GROUP CENTER

On 4 August, with his personal pilot, Hans Baur, at the controls of *Immelmann III* (a large Focke-Wulf Fw 200 "Condor" four-engine transport), Hitler flew to Bock's headquarters at Borisov. Accompanying him were GFM Wilhelm Keitel,

Chief of Staff at OKW; General Alfred Jodl, Chief of the OKW Operations Branch; and Oberst Rudolf Schmundt, his chief adjutant.[28] Upon arrival, they were greeted by Bock, his chief of staff, and his chief operations officer. Also present were Hoth, Guderian, and *Oberst* Heusinger, the latter no doubt operating as "eyes and ears" for Chief of the Army General Staff Halder.

Hitler began by warmly congratulating the army group commander on his "unprecedented successes" in the east. In an unusual move, he then proceeded to question each of his generals—Bock, Hoth, Guderian—separately, enabling him to gauge their opinions individually and in such a manner that none of the men knew what the others had said. If the dictator was expecting any support for his line of reasoning, it was not forthcoming on this day, as each of the generals hewed closely to Halder's position on the preeminent importance of Moscow.

Following the generals' individual audiences with the Führer, the entire group was brought together, and Hitler proceeded to lecture them: What would determine the future course of operations was the requirement to occupy those regions deemed "essential" (*lebenswichtig*) to Soviet Russia's survival; in this context, he laid out three alternatives in order of priority. His top priority remained Leningrad—with its "exclusive" factories for the production of heavy tanks (*alleinige Produktionsstätte für schwerste Panzer*)—along with seizure of the Baltic coast and elimination of the Soviet Baltic fleet. In second place was the south of Russia, in particular the Donbas (Donets Basin), south of Khar'kov, in the eastern Ukraine; this vital area, Hitler insisted, made up the "entire basis of the Soviet economy," and its capture would precipitate that economy's "sure collapse." To achieve this latter objective, Hitler was pondering the dispatch of "strong elements" of Bock's army group southward into the Ukraine.[29]

As for Moscow, it was still priority number three (*an dritter Stelle*) in the Führer's calculus; thus, he said, it was probably appropriate, for the time being at least, to stay on the defensive on the central front.[30] Bock countered that an immediate push toward Moscow would strike the main forces of the enemy, who was frantically assembling anything he could lay hands on before his army group; hence, it could lead to a "decision of arms" (*Waffenentscheidung*). Hitler listened intently but did not commit himself to a course of action.[31]

The conference then turned to other "more detailed questions." As Guderian recalled, the decision was made not to evacuate the El'nia salient "since it was not yet known whether this salient might not still be needed as a jumping-off point for an attack toward Moscow."[32] Both Hoth and Guderian seized the opportunity of Hitler's presence to lodge urgent pleas for the release of new tanks and replacement tank engines (the latter now "very worn as a result of the appalling dust") from current production; without new engines, they insisted, "wide-ranging operations" would no longer be possible. (The fact that the panzer generals had to plead with Hitler for new tanks and engines underscores the alarming extent of his micromanagement of the war.) Provided these requirements were met, and with a short period to rest and refit, Guderian was confident his panzer group could once more begin major operations by 15 August. Hoth was more cautious, suggesting he would be ready by 18–20 August.[33] The estimates of both Hoth and Guderian, however, were wildly off the mark, given the losses hitherto sustained and Army Group Center's growing logistical problems.

"Visibly impressed" by the panzer generals' pleas, Hitler authorized the release of 400 new tank engines (a month's production)[34] from depots in Germany, along with a pitifully tiny number of new tanks, 35 in all; beyond that, he refused to budge. When Guderian protested that his command alone required 300 new tank engines, the dictator demurred. Soviet losses, he claimed, were approaching those sustained by Imperial Russia in all of World War I, and this after just six weeks of war; besides, the success of future operations depended mainly on adopting the correct strategic approach, not haggling over a handful of tanks or spare parts. Thus, the diarist of 2 Panzer Group could only observe—and somewhat sheepishly at that—that even if the measures agreed to by the Führer did not compensate for the wear and tear on the panzer units, they at least "gave the troops something of the feeling that they were not forgotten"—a remarkable statement reflecting the dangerous degree to which the eastern front was being starved of new weapons and equipment, which Hitler was holding back for "future tasks."[35]

Two days later (August 6), Hitler flew to the command post of Army Group South, ensconced in a former Soviet military school in the dreary Ukrainian town of Berdichev. (Among the Führer's entourage was his diplomatic liaison officer, Ambassador Walther Hewel, who wrote in his journal, "We strolled through Berdichev. Ruined monastery church. Opened coffins, execution, ghastly town. Many Jews, ancient cottages, fertile soil. Very hot. Three hours' flight back.")[36] In his discussion with Hitler, GFM von Rundstedt was no more successful than his colleagues at Army Group Center in convincing the German warlord of the need to move on Moscow. Besides, the Führer's meteorologists had assured him that the dry weather would hold longer in the center than in the south, providing yet another reason for him to strike south first and to leave Moscow for later.[37]

HITLER MAKES HIS DECISION

After returning from Bock's headquarters at Borisov, Heusinger made a detailed report to Halder, for whom the Führer's continued inflexibility on the decisive question of how the campaign should go forward was a source of deep frustration and concern. The news that Moscow remained a tertiary priority for Hitler, behind Leningrad and the Ukraine, was a "bitter pill" for Halder, who was equally disturbed by the dictator's apparent inability to reach a final decision.

The dispute between Hitler and his generals would go on for two more weeks. In a last-ditch effort to turn Hitler around to his thinking, Halder directed Heusinger to prepare a memorandum marshaling all arguments for an immediate resumption of the attack toward Moscow. Sent by Brauchitsch to the Führer on 18 August, the memorandum "expressed more clearly than all previous ideas and drafts Halder's strategy during the preparatory and execution phase of Operation Barbarossa, which he now openly tried to realize against Hitler's wishes."[38] Simply put, the main thrust of the memorandum was that the annihilation of the Red Army around Moscow and the conquest of industrial resources in the region had to remain the primary objective of German military operations before the onset of poor weather in October. As he had before, Halder argued that the two other army groups (North and South) were still strong enough to achieve their objectives without the support of Army Group Center, which, the memorandum stated, would be able to assemble forty-two infantry divisions, thirteen mechanized divisions, and one cavalry division in time to begin the offensive in early September.[39]

Finally, on 21 August 1941, Hitler issued a new set of orders—drafted on his instructions by General Jodl of OKW—for the continuation of the campaign. They began by stating that "the Army's proposal for the continuation of operations in the east, of 18 August, does not conform with my intentions. I order the following: 1. The most important objective to be achieved before the onset of winter is not the capture of Moscow, but the occupation of the Crimea and the industrial and coal region of the [Donbas], together with the isolation of the Russian oil regions in the Caucasus. In the north, [it is] the encirclement of Leningrad and union with the Finns [*die Abschliessung Leningrads und die Vereinigung mit den Finnen*]." In the next paragraph, the document stipulated that the "uniquely favorable operational situation" resulting from Army Group Center reaching the line Gomel-Pochep was to be immediately exploited by a "concentric operation" involving the inner wings of both Army Groups Center and South to effect the encirclement of Soviet 5 Army in the area east of Kiev; this would free Rundstedt's army group to push eastward, beyond the Dnepr, to secure the vital industrial centers of Rostov and Khar'kov.[40]

One is struck by the palpable irony of this operational scheme: The advance of the right wing of Army Group Center (*Armeegruppe Guderian* and Weichs's Second Army) southward during the first three weeks of August (see chapter 5) had been undertaken—at least as far as GFM von Bock and his panzer generals were concerned—to clear the army group's southern (right) flank and secure jump-off positions for the drive on Moscow; and yet the success of these very maneuvers, coupled with the deplorable setup of Soviet Southwestern Front, facing Army Group South, had also created the conditions for a spectacular German success in the Ukraine, and Hitler was not about to let the opportunity pass.

THE ARMY HIGH COMMAND RESPONDS

Hitler's new orders arrived at the OKH late that evening, where they struck like a bomb. For Halder, the Führer directive of 21 August was "decisive" for the outcome of the campaign—decisive in the sense that it meant, or so he thought, the end to his plans and hopes for bringing the war to a successful conclusion in 1941. To Hitler's Army adjutant, *Major* Engel, it simply signified "a black day for the Army."[41]

It was not until early the next morning (0130 hours) that *Oberst* Heusinger's adjutant in the Operations Branch, *Hauptmann* von Münchhausen—relaxing in the officers' mess with several other OKH officers after a crab dinner—was handed a copy of Hitler's directive. He recorded his reaction—and that of his fellow officers—in his personal diary:

> We read it and were outraged because we immediately saw its decisive importance and knew what disappointment it would cause. It was signed personally by A. H. . . . This clearly means that an attack on Moscow this year will now probably no longer be possible! As *Generaloberst* Halder writes in a marginal note to the directive: "This order means that the majority of the German Army will remain bound up in Russia during Winter 41/42, and it will not be possible to carry out the planned operational intentions of the Army (and most likely of the *Luftwaffe* as well)." . . . Everyone is simply outraged. "That could mean losing the war!"[42]

Hauptmann Thilo (also in the OKH Operations Branch) agonized over Hitler's alarming (and growing) interference in the operational and tactical details of the eastern campaign; however, he was even more distressed by the failure of Hitler's military advisors at OKW and OKH to take effective action against the Führer's decision making. Thilo's diary entry of 24 August included frank observations on Hitler's increasing domination of the German officer corps, as well as on Germany's deteriorating strategic outlook:

> Yesterday [*sic*] the Führer, contrary to objections by OKH, released an order, which could (like his order before Dunkirk to halt the panzer units) have disastrous consequences for the <u>entire</u> campaign. . . .
>
> At the start of the war we underestimated the Russian; today we are overestimating him; every gap is causing serious jitters [*Nervenkrisen*] at OKW.
>
> What is deplorable is that nobody from the Führer's circle—C-in-C of the Army [Brauchitsch] certainly not—can resist any more. He [Hitler] is far too autocratic, even the old people . . . are frustrated (Göring recently just left the HQ for 14 days for this very reason!).
>
> If Moscow is not taken this year, then this winter we'll have the positional warfare [*Stellungskrieg*] our enemy wants, which will give him time and materiel (from the Moscow industrial region) for replenishment. Large elements of the *Luftwaffe* and the Army are committed to the east, while, without sufficient defenses in place, the English are able to bomb western and northern Germany. In

> the spring we'll be forced to attack once more against new Red forces, costing more blood and time.[43]

If younger General Staff officers at OKH like Münchhausen and Thilo were deeply disillusioned by the turn of events—and by the conspicuous lack of courage displayed by their superiors[44]—the German soldiers at the front, not privy of course to the inner workings of the High Command, reacted in a less complicated fashion to the abrupt shift in strategy: They were simply flummoxed, having no rational explanation for it. (As one eastern front veteran later put it, "The corporal's [Hitler's] wand waved over Army Group Center and turned it to stone.")[45] Indeed, for the men of Bock's army group, Moscow was *the* objective, and most were convinced its capture would bring a victorious conclusion to the war. The German soldiers' fixation on Stalin's capital city was reflected in their habit throughout the summer of 1941 of hanging signposts reading "TO MOSCOW" along the route of advance, as recounted by Guderian in his memoir: "On 13 August I visited the Desna front, to the east of Roslavl, on either side of the Moscow highway. With a heavy heart [*Wehen Herzens*] I saw how my soldiers, confident that they would soon be advancing straight toward the Russian capital, had put up many signposts marked 'TO MOSCOW.' The soldiers of the 137 Infantry Division, with whom I spoke at the front, would talk only of a rapid resumption of the move to the east."[46]

Despite Hitler's orders of 21 August, Halder still had a card to play. On 23 August, he flew to Bock's command post at Borisov, where he conferred with both Bock and Guderian. The ostensible purpose of the meeting was to discuss execution of Hitler's new attack orders. The three generals, however, had a more urgent task at hand—namely, hatching a "plot" in a final desperate foray to convince Hitler to support the operational planning of the Army for an attack on Moscow. According to Guderian, "We discussed at length what could still be done to alter Hitler's 'unalterable resolve.' We were all agreed that this new plan to move on Kiev must result in a winter campaign: this in its turn would lead to all those difficulties that the Army High Command had very good reasons for wishing to avoid." Guderian went on to explain why the turn south was untenable for his forces, among other things mentioning the "road and supply problems" that would inevitably accompany such a move, while also pointing out the exhausted state of his 24 Panzer Corps, which had been in almost continuous action since the beginning of the campaign. In fact, the thoroughly disgruntled panzer general went so far as to dismiss Hitler's proposed operation as a "crime."[47]

Bock suggested that Guderian accompany Halder back to Hitler's headquarters in East Prussia, where he would undertake a final attempt to change the dictator's mind—the thinking being that Guderian, as a general from the front, "could lay the relevant facts immediately before Hitler" in a uniquely powerful and persuasive way. The field marshal then put in a telephone call to Schmundt at the *Wolfsschanze*, requesting that Guderian be permitted to speak to the Führer. Later that afternoon, Guderian set off with Halder on his return flight, arriving at Lötzen airfield as darkness fell.[48]

The details of Guderian's dramatic encounter with Hitler at his evening situation conference on 23 August are well known and need not be reexamined at length. Simply put, when granted an opening, Guderian launched into an impassioned plea for continuing the advance on Moscow. Hitler, who had a special regard for the panzer pioneer and brilliant field commander, heard Guderian out; when he was finished, the Führer began to talk. He spoke of the vital necessity of seizing the raw materials and agricultural production of the Ukraine for the future prosecution of the war and of the importance of capturing the Crimea ("that Soviet aircraft carrier for attacking the Romanian oil fields"). It was at this point that Hitler rendered his notorious rebuke: "My generals know nothing about the economic aspects of war."[49]

Guderian listened in silence, refraining from opposition. After all, Hitler was surrounded by the usual cast of sycophants—OKW officers Keitel, Jodl, Schmundt, and the like—all nodding their approval of everything their Führer said. Inexplicably, neither Brauchitsch nor Halder had accompanied Guderian to the conference. The panzer general later justified his seeming acquiescence to Hitler's sharply opposing views by stating, "I did not then think it would be right to make an angry scene with the head of the German state when he was surrounded by his advisors."[50] Guderian, however, did manage to extract one concession from Hitler: His panzer forces were to be committed in their entirety to support Rundstedt's operations in the south and allowed to rejoin the Moscow axis after the battle east of Kiev had been won. In the final analysis, it seems Guderian was simply overawed in Hitler's presence, and the result finally put an end to Halder's cherished plans.

The next morning, Guderian reported to Halder, informing the Chief of the Army General Staff of his failure to convince Hitler and that the push into the Ukraine by Army Group Center would have to be carried out. Enraged by Guderian's apparent capitulation when confronted by the Führer firsthand, Halder heaped abuse on his colleague and, Guderian claimed, "suffered a complete nervous collapse [*Nervenzusammenbruch*]."[51] Halder, it seems, was particularly put out by Guderian's effort to ensure that the new operation was conducted from the start with adequate strength (i.e., with all of his armored forces, thus removing them, temporarily at least, from Bock's order of battle); moreover, he was bewildered by Guderian's volte-face after he had so sharply disagreed with Hitler's new plans during the conference in Borisov. The two men parted "without having reached agreement," their relationship having suffered a blow from which it would never recover. Guderian returned to his headquarters with orders to begin the drive toward Kiev on 25 August.[52]

5

Guderian Clears His Right Flank

As addressed in the preceding chapter, Hitler's ultimate decision to shift the main weight of his eastern armies to the wings, to the theaters of Army Groups North and South, was largely influenced by his emphasis on economic factors. Moreover, it had been his (arguably correct) conviction since late July that, before the drive on Moscow could be resumed, Army Group Center would have to clear its flanks of troublesome Soviet forces, which, if not destroyed, could seriously disrupt any push toward the Soviet capital. A memorandum released by OKW on 28 July ("Considerations and Instructions of the Führer") stated that the "most urgent task" (*dringlichste Aufgabe*) for Bock's army group was to clear its deep right flank by smashing the Soviet grouping around and north of Gomel. Hitler's order, also embodied in Führer Directive No. 34 (30 July), was to be carried out by Guderian's army group in cooperation with Weichs's Second Army. (Directive No. 34, it will be recalled, had also ordered Army Group Center to suspend its attack and go on to the defensive along the entire length of its expansive eastern front.)[1]

As Guderian's panzers headed south in adherence to Hitler's directive, the Soviets continued their fierce and wide-ranging counterattacks against Army Group Center that had commenced on 23 July. Although these attacks (orchestrated by Marshal Timoshenko) failed to achieve any operational—much less strategic—success, they did register unprecedented tactical successes that inflicted serious harm on Bock's army group, not only in terms of losses but also to German confidence and morale. In despair, Bock wrote in his diary on 24 August, "It [my eastern front] can't hold much longer the way things look now. I am being forced to spread the reserves that I have so laboriously scraped together for the hoped for attack behind my front just to have some degree of security that it will not be breached. If, after all the successes, the campaign in the east now trickles away in dismal defensive fighting for my army group, it is not my fault."[2]

Making matters worse for the frustrated field marshal was the paucity of replacements reaching his army group. On 2 August, *Generalmajor* Walter Buhle reported to OKH that Army Group Center had only received 23,000 replacements since the start of the Barbarossa campaign, a figure that did not begin to cover its actual losses (the situation was no better for Leeb's and Rundstedt's army groups). Buhle also reported on his visit to Guderian's group and its "clamor" for replacements for the panzer and infantry divisions. (As noted, the motorized infantry of both Guderian's and Hoth's commands had sustained particularly heavy losses during the bitter fighting along the rim of the Smolensk cauldron.) Bock's declining combat strength took another hit in mid-August: Alarmed by a sudden breakthrough on the right wing of Army Group North, Hitler ordered the transfer of Hoth's 39 Panzer Corps (12 PD, 18 ID [mot.], 20 ID [mot.]) to Leeb; on 16 August, the panzer corps began to move north from its rest areas between Smolensk and Dukhovshchina, stripping Army Group Center of badly needed tanks and panzer grenadiers.[3]

KRICHEV

In the second week of August, *Armeegruppe Guderian* was once again on the march, continuing the "southward tilt" it had begun with its victory at Roslavl and helping to close the widening gap between Bock's army group and Rundstedt's Army Group South. Yet, to have truly open flanks for the planned drive on Moscow, Guderian would—before any move on Gomel—first have to reduce the Soviet concentration around Krichev, southwest of Roslavl, where strong forces of the new Soviet Central Front were dug in. After briefly resting the three mobile divisions of Geyr's 24 Panzer Corps (3 PD, 4 PD, 10 ID [mot.]), Guderian was ready to strike.

Despite delays caused by muddy roads, complicating movement into their assembly areas, Model's 3 Panzer Division and Langermann-Erlencamp's 4 Panzer Division began their assault from positions east of Krichev on the morning of 9 August, while infantry of Wilhelm Fahrmbacher's 7 Army Corps screened the panzer corps' left flank. Always at the center of the action, Guderian accompanied the advance of 4 PD, whose attack, he stated in *Panzer Leader*, "went in as though it were a model attack on the training-ground: *Oberst* Schneider's artillery gave valuable support."[4] Also of interest are Guderian's next observations: "A significant indication of the attitude of the civilian population is provided by the fact that women came out from their villages on to the very battlefield bringing wooden platters of bread and butter and eggs and, in my case at least, refused to let me move on before I had eaten. Unfortunately, this friendly attitude toward the Germans lasted only so long as the more benevolent military administration was in control."[5]

Despite dogged enemy opposition and particularly poor road conditions due to bad weather (increasing fuel consumption by as much as 75 percent), the tanks and motorized infantry of 24 Panzer Corps smashed the defenses of Lt.-Gen. K. D. Golubev's 13 Army, sending his forces reeling southward in a desperate dash to avoid encirclement. Wheeling rapidly westward, the next day (10 August) Model's division seized the town of Klimovichi, encircling several divisions of 13 Army's 45 Rifle Corps in a pocket east of Krichev.[6]

Over the ensuing forty-eight to seventy-two hours, Model's 3 Panzer Division, supported by 7 Infantry Division[7] and elements of 10 ID (mot.), carved up the small pocket, while 4 Panzer Division set up a defensive screen above the town of Kommunary to prevent any attempts by Soviet forces outside the pocket to rescue the trapped divisions. By 13 August, the battle was over—despite repeated breakout attempts, the encircled forces of Golubev's 13 Army had been shattered; 16,000 *Rotarmisten* trudged into captivity, the Germans also capturing or destroying seventy-six guns, fifteen tanks, and one armored train (shot up by tanks of 4 PD).[8]

The modest victory, however, had also taken a toll on Geyr's panzer corps. On 11 August, 4 Panzer Division reported it was down to sixty-four available tanks, of which only twenty-five were Pz IIIs and eight were Pz IVs. Only days later, on the evening of 14 August, the panzer division's war diarist observed that the most recent fighting had been "very costly, also in materiel"; moreover, the men were "tired," the division "increasingly more worn out." The Russian tanks, he acknowledged, "especially the heavy ones, are good" (emphasis in the original).[9]

While Guderian had won another victory on the battlefield, he lost yet another round in his ongoing disputes over future operations: "On 15 August I was busy trying to persuade my superiors [at OKH and Army Group Center] not to exploit the success of 24 Panzer Corps by making them push on to Gomel. As I saw it such a march to the southwest would constitute a step backwards."[10] Guderian also argued that Geyr's panzer corps, which had not gone "a single day out of action" since the start of the eastern campaign, was "urgently in need" of being pulled from the line for rest, recuperation, and tank maintenance. His arguments fell on deaf ears.

GOMEL

From the perspective of GFM von Bock, an operation to seize Gomel had become a vital necessity from the moment the Soviet 21 Army had struck his army group's right wing in mid-July, recapturing Zhlobin and Rogachev along the Dnepr River and briefly threatening Bobruisk with a cavalry corps. Hence, when Guderian began his march southward across the Sozh River in the second week of August (culminating in the successful Krichev pocket battle), the field marshal seized the opportunity to eliminate once and for all Red Army forces between the Dnepr and the Sozh by means of an ambitious envelopment maneuver against Gomel—Weichs pressing in from the northwest and west and Guderian from the northeast.[11]

Generaloberst von Weichs's Second Army (seventeen divisions in five army corps and a special provisional corps) was positioned astride the Dnepr and Sozh Rivers, forming the heavily refused right wing of Army Group Center. Delayed by shortages of artillery shells, muddy roads, and other factors, Weichs was forced to postpone his drive on Gomel three times. Finally, shortly after dawn on 12 August, he began his offensive, his left wing (12 and 13 AKs), supported by a powerful preparatory artillery barrage, Stukas, and bomber units, pushing southward between the two rivers and making good progress on this first day. The next day (13 August) Second Army's right wing, 43 Army Corps, under command of *Gen.d.Inf.* Gotthard Heinrici, joined the assault, forging several bridgeheads on the eastern bank of the Dnepr, northwest of Gomel; with the Soviet defenders capable of nothing more than "local resistance" (*örtlichen Widerstand*), by nightfall Weichs's attacking army corps had broken through along the entire enemy front. At certain points, however, the defenders hurled back the attacking German infantry and inflicted heavy losses on them. In the assault on Kostjaschovo, half of a German battalion was wiped out by the large, well-concealed Soviet force defending the town: Displaying excellent fire discipline, the Russians had waited until the advancing Germans were barely ten meters away before opening fire; one company was reduced to thirty-five men.[12] The success of the attackers was also dampened by the loss of *Generalmajor* Kurt Kalmukoff, the commander of 31 Infantry Division (12 AK): As he drove out to visit his regiments, his vehicle struck a Russian mine, instantly killing the general and his adjutant.[13]

By 14 August, Weichs's infantry corps (much to the delight of GFM von Bock) had surrounded the bulk of 63 and 67 Rifle Corps (at least six rifle divisions) of Lt.-Gen. V. M. Gordov's 21 Army in a *Kessel* on the eastern bank of the Dnepr southeast of Rogachev (and northwest of Gomel). The next day (15 August), OKH directed Guderian to support the rapid advance of Second Army by continuing to push southward with 24 Panzer Corps and slipping in behind 21 Army to block its potential escape to the east. (At this time, the panzer forces of Geyr's corps, milling about in the area of Klimovichi and Kommunary, were roughly midway between Roslavl and Gomel and some 60 kilometers north of Unecha, a key rail junction astride the vital Gomel-Briansk-Moscow railroad line.) By late 16 August, Weichs's infantry had reached the northern outskirts of Gomel, forming "an anvil against which the divisions of Geyr's 24 Panzer Corps could strike like a hammer to encircle Soviet forces now caught in a deep salient northeast and east of the city."[14]

Events continued to unfold rapidly. While Langermann-Erlencamp's 4 Panzer Division had already captured the town of Kommunary (115 kilometers northeast of Gomel), on 16 August, the advance detachment of Model's 3 Panzer Division took the road intersection at Mglin, 30 kilometers north of Unecha. On 17 August, Model's splendid tank crews and panzer grenadiers, facing only desultory Red Army resistance, seized the important rail junction at Unecha.[15] Meanwhile, Soviet General Gordov's two encircled rifle corps sought to breakout to the south and southeast, toward the defenses around Gomel proper, compelling Weichs to commit strong forces to contain the pocket; by 17/18 August, the encircled Soviet divisions, hammered by repeated German blows along the perimeter of the pocket, had either been annihilated or surrendered, with only small groups of soldiers managing to make their escape. During the fighting, the C-in-C of Soviet 63 Rifle Corps, Maj.-Gen. L. G. Petrovsky, perished outside the village of Skepnia. "In an act of chivalry rare on the eastern front," the Germans buried the valorous Russian general with full military honors, erecting a cross over his grave with an inscription bearing witness to his bravery.[16]

To strengthen his advancing forces, Guderian now committed Lemelsen's 47 Panzer Corps to the operation, dispatching its 29 ID (mot.) toward Briansk to screen his army group's eastern flank along the Desna River and its 17 Panzer Division to reinforce 3 PD as it rumbled southward from Unecha; by nightfall, 18 August, lead elements of Thoma's 17 PD were closing in on Pochep, 50 kilometers east of Unecha. Continuing their southward plunge, by 22 August, the two panzer corps—as depicted on the situation map of the OKH Operations Branch—had reached the line (running east-west) Pochep (17 PD)–Starodub (3 PD)–Klintsy (10 ID [mot.])–Surazh (10 ID [mot.]). Guderian's lightning advance had carved out a 115-kilometer-wide and 120-kilometer-deep salient south of the Sozh River between Lt.-Gen. A. I. Eremenko's Briansk Front and Lt.-Gen. M. G. Efremov's Central Front, threatening the latter with encirclement east of Gomel.[17]

In his personal diary on 22 August, *Gen.d.Pz.Tr.* Lemelsen (47 PzK), no doubt deeply gratified by the fine showing of his men, put down his thoughts on the (putative) superiority of the German soldier vis-à-vis his gritty Russian opponent:

> In general, the superiority of the German soldier over the Soviet forces is becoming increasingly noticeable, especially since the divisions now appearing are mostly newly activated units of poorly trained soldiers who have little combat value; they fight only out of fear of their commissars. From the division's command post I drove in my vehicle through the most amazing dust to Pochep and Russaka to the church tower there, which provided a view deep into enemy territory. The church was a gruesome sight, utterly ravaged and abused, and in it, as in Smolensk, an anti-Christian museum with the nastiest of pictures.[18]

With the elimination of the Gomel pocket, Weichs's Second Army had cleared all Soviet forces between the Sozh and Dnepr Rivers, satisfying (as noted above) a key objective of GFM von Bock. In a letter to his family on 18 August, *Gen.d.Inf.* Gotthard Heinrici, whose 43 Army Corps had played a major role in the victory, outlined the results of the battle with satisfaction; the parallels to Lemelsen's diary entry are manifest:

> [The defeat at Gomel] is a very heavy blow for the Russian, who is now fighting only with pieced-together units, possesses barely any cohesive divisions, and who had to abandon an as yet unknown amount of artillery and vehicles in the forests. Operationally, this means the collapse of the southern half of his central front and is causing far-reaching consequences. We can, therefore, look back on the past 10–12 days with satisfaction.
>
> For me personally, they were not easy. We had to overcome very critical situations and sometimes the strain was ratcheted up to the maximum. It is also not particularly pleasant to drive through the countryside alone time and again, with only a paltry escort, through kilometer-long forests, always with the possibility of running into Russians. For the fronts are so far stretched, and so permeable, that friend and foe are often mixed up together.[19]

Encouraged by the victory, Heinrici ended his letter with an uplifting observation: "There's a severe crisis looming over there. The collapse is beginning to gather pace" (*Es kriselt drüben stark. Der Zusammenbruch beginnt sich anzubahnen*).[20]

Again supported by Loerzer's 2 Air Corps, infantry of Second Army now pushed directly into Gomel. In a desperate bid to defend the city, Lt.-Gen. Gordov threw industrial workers—according to Bock, armed with little more than shotguns—into the house-to-house fighting; at 1500 hours, 19 August, Second Army reported the capture of the city.[21]

The loss of Gomel forced the surviving elements of Gordov's 21 Army to retire toward the east and southeast; as they did so, they were intercepted by the forces of Geyr's and Lemelsen's panzer corps, which had built strong blocking positions in two parallel north-south lines—the first extending from Surazh to Klintsy (10 ID [mot.]); the second, farther east, running from Mglin to Starodub (3 PD, 4 PD, and elements of 17 PD).[22]

Thus ended two weeks of highly successful operations along the right flank of Army Group Center; in fact, from 9–21 August 1941, the combined German victories at Krichev and Gomel had yielded another 78,000 Russian prisoners and resulted in the capture or destruction of 144 tanks, 700 guns, thirty-eight aircraft, and two armored trains. Soviet 13 and 21 Armies and, with them, Soviet Central Front had been routed and destroyed (*geschlagen*)—a total of seventeen rifle divisions, one motorized division, two tank divisions, five cavalry divisions, and two air landing brigades largely disappearing from the Red Army order of battle.[23]

From an operational perspective, the capture of Gomel (and the destruction of Soviet forces in its vicinity) had far-reaching consequences: Along with removing the persistent threat to Army Group Center's southern flank, it helped bring about the collapse of Soviet forces west of the Dnepr and Desna Rivers. The loss of Gomel was at least partially responsible for major withdrawals conducted by Col.-Gen. M. P. Kirponos's Southwestern Front in the Ukraine, particularly of the front's 5 Army from its positions west of the Dnepr around Korosten, where its stubborn resistance had held up the advance of Army Group South on Kiev for several weeks. As a result, *Generaloberst* von Kleist's 1 Panzer Group was able to cross the Dnepr at several points in late August.

As for Bock, he was ebullient about his recent successes and convinced that conditions for a resumption of the advance on Moscow were now falling into place. On 19 August, he recorded his thoughts in his diary: "In the evening I once again made Weichs aware that no time must be lost! For now it might come to pass that, after Second Army's victory, and after the success of the planned attack on Velikie Luki on Ninth Army's northern wing, which is imminent, the entire army group can attack to the east!"[24]

Of course, as we have seen, the German dictator and warlord Adolf Hitler had a very different operational scheme in mind; thus, Guderian would continue his push to the south, into the Ukraine, where even greater success awaited him. And, once again, his attack would be led by Geyr's now seriously depleted 24 Panzer Corps.

6

The Kiev Cauldron Battle

While Army Group Center on Hitler's orders had suspended its drive toward Moscow at the end of July, on both wings of the eastern front, the *Ostheer* continued to register significant gains toward far-flung objectives.

On 10 August, GFM Ritter von Leeb's Army Group North launched a general attack on Leningrad, supported by the Stukas and medium bombers of Air General Wolfram Freiherr von Richthofen's 8 Air Corps (recently transferred to Leeb's army group from Army Group Center). Despite tenacious Russian resistance, Leeb's panzer units soon burst into the open country beyond the Luga River—Leningrad's outermost defensive line about 100 kilometers from the city. By the end of August, attacking German forces had cut the last rail line from Leningrad to the east at Mga, while *Gen.d.Pz.Tr.* Rudolf Schmidt's 39 Panzer Corps (also recently shifted from Bock's army group) was barely 25 kilometers from the city. On 3 September, German long-range heavy artillery (240mm) opened fire on Leningrad for the first time, while panzer and motorized units clawed their way through the enemy's extensive and concentric lines of defense,[1] *Gen.d.Pz. Tr.* Hans Reinhardt's 41 Panzer Corps reaching the city's suburbs by 5 September. On 9 September, the *Luftwaffe* began to pound Leningrad with round-the-clock bombing missions; the next day (10 September), the badly understrength 1 Panzer Division penetrated Soviet defenses on the Dudergof heights, barely 10 kilometers southeast of Leningrad. (From this tactically vital patch of ground, the Germans could see the city, with its gleaming golden cupolas and towers, spread out before them; warships were visible in the port, lobbing their shells at German targets.) Yet the attackers would get no farther, for Hitler had already decreed (5 September) that most of Army Group North's armor was to be transferred to Army Group Center to support the impending drive on Moscow.[2]

In the Ukraine, GFM Gerd von Rundstedt's Army Group South was also on the move. Following the reduction of a large Soviet pocket at Uman where, by 8 August, *Generaloberst* von Kleist's 1 Panzer Group had destroyed over twenty Soviet divisions and netted 103,000 prisoners (along with 858 guns and 317 tanks),[3] the tank units drove on toward Kirovo and Krivoi Rog (the iron ore center of European Russia), capturing the latter on 14 August. Exploiting Kleist's success, Rundstedt moved to clear Red Army forces from the entire western bank of the Dnepr River. Although the Soviet salient at Kiev held firm, by 1 September, Army Group South had secured several bridgeheads across the river—above Kiev (Sixth Army), at Dnepropetrovsk (1 Panzer Group), at Berislav (Eleventh Army), and at Kremenchug (Seventeenth Army).[4]

While Rundstedt sought to expand his Dnepr bridgeheads, Guderian's 2 Panzer Group had begun its plunge into the eastern Ukraine. (Note: On 22 August, Guderian handed over 7, 9, and 20 Army Corps to Kluge's Fourth Army, thus losing his status as an army group commander.) By early September 1941, Germany's hope for a spectacular victory rested largely on the panzer general's shoulders: Would he succeed, with his exhausted and weakened forces, in driving through the rich, black soil of the Ukraine and linking up with Kleist's panzer group behind Kiev, sealing the fate of Soviet Southwestern Front? Put another way, did the German panzer forces still have the strength to push through to their objectives despite the grinding attrition of men and machines, burgeoning logistical difficulties, and, of course, stiffening Red Army resistance?

SITUATION REPORT I: ATTRITION

On 7 August, GFM von Bock, in his journal, had expressed serious doubts about the short-term future prospects of his army group. He questioned how it would be possible to conduct a major new operation (he was thinking Moscow), given the "slowly sinking fighting strength of our constantly attacking forces." Yet he consoled himself by insisting that "things are undoubtedly even worse for the Russians!"[5] (In the weeks and months ahead, as the prospect of victory over Soviet Russia in 1941 slipped away, this rationalization—however bad *we* have it, *they* must have it worse!—would become a guiding "principle" behind German operations.)

Throughout August and into September, Army Group Center continued to experience unsustainable losses in both personnel and equipment. Bock's divisions were, collectively, sustaining about 3,000 casualties per day (ca. 40 percent of the estimated 7,300 casualties incurred daily across the entire eastern front).[6] The army group's officer losses were alarming, averaging roughly 80 per day through August 1941 (out of slightly more than 200 daily across the entire front).[7] By 31 August, the army group had registered some 50,000 dead out of about 126,000 fatalities throughout the *Ostheer*,[8] whose total losses (dead, wounded, missing) had climbed to half a million men. In general, combat strength of the infantry divisions in the east had plunged, on average, by 40 percent and that of the panzer units by fully 50 percent.

Reserve manpower (*Marschbataillone*) from the Replacement Army was now reaching the front, but their numbers were far from sufficient to cover all losses;[9] by the end of August, the eastern armies collectively showed a deficit of more than a quarter million men. And the outlook for the future was bleak: As Chief of the Army General Staff Halder noted on 26 August, "After 1 Oct. we shall have exhausted practically all our replacements." Making matters worse was that German fatal losses in the east (all combat arms) would be even higher in September (51,033) than they had been in August (46,066), bringing the aggregate figure through 30 September 1941 to 185,198; of these, an overwhelming majority, about 174,000 (94 percent), must be attributed to the ground forces—Army (90 percent) and Waffen-SS (4 percent).[10] Once again, assigning approximately 40 percent of these fatal losses to Army Group Center (the largest of the three army groups) indicates that, through the first 101 days of the campaign, Bock's divisions had sustained approximately 70,000 dead—grievous losses that fell disproportionately on the combat infantry.

In addition to the extravagant personnel losses, the panzer divisions had continued to see their tank strength decline precipitously. During August, both Hoth and Guderian attempted to pull their forces out of the line to rest and refit; the results, however, were far from satisfactory. The refitting process was disrupted by the inexorably expanding demands of the front, which often conspired to delay the withdrawal of the tank and motorized units and thus sorely limited their time for rest and recuperation. Moreover, frustrating delays in the delivery of spare parts, particularly the urgently needed replacement engines, 400 of which Hitler had promised the two panzer generals at the conference at Borisov on 4 August (a number Guderian had brushed off as "totally inadequate"), posed an additional handicap. (Sometime in mid-August, Army Group Center became privy to the fact that only 150 tank engines were actually earmarked for Hoth and Guderian, and these had yet to be delivered.) Given this dismal state of affairs, on 22 August, the army group put down in its diary that "the armored units are so battle-weary and worn-out that there can be no question of a mass operative mission until they have been completely replenished and repaired."[11]

Under such challenging circumstances, the panzer troops did what they could to complete their technical refitting; despite their efforts, as of 4 September, only 34 percent of the tanks within Army Group Center were considered combat capable, and this at a time when Guderian had already begun his advance south into the Ukraine. Specifically, Hoth's group reported 41 percent of its tanks and Guderian's group just 25 percent of its panzers as operational (*einsatzbereit*). Hoth's three panzer divisions possessed 320 operational tanks—7 PD (130), 19 PD (102), and 20 PD (88)—with 196 still under or awaiting repair (267 tanks were total losses). By comparison, Guderian's four panzer divisions had just 190 battle-ready tanks between them: 3 PD (41), 4 PD (49), 17 PD (38), and 18 PD (62).[12] This total of 510 tanks stands in stark distinction to the more than 1,800 tanks with which the two panzer groups had begun Operation Barbarossa on 22 June 1941.

Indicative of just how ruthlessly Hitler had starved his eastern armies after the start of the campaign—almost all current production of tanks and other key weapons was being held back to build new divisions for post-Barbarossa tasks—is the fact that, while the *Ostheer*'s four panzer groups had, by 31 August 1941, lost 1,488 tanks in aggregate, they had received but 96 replacements from new production of 815 tanks during the June-August period.[13] Moreover, the loss of tanks due to the unavailability of spare parts was often greater than losses from combat. The shortages of spares became such a frustration that the troops sometimes acted on their own initiative, slipping off to Germany to obtain parts and equipment that had failed to arrive via official channels.

Before moving on to logistics, I should note that the *Luftwaffe*'s support of Army Group Center was also plagued by remorseless attrition. During the late summer of 1941, this support was provided solely by Loerzer's 2 Air Corps of Kesselring's 2 Air Fleet, which, on 6 September, numbered just 240 operational combat aircraft (141 bombers, 55 dive-bombers, 44 fighters). Of course, a single, modestly resourced air corps was utterly incapable of covering the 700-kilometer front of Bock's army group; hence, it focused its efforts at the *Schwerpunkt* of army group operations—for instance, along the southern wing (Gomel region) and then in support of Guderian's drive into the Ukraine in late August and September. This left Bock's sprawling eastern front largely devoid of air cover, leading Ninth Army to complain on several occasions in mid-August that the Soviet Air Force had gained complete air superiority (*Luftüberlegenheit*) in the army's entire area of responsibility.[14] Not until late September would Richthofen's 8 Air Corps—its forces now "tired and depleted"—return from the sector of Army Group North to take part in Operation Typhoon.[15]

SITUATION REPORT II: LOGISTICS

As Army Group Center drove deeper into Soviet Russia, German logisticians shifted the supply depots forward in several bounds behind the advancing spearheads. Established by mid-July 1941, the Dnepr Supply District (*Versorgungsbezirk Dnepr*) was intended to sustain operations of the mobile units as far as Moscow. Indeed, by this date, the string of depots had been extended as far east as Polotsk-Lepel-Borisov-Bobruisk; a depot was established by the end of July at Orsha and another by the beginning of August at Smolensk—both along the main route toward Moscow. On the southern flank, a major supply center was built up at Gomel following its capture in mid-August; in the north, the depots were pushed forward to Nevel, Vitebsk, and Toropets by September 1941. Supply bases were also constructed at Mogilev and Roslavl, the latter close behind the front.[16]

Building these depots was one thing; stocking them with the immense quantities of materials they needed—for instance, ammunition, POL (petroleum, oil, and lubricants), and spare parts—to sustain current operations *and* amass stockpiles for future operations was quite another. Although the initial leap of German forces to the Dvina-Dnepr river lines in early July 1941 had been effectively supported by Army Group Center's *Grosstransportraum* (its organic truck-borne hauling capacity), the sustainment of operations beyond that point depended in large measure on the primitive Russian rail infrastructure. In this context, German logisticians were guilty of two highly flawed assumptions: (1) operations beyond the Dvina-Dnepr Rivers would mostly entail the mopping up of residual Red Army forces that had escaped encirclement and destruction west of the river lines, and (2) to support these operations they would be able to rely heavily on captured Soviet rail lines, locomotives, and rolling stock (thereby limiting the need to convert the lines from Soviet to European standard gauge). Both assumptions proved patently false.[17]

As soon became apparent, not only did the Soviets manage to maintain large, intact, and constantly nourished combat forces (despite a series of catastrophic defeats resulting in enormous human and material wastage), but they were also able to destroy rail lines and key rail installations as they withdrew while evacuating most of their locomotives and rolling stock. On 2 August, *Generalleutnant* Rudolf Gercke, Chief of *Wehrmacht* Transport, informed Halder that the "numerical scarcity" of captured Soviet locomotives and rolling stock was seriously impeding the supply of the Army in the east. The Germans were thus forced to undertake a major effort to re-lay the lines and restore them to operating condition. Efforts to advance the railheads went forward deliberately, albeit much too deliberately to overcome the Army's growing shortages. By 16 August, German railroad troops (*Eisenbahntruppen*) had converted the railway gauge to Orsha and Smolensk; in late August, the German railway reached Gomel in the south and was soon extended eastward to Roslavl; in the north, a standard-gauge track was pushed through Vitebsk to Toropets by September.[18]

Although the advance of the rail lines marginally improved the supply situation, the daily throughput of trains remained well below what was required to satisfy all the needs of the army group. In August, Bock required twenty-four supply trains per day to meet existing requirements and six more to build stockpiles for a resumption of the advance (thirty trains in all); Gercke, however, could promise only twenty-four, and in practice the army group seldom received more than eighteen trains per day during the month.[19] In September, too, the daily throughput of trains failed to meet requirements. Contributing to the shortfall was the nascent yet growing partisan movement, which was beginning to destroy rail lines, installations, and trains with alarming frequency.

Bridging the gap between the railheads and the troops at the front was the motorized transport of the *Grosstransportraum*, which, on 22 June 1941, had amounted to 25,000 tons of organic hauling capacity in Army Group Center. From the beginning, however, the incessant demands made upon the truck transport regiments and battalions led to alarming and unsustainable loss rates. The thousands of kilometers covered by the motorized (truck) transport on the appalling Russian roadways inevitably resulted in a rapid deterioration of the vehicles; moreover, the consumption of both fuel and oil was well above prewar calculations, while spare parts (particularly tires) were difficult to obtain. Under such conditions, actual hauling capacity rapidly dipped well below expectations; in fact, after only a few weeks of fighting, the army group had lost one-third or more of its trucks—a situation exacerbated by the fact that facilities for making major repairs were not brought forward but remained behind in Poland, or even in the Reich itself. Yet, despite the hopes of the Army High Command that the advance on Moscow would "bring about the last and decisive act of Operation Barbarossa," insufficient effort was made to concentrate all available truck transport behind Army Group Center; in late August, 5,000 tons of hauling capacity were even withdrawn and transferred to Army Group South to help build up its base of supply.[20]

Facing such a dismal state of affairs, by August/September 1941, Army Group Center (and the *Ostheer* writ large) was running short of a "laundry list" of items essential for the conduct of modern, mechanized warfare. Even the most basic items of a soldier's personal kit were now often in short supply. On 2 September, Dr. Heinrich Haape, a battalion doctor in a German infantry division, wrote a letter to his fiancée that is illustrative of the increasingly adverse conditions faced by the *Landser* at the front:

> You simply cannot imagine how we live here in such miserable conditions—in wet, damp, cold dugouts, foxholes, or temporarily in pitiful wooden lean-tos. No culture, not even the simplest contrivances of civilization can be found here. And we are constantly threatened by the enemy, by shell fire or attack. No variety, whether in life here or in the food. No vegetables, no fruit. Legumes for soup, potatoes with meat or canned food comprise, in the permanent, monotonous recurrence of the stew, our meals.
>
> Please don't think that I'm moaning to you in writing this—if it came to it, I would gladly bear even more privations, but I want nothing more than sympathy for the wish list I'm going to write down now! There are no shops here, nothing to buy. Razor blades, comb, toothpaste, skin cream, soap, nail cleaner, writing paper, fountain pen, ink, *Frankfurter Zeitung*, *Koralle* [an illustrated magazine], card games, tobacco, all kinds of sweets, pocket handkerchiefs, etc.[21]

Truly troubling were the serious shortages of ammunition and POL. The daily requirement of Bock's divisions for artillery shells and mortar rounds was enormous—through the end of 1941 the army group expended an average of 1,075 tons per day of ammunition of all types and calibers—and during the heavy defensive fighting from late July to early September 1941, the need for munitions was well above average. These defensive battles had hardly begun when, on 1 August, the field marshal complained in a telephone conversation with the Army quartermaster general that the shortages of munitions previously described as "serious" were, following a week with no improvement, "gradually becoming a crisis."[22]

Hauptmann Münchhausen (OKH Operations Branch) noted in his journal in early August that the "supply problem is becoming more and more difficult. . . . [The Russians] also have plenty of artillery and a lot of shells, which we can't manage to move up" (emphasis in the original). A few days later, he noted the "constant shortage" of artillery shells in the El'nia salient, while the Russian forces attacking there were "extravagantly" (*verschwenderisch*) supplied.[23] (As noted in chapter 3, in a discussion with Bock on 14 August, Guderian informed his superior that, in his view, a key prerequisite for continuing to hold the El'nia salient was to greatly increase the flow of munitions, and if this could not be done, the salient should be abandoned.) Simply put, the shortage of shells—on 10 September only fifteen trainloads of shells for standard 150mm medium field howitzers would be available for the entire eastern front[24]—was preventing Bock from compensating for the absence of strategic reserves and the attrition of his forces with adequate firepower. The situation of 26 Infantry Division was typical. In a postwar study of the division's artillery regiment (26 AR), a former German general recalled the frustrations created by the shortages:

> Our ammunition supply was insufficient. During pre-war maneuvers the expenditure of ammunition had been calculated as one unit of fire per day of major operations. For the regiment, that meant 8,100 rounds for light howitzers, and 1,800 rounds for medium howitzers.[25] Nevertheless, when our light howitzers fired only 3,000 rounds, and our medium howitzers only 600 rounds—i.e., about one-third of a unit of fire—during critical days like 22 and 27 August, we experienced serious difficulties. [In August 1941, the division was assigned to General Adolf Strauss's Ninth Army on the left wing of Army Group Center.]
>
> The shortage of ammunition forced us to conduct our artillery operations in far too passive a manner. There was hardly enough ammunition for satisfying requests from the infantry for direct fire support and for neutralizing definitely identified assemblies of enemy forces, particularly in view of the fact that requests from the badly and constantly pressed infantry were very numerous.
>
> For an active conduct of fire that would seek out and crush the enemy in his rear area, his probable bivouac sites, his headquarters, and similar installations, we lacked the necessary ammunition. An active conduct of fire along those lines would have been highly desirable especially in that situation. Moreover, we had

> all the signal and survey facilities needed for such a conduct of fire. . . . The ammunition shortage . . . completely prevented . . . the translation into practice of the modern principles of leadership set forth in the German instruction manual D-201 and taught in the artillery schools. We were forced to revert to artillery tactics of days long past.[26]

It did not help that vital ammunition trains were becoming "lost" in the Warsaw supply catchment area, with days often elapsing before they were once again located and sent on their way.[27] Moreover, the shortsighted decision of German military authorities in the period preceding the start of the Russian campaign to drastically throttle back ammunition production was finally coming home to roost with a vengeance.[28]

To address the growing crisis, priority was given to ammunition supply at the beginning of August, but this could only be accomplished by making drastic cuts to the supply of fuel and rations. On 21 August, Bock was informed that Guderian, "for reasons of materiel and fuel," could advance no farther toward Gomel.[29] During a conference on 30 August, *Generalmajor* Eduard Wagner, Quartermaster General of the Army, explained that both Army Groups Center and South had a "critical fuel shortage" and that replenishment would be impossible due to the serious problems with the railways.[30] Yet replenishment was critical, for the difficult terrain (and, increasingly, the poor weather) had raised fuel consumption well above the previously calculated fuel quotas, meaning that more fuel trains were needed than originally envisaged by German logisticians. In September 1941 alone, however, 120 approved fuel trains were unable to reach the front because of continuing transport problems on the railway. Thus, it is hardly surprising that, in mid-September, GFM von Kluge (C-in-C Fourth Army) felt compelled to complain, "The Army lives from hand to mouth, especially as regards the fuel situation."[31]

It was against this backdrop of crippling shortages of most every kind (tanks, infantry, shells, spare parts, fuel, food, etc.) that Guderian and his panzer group began their journey deep into the eastern Ukraine in late August 1941. Yet, despite the pronounced shortfall of resources, the panzer general was but weeks away from the greatest victory of his long and storied military career. This time, however, it would be no seamless blitzkrieg for Guderian and his panzer troops; rather, the push south would be a ponderous, methodical grind—illustrative of the brittle condition of his forces, desperate Soviet opposition, and, of course, his growing logistical problems. Assisted once again by *Generaloberst* Maximilian Freiherr von Weichs's Second Army, Guderian's panzer group would manage to eke out a victory while advancing on a broad front with a long, weakly defended open (eastern) flank that would trouble him greatly. In other words, his impending Ukrainian victory was in no way rapid, uncomplicated, or inexpensive in either men or machines.

GUDERIAN DRIVES SOUTH

The day after returning from Rastenburg, where Hitler had rejected his appeals to continue the advance on Moscow, Guderian, on 25 August, began to move south. In the van was Geyr's 24 Panzer Corps, with Lemelsen's 47 Panzer Corps covering the panzer group's open flank against Soviet Briansk Front. Guderian's first objective was the town of Konotop, roughly 150 kilometers due south of his start line (and about 200 kilometers northeast of Kiev).

Although two days before at the Wolf's Lair Hitler had promised Guderian his entire panzer group for the operation, Vietinghoff's 46 Panzer Corps was withdrawn from Guderian's command and put in reserve behind Kluge's Fourth Army. To Guderian, this was a "grievous disappointment." (And it is conceivable that a spiteful Halder, still furious over the panzer general's "betrayal" during his audience with the Führer, had played a role in the decision.) Doubtful that he possessed sufficient strength to complete his mission, he would repeatedly petition army group for release of 46 Panzer Corps to him. Yet Guderian's persistent demands for reinforcements and resupply only served to further alienate Bock, even if he ultimately acquiesced. Unbeknownst to Guderian, Bock, frustrated and disillusioned with his willful subordinate, would initiate discussions with OKH for Guderian's possible removal. Fortunately for Guderian, his remarkable achievements in the Ukraine would manage to stay the field marshal's hand. And yet, as noted by Russell A. Hart in his excellent biography, "time was now running out for Guderian."[32]

Guderian's tanks and motorized infantry struck Soviet Central Front, driving it back in disorder toward the Desna River. That same day (25 August), the STAVKA ordered up a new series of strikes along the front of Army Group Center. In this third (and most ambitious) of the "Smolensk counteroffensives," Lt.-Gen. A. I. Eremenko's Briansk Front was to advance right into the teeth of Guderian's forces, smash his panzer group, and reestablish a stable defensive front north of Kiev; to accomplish these objectives, Eremenko was to attack the advancing German columns along a broad front as Guderian's vulnerable eastern flank stretched southward. To provide centralized direction for its new operation, the Soviet High Command disbanded the Central Front—its situation already precarious—and unified its forces under Eremenko, assigning him responsibility for much of the Central Front's former operational area. In the days that followed, Eremenko sought tenaciously to destroy Guderian's group; however, as was so often the case with major Soviet counteroffensives in the summer of 1941, his operations were characterized by poorly organized attacks, inexperience at the tactical level, and a plethora of other problems that, in the end, would lead to failure. Conversely, the Soviet general's relentless assaults (strongly supported by airpower) would at times inflict serious losses on 2 Panzer Group while disrupting the tempo of Guderian's operations, in the process lengthening the course of the battle for the Ukraine and delaying the eventual German thrust toward Moscow.[33]

On the early morning of 25 August, Guderian visited his 17 Panzer Division (47 PzK) to accompany the division's attack across the Sudost River and its tributary, the Rog, directly to the south: "I drove along a terrible sandy track, a very bad road, and a number of my vehicles broke down. As early as 1230 hours I had to signal from Mglin for replacements of armored command vehicles, personnel lorries, and motorcycles. This was a grim omen for the future." At 1430 hours, he finally reached the command post of *Generalmajor* von Thoma's 17 PD, five kilometers north of Pochep. To acquire a personal impression of the enemy, "I went up to the front line, where Rifle Regiment 63 was attacking, and participated in a part of their attack on foot."[34]

Early the next day (26 August), Guderian, accompanied by his adjutant, *Major* Büsing, visited an advanced artillery observation post (O.P.) on the northern bank of the Rog: "I wanted to see the effect of our dive-bomber attacks on the Russians' river defenses. The bombs fell where they were supposed to, but their actual effect was negligible. On the other hand, the psychological impact of the dive bombing on the Russians was considerable; they kept down in their foxholes and as a result we crossed the river almost without casualties." While at the O.P., Guderian experienced another close brush with injury or death: "Owing to careless behavior on the part of an officer our presence in the O.P. became known to the Russians and we were subjected to well-aimed mortar fire. A shell landing very close to us wounded five officers, including *Major* Büsing, who was sitting close beside me. It was a wonder that I remained unhurt."[35]

After observing his troops crossing the Rog and the completion of a bridge over the river, Guderian drove that afternoon through Mglin to Unecha, where his headquarters was now located. While underway, he received an electrifying signal: In a daring maneuver, tanks of Model's 3 Panzer Division—once again in the van of Guderian's panzer group—had succeeded in taking intact the vital 800-meter-long bridge over the Desna River just east of Novgorod-Severskii. In a coup de main, a carefully selected combat team composed of a company of motorized infantry, a tank platoon, and a section of engineers had burst into the town "without regard for anything but speed." Led by three lieutenants, the detachment seized the bridge, neutralized its guards, and defused the explosive charges while the remainder of the *Kampfgruppe* cleared out Soviet resistance in the center of the town. It all happened with such lightning speed that the Russian artillery (whose fire had lodged a shell splinter in Model's hand the previous day) barely fired a shot. *Leutnant* Georg Störck, who had "personally removed the detonator from the bomb planted in the center of the main bridge and then held off a Soviet counterattack, threw himself down in exhaustion as the first panzers and half-tracks sped across to secure the far bank."[36]

Observed Paul Carell, "The much-feared Desna position, the gateway to the Ukraine, had been blasted open. A handful of men and a few resolute officers had decided the first act of the campaign against the Ukraine. Russia's grain areas lay wide open ahead of Guderian's tanks. Under a brilliant sunny later-summer sky they rolled southward."[37]

At once, Model sought to expand his bridgehead—as he exclaimed at the time, "this bridge is as good as a whole division"[38]—by ordering his entire division across the Desna, leaving the task of covering his rear to Wilhelm von Loeper's 10 Motorized Division (24 PzK). An advance detachment of Loeper's division had, by 28 August, seized a second crossing over the Desna 50 kilometers to the southwest at Korop. Over the next few days, however, 10 ID (mot.) was fiercely counterattacked by superior Soviet forces, requiring the intervention of its Field Bakery Company to save elements of the division from being completely overrun.

As always, Guderian was a whirlwind of activity. On 29 August, at Novgorod-Severskii, he lifted off in his *Fieseler Storch* spotting and liaison plane and "described a bold arc over the Russian front." Above the Soviet lines—right above Eremenko's divisions attacking the German Desna bridgehead—he "dipped down low, then banked," crossed back over the river, and returned to his command post at Unecha. The time was almost 1800 hours:

> Guderian had been to see his 3 and 4 Panzer Divisions, which were trying to extend their bridgehead in order to continue their thrust to the south. But the troops were pinned down. He had also been to [47 Panzer Corps] whose 10 Motorized Infantry Division and 17 and 18 Panzer Divisions were busy repelling fierce Soviet attacks from the flank. The situation there was not too rosy either. Too much was being demanded of the men. They were short of tanks and short of sleep.
>
> Next to Guderian sat *Oberstleutnant* Bayerlein [Guderian's Ia, or chief of operations], the situation map spread out on his knees. Thick red arrows and arcs on the map indicated the strong Russian forces in front of the German spearheads and along their flanks. "Eremenko is going all out to reduce our bridgehead," Guderian was thinking aloud. "If he succeeds in delaying us much longer, and if the Soviet High Command discovers what we are trying to do . . . the whole splendid plan of our High Command could misfire."
>
> Bayerlein confirmed the anxieties of his commander. "I was on the phone to Second Army yesterday. Freiherr von Weichs seems to be worried about it, too. *Oberstleutnant* Feyerabend, their chief of operations, has had reports from long-range reconnaissance about the Russians beginning to withdraw from the Dnepr front below Kiev. At the same time, work has been observed in progress on positions in the Donets area."
>
> "Well, there you are." Guderian was getting heated. "[The Soviets learned their] lesson at Uman. [They're] slipping through the noose. Everything now depends on which of us is quicker."

> But Guderian and Weichs need not have worried . . . [for] Stalin would not hear of a withdrawal. On the contrary, he squeezed another 28 major formations into the already packed river-bend. Whatever came off the assembly lines of the famous tank factories in Khar'kov was thrown into the Dnepr bend—the modern T-34s, the T-28s . . . heavy artillery, and multiple mortars.[39]

Guderian again cooperated with Bruno Loerzer's 2 Air Corps, which furnished his advancing panzers with vital ground support. On 27 August, Loerzer's air forces put up 220 sorties (including 180 Stuka sorties) in support of 17 Panzer Division. Three days later (30 August), Thoma's division was struck by more than ninety Soviet tanks, among them many super heavy KV-1s. "German intelligence about Soviet strength in the area had been very poor and the sudden appearance of so many Soviet tanks caused great alarm within Lemelsen's 47 Panzer Corps. There were fears that the corps, operating on the eastern bank of the Desna River, might be split in two as the Soviet attack drove two kilometers into the German line."[40]

The next day (31 August), Thoma counterattacked without success, as recorded in the panzer corps' *Kriegstagebuch* (war diary): "Numerous tanks of the heaviest variety, which our guns cannot penetrate, shoot with superior weapons from well-camouflaged positions at our advancing panzers. This causes considerable losses, among them 11 destroyed [German tanks]."[41] Only by committing his other panzer division (18 PD) to the battle, along with air support, was Lemelsen able to stabilize the situation while inflicting punishing losses on Eremenko's forces. However, in the two-day contest, 17 PD alone had twenty tanks destroyed and others damaged. "Once again the heavy model Soviet tanks reflected their superiority, even in the absence of adequate supporting arms. Indeed, all along the eastern front these colossal machines had developed a fearsome reputation within both the German panzer and infantry divisions. . . . The helplessness of the German troops against this unparalleled weapon was summed up by a battle report [of] 4 Panzer Division: 'Now one field gun opens fire and fires to the last shell. Then it is run over and crushed by a 52-ton tank.'"[42]

Despite such bitter and costly battles, Soviet resistance, for the most part, "varied from haphazard to non-existent." A more formidable challenge to Guderian's forces was the primitive roadways along the line of advance. As recorded in German war diaries, the "roads" south of Roslavl hardly deserved the name:

> Typically they consisted of little more than sandy farm tracks, more accustomed to the light traffic of small horses and peasant carts. The advent of dozens of tanks and hundreds of heavily loaded trucks soon turned them into quagmires, even in the absence of rain. In the 4 Panzer Division's sector south of [Unecha] the trucks were constantly getting bogged down and those that could not be dug out had to be pulled out with tractors. The war diary of Lemelsen's 47 Panzer Corps

> noted that movement was "exceedingly slow and difficult." Indeed, the many small streams that crisscrossed the area and could not be skirted were even more of a problem than the dire state of the roads. Their bridges had to be reinforced or rebuilt as they were too weak to support the traffic, and in the worst affected areas even the deployment of all the available engineering units could not avert hours of delay.[43]

Nevertheless, on Guderian's right wing, by 1 September (as depicted on the situation map of the OKH Operations Branch), both 3 and 4 Panzer Divisions (24 PzK) were clear of the Desna and advancing on the town of Konotop—the first objective of Guderian's panzer group—now just some 50 kilometers to the south (linear distance);[44] by moving beyond the river barrier, the German armor had reached the relatively open Ukrainian countryside.

Despite Model's success at Novgorod-Severskii, Guderian was less than enamored with the overall pace of the advance, which he attributed in large measure to the unsavory situation on his flanks, both of which were under attack by Eremenko's Briansk Front. Only the presence of Vietinghoff's 46 Panzer Corps, he believed, would get him moving again; thus, he insisted—repeatedly—that the panzer corps be returned to him at once. On 27 August, Chief of the Army General Staff Halder, in his diary, noted a telephone conversation he had with GFM von Bock: "Guderian rages that he's not making progress, because he's being attacked in both his right and left flanks [*Guderian tobt, er käme nicht vorwärts, weil er von rechts und links in der Flanke angegriffen sei*], and he is demanding that the other three units of his group be sent to him. Bock feels unable to do so because he must keep a reserve. I am of the same opinion and request him not to give way to Guderian. . . . In addition, I ask him to keep a tight rein on Guderian."[45]

The same day (27 August), *Generalleutnant* Friedrich Paulus (Halder's chief assistant) paid a visit to Guderian's headquarters. The panzer general seized the opportunity to again push for additional forces. Moreover, he claimed that Weichs's Second Army was advancing to the southwest and, as a result, had become separated from the right flank of 24 Panzer Corps; in fact, there was now a 75-kilometer gap. Guderian also stressed that the left (eastern) flank of Geyr's corps was "similarly insecure and, instead of being guarded, was merely under observation." The best solution, Guderian insisted, was nothing less than the transfer to 2 Panzer Group of Weichs's 13 and 43 Army Corps along with the 1 Cavalry Division. Once again, he repeated his request that Vietinghoff's 46 Panzer Corps be deployed to cover the panzer group's left flank. While Paulus agreed to support Guderian's position, his visit had also "provided a convenient means of bypassing Army Group Center and directing the appeal to Halder at the OKH."[46]

Guderian, however, did not stop there. That evening he made repeated calls to Bock's chief of staff, *Generalmajor* Hans von Greiffenberg, demanding reinforcements. In his diary, Bock commented that Guderian was "very agitated" and that he "berated his neighbor on the right [i.e., Weichs], who was advancing in the wrong direction, as a result of which his right and left flanks were being attacked. As expected, this was followed by the demand for the release of 46 Panzer Corps, which is in reserve southeast of Smolensk!"[47] Bock then conferred with Halder, and the two quickly reached agreement: They shared serious concerns about the situation on the army group's long and increasingly fragile eastern front, which was buckling under the strain of the latest Soviet counteroffensive; more to the point, they failed to grasp how Vietinghoff's corps could provide any tangible support to Guderian's panzer group, given the great distances it would have to cover across the frightful road net in the region. Indeed, Bock noted in his diary that he had "no idea whatsoever what Guderian was supposed to undertake with 46 Panzer Corps." Eventually, Brauchitsch was consulted, and he, too, agreed that, for the moment, the release of the panzer corps could not be considered. As for Guderian, he simply dismissed the decision of his superiors as resulting from "the general animosity toward myself that reigned in those quarters."[48]

Guderian's incessant lobbying finally lodged a modest success when the panzer general's chief operations officer, *Oberstleutnant* Bayerlein (about to depart Russia for North Africa), convinced Bock that 2 Panzer Group's spearheads needed to be reinforced by fresh forces. On 30 August, Bock thus decided to send Guderian *Oberst* Hörnlein's reinforced Infantry Regiment *Grossdeutschland* (recently pulled from the El'nia salient). Bock believed he could risk doing so because 267 Infantry Division (from Second Army) had just arrived in Roslavl. However, as he noted with disgust in his diary, "The penalty was not long in coming! The enemy has broken into our lines south of the El'nia salient. Kluge [Fourth Army] described the penetration as 10 kilometers in depth with heavy tanks and asked that [267 ID] and elements of 10 Panzer Division [46 PzK] be placed at his disposal to clear up the affair. I gave him both divisions. . . . Here is proof that I cannot give more forces to Guderian without endangering my eastern front."[49]

According to Bock, the next day (31 August) "began with new demands from Guderian for the rest of 46 Panzer Corps. . . . During the midmorning I received a lengthy radio message from Guderian, unpleasantly worded, in which he not only repeated his familiar wishes, but broadened them to include all of the army group's mobile units. My response was that I would decide if and when additional forces could be sent to him based on the overall situation on the army group's front. I rejected his request that the Führer decide."[50]

As for Halder—with Guderian's recent failure (at the Wolf's Lair) to enlist Hitler for an immediate drive on Moscow still fresh in his mind—he had no sympathy for the panzer general's situation, which, in Halder's view, Guderian had brought upon himself:

> The morning picture is dominated by a decidedly uncomfortable development in Guderian's group [i.e., this is most likely a reference to the incident involving 10 ID (mot.) described above]. Carrying out his drive as a flank movement along the full length of the enemy front, he squarely invited heavy attacks into his eastern flank; then his advance, striking far to the east and leading him away from Second Army, produced a gap that was exploited by the enemy for attacks also from the west. These two developments had reduced his power to strike south to a point where his movements are paralyzed. Now he is blaming everyone in sight for his predicament and hurls accusations and incriminations in all directions.[51]

That afternoon (31 August), following a telephone call with Bock, Halder jotted in his diary that "personal relations between Hq. of army group and Guderian are increasingly deteriorating. Guderian is striking a tone that Bock cannot tolerate on any account. He even appeals to the Führer for a decision concerning the leadership. This is unparalleled cheek!"[52]

Be that as it may, with the arrival of another infantry division from Second Army—255 ID was just reaching Bock's eastern front behind Strauss's Ninth Army, which was being heavily engaged by Soviet forces—the field marshal finally agreed to send Guderian the bulk of 46 Panzer Corps.[53] By 3 September, SS-*Gruppenführer* (Maj.-Gen.) Paul Hausser's SS *Reich* Division was reaching the front of Geyr's 24 Panzer Corps (Machine Gun Battalion 5, arriving from Roslavl, was placed under Hausser's command), while Vietinghoff's headquarters had also been sent to Guderian along with half of its *Korpstruppen* (GHQ troops).[54]

Yet, just as it seemed the Gods of War were once more smiling down on Guderian, on the evening of 3 September, a terrific thunderstorm struck the panzer group's area of operations and, as one panzer corps war diary put it, "With one stroke all large-scale movements became impossible." It was the beginning of a bad-weather period that would continue for two entire weeks. Naturally, the weather—and the resulting condition of the roads—had a deplorable impact on the supply situation. On 4 September, the war diary of the quartermaster general for *Panzergruppe* 2 noted, "On account of the transportation difficulties from the unfavorable roads and weather conditions, the general supply situation is in question."[55]

Further exacerbating the resupply of the panzer group was the fact that the truck-borne supply columns were having to bridge ever-greater distances between the railheads and frontline formations; moreover, by early September, an alarming number of supply trucks had broken down due to the corrosive effects of the primitive Russian roadways with their ubiquitous clouds of dust that clogged air filters and ruined engines. It is thus no surprise that 2 Panzer Group was now experiencing significant shortages of supply trucks (and supplies).

Most affected by the miserable roads and weather was Geyr's 24 Panzer Corps (Guderian's spearhead). On 4 September, the constituent 3 Panzer Division recorded that the roads "could no longer be driven on" and that along the supply route many trucks were bogged down hopelessly in mud; indeed, since crossing the Desna at Novgorod-Severskii, Model's tanks had barely covered a further 55 kilometers.[56] Guderian spent the day at the front with Langermann-Erlencamp's 4 Panzer Division, "where I also found General Geyr. It took me four and a half hours to cover [some 70 kilometers], so softened were the roads by the brief fall of rain."[57]

Several days later (10 September) 3 Panzer was reporting that its fuel supplies were "very critical." Driving again to the front, Guderian visited Model that day: "On the Seim bridge we were attacked by Russian bombers, on the road we were shelled by Russian artillery. As a result of rain the condition of the road had still further deteriorated and it was dotted with vehicles hopelessly stuck in the mud. It was impossible for the columns to observe their customary march discipline and they were badly straggled out."[58]

Meanwhile, by 6 September, "Papa" Hausser's SS *Reich*, deployed on the far right wing of 24 Panzer Corps, had largely succeeded in plugging the gap between 2 Panzer Group and Weichs's Second Army.[59] During the morning, lead elements of SS *Reich* (SS IR "*Der Führer*") reached the Desna south of Sosnitza, where they were rapidly reinforced by a platoon of assault guns and provided with artillery support. Continuing to advance, a battalion of SS infantry struck a Soviet column near the town of Mena, inflicting serious casualties on the defenders; fearing impending encirclement (elements of Second Army were attacking from the west), strong Russian forces began to withdraw southward across the railroad bridge over the Desna at Makoshino. On the outskirts of the town, the Soviets set up a defense anchored by two armored trains, which sought to hold open the crossing over the roughly sixty-meter-wide river.[60]

The mission of capturing (intact) the railroad bridge in a coup de main and seizing a bridgehead on the south bank of the Desna fell to SS *Reich*'s (reinforced) motorcycle battalion (*Kradschützen-Bataillon*). A Stuka attack on Makoshino—and on the north and south bank at the railroad bridge—had been ordered by 2 Panzer Group for early that afternoon; when it failed to materialize, Guderian, who was at the command post of SS Infantry Regiment "*Der Führer*," grew impatient and personally ordered the motorcycle battalion to put in its attack across the bridge without air cover. In response, the SS battalion—taking advantage of a sudden onset of good weather that had dried out the sandy roads—motored at high speed through unreconnoitered enemy territory. Exploiting the element of surprise, and despite taking fire from one of the Soviet armored trains, the lead motorcyclists—supported by two assault guns, two armored cars, and *Der Führer*'s motorcycle company—advanced through the town and up to the railroad line.[61]

Despite dogged enemy resistance, the *Kradschützen*, aware that Soviet engineers across the river could detonate the structure at any moment, dashed at full speed across the bridge. Before the Russians could react, the SS vanguard—the machine gunners in the sidecars raking the area with fire—burst through the enemy barricades. Behind the motorcycle battalion two audacious SS officers and a handful of anti-tank troopers crossed the large railroad bridge and "in a single, bold rush, tore the fuses from the demolition charges [and] wiped out the Russian demolition party." In doing so, they secured the tactically important bridge and helped to establish a small perimeter on the south bank of the Desna.[62]

The day, however, would end tragically for the motorcycle battalion of SS *Reich*. For it was at this juncture, late that afternoon, that the Stuka dive-bombers promised for several hours earlier finally appeared above the battlefield—three squadrons of them totaling twenty-seven aircraft. Despite signal flags and flares, they dropped their loads on Makoshino and on both the north and south banks of the Desna at the bridge:

> The town then disappeared in an inferno of swelling smoke and fire as the howling Stuka bombs burst in mighty detonations. The bombs not only hit the enemy, but also had a devastating effect on the *Kradschützen* fighting in the center of the town. The shocking outcome of that Stuka attack for the motorcycle battalion was 10 dead and 30 severely wounded. . . .
>
> Many curses were screamed at the Stukas. . . . A combination of tragic circumstances and misunderstandings had evidently led to this misfortune. No unit carries a charm that guarantees protection from such accidents in a war of movement with rapidly changing fronts. . . .
>
> Some good did, however, result from the Stuka attack. It considerably aided the advance across the bridge and the defense of the small bridgehead on the south bank. With it, the last resistance in Makoshino was broken and both of the armored trains were finally eliminated.[63]

Helmut Günther, a dispatch rider in SS *Reich*'s motorcycle battalion, was witness to the carnage caused by Loerzer's Stukas. His account underscores the awesome destructive power of the *Luftwaffe*'s Ju 87 dive-bomber:

> When we arrived at the site where I had left the temporary battalion command post, it presented a desperate picture. Gigantic craters within a radius of 50 meters, collapsed buildings, uprooted trees. The building where the men of the communications platoon had set up their radio stations had disappeared. Wherever you looked, it was a heap of ruins [*Überall, wohin man schaute, ein Trümmerhaufen*]. . . .
>
> I dismounted from my [motorcycle] and only then really saw what had happened: Right in front of me was Nickel's head. His body hung about eight meters away on a pole. Everywhere there were parts of the fallen—here a leg, there an arm. It was horrible! Words cannot describe all that I saw there.[64]

In his memoir, Guderian failed to mention this horrendous "friendly-fire" incident (and such incidents were quite common for both sides across the eastern front). He merely noted that he had spent the day with SS *Reich* and that he had "gone to some trouble to provide air support" for its attack on the railway bridge over the Desna near Makoshino. On his way to Hausser's headquarters, his staff convoy had driven through Russian artillery fire on several occasions but sustained no casualties or damage; once there, he issued orders for the Desna bridgehead to be "sufficiently enlarged so that the division might attack from the bridgehead toward the west bank of the Seim and thus help 24 Panzer Corps to cross that river."[65]

LINKUP AT LOKHVITSA

Despite the rain and the barely traversable roads; despite his exhausted and badly weakened panzer forces—not to mention the often tenacious, if largely uncoordinated enemy resistance—despite all that, *Generaloberst* Guderian, an indefatigable leader of men, constantly at the forward edge of battle with his troops, sharing in their hardships and their dangers, would manage to will his way forward deeper into the Ukraine, having received a boost from the reinforcements finally released from Army Group Center. Indeed, with the few remaining tanks of Model's 3 Panzer Division in the van, Guderian kept his eye firmly on the prize: a spectacular linkup with Rundstedt's Army Group South east of Kiev, well behind the front of Col.-Gen. M. P. Kirponos's Southwestern Front. The Battle of Kiev was finally taking shape.

Since seizing the bridge over the Desna at Novgorod-Severskii in late August, Geyr's 24 Panzer Corps had been slow to exploit its success, advancing deliberately toward Konotop, about 80 kilometers south of Novgorod-Severskii (linear distance). By the evening of 6 September, advance elements of 3 Panzer Division were nearing the town (Model would bypass it as he continued to push south), with 4 PD still somewhat farther back. In the days that followed, Guderian's spearheads, having struck a weak spot in the Soviet lines (the seam between 13 and 21 Armies of the Briansk Front),[66] began to achieve a measure of operational freedom. On 7 September, 24 Panzer Corps established bridgeheads on the south bank of the Seim River; two days later (9 September), Guderian was at the front with 4 Panzer Division, observing as elements of its 12 and 33 Rifle Regiments advanced on Gorodishche; this time, Loerzer's dive-bombers "gave effective support to the spearheads of the rifle regiments and of 35 Panzer Regiment." Meanwhile, Eremenko's Briansk Front, after more than two weeks of furious combat, was beginning to break up and lose cohesion. As a result, dangerous gaps were opening in its lines.[67]

Also on 9 September, GFM von Bock at Army Group Center noted that *Generaloberst* von Weichs's Second Army (on Guderian's right) "is making very good progress. Chernigov has been taken. 2 Panzer Group also made significant progress in the direction of Romny. Only weak enemy forces on its eastern flank."[68]

On 10 September, Loeper's 10 ID (mot.), continuing the panzer group's relentless push, seized Konotop, while Model's 3 PD, in a bold thrust, in pouring rain, deep into the Red Army's rear area behind Kiev, captured the tactically vital town of Romny, taking intact its two bridges over the Romen River. The Soviets, however, despite the valorous efforts of Eremenko's fading Briansk Front and repeated attacks from the air against Model's forces, strung out along muddy roads, could now do little to check the German advance.

Yet, even as Guderian registered the successful outcome of these battles, he was acutely aware of the brutal, cumulative effect of his relentless operations on his forces. As he later recalled, "[T]he limited combat strength of all units showed how badly they needed rest and recuperation after two and a half months of exhausting fighting and heavy casualties. Unfortunately there could be no question of that for the time being."[69]

Events continued to unfold rapidly. On 12 September, in the sector of von Rundstedt's Army Group South, *Generaloberst* von Kleist's 1 Panzer Group, having assembled the requisite supplies and built a suitable bridge, pushed northward out of Seventeenth Army's bridgehead at Kremenchug with its 48 Panzer Corps. The same day, at the request of Army Group South, Bock instructed Guderian to drive for the town of Lokhvitsa (ca. 45 kilometers southwest of Romny) and to link up there with the tanks of Kleist's panzer group. On the cusp of another historic victory, the tension at Bock's command post was palpable: "At noon came the news that the enemy is streaming east out of the more than 200-kilometer-wide gap between Kremenchug and Romny in dense columns. Immediately afterward, three telephone calls were received from Army Group South within a half hour, asking if Lokhvitsa had been reached yet."[70]

Aware now for days that his forces in the Ukraine faced imminent disaster, on 9 September, Marshal S. M. Budenny, Commander, Southwestern Direction (in overall control of Southwestern and Southern Fronts), asked Stalin for permission to abandon Kiev and pull back to less exposed positions. Stalin flatly refused. Two days later (11 September), Budenny appealed again to Stalin to begin "a general withdrawal" from Kiev; for his efforts, Budenny was dismissed and replaced by Timoshenko. Determined to defend the city, the Soviet dictator telegraphed the commander of Southwestern Front, Col.-Gen. M. P. Kirponos: "Kiev is not to be given up and the bridges are not to be blown without STAVKA authority. Kiev was, is and will be—Soviet. No withdrawal is allowed. Stay and hold, and if necessary die! Out!"[71]

Over the next two days, the converging spearheads of Guderian's and Kleist's panzer groups fought their way toward each other. On the morning of 13 September, Model's badly attenuated panzer forces seized Lokhvitsa, along with its bridge over the Sula River. To the south, advance elements of 1 Panzer Group's 16 Panzer Division—led by the gritty, one-armed *Generalmajor* Hans Hube—after refueling during the night, stormed the town of Lubny, unleashing a barrage of rockets (dubbed "Stukas on foot" by the *Landser*) whose smoke temporarily confused and blinded the Russian defenders. Yet here, a tantalizing 40 kilometers from Model's men at Lokhvitsa, Hube's panzer troops would be stopped by a fanatical wall of resistance. Although the town was defended by detachments of NKVD, an anti-aircraft unit, and a hastily assembled workers' militia, the local Soviet field commander exhorted the entire population to arms; soon the Germans were also being fired upon by civilians (according to German reports, mostly women) from rooftops, out of cellar windows, and from behind makeshift barricades. German tanks were targeted at close range by Molotov cocktails. The "eerie fighting" would go on throughout the night and into the next day, tying down Hube's forces and forestalling any further advance.[72]

With 16 Panzer Division suddenly immobilized, the final act of the drama would (appropriately) be left to Model. The next day (14 September), without authorization (perhaps even against the orders of his corps commander),[73] he launched a small battlegroup on a daring raid south from Lokhvitsa toward Lubny and union with Hube's 16 PD.[74] At 1300 hours, a handful of tanks and armored scout cars passed through the German picket lines near Lokhvitsa, escorted for a short while by a clutch of Stuka dive-bombers. The countryside stretched far to the horizon, and just ahead were the "dark outlines" of a wood:

> The weather was sunny and clear, the roads were firm, and there were only a few muddy patches. Additionally, it was Sunday—appropriate "riding weather" or "panzer weather." The tanks soon left behind the forward security of the advance guard near Iskovtsy-Senchanskie and had before them the wide and lightly undulating Ukrainian land and, in some places, the enemy, who we knew was still well armed.
>
> After a three-hour trip, the first town emerged on the left. A Russian transport column was on the road. As the German vehicles approached, the Soviets abandoned their horse carts and fled into the nearby field of sunflowers. As we moved on, the enemy supply wagons crossed the road. The machine guns spoke again. We advanced further. It was the Soviets [once more]. This time it was an enormous column of batteries, supply trains, construction battalions, guns, horse carts, and tractors, with Cossacks and two combat vehicles riding in between. The machine guns howled anew, shooting a passage through the Russian column, and the tanks raged with great speed into the middle of [a] stream.
>
> *Oberleutnant* Warthmann and his men understand only one thing: forward! Thus, the vehicles rolled endlessly through the ravines, swampy lowlands, through the forests and fields and over many brittle wooden bridges. By and by, the column came upon Tichi across the Sula—the halfway point! Suddenly, the division radio spat to life. The friendly vehicles were located in a ravine, however, as they moved further toward an open area, radio contact was made—and we could hear General Model and Major Pomtow breathe a sigh of relief back in Romney, as they heard: "As of 1602 hours, we were on the hills of Luka."[75]

The day was drawing to a close when, suddenly, the combat group lost radio contact with the division. To the south, through their binoculars, the men could make out the silhouette of a town against the evening sky; clouds of smoke lingered over the houses, while machine-gun fire and the thud of artillery shells striking their targets could be heard. The town was Lubny, and, nearby, the panzer troops of Hube's 16 PD were tensely awaiting their arrival:

> Cautiously the armored scout cars accompanying the tanks picked their way across a vast cornfield with the harvested grain piled in stooks. They dodged from one stook to the next. Suddenly an aircraft appeared overhead. "Look—a German reconnaissance plane!" "White Very light!" [*weisse Leuchtkugeln!*] Warthmann commanded. With a whoosh the flare streaked up from the turret of the tank. White signals always meant: Germans here. A tense moment. Yes, the plane had seen it. He dipped down low. He circled. He circled again. "He's touching down!" And already the machine was rolling to a stop among the stooks in the cornfield—right among the enemy lines. There was much laughter and hand-shaking.
>
> Today nobody knows who those three resolute airmen were. They informed *Oberleutnant* Warthmann about the situation at the front: less than [10 kilometers] away were units of Kleist's 16 Panzer Division. A moment later the aircraft took off again. Warthmann's men could see it dip down low beyond the wide ravine, dropping a message.[76]

"*Panzer marsch!*" Warthmann's combat group drove on, across the ravine and up the far bank. Having braved a gauntlet of Soviet forces desperately trying to escape encirclement, they finally reached a point just north of Lubny. Once again, white Very lights were exchanged, this time between Model's men and a company of combat engineers of Hube's 16 Panzer Division. Shortly thereafter, Guderian's command post received a brief radio message: "14 Sep 1941, 1820 hours, 1 and 2 Panzer Groups establish contact." In anticipation of success, Model ordered that the password for his troops on this day be "Tannenberg."[77]

Oberleutnant Warthmann crossed a brook in his vehicle and entered Lubny; a short while later he reported to *Generalmajor* Hube. In an orchard nearby, concealed among trees and hedges, the armored vehicles with the white "G" (Guderian) and white "K" (Kleist), the lead elements of two powerful panzer groups, stood side by side. "The sky was alive with the flashes of artillery and the howling of [rocket batteries]. The curtain was being rung up on the last act of the greatest battle of encirclement in military history."[78]

In fact, Model's linkup with Kleist's panzer group was less real than symbolic, given that Soviet forces were still scattered about the wide-open spaces. The next morning (15 September), however, his 3 Panzer Division established "conclusive physical contact" with major elements of *Generalleutnant* Alfred Ritter von

Hubicki's 9 Panzer Division (1 Panzer Group) due south of Lokhvitsa. Trapped inside their armored jaws and facing certain destruction was the entire Soviet Southwestern Front. "The 'Battle of Kiev,'" Bock exulted, "has thus become a dazzling success." Yet the field marshal then "sounded a far more demurring tone, questioning the cost of Hitler's battle in the south and what it meant for, as Bock saw it, the essential goal of the campaign."[79] As he confided in his diary, "[T]he main Russian force stands unbroken before my front and—as before—the question is open as to whether we can smash it quickly and so exploit this victory before winter comes that Russia cannot rise again in this war."[80] Yet, if Bock was beset by a certain ambivalence, there was jubilation at Hitler's *Wolfsschanze* headquarters. Joseph Goebbels, Hitler's propaganda minister, noted in his journal on 16 September that his Führer was in the best of moods and looked to the future with confidence and conviction.

Despite the desperate situation now facing all of Soviet Southwestern Front, Stalin still refused to bow to reality and order a breakout to the east. As the delusional Soviet dictator assured his Chief of the General Staff, Marshal Boris Shaposhnikov (who had replaced Gen. G. K. Zhukov as chief in August 1941), the situation now required from commanders at all levels "extreme coolness and steadfastness," while panic was to be avoided. Not until very late in the evening on 17 September did the STAVKA signal General Kirponos that Stalin had finally authorized a withdrawal from Kiev, but it was already too late for the Soviet armies trapped inside the bulging pocket. On 19 September, Kiev finally fell to GFM Walter von Reichenau's Sixth Army, German troops hoisting the Reich battle flag (*Reichskriegsflagge*) above the citadel within the city. The day before, in anticipation of Kiev's capture, *Gefreiter* Hans Roth had written,

> Our 21 and 30.5cm cannons have been firing onto the Russian defense lines around the outskirts of the city for the last 24 hours. There are rolling attacks from our Stukas. A dark, black cloud hangs over the city after a few hours. These guys deliver precision work. According to orders, the residential neighborhoods of the city are not to be attacked. They are to attack the fortress, the train stations, ammunition depots, and the Dnepr bridges. Orders for the general attack arrive in the afternoon. Tomorrow is the day. Guys, prepare for the mass grave! You can live out your hatred against the city that has been right in front of your faces for weeks, though as of yet unattainable. Tomorrow—finally, finally!!!![81]

Several days after the capture of Kiev, *Gefreiter* Roth described in striking detail the diabolical nature of Red Army defenses on the outskirts of the city, which had been under siege by the Germans since mid-July. His account offers a graphic illustration of the "art of war" as practiced by the Red Army in the late summer of 1941:

Early on September 19 we penetrated the heavily armed outer ring of the city. The enemy, by far not as strong as we had assumed, was defeated in bloody, close combat, and by 0900 hours we had already reached the western part of the city. The Reds have quit their attempts at heavy street fighting. At the same time strong assault parties attacked the citadel from the direction of Lysa-Hora, and by 1100 hours Nazi swastikas were raised there.

By noon we are in the center of the city, no shots are heard; the wide streets and squares are abandoned. It is eerie. The silence is making us nervous, for it is hardly believable that such a large city has fallen into our hands in such a short amount of time. . . . What does this western defense line, which Budenny depended upon just like the French did with the Maginot Line, look like? It's not a common line of bunkers; no, it is a collection of diabolic resources, which can only be conceived by the brain of a paranoiac. I will try and describe some of these horrific death zones that we passed through while intensely fighting on September 17, 18 and 19:

To the rear of Gatnoje, there are fields of cooperatives, vast vegetable farms. They lie there harmlessly in the sun. Who would believe that hiding among those plants is the most horrific death: a high voltage current! Atop the vegetation is a webbing of fine-caliber wire the length of several kilometers. This rests on thin, isolated metal poles, which are all painted green; a deadly net of high current, which is run by a power plant in a bunker. It is so well camouflaged that we recognize it unfortunately much too late, only after continued accumulation of losses.

Then there are the devil's ditches, lined up in great depth, several hundred meters long. They are mined, and when a single land mine is tripped, entire fields, which are connected underground by detonation channels, explode. At the same time, water pipes explode and rapidly flood the area two meters deep.

There are even a few more goodies that happen to be just lying around, seemingly random objects that are interesting to every soldier: watches, packs of cigarettes, pieces of soap, etc. Each of these objects is connected to a hidden detonator. If the soldier picks any of these objects up, he starts the ignition and detonates a mine or an entire minefield.

In this category also belong well-hidden trip wires, which cause contact mines to explode. These monsters jump up 3/4 of a meter and explode. . . . There are other areas where hidden among trip wires are thousands of knife-sharp steel spikes, which are poisoned and cause the injured to die a horrible death ten minutes later. All of the defensive belts are littered with automatic flamethrowers, which are activated by pressure.

Well—just imagine, among all these devilish things there are still normal battle installations: two-story bunkers, automatic weapons stands, ditches, kilometers of barbed wire, tank barriers, in addition to the average mined streets and paths. Add to that infantry mines, booby traps, ban mines, vehicles mines. And now, just imagine this whole hellish apparatus during combat; this is their defense against our attack. . . .

> Mine dogs: we shot about a dozen of these German shepherds alone near Schuljany. The animals carry a device with explosives on their back. According to a prisoner who has trained these dogs, they are made to attack tanks and other vehicles with their load of 3 kilos of ammunition.[82]

According to one observer at Hitler's East Prussian headquarters, the seizure of the Ukrainian capital by Rundstedt's Army Group South (after two long months of waiting) elicited "immense joy" [*riesige Begeisterung*] within the Wolf's Lair.[83]

THE KIEV CAULDRON BATTLE

In the days that followed, the tank crews and panzer grenadiers of *Panzergruppen* 1 and 2 compressed the gigantic pocket from the east, while the infantry of the Seventeenth, Sixth, and Second Armies did so from the south, west, and north; overhead, the fighters, dive-bombers, and bombers of the *Luftwaffe* decimated Soviet troop and vehicle columns inside the cauldron, while systematically interdicting rail lines leading into the pocket to block the arrival of reinforcements and disrupt lines of retreat.[84] (Note: The initial pocket was shaped like an isosceles triangle with sides 500 kilometers long, embracing an area of 135,500 square kilometers.)[85]

During the period from 13 to 19 September, 24 Panzer Corps alone reported capturing 31,000 Red Army soldiers, 190 guns, 23 tanks, and 23 anti-tank guns. In a single day (19 September), Kleist's panzer group took 12,000 prisoners of war while destroying or capturing 277 artillery pieces and 44 tanks. "The amount of prisoners and booty is never-ending," marveled a soldier in 16 Panzer Division (18 September). "This morning a procession of prisoners passed by us and it took almost half an hour before they had all marched past us. There were at most 10 German soldiers accompanying these endless rows as an escort party. All the different faces and caricatures to be seen there would make a mockery of any [attempt at] description. We can assume that it [the war] will soon be done, let us hope for the best."[86]

Inside the pocket, the situation resembled an apocalypse for the defeated Soviet soldiers fleeing for their lives to the east. According to a trapped Red Army major, "All around, wherever you look there are German tanks, sub-machine guns or machine-gun nests. Our unit has already been defending on all sides for four days within this circle of fire. At night the surrounding ring is clear to see, illuminated by fire that lights up the horizon."[87]

Contributing to this hellscape were the unremitting assaults of the air forces of both Bock's and Rundstedt's army groups. Among the *Luftwaffe*'s favorite targets were the vast wooded areas inside the pocket and close to the main roads, which were suspected—and rightly so—of harboring large masses of Soviet troops, horses, and equipment. From 12 to 21 September, one of the *Luftwaffe* formations supporting Army Group South, 5 Air Corps, alone flew 1,422 sorties and dropped 567,650 kilograms of bombs and ninety-six Type-36 incendiary bomb clusters, inflicting untold destruction on Soviet soldiers, weapons, and equipment.[88] According to one Russian account, pure birch forests, which "I never before or after saw," were consumed in flames as a result of the incendiary bombs dropped by German planes. "The burning grayish-white trees were turning reddish, as if blushing and ashamed of what was going on." Observing the inferno, he became aware of a "peculiarly pungent" smell: "For the first time, I smelled burnt flesh."[89]

By 24 September, the fighting in the pocket was over. A doctor with 3 Panzer Division surveying the battlefield reported his impressions: "A chaotic scene remained. Hundreds of lorries and troop carriers with tanks in between are strewn across the landscape. Those sitting inside were often caught by the flames as they attempted to dismount, and were burned, hanging from turrets like black mummies. Around the vehicles lay thousands of dead."[90]

Six Soviet armies (5, 21, 26, 27, 38, and 40) were either wholly or partially annihilated in the immense cauldron battle, eliminating fifty Soviet divisions from the Red Army order of battle. In sum, the Germans claimed to have captured 665,212 prisoners while seizing 824 tanks and 3,018 guns in the operations of Army Groups Center and South since late August 1941—the large majority of the POWs, more than half a million, attributed directly to the Kiev *Kesselschlacht*.[91] Among the Soviet soldiers who perished in the cauldron was Kirponos himself: At dawn, 20 September, about 12 kilometers southwest of Lokhvitsa, the general's column, about 1,000 strong, was ambushed and encircled; that evening, already wounded, Kirponos was struck in the head and chest by mine splinters. "He died in less than two minutes."[92]

Of course, the fighting had been far from one-sided. As early as 15 September, the panzer regiment of Model's 3 Panzer Division had been reduced to just ten serviceable tanks (one Pz IV, three Pz IIIs, and six Pz IIs). Moreover, many German units paid a heavy price attempting to hold back the furious and repeated (and often successful) Russian breakout attempts. East of Piriatin, in the sector of *Generalleutnant* Erich Clössner's 25 Motorized Infantry Division (Army Group South), Soviet troops fought fanatically and, by 19 September, had overwhelmed one of the division's infantry regiments and broken through its defensive perimeter. Racing to the regiment's relief, the panzer regiment of 9 Panzer Division managed to recapture the town of Melechi the next day, but German bodies were scattered everywhere. Refusing to take prisoners, not only had the withdrawing Russians killed every German unfortunate enough to get in their way, but many of the captured *Landser* had been gruesomely mutilated. About the same time, on a different Ukrainian battlefield, more than 100 German soldiers were found hung by their hands from trees; their feet had been doused with gasoline and set on fire, resulting in a slow, unimaginable death. Apparently, this barbaric act was not a solitary case; indeed, it was a method of killing known to the Germans as "Stalin's socks."[93]

Of course, atrocities of all kinds were committed by both sides throughout the eastern campaign. Criminal, or simply treacherous, behavior by one side begat more such behavior by the other; thus, from the very outset, a brutal dialectical logic of atrocity and reprisal resulted in a surging spiral of violence that, as the summer of 1941 progressed, dramatically accelerated incidents of extrajudicial killings by both combatants. In his memoir, Nicolaus von Below, Hitler's *Luftwaffe* adjutant, recalled that dispatches submitted in August by Army Group South included reports of atrocities committed by Soviet troops:

> They were so appalling that even Hitler was doubtful, and he sent me to Nikolayev to check with the 16 Panzer Division. I spoke there with General Hube [the division commander] and a very good friend of mine, Udo von Alvensleben. They described to me the discovery of the corpses of more than 100 murdered soldiers of 6./Rifle Regiment 79 at Grigovo station. At another place German prisoners had been drawn and quartered alive. Our troops had responded accordingly.[94]

REFLECTIONS ON THE BATTLE OF KIEV

From its purely material outcome—avoiding any judgment of Hitler's reasons for turning south in the first place, away from Moscow—Germany's staggering triumph in the Ukraine in the late summer of 1941 signified, by any measure, one of the most successful campaigns in the military history of the modern era. Something approaching a million Soviet troops were killed, wounded, or captured; thousands of tanks, vehicles, and artillery pieces of all calibers were destroyed or taken as booty—the numbers defy the imagination. While historians have debated for decades the strategic significance of the Battle of Kiev, the decisive role played by *Generaloberst* Guderian in its eventual outcome cannot be disputed. What he accomplished in a short few weeks, given the many factors that had conspired against him and his panzer troops, remains to this day a brilliant exposition of the art of war. In fact, Guderian's achievements in the Ukraine in late August and September 1941 marked the pinnacle of a military career spanning nearly four decades (1907 to 1945) and two world wars.

One must not, however, overlook the role played by Fortuna—the Roman goddess of fortune and good luck—in the outcome of the Battle of Kiev. In other words, neither Hitler, nor his General Staff, nor Guderian could have possibly anticipated being handed a triumph far exceeding what their exhausted panzer forces could have accomplished without Joseph Stalin's obstinacy and incompetence. As we have seen, Kirponos's Southwestern Front had been slowly and methodically encircled since late August 1941; yet Stalin strictly forbade him to withdraw his forces to safety or even to redeploy them in such a manner as to mitigate the danger. While many top Red Army officers tried to bring Stalin to reason and avoid the impending disaster, the Soviet dictator had remained steadfast in his desire to hold Kiev at any cost.

At his Wolf's Lair, Adolf Hitler viewed the magnificent triumph of German arms in the Ukraine as a total vindication of his strategic thinking vis-à-vis Halder, Bock, Guderian, and others among his General Staff and field generals. In exultation, he called the Battle of Kiev "the biggest battle in the history of the world." And now that Army Group Center's eastern flank had been cleared of the enemy, the dictator was finally ready to complete the march on Moscow that had been suspended for eight long weeks. In fact, in early September, he had issued a new Führer directive calling for preparations to be completed for a resumption of the offensive along the Moscow axis by the end of the month. If the new operation was successful—and why shouldn't it be, given the glorious victories taking shape at both Leningrad and in the Ukraine—the war in the east might still be brought to a triumphant conclusion before the end of 1941. Thus, Hitler once again looked toward the eventual outcome of his eastern campaign with renewed confidence.

(Note: While the battle in the Kiev cauldron was still raging, Guderian "hit upon a new idea" that served to illustrate his obdurate determination to satisfy his own needs regardless of the needs of others. Simply put, the shortages of trucks and their replacement parts within his panzer group were long-standing concerns well known to the panzer commander. Nevertheless, his urgent pleas for relief had largely been ignored. In the absence of any meaningful number of replacement vehicles or parts from depots in Germany, securing captured Soviet trucks [particularly American-manufactured Ford heavy trucks] became a priority for German field commanders, and Guderian was determined to secure the "lion's share" of the booty from the Kiev cauldron. Only weeks before, in the wake of the Battle of Smolensk, competition for Soviet trucks had become so intense that Guderian's requisition squads actually exchanged fire with elements of German 8 Army Corps. Now, with the need for replacement trucks more pressing than ever, Guderian's headquarters asked Army Group Center to secure an order from Army Group South granting 2 Panzer Group priority for all captured vehicles within the Kiev pocket. While it remains unclear what became of the panzer general's request, most likely GFM von Bock, wishing to avoid an unnecessary dustup with Rundstedt's army group, simply rejected the idea out of hand.)

Guderian visits the command post of one of his panzer regiments (August 1941). The caption of the German propaganda company (PK) reads, "The general is always to be found at the very front line." Indeed, as this study illustrates, leading from the front resulted in several close brushes with injury or death fo the panzer general. (Bundesarchiv, Bild 183-L19885/Huschke/CC-BY-SA 3.0, via Wikimedia Commons)

Guderian in his half-track command vehicle (SdKfz 251/3) on the eastern front (early September 1941). On the back of the photograph is written, "On the battlefield south of Baturin . . . in conversation with Lüttwitz, Cdr. Rifle Rgt. 12 [4 PD]." (Bundesarchiv N 802/30)

uderian observes a Pz II tank belonging to 35 Panzer Regiment (4 PD) as it rolls along a dirt road eptember 1941). One can easily imagine what a few hours of rain could do to turn such a road into n impassable mass of muck and mire. Sudden outbursts of rain were not uncommon in the summer of 941. (Bundesarchiv N 802/48)

anzer III tanks of *Generalmajor* Walther K. Nehring's 18 Panzer Division advancing south into the kraine. The tank in front is an "F" model (*Ausführung F*) with a 37mm main armament and twin coaxial achine guns. (Note the memorial cross painted on the driver's armored visor.) On Hitler's orders, and gainst his own fierce desire to continue the advance on Moscow, Guderian began his drive into the kraine on 25 August 1941. (Jason Mark/Leaping Horseman Books)

Gen.d.Pz.Tr. Joachim Lemelsen (C-in-C 47 PzK) (date, location unknown). The panzer general wa awarded his Knight's Cross on 27 July 1941. This study has repeatedly made use of the detailed journa kept by Lemelsen throughout Operation Barbarossa. At least twice early in the campaign, he felt com pelled to issue orders to his men not to shoot POWs or Russian civilians.

Guderian in conference with the commander of 3 Panzer Division, *Generalleutnant* Model, the latter Knight's Cross clearly visible (9 August 1941). Model would rise rapidly through the ranks to becom the commander of 41 Panzer Corps in October 1941 and commander of Ninth Army in January 194 (Bundesarchiv N 802/30)

oldiers of the elite Infantry Regiment "*Grossdeutschland*" leave the *Panzerrollbahn* and advance into a rested area in an effort to clear it of enemy snipers. From the very start of the Russian campaign, the biquitous Soviet snipers, often equipped with excellent automatic rifles with telescopic sights, struck me and again with lethal impact—picking off the drivers of supply vehicles, officers, and messengers on otorcycle. A German officer wrote to his wife on 11 July 1941, "Unfortunately, [Russian] snipers firing om concealed positions cause us endless problems." (Bundesarchiv, Bild 183-L28188/CC-BY-SA 3.0, ia Wikimedia Commons)

Concealed in high vegetation, German forward observers (*vorgeschobene Beobachter*) use their field radio to direct the fire of an artillery battery (location/date unknown). The photograph was gleaned from a book published in Berlin in 1944 (*Artillerie im Osten*); the caption reads, "Radio and telephone operators in the artillery must be really something [*ganze Kerle sein*]. Without the communications net, outfitted with the latest technical accoutrements, the effective use of modern artillery would be unthinkable."

A German 88mm multipurpose gun in action somewhere on the eastern front. At the beginning of Ba barossa, the famed "88s" were often the only tool available in the German arsenal that could effectivel challenge the new Soviet T-34 and KV-1 tanks. The weapon, however, had a high profile (making vulnerable to enemy fire) and took time to move into position and prepare for firing. With the office standing heroically on part of the gun carriage, the picture almost looks staged.

A much closer view of a German 88mm gun. Throughout the summer and fall of 1941, Guderian's panze group/panzer army was supported by the flak guns of *Generalmajor* Walther von Axthelm's I Flak Corp whose "88s" provided Guderian's troops and tanks with much-needed support against the heavier Sovie T-34 and KV-1 tanks. (Bundesarchiv N 802/125)

young soldier salutes his commander (July or August 1941). Whatever Guderian's faults as a general nd a man—and they were legion—he cared deeply about his men, a fact clearly discernable from let- rs to his wife, Margarete. (Bundesarchiv, Bild 101I-139-1112-17/Knobloch, Ludwig/CC-BY-SA 3.0, via ikimedia Commons)

main dressing station (*Hauptverbandplatz*) on the eastern front. By 31 December 1941, the *Wehrmacht* d sustained some 300,000 fatal losses in their failed Barbarossa venture. As Chief of the Army General aff *Generaloberst* Franz Halder noted in his journal in November, the German Army would never com- etely recover from its losses in the east in 1941. (Stackpole)

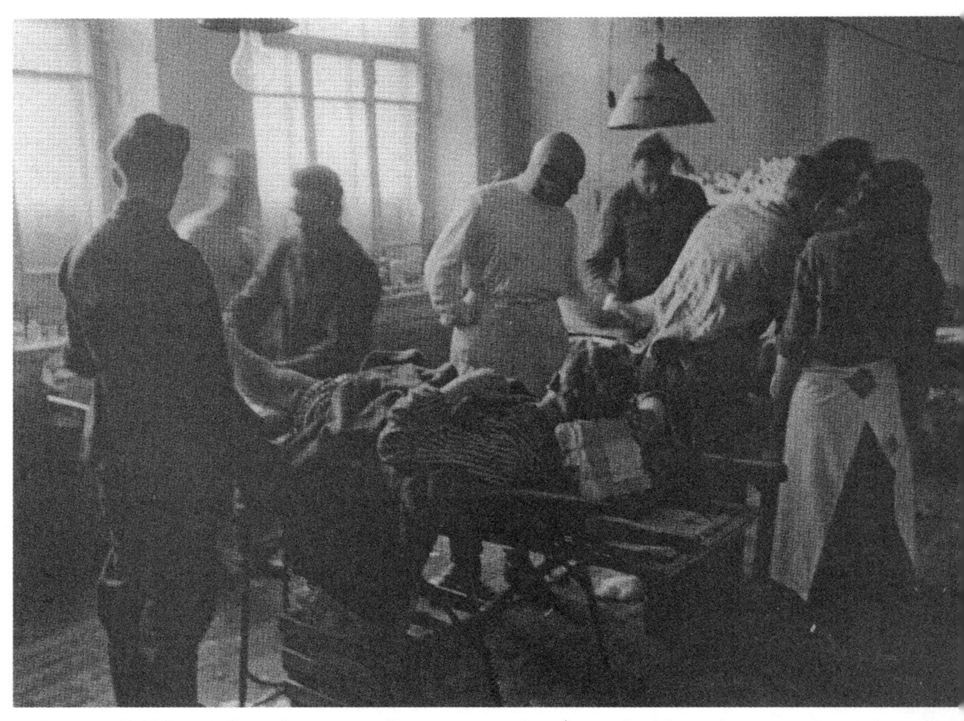

A German field hospital on the eastern front. Among the most valuable and respected members of th German Army were the so-called *Sanis* (*Sanitäter*), the medical personnel. According to internation law, medical personnel were noncombatants and were not to be armed; on the eastern front, howeve where both sides violated the laws of war with impunity, German medical personnel frequently carrie side arms. Throughout the war, despite enormous strains on available resources, the quality of Germa medical care remained remarkably high, even in the most primitive conditions; in fact, a wounded soldi who made it to a field hospital had a 98.5 percent chance of surviving—a testimony to the dedicatic and professionalism of German front doctors and nurses. (Stackpole)

he graves of three *Landser* of Guderian's panzer group, killed in action on 13 September 1941 and laid rest in the town of Yampoly. A year later, the trio were reinterred in a *Heldenfriedhof* (heroes' cemtery) in the village. Birch crosses such as these—each one denoting the death of a German soldier—were biquitous across the eastern front in 1941. (Jason Mark/Leaping Horseman Books)

Heldenfriedhof for German soldiers who died in Field Hospital 29 (*Feldlazarett* 29) while it was based Karachev. Most of the dead men belonged to 29 ID (mot.), but there were several from 17 and 18 PDs. otes historian Jason Mark, "The elaborate memorial was in fact just a repurposed Soviet monument: statue of Lenin was toppled and replaced by this large Iron Cross and his name covered by a plaque earing the words 'Unseren Helden' [to our heroes]." (Jason Mark/Leaping Horseman Books)

A flight of Ju 87B Stukas over the eastern front. During his push south into the Ukraine, Guderian agai cooperated with Bruno Loerzer's 2 Air Corps, which furnished his advancing panzers with vital groun support. In his memoir, the panzer general made several references to effective support from Stuka div bombers during the Battle of Kiev.

A flight of He 111 medium bombers. While Stukas pounded Soviet troop concentrations, German boml ers systematically interdicted rail lines leading into the Kiev cauldron to block the arrival of reinforc ments and disrupt lines of retreat. (Although this photograph was shot in southern Russia later in the wa it reveals the graceful lines of this warplane, which, by the start of World War II, was already approachir obsolescence.) (Bundesarchiv, Bild 101I-641-4548-24/Wanderer, W./CC-BY-SA 3.0, CC BY-SA 3.0 D via Wikimedia Commons)

esults of the interdiction of Soviet railways by the *Luftwaffe* (summer 1941). In his memoir, GFM lbert Kesselring praised 2 Air Corps for its "decisive impact" (*ausschlaggebende Wirkung*) in the Kiev *esselschlacht*.

German 105mm K18 cannon in a firing position on the open steppes of Russia (summer 1941). The lo elevation of the cannon suggests a direct-fire support mission, perhaps against enemy armor at long rang or in support of a tank attack. The K18 was capable of firing a 33.4-pound shell a maximum distance some 19,000 meters. (Stackpole)

A German heavy machine gun crew (with supporting troops) poised for action in what appears to be a urban environment (September 1941). For a breakdown of the organization, personnel, weapons, an equipment of a "typical" German 1941 infantry division, see appendix D. (National Digital Archive public domain, via Wikimedia Commons)

\dvance elements of 29 ID (mot.) deployed in open order (late August 1941). They are trying to reach the hree-span railway bridge across the Desna that is visible on the horizon. (Note: This is not the 800-meter-ong bridge over the Desna near Novgorod-Severskii captured in a coup de main by Model's 3 Panzer)ivision on 26 August.) (Jason Mark/Leaping Horseman Books)

A Red Army tank trap south of Mogilev in Belorussia (19 August 1941). In the background a typical Russian peasant village. It was at Mogilev that Guderian's panzer group trapped major elements of Soviet 13 Army in mid-July. (U.S. National Archives)

Generaloberst Guderian (sitting) at a field command post discussing situation at the front with another general (August 1941). (Falk, public domain, via Wikimedia Commons)

Generalmajor von Boltenstern (second from right), C-in-C 29 ID (mot.), briefs Panzer General Lemelsen (wearing glasses) about his division's situation on 29 August. The division, at the Desna River, formed part of the long eastern flank of 2 Panzer Group. (Jason Mark/Leaping Horseman Books)

Adolf Hitler meeting with his troops on the eastern front. The German dictator visited the headquarters of both Army Groups Center and South during the first week of August 1941 to discuss the next phase of operations in the east. Neither GFM von Bock nor GFM von Rundstedt succeeded in convincing their Führer to continue the attack toward Moscow instead of sending Guderian into the Ukraine.

A German radio station (*Funkstation*) situated in a roadside ditch on the central front (late July 1941). The caption of the Propaganda Company reads, "From here the command posts [*Gefechtsstände*] receive information about the progress of the supply columns and the formations that are following on the road." (U.S. National Archives)

Terrific photograph of a German assault gun (StuG III) in front of a village after crossing the Dnepr Rive (2 September 1941). "The *Sturmartillerie* [assault gun] is our ultimate weapon [*letzte Waffe*]," wrote a artillery officer fighting in the El'nia salient (east of Smolensk) in a letter to his wife on 30 August 1941 "They are tanks with a gun, only they are open on top and so they shoot with the aid of a scissors tele scope! The armor plating is very good! I learned to appreciate this weapon during the infantry attacks— every battalion was allocated two assault guns, they would lead the way and the infantry would advanc under their protection. They use shells that are good for combating and shelling tanks." (Bundesarchiv B 145 Bild-F016202-23A/CC-BY-SA 3.0, via Wikimedia Commons)

German infantry on the outskirts of Kiev. Although elements of Army Group South had reached the out skirts of the city by mid-July 1941, it would not be captured by GFM Walter von Reichenau's Sixth Army until 19 September. The diabolical nature of Red Army defenses screening the city is described in fulsome detail by *Gefreiter* Hans Roth in chapter 6. (Stackpole)

Elements of *Generaloberst* Ewald von Kleist's 1 Panzer Group of Army Group South advancing through a Russian village (September/October 1941). Note the "K" for Kleist behind the turret of the closest tank. In mid-September, the spearheads of Kleist's and Guderian's panzer groups would link up east of Kiev, initiating the most spectacular cauldron battle of the summer campaign. (Britannica.com)

Generaloberst Guderian (foreground) with a clutch of officers watching an attack go in near Lokhvitsa (15 September 1941). It was near this town that the forwardmost elements of Model's 3 Panzer Division made physical contact with Kleist's panzer group to finally close the trap around the Soviet Southwestern Front. (Bundesarchiv N 802/48)

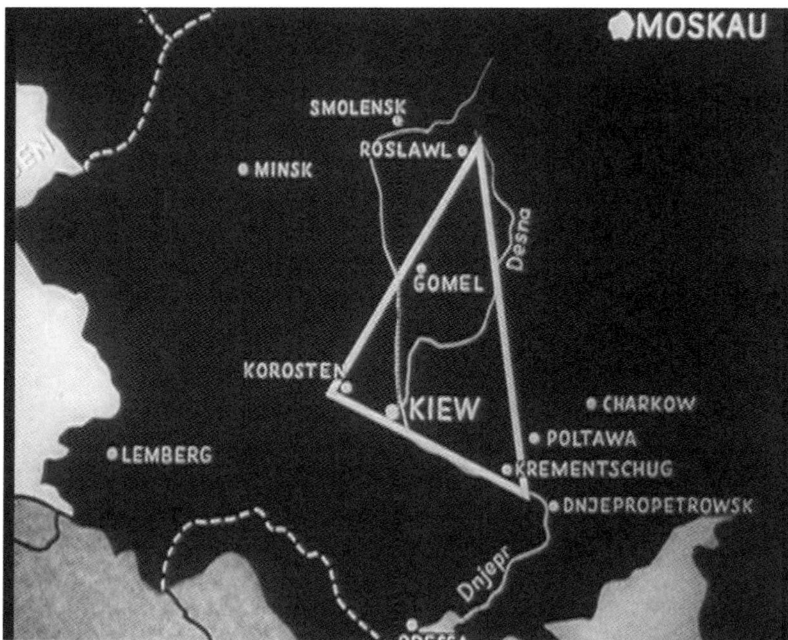

Graphic showing the extent of German encirclement operations from Roslavl to Kiev (August/September 1941) The pocket was shaped like a huge triangle with sides 500 kilometers long embracing an area of 135,500 square kilometers. (*Deutsche Wochenschau*, Nr. 577)

Destroyed or abandoned Soviet guns and two faithful horses that perished inside the Kiev cauldron (late September 1941). In addition to losing fifty divisions, the Red Army lost hundreds of tanks and thousands of artillery pieces. (*Deutsche Wochenschau*, Nr. 577)

The ruins of Kiev (September 1941). As noted by eastern front historian David Stahel, "The climactic battle of Kiev in late August and September 1941 was an epic of human endurance, strategic uncertainty and ceaseless carnage. When German troops entered the city they were surprised by a series of explosions of Soviet radio-controlled mines in the center of Kiev from 24 September onward. The mines, which caused massive fires and killed an estimated 200 Germans, were not extinguished until 29 September; they provided German authorities with the pretext to commence the slaughter of more than 30,000 Jews at Babi Yar the same day." (Public domain, via Wikimedia Commons)

Guderian as seen on *Deutsche Wochenschau*, the German weekly newsreel, in September 1941. Although the newsreels offered a sanitized version of the war in the east, they still evoked anxiety in more than a few German moviegoers. As *Frau* "K.B." wrote to a loved one at the front, "Through the *Wochenschau* we do get a small idea of what is going on in the east and, believe me, this snippet arouses so much horror in us that we would dearly love to close our eyes just to let some images roll by unseen." (*Deutsche Wochenschau*, Nr. 578)

Soviet prisoners of war en route to Germany (ca. October 1941). Six Soviet armies were wholly or partially destroyed in the Kiev cauldron battle. All told, the Germans claimed to have captured more than 650,000 Red Army soldiers in the operations of Army Groups Center and South since late August 1941—the large majority of the POWs, more than half a million, attributed directly to the Kiev *Kesselschlacht*.

Part III

OPERATION TYPHOON

FROM TRIUMPH TO DEFEAT

Following his splendid foray into the Ukraine, *Generaloberst* Guderian began at once to regroup, reorganize, and partially re-equip his forces for the resumption of the attack toward Moscow. Convinced that the fall of the Soviet capital would bring the Soviet state to collapse, he shifted his group northward into its assembly areas in record time—a remarkable feat of administration and organization.[1] With his attack on the right wing of Army Group Center earmarked to begin on the final day of September, there was virtually no time for the rest and recuperation of his exhausted troops or for maintenance and repair of worn-out tanks and vehicles.

Operation Typhoon began in spectacular fashion for Guderian and along the entire front of GFM von Bock's army group, as the three panzer groups committed to the operation immediately broke through in their respective sectors. In just two days, Guderian's tanks and motorized infantry lunged more than 200 kilometers to Orel, seizing the city off the march. Once again cooperating with Weichs's Second Army, his forces enveloped a large Soviet grouping around Briansk, while farther north, an even larger pocket took shape at Viaz'ma on Bock's left wing. With an enormous gap ripped in the Soviet front, Hitler and his High Command believed final victory to be at hand.

Yet sterner trials awaited. In the south, Guderian's advance soon slowed dramatically, the result of perennial problems of supply and a serious tactical setback at Mtsensk, where Second Panzer Army (Guderian's command had been upgraded to army status) encountered large numbers of T-34 and KV-1 tanks. Outclassed and outfought, Guderian—now possessing fewer than 300 tanks—temporarily halted his advance.

Although the pockets at Viaz'ma and Briansk were gradually cleared of Soviet troops (yielding another haul of well over half a million POWs), the fall rains soon turned the roads into bottomless pits of mud, slowing the German advance to a crawl. On 30 October, Bock suspended his offensive along the entire front of his army group—he would await the arrival of freezing weather conditions to harden the roads before resuming his attack. Guderian's spearheads, meanwhile, had reached the strategically pivotal town of Tula (272,000 inhabitants)[2] but had been stymied in their initial attempt to seize it by determined Soviet resistance.

Bock resumed his offensive in mid-November, but his exhausted and eviscerated forces—infantry companies had, in many cases, been reduced to less than 50 combatants, while the panzer units possessed but a fraction of their original combat power—once again failed to reach their coveted objective in the face of stiffening Red Army resistance. While Guderian managed modest progress on his right wing, he remained bogged down around Tula, unable to seize it. With Army Group Center's lead units a tantalizing 25 to 30 kilometers from the outskirts of Moscow, Bock had no choice but to break off his operations for good on 5 December 1941.[3]

That same day, in arctic weather conditions, the Soviet High Command unleashed a major counteroffensive that would threaten the remnants of GFM von Bock's dangerously overextended army group with annihilation in the weeks that followed. Racially and ideologically dismissive of their enemy's capabilities, senior German generals (Guderian among them) at first underestimated the scale and scope of the Soviet attack.

If Army Group Center's situation had become suddenly desperate, Guderian bore his fair share of the responsibility for that: His final, futile push toward Moscow had left his panzer army unevenly deployed and vulnerable to counterattack. Moreover, in the ensuing weeks, he repeatedly (and surreptitiously) violated superiors' orders by conducting unauthorized withdrawals that, ultimately, would lead to his dismissal the day after Christmas. While Guderian would later hold other leading positions in Hitler's military hierarchy, the panzer leader would never again command an army on the field of battle.

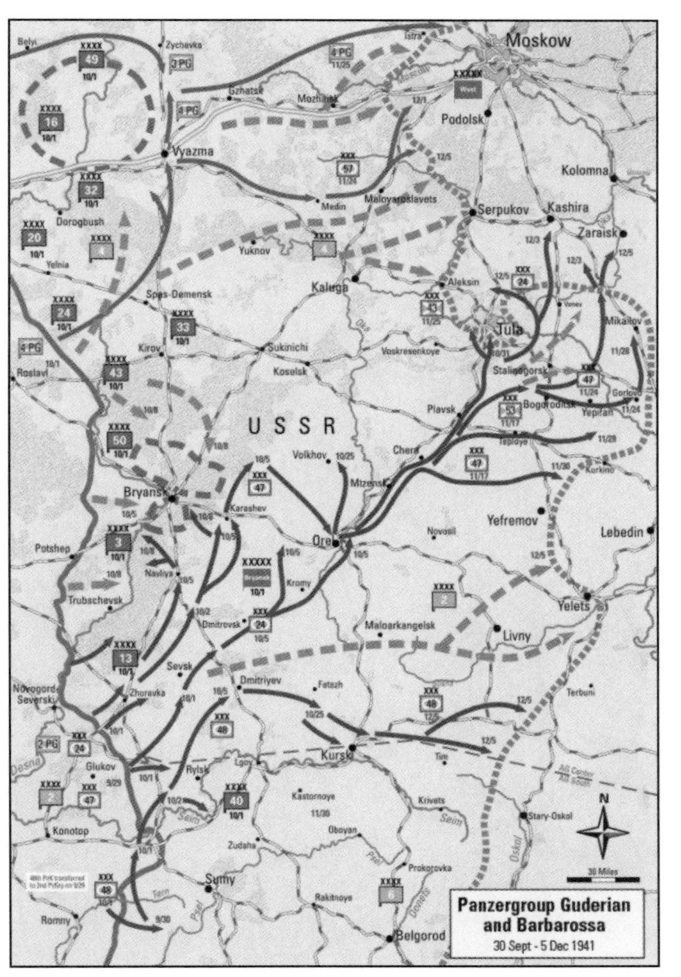

Operations of 2 Panzer Group/2 Panzer Army: 30.9.1941–5.12.1941

7

Operation Typhoon

The Plan

Since mid-July 1941, the Soviets had conducted a series of major counteroffensives in an effort to disrupt, even destroy, Army Group Center. If, in general, these Soviet counteroffensives were poorly organized and executed, lacking adequate air support and supply, they had grown progressively larger in scope and duration and more serious in terms of their impact on GFM von Bock's army group. In the second week of September, however, they finally petered out in exhaustion with the conclusion of the "Third Smolensk Counteroffensive," of which the attacks of Lt.-Gen. A. I. Eremenko's Briansk Front against Guderian's 2 Panzer Group had been an integral part.

The most noteworthy success gained by the Soviets in these attacks was forcing the Germans to finally abandon the El'nia salient,[1] which, after weeks of costly fighting, had become an unbearable drain on German manpower. The evacuation was complete by 5 September, with the Red Army occupying the town of El'nia the next day.[2] The Soviet victory, modest though it was, marked the "first occasion when Soviet forces successfully penetrated prepared German defenses and regained a sizeable chunk of occupied territory."[3] But the Red Army had paid dearly for its offensive strategy, sustaining absolutely brutal losses in men and materiel (at El'nia alone, of 103,200 men committed to the operation, the Soviets lost 31,853—10,701 killed, captured, or missing and 21,152 wounded); hence, when Operation Typhoon (*Taifun*) struck at the beginning of October, Soviet forces along the Moscow axis were far weaker than they had been just a month before, the average strength of many Red Army rifle divisions having been reduced to only about 3,000 men.[4]

The relative pause in the fighting along Bock's eastern front (facing Moscow) gave the infantry of his Fourth and Ninth Armies—as well as his few remaining mobile units stationed north and south of Smolensk—a brief but badly needed period for rest, recuperation, and maintenance. For the first time in weeks, the

Landser were able to clean weapons and equipment, tend to personal hygiene, catch up on letters to loved ones at home, and, most importantly, get some rest and sleep. In general, the soldiers on both sides returned to the less eventful routines that characterized quieter periods at the front, engaging in regular patrolling, conducting occasional local assaults, and reinforcing their rifle pits and bunkers. With daily requirements for shells, fuel, spare parts, and other critical resources now dramatically reduced, the German quartermasters finally began to replenish their supply depots for the impending march on Moscow.[5]

DIRECTIVE NO. 35

On 6 September 1941, Adolf Hitler, satisfied that operations on both the northern (Leningrad) and southern wings (the Ukraine) of the eastern front were going according to plan, issued Directive No. 35, ordering the attack of Army Group Center toward Moscow to begin "at the earliest possible moment (end of September)." What the Germans called the "Timoshenko Army Group" (*Heeresgruppe Timoshenko*) was to be "defeated and annihilated in the limited time that remains before the onset of winter weather." This was to be accomplished by destroying Soviet forces east of Smolensk in a vast pincer movement (*Umfassung*) in the "general direction of Viaz'ma, with strong [concentrations] of armor on the flanks."[6]

Hitler's directive also made clear that only after Soviet forces in front of Moscow had been "defeated in these highly coordinated and closely encircling operations of annihilation" (*Vernichtungsoperation*) was Bock's army group to begin a general advance on Moscow, with its right flank anchored on the Oka River, its left on the upper Volga. In other words, Typhoon was to be carried out in two distinct phases; more importantly, as the directive clearly stipulated, the primary objective of Typhoon was not Moscow but the destruction of the Red Army.[7]

While Hitler and his General Staff looked forward confidently to the "final battle of the year"—convinced as they more or less were that "the war against the Soviet Union could in fact be ended with one more major offensive"[8]—on 5 September, that is, on the day before Hitler issued his new directive, *Oberstleutnant* Hellmuth Stieff, one of the more enlightened intellects assigned to the Army High Command compound in the Mauerwald (just outside the Führer's *Wolfsschanze* headquarters in East Prussia), wrote a letter to his wife. In it, he commented darkly on the increasingly precarious predicament of Bock's army group, offering a sobering counterpoint to the prevailing conventional wisdom:

> The eastern front of [Army Group Center] has been involved in the heaviest defensive fighting on the scale of the World War (up to 300 enemy batteries in a single corps sector) for days, even weeks, during which there have been serious daily breaches [of the HKL] and in the course of which the combat strength of our divisions has melted away like snow in the sun. The tragic thing in all this is that our troops are suffering chronic ammunition shortages due to transport issues.

> The situation there is on the razor's edge [*auf des Messers Schneide*], because we have no more reserves. Hopefully the Russian will run out of steam first; otherwise there's the distinct danger of losing Smolensk.[9]

PLANNING AND PREPARATIONS

The main planning for Operation Typhoon was done by the Army High Command (OKH) along with Bock's Army Group Center—all plans, of course, subject to the Führer's final approval. Because preparations for the offensive would go through the end of September, Bock's army group and subordinate commands had sufficient time to plan the new operation in great detail and to test its validity in map exercises. While the German intelligence appreciation of Soviet troop dispositions before Moscow had significantly improved, it was still far from perfect. Soviet Western Front was estimated to consist of 70 to 100 divisions, and, as it turned out, this estimate was not far off the mark. Nothing, however, was known about the size and strength of Russian armies in rear areas, although the hastily constructed lines of defense in front of Moscow were easily detected by German aerial reconnaissance.

As the days passed and the planning continued, the significance of the impending operation grew in stature. Indeed, despite the successes at Leningrad and in the Ukraine, it was becoming increasingly evident that Soviet Russia had yet to be subdued and that it would take another great effort to finish her off. Gradually, German thinking congealed around the conviction that it was not enough to simply seek elimination of the large Soviet force concentrations opposite Army Group Center; rather, Moscow became the ultimate objective and, erroneously to be sure, was ascribed a decisive importance for bringing the war to an end. As was so often the case with German planning, the coveted objective was, from the outset, thought to be attainable and, thus, unaffected by questions concerning its ultimate viability. The available forces would simply have to "take whatever measures are necessary" to achieve their stated goal. In September 1941, it was not just Hitler and his OKW who were guilty of such a distorted outlook but also the OKH and many of the field commanders, among them Bock and Guderian.

On 16 September, Bock issued his operational orders for Typhoon for the three panzer groups now assigned to his command—*Panzergruppe* 2 (Guderian), *Panzergruppe* 3 (Hoth), and *Panzergruppe* 4 (Hoepner).[10] Their mission was to destroy the Soviet Western, Reserve, and Briansk Fronts by means of broad envelopment operations and, in doing so, prevent the withdrawal of enemy forces in good order toward Moscow. The *Schwerpunkt* was with Hoth's and *Generaloberst* Erich Hoepner's panzer groups: striking from positions north and south of Smolensk, respectively, they were to join hands at the town of Viaz'ma, thus placing their spearheads barely 200 kilometers (linear distance) from the outskirts of the Soviet capital.[11]

Given the limited time remaining before the start of Typhoon, a major redeployment of Guderian's panzer group (upon its return from the Ukraine) was considered too demanding; hence, it was to attack from the south, on the far-right wing of the army group, where it was to operate in a certain degree of exclusion. Specifically, the panzer group's left wing was to envelop Soviet forces in the Desna bend near Briansk—once again in cooperation with Weichs's Second Army—while the main weight of the attack (*Schwerpunkt*) was to the northeast toward Orel.[12]

As was typically the case, there were disagreements between the principal decision makers, with Bock having initially proposed a deeper encirclement to the east of Viaz'ma, while Hitler and Halder championed a shallower one aimed directly at the town. Yet the idea of Bock's army group launching another operation of the depth it had achieved in the great cauldron battles of the summer was simply unrealistic, given the stark decline of his forces since 22 June. Thus, Bock's "grand solution" was rejected. On 17 September, Bock—still piqued about the "very narrow scope of attack imposed on me"—submitted his operational plans to Halder.[13] In the meantime, the army group had begun to assemble operational staffs, formations, and Army troops for the impending operation that, on 19 September, received the cover name "Typhoon."[14]

Among the many challenges facing the C-in-C of Army Group Center as he prepared for his "decisive" battle was ensuring the timely transfer to his army group of units still assigned to Army Groups North and South that were earmarked for Typhoon. The redeployment of these units placed an enormous strain on an already overburdened transportation system; moreover, by mid-September, it was becoming apparent that many of these formations were going to be tied down longer than expected by the operations east of Kiev and the ongoing attack on Leningrad. Bock was particularly worried about the redeployment of several mobile divisions from Leeb's army group; in the third week of September, these units were still actively engaged on the Leningrad front and thus would only reach their final assembly areas for Typhoon at the last moment. In general, achieving concentration of forces (of the mobile units in particular) would require ambitious strategic redeployments that would tax the strength of affected units while limiting time for rest and refitting.

On 20 September, Bock moved his headquarters from Borisov to an abandoned orphanage in Smolensk, putting him much closer to the front. On 24 September, he hosted the final planning conference there. ("It is time!" Bock exulted in his diary that day.)[15] Among those in attendance were GFM von Brauchitsch (C-in-C of the Army), Halder, and Kesselring (C-in-C of 2 Air Fleet), along with the commanders of the armies and panzer groups. Together, one last time, they pored over operational plans and objectives. At the end of the conference, the decision was made to launch the new offensive on 2 October. While Hoth had proposed beginning the attack on 3 October, he was overruled; Guderian, however, requested and was granted permission to start his assault two days earlier (30 September). Guderian claimed that this would enable his panzer group to reach the "good roads" around Orel before the "mud set in and to secure the transverse Orel-Briansk road so that I might have a decent supply route"; the early start, he argued, would also create the opportunity for additional air support before the main attack went in: "I could only expect strong air support if I could arrange for the bomber missions to be flown two days before the attacks by the other armies of Army Group Center were due to start."[16] "It suits me fine," wrote Bock in his journal, "if [Guderian] has a head start, for he is still so far from the right wing of the main attack that his advance cannot have a direct influence until four or five days later."[17]

On 26 September, Bock formally released the general attack order for Typhoon (*Heeresgruppenbefehl für den Angriff*) to his armies and panzer groups; it began, "Following a long period of waiting the army group once again is moving to the attack." The next day (27 September), he set the time for unleashing the main attack at 5:30 a.m., 2 October.[18] "Somewhat hurried," he wrote in his diary, "but we have no time to lose."[19] On the same day *Hauptmann* Thilo (OKH Operations Branch) noted in his diary with a certain perspicacity, "[For Army Group Center] and South it has now become a race with the winter, whose precursor, 'bad weather,' will smother all operations in mud for 6–8 weeks."[20] Bock's Ninth Army had already gotten a foretaste of what the impending "bad weather" (i.e., the fall rainy season—the so-called *Rasputitsa*) held in store, when in late August and early September a period of heavy rains disrupted operations and exercised an "almost crippling" effect on the morale of both officers and men. "For the first time," noted the army's war diarist, "we became fully conscious just how much operations under the impracticable conditions in Russia depend upon the weather."[21] Yet, no matter, for German planners assumed that Typhoon, and with it the eastern campaign, would be finished by the end of November, at which time they could finally begin to return most of the Army to Germany to be rested and re-equipped.

As German intelligence continued to provide updates on the Soviet order of battle and dispositions opposite Army Group Center, on 29 September Bock requested that 2 Air Fleet immediately begin to take out all major rail junctions (*Eisenbahnknotenpunkte*) behind the enemy front to disrupt and delay Soviet troop movements.[22] In response, Kesselring's *Luftflotte* 2 conducted several heavy attacks against these designated objectives and also struck enemy airfields.

By 1 October (D–1), the enormous aggregation of ground forces earmarked for the offensive had reached their jump-off positions. All was now set for the final push and, so it seemed, for a decisive German victory.

GUDERIAN PREPARES FOR TYPHOON

After three months of almost continuous movement and combat, Guderian's exhausted tankers and mechanized infantry were badly in need of rest and time to repair worn-out vehicles and equipment. But the ambitious timetable for Typhoon would not allow for it: "Only three days could be allotted to the gallant troops for this purpose and even this short period for rehabilitation was not vouchsafed to all units."[23] Thus, his battered and depleted formations were about to embark on another great offensive for which they had little time to prepare. Yet Guderian's panzer group was hardly the exception. Walter Chales de Beaulieu, Chief of Staff of Hoepner's 4 Panzer Group, recalled after the war that, prior to the start of Typhoon, his forces "had little or no rest and must join the new battle directly from a tiring march."[24]

On 20 September, the tank regiments of 3 and 4 Panzer Divisions (24 PzK) were ordered—regardless of their situation—to break off at once from the fighting around Kiev and be prepared to depart for their new assembly areas by the next day at the latest. Regrouping for the new operation, the main concentration area for *Panzergruppe* 2 was around and to the north of Glukhov (some 150 kilometers west of Kursk). It was here, on the right wing of Bock's Army Group Center, that Guderian would assemble his armored fist—the four panzer divisions of Geyr's 24 Panzer Corps and Lemelsen's 47 Panzer Corps.[25]

Guderian's forces underwent a major reorganization for the new campaign. While he relinquished his 46 Panzer Corps (turned over to Hoepner's group), assigned to his command were two infantry corps with six infantry divisions and one cavalry division (34 and 35 AK), along with *Gen.d.Pz.Tr.* Werner Kempf's 48 Panzer Corps (9 PD, 16 ID [mot.], and 25 ID [mot.]), the latter joining Guderian from Rundstedt's Army Group South. All told, his panzer group now comprised 16 divisions (5 panzer, 4 motorized, 6 infantry, and 1 cavalry division).

In his postwar study, Guderian's chief of staff, *Oberst* Kurt Freiherr von Liebenstein, stated that the personnel strength (*Gefechtsstärke*) of the panzer and motorized divisions was now about 75 percent of what it had been on 22 June. The total number of combat-capable tanks was about 400, including a last-minute consignment (*Neuzuweisung*) of 85 replacement tanks[26] and a large number of tanks that the workshop companies of Model's 3 Panzer Division had "coerced" into working order by means of cannibalization and a few replacement engines arriving from Germany. (Hitherto, since the beginning of the eastern campaign, Guderian had received just thirty replacement tanks, all going to Nehring's 18 Panzer Division.) General headquarters (GHQ) troops assigned to 2 Panzer Group for Operation Typhoon included *Nebelwerfer* Regiment 53 (three battalions), Machine Gun Battalion 5, and an Army flak battalion (Fla-Btn. 602).

To provide for the requisite air support, Guderian consulted with GFM Kesselring. Simply put, Loerzer's 2 Air Corps (reinforced by elements of 4 Air Fleet from Army Group South) was to cooperate with Second Army but primarily with Fourth Army and *Panzergruppe* 2. Also deployed in Guderian's area of operations was the *Luftwaffe*'s I Flak Corps, which was to be used as "reinforcement and assault artillery," that is, in a ground support role. (Since the beginning of the eastern campaign, I Flak Corps had destroyed 314 Russian planes and some 3,000 tanks.)[27]

To carry out his attack, Guderian concentrated the bulk of his armor in a powerful wedge formation (*mächtigen Keil*). Geyr's 24 Panzer Corps, beginning its assault from Glukhov—and representing the panzer group's main effort—was to advance via Sevsk to Orel, a major Soviet rail junction some 200 kilometers (linear distance) from its start line. (At Geyr's disposal were the best roads in the region.) To Geyr's right, Kempf's 48 Panzer Corps, with its single panzer division (9 PD) in the van, was to attack northeast from Putivl, just under 50 kilometers (linear distance) east of Konotop. (Kempf's spearheads would eventually turn south toward Kursk.) On Geyr's left, Lemelsen's 47 Panzer Corps, advancing from Shostka (northwest of Glukhov), was to strike out to the east (its right wing anchored on Sevsk), then turn north and, in conjunction with Weichs's Second Army, encircle and destroy Soviet forces around Briansk. The six infantry divisions of General Metz's 34 and General Kaempfe's 35 Army Corps, which were to protect the flanks of 2 Panzer Group, were still in transit when Guderian began his attack.[28]

The panzer leader and his lieutenants were convinced that, when finally unleashed to begin this "final battle of the year," they would successfully complete the drive on Moscow they had so confidently begun on 22 June 1941. *Generalmajor* Walther K. Nehring (18 Panzer Division) calculated that, from an examination of captured Soviet staff maps, he would require a fifteen-day logistical capability to sustain his operation to the very gates of the Soviet capital.[29] Perhaps the dutiful general was unaware that Guderian—as he noted in his memoir—was disappointed with his allotment of fuel for the forthcoming offensive. Indeed, as his chief of staff recalled, "It was already foreseen at the start of the operation that the supply of fuel would not correspond to the operational requirements [*den operativen Forderungen nicht entsprechen werde*]."[30]

THE CORRELATION OF FORCES

German Forces

By the end of September, GFM von Bock had assembled an impressive order of battle for Typhoon. Along a front of 760 kilometers, his assault forces encompassed some 1.75 million men arranged into three armies and three panzer groups with seventy-two-plus divisions, among them fourteen panzer and eight motorized divisions. (Four security and two infantry divisions, which operated in the army group's hinterland, are not included in these numbers.) These forces boasted some 4,100 guns (1,022 light, medium, and heavy batteries) and 1,400 tanks (excluding assault guns).[31] Bock's tank forces, in fact, had been more than doubled with the arrival of the *Wehrmacht*'s last two panzer divisions from Germany (2 and 5 PDs with about 450 tanks total), as well as the addition of some 300 tanks from new production. In the aggregate, these forces made up the largest armada the *Wehrmacht* had ever assembled for a single battle, and with Richthofen's 8 Air Corps having finally returned from Army Group North, it was supported by 1,000 aircraft of Kesselring's 2 Air Fleet (including 292 medium bombers, 210 dive-bombers, and 279 fighters).[32]

Although impressive on paper, the figures for Bock's army group cited above are not quite what they seem. Despite the partially successful efforts to enhance the striking power of the panzer divisions, virtually all of Bock's divisions remained understrength, some significantly so; hence, in terms of fighting ability, they were no longer the divisions they had been at the start of the campaign.[33] Moreover, despite modest improvement in the logistical outlook in the second half of September (after the Soviet High Command had broken off its offensives), the army group's ability to effectively sustain its offensive for more than a short period remained in doubt due to the inadequacies of the rail network and the serious diminution of supply trucks.

Soviet Forces

When Typhoon commenced, the attacking forces of Army Group Center were faced by three Soviet fronts: Western Front (six armies), commanded by Col.-Gen. I. S. Konev (he had taken command of the front from Timoshenko on 10 September) and defending from Lake Seliger to south of Iartsevo; Reserve Front (six armies), commanded by Marshal S. M. Budenny and echeloned in depth from north of El'nia to east of Roslavl; and Briansk Front (three armies and one operational group), commanded by Lt.-Gen. A. I. Eremenko and deployed from east of Roslavl southward to the Seim River. The three fronts, which made up some 40 percent of the Red Army's entire combat strength from the Baltic to the Black Sea, numbered 1.25 million men, supported by 7,600 guns and mortars, 990 tanks, and 667 combat planes.[34]

Yet, like those of the Germans, these Soviet forces had weaknesses. The divisions allocated to the three Soviet fronts were an amalgam of veteran formations worn down in previous battles and new, poorly trained, inadequately outfitted People's Volunteer Formations. Most of the rifle divisions—the backbone of the Red Army—were at half strength (5,000 to 7,000 men), while many suffered from a paucity of artillery and machine guns. Of Konev's 479 tanks, less than 50 were new KV or T-34s, and all three fronts were characterized by severe shortages of trained officers, modern aircraft, and effective anti-aircraft and anti-tank weaponry.[35]

The Soviets' complex command structure, coupled with the constant reshuffling of commanders between front and direction commands, elicited an atmosphere of confusion and uncertainty. All of these headquarters lacked proper numbers of trained staff officers and long-range radios. In any case, due to the widespread fear of German signal-intercept operations, many Soviet commanders avoided the use of radios, content to rely on liaison officers to pass on their orders to higher and lower headquarters. Such a system, of course, was "slow and tenuous," and communications collapsed rapidly once Typhoon began.[36]

Finally, a brief examination of the Soviet intelligence appreciation of German intentions is in order: Since mid-July, the Soviets had been building a series of concentric defensive lines to protect their capital; these fortified regions, in particular the Mozhaisk Defense Line, were 40–50 percent complete by 30 September. Stalin and the STAVKA had expected the "final assault" on Moscow to begin in late August, and when it failed to materialize, they began to relax their guard. They grew confident, as the days grew shorter and bad weather approached, that the Germans would not attempt another major offensive following the Battle of Kiev. Reinforcing their perceptions was the failure of Soviet intelligence to detect the movement of much of *Panzergruppe* 4 from Leeb's to Bock's army group and the rapid return of Guderian's *Panzergruppe* 2 from the Ukraine; thus, they continued to believe that the bulk of German armor was still in the north and south—and not (as it was) in the center of the German front with Bock's army group. Once Typhoon got underway, several days would pass before the Soviets grasped their error.

TYPHOON ABOUT TO BREAK

As the increasingly cool September days slipped by, a palpable air of excitement began to grip the battle-hardened veterans of Army Group Center, as the front was once again jolted into purposeful activity. New units, weapons, and equipment were now arriving in vast quantities, and rumors filled the air. As one veteran recalled,

> There was something in the air, but nobody could say what it was. A kind of feverish bustle pervaded the troops and the command posts. There were secret orders and there was extensive reconnaissance. The digging of trenches or improvement of the positions were largely ignored. Only the most essential was done to the positions. The troops pricked up their ears when suddenly new cipher documents for radio traffic were distributed. Then it became clear to many that it could only mean an attack in an eastward direction."[37]

A soldier with Bock's army group posted a letter to his wife (29 September): "Bobi, don't be cross if, from tomorrow, I can't write to you every day; I did already write you that things will get rolling again soon. The second push is starting. Hopefully, it's the last one. The prisoners that we took last night come from the Urals. So things must look pretty dire on the other side. It looks like these are their last reserves. And so now it's off right into the middle of things. Kiev is over. Now it's Center's turn again. The grand finale will soon be played in the east. We are placing all our hopes on the coming four weeks."[38]

On the eve of the assault, *Unteroffizier* Helmut Pabst observed the mighty buildup of forces with obvious wonder:

> What news there is we piece together like bits of a mosaic. Somebody has seen the tanks, the yellow ones that were meant for Africa. [Note: The reference is to 5 PD, whose tanks had been painted in desert colors for shipment to North Africa until assigned to Typhoon.] Now they've turned up here. Someone else has seen assault guns. And a man from the *Nebelwerfers* appeared by mistake. All kinds of special weapons—lots of them—guns of every caliber; they are all being concentrated in this sector. It's piling up inexorably like a thunderstorm. It is the sword above the calm—the drawing of breath for a stroke that may be bigger than any we have seen yet. We don't know when it will start. We only feel the veil over the calm getting thinner, the atmosphere gathering tension, the approach of the hour when it will only need a word to let loose hell, when all this concentrated force will spring forward.[39]

As for Guderian's group, it had, of course, not enjoyed the weeks of relative quiet that had favored Bock's eastern front throughout most of September. As explained, following its exemplary role in the Battle of Kiev, it had raced out of the Ukraine and rapidly redeployed along Bock's right wing in record time. Indeed, after frantic regrouping, Model's 3 Panzer Division had retraced its steps, making its way back across the Sula and the Seim almost 100 kilometers to Glukhov, arriving at the town on 29 September. The brilliant panzer general—who in early 1944 would become the second-youngest field marshal in the German Army (after Erwin Rommel)—received his new orders posthaste: His attack was to go in the next morning.

8

The Final Desperate Push

Shortly before Typhoon began, Adolf Hitler, as he had done only hours prior to the start of the Barbarossa campaign, released a grandiloquent proclamation to his assembled soldiers: "Today begins the last great decisive battle of this year [*letzte grosse Entscheidungsschlacht dieses Jahres*]. In it, we will destroy the enemy and, in so doing, England, the instigator of this whole war. . . . We are thus lifting from Germany and Europe the danger that has hovered over the continent ever since the times of the Huns and later the Mongol invasion."[1]

At first light on 2 October 1941, following a short artillery barrage that blanketed the front in a dense smokescreen, the bulk of Army Group Center surged across the main battle line from their positions southeast of Smolensk (4 PzGr and Fourth Army) and northeast of the city (3 PzG and Ninth Army). Striking with overwhelming force at critical points along the army group's 700-kilometer front, both panzer groups shattered Soviet defenses in their sectors and began to drive into Soviet-held territory, the initial objective being to close a ring around a large Soviet grouping between Viaz'ma and Dorogobuzh. Overhead, the squadrons of Kesselring's 2 Air Fleet thrashed the forward enemy lines and targets behind the front, the pilots and air crew of Richthofen's 8 Air Corps flying an average of four (and as many as six) sorties on this day.[2]

As one *Landser* observed, it was "the most beautiful, sunny, fall day,"[3] and the men were thrilled to once again be on the attack. Another, an unknown soldier in 5 Infantry Division, described the start of the assault in his diary: "A few minutes more and the hands of the watch read 0600. Now it's time. All at once, the entire front roars. It's as if all hell has been let loose. You can't hear yourself think any more. But the thunder rolls on from thousands of barrels. It doesn't stop. Then the planes come, which we've not seen in such a long time. In groups of up to 30 airplanes, the Stukas soar over and above us, heavily laden with bombs."[4] *Unteroffizier* Helmut Pabst watched the assault go in on the front of Adolf Strauss's Ninth Army:

> 0600. I jump on top of a dugout. There are the tanks! Giants rolling slowly toward the enemy. And the planes. One squadron after another, unloading their bombs across the way. Army Group Center has launched its attack.
>
> 0610. The first *Nebelwerfer* salvo. Dammit, it's really something seeing; the rockets leave a black trail, a dirty cloud that drifts slowly away. The second salvo goes off! Red and black fire, then the projectile emerges from the cone of smoke. You can see it clearly as soon as the rocket burns off: the things fly straight as arrows through the morning air. None of us have seen it before. Reconnaissance planes come flying back low over the lines. Fighters are circling overhead.
>
> 0645. Machine-gun fire ahead of us. It's the infantry's turn.
>
> 0820. Tanks roll by, close to the gun position. A hundred have gone by already, and they're still coming on. Where there was a field 15 minutes ago there's now a road. Five hundred yards to our right assault guns and motorized infantry come on without a pause.[5]

With his tanks and infantry at last on the road to Moscow again, Bock was elated. His diary entry for the day began "The army group went to the attack according to plan [*Die Heeresgruppe tritt planmässig zum Angriff an*]. We advanced so easily everywhere that doubts arose as to whether the enemy had not in fact decamped. I drove to 4 Panzer Group's command post, from where one has a smashing view of the Fourth Army's battlefield, then to the Desna."[6]

The next day (3 October), a jubilant Führer, buoyed by the initial success of the new offensive, traveled to Berlin in his special train, *Amerika*. After lunching with his staff at the Reich Chancellery, he drove through throngs of cheering Berliners to the *Sportpalast*, where he gave an inspired speech to open the annual Winter Aid (*Winterhilfswerk*) campaign. It was, in fact, "one of the most stirring speeches of his life," delivered "wholly *ex tempore*."[7] Of the successes of his armed forces in Russia, he exclaimed, "If people now talk of lightning [*Blitz*] wars, then it is these soldiers who are responsible for it; their achievements are like lightning, because never in history have there been advances like these."[8] To rapturous applause he declared, "The enemy is already broken and will never rise again." (*Dieser Gegner ist bereits gebrochen und wird sich nie mehr erheben.*)[9] Within an hour, Hitler's special train was shepherding him back to his dreary East Prussian compound. Final victory in the east seemed all but certain.

BLITZKRIEG TO OREL

On 0600 hours on 30 September, Guderian put in his attack along the Orel axis, his armor supported by the Bf 109s of *Jagdgeschwader* 51 (JG 51) from their bases southeast of Smolensk[10] and by swarms of dive-bomber and destroyer aircraft

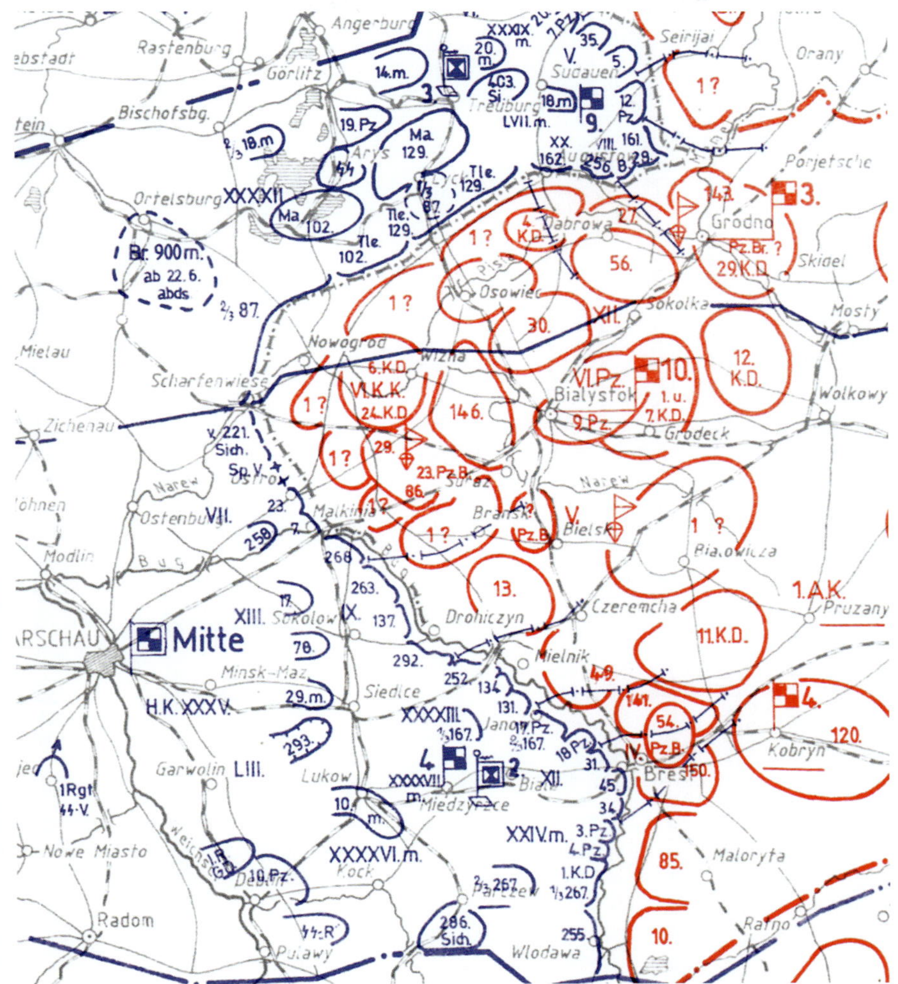

1 Deployment of Army Group Center for Operation Barbarossa (evening, 21.6.1941)

"*Barbarossa*: In the night of 21/22.6. OKW transmits the code word '*Dortmund*.' Thereby is the start of the attack finally ordered for 22.6. The order is passed on to the army groups. The closing up [of the forces] into their assembly areas proceeds according to plan [*planmässig*]." Schramm (ed.), *Kriegstagebuch des OKW*, Bd. I, 417.

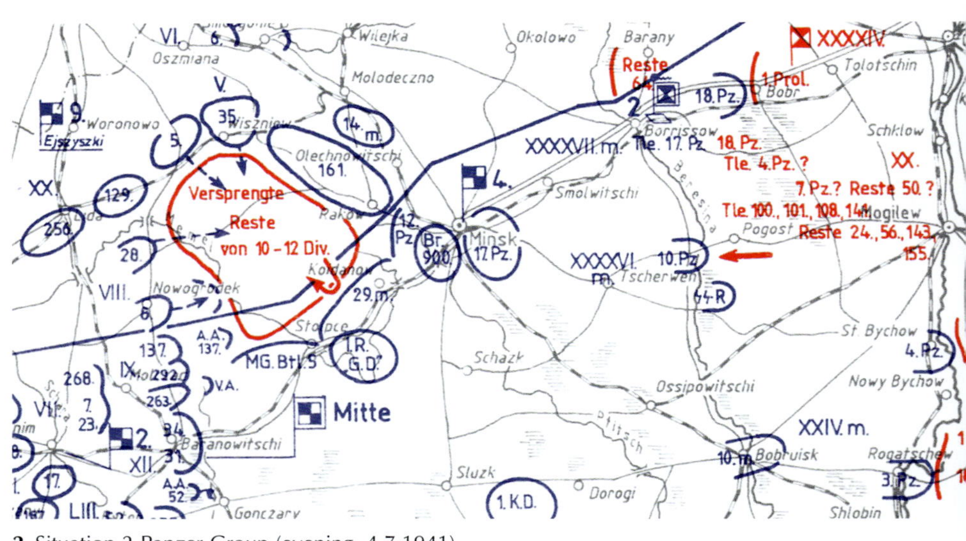

2 Situation 2 Panzer Group (evening, 4.7.1941)

"*Osten*: . . . In the sector of *H.Gr.Mitte*, Second and Ninth Armies clear the battlespace of dispersed enemy elements. Enemy resistance is growing stronger against 4 Panzer Army; on the primary thoroughfares and at [river] crossing points the enemy is putting up stubborn [*hartnäckig*] and organized resistance." Schramm (ed.), *Kriegstagebuch des OKW*, Bd. I, 427.

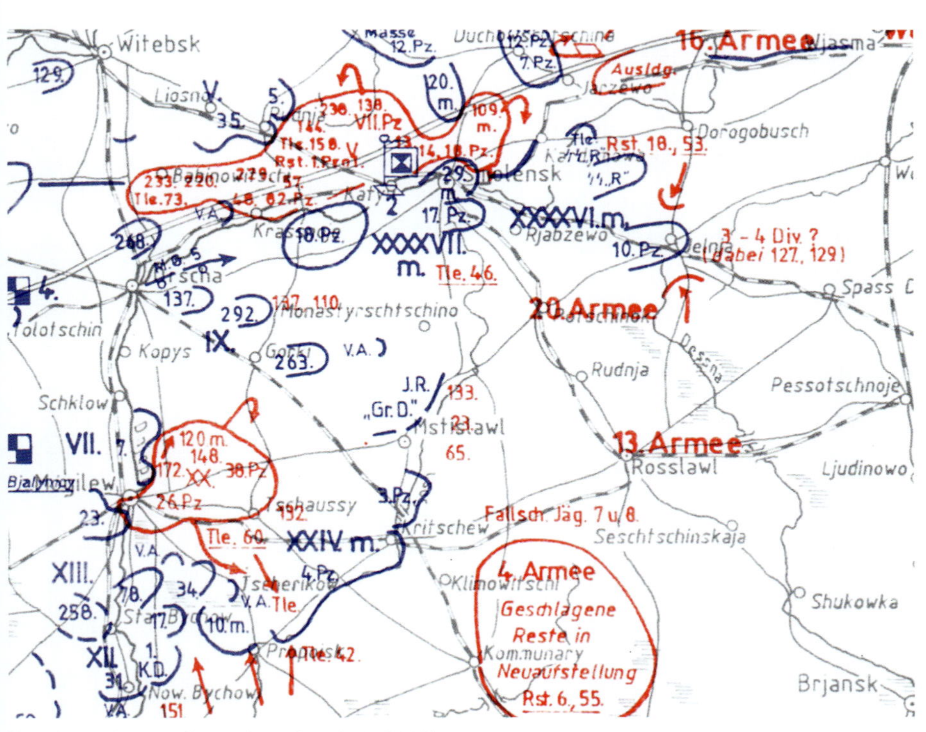

3 Situation 2 Panzer Group (evening, 20.7.1941)

'*Osten*: . . . In the sector of *H.Gr.Mitte* the enemy is conducting strong relief attacks [*Entlastungsangriffe*] against the forces of 4 Panzer Army at Propoisk and Smolensk. . . . A continuation of these enemy relief attacks, especially against Smolensk, is to be expected." Schramm (ed.), *Kriegstagebuch des OKW*, Bd. I, 438.

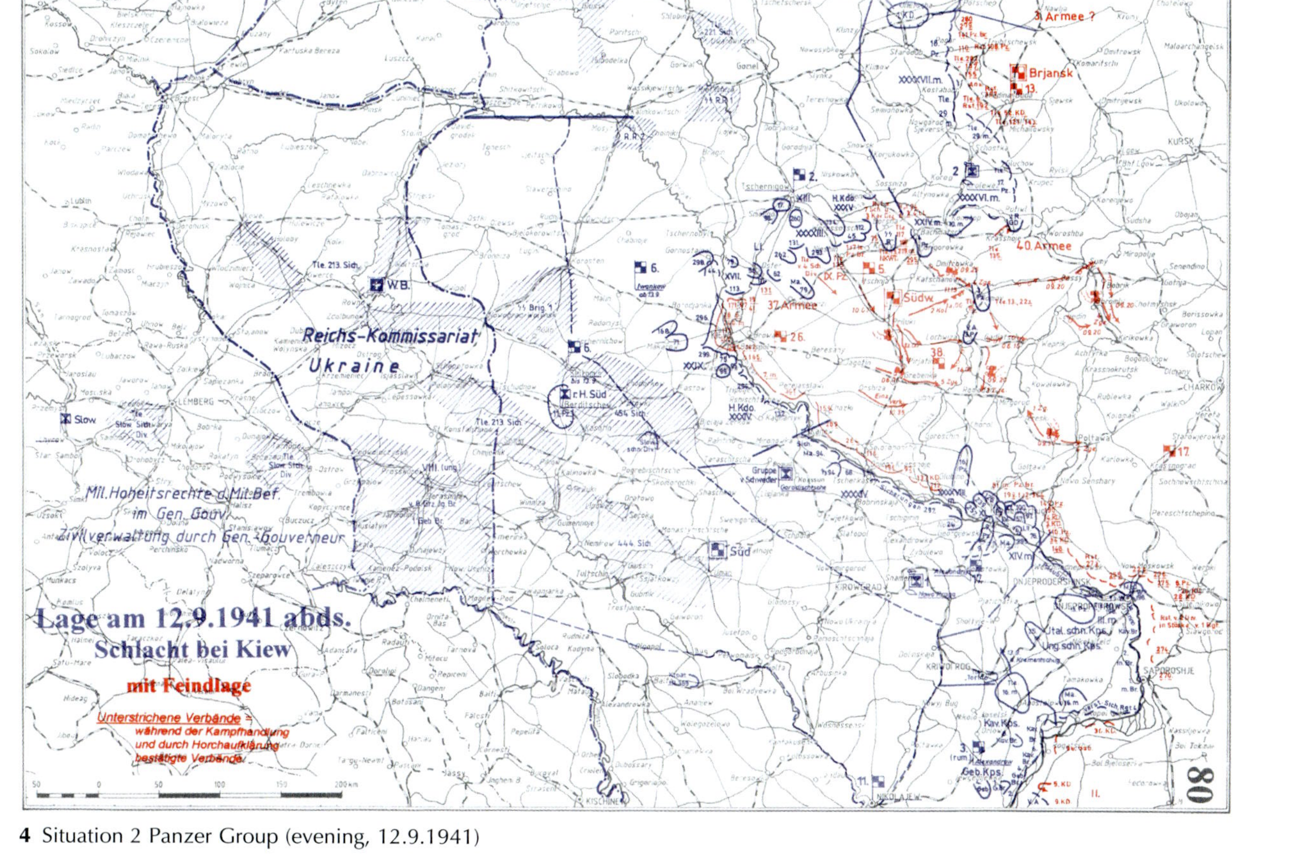

4 Situation 2 Panzer Group (evening, 12.9.1941)

"*H.Gr.Mitte*: . . . In sector of 2 PzGr the enemy continues to put up stubborn resistance against the right wing of 24 PzK. An advance detachment [*Vorausabteilung*] of 3 PD seizes intact the bridges over the Sula directly north of Lokhvitsa. . . . *Wetter*: In the southern sector of the army group, the continuous rain further degraded the condition of the roads and impeded the operations of *Luftflotte 2*."

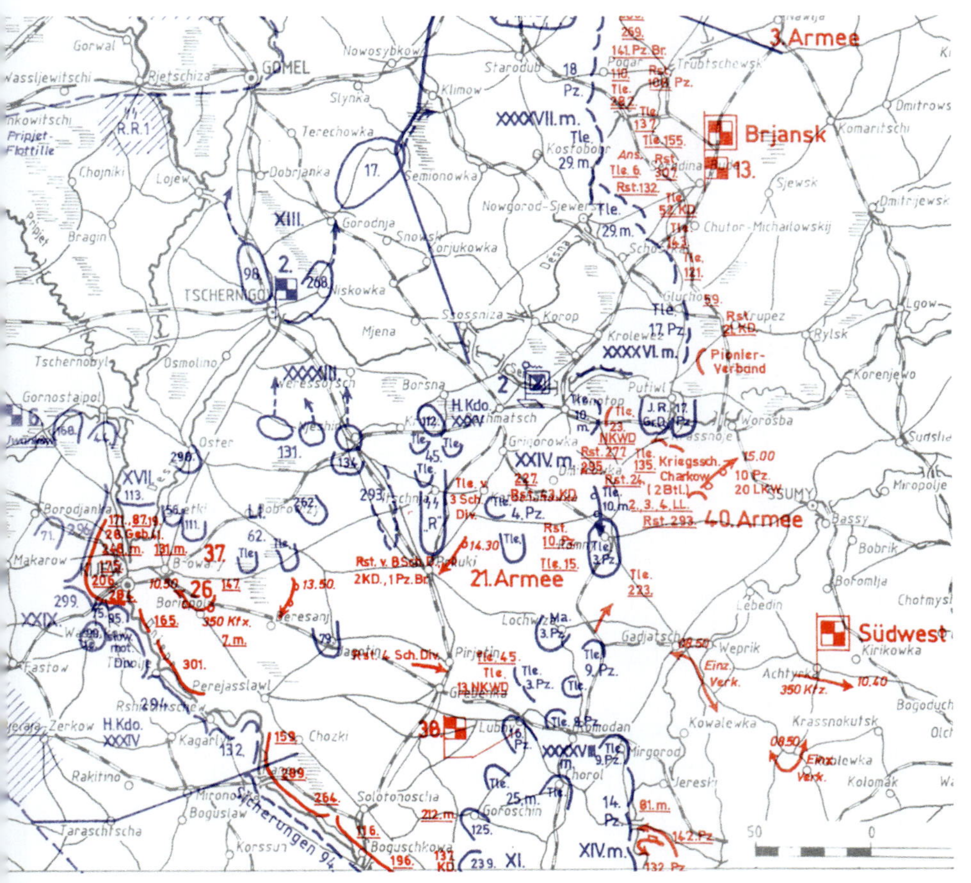

Kiev Cauldron Battle (evening, 15.9.1941)

H.Gr.Mitte: . . . 2 PzGr continues to fight against strong enemy rearguards [*Nachhuten*], some of which re putting up tenacious resistance. . . . In the cauldron [*Kessel*], the [enemy] columns and [troop] oncentrations around Prikuli point to stronger pressure on both sides of Lokhvitsa in the coming days." Tagesmeldungen der Operations-Abteilung des GenStdH," in Schramm (ed.), *Kriegstagebuch des OKW*, d. I, 637.

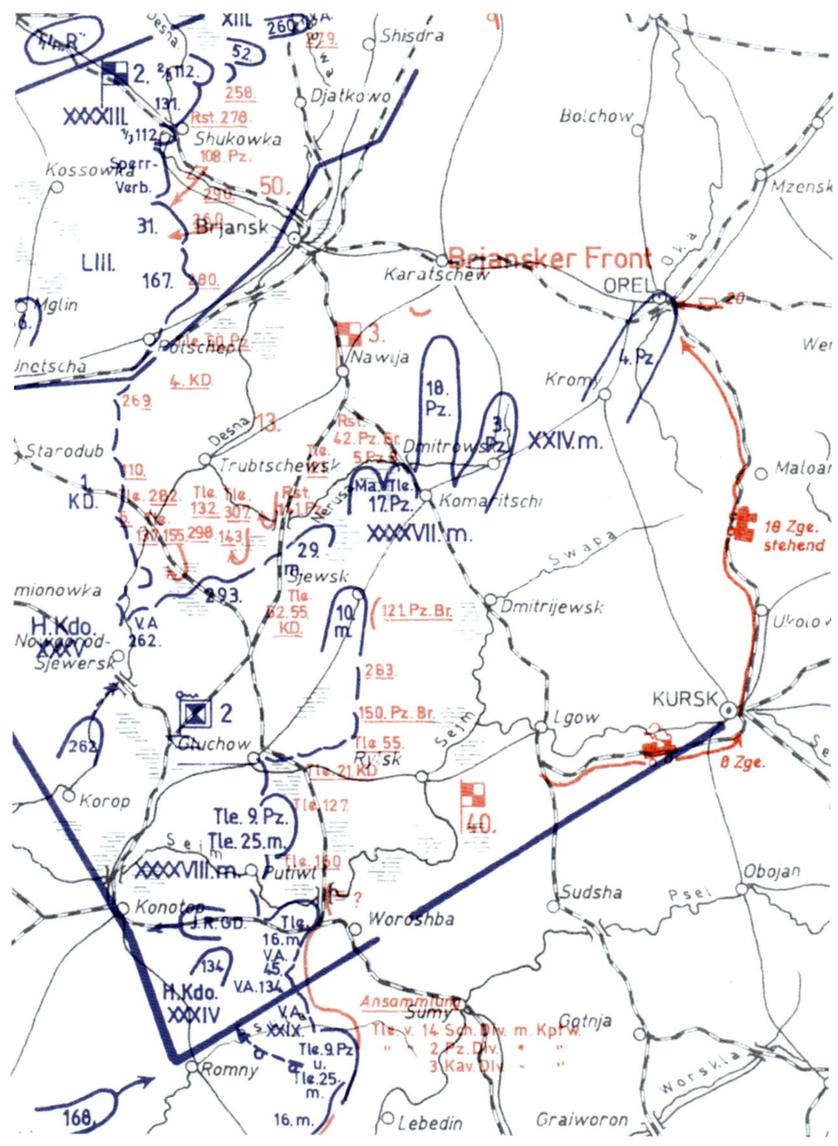

6 Situation 2 Panzer Group (evening, 4.10.1941)

"*H.Gr.Mitte*: 2 PzGr: . . . 24 PzK continues to close ranks. Mass of 4 PD in Orel. The left wing of the corps is advancing rapidly north of Dmitrowsk. Elements of 47 PzK thrust across [one river barrier and force a contested crossing over another]. On the right wing and in center of Second Army in part considerable enemy resistance [*erheblicher Feindwiderstand*]." "Tagesmeldungen der Operations-Abteilung des GenStdH," in Schramm (ed.), *Kriegstagebuch des OKW*, Bd. I, 677.

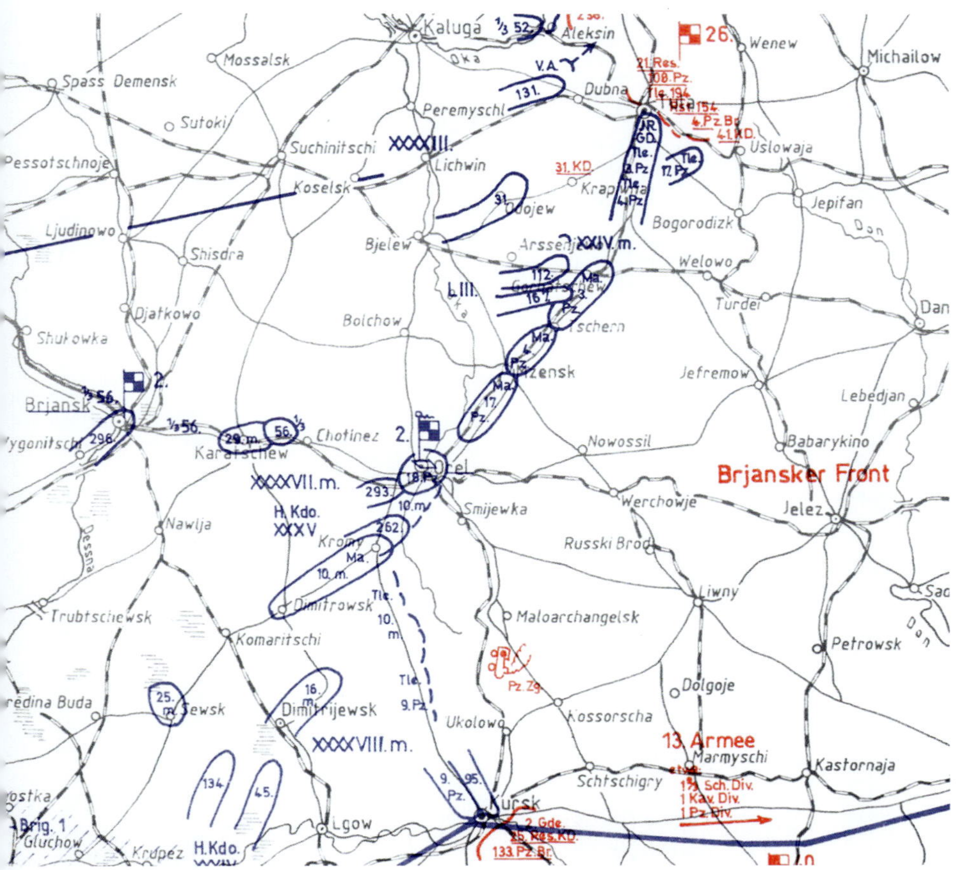

Situation 2 Panzer Army (evening, 2.11.1941)

H.Gr.Mitte: Second Army: In the morning hours, 48 PzK pushed into Kursk from the west and north with PD and 95 ID. By evening, the town was firmly in [German] hands. In the sector of Second Panzer Army ere were no special events [*keine besonderen Ereignisse*]. . . . *Wetter*: overcast, rainy. Road conditions ill bad." "Tagesmeldungen der Operations-Abteilung des GenStdH," in Schramm (ed.), *Kriegstagebuch es OKW*, Bd. I, 737–38.

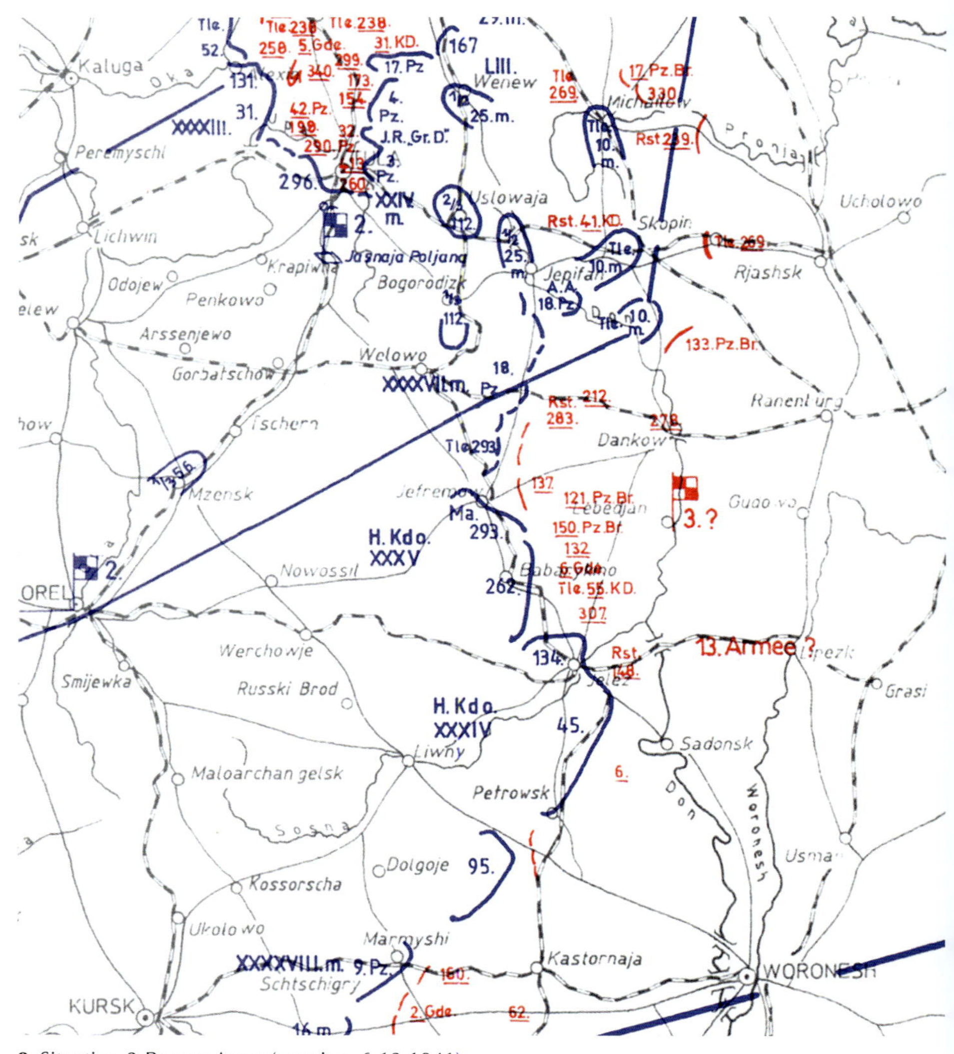

8 Situation 2 Panzer Army (evening, 6.12.1941)

"*H.Gr.Mitte*: . . . On the eastern front of Second Panzer Army negligible combat activity [*Gefechtstätigkeit*]. Enemy attacks against its northern front were repelled. Northeast of Tula 4 PD repulsed strong enemy attacks from northern direction. The division was withdrawn to a [defensive] line at and northeast of Kischkino. Due to icing [*infolge Vereisung*], a large number of vehicles and guns were destroyed and left behind. . . . In sector of 43 AK, 31 ID fell back to its jump-off position [*Ausgangsstellung*]. . . . *Wetter*: strong frost, mostly clear, cold up to –38 Celsius." "Tagesmeldungen der Operations-Abteilung des GenStdH," in Schramm (ed.), *Kriegstagebuch des OKW*, Bd. I, 796–97.

(*Stuka- und Zerstörergruppen*). The weather was cool, with scattered showers. Concentrated on a narrow front, his 24 and 47 Panzer Corps struck Maj.-Gen. A. N. Ermakov's operational group on the Briansk Front's left wing, just as the Soviet general was preparing an attack of his own. Stunned by the sudden German assault, Ermakov's five divisions fell back in disorder; in so doing, they exposed the left flank of Maj.-Gen. A. M. Gorodniansky's 13 Army. By day's end, Guderian's panzers and motorized infantry had driven a wedge 15 to 20 kilometers in depth between Soviet 13 Army and Group Ermakov.[11]

With the Soviets slow to react—at Lt.-Gen. A. I. Eremenko's Briansk Front HQ, the German attack was assessed as merely a diversion—Guderian's spearheads continued to drive rapidly through the heavily wooded terrain. On 1 October, Geyr's 24 Panzer Corps seized the town of Sevsk (on the Orel axis) while Lemelsen's 47 Panzer Corps began to wheel to the north into the rear of 13 Army. Although Ermakov counterattacked in an effort to close the breach, he did so in a piecemeal fashion without adequate armor and air support. Recalled Guderian,

> We had succeeded in breaking through the enemy front. The advance was energetically pursued, so far as the fuel situation would permit. I drove from Glukhov, through Essman, to 4 Panzer Division at Sevsk. On the side of the road lay shot-up Russian vehicles of all sorts, a further proof that the enemy had been surprised by our attack. On a hill surmounted by a windmill, just off the road of the advance, I saw Generals [Geyr and Langermann]. Considerable elements of [4 PD] had already reached Sevsk. The countryside showed traces of fierce fighting. There were dead and wounded Russians to be seen, and during the short walk to the windmill I and my companions found 14 unwounded Russian soldiers hiding in the long grass, whom we made prisoners; among them was an officer who was still engaged in talking to someone in Sevsk on a telephone.[12]

On 2 October, the attack, as Guderian put it, "was resumed with violence." With Bf 109s of Loerzer's 2 Air Corps overhead, "a complete breakthrough was achieved and [13 Army] was thrown back to the northeast."[13] So far, casualties had been light and, on this day, Langermann-Erlencamp's 4 Panzer Division captured Kromy, thus reaching the metaled road to Orel. At the same time, on Guderian's left, Weichs's Second Army had broken through the Soviet Sudost-Desna position despite robust enemy opposition.

On 3 October, lead elements of 4 PD (despite unceasing attack from the air),[14] having pushed deep behind the Soviet front, captured Orel (a strategic road and railway junction) in a coup de main, while also seizing large quantities of fuel and rations. In an astonishing act of audacity—and initiative—so typical of the German panzer forces early in the war, the city of 120,000 inhabitants was seized by 6./Pz.Rgt. 35 with just four tanks. Unsupported, the handful of tanks, commanded by *Oberleutnant* Arthur Wollschlaeger, stormed into the city and, by late afternoon, had secured the key bridge over the Oka and the main railway station, in the process knocking out a number of Russian flak guns. The shock effect on the local population was so great that resistance never materialized. (As Guderian recalled, "Our seizure of the town took the enemy so completely by surprise that the electric trams were still running as our tanks drove in.")[15] Following their remarkable "panzer raid," the diminutive "panzer group" was able to hold their positions for several hours until reinforcements finally reached them. Orel, some 240 kilometers from 2 Panzer Group's jump-off point just four days before, had been captured with hardly a shot fired.[16]

Immediately after the city's capture, its airfield became a base for dive-bombers and fighters, as well as a supply center from which to furnish fuel for Guderian's tanks, trucks, and armored fighting vehicles. It would become a popular target of Soviet aerial attacks.

The loss of Orel was a devastating blow to the Soviet Briansk Front, whose primary lines of communications ran through the city; thus, Eremenko rapidly lost contact with many of his formations and with the STAVKA in Moscow. Conversely, for Guderian's 2 Panzer Group, it appeared that Operation Typhoon had got off to a very good start indeed:

> In many respects the success at Orel raised hopes that Moscow could in fact be taken in the coming days and weeks. Yet Orel was the exception, not the rule. The advance had already almost exhausted Guderian's entire stock of fuel, while the weather had remained excellent and the roads were, at least in parts, well above average for the Soviet Union. The complications of continuing major operations in the east during the Russian autumn were as yet unknown to the *Ostheer*. . . . Wagner, the army quartermaster-general who was in charge of the *Ostheer*'s deeply troubled logistical apparatus, wrote in a letter on the same day (3 October): "I think that a great success, that is to say the decisive one, will be achieved in four weeks." Perhaps the Germans had lost their fear of the Russian winter and the vastness of the Soviet Union, or maybe it had merely been supplanted by faith in Hitler's maxim: "To the German soldier nothing is impossible!" In either case, Typhoon's success and easy victories were to be short-lived.[17]

BRIANSK CAULDRON I: FORMING THE POCKETS

On 3 October, on Guderian's left wing, the tanks of 47 Panzer Corps (17 and 18 PDs) rolled northward toward Karachev, deep behind Soviet 13 Army and into the rear of Maj.-Gen. Ia. G. Kreizer's 3 Army, threatening the entire Briansk Front with encirclement. Eremenko countered by attacking toward Seredina Buda (ca. 30 kilometers west of Sevsk) with two rifle divisions in an effort to halt Lemelsen's rampaging panzers, but soon found himself hard-pressed by the overwhelmingly superior German forces; facing extreme pressure on his front, flank, and rear, the Soviet general requested permission to withdraw to new positions, but his petition was denied by Marshal Boris Shaposhnikov (Chief of the Soviet General Staff).[18]

If the weak divisions of the Briansk Front were unable to slow the slashing pace of Guderian's panzer forces, the brave pilots and crews of the resurgent Soviet Air Force (VVS)[19] were more than willing to step into the breach. Despite the growing lateness of the year, flying conditions were still good—an advantage to both sides—and the German panzer spearheads were inevitably a prime target of Soviet combat planes. Noted Guderian on 5 October,

> On this day, as it happened, I gained a vivid impression of the liveliness of the Russian Air Force. Immediately after I had landed at Sevsk airfield, where 20 German fighters had also just come in, the Russians bombed it; this was followed by an air attack on the corps headquarters that sent the glass in the windows flying about our ears. I drove at once along the road of advance of 3 Panzer Division. Here too we were subjected to a series of bombing attacks by small groups of from three to six Russian bombers; but they flew high and their aim was consequently pretty inaccurate. The [2 Air Fleet] promised us stronger fighter cover for the 6th, so we could reckon on an improvement of the situation.[20]

Despite the valiant efforts of the VVS, the situation rapidly went from bad to worse for the unfortunate Eremenko. The lack of good radio communications, coupled with poor (or nonexistent) coordination between units, robbed the Briansk Front commander of his situational awareness, allowing Guderian's tankers and panzer grenadiers to easily outmaneuver their adversary. On 6 October, a company-size *Kampfgruppe* of 17 Panzer Division (13 tanks, four SPWs with a platoon of infantry, and two SP 20mm flak guns) was dispatched due west, bearing down on Briansk from behind. Eremenko was oblivious to the danger until the German battlegroup suddenly showed up right outside his headquarters (11 kilometers south of the city) and captured it after a sharp firefight. Although wounded, Eremenko was able to narrowly escape capture despite remaining at his command post until German tanks were barely 200 meters away (on 13 October, he would be wounded again in a German air strike and evacuated to Moscow).[21]

Continuing its rapid push, 17 Panzer Division, once again commanded by *Generalleutnant* Hans-Jürgen von Arnim,[22] seized a bridge over the Desna River that evening; the next morning (7 October), the division stormed into Briansk and captured the town of 87,000 in a coup de main. In a single stroke, a small German tank force had decapitated the leadership of the Briansk Front. Yet, despite its impressive performance as the spearhead of Lemelsen's 47 Panzer Corps, by 5 October 17 PD was down to just thirty operational tanks—one data point among many illustrating that for Guderian's panzer forces, and for Army Group Center writ large, the "margin for error was sometimes smaller than it appeared."[23]

Meanwhile, Nehring's 18 Panzer Division was linking up with infantry of Weichs's Second Army near Zhizdra to the northeast. The masterful operations of Lemelsen's two panzer divisions had resulted in the trapping of three Soviet armies. Briansk Front was now, in effect, split in two—Maj.-Gen. M. P. Petrov's 50 Army encircled at Diat'kovo; Kreizer's 3 Army, along with Gorodniansky's 13 Army, trapped in the area around the town of Trubchevsk south of Briansk. In recognition of its outstanding performance since the beginning of Barbarossa, Guderian's panzer group was upgraded in status to a panzer army on 6 October.[24]

In his diary, *Unteroffizier* Robert Rupp (17 PD) described his experiences inside the town of Briansk on 7 October. He and his comrades were engaged in brutal and costly combat in an urban setting while also pilfering fur coats from a Russian military barracks, for the weather was now uncomfortably cold, and the men were still without their winter clothing:

> We are to mop up inside the town. It's very cold. We sit around for a while. Tanks roll up along with personnel carriers. I meet up with the battalion commander and *Oblt.* Ostermeier, chief of the 9th Company, who suffered many losses in the street fighting. He won't send any more men into the city, because hardly anyone comes back in one piece. Partisans. Molotov cocktails. A hit by an anti-tank gun on one of the personnel carriers killed nine men. Our tanks inside the town can't do it all on their own. We don't want to fire high-explosive shells [*Sprenggranaten*] into the houses—there are too many civilians inside.
>
> We are ferried across the river [the Desna] in boats and go ashore at an embankment. A Russian [emerges] from the canal shaft, sopping wet, wounded, bleeding, and cries because he hasn't received a dressing. A difficult hour. We begin a mopping-up action. Tanks are in the town. Many of the houses are on fire or badly shot up. We clear the houses; doors and gates are opened and searched. . . . The company occupies a military barracks. Inside the clothes closet there are fur coats. Nöth gets hold of two marvelous sheepskin fur coats for us. Blankets are also found and lots of honey. I find a flute and an exercise book, which I take with me.
>
> It's getting dark so we move out. Many of us are outfitted with fur coats. The Second Battalion got the most of them, because they were the first ones into the town. Some of the officers also have fur coats. The commander offers 50 *Reichsmarks* for just one coat, but he gets no takers! We occupy a position on the edge of a settlement. The houses are really nice, true to the old way of building them. They are made totally out of wood, and only covered with clear slate. . . . Inside they are very clean [but] all the houses are deserted, so we have to blast the doors open. But before we can get comfortable, a messenger shows up: We have to move on. The company has a special assignment [*Sonderauftrag*]—seize some high ground and hold it. Once again, no sleep. Once again, a cold night. Stupidly, I didn't bring my fur coat with me but left it with the baggage train.[25]

Late on 8 October, Eremenko's eviscerated armies finally began to withdraw. In the days that followed (see "Briansk Cauldron II: The Pockets Cleared,"), significant elements of all three armies would succeed in escaping through the German blocking positions, for once again Guderian was more concerned with pushing on toward far-flung objectives than with committing his modest forces to encirclement rings, which, from his perspective, only impeded his progress.

Meanwhile, GFM von Bock's Army Group Center was also effectuating spectacular progress with its main attack some 200 kilometers to the north. Here, the powerful armored prongs of Bock's two other panzer groups had made short work of the Soviet defenses east of Smolensk and plunged deep into the Russian hinterland. On 4 October, Army Chief of Staff Halder observed with satisfaction that the offensive was "developing on a truly classic pattern."[26] On the morning of 7 October, the lead elements of 3 Panzer Group (now led by *Gen.d.Pz.Tr.* Hans Reinhardt) and *Generaloberst* Erich Hoepner's 4 Panzer Group—7 PD and 10 PD, respectively—joined hands at Viaz'ma, encircling four armies and part of a fifth of Soviet Western and Reserve Fronts. In anticipation of the linkup, Hoepner had written to his wife the day before, "We had good weather from 2 October until yesterday. Today, it's cold and windy. The situation is developing well. Tomorrow, I hope to be able to shake hands with Hoth, who is coming from the northwest. By then, almost 30 of Timoshenko's divisions ought to have been encircled. The approach taken was not the one I suggested, otherwise more would have been captured."[27]

In less than a week's time, Bock's infantry armies and panzer forces had ripped a 500-kilometer-wide breach in the Soviet front,[28] encircling dozens of Red Army divisions and hundreds of thousands of *Rotarmisten*. Elated by their success, the Army High Command (7 October) ordered the field marshal to begin the pursuit of the beaten enemy toward Moscow. So caught up was Hitler in the unfolding drama that he did not eat that day, which General Jodl (OKW) characterized as the "most crucial day of the whole Russian war," comparing it with Königgrätz, the decisive battle of the Austro-Prussian War in 1866. The next day (8 October), Jodl "repeated his triumphant verdict: 'We have finally and without any exaggeration won this war.'"[29] The day after that (9 October), the Reich Press Chief, Dr. Otto Dietrich—to be sure, not without Hitler's imprimatur—proclaimed to the world that, with the "smashing" (*Zertrümmerung*) of the Red Army before Moscow, "the campaign in the east has been decided."[30]

At Bock's headquarters in Smolensk, the verdict was about the same. Indeed, on 8 October, the war diary of Army Group Center noted, "Enemy Situation: Today as well the impression exists that at present the enemy has only weak forces available with which to contest the further advance of the army group on Moscow."[31] Far off at the front, however, the reality wasn't quite as reassuring to the soldiers doing the fighting and dying. As Guderian recollected,

> General [Geyr] informed me that the enemy opposite 4 Panzer Division had been reinforced. . . . The 4 Panzer Division's task for 9 October was to take Mtsensk. Descriptions of the quality and, above all, of the new tactical handling of the Russian tanks were very worrying. Our defensive weapons available at that period were only successful against the T-34 when the conditions were unusually favorable. The short-barrelled 75mm gun of the Panzer IV was only effective if the T-34 were attacked from the rear; even then a hit had to be scored on the grating above the engine to knock it out. It required very great skill to maneuver into a position from which such a shot was possible. The Russians attacked us frontally with infantry, while they sent their tanks in, in mass formation, against our flanks. They were learning. The bitterness of the fighting was gradually telling on both our officers and men. . . .
>
> For the first time during this exacting campaign, *Oberst* Eberbach gave the impression of being exhausted, and the exhaustion that was now noticeable was less physical than spiritual. It was indeed startling to see how deeply our best officers had been affected by the latest battles. What a contrast to the high spirits in evidence at the OKH and at Army Group Center![32]

THE SOVIET LEADERSHIP RESPONDS

The sheer speed and violence of the German attack had resulted in a breakdown of communications at all levels of the Soviet command system. Not only the front formations but the STAVKA as well seemed utterly ill informed about the real situation at the front. Then, on Sunday morning, 5 October, a Soviet fighter plane spotted a 24-kilometer-long German armored column moving undisturbed along the Warsaw highway from Spas-Demensk toward Iukhnov, about 175 kilometers southwest of Moscow. When he reported back, nobody believed him. He was ordered to fly out again and confirm; this time, he saw the German column approaching Iukhnov itself and, as if to add emphasis to his report, returned to base with damage from anti-aircraft fire. This was enough for Colonel Sbytov, Air Commander of the Moscow Military District, so he passed on the urgent intelligence to his superiors. For his efforts, he was accused by the NKVD of "encouraging panic" and his staff threatened with court-martial and execution. After a third reconnaissance mission confirmed that the Germans had now entered Iukhnov, Stalin was informed.[33]

Thus began the Soviet dictator's "Black Sunday." He ordered a withdrawal to the Mozhaisk Defense Line[34]—still incomplete but festooned with gun positions, anti-tank obstacles, dragon's teeth, and barbed wire—but with most of his armies now trapped at Viaz'ma and Briansk, at first he could only try to secure the line's most vital points with an ad hoc grouping of officer cadets, "destroyer" battalions, People's Militia, and NKVD and police units. It was also on this dreadful day, when the front before Moscow appeared to be crumbling, that Stalin dispatched an urgent order to General G. K. Zhukov (former Chief of the General Staff), recalling him from Leningrad and appointing him commander of the Western Front, with overarching responsibility for the defense of Moscow and its environs (on 10 October, the STAVKA combined the remnants of Western and Reserve Fronts into a new Western Front under Zhukov's command).

General Zhukov, who had managed to stabilize the situation at Leningrad, was now tasked to do the same on the approaches to Moscow. He immediately asked Stalin to begin to shift large reserves toward the Soviet capital; as a result, the State Defense Committee (GKO), the Party's Central Committee, and the Supreme Command took measures to halt the German advance. Troop movements got underway on 7 October to reinforce the concentric defensive belts west of the city. All told, fourteen rifle divisions, sixteen tank brigades, more than forty artillery regiments, and other units were siphoned from the STAVKA strategic reserve and adjoining fronts; these forces, however, badly understrength, amounted collectively to only about 90,000 men. Remnants of Soviet formations that had escaped the German encirclements were also shepherded into the defensive lines. Of course, this patchwork of formations was clearly inadequate to conduct a reliable defense, but it was all that could be mustered at the moment.[35] On 5 October, however, the STAVKA had ordered the formation of ten reserve armies east of Moscow.[36]

Stalin, clearly agitated by the unfolding disaster, asked Zhukov, "Are you sure that we will hold Moscow? I ask you about this with a pain in my soul. Tell me truthfully, as a communist." Zhukov's response, reflecting his uncompromising nature, was blunt and to the point: "We will, without fail, hold Moscow."

SETBACK AT MTSENSK

If, as Halder suggested, Typhoon was taking an altogether classical course, so too were those vexing logistical problems once more coming to the fore. Before Guderian could even contemplate driving north toward Tula, a factory town and the key to Moscow's southern defenses, he first needed to contend with his near-absent fuel reserves. After capturing Orel, Langermann-Erlencamp's 4 Panzer Division was temporarily unopposed on the road to Tula (175 kilometers to the northeast); yet, because of fuel shortages, he was unable to exploit his advantage. *Gen.d.Pz. Tr.* Geyr complained bitterly to Guderian about the bad fuel situation (*schlechte Betriebsstofflage*); moreover, the stocks of captured fuel were unfortunately small. On 5 October, Guderian lodged an urgent appeal with GFM Kesselring (2 Air Fleet) for 500 cubic meters of fuel (about 100,000 gallons) to be flown to an airfield at Orel, but the best the *Luftwaffe* field marshal could manage was 70 to 100 cubic meters the next day. Yet, as both Guderian and Geyr knew all too well, the future extent of their advance would depend in large measure on the availability of fuel.[37]

On 6 October, having received just enough fuel, the tanks of 4 Panzer Division resumed their march toward Tula;[38] however, after advancing less than 50 kilometers, they ran headlong into large numbers of Soviet T-34 and KV-1 tanks near Mtsensk. As one biographer of Guderian put it, "This was an awesome moment." And indeed it was: For the first time, the Germans encountered "in a big way" the threat that Guderian and Nehring (18 Panzer Division) had first confronted on the road to Smolensk in early July.[39] To put it bluntly, the tanks of 4 Panzer Division (the vanguard of *Kampfgruppe Eberbach*) were outfought by the T-34s and KV-1s of Maj.-Gen. D. D. Leliushenko's 1 Guards Rifle Corps, which displayed a tactical proficiency Guderian's panzer troops had yet to encounter.[40] In fact, 4 Panzer "had been dealt a crippling blow by an expertly managed Soviet counterstroke. . . . Now young Soviet commanders were learning that headlong attacks into prepared German positions were rarely successful and, as the war diary of 4 PD noted: 'The Russian was very skilled in directing his tanks, pulling back often, only to appear again in a flanking attack. In the course of the afternoon his heavy models inflicted heavy losses.'"[41]

Among the "heavy losses" sustained by Langermann-Erlencamp's stunned panzer troops were ten tanks (six a total loss, four damaged) and five artillery/flak guns; personnel losses amounted to ten killed and thirty-three wounded. Soviet T-34s and KV-1s, concealed among stands of birch trees in a tactically superior position, had struck the unsuspecting German vanguard with a barrage of 76.2mm anti-armor rounds, opening fire from outside the effective range of the panzers, whose shells ricocheted harmlessly off the thickly armored Soviet tanks. Several of the less well-armored and undergunned Panzer IIIs and IVs were split open by the heavier Russian tank shells; the complete commander's cupola flew off from one frontal hit. A battery of multipurpose "88s," supported by several light and medium field pieces, succeeded in destroying or damaging several T-34s (but paid a heavy price in doing so). And although 4 Panzer Division managed to knock out seventeen Russian tanks, it was the Red Army that held the field.[42]

Not only did the Soviet attack compel a German panzer division to lurch back in defeat, but as even the Germans acknowledged, the Soviets did not achieve their victory through numerical superiority. According to German estimates, the Russian tank force had amounted to about forty-five tanks (all models, including some BT light tanks), while 4 Panzer had fielded some fifty-six operational tanks on the eve of the battle. In addition, the Germans had advanced with a motorcycle infantry battalion (*Kradschützen-Bataillon*) and an 88mm flak battery, while a battalion of *Nebelwerfer* multiple-rocket launchers and two artillery battalions had furnished fire support. Much of this supporting force also sustained losses during the ensuing engagement.[43]

Some two weeks after the jolting setback at Mtsensk, *Generalmajor* von Langermann-Erlencamp submitted a disturbing analysis of his 4 Panzer Division's recent battles. Due to its trenchant insights—among them, recognition of the growing sophistication of Red Army tank tactics—it is excerpted here at length:

> In its battles, the 4 Panzer Division frequently encountered heavy Russian tanks. At first only a few appeared and could be driven off by concentrated artillery fire or bypassed. In a few especially favorable cases single heavy tanks were destroyed by direct hits from artillery.
>
> After taking Orel, the Russians employed their heavy tanks *en masse* for the first time. In several engagements it came to very hard tank battles, because the Russian tanks no longer let themselves [be] driven off by artillery fire.
>
> For the first time during the campaign in the east, in these battles the absolute superiority of the Russian 26-ton and [47]-ton tanks [T-34 and KV-1, respectively] over our Pz.Kpfw.III and IV was felt.
>
> The Russian tanks usually formed in a half circle, open[ed] fire with their 7.62cm guns on our panzers already at a range of 1,000 meters and deliver[ed] enormous penetration energy with high accuracy.
>
> Our 5cm [Pz III] tank guns can achieve penetrations only on vulnerable locations under very special favorable conditions at very close ranges under 50 meters. Our panzers are already knocked out at a range of several hundred meters. . . . The accuracy and penetration ability of the Russian 7.62cm tank guns are high.
>
> In addition to the superior weapons effectiveness and stronger armor the 26-ton [T-34] is faster, more maneuverable, and the turret traverse mechanism clearly superior. [Its] wide tracks allow wading of fords that can't be crossed by our panzers. The ground pressure is somewhat better than ours, so that in spite of the larger weight of the Russian tank the same bridges can be crossed as by our panzers. . . .
>
> The available facts and, above all, the impression that the Russians are aware of the technical superiority of their tank force must work out in time to be detrimental to our *Panzertruppen*. The previous attack energy and spirit will be weakened and lost due to a feeling of inferiority. The panzer crews know that they can already be knocked out at long range by enemy tanks and that they can achieve only a very minimal effect on enemy tanks in spite of the *availability of special ammunition*[44] fired at close range. (Author's emphasis)[45]

Langermann-Erlencamp goes on to explain, in quite sobering terms, how neither the 88mm gun nor the 105mm (10cm) artillery piece—both capable of being highly effective in an anti-tank role—was capable of dealing alone with the deadly challenge posed by the heavy, well-armed, and well-armored Russian tanks:

> Combating the Russian tanks with the 8.8cm flak or the 10cm guns can never by themselves be sufficient. Both guns are ponderous in comparison to the fast tanks and in most cases are already spotted, taken under fire and destroyed as they try to get into firing position. Alone in the one tank engagement between Orel and Mtsensk, two 8.8cm flak guns and a 10cm gun (all of the heavy defensive weapons

that were employed) were shot up and overrun. In addition these big-as-a-barn-door, unarmored guns present much too large and easily acquired targets.

From these experiences, our panzer forces must again be perfected in the shortest time so that the German soldier of today doesn't face the heavy tanks with the same primitive methods as in 1917 and 1918.[46]

The situation so alarmed Guderian that he temporarily abandoned the planned "rapid advance on Tula." In his memoir, he referred to 4 PD's "grievous casualties," while indicating that "this was the first occasion on which the vast superiority of the Russian T-34 to our tanks became plainly apparent."[47] (In fact, the superiority of the T-34 had been manifest from the very start of the war; yet the tank's many technical advantages had largely been negated by crew inexperience and poor tactical deployment.) Observed Kenneth Macksey,

All at once the situation swung hard against the Germans and for the first time Guderian lost hope. The tale of woe that fills the pages of *Panzer Leader* sincerely reflects his feelings at the time. The advance died in its tracks and twitched only fitfully in the moments when the state of the roads and the surrounding fields permitted. . . . Moreover options were no longer open for changes of direction and the achievement of surprise. The Russians easily read German intentions and skillfully sited their blocking positions.[48]

Although the town of Mtsensk would be captured by the Germans in the days ahead, the unexpected and staggering defeat there would help to hold up the advance of Geyr's 24 Panzer Corps on Tula for a critical period.

THE FALL *RASPUTITSA*: THE ADVANCE STALLS

It was not only the shocking reversal at Mtsensk that had stopped Guderian in his tracks. By the second week of October, the autumn rains, known in Russia as the *Rasputitsa* ("the time without roads"), had set in across the eastern front, dramatically slowing the pace of Army Group Center's pursuit of its beaten Russian foes.

On the night of 6/7 October 1941, it snowed for the first time, and it did so right in Second Panzer Army's area of operations. "It did not lie for long," Guderian recalled, "and, as usual, the roads rapidly became nothing but canals of bottomless mud, along which our vehicles could only advance at a snail's pace and with great wear to the engines."[49] In his diary, *Leutnant* Georg Kreuter (18 PD) lamented, "It is snowing and miserably cold [*hundekalt*]. I ride my 'Ivan' [a horse], but often I have to walk him, so that I can get warm again. At night we hole up in stinking shacks along the road. The pleasant times [bivouacking] under the open sky are now finally over."[50] Another soldier, attached to an assault gun battery near Orel, recalled,

> It was snowing! The wind drove thick clouds of snowflakes across the earth and the ground was already covered in a thin sheet of snow. Even the assault guns parked outside on the road had taken on a curious appearance. They were completely white as if covered in icing sugar! I recorded this first snowfall in my diary and went back inside to lie down again. When I awoke in the morning and glanced outside, the snow had already gone. But as a consequence the road was covered in mud and the land around totally soaked.[51]

Winter was closing in, and *Generaloberst* Guderian put in a request for winter clothing—he had done so before—but was informed that his panzer army would receive it in due course; moreover, he was "instructed not to make further unnecessary requests of this type. Still, I repeated my demands on several occasions, but the clothing did not reach the front."[52] (In fact, trains with winter clothing and equipment had been sitting on rail sidings near Breslau and Kraków since late August, but with the breakdown of the German logistical system in the east in fall and winter, they would fail to arrive in time.)

On 9 October, the war diarist of the army group complained, "The movement of panzer units off the main roads is at the moment not possible as a result of the bottomless, bad roads, due to bad weather."[53] Due to the dangers posed by icing, poor visibility, and soggy runways, the sorties of 2 Air Fleet plunged precipitously, from 1,400 on 6/7 October to just 139 on 9 October. On 12 October, Guderian's panzer army complained of unimaginable difficulties, as its columns were now advancing at the rate of one kilometer an hour. The bad weather also disrupted movement of supplies and evacuation of wounded to the rear. Yet the worst consequences of the *Rasputitsa* would not be felt until after mid-October.[54]

On 11 October, Klaus K., a soldier with Army Group Center, described the abrupt turn in the weather: "We've had snow and frost for two days. . . . [I]t's gradually getting unpleasant here. The roads are in an unimaginable state. No structured foundations and the vehicles can barely get through. You simply can't write or describe it. You have to have seen it. You're just happy to have a roof over your head at night."[55]

As supply lines broke down under the strain, desperately needed fuel and ammunition had to be flown in by air. Tanks were withdrawn from the line to pull guns and ammunition trucks out of the axle-deep mud. Soldiers' uniforms and footwear rapidly deteriorated; some troops went for days without bread and were forced to live off the land and from such local food supplies as the Russians had not destroyed. Horses also suffered terribly, and many collapsed and died under the strain; "in some cases," the C-in-C of Army Group Center noted with obvious stupefaction, "24 horses are required to move a single artillery piece" through the muck and the mud.[56]

According to *Oberst* von Liebenstein's immensely valuable postwar study, the period from 6 to 23 October witnessed just two days (13 and 17 October) free of rainfall or snow in the sector of Second Panzer Army.[57] The sector of Werner Kempf's 48 Panzer Corps (on Guderian's right wing) was one of the worst impacted by the autumn rains; on 12 October, the corps' war diarist noted, "The divisions are all completely fixed [by the mud]," while in rear areas hundreds of vehicles were left stranded in the muck and mire. Most significant in terms of Guderian's immediate operational objectives was that the incessantly bad weather, the concomitant lack of fuel and other critical supplies, and the ongoing Soviet resistance at Mtsensk would paralyze the advance of his spearhead (Geyr's 24 PzK) for more than two weeks.

On 16 October, General Lemelsen (47 PzK) recorded his impressions of the travails of the marching infantry; the admiration he felt for these "foot sloggers" (*Fusslatscher*), who bore their burgeoning hardships stoically, was universal within the *Ostheer*:

> In flurries of snow, interspersed with rain, we then went back to Karachev on this dreadfully rutted route, through deep holes and ruts with standing water. On the way, we encountered the companies of the foot divisions, who were also participating in this cauldron. The poor men tramped wearily through the mire with shelter halfs hung round their shoulders, on which fell the snow and rain. And then they take up their position, dig their foxholes in the wet forest ground, and camp in them, freezing in the icy cold and wet night. It really is a silent heroism exhibited here by the German soldiers in addition to their achievements in marching and combat. And all of that after they've marched over 1,000 km from Warsaw, day in, day out. The demands that are made on the physical capabilities of our soldiers exceed even those of the World War. I was thoroughly ashamed of myself when, as darkness fell, I returned to my quarters completely frozen through, and was able to dry myself both outside and inside in a warm room with the help of a vodka.[58]

On 26 October, *Leutnant* Joachim H., serving in 131 ID (just assigned to Guderian's Second Panzer Army), wrote a letter offering a graphic depiction of the impact of the squalid weather on man and machine alike. The letter is typical of so many posted by the *Landser* during this period of the war in the east:

> By and large, this war is anything other than pleasing in comparison with the campaign in the west. Since 22 June, we have been constantly deployed with our division or at least on the march: We crossed over the 2,000-km-limit long ago. . . . Unfortunately, the weather has brought us considerable difficulties in the last ten days. That concerns provisioning above all. What with the sodden clay roads, simply no vehicle can get through anymore. It's just a good thing that the enemy resistance is already so weak that almost no artillery ammunition

> is necessary, otherwise we could get into the tightest of spots. For six days now, neither rations, nor fuel, nor mail has arrived. Just as little mail leaves. . . . So we have to "feed ourselves from the land," as our orders so nicely put it. When there's nothing to find, those are golden words. At least a large-scale cull of hens, ducks, and geese has begun already, and some *Kolchos* (farms) still provide honey, oats, flour, etc., so that we can even bake bread ourselves. Hopefully, there'll be a frost soon so that these provisioning difficulties stop.[59]

Weather notwithstanding, by mid-October, the panzer and infantry corps of Second Panzer Army had reached the following general positions: Hermann Metz's 34 Army Corps (far right flank), between Sevsk and the Seim River (near the left-wing boundary of Army Group South); Kempf's 48 Panzer Corps, closing in on Fatesh in preparation for a push toward Kursk; Geyr's 24 Panzer Corps, far to the north, along the road to Tula, but still bogged down at Mtsensk (despite finally capturing the town on 11 October); Lemelsen's 47 Panzer Corps, still in action along the encirclement rings in the Briansk region; and, finally, Rudolf Kaempfe's 35 Army Corps, in action against the southernmost pocket centered on Trubchevsk.[60]

BRIANSK CAULDRON II: THE POCKETS CLEARED

Since encircling Soviet Briansk Front in early October, Weichs's Second Army and elements of Guderian's panzer army had made considerable progress in eliminating the bulk of the three Soviet armies trapped in the pockets north and south of the town of Briansk (50 Army and 3 and 13 Armies, respectively). According to the situation map of the German Army's Operations Branch, by 13 October, the northern pocket had been compressed to a small area north of Karachev, while in the south a larger pocket remained.[61]

As in the earlier cauldron battles of Minsk, Smolensk, and Kiev, encircled Soviet troops, in smaller or larger groups, sought repeatedly to flee to the safety of their own lines and, while sustaining staggering losses, sometimes inflicted serious casualties on the often tenuous German blocking positions. As the war diary of Army Group Center recorded on 14 October, "Particularly violent [*besonders heftig*] and repeated breakout attempts by the enemy, resulting in bitter, costly fighting for both sides. . . . The main burden of the enemy attacks falls on 18 Panzer Division, Infantry Regiment *Grossdeutschland* (which has lost five company commanders, among them [a Knight's Cross holder]), 29 Motorized Division, and 134 Infantry Division."[62] And many Soviet troops did succeed in breaking out—all told, some 13,000 men from 3 Army, 10,000 from 13 Army, and about 10 percent of 50 Army escaped captivity. Contributing to their escape was the fact that the Briansk region was densely forested, full of primeval marsh, thickets, and undergrowth, making German efforts to comb out stragglers a very dangerous business. Yet Guderian himself had helped to "sabotage" his remarkable achievement by failing to allocate sufficient forces of Lemelsen's 47 Panzer Corps to seal off the Trubchevsk pocket. As a result, the trapped Soviet 3 and 13 Armies mounted a successful breakout assault that Lemelsen was unable to block, enabling parts of a half dozen Soviet rifle divisions to slip through the loose cordon and escape to friendly positions near Tula.[63]

On 15 October, Ernst Guicking, a soldier in Second Army, offered a glimpse into the pitiless nature of the combat within the Briansk *Kessel*: "Combing the forests. Past a destroyed Russian baggage train. Terrible sight. Shredded horses and men. Dead gun molls. A destroyed battery. 300 dead Russians. Unimaginable. This was the revenge of the Regiment '*Grossdeutschland*' for their two fallen Knight's Cross holders."[64] Two days later, he wrote,

> The Russian is being squeezed on all sides and is trying to break through here. We are tripping all over fallen Russians here. It is truly a horror [*Es ist das wahre Grauen*]. Yesterday, 3,000 prisoners, a never-ending number of fatalities. Many women among them. No battlefield can look worse. It has become a habit for us in the last ten days. We have got used to this horror. Fighting here together with the *Grossdeutschland* regiment. And wherever these men are, the forest roars. . . . Our successes are great. But our losses are also bitter and painful. Such dear and brave comrades lie here in the Russian soil. Fate has been merciful to us so far. Yesterday we buried two bearers of the Knight's Cross. They were from the *Grossdeutschland* regiment. I can't say anything about the bigger picture. . . . The Russian would rather freeze in his foxholes than surrender. . . . We have been deployed with a special assignment since 2 October and so far there has been not a single day without battle. . . . Our task in all this will soon be done. The cauldron is just about to burst. . . . Well, it will come to an end sometime soon. It can't be much longer.[65]

On 17 October, Second Army and Second Panzer Army reported that the cauldron battle north of Karachev had finally come to an end. Soviet resistance south of Briansk, however, was not put down until 23 October. According to contemporary German estimates, the pocket battles around Briansk yielded some 100,000 prisoners, while Maj.-Gen. M. P. Petrov (50 Army) was killed in the fighting. (Note: In his postwar study, *Oberst* von Liebenstein recorded that, between 30 September and 20 October, Guderian's panzer troops alone had taken a total of 108,000 prisoners while capturing or destroying 257 tanks, 763 guns, 79 Pak, 93 flak, and 19 aircraft.[66] Yet, Guderian's former chief of staff acknowledged that it had not been possible to completely clear the difficult wooded terrain around Briansk of all Soviet forces and that, in the years ahead, this area would become a major center of Soviet partisan activity.)

On 20 October, Soviet resistance inside the much larger Viaz'ma pocket finally flickered out, with the attacking German Fourth and Ninth Armies, together with *Panzergruppen* 3 and 4, collecting more than 600,000 POWs. In summation, the massive encirclement battles across the front of Army Group Center had destroyed the Western and Reserve Fronts while badly damaging the Briansk Front. According to estimates by historian David M. Glantz, the three fronts collectively lost seven of their fifteen armies, sixty-four of ninety-five divisions, eleven of fifteen tank brigades, and fifty of sixty-two attached artillery regiments; equipment losses amounted to 6,000 guns and mortars and 830 tanks. All told, about 1 million Red Army troops were lost in these battles, of which approximately 700,000 were taken prisoner by the Germans. "By any measure," concluded Glantz, "the results were truly catastrophic."[67] In an order of the day (*Tagesbefehl*), Bock noted the result of the Viaz'ma-Briansk cauldron battles and offered up praise to his men: "This difficult battle, too, you have come through with honor, and, in doing so, completed the greatest feat of arms of the campaign! [*grösste Waffentat des Feldzuges!*]."[68]

Yet these historic German victories had come at quite a cost for the armies and panzer groups of Army Group Center. In a letter to Bock on 18 October, the commander of 7 Panzer Division, *Generalmajor* Hans Freiherr von Funck, informed the field marshal that, on 11/12 October, his division had lost nearly 1,000 men; that an entire battalion had been "literally . . . wiped out" in its blocking positions north of Viaz'ma.[69] In a letter to an unknown recipient (27 October), *Major* Werner Heinemann, a battalion commander in 23 ID, made no attempt to conceal the almost preternatural dreadfulness of his experiences along the front of the fragile German encirclement ring at Viaz'ma:

> The recent events of 10–15 October in the encirclement of Viaz'ma were the worst strain on the nerves. On 10 [October] my battalion struck a withdrawing Russian division; we took 7,000 prisoners on this one day alone. But to float around quite literally like tiny little islands in the rear area of a hundred-fold superior enemy army, cut off from all supplies and communications, surrounded on all sides in the immense forests by desperately fighting Russians—those were bitter days.
>
> We really breathed down their neck . . . but for us leaders, left to rely entirely on ourselves, that was a dreadful strain; I stood alone with my battalion for 6 days, for days at a time without any radio link to my regiment. And back home they were all rubbing their hands and saying: "Great! 6 armies in a cauldron and over half a million prisoners!" What do they know about what that means! Because each [Russian] has a weapon in his hand and wants, come what may, to get out of the cauldron, to get back to <u>his</u> home. Our slender ring gave way here and there on dozens of occasions, and <u>we</u> were the ones encircled. My God, those nights in the forests, icy nights in biting frost and snow!" (Emphasis in the original)[70]

The bitterness expressed by *Major* Heinemann about the sanitized version of events being fed the German people by Goebbels's (and *Wehrmacht*) propaganda was also a common theme in the letters and diary entries of front soldiers in the fall of 1941. Indeed, *Leutnant* Joachim H. (131 ID), in the letter of 26 October cited above, lashed out at the chauvinistic patriotism (*Hurrapatriotismus*) typical of the radio and press reports on the current situation in the east. About such reports "one could only shake his head," he wrote. "Such twaddle certainly isn't going to affect our good morale, but we're hardly in the mood for singing. . . . It's also wrong to depict the Russian soldier as an enemy that can easily be beaten. *Der Russe* is a tough fighter, and would rather let himself be cut to pieces than give way [*lässt sich eher in Stücke hauen, als zu weichen*]. And that totally aside from his good weaponry, which meets all modern standards."[71]

One is reminded of the sobering warning of *Generalmajor* Walther K. Nehring (18 PD) all the way back in July—to wit, these high loss rates should not be allowed to continue "if we do not intend to victor ourselves to death."

TULA I: THE ADVANCE

On 7 October, after the debacle of the day before, Geyr's 24 Panzer Corps renewed its attempt to capture Mtsensk, some 50 kilometers northeast of Orel (linear distance). Once again, the spearhead of Langermann-Erlencamp's 4 Panzer Division—the battlegroup led by *Oberst* Heinrich Eberbach, commander of the division's panzer regiment (35 Pz.Rgt.)—was sent reeling back in defeat with "heavy personnel and materiel losses." On 9 October, after restocking fuel and ammunition, *Kampfgruppe Eberbach* tried for a third time to seize the town. Despite Stuka support, the battle ended in another frustrating setback for the Germans. As recorded in the *Kriegstagebuch* of 4 PD, "Forward movement along the route of advance was not possible because of the superior weaponry of the Russian tanks (around 25). No Russian tanks hit, unfortunately again some personnel and materiel losses (four panzers destroyed, a few damaged, one 88mm anti-aircraft gun, one 100mm cannon, one [personnel carrier], one artillery observer destroyed)."[72] The unequal contest had consumed fully half of Eberbach's ammunition, while his panzer regiment was down to just thirty combat-ready tanks with no gains to show for its painful losses.[73] As the results of the battle along the Tula axis indicated, at least some units of the Red Army were learning how to fight, even to outperform, the depleted forces of the *Ostheer*.

On 10 October, "fresh instructions" arrived from army group; these included the capture of Kursk (far to the southeast), the final "mopping up" of the Briansk pockets, and the resumption of the stalled advance on Tula. Taken together, these operational tasks threatened to scatter Guderian's Second Panzer Army along eccentric axes of advance; moreover, they were to be carried out immediately. Attempts by Chief of Staff von Liebenstein to inquire about the priorities to be assigned to these missions went unanswered. Simply put, Guderian was being asked to do too much with too little, and besides, major mobile operations were currently out of the question due to the debilitating effects of the rainy season. As if to underscore the point, he recalled, "The next few weeks were dominated by the mud. Wheeled vehicles could only advance with the help of tracked vehicles. These latter, having to perform tasks for which they were not intended, rapidly wore out. Since chains and couplings for the towing of vehicles were lacking, bundles of rope were dropped from [aircraft] to the immobilized vehicles. The supplying of hundreds of such vehicles and their crews had now to be done by the *Luftwaffe*, and that for weeks on end."[74]

That same day (10 October), the irrepressible *Oberst* Eberbach tried again to seize Mtsensk. The state of his *Kampfgruppe* was anything but encouraging. As he recalled, "The forces were exhausted, had suffered setbacks, were wearing wet uniforms and were chilled through and through"; also, few hand grenades were available, and ammunition for machine guns was in short supply.[75] This time, however, in a deft maneuver ("In the end, it was boldness and surprise in this situation that offered the only chance for success"),[76] Eberbach's tanks and infantry managed to outflank Soviet defenses and press on in to the town, in the process overrunning a battery of BM-13 rocket launchers and an anti-aircraft battery. The defending Soviets counterattacked immediately with tanks, but the tactical situation had now changed to their detriment. As Eberbach later wrote, "Our tanks had taken up concealed and covered positions behind houses and in the gardens and allowed the Soviets to approach to point-blank range. Three Russian tanks [T-34s] were knocked out; the rest pulled back."[77] By mid-afternoon, Eberbach's spearheads were solidly dug in at Mtsensk. With the capture of the town,[78] the Germans were still 120 kilometers (linear distance) from Tula—stalled by weather, serious logistical problems, and increasingly effective Red Army opposition.

Still shaken by his disastrous encounter with the new Soviet tank models and what it portended for the future of the campaign ("the prospect of rapid, decisive victories was fading in consequence"),[79] Guderian submitted a report to army group; in it, he urged that a commission be dispatched at once to his sector of the front and that it consist of representatives of the Army Ordnance Office and the Armaments Ministry, as well as tank designers and builders. He also proposed rapid production of an anti-tank gun with the penetrating power to knock out the T-34.[80]

By 16 October, ongoing attrition had reduced Guderian's panzer army to 271 tanks;[81] none of his five panzer divisions possessed more than 82 tanks (Model's 3 PD), while 4 Panzer Division had just 38 operational tanks, and 9 Panzer Division (48 PzK) had but 23.[82] (By 20 October, 9 PD, still a long way off from Kursk,[83] was reporting seven tanks ready for action!) Personnel losses had also been grim: During the first ten days of October, Second Panzer Army had sustained losses of more than 2,000 men; by 20 October, it lost an additional 2,300, bringing its total casualties since the beginning of Barbarossa to 45,643. And while the panzer army had received a number of replacements, they lacked the combat experience and toughness of the older men.[84]

Meanwhile, Guderian had written home to his wife, exulting that recent German operations had "now destroyed the great mass of the Russian army. There cannot be too many good [Soviet units] left." Betraying his ignorance of the seasonal conditions in Soviet Russia (the autumn rains were about to transform much of the terrain into a "sodden bog"), he continued, "Now we're hoping for good, dry weather, at least for 14 days; then the main task is probably achieved; otherwise, it could last much longer."

In his letters to Margarete at this time, the strong-willed and steadfast panzer general often adopted a very different tone, illustrating how the grinding rigors of the campaign in the east managed, over time, to wear down even the toughest of men. On 11 October, he noted his need to "unburden my heart to another human being." Although he seems to have enjoyed good relations with his staff, he wrote, "As an older person—I am ever more isolated and the young people increasingly keep their distance. In spite of the very nice way of life in my staff, I feel this more and more." Four days later (15 October), Guderian admitted to experiencing "many emotions" and found himself reflecting on "lovelier and generally more carefree times." He was also worried about the condition of his men, for whom "one must be a good example . . . and bring himself to merriment, a daily new struggle." Privately, his letters were slipping more and more into fantasies about his good life at home with Margarete, whose absence he seemed to sense more heavily with each passing day. This was in stark contrast to his portrayal of life at the front (21 October): "Here there is no personal touch, no spirit, no contentment. In this country, the beauty is just as tramped down as the spirit. Everything has become bleak, mechanical, heartless machinery, hideous and squalid, indescribably feeble. One has to have seen it to know what it's like."[85]

Yet, however downcast his private thoughts, Guderian had a war to win; thus he was soon again on the march. On 23 October, the panzer general—having finally brought up enough supplies and reinforced by elements of Lemelsen's 47 Panzer Corps (now free of their Briansk cauldron duties)—resumed his drive on Tula. Despite the continuing rainfall and the corresponding terrain challenges, he had no choice but to do so: He had gotten wind of the *Luftwaffe*'s intent to shift a large number of Kesselring's Stuka formations to the Crimea,[86] and he had to act before that happened. This time, Walter Model's 3 Panzer Division spearheaded the attack and managed to push its way through Soviet field positions northwest of Mtsensk that included bunkers with armored cupolas. Two days later (25

October), lead German elements captured the town of Chern, 28 kilometers northeast of Mtsensk but still 95 kilometers from Tula.

On 25 October, a planned reorganization of the right wing of Army Group Center took effect. The 34 and 35 Army Corps, along with Kempf's 48 Panzer Corps (less its 25 ID [mot.]), were transferred from Guderian's panzer army and reassigned to Weichs's Second Army. In exchange, Guderian received *Gen.d.Inf.* Gotthard Heinrici's 43 Army Corps (31 and 131 IDs) and *Gen.d.Inf.* Karl Weisenberger's 53 Army Corps (112 and 167 IDs). "The task of *2. Panzerarmee*," Guderian noted, "was now to advance on Tula, while the new Second Army was to head eastward: that is to say, we were once again going in divergent directions."[87]

Despite bad roads, blown bridges, minefields, and perpetual fuel shortages, progress along the Tula axis continued at a steady pace. Corduroy roads were laboriously constructed over long distances to ensure that the advancing troops would at least receive a minimum of supplies. To furnish his attacking forces with the requisite combat power, Guderian had consolidated the bulk of his remaining armor into the battlegroup led by *Oberst* Eberbach. His *Kampfgruppe*'s order of battle now comprised the panzer regiment of 4 Panzer Division, the panzer regiment of 3 Panzer Division, and a battalion of tanks from 18 Panzer Division (I./Pz.Rgt. 18), giving Eberbach a total of six *Panzer-Abteilungen* with some 150 tanks.[88] ("Panzer Brigade Eberbach" would continue to operate as Guderian's spearhead through late November.)

By 27 October, with a battalion of *Oberst* Walter Hörnlein's Infantry Regiment *Grossdeutschland* riding on the tanks and supported by the *Luftwaffe*, Eberbach's group had taken Plavsk (roughly 36 kilometers northeast of Chern) and advanced to a point just 33 kilometers south-southwest of Tula.[89] By October 29, the lead German tanks, taking advantage of some light frosts that hardened the ground, had bolted to within four kilometers of Tula.[90] Bitter fighting took place in Tula's suburbs and around the estate of Count Leo Tolstoy (which the Germans tried not to damage). Fallen *Landser* were buried next to the author's grave.

On 30 October, Eberbach, attempting to capitalize on the momentum of his thrust, tried to seize Tula in a rapid strike. At 0530 hours, he attacked with some sixty tanks and several battalions of infantry. Although Soviet defenses were thin—the city was garrisoned by militiamen and some anti-aircraft and NKVD troops—they mounted stubborn resistance, inflicting painful losses upon Eberbach's infantry (three company commanders were killed). Firing over open sights, Soviet 37mm anti-aircraft guns damaged several German tanks. Unable to advance into Tula without infantry support, his ammunition almost exhausted, Eberbach pulled his forces back to regroup. That night, major Soviet tank reinforcements began to arrive by rail, soon to be followed by three rifle divisions; the next day (31 October), the Russians counterattacked unsuccessfully in an effort to hurl back the Germans from the southern outskirts of the city. Nevertheless, *Oberst* Eberbach's "window of opportunity" had finally been slammed shut.[91]

While Eberbach's sudden push to the periphery of Tula was an impressive achievement, it would prove to be the capstone of Guderian's autumn offensive—his spearhead now stymied some 160 kilometers south of Moscow. Despite every effort, the Germans had failed to capture the city, which continued to block the road to the Soviet capital and could not be taken frontally; moreover, in addition to having geographical features that favored the defense, it boasted a heavy armaments industry that was able to supply the defending Soviet 50 Army (now commanded by Lt.-Gen. I. V. Boldin) directly from its factories. And just as Eberbach's battlegroup had reached the south end of Tula, 50 Army began to receive major reinforcements from Soviet reserves; soon it would be solidly dug in around the city with six rifle divisions and two tank brigades.[92]

Guderian's offensive had been carried beyond its Clausewitzian culmination point, thus becoming vulnerable to sudden reversal and defeat.[93] Hitler and his High Command (OKW and OKH), however, viewed the matter rather differently; indeed, as October turned to November and the rains of the *Rasputitsa* yielded to the arctic frosts of the Russian winter, they continued to be seduced by distant objectives and the unshakable conviction that their exhausted armies could still be lashed and driven to victory. Meanwhile, the troops of Heinrici's 43 Army Corps had, as of 29 October, failed to receive an issue of bread for almost ten days.[94]

On 31 October, Guderian wrote again to Margarete, "Our situation here is annoying [brought on] by scarcity of supply and heavy rainfall and the abysmal roads. Replenishment almost fails and the troops can only move with extreme slowness. We have nonetheless reached the southern outskirts of Tula, but we must close our ranks and take a deep breath before this important industrial city can be taken."[95] Unfortunately, the rain and frost would render the logistical situation of Guderian's panzer group around Tula even more precarious in the days ahead, as he became increasingly dependent upon captured horse-drawn *panje* wagons and armored half-tracks (SPW) to move even a bare minimum of supplies forward. As the temperatures plummeted, so too did the morale of the men, who were not prepared—mentally or materially—for living outdoors in freezing weather.

TULA II: THE FAILURE

By 30 October 1941, the worn-out formations of Army Group Center had come to a temporary halt along and east of the Mozhaisk Defense Line, their positions running (north to south) from Kalinin through Volokolamsk, Naro-Fominsk, and Aleksin (on the Oka River), to the outskirts of Tula; the army group's enormous front line then swung southwest to Orel, before heading due south to the outskirts of Kursk. Since the start of Operation Typhoon, GFM von Bock's divisions had advanced 230 to 260 kilometers closer to Moscow, with units of Fourth Army and 4 Panzer Group now little more than 50 to 75 kilometers from the Soviet capital. Conversely, Bock acknowledged that his army group's losses had become "quite considerable," with officer losses being such that more than twenty battalions were now commanded by lieutenants.[96] For the stern, austere field marshal it must have been but a small consolation that, on the morning of 2 November, elements of Weichs's Second Army—the remnants of 9 PD supported by 95 ID—finally succeeded in storming into Kursk and capturing the city by day's end.[97]

With the momentum of Typhoon broken and Army Group Center dangling at the end of an increasingly tenuous supply line some 1,000 kilometers in length, the culmination point of the entire Barbarossa project had been reached. In a letter to his wife, Hoepner (4 PzG) acknowledged the radical change in the situation: "The weather is so ghastly at the moment that all roads have become heavy. Everything has ground to a halt. It's not possible to move troops. Neither fuel nor ammunition or provisions reach the front. Aircraft can't start, because they either sink into the airfields or can't be supplied with fuel, or rain and fog make orientation impossible" (emphasis in the original).[98]

On 1 November, Bock gave vent to his growing frustration: "The situation is enough to drive one to despair and filled with envy I look to the Crimea, where we are advancing vigorously in the sunshine over the dry ground of the steppe and the Russians are scattering to the four winds. It could be the same here if we weren't stuck up to our knees in mud. . . . The Army High Command was again briefed on our desperate situation by [my Chief of Staff] Greiffenberg."[99]

"On 7 November," recalled Guderian in *Panzer Leader*, "we suffered our first severe cases of frostbite";[100] by mid-November, Army Group Center's total casualties from frostbite had climbed to 400 a day. Adding to army group's growing list of difficulties was that Kesselring's 2 Air Fleet headquarters, along with much of his air fleet, was withdrawn and transferred to the Mediterranean theater of war, leaving Bock almost entirely dependent on Richthofen's understrength 8 Air Corps for air support. The time had come to suspend operations, establish a strong winter defensive line, and build up strength to support a resumption of offensive operations in the spring. Instead, following a rather perfunctory debate, the Germans decided to make one final lunge for Moscow after stocks of ammunition and fuel were rebuilt and a permanent frost had set in (freezing the roads and making them again traversable).

The prime movers behind this badly ill-advised decision were Bock and Halder; moreover, the Chief of the Army General Staff, still convinced that the Red Army was on the verge of collapse, was, as late as the second week of November, still imagining objectives hundreds of kilometers beyond Moscow.[101]

German historian Johannes Hürter argued that the "catastrophe" for Germany did not begin with the Soviet winter offensive in December 1941; rather, it was the "fatal decision" to resume Typhoon in November: "The recklessness with which the final offensive on Moscow was ordered is incomprehensible, and the responsibility belongs not only to Halder, but even more to Bock, because this most important commander of the *Ostheer* was much closer to the reality of the front than was the Chief of the General Staff."[102]

The accumulation of stocks by Army Group Center proceeded at an agonizing pace. "The armies," observed Bock on 14 November, "are all complaining about serious supply difficulties in all areas—rations, munitions, fuel, and winter clothing. With the limited number of trains in use it is impossible to do anything about it. Naturally this has significantly complicated the attack preparations."[103] While Bock fretted, Zhukov was busy shoring up his defenses in the woods and hamlets along the approaches to Moscow. Fortifications were expanded and laid out in depth; in the first two weeks of November, Soviet forces around the capital received an additional 100,000 men, 300 tanks, 2,000 guns, and more anti-tank guns. In contrast, Bock's army group received no reinforcements at all during this period; not only that, but throughout this lull in the fighting, it continued to incur casualties in local battles unable to alter the strategic calculus. For example, from 10 to 13 November, Gotthard Heinrici's 43 Army Corps of Guderian's Second Panzer Army sustained 706 combat losses (killed and wounded) while also losing 180 men to frostbite.[104]

The final operational plan (approved by Hitler on 30 October) called for two mobile groupings to strike the flanks of Soviet Western Front, envelop Moscow from the north and south, and encircle Soviet forces by linking up well behind the Soviet capital near Orekhova-Zueva and Kolomna. Reinhardt's 3 Panzer Group and Ninth Army were to form the northern pincer, advancing through Klin and across the Volga-Moscow Canal. In the south, Guderian's panzer army was to drive northeast through Tula and Kashira to unite with its "sister" group. In retrospect, the objectives set by Hitler and the OKH were totally out of touch with reality. And certainly so at a time when Guderian's panzer divisions were (collectively) down to perhaps 200 operational tanks,[105] while the combat strength of his infantry averaged about fifty men per company.

On the "raw and misty morning" of 15 November 1941, Army Group Center began the final phase of Operation Typhoon. At first, Bock's tanks—painted white to blend with the landscape, now blanketed by a light, dry snow—made surprisingly good progress, even if the shortened days, low-hanging clouds, and occasional snow flurries restricted their air cover. And if the troops were unaccustomed to temperatures of −10°C to −20°C, at least the armor could now move cross-country over the frozen ground. But this, "the

Germans were uneasily aware, was not the real Russian winter. Fighting then would be altogether different."[106]

Guderian's attack, however, was preceded by a serious crisis, when elements of 112 Infantry Division (53 AK), in position south of Dedilovo protecting the panzer army's right flank, were suddenly overrun by fresh Siberian troops supported by tanks, resulting in a collective panic. This happened on 17 November. About it, he later wrote,

> Before judging their performance it should be borne in mind that each regiment had already lost some 400 men from frostbite, that as a result of the cold the machine guns were no longer able to fire and that our 37mm anti-tank gun had proved ineffective against the T-34. The result of all this was a panic, which reached back as far as Bogorodisk. This was the first time that such a thing had occurred during the Russian campaign, and it was a warning [*ernstes Warnungszeichen*] that the combat ability of our infantry was at an end and that they should no longer be expected to perform difficult tasks.[107]

As a result, Guderian's attack did not go in until 18 November, but when it did—with the *Luftwaffe* providing effective support—it also made good initial progress. Attempting to seize Tula in a pincer attack,[108] Guderian struck the seam of Soviet Western and Southwestern Fronts, the remaining tanks of Geyr's 24 PzK (concentrated in *Kampfgruppe* Eberbach) working their way forward deliberately in an effort to encircle Red Army forces defending the city from both the east and the west. After penetrating the Soviet defenses—German 88mm flak guns picking off several T-34s and KV-1s along the way—Geyr's panzers fanned out: 3 Panzer Division (now led by *Generalmajor* Hermann Breith)[109] turning inward toward Tula with fifty tanks, 17 Panzer Division (now assigned to 24 PzK) bolting north toward Venev with fifteen tanks, and 4 Panzer Division pushing toward Stalinogorsk with thirty-five tanks.[110] Also on this first day of the offensive, 4 PD captured Dedilovo and seized a bridgehead across the Upa River southeast of Tula. Farther to the southeast (on Guderian's long right flank) reconnaissance troops of Weisenberger's 53 Army Corps reached the western edge of Epifan' and the Don River.[111]

Guderian had launched his new attack with a total strength on paper of 12.5 divisions (including the reinforced IRGD); however, Second Panzer Army's actual combat strength amounted to barely 4 divisions.[112] Moreover, his army's mobility was now seriously degraded due to the loss of thousands of trucks and other motor vehicles. (As of 5 November, only 45 percent of trucks/motor vehicles [18,800] were fully operational, given a strength of 42,200 on 22 June 1941.) As each day passed, his thoughts and concerns turned ever more anxiously to the increasingly dire predicament of his panzer troops. His visits to the front revealed evidence of growing privations among the men, resulting from shortages of boots, shirts, socks—in fact, of winter clothing in general. Alarmingly, not simply rank-and-file soldiers but senior officers as well were now showing signs of exhaustion.

On 21 November, GFM von Bock, following the initial success of the renewed offensive on both flanks of his army group, committed his only reserve division to the fighting, influenced, it seems, by his recollections of the Battle of the Marne in 1914, when—in the German mythology of the Great War—the younger Moltke had seen victory torn from his grasp by his failure to commit his final battalions to battle. At this critical juncture, the increasingly exhausted field marshal seems to have been gripped by a "strange, ambivalent attitude"[113]—one moment convinced that a final push would destroy the enemy; the next seized by serious doubts about the ultimate outcome of the battle. Be that as it may, he could not have failed to notice that his divisions were literally crumbling before his eyes. As he put in his diary,

> Drove from Gzhatsk to 7 Army Corps. The Commanding General has been visibly affected by the heavy fighting and described the pitiful state of his divisions, whose strength is spent.
>
> Losses among the officers, in particular, are making themselves felt. Many second lieutenants are leading battalions, one first lieutenant leads a regiment, regimental combat strengths of 250 men, also the cold and inadequate shelter, in short: in his opinion the corps can do no more. I gave him a word of encouragement and said that I wasn't demanding major combat operations from him at present. . . .
>
> The whole attack is too thin and has no depth. Based on the number of divisions, as seen from the green table, the ratio of forces is no more unfavorable than before. In practice the reduced combat strengths—some companies have only 20 and 30 men left—the heavy officer losses and the overexertion of the units in conjunction with the cold give a quite different picture. Still, in spite of everything we might succeed in cutting off several enemy divisions west of the Istra reservoir. But it is doubtful if we can go any farther. The enemy can move everything he has to Moscow. But my forces are not up to a concentrated, powerful counterattack.[114]

That same day (21 November), Guderian paused briefly to pen a decidedly gloomy (and bitter) missive to his beloved Margarete:

> The icy cold, the lack of shelter, the shortage of clothing, the heavy losses of men and equipment, the wretched state of our fuel supplies, all this makes the duties of a commander a misery and the longer it goes on the more I am crushed by the enormous responsibility [*ungeheure Verantwortungslast*] that I have to bear, a responsibility that no one, even with the best will in the world, can share.

> The demands on the troops are enormous and their performance is admirable. There is no support from above. I must muddle along on my own. Yesterday I was on the brink of despair and my nerves were at an end. Today an unexpected battle success by the brave panzer divisions has given me new hope. Whether it continues remains to be seen. I have been at the front three days running in order to form a clear picture of the conditions there.[115]

On 24 November, Guderian got another temporary lift to his spirits when lead elements of 17 Panzer Division (24 PzK), now commanded by *Oberst* Rudolf-Eduard Licht, captured Venev (50 kilometers south of Kashira) despite serious enemy opposition, knocking out a large number of Soviet tanks in the process; however, 17 PD—its 39 Pz.Rgt. now down to just five operational tanks[116]—had reached the end of its combat effectiveness. (As panzer soldier Erich Hager, a tank radio operator in the division, scribbled in his diary, "Flak guns shot a lot of our tanks to pieces. . . . We've been quite disheartened today.")[117] Just as staggering is the fact that Eberbach's battle group (to which elements of 17 PD were attached) was now down to just thirty-two operational tanks.[118]

Ominously, as temperatures plunged, the panzer army's intelligence detected fresh Siberian troops detraining near Riazan', about 100 kilometers east of Kashira. In addition, Lt.-Gen. I. V. Boldin's 50 Army, defending doggedly at Tula, struck Guderian's front and flank with repeated counterstrokes. With his own troops running out of fuel, ammunition, and operational vehicles (just 108 combat-ready tanks),[119] the advance of his panzer army slowly jerked to a halt. The panzer general now pleaded for the offensive to be broken off, but neither GFM von Bock nor anyone at OKH had the authority to make such a decision without Hitler's imprimatur.[120]

Contributing to Guderian's growing list of challenges was the increasingly robust activity of Russian air forces. On 24 November, the war diary of Second Panzer Army recorded, "Intense enemy air activity. Attacks by bombers and low-flying aircraft occasioning casualties. The troops regret the absence of our own aircraft."[121]

Meanwhile, on 22 November, 35 Panzer Regiment (4 PD) had seized Stalinogorsk (40 kilometers southeast of Tula). Although Guderian had only intended to occupy the town to cover his right flank as he enveloped Tula, the Soviets "had other ideas." Mounting a major counterattack, they recaptured the town on 26 November, compelling Geyr at 24 Panzer Corps to commit elements of 6 Panzer Regiment (3 PD) to restore the situation. The ensuing battle, however, went badly for the Germans, with a company of tanks virtually destroyed after losing its commander, five Pz IIIs, and three Pz IVs. Once again, the Soviets were learning.[122]

As the fighting surged back and forth, by 25 November, in a bold advance, reconnaissance forces of Licht's 17 PD were just three kilometers south of Kashira[123]—and barely 100 kilometers (linear distance) southeast of Moscow—where they met strong enemy resistance. The next day, infantry of Weisenberger's 53 Army Corps, crossing the Don River southeast of Tula, fell upon the Siberian 239 Rifle Division, capturing forty-two guns and taking 4,000 prisoners. Simultaneously, 29 ID (mot.)[124] attacked the Siberians from the east and managed to encircle them.

The next morning (27 November), Guderian visited Lemelsen's headquarters,[125] where he learned that a crisis had arisen in the sector of 29 ID (mot.) during the night: Abandoning their heavy weapons and vehicles, the mass of the Siberian rifle division had managed to break out to the east, inflicting serious casualties on the weak German defensive perimeter. Guderian quickly made his way to the hardest hit of the regiments (71 IR):

> At first I was of the opinion that a failure of reconnaissance and security arrangements had been the cause of the misfortune. Reports by the battalion and company commanders, however, made it quite clear that the troops had done their duty and had been simply overwhelmed by numerical superiority. The great number of dead, all in full uniform and with their weapons in their hand, were grim proof of the truth of what I had heard. I did my best to encourage the badly shaken soldiers and to help them get over their misfortune. The Siberians—though without their heavy weapons and vehicles—had slipped away because we had just not had the strength to stop them. This was the most disturbing single factor of the day. The motorcyclists of [29 ID (mot.)] set off at once in pursuit, but in vain.[126]

For Guderian, 27 November brought another disturbing event. The Soviet 1 Guards Cavalry Corps, hastily assembled by Stalin and Zhukov—and including tanks, combat engineers, and a unit of the new BM-13 *Katyusha* (Little Kate) multiple-rocket launchers—infiltrated the badly scattered picket lines of 17 Panzer Division, counterattacked, and drove the Germans back from Kashira. In doing so, the Soviets had not only relieved the pressure on Tula but also put a definitive end to Guderian's advance on Moscow. Indeed, as Bock commented on the situation in his diary, it was a "black day for Second Panzer Army! . . . The enemy pushed very hard from the north through Kashira against the spearhead of Panzer Brigade Eberbach."[127]

In the final days of November, Guderian again turned his attention to Tula, whose capture was now his "most urgent task. . . . Until we were in possession of this communications center and its airfield we had no hope of continuing to advance either northwards or eastwards."[128] The panzer general planned to seize the city in a double envelopment, with Geyr's 24 Panzer Corps attacking from the north and east and Heinrici's 43 Army Corps from the west. Yet Guderian harbored no illusions about the task at hand. Like Army Group Center writ large, he was, in effect, running out of troops and weapons: 4 Panzer Division had just twenty-one combat-ready tanks and eighteen artillery pieces, while the corps artillery of 24 Panzer Corps could muster but twelve guns.

From 27 to 29 November, the remaining infantry of Gotthard Heinrici's 43 AK (31 and 131 IDs), holding a sector of Second Panzer Army's front northwest of Tula, at last succeeded in breaking through the Soviet defensive line at Aleksin and capturing the town. With this modest victory, however, the offensive power of the corps was finally broken. Two days later (1 December), the Russians began to counterattack. On the same day, Heinrici wrote to his wife,

> At the moment we are in dire straits [*in äusserster Bedrängnis*]. The enemy is wildly attacking our newly won positions. Our men are exhausted in the extreme. Moreover, it's −20 degrees [Celsius] and an icy north wind drives great clouds of snow across the landscape. The situation has hardly ever been so bad [*ist so übel wie kaum*] and we fear the most unpleasant consequences. What's most threatening about the situation is that our people have reached the end of their strength.
>
> On the northern front opposite Moscow Kluge [Fourth Army] has achieved very considerable successes. South of the city, by Tula, and in our area, Guderian keeps trying to do more with insufficient resources. We are the ones suffering. Only one thing is clear to us—that it can't go on like this much longer. Our losses are quite considerable. The demands upon the men [are] enormous [*die Beanspruchung der Leute übermenschliches*].[129]

On 2 December, under clear skies, with temperatures having plunged to −20°C in the sector of Second Panzer Army,[130] Guderian began his final assault on Tula, Geyr's 24 Panzer Corps again moving into action.[131] When the *Generaloberst* visited his forward command post at Yasnaya Polyana (seven kilometers south of Tula) to receive a status report, he learned that 3 and 4 PDs, supported by IRGD, had surprised the enemy and broken into their forward positions on the outskirts of the city; however, the attackers had failed to fully penetrate the Russian defenses. The next day (3 December), the attack went forward in a blizzard. Although the icy roads greatly hampered movement (the low for the day was −8°C),[132] the vanguard of Langermann-Erlencamp's 4 Panzer Division, supported by IRGD and getting in behind Tula, was able to cut the vital Moscow-Tula railway and capture six enemy guns before finally reaching the Tula-Serpukhov road (27 kilometers north of Tula),[133] approaching to within 15 kilometers of the forward positions of Heinrici's 43 Army Corps.[134] Given the circumstances, it was a profound tactical achievement, but it also signified the end of Geyr's strength and of his fuel supply as well.

While the attackers still sought to claw their way forward, on 4 December Soviet reinforcements began to arrive, threatening the exposed flanks of 24

Panzer Corps. Infantry Regiment *Grossdeutschland* came under attack, and its line shattered; unable to execute a fighting withdrawal, even this elite unit "broke and ran." The neighboring 3 Panzer Division recorded the disaster in its war diary: "A panic broke out, the town was lost, a part of Infantry Regiment *Grossdeutschland* was overrun and cut down, at times murdered. Others fled back through the forests to the southeast."[135] (In *Panzer Leader*, Guderian does not appear to mention this grim defeat of IRGD.) Similar scenes unfolded farther north, where *Oberst* Licht's 17 Panzer Division, holding the northern flank of Geyr's panzer corps, was also strongly attacked. In the sector of 3 Panzer Division, serious fighting had broken out in the wooded country east of Tula. Putting lipstick on a pig—to employ an amusing (yet appropriate) idiom—Guderian brushed off this disastrous day with a laconic remark: "Only limited progress was made on this day."[136]

As Guderian acutely realized, one of the "decisive factors" affecting the entire operation was whether Heinrici's 43 Army Corps still possessed sufficient strength to close the ring around Tula from the west and make contact with 4 Panzer Division north of the city. On 3 December, the panzer general visited Heinrici's headquarters at Griasnovo to make a personal assessment of the combat strength of his army corps. The next morning (4 December), Guderian drove to the headquarters of the 31 Infantry Division and, from there, to its 17 Infantry Regiment and to that regiment's Jäger Battalion (III./IR 17). He recalled the moment in his memoir:

> This was my old Goslar Jäger unit, where I had started my military career and whose 11th Company I had commanded in 1920–22. In lengthy conversation with the company commanders I raised the serious question of whether the troops still possessed enough offensive strength for the task that lay ahead of them. The officers did not attempt to hide their anxieties, but in answer to my question whether the troops could attack successfully they replied that they could. "We can knock the enemy out of his positions once more." [*Einmal wollen wir den Feind schon noch aus seinen Stellungen stossen.*] Whether the other units of 43 Army Corps were as energetic as my old Goslar Jägers remained unknown. But in any event the impressions I gained from this battalion decided me to try the attack once again.[137]

Having received his orders, *Gen.d.Inf.* Heinrici made his attack preparations, but he did not attack on this day (4 December). The thermometer dropped to −16°C.[138] *Luftwaffe* reconnaissance reported major enemy forces advancing south from Kashira, with vigorous Russian fighter screens preventing more detailed observation.

The bitter cold, the strong winds, and the deep snow made just about any activity physically and mentally exhausting. Without proper winter clothing and exposed to the dreadful (and deadly) indifference of nature, the men stripped dead *Rotarmisten* of their coveted winter coats—even sawed off their legs for their felt-lined boots—and stalked local villages to "requisition" whatever items of warmth they could lay hands on (in photographs of German soldiers from this period, they often look like gypsies—or perhaps mummies—their worn-out uniforms concealed beneath the most imaginative ensemble of peasant clothing [both men's and women's]). To keep their vehicles running, *Landser* often lit fires under them to warm the engines, even though this consumed precious petrol. To ensure proper functioning of their rifles, the men placed the rifle bolts in (comparatively) warm places, such as their pockets, and would "not insert them until the enemy had closed to within 50 [meters] lest the frozen component fail at the moment of truth."

> In such dangerously cold conditions, German units typically occupied trenches and firing lines during the day, and left only token forces during the night. Generally housed in nearby settlements, rats, disease, lice, and other vermin brought a whole new level of discomfort. The absence of appropriately warm, layered, and breathable clothing promoted dehydration, hypothermia, and slurred speech, as well as degraded judgment and coordination,[139] and impeded maintaining proper hygiene. Eating poor-quality food and snow only worsened these cold-weather maladies. To avoid unnecessary exposure during elimination *Landser* were known to cut flaps into their trouser rears. With heavy physical exertion that included digging trenches from the hard, frozen earth German soldiers soon became emaciated.[140]

If Heinrici had failed to attack, he did have time on 4 December to make an expansive entry in his personal journal. Without (hopefully) being guilty of "*Landser* pathos," I find that the general's observations lay out in staggering detail the immense trials now faced by the German soldier on the eastern front. He begins by noting that his men are without proper shelter (*Unterkunft*) from the arctic conditions; that the troops in the forwardmost villages are packed like sardines into the few available dwellings: "Everything here is so overcrowded, that 30 men are happy [to find] a single room. They can no longer lay down but will stand for hours just to keep themselves warm. To wash up or clean up—it's all impossible." All the men, it seems, are teeming with lice, and they itch and scratch themselves endlessly; as a result, many have suppurating wounds. Many others have bladder and bowel ailments from lying on the cold ground; they get not a moment's peace because of the constant urge [*Drang*] to relieve themselves. He continues,

> It's utterly impossible to find quarters for our reserve forces so they can intervene in timely fashion. We just put up with this, thinking that, should *der Russe* breach our line, he hopefully won't push into our rear areas.

> All the basics of tactics have been thrown overboard [*über den Haufen geworfen*] in this war. We fight on frontages that in the past would have seemed absurd [*unsinnig*] to anyone. We hold positions kilometers in length with companies that have a strength of 40 men. All the men up front are so on edge and stressed by these conditions that it all draws to a close.
>
> Everywhere I go I'm confronted by the same three complaints: Why did the panzer army let us attack, without giving us the assurance that they, too, would [support our attack]—with the result that our sacrifice (635 men in the 131 Div[ision], including sick, since 27.11), given our negligible strength, is intolerable and in vain? Why are the men getting marmalade, when what they most need in this cold weather is lard? Why were we sent with such deficient clothing into a winter battle, whose demands are enormous [*übermenschlich*]? Doesn't anyone know what it's like here? [*Weiss denn niemand, wie es hier aussieht?*][141]

At 0100 hours on 5 December, Heinrici finally stirred himself to act, putting in his assault with infantry of 31 ID supported by three still-operational assault guns and a few 105s of the corps artillery. (All that the *Luftwaffe* could manage in the cruelly cold weather was a handful of sorties.) Despite some initial progress—including the capture of two villages after hard fighting—the attacking force was soon brought to a halt by unexpectedly robust Russian resistance. Although combat losses had been tolerable (*erträglich*), the numerous cases of frostbite had so weakened Heinrici's corps that further offensive action was no longer possible.[142]

At the forward edge of battle, Guderian had personally marched with his troops to share their hardships.[143] His forces, however, ghostly shadows of the superb formations that had blitzed their way through Soviet Russia during the past summer, were at the end of their tether. In the sector of 29 ID (mot.), the Soviets were attacking with armor northeast of Venev; 24 Panzer Corps reported that strong enemy forces had broken through the front of 3 Panzer Division[144] northeast of Tula. The threat to the flanks and rear in the area north of Tula, along with the fact that Geyr's panzer corps was now largely immobilized due to the frost, unable to advance, raised the obvious question in Guderian's mind: Was it time to finally call off the attack? If the answer was affirmative, Guderian faced a serious dilemma: Dedicated positions, onto which he could pull back his troops to ride out the Russian winter, had not been constructed.[145] It was a glaring oversight.

In his memoir, Guderian leveled thinly veiled criticism at his nemesis, GFM von Kluge, for failing to render more support during these final days of offensive action. The positions of Kluge's Fourth Army southwest of Moscow stretched all the way to the Oka River (east of Kaluga) and the left wing of 43 Army Corps. As Guderian saw it, if elements of Kluge's army had attacked from the west, they might have succeeded in tying down significant Red Army forces, thus easing the way for the panzer general's final push. And yet, "the contrary happened.

Cooperation by Fourth Army was limited to an action by a fighting patrol two companies strong that, after completion of its mission, returned to its previous position. This episode had no effect on the enemy opposite 43 Army Corps. Fourth Army had gone over to the defensive."[146]

Guderian's suggestion that Kluge was halfhearted in his commitment to the final battles outside Moscow is unjust. In the first place, Kluge, beginning on 1 December, had launched a major attack on his left wing opposite Naro-Fominsk, where the Soviets had constructed a powerful defensive system of wooden and stone bunkers covered by countless mines. Fourth Army losses were high; indeed, on the first day, *Generalmajor* Wilhelm Ritter von Thoma's 20 Panzer Division[147] lost ten tanks to mines alone. Nevertheless, some significant penetrations were made before the attack finally collapsed in the face of heavy Soviet opposition. Second, Kluge's right wing (which, as noted, abutted the left wing of Heinrici's 43 Army Corps) was "both markedly weaker in aggregate terms and was starved of resources in order to support the attack on [his left wing]." Thus, it could have offered but little assistance to Guderian's final assault on Tula. As Kluge's chief of staff observed, committing the Fourth Army's right wing to battle when "so little could be expected of it was a dangerous proposition that led to hours of deliberation." Ultimately, the idea was dropped.[148]

On the night of 5 December, Guderian, having pored over his battle maps and read the reports from the front, did the only thing left for him to do: He broke off his offensive on Tula, a decision he reported to Army Group Center at 2220 hours.[149] He had decided to withdraw his forwardmost units to an interim defensive line:

> This was the first time during the war that I had had to take a decision of this sort, and none was more difficult. The fact that my chief of staff, Liebenstein, and my senior corps commander, General [Geyr], were in complete agreement did not make it any easier for me.
>
> During the course of the night I informed [GFM] von Bock of what I had decided. His first question was: "Where actually is your headquarters?" He imagined that I was in Orel and too far away from the fighting front. But that was one mistake that no panzer general ever made. I was close enough to the battle and to my soldiers to be able to form a clear judgment of both. . . .
>
> Our attack on Moscow had broken down. All the sacrifices and endurance of our brave troops had been in vain.[150]

9

Defeat and Dismissal

On 5 December 1941—At *Generaloberst* Heinz Guderian's forward command post south of Tula, on Count Leo Tolstoy's estate, the temperature suddenly plunged to −35°C.[1] Vehicles no longer started; engines froze while they ran; the breeches of artillery pieces froze shut; tank turrets froze solid; tank and artillery gun recoil mechanisms jammed; machine guns jammed; artillery fire became irregular (the gunpowder seemed to burn differently); the fins of mortar shells—if exposed too long to the cold—sometimes broke off when fired and got stuck in the tubes; radios quit functioning; motor oil thickened; batteries suffered from reduced effectiveness; and on it went. As a former German officer recalled, because of such incidents, the trust (*Vertrauen*) of the German soldier in his weapons was often badly shaken.[2]

With Army Group Center immobilized by the frost and having reached the end of its combat strength, GFM Fedor von Bock canceled the entire offensive, his broken divisions going over to the defensive in the positions they had reached. Since 15 November, they had advanced another 80 to 110 kilometers to the very threshold of Moscow. Indeed, Hans Reinhardt's *Panzergruppe* 3 and Erich Hoepner's *Panzergruppe* 4 were barely 25 to 30 kilometers from the outskirts of the Soviet capital, astride the Leningrad, Piatitskoe, and Volokolamsk roads; in the center, Fourth Army was within 40 kilometers of Moscow; in the south, Guderian's *Panzerarmee* 2 had been halted just short of Kashira, his handful of surviving tanks practically out of fuel.[3]

The "Situation East" (*Lage Ost*) map of the OKH Operations Branch illustrates just how close the Germans had come: Some two dozen of Bock's divisions were within 75 kilometers of the Soviet capital, and, as noted, many of these were much closer.[4] German officers nearest to Moscow could see the spires of the city through their field glasses or watch as the city's searchlights and anti-aircraft guns engaged the small packets of *Luftwaffe* bombers that sometimes circled overhead. Yet, after more than five months of uninterrupted combat, Bock's crippled army group—by 30 November having sustained more than 120,000 casualties since the start of Typhoon—no longer possessed the strength to advance another kilometer.[5] The Red Army, "contrary to expectations," had "halted the German juggernaut on the outskirts of Moscow."[6] (In a remarkable historical irony, Napoleon's *Grande Armée*, relying solely on the motive power of its soldiers' feet and horses, was able to occupy Moscow on 14 September 1812, just 84 days after crossing the Nieman River on 23 June and having advanced at an average pace of more than 10 kilometers per day; Hitler's *Wehrmacht*, however, needed 160 days—advancing at an average pace of just six or seven kilometers per day—to simply reach the outskirts of the Soviet capital with its panzer units.)

Suddenly engulfed in a winter crisis for which they were completely unprepared, GFM von Bock and his field generals—primary among them the panzer group commanders—"grappled with its dire implications." Unlike Hoepner, however, Guderian "was never prepared to admit any personal liability for underestimation or miscalculation; in his conception it was the senior Army leadership who bore all the responsibility."[7] In a missive to Margarete on 8 December, Guderian poured out his anger and frustration:

> We are facing the sad fact that the senior leadership has overdone things [*die obere Führung den Bogen überspannt hat*], did not want to believe the reports of the troops' declining combat strength, only made demands, did not make provisions for the harsh winter and was now surprised by the Russian cold of minus 35 degrees. The strength of the troops was no longer sufficient to carry out the attack on Moscow, so that, with a heavy heart, I had to resolve on the evening of 5 December to break off the unwinnable battle.[8]

"The gall of Guderian's accusation," averred military historian David Stahel, "is remarkable, given that he had advocated for the offensive at every stage, knowing full well—and choosing to disregard—the exhaustion within his ranks, the lack of supplies and the freezing conditions."[9] In *Panzer Leader*, Guderian even went so far as to credit himself with saving the situation because—on his own responsibility—he had ordered his Second Panzer Army to suspend its attack on 5 December, just hours before Bock's general halt order. "Had I not done so," he insisted, "a catastrophe could not have been avoided."[10] One can only wonder what difference a few hours would have made. Yet the salient point is this: "Once again Guderian had removed himself from any responsibility for the events impacting his panzer army."[11]

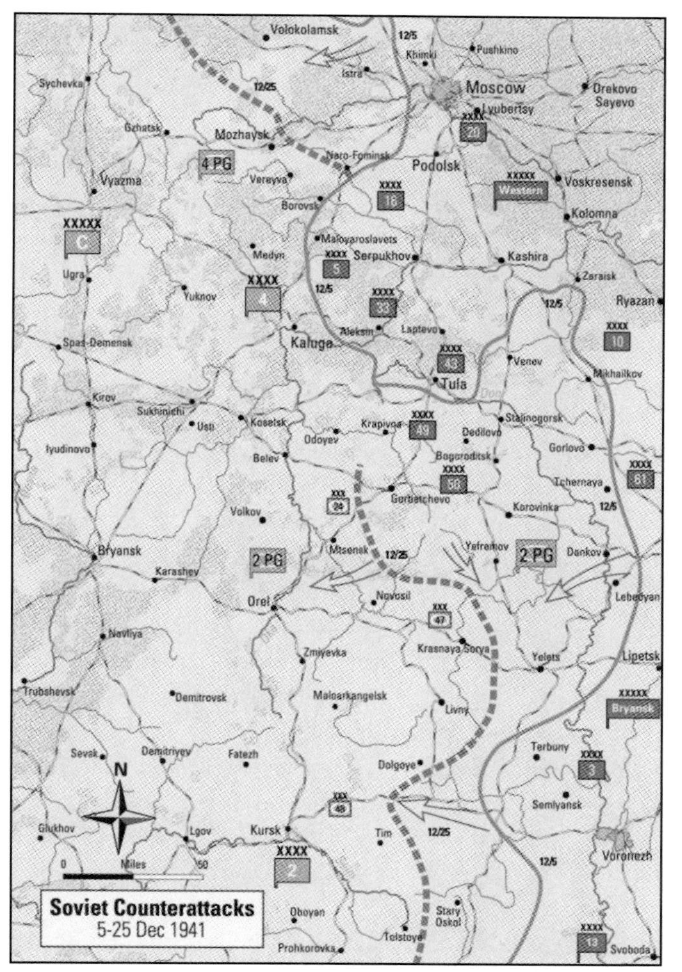

The Soviet Counteroffensive: 5.12.1941–25.12.1941

THE SOVIET COUNTEROFFENSIVE

German plans to spend a relatively quiet winter in their shelters and dugouts—while rebuilding their armies to resume the advance in the spring—were abruptly shattered on 5/6 December 1941, when the Red Army counterattacked the dangerously exposed flanks of Army Group Center in weather of −30°C and below. Caught completely off guard—German intelligence had failed to detect the buildup of substantial Soviet reserves—the depleted German divisions began to withdraw in a frantic effort to secure vital lines of communication and to avoid encirclement and annihilation. Bock's infantry divisions could often muster no more than twenty to twenty-five fighting men per rifle company, while the panzer divisions had disintegrated to a handful of tanks and retained little mobility. The already overburdened logistical system now completely collapsed, meaning that little in the way of food, fuel, weapons, and munitions reached the front.

By mid-December 1941, fighting had flared up along the entire front of Army Group Center, as Joseph Stalin and Gen. G. K. Zhukov—their initial assaults having removed the most immediate threat to Moscow—expanded the scope of their offensive. Paralleling the arrival of the most severe winter weather in memory,[12] combat across the front took on new characteristics. The Germans no longer held a cohesive line; rather, they began to cling to key towns and villages and to defend the handful of roadways and rail lines that were the sole arteries for major movements of troops and supplies. Masters of infiltration tactics, Soviet ski troops slipped between the German strongpoints, which often became surrounded, and streamed into the snow-covered landscape behind what was left of the German front. As noted, the arctic conditions played havoc with German weapons, which, for the most part, were more finely machined than those of their adversary and not designed to function in such extreme cold. Frostbite began to cause more casualties than action in battle, while sicknesses associated with the arctic cold, exhaustion, and lack of food took an increasing toll. Wounded German soldiers died from the shock of even minor wounds, while others froze to death on the way to rear-area dressing stations. A crisis of confidence spread across the front as the *Landser* looked to their generals for leadership, yet found them wanting.

Photos and newsreels from this period offer shocking images of withdrawing German soldiers, who, in their outward appearance, are unrecognizable compared to the confident warriors who had stormed across the German-Soviet frontier on 22 June 1941; having received little in the way of proper winter gear,[13] clad from head to toe in whatever clothing or rags they could lay hands on, they more closely resemble bands of marauding gypsies. As a rule, however, the deeply ingrained discipline of the German soldier enabled even badly mauled formations to maintain their cohesion despite the virtually unthinkable conditions at the front; moreover, the fear of capture—and summary retribution—by Red Army soldiers was a formidable motivating factor.

In a postwar history, Joseph Dinglreiter, a former officer in 17 Panzer Division, explained the concept of *innere Führung*—simply put, the care of the leader for his men—a battle-tested tradition of German armies long past:

> Mentioned here is an episode of an internal nature at the command post of II./40 [2nd Battalion, 40 Rifle Regiment] at Truchatschevka. The situation is worse than wretched. The mood of most of the men is subdued, if not to say depressed. The battalion doctor, who is also the regimental doctor, *Stabsarzt* [Captain, med.] Dr. Knoer, has his precious Bandoneon [concertina] wrapped in wool blankets. Dr. Knoer is a grand musician. . . . *Major* Eckart, the battalion commander, turns to him. "Lukas, take out your [instrument] and play the Tannhäuser Overture!" And he does just that. The music works wonders. The battalion commander, *Major* Eckart, and *Stabsarzt* Dr. Knoer, despite everything, are still of high confidence and morale [*bewegen sich trotz allem noch in den "Höhen"*]. As long as our leaders still have an open heart and mind for such uplifting music, then the troops can also take heart and have no need to despair. That is [what is meant by] "*innere Führung*."[14]

Yet there were also occasions when discipline collapsed, when the center did not hold. Dinglreiter described one such occasion:

> The morale [*Stimmung*] of the troops, who in the previous battles were committed to the attack, has suffered considerably due to the disengagement and withdrawal from Kashira to Mtsensk. In particular the *Kampfmoral* of the troops was badly affected by the many unpleasant scenes they've witnessed of other units. For example, on 14 December, near Ostrakovo, numerous weapons and other war materiel belonging to an infantry division (including 5 Light Field Howitzer 18s and 25 carbines) were found. Along with the equipment, which was scattered about aimlessly, there was a large number of horses that had been shot and were frozen together in clumps. . . . The overall picture was downright disturbing [*geradezu erschütternd*] and made an extremely bad impression on our men.[15]

Feldwebel Peter Stahl, a Ju 88 bomber pilot, described the desperate plight of the retreating *Landser* observed by *Luftwaffe* crews as they flew above the snow-draped battlefields: "We are offered a sorrowful view: long columns of our own soldiers strenuously stumbling back. Everywhere one can see abandoned vehicles, some half-covered with snow, and others just recently abandoned. As we fly past the columns and small groups of soldiers at low altitude, it is evident that they are half unconscious out of fatigue. They pay no attention to us. We pass by burning villages. The enemy won't be able to use them as living quarters when he pursues our troops. The entire horizon is filled with columns of black smoke. It is a merciless war."[16]

The pursuing Russians, however, had their own challenges with which to contend. While their offensive slowly ground its way forward—the average daily rate of advance of the Red Army's Western Front ranged from 4 to 15 kilometers per day between 6 and 25 December[17]—problems of poor leadership, inelegant tactics, and shoddy operational control were immediately apparent. Many of the attacking armies were composed of poorly trained and equipped reservists, while after the unprecedented equipment losses of the summer and fall battles, heavy weapons, such as artillery and tanks, were in short supply.[18] Conversely, the Red Army offensive received a boost from the Soviet Air Force (VVS), which now enjoyed complete superiority over the battlefield and behind the German front.

Yet, despite the unparalleled catastrophe, Army Group Center would bend but not break during the winter of 1941/42. Indeed, the Red Army—while committing more than seventy new formations of brigade or division size against Bock's army group in December 1941 alone[19]—consistently failed to crack German strongpoints in key cities and towns and was unable to interrupt primary road and rail communications for more than short periods, enabling vital supplies of food, fuel, and ammunition (and, eventually, winter clothing) to trickle through to the German defenders. In line with doctrine, German forces—at least what remained of them—counterattacked repeatedly, in the process encircling and later destroying several Soviet armies and operational groups that had broken through the brittle German lines. By February 1942, Army Group Center—and the eastern front as a whole—had largely weathered the storm (literally and figuratively).[20]

On 12 February, the German Army High Command promulgated its "Directive for the Conduct of Operations in the East after the Conclusion of the Winter." It began by observing that the worst of the crisis had passed and that the Red Army had been brought to a halt (*zum Stehen gebracht*) due to the "incomparable performance" [*unübertreffliche Leistungen*] and "unshakable will" of the German soldier.[21] In fact, despite pushing back German forces some 150 to 400 kilometers to the west,[22] as well as liberating sixty cities and hundreds of towns and villages, Stalin's counteroffensive had failed to achieve any of its primary objectives. Contributing significantly to the defensive victory of the *Ostheer* were (1) the remaining battle-hardened officers and NCOs, whose toughness, experience, combat skill, and, when required, ruthlessness held the remnants of their exhausted units together and made them fight; and (2) the remaining heavy weapons—artillery, flak, tanks, assault guns—deployed at pivotal sectors of the front and exercising an influence on tactical events well beyond their all too modest numbers.

By February 1942, however, Guderian was long out of the picture, having been relieved of his command in late December 1941 by his old nemesis, GFM Günther von Kluge, who had taken over for the ailing Bock as C-in-C of Army Group Center.

GUDERIAN AND THE DECEMBER CRISIS

On 6 December, acknowledging that his offensive was hopelessly stalled, Guderian had, without orders, withdrawn his forwardmost elements into temporary defensive positions in anticipation of the impending Soviet counterstroke. As noted, Guderian's final push toward Moscow had left his forces unevenly deployed and vulnerable to counterattacks against his now dangerously overextended right (eastern) flank.[23] At Tula, from 6 to 12 December, elements of Second Panzer Army were defeated in detail as both its flanks were "smashed in" by the advancing Red Army, forcing the Germans to fall back time and again while evincing increasing signs of demoralization. The panzer army also suffered from an alarming number of frostbite cases. Hermann Hoss, an *Oberleutnant* and signal officer in 4 Panzer Division, described the start of the retreat:

> It was midnight when the telephone called out shrilly. . . . The division commander wanted to speak to *Oberst* Eberbach. I didn't need to awaken him since he didn't sleep during those kinds of situations. He merely rested with wide-awake senses. From his answers, I could figure out the entire conversation. It was a complete and total order to retreat in order to save the lives of the men of the division, disregarding the materiel. The Russian winter offensive had erupted in full force [and] 4 Panzer Division was in the middle of the enemy and a self-made trap. All objections of our commander—the certain, immense losses in materiel, the immobile guns and tanks—all of them were useless. . . .
>
> Whatever could move was prepared for movement. We thoroughly destroyed everything else. The landline section's truck was already on fire; the signal equipment and the men were loaded on the command vehicle. My small *Stöwer* [staff car] was hooked up behind, since it would not go cross-country and through the deep snow. The routes through the ravines were impassable due to the ice. On the slope behind the village, the first few vehicles were already getting hung up and were unable to climb the hill. A flak crew attempted to bring its gun up the slope with a winch, but the cable tore as if it had been paper. On one of the 10.5-centimeter guns, the limbers broke off like glass, and the gun had to be blown up. We learned our lesson: Always stay on the high ground and avoid every defile. The advance guard was also coming back along the road. It had had to leave a lot of material behind.
>
> We went around the ravine, marched through the woods and were soon in Nefedova. Despite the cold, it was too hot for me, because I had to run next to the vehicle half the stretch and guide the driver so that we did not get stuck anywhere. The 10 men in and on the tank counted on me. In Nefedova, three large *Henschel* trucks from the engineers were burning. They did not have any chains and, as a result, were unable to climb the hill. We quickly reached the rail line at Revjakono. Once we were across, I had us stop for a short period. In the process, the *Stöwer* ran into the back of the tank and smashed in its radiator. I yelled at Fischer, but he could not help it—the brakes were frozen. Towing it any farther would have been pointless. It was tipped off the side of the road and set on fire.

> We continued on. . . . The snow cleats for the tanks, which had been flown in to Dedilovo, had broken off a long time ago. . . . When we reached the top of the hill it was dark. . . .
>
> The muzzle flashes of artillery pieces flamed into the twilight.[24]

During these desperate days, a STAVKA reserve outfit (10 Army) suddenly appeared on Guderian's eastern flank near the town of Mikhailov, routing the remnants of Joachim Lemelsen's 47 Panzer Corps. The 10 Army pushed 30 kilometers in two days, slashing across Guderian's lines of communication and seeking to link up with Soviet 50 Army advancing from Tula—an operation that, if successful, would result in the encirclement of Geyr's 24 Panzer Corps. Guderian responded promptly by ordering a rapid withdrawal and briefly forming a new front between Tula and Epifan'; however, when Marshal Semen Timoshenko's Southwestern Front pushed Second Army (situated south of Second Panzer Army) back toward Orel, Guderian was forced to retreat again, his troops abandoning artillery, vehicles, and other items of equipment along the way.[25]

Guderian's solution to this perilous state of affairs was "a prompt and extensive withdrawal to a line where the terrain was suitable to the defense." For him, the "obvious choice" was the "Susha [Zusha]–Oka position, which had been partially fortified in October. But this is exactly what Hitler refused to allow."[26] In anger, he lashed out at Hitler, OKH, anyone—other than himself—he held responsible for the miserable conditions at the front.

Bock was now beset by serious doubts about Guderian's ability to withstand the burgeoning crisis. On the morning of 9 December, he briefed Army Chief of Staff Franz Halder about his (Bock's) "strange conversation" (*merkwürdige Unterredung*) with Guderian. The panzer general had telephoned Bock the previous evening and described his situation "in the blackest terms":

> [In] doing so [Guderian] said that he could not conceal from me that, as he put it, a crisis of confidence [*Vertrauenskrise*] was taking hold. He asked for the hundredth time if those at the very top [the reference of course is to Hitler] were aware of this situation. . . . The conversation ended with me telling him that complaints were useless here, I could not give him reinforcements, either one held out or let himself be killed [*entweder man risse aus oder man liesse sich totschlagen*]. There were no other choices. Thus the only important thing was to see to it that everyone stubbornly held onto whatever he had to hold.[27]

On 10 December, Bock posted in his diary, "In response to Guderian's suggestion of a 'crisis in confidence,' Brauchitsch telegraphed all the Commanders-in-Chief of the armies, informing them that he, like the Führer, was completely informed about the situation but that the utmost had to be demanded of the forces in the field."[28]

The same day, Guderian wrote again to Margarete. It was a special day for the happily married couple: "Thirty years ago today, you agreed to become my dear wife and have made me immensely happy ever since." He went on to note conditions at the front: "Two days ago, I reported about my great worries. Unfortunately, they get worse with each passing day. It's not so much about my own army, which is still intact [*geschlossen*] and led by a firm hand, as it is, at least in part, about our considerably more vulnerable neighbor, whose fate naturally also affects mine. . . . The enemy, the size of his country, and the treacherous nature of the climate were considerably underestimated, and that's now taking its toll."[29]

From the perspective of Army Group Center, however, it was not so much a "firm hand" they were seeing from Guderian as an alarming proclivity to retreat, despite Bock urging him to hold his ground. As if that weren't enough, Bock's vexatious subordinate had been unwilling to attempt to close a 20-kilometer gap northwest of Tula—a Soviet breakthrough that split Heinrici's 43 Army Corps from Geyr's 24 Panzer Corps and through which Soviet forces were now advancing dangerously into the rear of the army group. Although both corps belonged to Guderian's panzer army, he refused to take any responsibility for the genuine crisis, leaving Kluge at Fourth Army to deal with it on his own. In a letter to his wife, he "disingenuously complained," "My northern neighbor [Fourth Army] ruptured again," and then suggested he could do nothing to help "because I cannot overturn the entire eastern front on my own."[30]

Bock tried (and failed) to convince the recalcitrant panzer general that the Tula gap needed to be addressed. On 15 December, after what he described as a "difficult conversation," the frustrated field marshal put in his journal that Guderian "refuses to acknowledge any possibility of closing it from the south."[31] For his part, Guderian blamed Kluge, claiming that the four battalions of an infantry division the latter had dispatched to his aid were "totally inadequate," and thus "the vital gap could not be closed."[32] It was to become a "wound in the side of Army Group Center, and the longer it went unattended the more it would fester; but neither at the time nor afterward would Guderian accept any responsibility for what was to transpire."[33]

Meanwhile, Guderian, in open defiance of his superiors, had continued his "rash flight" toward the Susha and Oka Rivers. On 13 December, he began to pull back from the Stalinogorsk-Shat-Upa line to a new temporary position along the Plava River. He justified his decision by insisting that neither Fourth Army nor 3 and 4 Panzer Groups were able to hold their positions; so he, too, had no choice but to withdraw. Of course, Guderian was hardly wrong about the predicament of Kluge's Fourth Army or of the panzer groups. Indeed, as the C-in-C of 4 Panzer Group, *Generaloberst* Hoepner, wrote to his wife at this time,

> The sound of the telephone is enough to make one jump. And it never stops ringing. Every day, we have to withdraw forces somewhere. Yesterday, the Russians broke through my southern flank, too. The counterattack we carried out today was unsuccessful. The fighting is taking place 30 km from here. The sheer number of Russians is smothering us. Their fighting spirit is low. But our people are exhausted, fall asleep on their feet, are so lifeless that they no longer take cover when the shooting starts. Frostbite is almost more common than bloody losses. Our position is desperately similar to that of Napoleon in 1812. The Russians were right when they claimed that the winter will bring us to a standstill. It is incredibly difficult to keep our nerves. The commanding generals are crying out for help. [*Gen.d.Inf.* Hermann] Geyer [9 AK] sends a written lament on an almost daily basis. In addition, Kluge and Bock are calling from behind, asking this and that, giving advice and issuing orders that cannot be carried out. Even [*Oberst* Walter Chales de] Beaulieu [chief of staff, 4 PzG] is developing a thick skin towards them and starting to get rude on the telephone. By the way, he is also so nervous that he can no longer sleep at night.[34] (Emphasis in the original)

Despite Guderian's insubordination, on 12 December Bock took the decision to give him control over the tottering Second Army (now led by *Gen.d.Pz.Tr.* Rudolf Schmidt, who had replaced the ailing *Generaloberst* von Weichs in mid-November), resulting in the formation of what Second Panzer Army's war diary proudly referred to as *Armeegruppe Guderian.* Not surprisingly, following this command reorganization—creating a unified command structure from Tula south to Kursk—Guderian became more amenable to providing support to Schmidt's Second Army (which, it seems, was Bock's principal rationale for undertaking the initiative in the first place).[35]

On 14 December, Guderian met with GFM von Brauchitsch in Roslavl (Kluge was also there). To attend the conference, he had to drive for twenty-two hours through a raging blizzard. After describing the condition of his army, the panzer general requested formal approval to withdraw to the Susha-Oka position. On his own accord, the ailing Brauchitsch—just days from being dismissed from his position as C-in-C of the Army—agreed. (Noted Guderian, "I could rightly assume that the Commander-in-Chief of the Army would inform Hitler of this decision; but subsequent events make it at least doubtful whether he did, in fact, ever do so.")[36]

On 16 December, Guderian reported to Army Group Center that the actual strength (*Ist-Stärke*) of his panzer army had been whittled down to just forty tanks.[37] The perilous condition of his troops at this time was recorded in the diary of *Oblt.* Beck-Broichsitter of IRGD, whose account also made clear that morale was still intact in this elite unit:

The fighting goes on only for the villages. Finding a warm shelter is all that matters. Whoever is left outside is lost. All night long we marched right through the fields. But you need to find an hour to sleep. Beside the roadway is a peaceful-looking village. About 30 civilians are standing around gawking at us. We just want to avoid combat and reach our objective. So we don't bother with it. As we learn later, the village was fully occupied.

We [reach a new village] and scour it for food [*organisieren*]. The coffee in our field canteens has frozen solid. The boy [*Pimpf*] thaws them out. We are done in and utterly wasted [*verkatert*].

With 200 grenadiers we are to occupy a front four kilometers in width.

Suddenly, on the high ground opposite the men, several forms emerged—Russian tanks, a whole pack of them, were attacking again. The German troops scrambled to occupy whatever defensive positions they could find, but they were hampered in this task by their extreme exhaustion. The account continued,

Oberst Hörnlein, the commander of *Grossdeutschland*, suddenly drove up in his vehicle as tank shells tore up the ground around him.

"What company?" "The third, *Herr Oberst!*" "Where are the others?" "That's all of them." Under [enemy] mortar fire he speaks with several of the grenadiers. He understands their dire situation. In the World War he was an infantry lieutenant; he's now experiencing his 7th year of war. He knows just how tough it all is. He gives us confidence.

Four [enemy] tanks move up [to a position] just 1,200 meters from us and shoot up the houses. They collapse and burn. A Pak from my 14th Company goes into position. It can be clearly seen. What's the point? One of the tanks is hit and burns; the other three all let loose: The Pak gun is a twisted and shot up wreck. The gunner, an old *Obergefreiter*, lies dead beside it. Once again, I've lost an old friend.

I'm being pursued by sheafs of fire from a Russian machine gun. I scurry from one shadowy place to another. On this long, clear surface my strength threatens to fail me. Trying to run through this snow is like a bad dream in which one is paralyzed and unable to move. . . . I look for an MG, a mortar, several of the grenadiers. [Holding] a position often depends upon a single NCO. For some time now we distinguish among the men based on their personal attributes, not their rank. I know most everyone in the battalion by name. [The assignment of] a tactical mission is often followed by: "It all depends here on you!"

Late in the night *der Russe* gives up. His fire becomes weaker. The tanks are gone. Now and then we still hear one growling in the distance.

Then the picture of the previous days repeats itself: Fall in, set the village on fire, check compasses, gather up equipment, march across the fields. The entire night through. Once again, we've done it. The Russian is powerless and stupid. He is only helped by his masses.

> Those typical [ideas] among people of sleep, awake time, food, and expenditure of energy are no longer valid for us.
>
> At home they are now buying Christmas trees.[38]

On 16 December, Guderian, now "racked by sciatica,"[39] composed his last known letter to his wife for 1941. Once again, he laid into the senior leadership (OKW/OKH) and accused them of all that had gone wrong in the campaign, "but revealingly, excluded Hitler from any blame and in fact cast the dictator as the solution to Germany's problems."

> I lie awake at night racking my brains [*zermartere mir das Gehirn*] about how I can help my poor men who have no protection against this terrible winter weather. It is horrific, unimaginable. . . . The complete underestimation of the enemy and the resulting recklessness with regard to preparations for the winter campaign in Russia have placed us in a very difficult position. How are we supposed to come out of this again, I don't yet know myself. In any case, we must act quickly and energetically, and at present there is no hint of this. I am only happy that the Führer is now at least in the picture[40] and will hopefully intervene with his usual vigor in the bureaucratized gears of the Army, the railways and other machinery.[41]

"Not only does this reflect Guderian's slavish devotion to Hitler," affirmed David Stahel, "who had without question been inextricably involved in the day-to-day decisions of the High Command, but more importantly, it underlines the panzer general's fundamental misunderstanding of Germany's predicament." Stahel went on,

> Apart from the fact that Hitler was not a good crisis manager, even if he had been, the systemic nature of the crisis unfolding on the eastern front had progressed well beyond any decisions Hitler might or might not make—a fact that Guderian's blind devotion could not grasp. There was simply no quick fix to the lack of trains arriving on the eastern front or the absence of winter equipment for three million men. Yet here again the primacy of National Socialist "will" as a catch-all solution to any problem allowed circles to be squared. In Guderian's mind, Hitler's iron conviction and indomitable will could deliver the impossible, a conclusion that should have been completely anathema to his General Staff training.[42]

Earlier in the day (16 December), Guderian, at his "urgent request," had met with Hitler's chief military adjutant, *Oberst* Rudolf Schmundt, at Orel airfield. They talked for an hour, Guderian laying out his situation in the gravest of terms and asking Schmundt to convey what he (Guderian) had said directly to the Führer. "I expected Hitler to telephone me during the night and to answer the proposals that I had made to Schmundt."

The telephone call from Hitler arrived at 0300 hours (17 December).[43] The German dictator—having finally taken charge of the deteriorating situation at Army Group Center by issuing his formal "halt order" the day before (see below)—ordered Guderian to stand fast, thus forbidding any further withdrawal. At the same time, Hitler promised to dispatch "replacements," but, according to Guderian, these (initially at least) amounted to a paltry 500 men—less than a full-strength battalion—to be flown in by air.[44]

Three days later (20 December), Guderian, still hoping to gain Hitler's approval to pull back his forces—which, of course, he was already quietly doing—made the long flight from the frozen front north of Orel to the Führer's East Prussian headquarters, touching down at Rastenburg airfield late that afternoon. With Wilhelm Keitel, Schmundt, and other officers of Hitler's entourage in attendance, the conference dragged on for five hours. (Neither Halder nor any other representatives of the Army High Command were in attendance. "And so, as on 23 August 1941, I stood in lonely opposition to the ranks of the OKW.")[45]

The conference began with Guderian describing the operational situation (*operative Lage*) of his Second Panzer Army and Second Army. He then spoke of his intention to withdraw both armies in short bounds (*abschnittsweise*) to the Susha-Oka position—an intention that Guderian had already expressed to GFM von Brauchitsch when the two had met at Roslavl on 14 December and which Brauchitsch had approved. Convinced that Hitler must have been informed of this, he was taken aback when the Führer shouted, "No! I forbid that!" (*Nein, das verbiete ich!*) In response, Guderian turned to his typical tactic in such difficult situations: "I informed him that the withdrawal was already in progress [*bereits im Gange sei*] and that there was no intermediate line at which it could be halted for any length of time before the rivers were reached. If he regarded it as important to preserve the lives of the troops and to hold a position throughout the winter he had no choice but to permit the withdrawal to be completed."

Hitler:[46] "If that is the case they must dig into the ground where they are and hold every square meter of land!"

Guderian: "Digging into the ground is no longer feasible in most places, since it is frozen to a depth of [1 to 1.5 meters] and our wretched entrenching tools won't go through it."

Hitler: "In that case they must blast craters with the heavy howitzers. We had to do that in the First World War in Flanders."

Guderian: "In the First World War our divisions in Flanders held, on the average, sectors [four to six kilometers] wide and were supported in the defense by two or three battalions of heavy howitzers per division with proportionately abundant supplies of ammunition. My divisions have to defend fronts of [20 to 40 kilometers] and in each of my divisions there are 4 heavy howitzers with approximately 50 shells per gun. If I use those shells to make craters I shall have

50 hollows in the ground, each about the width and depth of a wash tub with a large black circle around it. I shall not have a crater position. In Flanders there was never such cold as we are now experiencing. And apart from that I need my ammunition to fire at the Russians. We can't even drive stakes into the ground for carrying our telephone wires; to make a hole for the stake we have to use high explosives. When are we to get sufficient explosives to blast out defensive positions on the scale you have in mind?"

Hitler, however, was not to be moved and insisted on his order being carried out—"that we remain where we were."

Guderian: "Then this means taking up positional warfare in an unsuitable terrain, as happened on the western front during the First World War. In this case we shall have the same battles of material [*Materialschlachten*] and the same enormous casualties as then without any hope of winning a decisive victory. If such tactics are adopted we shall, during the course of this coming winter, sacrifice the lives of our soldiers, our non-commissioned officers and of the men suitable to replace them, and this sacrifice will have been not only useless but also irreparable."

Hitler: "Do you think Frederick the Great's grenadiers were anxious to die? [*Glauben Sie, die Grenadiere Friedrichs des Grossen wären gerne gestorben?*] They wanted to live, too, but the king was right in asking them to sacrifice themselves. I believe that I, too, am entitled to ask any German soldier to lay down his life."[47]

With Hitler and Guderian at loggerheads, the conference adjourned for the evening meal, the panzer general sitting beside the Führer and using the opportunity to inform him of the deplorable conditions at the front. "But the effect of my anecdotes was not what I had expected. Both Hitler and his entourage were plainly convinced that I was exaggerating." The discussion continued after the meal but only grew more acrimonious. When Guderian—having failed to change Hitler's mind—finally left the conference room, he overheard the dictator say to Keitel, "I haven't convinced that man!" (*Diesen Mann habe ich nicht überzeugt.*)[48]

Four days prior to his dramatic encounter with Guderian at the *Wolfsschanze*, Hitler had decreed his (still) controversial "halt order" (*Haltebefehl*),[49] forcing the divisions of Army Group Center to stand fast where they were and to retreat no farther, even when threatened with encirclement by attacking enemy forces.[50] On 18 December, in a teletype message (*Fernschreiben*) to the army group, the dictator amplified his order, noting that attempted withdrawals would only lead to the total loss of heavy weapons and equipment; hence, army and corps commanders—and officers in general—were to personally rally the troops to fanatical resistance (*fanatischen Widerstand*) in their existing positions. To stiffen their defenses, replacement battalions were to be rushed to the front by means of rail and air transport; moreover, several divisions from *Generaloberst* Friedrich Fromm's Replacement Army were to be dispatched to Army Group

Center, along with five infantry divisions from France (the latter from 1 January to 1 February 1942).[51]

Many frontline generals—among them, certainly Guderian—were strongly opposed to the halt order, instead clinging to their bedrock doctrinal belief in the primacy of maneuver warfare (in this case, including retrograde movements to withdraw to more defensible positions). Yet, as argued by Guderian biographer Russell A. Hart,

> Given the immobility of the German Army—owing to lack of transport and minimal winter equipment—the only viable action was to stand fast in fortified village hedgehog defenses and weather the Soviet storm as Hitler demanded. Any time German forces had fought delaying withdrawals they had found it difficult to disengage from the enemy—who were better equipped for winter warfare—without suffering appreciable losses, particularly heavy weapons that had to be abandoned for lack of transport and fuel. Hitler was usually poor at strategic decision making, but he was right this time, although this would have disastrous consequences for the future. The problem with the retreat Guderian desired was that it would have turned into a rout since his attenuated, ill-supplied forces, ill-equipped for winter maneuver, were simply incapable of the operational maneuver he continued to advocate. The "stand fast" orders Hitler gave thus helped save the Second Panzer Army from destruction.[52]

Hitler's decision was indeed the correct one—in fact, it was the *only* decision that had a chance of saving not only Guderian's exhausted forces but all of Army Group Center from annihilation. In other bold initiatives taken at this time, Hitler, on 19 December, accepted the resignation of GFM von Brauchitsch—sick, exhausted, utterly demoralized, and increasingly despised by the Führer—and assumed direct operational command of the Army. He then began to relieve tired, sick, and worn-out general officers at the front—among them GFM von Bock and, of course, Guderian himself—and to fill their posts with fresher and more effective officers.[53] These bold initiatives—one and all a reflection of Hitler's iron will and determination to take direct control of operations in the east[54]—began to lift morale and fill the vacuum in leadership, helping to prevent the disintegration of the embattled remnants of Army Group Center.

Hitler's *Haltebefehl* hit Guderian hard, and his reaction to it illustrates just how close he had come to the end in both body and mind. The *Generaloberst* had a "well-deserved reputation as a headstrong, independent commander whose success reflected his innovation and boldness, but he also had a predisposition for disloyal, egocentric, and intransigent behavior."

> Hitler's halt order evoked all these emotions in Guderian, and with the demands of his men uppermost in his mind, the panzer general was in no mood to take orders he did not agree with. For the first time in the war there is also evidence

that Guderian was struggling emotionally, no doubt compounded by his months of unrelenting activity—including a number of near death experiences while visiting the front. His formerly towering self-confidence had become a facade. When Richthofen visited Guderian at the beginning of the Soviet offensive, he alluded afterward in his diary to the shattered man he encountered: "To Guderian. Very open discussion. He is only externally hard, otherwise made of jelly. I actually wanted to be consoled by him and instead had to do it myself for him! Bitter and difficult." Likewise, Schmidt, who had daily contact with Guderian, observed on 19 December that the once "great optimist" had reached the "end of his hopes." In Guderian's letters to his wife the intractable situation at the front seemed to gnaw at him, and the ever-present feeling of helplessness was compounded by the genuine affection he felt for his men.[55]

GUDERIAN'S DISMISSAL

Following his discouraging audience with Hitler, the next day, Guderian flew back to Orel, where he continued to withdraw in flagrant defiance of the dictator's order. Two days before (19 December) GFM von Kluge had replaced Bock as commander of the army group. With Kluge, of course, "new squabbles" broke out immediately. As before, the major issues were Guderian's ongoing insubordination, his reluctance to do his part to close the festering Tula gap, and his persistent refusal to accept any personal responsibility for the crisis at hand. (Moreover, during December, Guderian had used Hitler's personal adjutant [Schmundt] and others as backdoor channels to convey his concerns to the Führer and to the Army High Command.) Kluge soon reached the same conclusion as his predecessor: Guderian had lost his nerve.

It had also become apparent to GFM von Kluge and his staff that Guderian—determined as ever to fight the war in a manner that he, and he alone, saw fit—was covertly withdrawing one regiment from each of his panzer army's forward divisions all the way back to the Oka River, where he was building a new defensive front: "It was an unmistakable prelude to the wholesale retreat of the Second Panzer Army all the way back to the southern reaches of Bock's old *Königsberg* Line. The audacity of what Guderian was attempting was measured not just by the degree of his defiance, bordering on open rebellion against the High Command, but by the implications for Army Group Center's ability to maintain a cohesive line. Presumably, Guderian had simply given up on this. . . . In any case Kluge was outraged."[56]

In the final days before Christmas, the commander of *Armeegruppe Guderian* was once again at the front, visiting with the divisions of Lemelsen's 47 Panzer Corps and dealing with Russian penetrations of his army's positions. On Christmas Eve, he visited several military hospitals "to bring a little good cheer to many a brave soldier. But it was a heart-rending business. I spent most of the evening working alone; later Liebenstein, Büsing, and Kahlden came to see me and we spent a short time together in comradely fashion."[57]

The final straw for Guderian came on 24/25 December. As he explained it, that night *Generalleutnant* Wilhelm von Loeper's 10 ID (mot.) gave up Chern (northeast of Mtsensk) when it was unable to hold off a Soviet enveloping attack. (With the loss of the town, elements of Guderian's army group had been thrown back as much as 150 kilometers since the start of the Soviet counteroffensive in early December.) Guderian insisted that he "immediately reported this misfortune" to Army Group Center, but Kluge accused him "in violent terms" of having ordered the evacuation of Chern, and having done so the day before. According to Guderian, the exact opposite was the case, and he "angrily denied" the field marshal's "unjust accusations."[58]

GFM von Kluge, however, wasn't buying it and was, no doubt, now convinced the time had come to rid himself once and for all of the nettlesome Guderian. On Christmas Day, Kluge telephoned Halder, telling him that he (Kluge) could no longer work with Guderian. Kluge then gave the General Staff chief an ultimatum: "Either he or I." Kluge justified his demand by offering a final tribute to the panzer leader's achievements: "I have the greatest respect for *Generaloberst* Guderian and he is a fantastic commander, *but he does not obey*. In this situation, I can only transmit and execute the Führer's orders if I can rely on my army commanders" (author's emphasis). Kluge made clear to Halder that the issue was Guderian's blatant defiance, not his strategic assessment. "I am basically entirely on Guderian's side," he told Halder; "one cannot simply let himself be slaughtered, but he must obey and keep me oriented."[59]

Following his discussion with Kluge, Halder[60] spoke to Hitler, who immediately authorized Guderian's dismissal. According to the dictator's Army adjutant, Gerhard Engel, it had been clear to Hitler for days that Guderian could no longer lead. Hitler's *Luftwaffe* adjutant, Nicolaus von Below, stated that the Führer now considered Guderian to be *völlig durchgedreht*, which, in context, may perhaps best be translated as "on the verge of a breakdown." More to the point, however, is that when confronted with failure, Guderian often "reacted with despondency and gloom," and December 1941 was his lowest ebb.[61]

Guderian wasted little time in going after Kluge, a professional colleague—and a fine general in his own right—who clearly had become a lightning rod for much of Guderian's frustration. He bitterly accused the new C-in-C of Army Group Center of treating him in a fully unjustified manner. Guderian also insisted that he put in, on his own, a request to be relieved of command, only to be beaten to the punch by Kluge: "On the morning of 26 December I was informed that Hitler had transferred me to the OKH officers' reserve pool. My successor was to be the commander of Second Army, General Rudolf Schmidt."[62]

On 26 December, Guderian bade farewell to his devoted staff and issued a short order of the day to his troops:

> *Soldaten der 2. Panzerarmee!* The Führer and Supreme Commander of the Armed Forces [*Oberste Befehlshaber der Wehrmacht*] has today relieved me of my command. At this time when I am leaving you I remember our six months of battle together for the greatness of our land and the victory of our arms, and I recall with honor and respect all those who have bled and died for Germany. From the bottom of my heart I thank you, my comrades-in-arms [*Kampfgefährten*], for the trusty devotion and true comradeship that you have at all times shown during these long months. We have been together in success and in adversity and my greatest joy has lain in my chances to help you and to protect you.
>
> . . .
>
> Heil Hitler!
> signed, Guderian[63]

Guderian's words were heartfelt. Whatever his failings as a soldier and as a man, there is no doubt that he cared deeply for his men, who, in turn, not only loved and honored their commander but also believed he had always acted in accordance with their best interests. A rumor, albeit unconfirmed, circulated among the men along the front that Guderian cried when he learned he was being dismissed from his Second Panzer Army command. Another panzer leader, Hermann Balck, recalled that the news "hit everybody very hard." *Oberst* Eberbach, who had fought his way across Soviet Russia with Guderian, described him as a commander "with whom everyone had felt a kinship." Joachim von Lehsten, another officer of Guderian's, wrote, "All our commanders—at divisional, regimental and battalion level—were talking about it. It was an absolute disaster—our soldiers found Hitler's action incomprehensible. Everyone respected and admired this man; a remarkable leader of outstanding ability."[64] *Gen.d.Pz.Tr.* Lemelsen, who had also served alongside Guderian from the beginning of the Russian campaign, went so far as to send a request to GFM Keitel (OKW), asking that Guderian be reinstated (to no avail).[65]

On 27 December, Guderian departed the front, and while major roles still awaited him in Germany's armed forces, he never again served as a commander in the field. On New Year's Eve—via Roslavl-Minsk-Warsaw-Posen—he arrived in Berlin.

Tanks and trucks of 17 Panzer Division in an assembly area. Commanded again by *Generalleutnant* Hans-Jürgen von Arnim (he had been wounded in late June), the division played a major role in the encirclement of Soviet forces at Briansk. (D. Garden and K. Andrew)

Stuka dive-bombers heading to the front on 2 October 1941, the first day of Army Group Center's drive toward Moscow (Operation Typhoon). (H. Sohn)

A German 150mm *Nebelwerfer* rocket launcher on the central front (summer 1941). For many German soldiers, the first day of Operation Typhoon was their first exposure to the relatively new and devastating weapon, which they observed with great curiosity. As one soldier recalled, "0610. The first Nebelwerfer salvo. Dammit, it's really something worth seeing; the rockets leave a black trail, a dirty cloud that drifts slowly away. The second salvo goes off! Red and black fire, then the projectile emerges from the cone of smoke." (U.S. National Archives)

Example of the "black trail" of smoke left behind by the *Nebelwerfer* rockets. These massive plumes of smoke betrayed the location of the *Nebelwerfer* battery and could result in serious losses from Soviet counterbattery fire if the battery did not change position rapidly. (U.S. National Archives)

A dramatic photograph of a supply column of Guderian's panzer group at a stop. There is clearly serious combat going on up ahead! (n.d.) (Bundesarchiv N 802/125)

Soviet bunker near the Desna captured on 2 October 1941. The next day, at the *Sportpalast* in Berlin, a jubilant Hitler declared to rapturous applause, "The enemy is already broken and will never rise again." (U.S. National Archives)

German tanks and other vehicles advancing on the town of Viaz'ma. On the morning of 7 October, the lead panzer divisions of 3 and 4 Panzer Groups joined hands at Viaz'ma, encircling four Soviet armies and part of a fifth of Soviet Western and Reserve Fronts. (Fotoafdrukken Koninklijke Landmacht, CCO, via Wikimedia Commons)

On 3 October, lead elements of 4 Panzer Division, having broken into open terrain and raced more than 200 kilometers from their start line, captured Orel (a strategic road and railway junction) in a coup de main, also seizing large quantities of fuel and rations. This is how the town looked after the fighting. (D. Garden and K. Andrew)

Guderian sitting in the passenger seat of his personal car accompanied by elements of his command echelon (n.d.). Note the small insignia on the left rear fender that denotes it is an army commander's vehicle, making it part of Guderian's *Befehlsstaffel* (command echelon). The vehicles on the right most likely belong to Boltenstern's 29 ID (mot.), as the large white marking—while not clear—is reminiscent of a regimental marking of the division. (Bundesarchiv N 802/30)

Elements of a panzer division advancing toward Moscow (October 1941). The lead tank is a Panzer III "G" model. The Panzer III was the *Wehrmacht*'s main battle tank in 1941. (National Digital Archives, public domain, via Wikimedia Commons)

Another image of Pz IIIs (*Ausführung G*) on the central front during Operation Typhoon. The *Ostheer* began the eastern campaign with 979 Pz IIIs across its three army groups; of these the majority were the "up-gunned" 50mm L/42, the remainder being outfitted with a 37mm main armament. (National Digital Archives, public domain, via Wikimedia Commons)

The Führer at one of his daily military conferences at his *Wolfsschanze* headquarters in East Prussia (October 1941). To Hitler's right (hands on the map table) is GFM von Brauchitsch (C-in-C of the Army); to Hitler's left is GFM Keitel (Chief of OKW); the tall officer against the wall is *Generalleutnant* Friedrich Paulus (Deputy Chief of Staff for Operations [OQu1] in OKH). (Bundesarchiv, Bild 101I-771-0366-02A/ CC-BY-SA 3.0, DE, via Wikimedia Commons)

German StuG IIIs on the central front (October/November 1941). (Bundesarchiv, Bild 101I-140-1212-04A/Götze/CC-BY-SA 3.0, via Wikimedia Commons)

Graphic image of tank-on-tank combat—a destroyed Pz IV almost adjacent to a knocked-out Soviet T-34. On 6 October, near the town of Mtsensk, 4 Panzer Division ran headlong into a pack of Soviet T-34 and KV-1 tanks. As one Guderian biographer put it, "This was an awesome moment." And indeed it was: For the first time, Guderian's panzers were clearly outfought, sustaining significant losses. In fact, 4 PD "had been dealt a crippling blow by an expertly managed Soviet counterstroke."

A knocked-out Panzer III belonging to 18 Panzer Regiment (18 PD). Notice the dark black arrow pointing to a dark circle placed around the spot where the enemy shell entered the tank. (German War Graves Commission)

A column of German tanks (led by a Pz IV) on the move (October 1941). The first snow fell in the sector of 2 Panzer Group on 6/7 October. "It did not lie for long," Guderian wrote, "and, as usual, the roads rapidly became nothing but canals of bottomless mud, along which our vehicles could only advance at a snail's pace and with great wear to the engines." (Bundesarchiv, Bild 101I-268-0185-02A/Böhmer/CC-BY-SA 3.0, DE, via Wikimedia Commons)

Two dozen *Landser* struggle to pull a vehicle through the mud and muck of the fall rainy season in Russia. By the second week of October, the autumn rains, known in Russia as the *Rasputitsa* ("the time without roads") had set in across the eastern front, dramatically slowing the pace of Army Group Center's pursuit of its beaten Russian foes. (Note: The Swastika flag was used by German forces across the eastern front to reduce incidents of "friendly fire" involving the *Luftwaffe*. However, despite such precautions, such incidents were quite common in all armies throughout World War II.) (Bundesarchiv, Bild 146-1981-149-34A/CC-BY-SA 3.0, DE, via Wikimedia Commons)

A German supply truck is hopelessly stuck in the mud and goo of the Russian fall rainy season. The mud produced in just a few hours of rain was sufficient to transform a typical Russian road into an utter quagmire, with all concomitant consequences. (H. Wijers)

Panzer soldiers of 18 Panzer Regiment (18 PD) pulling their tanks through the mud. It does not take much imagination to see how such conditions slowed the German advance and exhausted the troops. Of course, it is also true that the Russians had their own challenges with the rain of the *Rasputitsa* and the arctic cold and snow that followed in the weeks ahead. (German War Graves Commission)

Vehicles of Second Panzer Army crossing over a corduroy road (fall 1941). On both the staff car and the motorcycle/sidecar combination directly behind it, the "Gs" for Guderian's panzer army are clearly visible. (Note: Guderian's 2 Panzer Group was upgraded to Second Panzer Army in early October 1941). (Jon Davidson)

Supply trucks of Second Panzer Army (fall 1941). The mobility of Guderian's forces was now seriously degraded due to the loss of thousands of trucks and other motor vehicles. By 5 November, only 45 percent of trucks/motor vehicles (18,800) in his army were fully operational, given a strength of 42,200 on 22 June 1941. (Bundesarchiv N 802/125)

In the cauldron battles of Kiev, Briansk, and Viaz'ma in September/October 1941, the Germans captured more than 1.25 million Red Army soldiers. Overwhelmed by these masses of prisoners, German rear area services were not prepared to feed, house, or transport them. Most of the prisoners captured in 1941 were moved west, toward the POW pens that awaited them, in forced marches; these often continued for weeks, under catastrophic conditions over hundreds of kilometers, resulting in the deaths of tens of thousands along the roads leading to the camps. Exhausted, starving, and wounded, those prisoners who weakened and fell behind were shot dead, even in large cities such as Minsk or Smolensk. (Stackpole)

A German communications tower—which rather looks like a Tower of Babel!—pointing the way to Tula. The photograph has been marked with a black arrow (center left)—no doubt pointing out something important to someone. (German War Graves Commission)

Soviet 85mm anti-aircraft gun on the Proletarian Bridge in Tula (October 1941). Despite clawing their way to the outskirts of this strategically significant town, Guderian's weak and exhausted forces were unable to close the ring around Tula. On the night of 5 December, the panzer general—admitting defeat—broke off the attack on Tula for good, having decided to pull back his forwardmost units to an interim defensive line. (http://waralbum.ru/2708/, public domain, via Wikimedia Commons)

oldiers in a passenger car belonging to Guderian's panzer forces stop for a photograph. Behind them is a ice image of a Panzer II (the crew in their black uniforms atop the tank). As seen in many photographs of z II tanks, the 20mm L/55 main armament and 7.92 machine gun are wrapped in some kind of material, nost likely to keep dust, dirt, and mud from getting inside the barrels.

group of Panzer IV tanks moving down a road in the snow (October 1941). The *Ostheer* began the ussian campaign with just 444 Pz IVs in its order of battle—more proof that Hitler's eastern armies were eriously underpowered, given the enormity of the mission. (Bundesarchiv, Bild 101I-268-0185-03A/ öhmer/CC-BY-SA 3.0, DE, via Wikimedia Commons)

A platoon of Panzer III tanks advancing across snow-covered terrain. GFM Fedor von Bock had temporar ily suspended Operation Typhoon at the end of October; in mid-November, after the ground had finall hardened due to the colder weather, the attack was resumed by the mobile groupings on either wing c Army Group Center (Guderian's Second Panzer Army forming the right wing). Although the new offensiv initially made progress, it soon collapsed in the face of stiffening Soviet resistance. On 5 December 1941 Bock suspended the attack all along the front of his army group. (Stackpole)

German tanks in an arctic landscape. By December 1941, German offensive operations had been pushe well beyond their Clausewitzian culmination point—that is, the point where the strength and resource of the attacker are suddenly superseded by those of the defender. (H. Sohn)

German horse-drawn supply column moving through light snow into a Russian town (n.d.). Only
bout 20 percent of the *Ostheer* was composed of panzer or motorized divisions; thus the vast majority
f the German *Landser* marched across Russia on foot, supported at the start of the campaign by more
ian 600,000 horses. (The signs on the lower right point the way to a maintenance company [*Werkstatt-*
omp.] and a field hospital [*Feldlazarett*]). (U.S. National Archives)

battery of 105mm light field howitzers (le.FH 18) in an exposed firing position. The ground was so hard
iat explosives had to be used to dig trenches or gun emplacements. When explosives were unavailable
r deployment was required posthaste, the guns were placed out in the open, making them vulnerable
counterbattery fire. A German military publication in 1943 called the artillery the "backbone of the
ont" (*das Rückgrat der Front*), and indeed it was. During 1941/42 alone—despite habitual shortages of
iells—the German artillery in Russia would expend more than 60 million rounds—preparing the way
or the infantry in attack and shouldering much of the burden in defense. (Stackpole)

German armor advancing from the Kalinin region southward toward Moscow (most likely Novembe 1941). The harshness of the Russian winter landscape is graphically evident in this photograph. On November frost set in on the central front and continued (with snowfalls) until 7 November. For the fir time, on 6 November, the Volga had an unbroken covering of ice. On 8–9 November, another thaw se in. The cold season finally began in earnest on 10 November, and by the evening of 11 November th temperature had plunged to –10ºC. (Hans Boucsein)

A knocked-out Soviet T-34/76 near Moscow (late 1941). Soviet tank losses in 1941 amounted to mor than 20,000. From 30 September to 5 December 1941, average *daily* losses of Red Army forces opposi Army Group Center amounted to 9,825 men, 42 tanks, 57 artillery pieces and mortars, and four aircra (Jon Davidson)

German heavy machine gun position (winter 1941/42). In the arctic conditions of one of the coldest ussian winters ever recorded, the finely engineered German MG 34s often jammed or failed to fire at all. ɔ avoid potentially catastrophic malfunctions, machine gunners would often carry the bolt assemblies their pants pockets to keep them warm or, if possible, place their MGs inside houses until needed for ɔmbat. Because lubricants froze inside the weapons, it was soon discovered that the MGs would fire ore reliably if dry-cleaned of all lubrication. (U.S. National Archives)

ements of 29 ID (mot.), now commanded by *Generalmajor* Max Fremerey, retreating in December 1941. handful of cars and motorcycles still functioned. Most of the men walked, while those ill, wounded, infirm were allowed to be transported. With the destruction of so many of the division's vehicles, the ɔrse-drawn sleighs gained vital significance. (Note: Looking at the horizon one might conclude the men ere heading off into oblivion, and many undoubtedly were.) (Jason Mark/Leaping Horseman Books)

German troops in winter quarters somewhere between Orel and Kursk (December 1941). Due to his re
fusal to stop pulling back his forces, Guderian would be removed as commander of Second Panzer Arm
on 26 December 1941. While he later served Hitler's Third Reich in important staff positions, he wou
never again serve as a commander in the field. (Jon Davidson)

Epilogue

This brief study of *Generaloberst* Heinz Guderian and his panzer troops in Operation Barbarossa began by posing a vexing question: How was it possible that, with each spectacular victory secured by Guderian and his men along the road to Moscow, the prospect of final victory over the Red Army and the Soviet state seemed to slip further from their grasp? After having explored in some detail the operations of Guderian's forces throughout this decisive period of the Russian campaign, some answers to this paradox have emerged; they offer a window not only into the ultimate failure of Guderian's operations but into the collapse of Hitler's war of annihilation (*Vernichtungskrieg*) against the hated "Jewish-Bolshevik" enemy writ large.

What comes to mind posthaste is that Guderian's forces—and those of the entire *Ostheer* across the vast expanse of European Russia—were simply too weak to accomplish the Herculean tasks assigned to them by Hitler and his High Command. From a macro perspective, this was due, in large measure, to the fact that armaments production—even in the months preceding the start of the Russian campaign—had continued to limp along at an inexplicably leisurely pace; for example, in the first six months of 1941, German tank production amounted to an average of less than 220 units per month and would not reach a monthly average of 400 units until the spring of 1942.[1] Another data point: "In artillery alone, the paradoxical situation arose that in June 1941 the eastern army could only deploy [7,146] guns of all calibers, whereas during the campaign in the west in 1940 there had been 7,378 guns available on a considerably narrower front."[2]

Whether due to an unfathomably slipshod strategic analysis or perhaps simply to hubris, the impending confrontation with Soviet Russia did not result in the increases in production clearly required by the Army.[3] Fatally dismissive of the Russian colossus, Hitler and his General Staff—convinced they would be sufficiently prepared with stocks of weapons on hand for a blitzkrieg campaign of short duration—thus forfeited a singular opportunity between July 1940 and June 1941 to ramp up armaments production for Operation Barbarossa. Moreover, dramatic shifts in production priorities decreed by Hitler in mid-July 1941 (to prepare the Reich for its post-Barbarossa tasks; i.e., the second phase of the dictator's plan to achieve global power status) would have "disastrous consequences" by late in the year.[4] Yet, even *before* the start of the eastern campaign, the German armaments industry had made massive cuts to the output of ammunition, which began to affect German operations as early as August 1941 and would culminate in drastic shortages of critical types of ammunition (particularly of artillery shells) on the eastern front in fall/winter 1941/42.

As posited by the late English historian Paul Johnson, Operation Barbarossa "was to be the last *Blitzkrieg*."

> It was cut to the bone. Even in 1941 Hitler was not prepared to put the German economy on a full war-footing. Since the occupation of Prague [March 1939] he had become suspicious of the will of the German people to wage total war, and he was reluctant therefore to drive women into the war-factories or to cut civilian production and consumption more than was absolutely necessary to attain his military objectives. As a result, *Barbarossa was seriously underpowered* in terms of the magnitude of its objectives. (Author's emphasis)[5]

In the opening months of the campaign, the precious few German mobile units in the east (amounting to less than 25 percent of the entire Barbarossa force structure) were largely denied the replacements of men and materiel they needed to cover their crippling losses. Hitler and his General Staff, convinced they were on the verge of a decisive victory after just a few weeks of fighting, elected to hold back most new production of tanks, engines, and other vital items of equipment from their eastern armies and, instead, to use them to create new divisions earmarked for the farcical military adventures that were to follow in the wake of Barbarossa's success. Although the *Ostheer* had gone into the eastern campaign with 3,600 tanks and assault guns, some 2,100 armored fighting vehicles were recorded by the *Generalquartiermeister* of OKH as "out of action" on 10 November 1941; moreover, less than 30 percent (600) of these losses had been replaced since 22 June (and, of course, many of the replacement tanks and assault guns had also been put out of action by 10 November, meaning that Army Group Center was especially hard hit, for in the fall of 1941 it had three of the four panzer groups/ panzer armies in its order of battle). In an "Assessment of the Combat Power of the Eastern Army" (*Beurteilung der Kampfkraft des Ostheeres*) of 6 November, OKH concluded that the actual combat capability of a panzer division had been reduced to just 35 percent of its normal strength.[6]

As for Guderian, there is the astonishing fact that he began Operation Barbarossa with fewer tanks than he had at the beginning of the French campaign in 1940—even though his panzer group in Soviet Russia would operate on frontages as much as four times wider than he had experienced in France, while in the east the distances to be covered would be enormous compared to 1940. Such fundamental factors, coupled with the relentless attrition of men and machines due to the almost constant combat action and the wastage caused by often highly adverse geographical and atmospheric conditions—to say nothing of the failure of the Army High Command to make good his losses in the field—meant that, by late fall, Guderian possessed nowhere near the resources he needed to bring significant operational—or even relatively minor tactical—situations to a satisfactory outcome.

Guderian's operations were also hamstrung by the failures of the German military in the crucial (yet imprudently neglected) fields of intelligence and logistics. In his controversial tome *Hitler's War* (1977), English journalist and historian David Irving observed, "Probably no major campaign has ever been launched upon less intelligence. The services had furnished Hitler—to say nothing of their lower commands—with only the most inadequate information on the Russians. They were certain of only one thing: the German fighting man's inborn superiority. All else was the product of rumor, speculation, and fragile calculations. . . . This lack of proper intelligence was the root cause of the ultimate disaster."[7] Early on in the eastern campaign, Guderian was surprised to encounter a second echelon of Soviet armies along the Dnepr River, for which neither he nor the German General Staff had been prepared; months later, in early December 1941, he received no warning from German intelligence about the impending Soviet counteroffensive. Simply put, the monumental failures of German military intelligence before and long after 22 June 1941, coupled with racial and ideological prejudice against the Slav *Untermensch*, resulted in a fatal underestimation of the Red Army and the Soviet state[8]—a nasty quirk that would continue throughout the war (although German intelligence analysis did rather improve after Richard Gehlen took over at Foreign Armies East in the spring of 1942).[9]

As for logistics, although the supply and transportation problems that had to be mastered in a war with Soviet Russia staggered the mind, German logisticians, led by the Army quartermaster general, consistently fell back on facile and overoptimistic assumptions about what could be accomplished in this realm. From the start, however, it was apparent that the Army's supply system would be incapable of effectively sustaining an advance of more than 500 kilometers beyond the eastern frontier—but no matter, for the campaign would be over, or so it was thought, before supply became a significant issue. And yet, in a matter of weeks, the resupply of Army Group Center with fuel, munitions, and other necessities of war was becoming a growing challenge; by late fall, the entire logistical system was in a state of collapse. Indeed, the paralysis of Guderian's forces in the Tula-Kashira sector was due in part to fuel shortages that could not be overcome; in general, the operations of his Second Panzer Army throughout this final phase of Operation Barbarossa were repeatedly crippled by shortages of most every kind.

Yet, as this study has often emphasized, Guderian's own responsibility for the ultimate failure and defeat of his forces looms large. Like Hitler, OKH, OKW, and many of his fellow field generals, Guderian embraced a *Russland-Bild* (image of Russia)[10] that made him racially and ideologically dismissive of Red Army capabilities. After the victories over Poland and France, it was inconceivable to him that Germany could lose a war with Russia. Thus, while acutely aware of the unique challenges posed by the Soviet Union, he fully supported the Barbarossa adventure, convinced as he was that it could only end in triumph. Just like Hitler and his immediate circle of political and military advisors, Guderian was more than willing to bid *va banque*[11]—to put Germany's fate (and his own) on the line by taking a leading role in an enormous military enterprise from which Zeus himself might well have recoiled.

When it all ended in failure and a new (defensive) phase began, Guderian's shortcomings became manifest. In the weeks leading up to his relief, he had "proved too prone to retrograde movement with forces incapable of such action. This reflected his persistent belief in the superiority of maneuver. Moreover, Guderian was simply not a very effective defensive commander. He had not trained for or studied defense and considered it to be by far the inferior posture."[12] (In a letter to his wife, General Heinrici wrote on 19 December, "From today we are no longer part of Guderian's but of Kluge's army. We are pleased about that, because the leadership was not clear and good.")[13] The God of War having turned against him, Guderian grew melancholy. He refused to accept his own responsibility for the failure of the Barbarossa campaign, instead casting blame on anyone but himself and his shortcomings as a commander.

Of course, it must also be underscored that between the world wars Guderian was one of the pioneers of modern maneuver warfare (albeit not to the extent he later claimed) and became one of its foremost and ablest practitioners. Given the formidable challenges posed by the Red Army and the extent of the Russian European landmass, Guderian was convinced that constant movement was a vital prerequisite of victory: It would enable his panzer troops to push deep behind enemy lines, sowing disruption and confusion and paralyzing enemy command and control by disrupting their "OODA loop."[14] The acronym stands for "Observe, Orient, Decide, Act," and denotes the process by which an organism (either an individual or a group) reacts to an event. According to the concept (invented by a U.S. Air Force fighter pilot), the key to victory is to create situations whereby one can make appropriate decisions and take appropriate action before an opponent can react. Guderian understood this concept instinctively; in fact, it formed the very basis of his doctrinal thinking as one of the key founders of the German panzer troops in the late 1930s.

While Guderian sought success (and safety) in movement, actual combat was to be avoided when at all possible. When battle did come, he prioritized, in true Clausewitzian fashion, gaining overwhelming superiority at the decisive point(s). In the context of maneuver warfare, this meant deploying his tanks and motorized infantry *en masse* in accordance with his motto "Not in driblets but in mass!" (*Nicht kleckern sondern klotzen!*)

Guided by these and other canons of early 1940s maneuver (blitzkrieg) warfare, Guderian and his panzer troops slashed their way through central Russia, then into the Ukraine, registering one remarkable victory after another. Fully aware that the realities of time, space, and resources did not favor him, Guderian relentlessly pushed his soldiers to (and sometimes beyond) the limits of human endurance; indeed, the panzer general's solution to the unprecedented challenges posed by the Russian theater of operations was simply to drive himself and his men even harder than in previous campaigns.

Yet Guderian, in his obsession with speed and maneuver, clearly overestimated the operational significance of both in the unique battlespace of Soviet Russia. He failed to realize that the Red Army was much less sensitive to being enveloped and surrounded than his adversaries of 1939/40 and, perforce, would continue to resist despite immense losses and long after any possibility of relief or escape had vanished. It is thus not unreasonable to posit that Guderian did not, in fact, truly understand the fundamental character of the war on the eastern front, convinced as he was that the Russians—like the Poles and the French before them—could simply be overrun and defeated by speed and maneuver alone.[15] (Yet, to be fair, the same criticism could easily be made of Hitler, his High Command, and many [most?] of the *Ostheer*'s field generals fighting in the east in 1941.)

Leading from the front—on one occasion, at least, even operating a machine gun—Guderian was repeatedly exposed to enemy fire and had several narrow escapes. While such a leadership style was expected of a panzer general, it inevitably began to take its toll. Early on, "even Guderian came to recognize the great strain he was under. But, like most Germans, he naively continued to believe that the enemy was nearly broken and one last great offensive exertion would see Germany emerge triumphant. Amazingly, Guderian told Hitler on 4 August that the Red Army was scraping the proverbial bottom of its manpower barrel. Yet his frequent trips to the front must have revealed to him that such a perception was illusory."[16]

When assessing the leadership style of Guderian—and of other top panzer generals (Hoth, Hoepner, Geyr, Lemelsen, Schmidt, Manstein, etc.) for that matter—one must bear in mind the enormous pressure they were under. The success or failure of the Barbarossa gamble would largely hinge on their ability to carry out their mission of encircling and destroying the bulk of Red Army forces in a blitzkrieg campaign of mere weeks' duration, before the Russian colossus could mobilize and deploy its millions of trained reservists. By early August 1941, however, with the failure to rapidly bring the Battle of Smolensk to a close, it was becoming apparent—at least to the more contemplative among Hitler's officer corps—that the *Ostheer*'s panzer forces had failed in their mission and that the war might well be lost. It was certainly apparent that the blitzkrieg had come to an end; that the war in the east would be a long war. And such a war would be a war of attrition, dominated not by tactical or operational ingenuity but by the cruel calculus of production, industrial capacity, and material and manpower reserves. Guderian, of course, understood all this, and it was precisely this outcome that he had sought so desperately to avoid.

In his foreword to the English edition of Guderian's memoir, B. H. Liddell Hart maintained, "[Guderian] possessed most of the qualities that distinguished the 'Great Captains' of history—*coup d'oeil*, a blend of acute observation with swift-sure intuition; the ability to create surprise and throw the opponent off balance; the speed of thought and action that allows the opponent no chance of recovery [the 'OODA loop' concept described above] . . . [and] the power to win the devotion of troops, and get the utmost out of them."[17]

While all of that is true, Guderian remained a deeply divisive figure, a man of towering ego and ambition determined to perform *his* mission on his own terms, even to the point of insubordination; hence, it hardly surprises that he was viewed by many colleagues with a "mixture of suspicion and animus." According to one fellow general, Guderian was "a good tank man" but "no great personality" for he was "terrifically impulsive." Even General Geyr, whose 24 Panzer Corps fought under Guderian throughout the summer and fall of 1941, seems to have entertained a "low opinion" of his superior's character.[18]

Of course, Guderian also had his admirers—recall, for example, the remarks of *Oberstleutnant* Karl-Henning von Barsewisch, Guderian's *Luftwaffe* liaison (chapter 3). Friedrich von Mellenthin, a former German general who also fought on the eastern front, affirmed in his postwar appraisal of Guderian, "[His] almost frenetic urge to advance was certainly somewhat disconcerting to his superiors, but he never acted without due reflection. In spite of his temperament . . . [he] always made due allowance for his own capabilities and the potential of his own troops. . . . Success was Guderian's justification, and his troops followed him with enthusiasm and without hesitation."[19] In a publication in June 1988, honoring Guderian on the centennial of his birth, military historian Dr. Günter Roth went so far as to praise the panzer general for the superior operational judgment (*operatives Urteilsvermögen*) and strength of character (*Charakterstärke*) he had demonstrated by disregarding Hitler's halt orders in the final weeks before his dismissal.[20]

Despite his obvious talents, Guderian was not a military leader endowed with conspicuous strategic insight, the capture of the Soviet capital becoming an idée fixe that blinded him to the insurmountable challenges of the war in the east. (In this, of course, he was hardly alone, as other top generals—such as Brauchitsch, Halder, Bock, and Hoth—also placed their hopes for a successful outcome on the capture of Moscow.) He was also often anything but a "team player." During the cauldron battles of Belostok-Minsk (June-July) and Smolensk (July-August), he was concerned less with following Bock's orders to seal the pockets than with driving on farther east, toward his coveted goal: Moscow. Moreover, it was his blatantly disobedient behavior that, in the end, would get him dismissed from his command in late December 1941.

In the final analysis, Guderian's failure—and the failure of the Barbarossa campaign writ large—was foreordained. The point is simple yet germane: In terms of geography and resources, Nazi Germany was a mid-level power of about 80 million people (1939); conversely, Soviet Russia occupied one-sixth of the Earth's land surface, possessed a population of 190 million (1941), and, since the early 1930s, had built by far the world's largest military. With the failure of Operation Barbarossa to reach a rapid decision, the Soviets were given the time they needed to assemble and place dozens of new armies in the field; by the end of December 1941, the Soviet mobilization system had astonishingly generated more than fifty new field armies composed of many hundreds of new rifle, tank, and cavalry units.[21] And it was these fresh formations that ultimately stopped the *Ostheer*'s weakened and largely unreplenished forces at the gates of Moscow.

Between June 1941 and May 1945, the Soviets committed more than thirty million men to their "Great Fatherland War" (outfitted with numbers of tanks, trucks, guns, and planes that dwarfed what the Germans could muster), while the *Wehrmacht* barely managed to assemble ten million soldiers inside the borders of the Soviet Union. To conduct a successful attack, military theorists posit a 3:1 ratio in favor of the attacker. What a heavy irony it is that, in Hitler's titanic struggle against Stalin's Soviet state, that ratio was turned on its head.

For a while at least, in the opening phases of Operation Barbarossa, Panzer Leader Heinz Guderian, the protagonist of our story, was able to defy this fatal correlation of forces through the power of his will and his extraordinary generalship. Yet victory in modern total war goes to the side with the greatest resources, both human and material; in World War II that side was not Adolf Hitler's National Socialist Germany. And with the entry of the United States into the war in December 1941, Hitler's "Thousand-Year Reich" suddenly found itself hopelessly ensnared in a global conflict against an Allied coalition marshaling some 75 percent of the world's resources.[22] The outcome was no longer in doubt.

* * *

As I was editing this manuscript, I stumbled across a fascinating—and more than a little ironic—document in the late Dermot Bradley's biography of Guderian. It is a letter to Guderian from *Grossadmiral* Karl Dönitz, the C-in-C of the *Kriegsmarine* and Adolf Hitler's chosen successor to lead Germany after his death. The letter was written on 9 May 1945, just hours after GFM Wilhelm Keitel (Chief of Staff of OKW) had signed a final German instrument of surrender at the Soviet Army headquarters in Berlin-Karlshorst:[23]

> *Lieber Generaloberst* Guderian!
>
> Now that, as of today, the war has reached its end, I am thinking particularly of the tank weapon and its creator [*gedenke ich besonders der Panzerwaffe und ihres Schöpfers*]. In countless battles this weapon was in action at the critical points [*Brennpunkten*]—in the attack and, at the end, in defense. It was the sharp sword [*scharfe Schwert*] in the hand of the leadership.
>
> What you have given to the *Panzerwaffe*, in spirit, training, organization, and the most modern weaponry, now belongs to history. Your name has become, well beyond the framework of the *Wehrmacht*, an idea [*Begriff*] for the German people that will lift up coming generations.
>
> I fondly remember the time that we worked together and offer you my comradely greetings.
>
> Your Dönitz
> *Grossadmiral*[24]

Postscript

Throughout 1942, Guderian would remain on the unassigned officer reserve list; hence, he took no part in the Russian campaign that summer that ended with Friedrich Paulus's Sixth Army—the largest army the *Wehrmacht* had ever put in the field—trapped in a *Kessel* at Stalingrad. "Embittered" by the "unfair treatment" that had culminated in his dismissal, in early January 1942, he requested that a military court of inquiry be established to examine his past conduct: "This would have led to the refutation of the charges that [GFM] von Kluge had made against me and would have made clear the reasons underlying my past behavior. My request was turned down by Hitler. I was not informed on what grounds he did this."[1]

In his memoir, Guderian does not dwell on the year 1942, to which he devotes but a few pages. He had good reasons to omit the details of his activities at that time, since they did "not reflect well the self-image he wished to depict."[2] In late March, on the advice of his doctor, he and Margarete went to Badenweiler for a four-week cure, his heart problems having worsened due to the insufferable strain of the final months on the eastern front. ("The peacefulness of the beautiful countryside in spring and the medical baths of the little spa combined to soothe both heart and soul.") Still, his heart problems failed to improve, and in late November 1942 he suffered a complete collapse (*vollständigen Zusammenbruch*); he was almost "totally unconscious for several days and could take no nourishment." He would recover slowly.[3]

He also spent time looking for a house where he and Margarete could live following his retirement. His house-hunting prospects dramatically improved in the spring of 1942, when he accepted a secret payment of 1.25 million marks from Hitler—in effect, a massive bribe equivalent to more than fifty years' salary for an officer of Guderian's rank and seniority. (In fact, it signified the largest single bribe that Hitler ever gave to any of his field commanders. And a bribe it was meant to be, for the Nazi dictator had grown increasingly distrustful of his senior generals and used the money to hold them in line.) In October 1942, Guderian purchased a 2,500-acre rural estate of excellent farmland in the town of Deipenhof, but not before the Polish owners were forcibly evicted.[4]

He would languish for over a year without an appointment until Hitler called him back to service in late February 1943 as Inspector General of Armored Troops; in this capacity, he sought to increase the combat efficiency of the panzer divisions, developing new tables of organization for these formations and re-equipping them with the latest tank models. Prior to the July 1944 *Attentat* against Hitler, Guderian was asked to join the conspirators; although loyalty to his Führer kept him from doing so, he did not betray the plotters. In its aftermath, he was appointed to the Court of Honor, which expelled those officers thought to have been involved in the plot so they could be handed over to Roland Freisler and his notorious People's Court (*Volksgerichtshof*).

Following the failed bomb plot, the still-dazed Hitler elevated Guderian—who had deftly covered his tracks to avoid suspicion—to Acting Chief of the General Staff. In this capacity, however, Guderian's duties were restricted to advising Hitler on the eastern front (all other theaters of war being the responsibility of the OKW). On 29 July, in a basic order to all General Staff officers, Guderian demanded that each of them fulfill the role of a National Socialist guidance officer (*Nationalsozialistischer Führungsoffizier*, or NSFO) to strengthen the ideological orientation of the Army; moreover, they were to demonstrate their exemplary attitude on political issues and to do so publicly. Guderian also ordered that, in the assessment and selection of General Staff officers, personal qualities ("character" and "heart") were to receive priority over intellect.[5]

As Chief of the General Staff, Guderian "repeatedly demonstrated his lack of supreme command ability by routinely denigrating both the strategic importance and the resource needs of the other theaters. To Guderian, the war was the eastern front."[6] Of course, the mercurial panzer leader repeatedly came into conflict with an increasingly quarrelsome and deluded Hitler; thus, on 28 March 1945, he was relieved of command and sent home on sick leave.

He and Margarete retired to Munich, where he underwent further heart treatment. In the final days of the war, Guderian, ever dutiful,[7] rejoined his Inspector General of Armored Troops headquarters, which had been evacuated to the Tyrol, resuming his responsibilities. On 10 May 1945, he was taken captive by the Americans and released on his sixtieth birthday, 17 June 1948.[8]

From his birth on 17 June 1888 (two days after Wilhelm II had become Kaiser), the arc of Guderian's life had been shaped by the unprecedented upheavals of the first half of the twentieth century, which had seen him participate in two world wars and serve three separate masters: the Kaiser's Imperial Germany, the Weimar Republic, and Hitler's totalitarian Germany. After the Allied occupation of western Germany, he lived out his final years in the fledgling Federal Republic (*Bundesrepublik*) of the New Germany. Following publication of his highly influential memoir, *Panzer Leader*, by the Kurt Vowinckel *Verlag* (publishing house) in 1951, he passed away on 14 May 1954 at the age of sixty-five in Schwangau bei Füssen, Bavaria, West Germany.

Appendix A

Equivalent Military Ranks[1]

(German/American)

OFFICER RANKS

Generalfeldmarschall	Field Marshal
Generaloberst	General
General (der Infanterie, etc.)	Lieutenant General
Generalleutnant	Major General
Generalmajor	Brigadier General
Oberst	Colonel
Oberstleutnant	Lieutenant Colonel
Major	Major
Hauptmann or Rittmeister	Captain
Oberleutnant	First Lieutenant
Leutnant	Second Lieutenant

NONCOMMISSIONED OFFICERS (NCOS)

Stabsfeldwebel	Sergeant Major
Oberfeldwebel	Master Sergeant
Feldwebel	Technical Sergeant
Unterfeldwebel	Staff Sergeant
Unteroffizier	Noncommissioned Officer

ENLISTED MEN

Stabsgefreiter	Administrative Corporal
Obergefreiter	Corporal
Gefreiter	Lance Corporal
Obersoldat	Private 1st Class
Soldat (Schütze)	Private (Rifleman)

MEDICAL RANKS

Oberstarzt	Colonel (med.)
Oberfeldarzt	Lieutenant Colonel (med.)
Oberstabsarzt	Major (med.)
Stabsarzt	Captain (med.)
Oberarzt	First Lieutenant (med.)
Assistenzarzt	Second Lieutenant (med.)
Unterarzt	NCO (med.)

Appendix B

2 Panzer Group Order of Battle (22.6.1941)[1]

Bfh.:	*Gen.Oberst* Guderian
Chef d.St.:	*Obst.i.G.* Frhr. v. Liebenstein
Ia:	*Obstlt.i.G.* Bayerlein

46 *Panzerkorps*

Kom. Gen.:	*Gen.d.Pz.Tr.* v. Vietinghoff gen. Scheel
Chef d.St.:	*Obstlt.i.G.* v.d. Burg
SS "R:"	*SS-Gruppenführer* Hausser
10 PD:	*Gen.Lt.* Schaal
IR "GD:"	*Oberst* v. Stockhausen

47 *Panzerkorps*

Kom. Gen.:	*Gen.d.Pz.Tr.* Lemelsen
Chef d.St.:	*Oberst.i.G.* Bamler
18 PD:	*Gen.Maj.* Nehring
17 PD:	*Gen.Lt.* v. Arnim
29 ID (mot.):	*Gen.Maj.* v. Boltenstern
167 ID:	*Gen.Lt.* Schönhärl

12 *Armeekorps*

Kom. Gen.:	*Gen.d.Inf.* Schroth
Chef d.St.:	*Obstlt.i.G.* v. Waldenburg
34 ID:	*Gen.Lt.* Behlendorff
45 ID:	*Gen.Maj.* Schlieper
31 ID:	*Gen.Maj.* Kalmukoff

24 *Panzerkorps*

Kom. Gen.: *Gen.d.Pz.Tr.* Frhr. Geyr v. Schweppenburg
Chef d.St.: *Oberst.i.G.* Schilling
1 Kav.-Div.: *Gen.Maj.* Feldt
267 ID: *Gen.Maj.* v. Wachter
4 PD: *Gen.Maj.* Frhr. v. Langermann u. Erlencamp
3 PD: *Gen.Lt.* Model
10 ID (mot): *Gen.Lt.* v. Loeper
255 ID: *Gen.Lt.* Wetzel (2 PzGr reserve)

General HQ Units (*Heerestruppen*):[2]

Assault Gun Battalions 192 and 201 (12 AK)
4 105mm cannon battalions (2 to 12 AK; 1 each to 24 PzK and 47 PzK)
1 mixed artillery battalion (47 PzK)
4 150mm medium howitzer battalions (2 to 12 AK; 1 each to 24 PzK and 47 PzK)
4 210mm heavy howitzer battalions (1 each to 12 AK, 24 PzK, and 47 PzK; 1 directly controlled by 2 Panzer Group headquarters [*z.V.Pz.Gr.*])
1 210mm heavy howitzer battalion (limited mobility) (12 AK)
1 150mm cannon battalion (*z.V.Pz.Gr.*)
2 *Nebelwerfer* rocket projector battalions (12 AK)
1 *Nebelwerfer* rocket projector regiment (47 PzK [less one battalion]; 1 battalion to 24 PzK)
Machine Gun Battalion 5 (*z.V.Pz.Gr.*)
3 anti-tank battalions (2 mot., 1 SP) (1 each to 12 AK, 24 PzK, and 47 PzK)
2 flak (*fla*) battalions (1 12 AK; 1 *z.V.Pz.Gr.*)
Flamethrower Tank Battalion 100 (*Pz.Abt.[F]100*) (47 PzK)[3]

Appendix C

Order of Battle of a (Notional) German Panzer Division (June 1941)[1]

Division HQ with Map Section (2 le.MG)
Panzer Brigade Staff with
  Signal Platoon, Light Tank Platoon (3 Pz III command tanks, 5 Pz II)
2 Panzer Battalions,[2] each with
  1 HQ Company (2 Pz III command tanks, 5 Pz II)
  2 Light Tank Companies (each with 17 Pz III, 5 Pz II)
  1 Medium Tank Company (14 Pz IV, 5 Pz II)
2 Rifle Regiments (mot.), each with
  HQ Company (Signal Platoon, Combat Engineer Platoon, Motorcycle Platoon, 3 le.MG)
  2 Rifle Battalions each with
    3 Rifle Companies (each with 18 le.MG, 2 s.MG, 3 le.GrW)
    1 MG Company (8 s.MG, 6 s.GrW)
    1 Heavy Company (3 37mm Pak, 2 le.IG, 4 le.MG)
  1 Infantry Gun Company (2 s.IG, 4 le.IG)
1 Motorcycle Battalion with
  3 Motorcycle Companies (weapons same as rifle battalions)
  1 Motorcycle-MG Company (same as above)
  1 Heavy Company (same as above)
1 Medium Infantry Gun Company (Self-propelled)
  Only for 1, 2, 5, 9 and 10 PDs (6 s.IG [SP])
1 Armored Reconnaissance Battalion (mot.) with
  Staff and Signal Platoon (2 le.MG)
  1 Armored Scout Company (10 KwK 20mm,[3] 25 le.MG)
  1 Motorcycle Company (18 le.MG, 2 s.MG, 3 s.GrW)
  1 Heavy Company (same as in rifle battalions)
  1 Reconnaissance Column (3 le.MG)

1 Artillery Regiment (mot.) with
- Staff and Signal Platoon
- 2 Light Artillery Battalions each with
  - 3 Light Field Howitzer Batteries (each with 4 105mm le.FH, 2 le.MG)
- 1 Medium (*schwere*) Mixed Artillery Battalion with
  - 2 Medium Field Howitzer Batteries (each with 4 150mm s.FH, 2 le.MG)
  - 1 100mm Gun Battery (4 100mm cannon, 2 le.MG)

1 Anti-tank Battalion[4] (mot.) with
- Staff and Signal Platoon
- 3 Anti-tank Companies (each with 8 37mm Pak, 3 50mm Pak, 6 le.MG)
- 1 Flak Company[5] (SP) (8 20mm flak, 2 20mm *Vierling Flak*)

1 Armored Combat Engineer Battalion (mot.) with
- 2 Light Combat Engineer Companies (each with 9 le.MG)
- 1 Armored Combat Engineer Company (Pz I,[6] 6 SPW[7] with 280/320 rocket projectors)
- 1 Bridging Column "B" (mot.)
- 1 Bridging Column "K" (mot.)
- 1 Light Combat Engineer Column (mot.)

1 Armored Signal Battalion (mot.) with
- 1 Armored Telephone Company (2 le.MG)
- 1 Armored Radio Company (13 le.MG)
- 1 Light Armored Signal Column

1 Field Replacement Battalion

Supply and Rear Area Services, including

Motor Vehicle Supply Columns

1 Supply Company (mot.)

3 Maintenance and Repair Companies (mot.)

2 Medical Companies (mot.)

3 Ambulance Platoons (mot.)

1 Bakery Company (mot.)

1 Butchery Company (mot.)

1 Ration Supply Office (mot.)

Military Police (mot.)

Field Post Service (mot.)[8]

Appendix D

292 Infantry Division

Organization, Personnel, Weapons, and Equipment (June 1941)

Details on the 292 Infantry Division are provided here as an example of a "typical" German infantry division on the eve of Operation Barbarossa. The division was mobilized in the 8th Wave and formed in February 1940 on the Troop Training Grounds (*Truppenübungsplatz*) Gross-Born, in Military District II (*Wehrkreis* II); it was considered to be fully combat capable. At the start of Barbarossa, 292 ID was assigned to GFM von Kluge's Fourth Army. Throughout the summer and fall of 1941, it saw major action in the central sector of the eastern front. Beginning in July 1941, 292 ID was temporarily assigned to Guderian's command and saw action at Roslavl and in the bitter defensive fighting at El'nia, east of Smolensk. The division also took part in Operation Typhoon, the assault on Moscow.

Combat strength (*Gefechtsstärke*):[1]

- Officers: 269
- Civilian officials: [2]7
- NCOs: [3]1,553
- Enlisted personnel: 9,712

Ration strength (*Verpflegungsstärke*):[4]

- Officers: 358
- Civilian officials: 85
- NCOs: 2,196
- Enlisted personnel: 12,510
- Horses: 5,729

Organization

- 292 Mapping Detachment (mot.)
- 507 Infantry Regiment

1 Signal Platoon
1 Pioneer Platoon (3 le.MG)
1 Regimental Band
3 Infantry Battalions, each with
3 Rifle Companies (9 le.MG, 2 s.MG, 3 le.GrW each)
1 Heavy Company (8 s.MG, 6 s.GrW)
13 Infantry Gun Company (2 s.IG, 6 le.IG)
14 *Panzerjäger* (AT) Company (mot.) (12 le.Pak, 4 le.MG)
1 Mounted (horse) Reconnaissance Platoon
1 Light Infantry Supply Column

508 Infantry Regiment
(same as 507 IR)

509 Infantry Regiment
(same as 507 IR, but no regimental band)

292 *Panzerjäger* (AT) Battalion
1 Signal Platoon (mot.)
3 *Panzerjäger* Companies (mot.) (12 le.Pak, 6 le.MG each)

292 Bicycle Squadron
1 Bicycle Squadron (12 le.MG)
1 *Panzerjäger* Platoon (3 le.Pak, 1 le.MG)

292 Artillery Regiment
3 Battalions (1, 2, and 3), each with 3 Batteries (4 le.FH, 2 le.MG each)
1 Battalion (4) with 3 Batteries (4 s.FH, 2 le.MG each)

292 Replacement Battalion (*Feldersatz-Bataillon*)
3 Companies

292 Signal Battalion
1 Radio Company (mot.)
1 Telephone Company (mot.)
1 Signal Supply Company (mot.)

292 Pioneer (Combat Engineer) Battalion
2 Pioneer Companies (9 le.MG each)
1 Pioneer Company (mot.) (9 le.MG)
1 Bridging Column "B" (mot.) (*Brüko "B"*)
1 Engineer Supply Column (mot.)

Divisional Supply Troops
Several Light Columns (mot.)
Light Fuel Column (mot.)
Maintenance Platoon (mot.)
Supply Company
Divisional Administration
Field Bakery

Butcher Detachment (mot.)
Medical Company
Medical Company (mot.)
Field Hospital
Ambulance Companies (2)
Veterinary Company
Military Police Troop (mot.)
Field Post Office (mot.)

Total Available Weapons (*Verwendungsbereite Waffen*)[5] (included the following):

le.MG	384
s.MG	108
Pz.B.	93
le.GrW	79
s.GrW	53
le.IG	18
s.IG	6
le.Pak	43
m.Pak	6
le.FH	36
s.FH	12

Appendix E

2 Panzer Group Order of Battle (30.9.1941)[1]

47 *Panzerkorps*
Kom. Gen.: *Gen.d.Pz.Tr.* Lemelsen
29 ID (mot.)
17 PD
18 PD

24 *Panzerkorps*
Kom. Gen.: *Gen.d.Pz.Tr.* Frhr. Geyr v. Schweppenburg
3 PD
4 PD
10 ID (mot.)

48 *Panzerkorps*
Kom. Gen.: *Gen.d.Pz.Tr.* Werner Kempf
9 PD
25 ID (mot.)
16 ID (mot.)

34 *Armeekorps*
Kom. Gen.: *Gen.d.Inf.* Hermann Metz
45 ID
134 ID

35 *Armeekorps*
Kom. Gen.: *Gen.d.Art.* Rudolf Kaempfe
95 ID
296 ID
262 ID
293 ID
1 Kav.-Div.

Partial list of General HQ Units (*Heerestruppen*):

- *Nebelwerfer* Regiment 53 (3 battalions)
- Machine Gun Battalion 5
- Army Flak Battalion 602
- PzG Signal Regiment 2
- Engineer Battalion 635 (mot.)
- Bridge Building Battalion 159
- 3 Bridge Columns "B"
- 2 road construction battalions
- 2 reconnaissance squadrons

(Note: I Flak Corps,[2] with its 88mm guns in a ground-support role, also supported the attack of 2 Panzer Group [*auf Zusammenarbeit angewiesen: Flak-Korps I*].)

Appendix F

Panzermänner in Operation Barbarossa[1]

A General Overview

CHARACTERISTICS OF THE PANZER ADVANCE (*VORMARSCH*)

In a staff report on 17 June 1941, 24 Panzer Corps observed that its great objective, the Soviet capital of Moscow, lay precisely 1,040 kilometers to the east. As the officers in this powerful, battle-tested formation no doubt fully understood, a successful outcome to the campaign would hinge almost entirely on their ability—and that of the other panzer corps, which together made up the hard edge of the *Ostheer*—to carry out the missions laid out for them in the Barbarossa directives. Hitherto, the panzer units of the *Wehrmacht* had enjoyed a rather good run. Harnessing mobility, firepower, radio communications, and combined-arms tactics—perhaps the most striking example of the "unparalleled profusion" of revolutions in military affairs (RMAs) originating in the interwar period between 1919 and 1939—along with a leadership culture that, in the best traditions of the Elder Moltke, sought to push responsibility for critical decision making on the battlefield down to the lower ranks (*Auftragstaktik*), the *Panzermänner*, in their crisp, black uniforms, had shattered Germany's more conventional opponents in swift succession, from the plains of Poland, across the fields of France, to the rugged landscape of the Balkans. To be sure, Russia posed their greatest challenge yet; still, most were confident the campaign would progress no differently than those during the first twenty months of war.

In hindsight—if not to Hitler, OKW, and OKH in the spring of 1941—it is all too apparent that Operation Barbarossa, and the key operational concept it embodied, signified a risk of immense proportion. Indeed, if one considers the relative paucity of operational and tactical intelligence on which the campaign was based, it becomes clear just how daring—perhaps foolhardy—was the mission assigned to the panzer corps: to push hundreds of kilometers beyond the frontier, deep into the enemy's hinterland, without regard for their flanks or rear, while encircling and destroying an enemy known to be much larger numerically. Nonetheless, as executed on 22 June, the concept seemed at first to work out brilliantly, the eastern blitzkrieg functioning, in the words of historian Christian Hartmann, with an "uncanny efficiency and speed."[2]

With permanent support from GHQ units (*Korpstruppen*)—assigned, yet not organic, to the panzer corps, including flak artillery, medium and heavy motorized artillery battalions, assault gun units, *Nebelwerfer* rocket-projector batteries, and so forth—and the bulk of *Luftwaffe* fighters, bombers, and dive-bombers carving up the enemy before them, the tank and motorized divisions smashed through the Soviet frontier defenses and drove east toward their initial objectives. In his novel *Moscow*, published shortly after the war (1953), German author Theodor Plievier captured the essence of the German armored onslaught into Soviet Russia:

> The stream of tanks thundered over the bridge. The infantry lying at the side of the road were covered with dust. When there was a halt the men of Gnotke's platoon could have a good look at the tanks. Only the driver sat inside, the crew sat on top—the commander on the edge of the turret with his headphones on, the others behind him.
>
> "Look at that, they've got all their gear hanging on the outside." "Of course, everything goes bad in the heat with the stink of oil." Cooking utensils, drinking water, sacks of bread and rations—they all hung dangling on the walls of the tanks. Behind there were the gasoline tins, and no tank was without its boards and beams, its wooden matting to lay on soft patches. Then there were tanks with trailers.
>
> "Like gypsies," remarked one of the infantrymen.
>
> The column went on, there was a halt, and then it started again, rolling ahead at 10 miles an hour. An armored division had about 5,000 vehicles; spaced out at the regulation interval with all the auxiliary units, it would cover more than a 100 miles. . . .[3]
>
> There was no sign of the sun, which must be sinking, for all this rattling and roaring and whining and screeching that crept by blotted out the day. The long stream of armor and the long wake of thick dust it stirred up stretched as far back as the Bug and over the Bug far into the heart of Poland. . . . So it rolled on along the road through Brest-Litovsk, Minsk and Smolensk, rolled along the military highway to Moscow—the highway they had seized and would now irresistibly sweep clear.[4]

The greatest German successes developed on the central axis, where Army Group Center—unlike Army Groups North and South—had two tank groups at its disposal. Despite a negative correlation of forces (about 1:1.6) at the outset of the campaign (more than 1,800 tanks of Army Group Center facing 2,900 tanks of Soviet Western Front), the *Panzergruppen* of Hermann Hoth and Heinz

Guderian repeatedly demonstrated their tactical superiority over the Red Army, which was patently overmatched by the new techniques of modern mobile warfare. A key point, however, all too often overlooked in accounts of the stunning series of victories registered by German forces in the summer of 1941, is that their success was as much the result of Soviet unpreparedness (shortfalls in training, weapons, ammunition, logistics, etc.) as it was the outcome of the operational and tactical supremacy of the *Wehrmacht*. For example, only 383 of the Western Front's tanks were modern T-34 and KV models; the rest were superannuated T-26 and BT light tanks. Many of the T-34 and KV tank crews had received little to no training prior to 22 June; photographs abound of T-34s abandoned in swamps and bogs, having been driven off the roads by the relentless attacks of German combat planes enjoying total supremacy in the air. On the front of Army Group North, many Soviet KV tanks—victims of clogged oil filters and transmission failures—broke down en route to the battlefield.

In one remarkable incident outside the town of Raseinai on 24/25 June (sector of Erich Hoepner's 4 Panzer Group), an attack by two battalions of rampaging T-34s and KV-1s was brought to a halt only because the Soviet tanks—much to the astonishment of the defending Germans—ran out of fuel and failed to make use of their main 76.2mm armament (the tank guns had not yet been bore-sighted; thus their crews had orders to ram the advancing panzers), enabling German sappers to eventually neutralize them with satchel charges.[5] When the T-34s and KV-1s did get properly into battle, the lack of training meant poor marksmanship and clumsy tactical control. And still, the heavy Soviet tanks had "thrown a fright" into the Germans, "mastered, finally, only by the attitude and discipline of the officers."[6]

Another problem for the Red Army was its lack of effective anti-tank technology, the majority of its 14,900 AT weapons being underperforming 45mm guns.[7] Yet, despite being unprepared on so many levels for the unprecedented German assault, the Red Army (for the most part) fought across the entire eastern front with a tenacity, courage, and level of violence in the attack that uniformly stunned the German invaders.[8]

Following the successful execution of the opening battles of encirclement at Belostok-Minsk in early July 1941, the tanks of Army Group Center breached the Dvina-Dnepr river lines—the crossing of the Dnepr by 24 Panzer Corps alone supported by 333 *Luftwaffe* aircraft. Fighting and marching without surcease, the German mechanized units smashed division after enemy division; by 13 July, for example, 17 Panzer Division (47 PzK.)—"this brave division," as Guderian called it—had alone knocked out 502 Russian tanks.[9]

What it was like to fight and die in a tank is described in exacting detail by former British Army Colonel Robert J. Kershaw:

> Panzer crewmen have a different battle perspective compared to infantry on their feet. Scenery, as a consequence of greater mobility, changes quickly and more often. Maps are read from a different vista in terms of time, distance and scale. Panzers quickly crossed maps. Infantrymen saw each horizon approaching through a veil of sweat and exhaustion. . . . A new horizon for the tank soldier meant an unknown and, very likely, a threatening situation. His was an impartial war, fought at distance. Technology separated him from direct enemy contact: he normally fought with stand-off weapon systems at great range. When direct fighting did occur, it was all the more emotive for its suddenness and intensity. . . .
>
> Little can be seen from the claustrophobic confines of a tank closed down for battle. Fighting was conducted peering through letter-box size—or smaller—vision blocks in a hot, restricted and crowded fighting compartment with barely room to move. Each report from the main armament or the chattering metallic burst of turret machine gun fire would deafen the crew and release noxious fumes into the cramped space. Tension inside would be high, magnified throughout by a prickling sense of vulnerability to incoming AT round strikes, anticipated at any time. These projectiles were easily seen flying about the battlefield as white-hot slugs, with the potential to screech through a fighting compartment and obliterate all in its path. The kinetic energy produced by the strike set off ammunition fires, searing the fighting compartment in a momentary flash, followed by an explosive pressure wave blasting outward through turret hatches, openings or lifting the entire turret into the air. An external strike by a high-explosive (HE) warhead would break off a metal "scab" inside; propelled by the shock of the explosion, this would ricochet around the cramped interior of the tank. The results were horrific. Flesh seared by the initial combustible flash was then lacerated by jagged white-hot shrapnel, which in turn set off multiple secondary explosions.
>
> Tank crewmen were muffled to some extent from battle noises outside the turret, because the screams were dulled by the noise and vibration of the engine. Human senses were ceaselessly buffeted by violent knocks and lurches as the tank rapidly maneuvered into firing positions. Dust would well up inside upon halting, and petrol and oil smells would assail nostrils during momentary pauses.[10]

Gefreiter Erich Hager, a tank radio operator in 17 Panzer Division, experienced firsthand the horror of having the tank in which he was fighting destroyed in combat. During the initial days of the war, he took part in major tank-versus-tank combat and, despite some difficult moments, survived unscathed. On 28 June 1941, however, southwest of Minsk, Hager and his crew's good fortune finally ran out. In his diary, meticulously crafted in German *Sütterlin* script using a Russian school notebook, Hager recorded the harrowing event:

> 28 June [1941]:
>
> Everything keeps moving. . . . We get 60 liters of fuel from the half-tracks and drive on through the line of bunkers. Receive fire and transmit okay. Get stuck in the mud, also *ObLtn.* Zinschütz. Our company commander pulls us out. We

> get in, get the shells, and get to the rendezvous point. Drive through the burning town that has been destroyed by Stukas. Outside the bunker there is Pak (anti-tank) artillery. We fire at everything and drive on. Once again, there is firing from the left and the right. The Russians are hiding and firing from an ambush. There has never been a war with so many snipers, civilians among them. . . .
>
> We drive on in the lead and come to a village. Heavy firing there. We come to a corner and here it happened: Three shells from not more than 20–30 meters away struck our tank. Driver *Uffz.* Wedde is dead. . . . We bale out as the tank is already on fire. We get out with only what we have on us. It was so quick. . . .
>
> Shells struck the driver and just missed me. I can only speak of luck that I didn't get hurt. I'm so sorry about Wedde. He didn't make a sound. He must have been killed outright.[11]

Hager and the other survivors took refuge in a ditch, where they lay in the mud for three-quarters of an hour while the Russian fire continued. Pinned down, with hostile forces all about them, they were unable to get away: "We see our last hour coming." At the final moment, however, Hager and his comrades were rescued by a German infantry patrol. Having lost contact with their tank company, they stayed with the infantry the next day (29 June); outfitted by their hosts with helmets and rifles, they fought as infantry. On 30 June, they moved out to find their unit: "At 12.00 we find Sch . . . [illegible] with his tank. We get on top and ride with him. All of a sudden *Uffz.* Hertlein comes up behind us with three pals. He turns completely pale. No one believed we were still alive. The whole company gathers together. We had been reported as dead and signed off by the boss. There is great joy."[12]

Still deeply affected by the tragic events of 28 June—the loss of a valued comrade—Hager returned to the site of his destroyed Panzer IV. Other knocked-out German tanks were also there, and he snapped photos of them. In his diary, he expressed shock at the damage sustained by his tank and the others—their armor plating stripped away by the impact of the shells. The driver, Wedde—"they found one good body part [of him]"—and the other dead panzer soldiers were buried in simple, raised, rectangular graves, each one carefully adorned with the dead comrade's helmet, flowers, and a wooden cross.

Bolting past the Dnepr-Dvina River barriers, the enveloping arms of 2 and 3 Panzer Groups linked up again, this time around Smolensk, some 600 kilometers from the frontier, forging a second spectacular battle of annihilation on the central front. On 16 July 1941, Guderian's motorized troops stormed into Smolensk; by 5 August 1941, some 300,000 more Soviet soldiers were marching into the German prisoner of war pens.

The principal catalyst behind these extraordinary victories along the central axis was, of course, the panzer generals themselves—Guderian, Hoth, Schmidt, Geyr, Lemelsen, Model, Funck, Nehring, Harpe, et al. To a man, they fully understood that victory hinged less on engaging the enemy in combat than on the rapidity of their movement. Immense distances needed to be overcome and vital objectives secured in a matter of weeks—while the weather was good and before the Russians were able to mobilize their vast resources of men and materiel. As mentioned, on the eve of the campaign, Guderian had exhorted his tankers to be on the move day and night, without repose, without concern for threats to their flanks—to push on as far as their fuel would take them. "The main thing," he assured them, "is to advance far, and to shoot little." An officer attached to 4 Panzer Division confided in his diary, "We shall be constantly on the march. There will be no stops. We will only rest during periods of refueling. We will take our meals either while on the march or during the short refueling pauses. There is only one objective—Moscow!"[13]

From 22 June onward, the pace of operations was remorseless, the panzer generals pushing their men, tanks, and vehicles (and often themselves) to the limits of their endurance. An account by a veteran of 19 Panzer Division amplifies this point while also underscoring other common characteristics of the panzer *Vormarsch*—such as the Soviet tactic of slashing at the flanks of the German armored columns, which, advancing far ahead of the foot infantry, sometimes became temporarily cut off or outran their logistical support:

> After a few days' marching, the march route of 19 PD swung from "P 1" (*Panzerstrasse* 1)[14] toward the south. . . . Here, the motorcycle riflemen marching at the front met stiff enemy resistance and were also attacked from the flanks. A bridgehead that had been established over the river Gavia was temporarily abandoned. The remaining divisional elements were cut off from the elements located further forward by enemy units attacking from the flanks, so the [forward troops] could not at first receive support from heavy weapons. The platoon leader of one infantry gun platoon writes:
>
> "Like an angel, an observer from the artillery suddenly turned up! A few moments later, the first shells exploded in the ranks of the enemy. Under the battery's cover fire, the platoons were able to withdraw to the near side river bank and to be immediately redeployed."
>
> . . . The division then deployed in battle formation. Upon their arrival, the individual batteries immediately got themselves ready to fire. And with that ended the grueling, nerve-wracking, tension-laden, hot days of the first days of the advance. Up to that point, nobody had been either able or permitted to sleep a wink, which, however, would not have been bearable any longer.
>
> A report on this:
>
> "I had managed to keep myself awake for up to five days. Then my eyelids ineluctably dropped. Evidently there was a limit to the amount of sleep deprivation and desperate wakefulness that human beings could bear. The result was that we entered into our first action utterly exhausted, dripping with sweat, filthy, and otherwise provided with only meager rations."[15]

Despite the measures taken to make the mobile units largely self-sufficient for the first days of the campaign, the speed and depth of the advance meant that the panzer corps had soon left their support elements far behind. On occasion, fuel for tanks and vehicles had to be rushed forward in emergency airlifts, while soldiers often foraged for food to supplement their meager rations, an activity described in another anecdote involving 19 PD; like so many of the personal accounts in this narrative, it offers fascinating ancillary insights as well:

> On one of these days, at the entrance to a Lithuanian village, *Oberleutnant* Lewerenz (7./AR 19) had commissioned me to take care of the necessary provisioning, because our field kitchen had not kept up. The "iron" rations were not to be touched. With a sidecar-motorcycle, I drove through the strung-out village and started by asking at the last house for bread, which was willingly given to me. After they had handed over the bread they had available, all the villagers directed me to the village grocer, who had built his wooden house in the shape of a rectangular fort with a courtyard. At my knock, a bearded, rather portly grocer in a black kaftan appeared, who declared in Yiddish: "I not have bread." Since he had been described by the other villagers as the wealthiest, but also the most miserly—which I found to be true—I shoved this fatso to one side and took a look at his warehouse, in which lay whole sacks of everything that our field kitchen could possibly need, just no baked bread. After loading the sidecar with round, strangely sour-tasting loaves of bread and eggs from the other villagers, I returned to our battery.[16]

Advancing mostly in ad hoc battlegroups—their columns strung out for 50 kilometers or more over the inadequate Russian road net—the German tank crews, motorized infantry, and supporting combat units marched and fought for weeks on end, often without any badly needed breaks for rest, replenishment, or maintenance. By mid-August 1941, 24 Panzer Corps had yet to have a single day out of action, and despite its desperate need for rest and maintenance and Guderian's pleas, OKH ordered its operations to continue. No twenty-first-century "postmodern" Western army would dare to even contemplate demanding of its soldiers what the Germans demanded of theirs (mobile troops and infantry alike) during the summer of 1941 in Russia.

GERMAN PANZER GENERALS LED FROM THE FRONT

Observed historian and former Swiss tank corps officer Rudolf Steiger, "When commanding armored units in particular, the situations change so rapidly, and the opportunities to make use of good luck pass so quickly that commanders should not confine themselves to posts far behind the lines."[17] As we have seen, German panzer generals led from the front. A glance at Guderian's memoir underscores this principle: The fifty-three-year-old general was a whirlwind of purposeful activity, driving from one corps or divisional headquarters to the next, consulting with key subordinates, collecting information, issuing orders, and accompanying his troops at the point of the advance. It is thus no surprise that Guderian would experience several narrow escapes from death or capture from the very beginning of the eastern campaign.

Guderian, of course, was not the only German panzer general whose propensity to fight from the vanguard resulted in close scrapes or even serious injury in the summer of 1941. General von Arnim was wounded in late June 1941 and forced to relinquish command of 17 Panzer Division; General Model, the tempestuous commander of 3 Panzer Division—who "kept turning up, monocle in place and cursing, at every crisis point"[18]—had a close call on 24 June, when the armored car he had only just vacated was obliterated by Russian artillery fire. General Schmidt, Commander, 39 Panzer Corps, barely escaped from a dangerous encounter caused by his own reckless behavior on the fourth day of the war; on 25 June, with his tanks advancing southeast from Vilnius toward Minsk, Schmidt personally led a terrain reconnaissance (*Erkundungsvorstoss*) at the head of his troops. In an article that appeared in a German newspaper several days later, Hans Hertel, an officer on the staff of the panzer corps, wrote about the incident:

> The troops had continued their attack the following morning at undiminished speed and boxed their way through the enemy resistance everywhere. But the rapid tempo was still not enough for the general of these troops [i.e., Schmidt]. He knew that speed was everything in this offensive. So he gave the order: forward, at any cost! [*Vorwärts um jeden Preis!*] And then began an unprecedented chase. The general, accompanied by only a very few forces from a reconnaissance battalion and a few men from his staff, positioned himself personally at the spearhead, driving ahead in an open jeep in order to reconnoiter the best march routes.[19]

Yet the daring expedition into territory still teeming with Russians quickly turned sour. Schmidt and his small party were soon fighting for their lives, having been ambushed and surrounded by the Russians in a wooded area near Molodechno, with the general trapped in a ditch beside the road. Despite being assaulted from three sides by Soviet troops, collectively voicing their bone-chilling cries of "Urrah!," General Schmidt, keeping his composure, ordered his men to break out through the enemy lines. Under cover of darkness, Schmidt and his small party somehow managed to extricate themselves from their existential predicament and, early the next morning, linked up again with friendly troops.

At the conclusion of his article, *Ordonnanzoffizier* Hertel praised the general for the example he had set for his men. Schmidt's biographer, however, offered a rather different perspective on the general's behavior that day:

> Well, it's open to debate whether a reconnaissance foray by a corps commander is an encouraging example from a military point of view. If a general appears at the front with his troops, then he is providing his soldiers with a good example.

> However, if he ventures into the territory of enemy forces with only very weak cover, then in my opinion that's reckless and, in view of the unnecessary losses that could incur, irresponsible. After all, the corps could have lost its leader in that venture. . . . Guderian's leadership principles—that a panzer general should lead from the front—were taken too far here. But even Guderian and other German generals had already exposed themselves to similar situations. It was, to be sure, in the mentality of the Prusso-German officer corps to lead their soldiers by example, and, in doing so, to occasionally disregard responsibility for their men and even themselves.[20]

Many months later, Hertel would compose the following account, revealing the "method" in Schmidt's "madness."

> By the onset of winter 1941, the officer corps of 39 Pz.Korps had, in percentage terms, suffered double the fatalities of the enlisted soldiers. Such losses cannot be replaced in the long run, certainly not in terms of their quality: in view of the expected long duration of the war, they were not objectively justifiable, but they were the great secret for the exemplary discipline and admirable performance of the troops.
>
> At 39 Pz.Korps, the corps commander [Schmidt] is always right at the front, the chief of staff leads further back. The commander is always right there where the action is. He knows from the experiences of the First World War that a body of men only remains intact if the officers set a good example. On the first day of the Russia campaign, he crossed over the frontier with the combat engineer spearhead; during panzer attacks, he drives ahead of the panzers in an open command car. He gives no quarter to officers who fail, even in the slightest, to maintain their bearing and sends them straight home. This all gets round very quickly and all the soldiers have real trust in their "Papa" Schmidt. Yet he's not some sort of dare-devil with a "sore throat" (this means a desire for medals to wear round the neck, e.g. the Knight's Cross and so on), or consumed by some sort of abnormal ambition. He certainly isn't some sort of chauvinist, more like a cosmopolitan, but really properly rooted in Germanness.[21]

There is an amusing postscript to the incident of 25 June 1941. From the shot-up and abandoned vehicles of Schmidt's reconnaissance party, the Soviets had salvaged a clutch of documents. That evening, Moscow radio made a special announcement, declaring the complete destruction of German 39 Panzer Corps and the death in battle of General Schmidt. During the announcement, the names of all German officers ostensibly killed in the action—among them, Hans Hertel—were read out. The next morning, the same report was aired by the British Broadcasting Company's German-language broadcasts. At home, in Weimar, Germany, Frau Schmidt received a sympathy visit from an acquaintance, appropriately attired in a black suit and top hat. Even the Commander-in-Chief of the Army, *Generalfeldmarschall* von Brauchitsch, was sufficiently alarmed by the foreign radio reports to place a telephone call to the staff of 39 Panzer Corps. To put the rumors to rest, special reports were promulgated by the German press, while General Schmidt was interviewed by a Dr. Ernst from Radio Cologne (*Reichssender Köln*) on the captured airfield at Molodechno.

T-34S, KVS AND "STALIN ORGANS"

While the T-34s and KVs were relatively few in number and, for the most part, poorly led, they did force the Germans to take notice; in fact, they administered a collective adrenal shock to the soldiers of the *Ostheer*.[22] As for Guderian, he at once recognized the superiority of these new Russian tanks over existing German models, and it disturbed him.

On the first day of the war, 7 Panzer Division had been roughed up on its approach to Olita by T-34s fighting in hull-down positions; on 6 July, a tank battalion of 3 Panzer Division suffered heavy losses from a handful of well-concealed T-34s during combat along the Dnepr river line. Three days earlier (3 July), Nehring's 18 Panzer Division, advancing on Tolochino from its bridgehead over the Berezina at Borisov, had its first encounter with both T-34 and KV tanks; an officer in the division's 18 Panzer Regiment described the division's rude introduction to the T-34 at this time:

> Early morning 0700 hours, between Borisov and Tolochino, *Panzeralarm*. From the right comes a Russian tank battalion at "full speed" and attacks us. *Hauptmann* Kirn, with the 1st Battalion, fires furiously, but all hits simply slide off: the first T-34s. Horror grips us. Only a wet field separates us from the Russians. They drive at full throttle into the marshy ground and 11 T-34 tanks get stuck. The remaining tanks turn back, luckily for us. Now we wear the others down with our firing; they slowly climb out and we take 11 tank crews prisoner, with their commander and adjutants. The Russian commander is deeply impressed.[23]

In a diary entry on 25 July 1941, *Major* "S.," a tank battalion commander in 20 Panzer Division, vividly illuminated the visceral shock evoked by these early encounters with Soviet T-34 and KV tanks. On this day, *Major* "S." and his battalion took part in a harrowing engagement against a heavy Soviet tank brigade. After expending their armor-piercing rounds on a KV-1, to no effect, the major and his crew discovered that their tank's engine would no longer turn over. Immobilized and out of shells, they abandoned their machine. Evading the Russian tank's machine-gun fire in a desperate "cat and mouse" game, they managed their escape.

> Gradually, a reaction of nervous tension made itself felt amongst us. Somewhat exhausted, we went a little way back along the road, up to a street attendant's cottage, where we sat down on a bench to rest. From there we had a good overview of the battlefield in the sunken ground. We saw both our own and enemy

> tanks that had been put out of action, but none combat ready from either party. About 100 meters away from us stood a burning T-34, which, as was later ascertained, had been shot into flames by the commander of 6th Company. Half an hour later it blew sky high with a dull crack, flinging the turret 30 meters away. Further back at the forest edge we saw a T-34 that had rammed one of our Panzer IIs. It had even climbed up it and then not been able to free itself. From a distance it looked like the mating of two dinosaurs. This scene was later referred to in the regiment as the panzer wedding.
>
> Of course some of my men had suffered a shock, as they were taken completely by surprise and attacked right up close by an opponent clearly superior in terms of weapons and armor plating. And even more so when they discovered that they had hardly any impact with their own little tank guns. Who could hold that against them? One non-commissioned officer drove back into the area of Combat Echelon B with his tank, which had been severely damaged in the fight. There, sinking down exhausted next to *Oberleutnant* K., he told the following about his experience:
>
> "*Herr Oberleutnant*, it was terrible! One [of the Russian tanks] just advances up to me, I'm firing and firing, armor piercing shells, high explosive shells, with the machine gun. Hit after hit, but he doesn't notice any of it. And he's coming ever closer, his shots missing us by a hair's breadth. Shoots again, the shot tears the track shield from my tank. I can calculate when he will have the next huge shell in his barrel, then he will hit home. I'm only 30 meters away from him, and then another tank comes at me from the side, its barrel pointed at me. That's when my driver puts his foot down and we drive off between the two of them with gusto. They are better armored, better armed, and faster, what else could we have done? Look how I'm shaking!"[24]

Major "S." went on to explain how the German panzer crews not only survived but, more often than not, emerged victorious from such encounters in the summer of 1941: "If the Russian tank soldiers had had good leadership and the proper conduct, the destruction of my battalion would have been unavoidable. . . . To be precise, the difficult fighting of that day in a near hopeless situation was overcome by the fighting spirit, greater marksmanship, and quick responses of the German tank crews [*Panzermänner*] of all ranks."[25]

In his postwar manuscript, Kurt Werner Andres, in July 1941 a nineteen-year-old motorcycle messenger in 21 Panzer Regiment (20 PD), provided additional insight into the reasons behind the success of the German panzer crews in the summer of 1941:

> The diary entries [of the panzer crews] show clearly on the one hand the surprise of the German panzer crews at the appearance of the first T-34s and KV-1s on the battlefield and, on the other hand, the better fighting spirit, the quicker reactions, the mental flexibility in the midst of battle, and, not least, the [superior] marksmanship of the panzer crews. "Battle between Pak and tank, and tank and

> tank is like a duel, he who fires faster and more accurately will be the victor," so *Major* S. in his diary entry of 25 July 1941.
>
> In the context of blitzkrieg warfare, it was of decisive importance to deploy panzer units *en masse* in accordance with the motto of *Generaloberst* Heinz Guderian (1888–1954): "Not in driblets but in mass!" [*Nicht kleckern sondern klotzen!*] In contrast, at the beginning of the campaign, the Soviet tank tactics stood out by allocating their tanks to the individual infantry companies. This was surprising, because following the capture of Minsk, on 30 June 1941, we found in some officers quarters a film projector and several rolls of film that showed, among other things, in the form of a training film, the German panzer tactics during the French campaign.
>
> *Oberleutnant* K. in his diary entries of 27 July 1941: "The Russian leadership is not employing [its armored vehicles] operationally in large masses, a tactical plan cannot be discerned, and so their use is being frittered away in individual actions. It is incomprehensible, but it has always been like this. We would hardly have survived these days if the Russian, who shows himself as an individual to be brave and determined, had been well led."[26]

Despite the obvious superiority of Soviet T-34 and KV tanks, they remained more of a novelty—albeit a sobering one—than an existential threat to the panzer crews and their commanders in the summer of 1941. (Numerous photographs from the period show curious German soldiers closely examining, even crawling about, the tanks.) Nevertheless, it is a truism that soldiers in all armies, at all times, are badly shaken whenever confronted by the fact that their opponent possesses weapons of superior quality; as the accounts above illustrate, this was certainly true of the *Panzermänner* in Soviet Russia. Not until early October 1941, however, at the start of Operation Typhoon (the final advance on Moscow), did the alarm bells go off, when Langermann-Erlencamp's 4 Panzer Division (a component of Guderian's 2 PzG) was badly mauled by large packs of well-led T-34s south of Mtsensk. "This was the first occasion," acknowledged Guderian, "on which the vast superiority of the Russian T-34 to our tanks became plainly apparent. The division suffered grievous casualties. [*Die Division hatte betrübliche Verluste.*] The rapid advance on Tula that we had planned had therefore to be abandoned for the moment."[27]

Another new Soviet weapon, the highly secret BM-13 *Katyusha* (Little Kate) solid-fuel multiple-rocket launcher, was first used in mid-July 1941—against German forces fighting west of Smolensk. On 13 July, 17 Panzer Division captured the critical rail junction of Orsha, southwest of Smolensk. The next day, the railroad station there was overflowing with *Wehrmacht* trains and supply transports; these were taken under fire by a battery of *Katyushas* in the first battlefield test of the weapon system. The battery fire began in mid-afternoon and lasted fifteen to twenty minutes; about 100 132mm-caliber rockets struck the rail yards, blowing up German ammunition trains and fuel tank cars and turning the yards into a blazing inferno.[28]

On 15 July 1941, the *Katyusha* battery was again in action, this time against 12 Panzer Division at Rudnia,[29] midway between Smolensk and Vitebsk. About this action Soviet General A. I. Eremenko later wrote,

> We tried out this superb weapon at Rudnia, northwest of Smolensk. In the afternoon of 15 July, the earth shook with the unusual explosion of jet mines [rockets]. Like red-tailed comets, the mines were hurled into the air. The frequent and dazzling explosions, the like of which had never been seen, struck the imagination. The effect of the simultaneous explosion of dozens of these mines was terrific. The Germans fled in panic, and even our own troops near the points of the explosions, who for reasons of secrecy had not been warned that this new weapon would be used, rushed back from the front line.[30]

Despite the infernal racket made by multiple explosions, the Germans soon discovered that the rockets were not particularly accurate and the fragmentation effect was poor. The *Katyushas* were most effective as an area weapon—against troops caught in the open and lightly skinned vehicles. Against tanks, the rockets had little effect except for a rare and fortuitous direct hit. That the weapon could be extremely lethal, however, especially against troops unfamiliar with it, is beyond question. Recalled a former *Gefreiter* with 14 Infantry Division (mot.) in a letter to me,

> We weren't so afraid of . . . the Stalin Organ. The casing was not thick, so the fragmentation effect was not great, but—large fragments, half shells lay around plentifully enough. A lot of earth was moved, but the deafening sound [*Krach*] was the biggest thing about it! You could see them approaching, but then, with time, we got wise to it: don't lie on the ground—like with artillery shells—stand ready, and then kick upward with the shifting sand or soil. In the beginning, we had too many losses to the Stalin Organ because everyone instinctively hit the ground inside their trench, and then they were buried by the soil movements and suffocated!
>
> Once, they shouted out over the trench loudspeaker: "Early tomorrow morning we will deploy the new 320mm rocket projector! None of you will survive the day tomorrow, so: Change sides tonight!" The 320s came and they came frequently after that—and I'm still alive today![31]

In the summer of 1941, the BM-13 multiple-rocket launcher saw only limited action. Yet, as many German war diaries and *Landser* accounts reveal, this would change dramatically in the fall of 1941, when the Red Army began to employ the weapon often and to great effect on the central front outside Moscow.

THE INEVITABLE OUTCOME: REMORSELESS ATTRITION

In mid-July 1941, *Oberstleutnant* Smilo Freiherr von Lüttwitz, Commander, 12 Rifle Regiment, took part in a commanders' conference on the outskirts of a village somewhere beyond the Dnepr River. The regiment belonged to Langermann-Erlencamp's 4 Panzer Division, one of the most elite units of the *Wehrmacht*. The conferring officers were perched on several benches beneath a large apple tree in an orchard. It was a peaceful, idyllic scene. Suddenly, a shell from a heavy Russian gun burst atop the apple tree.

> [*Oberst* Dietrich von] Saucken and 4–5 others were critically injured, one of them died very soon after. Ecker and I, who sat right in the middle of all of them, were thrown a long way clear by the air pressure, but not even scratched, an utter miracle! We immediately helped the severely wounded. I put pressure on the artery of an *Oberleutnant*, whose leg was ripped off, until the doctor eventually came. On the way back to the regiment, we washed off the blood in a puddle, great quantities of blood that plastered our entire uniforms.[32]

Scenes such as this were common in Russia in the summer of 1941. Injury and death, when they came, were often sudden and unexpected.

In assessing the attrition of German mobile forces in the summer of 1941, it is instructive to begin with Carl von Clausewitz. Generally speaking, the debilitating effects of bad weather, terrain, poor roads, poor maps, tank and vehicle breakdowns, accidents, tactical errors, supply problems, human exhaustion and frailty, the unforeseen, and other phenomena too numerous to adumbrate all fall under the rubric of friction, the "only concept," wrote Clausewitz, "that more or less corresponds to the factors that distinguish real war from war on paper."[33] The cumulative impact of such factors, coupled with inexorably hardening Russian resistance—by late July/August 1941, coordinated counterstrokes were underway across the central axis of the German advance—was to alarmingly attrit the panzer forces of both Hoth and Guderian while significantly slowing their pace of operations.

From the outset, the unexpected requirement to fight the cauldron battles to the bitter end—the result of tenacious Russian resistance—disrupted the advance of the panzer corps and caused serious casualties (29 ID [mot.] alone losing forty-seven officers in late June 1941 while covering the sector of the Belostok-Minsk pocket west of Slonim). As Robert J. Kershaw observed,

> The need to fight encirclements to annihilation had not happened before in [World War II]. It broke the tempo of Blitzkrieg. An ominous portent of the future had been the vicious battle for the citadel of Brest-Litovsk in the first days of the campaign. . . . Encirclement battles at Minsk and Smolensk consecutively tied down more than 50% of the offensive potential of Army Group Center. In the west, creative General Staff planning had split and outmaneuvered the allied

> armies, which capitulated. The Russians doggedly fought on, whatever the cost. Inspired maneuver alone would not suffice to win battles on the new eastern front. The savaged opponent had first to be finished off, a time-consuming and costly affair. German "fast" motorized or panzer divisions were not configured for this development and were unpracticed in defense. They were badly mauled penning their fanatical opponents, waiting for the arrival of the infantry who were to administer the *coup de grace*.[34]

Racing eastward, the panzer corps were soon as much as 150 to 200 kilometers ahead of the foot infantry. Adeptly exploiting this vulnerability in the configuration of German forces—that is, the ever-widening gap between the mechanized spearheads at the tip of the advance and the foot infantry bringing up the rear—the Russians tore repeatedly at the open flanks of 2 and 3 Panzer Groups. To counter their growing isolation, the armored combat teams improvised new defense and security measures—such as all-around defense (*Rundumverteidigung*)—that were often not even mentioned in German field manuals. The farther east the Germans advanced, the greater the length of the front became; because the front was often thinly held and far from contiguous, many gaps opened up, enabling Soviet forces, time and again, to attack and destroy rear-area services and supply columns—missions also undertaken by Russian stragglers and partisans behind the front. In mid-July 1941, the diary of an officer in 18 Panzer Division noted a Soviet ambush of the division's field hospital in Dobryn, resulting in heavy losses.

Because the mobile units were constantly on the move at and beyond the forward edge of battle, sometimes becoming intermingled with, or even cut off by, Red Army forces, they were vulnerable to accidental attack by their own forces. In fact, such "friendly-fire" incidents may well have contributed more to the attrition of the German armored forces than has been hitherto recognized. Recalled Kurt Werner Andres (20 PD), "Grievous [*bitter*] were the losses resulting from the fire of our own weapons. In the excitement of the moment, it was not unusual for German tanks, mistaken for those of the enemy, to be knocked out [by friendly fire]."[35]

In modern warfare, with the antagonists normally separated by great distances and employing horrifically destructive weaponry, getting killed or wounded by one's own troops with weapons intended for the enemy is an all too common occurrence.[36] In World War I, Adolf Hitler's own regiment, the Bavarian Reserve Infantry Regiment 16 (the so-called List Regiment), became a victim of friendly fire on its first day of combat in October 1914, during the First Battle of Ypres.[37] Paul Fussell, the late American cultural historian, discussing the large number of friendly-fire incidents involving Anglo-American troops between 1939 and 1945, saw in these and other types of deadly "blunders, errors, and accidents something very close to the essence of the Second World War."[38]

While several examples of such incidents among the troops of Army Group Center have been outlined in the preceding narrative, a few more will serve to reinforce this serious yet neglected topic. In his personal diary, *Leutnant* Georg Kreuter (18 PD) noted that a "high percentage" of his unit's losses on 22 June were the result of friendly artillery fire.[39] On 1 August, Guderian was caught in a *Luftwaffe* bombing attack, in which the "first bomb burst 5½ yards from my car"; the bombing caused "heavy casualties."[40] Several weeks later, as 2 Panzer Group drove south, into the Ukraine, the 2 SS Motorized Infantry Division *Reich* was set upon by more than two dozen Stuka dive-bombers, whose bombing runs left ten dead and more than thirty wounded Waffen-SS soldiers in their wake (see chapter 6).

The swift pace of the advance also meant that signal communications—radio and telephone—were becoming more difficult to maintain while vital lines of supply grew longer and more vulnerable. By the time of the Smolensk operation (July-August 1941), logistical problems were beginning to affect operations, in part because conversion of the rail lines from Russian broad gauge to European standard gauge was not proceeding with the requisite dispatch. Shortages of spare parts were now appearing, as were breakdowns in the delivery of supplies. Observed Kenneth Macksey,

> At this time in the German diaries, for example, that of the Chief of Staff of 2 Panzer Group, tales about the chaotic arrival of stores begin to appear. Mud shields arrived, but not vital parts for vehicles. On occasions concrete practice mortar rounds came forward instead of the real article. This was typical of what was happening.
>
> There was, therefore, a sort of steady decay: not total breakdown or anything like that, but things were not as good as they might have been, and this was beginning to restrict operations and make people more cautious. They looked over their shoulders, wondering whether tomorrow's supplies would arrive. Also, with the much more intense battles, ammunition expenditure was far higher than expected.[41]

Seriously exacerbating this slow, "steady decay" was the fact that the losses of the panzer groups (both personnel and materiel) were not being made whole. On 4 August 1941, when Guderian reported to Hitler at the headquarters of Army Group Center, in Borisov, he reminded his "Führer" that only an "unbroken, steady stream" of new tanks, engines, and replacement parts—as well as aircraft—could keep the offensive going. Hitler replied that he needed all the new tanks and planes for "future tasks." Grudgingly, the dictator agreed to supply a month's production of new tank engines, nothing more. Other than that, Guderian's panzer group and the rest of the tank forces would have to make do with what they had.

What they had, however, was, after six to eight weeks of continuous operations, markedly less than what had made up their orders of battle on 22 June 1941. Figures on tank and personnel strength for several of the panzer divisions of Army Group Center amplify this point:

- 3 Panzer Division, having entered the campaign with more than 200 tanks, had just 86 tanks in a combat-ready state on 30 July 1941 (with some 50 more in the workshops for repair).[42]
- 4 Panzer Division, by late July, had 49 tanks ready for action (out of an initial complement of 177), with 83 more considered repairable. By mid-August, the division's motorized rifle companies had lost 50 to 70 percent of their combat strength, with many of "the best fighters" among the casualties. By 31 August 1941, the division had suffered a total of 2,325 casualties (dead, wounded, missing), while receiving only 528 replacements.[43]
- 7 Panzer Division, on 21 July 1941, reported a combat strength of 118 tanks, with 96 others under repair. To maintain its combat effectiveness, the division broke up one of its three tank battalions to keep the remaining two at effective strength. The division had begun Barbarossa with 265 tanks.[44]
- 10 Panzer Division, which had possessed 182 tanks on 22 June (including 45 Pz IIs, 105 Pz IIIs, and 20 Pz IVs) had just 5 Pz II and 4 Pz III tanks fully combat capable on 20 July 1941. An additional 25 Pz IIs, 38 Pz IIIs, and 3 Pz IVs (many with minor engine damage due to a lack of oil) were considered capable of performing a defensive mission. Roughly 100 of the division's tanks required maintenance and repair.[45]
- 18 Panzer Division, which began the campaign with 218 tanks, had been reduced to 83 operational machines by 11 July—losses due, in part, to costly encounters with superior T-34 tanks. The division had also lost 2,279 men, more than 13 percent of its manpower, in barely twenty days—an unsustainable loss rate of more than 100 men per day. By 18 July, 18 PD had lost more than 75 percent of its armor as well as almost half its anti-tank guns; by late July, the division had sustained 765 dead (among them 63 officers), 1,968 wounded, and 377 missing (including units temporarily under the division's control). The division was so exhausted it was pulled out of the line for several weeks, undergoing rest and replenishment in the forests southeast of Smolensk.[46]
- 20 Panzer Division, by 26 July 1941, had incurred a total of 2,085 casualties, for an average daily loss rate of 60. These losses embraced fully 35 percent of the division's officers, 19 percent of NCOs, and 11 percent of rank and file (compared to their respective marching-out strengths).[47]

On 25 July 1941, General Lemelsen, C-in-C, 47 Panzer Corps, noted in his diary that his three divisions (17 PD, 18 PD, 29 ID [mot.]) had sustained an average of 2,200 casualties since the start of the campaign, while also losing up to 50 percent of their motor vehicles. "My divisions urgently require replenishment, but where it will come from no one knows," he wrote dejectedly.[48] Losses of officers, Lemelsen observed several days earlier, had been lamentably high:

> 16.7.[41]:
>
> Yesterday evening, 29 [ID (mot.)] captured Smolensk despite fierce resistance. The 71 IR in particular distinguished itself here. House after house had to be taken with "cold steel" [*mit blanker Waffe*] and hand grenades, and in a city of 150,000 inhabitants, that's quite something.
>
> The losses were considerable as a result. Many graves lined the road as I drove to Smolensk early this morning, including a large number of the most capable young active officers from 15 IR who had, until now, taken part in the entire war without injury. It's a real shame. "Fallen for Greater Germany" stands simply on the plain crosses. I even found the grave of *Leutnant* Keitel from 29 AR, the son of the Field Marshal, on that road today. Our best officers are dwindling away in this cruel war, which is so very different to that against Poland or even that in the west.[49]

The grinding attrition, particularly among officers (and NCOs), and the congealing Red Army resistance were becoming growing concerns to the German Army High Command. Moreover, the first, quiet doubts about the future course of the campaign were beginning to emerge, as revealed by a diary entry of *Hauptmann* Georg Heino Freiherr von Münchhausen, adjutant to *Oberst* Adolf Heusinger (Chief, OKH Operations Branch), in early August 1941: "The Russian has put up really strong forces opposite the eastern front of Army Group Center! And all those reserve armies behind them. Will we manage to smash him before Moscow? The supply problem is becoming increasingly difficult for us, the losses in the panzer groups due to the attrition of materiel will continue to rise, even after replenishment, and the troops are increasingly battle weary [*abgekämpft*]. And above all the high number of losses among the officers!"[50]

By late July 1941, the panzer generals at the front, and many of their officers and men, were also starting to question how much longer they could endure the high attrition rates yet continue to fight effectively. As General Nehring, C-in-C, 18 Panzer Division, recalled in an article published in 1961, "Four weeks of storming forth without pause, with their immense exertions and hardships, had their effect on both men and materiel. Very softly the question began to arise: 'How can this continue?'" (*Wie soll es weitergehen?*)[51] As early as 11 July 1941, Nehring, sounding the alarm on the dangerous attrition in his division, had warned that the high loss rates should not be allowed to continue "if we do not intend to victor ourselves to death" (*wenn wir uns nicht totsiegen wollen*).[52] Weeks later, on 22 August, Army Group Center acknowledged in its war diary, "The armored units are so battle weary and worn out that there can be no question of a mass operative mission until they have been completely replenished and repaired."[53] Yet, in spite of the battle weariness, major operations went on; not only the panzer corps of Army Group Center, but the *Ostheer* as a whole, continued to consume diminishing resources in constant marching and fighting—as the battle lines grew in length, the combat increased in intensity, and replacements of men, machines, and materiel failed to reach the front in sufficient numbers.

Despite the heavy losses and the many unforeseen challenges, the morale of the panzer troops remained remarkably high. In a letter to his father, tank gunner and reserve officer candidate Karl Fuchs (7 PD) gushed with pride about his and his unit's accomplishments during the opening weeks of the campaign:

> 24 July 1941:
> Dear Father
>
> It's been quite a while since you wrote to me and informed me of your transfer. When I received your letter, we were already on the march against the enemy. The weather was incredibly hot, and dust and dirt were our constant companions. From the north of East Prussia we advanced over Kalvaria to Olita. There I was involved in the biggest tank battle in history! The enemy was thrown back with heavy losses. Immediately we pursued them. On the third day of the campaign we reached Vilnius. The Lithuanian civilians had staged an incredible reception for us. We were literally showered with flowers!
>
> After a day's rest we continued in the direction of Minsk. I was always up front in my tank, creating gaps in the enemy lines. Special radio announcements reported our accomplishments. When we heard them outside of Minsk, we were overwhelmed. Our company was given special orders and we carried them out to everyone's satisfaction. For a week, during our attack of Lepel and further on in Vitebsk, I was always in the lead with my tank. I will never forget those battle experiences.
>
> Now we are already on the other side of Smolensk. . . . For me the battle itself is the biggest adventure and experience. During our attack on Minsk I received the Tank Assault Medal and I have been recommended to receive the Iron Cross, Second Class. Yes, we're moving forward toward victory and peace.
>
> I hope that you are in the best of health. I greet you with our old battle cry: Germany, Sieg Heil!
>
> Your loyal son, Karl[54]

On the evening of 21 November 1941, during a skirmish with Russian tanks, Karl's tank was knocked out, and he was killed. Roughly a year and a half later (18 June 1943), his widow, Helene Fuchs, received a correspondence from a major in her husband's former unit; it contained the silver Tank Assault Medal that Karl had so proudly earned.

Appendix G

German Army Organization and Weaponry (June 1941)

Because the narrative portion of this book focused on the combat leadership of Panzer General Heinz Guderian and the operations of his 2 Panzer Group (Second Panzer Army), issues of unit organization and the individual capabilities of German weapons systems were rarely addressed. The purpose of this appendix is to remedy those lacunae in the main text.

As discussed at some length in the epilogue, during the critical period between July 1940 and June 1941, neither Hitler nor his military staff were prepared to assign to their planned confrontation with Soviet Russia—the burden of which was to be carried by the Army—the priority it deserved.

The outcome of a German military culture dominated by strategic myopia, collective hubris (anything was possible for the German soldier!), and racial contempt for its Slavic enemy was that the *Ostheer* crossed the German-Soviet frontier on 22 June 1941 with "alarming shortfalls"—in armor-piercing weapons, field artillery, and infantry field pieces, to name a few—that seriously compromised the firepower of the infantry. Some eighty-four infantry divisions—and several motorized infantry divisions as well—were outfitted with all types of foreign vehicles (mainly of French origin), while captured weapons were used to partially outfit the anti-tank units. The armored forces went into combat with hundreds of obsolete tanks, as well as large numbers of armored fighting vehicles of Czech origin. While these and other types of foreign equipment were by no means necessarily inferior to German standards, they added to the bewildering multiplicity of types[1] in the German Army, complicating already existing challenges in the areas of ammunition, spare parts, and maintenance. Were it not for the use of captured materiel, however, it would scarcely have been possible to equip the expanded German Army of 1941 for Hitler's war in the east. Indeed, in the summer of 1940, the OKH had recognized that captured stocks of weapons, vehicles, and other equipment were a "vital prerequisite" for the deployment of the *Ostheer*.[2]

As outlined below, Germany's military leadership made significant qualitative improvements to their ground forces in the year separating the victory in the west from the start of Barbarossa. And yet the inescapable conclusion is that the order of battle assembled for war against Soviet Russia was not much more imposing than that committed to the campaign in the west in 1940, while the "patchwork quilt" of weapons, vehicles, and equipment collected for the Russian campaign suggests that "Hitler's eastern army resembled a pieced-together, mismatched construction—not the imposing, purpose-built, uniformly-equipped war machine often portrayed in the immediate post-war literature."[3] Again, the proximate cause for what, in hindsight, seems scarcely fathomable is a German military culture that—after nearly two years of unbroken victories—had lost its professional bearings and, perforce, exhibited too little curiosity and concern about its future adversary in the east. To sharpen the point: The German generals' approach to Barbarossa reminds us "why war must be carefully planned and thoroughly researched prior to opening the latches that secure Hell's gates."[4]

THE (FOOT) MARCHING INFANTRY

The foot infantry, dependent largely upon horse-drawn transport, continued to dominate the force structure of the German Army of 1941, accounting for close to 75 percent of its more than 200 divisions. Despite the "headlines" grabbed by the panzer divisions, it was the infantry that shouldered the principal burden on the battlefields in all theaters of operation, just as it had in the Great War of 1914/18. The typical infantryman on the eastern front lasted only a matter of weeks before being wounded or killed. Many were wounded repeatedly, only to return time and again to their units, until finally being killed or taken prisoner. Yet the German infantry "fought with impressive tenacity and effectiveness throughout World War II, even after their units had sustained extreme losses."

> Statistical analyses have concluded that German troops typically inflicted 50 percent greater casualties on their opponents than they suffered in return, regardless of whether they were attacking or defending, even in the face of overwhelming Allied numerical advantages and air superiority later in the war. One of the most basic elements of this phenomenal military fighting power was unit cohesion: the ability of German soldiers to stick together and to continue operating as an integrated team despite devastating losses, long after the point where other forces would have dissolved into a mass of individuals driven by panic and the mere instinct of self-preservation. German soldiers also showed a remarkable capacity to regroup and form *ad hoc* battlegroups composed of stragglers and survivors of various units.[5]

During World War II, the German armed forces organized, trained, equipped, and sent into battle 389 infantry divisions.[6] According to standard German practice, these divisions were created in "waves" (*Welle*), with no fewer than thirty-five waves created throughout the war. As a rule, each wave was characterized by (mostly) minor differences in weaponry and equipment, while organization tended to be more standard. At full strength in 1939, a "first wave" infantry division with highest priority for materiel possessed more than 5,000 horses but fewer than 600 trucks. The "haphazard process" of rearmament from 1933 to 1939 had precluded any attempt to expand the German automobile industry sufficiently to motorize a mass army. The German Army had responded by building for its foot infantry a family of state-of-the-art horse-drawn wagons, outfitted with such refinements as ball-bearing wheels and rubber tires. The only fully motorized elements in German infantry divisions were the anti-tank companies and battalions, for which it was imperative to move fast enough to counter enemy armor. Signal and reconnaissance units also had some motorized elements; however, the latter continued to mount some of its soldiers on bicycles.

The total strength of an infantry division in June 1941 was about 17,000 men. The core of the division was its three infantry regiments, each comprising approximately 3,000 men. Each regiment, in turn, broke down into three battalions, each of four companies—three rifle companies and one machine-gun company. The infantry regiments were also equipped with a company of light and medium infantry guns and an anti-tank (*Panzerjäger*) company. Complementing the three infantry regiments in each infantry division's order of battle were an artillery regiment, an anti-tank battalion (outfitted with the same weapons as the regimental anti-tank companies, only more of them), a reconnaissance battalion, and a combat engineer battalion, along with signal, medical, veterinary, administrative, and supply services.

Standard weapons of the rifle company included (1) the Mauser 98K bolt-action rifle, the standard German infantry weapon throughout the war (caliber: 7.92mm; feed: five-round clip;[7] effective range: ca. 725 meters); (2) machine pistols (typically for NCOs and officers), the most common type being the *Machinenpistole* 40 (MP 40), with a thirty-two-round magazine and practical rate of fire of 180 rounds per minute; (3) machine guns, primarily the MG 34 (caliber: 7.92mm; feed: belt or drum; rate of fire: 900 rounds per minute (cyclic); practical rate of fire: 100 to 120 rounds per minute as le.MG, 300 as s.MG; effective range: as le.MG, ca. 550–725 meters, as s.MG, ca. 1,800–2,300 meters); (4) light and medium mortars (50mm le.GrW 36 and 81mm s.GrW 34); and hand grenades.[8]

The building block of the rifle company was the squad (*Gruppe*), a ten-man unit built around its light machine gun (le.MG 34). The squad leader (NCO), originally armed with a rifle, had by 1941 been equipped with an MP 40, bringing a major boost in firepower. The machine-gun company (actually a heavy weapons unit and always the last numbered company in a battalion; hence the fourth, eighth, and twelfth companies, respectively, in the three infantry battalions of an infantry regiment) was outfitted with heavy machine guns (s.MG 34) and medium mortars, giving it a good mix of flat and high-angle weapons.

The infantry gun company (the thirteenth company in a regiment) comprised six 75mm light (le.IG 18) and two 150mm medium guns (s.IG 33); these weapons, sometimes referred to affectionately as "house artillery" (*Hausartillerie*) by the *Landser*,[9] provided the regimental commander with serious organic firepower. The le.IG 18, which fired either high-explosive (HE) or hollow-charge rounds, had a maximum range of almost 3,600 meters. The s.IG 33 was a standard infantry weapon that could be used for both high- and low-angle fire; it fired high-explosive and smoke projectiles and had a maximum range (HE) of 4,700 meters.[10]

The anti-tank company (a regiment's fourteenth company) was still outfitted primarily with the 37mm anti-tank gun (Pak 35/36)—a weapon that had failed dramatically against heavier Allied armor in 1940 and was now basically obsolete. In response, the Army had introduced a 50mm anti-tank gun (Pak 38), which, by June 1941, was only beginning to reach the forces in the field in dribs and drabs. As a result, some divisions also received French 47mm anti-tank guns as a stopgap measure. The problem, however, was that none of the AT guns in the inventory of the German Army in 1941 were effective against the heavily armored Soviet KV-1 and T-34 tanks. The 37mm gun—useless against these enemy tanks except perhaps at point-blank range—was labeled (quite contemptuously) by the *Landser* as the "Army doorknocker" (*Heeresanklopfgerät*).[11] The inefficacy of their anti-tank weapons forced the Germans to resort to radical measures in an effort to neutralize a T-34 or KV-1: a lone soldier—in what the Germans might have called an act of *Draufgängertum*[12]—stalking the enemy tank and attacking it with grenade bundles, Teller mines, or other explosives that had to be affixed to the tank, the soldier often having to climb up the tank and expose himself in the process, an obviously perilous procedure that often ended in injury or death.[13]

An infantry division's artillery regiment—its soldiers with their red piping arm insignia—would play an indispensable role in the fighting of 1941. A German military publication in 1944 called the artillery the "backbone of the front" (*das Rückgrat der Front*),[14] and indeed it was. During 1941/42 alone—despite habitual shortages of shells—the German artillery in Russia would expend more than sixty million rounds[15]—preparing the way for the infantry in attack and shouldering much of the burden in defense. The standard artillery regiment was composed of four battalions, each of three batteries, with each battery having four guns. The first three battalions were equipped with a total of thirty-six 105mm light field howitzers (le.FH 18), while the fourth battery normally boasted twelve 150mm medium field howitzers (s.FH 18), making for forty-eight pieces in all. Designed by Rheinmetall in 1929/30 and introduced into service in 1935, the le.FH 18 was the standard German divisional fieldpiece and in operation throughout the war; it had a muzzle velocity of 470 m/sec and a maximum range of more than 10,500 meters (firing an HE shell).[16] The backbone of the medium artillery, the s.FH 18 was developed between 1926 and 1930—the howitzer built by Rheinmetall and the gun carriage by Krupp. It possessed a muzzle velocity of 495 m/sec and could launch a high-explosive shell out to 13,250 meters.[17] All of a regiment's artillery was, of course, horse drawn, the regiment possessing more than 2,000 horses for the task.

Whatever the weak points of a German infantry division, its aggregate firepower was immense (appendix D provides a detailed breakdown of the small arms, mortars, Pak, etc., of a typical 1941 division). Indeed, the infantry divisions earmarked for the eastern front would begin the Russian campaign with several potent new weapons systems now entering service in significant numbers (if not yet organic to the infantry divisions themselves). Among them were the 20mm *Vierling Flak*; the 150mm *Nebelwerfer* 41 rocket projector; the 280mm and 320mm rocket projector (28/32cm *schweres Wurfgerät* 40/41); and, most notably, the assault gun, or *Sturmgeschütz*. The *Vierling Flak* was an anti-aircraft gun boasting four 20mm cannon on a single mount; with a practical rate of fire of 800 rounds per minute, it was an utterly devastating weapon against ground targets. The *Nebelwerfer*, a six-barreled rocket launcher, hurled an HE shell nearly 7,000 meters, also with devastating effect. The 280mm (HE) and 320mm (incendiary) rockets were fired from wooden crates mounted on the sides or rear of a half-track vehicle; the impact of a large number of these weapons arriving simultaneously at their target was horrific. The range of the rockets, which the troops dubbed *Stuka zu Fuss* (Stukas on foot), was about 2,000 meters.[18]

In Operation Barbarossa the Germans were to make the first large-scale use of a highly effective new weapon: the StuG III (*Sturmgeschütz*) assault gun.[19] By June 1941, some 375 assault guns had been produced, 250 of which were committed to the eastern campaign in eleven battalions and five separate batteries.[20] The main armament of the StuG III was a short-barreled 75mm L24 gun mounted on the chassis of a Panzer III tank. Because the weapon system had no turret (the 75mm gun was built directly into the hull), it had a low silhouette, enhancing survivability. The assault gun had been commissioned to provide close armor support to the infantry; yet, as the eastern campaign progressed, it performed with increasing efficacy in an anti-tank role. Those infantry divisions fortunate enough to be assigned a battery or company of assault guns would come to greatly appreciate the weapon, while the Russians would come to fear it. "The *Sturmartillerie* [assault gun] is our ultimate weapon [*letzte Waffe*]," wrote an artillery officer fighting in the El'nia salient (east of Smolensk) in a letter to his wife on 30 August 1941: "They are tanks with a gun, only they are open on top and so they shoot with the aid of a scissors telescope! The armor plating is very good! I learned to appreciate this weapon during the infantry attacks—every battalion was allocated two assault guns; they would lead the way and the infantry would advance under their protection. They use shells that are good for combating and shelling tanks."[21]

PANZER AND MOTORIZED DIVISIONS

If the foot infantry dominated in numbers, it was the panzer and motorized formations that were to dominate on the field of battle—across the open plains and steppe lands of Soviet Russia. While the mobile units made up but a small fraction of the *Ostheer*, it was the panzer generals—Kleist, Guderian, Hoth, Hoepner, et al.—who were to carry out the deep encircling operations designed to crush the Red Army and pave the way to victory in a mere matter of weeks. Failure of their "deep battle" operations was not an option, for it would mean failure of the entire Barbarossa enterprise.

From 1 April 1940 to 1 June 1941, the inventory of German armored fighting vehicles (AFVs) had climbed modestly—from 3,387 (all models) to 5,694 (all models). The latter figure, broken down by AFV type, reveals the following:

877 Pz I
1,157 Pz II
187 Pz 35(t)
754 Pz 38(t)
1,440 Pz III
572 Pz IV
330 armored staff cars
377 StuG III

Of these AFVs, 3,648 were deployed in the east on 22 June 1941:

281 Pz I
743 Pz II
157 Pz 35(t)
651 Pz 38(t)
979 Pz III
444 Pz IV
143 armored staff cars
250 StuG III[22]

To accurately assess the nature of the war in the east, it is necessary for one to acquire a rudimentary awareness of the technical means by which it was fought. Since the primary protagonist of the operational concept of blitzkrieg was clearly the tank, the technical specifications of each model in the German inventory are briefly outlined below.

Panzer I: This vehicle was the lightest, and most lightly armed, of all German tank models in use in 1941. First introduced in 1934, it was intended as an interim vehicle for rapid building and training of Germany's nascent tank arm. The Pz Kpfw I[23] weighed between five and six tons, was equipped with two 7.92mm machine guns, and had an armor thickness of just thirteen millimeters. It had first seen action in the Spanish Civil War and, thereafter, in the early campaigns in World War II. Yet, even in Spain, its deficiencies—armament and protection—had become apparent, and by 1941 the tank was clearly obsolete. Nevertheless, 281 of these tanks were assigned to the Barbarossa strike force. Only thirteen days into the campaign, *Generalmajor* Ritter von Thoma, returning from an inspection tour of 3 Panzer Group, informed Chief of the Army General Staff Halder that the Pz I had become a "burden" to the troops; that it should be removed from active service in the east and used for protection of the home front, coastal regions, and as a training vehicle.[24]

Panzer II: Due to the slow development and production of the new medium tanks the German Army required in the mid-1930s, the Pz II was introduced as another interim AFV. First issued in 1936, it had a three-man crew, a main armament of one 20mm L/55 gun, and a 7.92 MG. Several variants of the tank—which had somewhat better armor protection and were slightly heavier than the original model—had been introduced by 1941. Nearly 750 of these tanks would see duty with the four panzer groups operating in Russia in 1941—most of them assigned to the light tank companies. Like the Pz I, the Pz II was already out of date; yet, together, these two models made up more than 1,000 of the tanks (28 percent) in the Barbarossa force structure.[25]

Panzer 35(t): Following the occupation of Czechoslovakia in 1939, the Army benefited from that country's arsenal of high-grade weapons and its impressive armaments industry. The Czech tank industry was particularly valuable, for it had produced vehicles clearly superior to the early German tanks. The heavier of the two Czech tank models was redesignated the Pz 35(t) by the Germans; it boasted 25mm armor plating, a 37mm main armament, and two 7.92 MGs. Unfortunately, the tank's armor was riveted, not welded like German tanks, and the rivets had the disturbing tendency to pop out under the impact of a heavy shell, sending rivet shanks swirling through the inside of the tank as secondary projectiles. By June 1941, the tank was in decline, and the only unit so equipped was 6 Panzer Division, which had all 157 of them.[26]

Panzer 38(t): This tank was the Czech follow-on design to its Pz 35(t). While lighter than its predecessor, it was eventually outfitted with thicker armor plate. The tank's main armament was also a 37mm gun, supported by two 7.92 MGs. After seizing the Czech stocks, the Germans adapted the tank to fit a four-man crew, adding a gun loader to the driver, radio operator, and commander/gunner. The tank was extremely reliable mechanically, with its durable chassis also providing a base for later variants in design, among them the tank hunters (*Panzerjäger*) Marder III and Hetzer. Indeed, the Pz 38(t) represented the best of the German light tanks in June 1941, and 651 of them were assigned to the Barbarossa order of battle, the lion's share going to Hermann Hoth's 3 Panzer

Group.[27] Yet, for all its attributes, the tank was still a light tank, and on the eastern front it also failed when pitted against Soviet T-34s and KV-1s and the heavier-caliber artillery of the Red Army. The tank's attrition rate was correspondingly high, the heavy losses amplifying the basic weakness of the *Ostheer*'s tank forces, upon which so much depended—that being that more than 50 percent of all the armor assembled for the campaign were light tanks that were largely obsolete.

Panzer III: The first experimental models of this medium tank—disguised as a "medium tractor"—were ordered by the German Army as early as 1934, with the first few examples being produced by 1937.[28] The Pz III was one of the two tanks (the other being the Pz IV) specifically developed for the new armored units of the *Wehrmacht*. It was envisaged as *the* main battle tank—that is, the "anti-tank" tank—of the German armored forces and was to be outfitted with a high-velocity armor-piercing shell. However, when it first appeared, its version of the 37mm gun proved less than adequate. The weapon system experienced other "teething" problems as well in its initial iterations, and following a complete redesign of the suspension system, the "E" model (*Ausführung E*) of the Pz III went into series production in December 1938. Several more series were designed and manufactured over the next few years, with a new main armament—a more powerful 50mm L/42 gun—finally becoming standard in the "G" series, 600 of which were manufactured between April 1940 and February 1941. This model of the Pz III, with an armor thickness of up to 37mm, also had two 7.92 MGs and weighed about twenty tons. It was operated by a five-man crew. The final Pz III upgrade to be undertaken before the launch of Barbarossa was the "J" series, which began production in March 1941 and thickened the basic hull armor to 50mm. All told, just under 1,000 Pz IIIs were allocated to the eastern strike force; of these, the majority was equipped with the "upgunned" 50mm L/42 main armament, providing the tank forces with a significant boost in firepower and, in fact, "bringing the first real backbone to the panzer divisions."[29]

It should be pointed out that Hitler, apparently, had wanted the Pz III upgraded with an even longer-barreled 50mm gun, which would have had a greater muzzle velocity. As Panzer General Guderian noted in his memoir,

> On the basis of the experience gained during the western campaign, Hitler ordered a tank production of 800 to 1,000 units per month. However, the Army Ordnance Office reckoned that the cost of this program would be about two milliards [billions] of marks, and that it would involve the employment of 100,000 skilled workers and specialists. In view of these heavy expenses Hitler unfortunately agreed to the abandonment of this plan for the time being.
>
> Hitler also ordered that the 37mm gun in the Panzer III be replaced by a 50mm L60. In fact it was the 50mm L42 that was used, a gun, therefore, with a considerably shorter barrel. Hitler was apparently not immediately informed of this modification to his directive on the part of the Ordnance Office; when, in February

> of 1941, he learned that his instructions were not being carried out even though all the technical requirements were at hand, he became extremely angry [*wurde er sehr ärgerlich*] and he never forgave the responsible officers of the Ordnance Office for this high-handed act. Years later he was to refer to it.[30]

Panzer IV: This model, the final one to take part in the invasion of Russia, had first entered production in 1936. All series manufactured prior to June 1941 ("A" through "F"), were outfitted with a short-barreled 75mm L24 main armament. Originally, the Pz IV had been conceived as a close-support weapon and, thus, as a complement to the Pz III main battle tank. However, its success in the Polish and French campaigns—and later against Allied and Soviet vehicles—soon led to its active use as an "anti-tank" tank as well. The final version to enter production before the start of Barbarossa was the "F" series (April 1941), with generally increased armored thickness for added protection. The tank, operated by a crew of five and equipped with two 7.92 MGs as secondary armament, weighed about twenty-six tons. Various models of the Pz IV would see combat throughout the war; with a total production run of about 9,000, the Pz IV would make up the backbone of the German armored force in World War II.[31] Nearly 450 Pz IVs were assigned to the Barbarossa tank fleet.

REORGANIZATION AND EXPANSION OF THE MOBILE FORCES

Even before the end of the campaign in the west in 1940, the Army High Command had contemplated a major reorganization and expansion of its panzer and motorized divisions. The initial target figure of twenty-four panzer and twelve motorized divisions drafted in May 1940 had, by the middle of June, been reduced to the final figure of twenty panzer and ten motorized divisions.[32] The new divisions—ten tank and eight motorized divisions—were established in the fall of 1940 and spring of 1941; at the same time, the existing ten panzer divisions were reorganized and partially re-equipped. In the course of this major undertaking, the OKH was guided by the experiences of the French campaign, while also seeking to make the panzer divisions more uniform in organization—an intent only partially realized. Before Operation Barbarossa, the plan was altered only by the creation of the 5 Light Division (mot.) in early 1941, which was intended as the blocking force (*Sperrverband*) for North Africa; following its arrival in Libya, it was redesignated as 21 Panzer Division on 21 August 1941.[33]

Due to the anemic production of tanks in 1940/41, the only way to double the size of the panzer force was by greatly reducing the number of tanks in each division. As a result, each panzer division was reduced in size to a single panzer regiment (of two or three tank battalions), whereas in 1940 six of the ten existing panzer divisions had possessed two tank regiments. While this measure was partially offset by phasing out hundreds of obsolete Pz Is and Pz IIs and re-equipping the panzer divisions with more medium Pz IIIs and Pz IVs, it still reduced them to the outer limit of the minimum number of tanks needed to operate effectively. In fact, the *average* number of tanks in the panzer divisions plunged from 258 in 1940 to just 196 after the reorganization and expansion, while the *actual* number of tanks assigned to the divisions ranged from a mere 147 to 299.[34]

The contraction in the number of tanks was ameliorated by outfitting each panzer division with a second motorized infantry regiment, while a motorcycle battalion (*Kradschützen-Bataillon*) was also added to each division's table of organization. In addition to the partial change out in tank models, the panzer divisions were beneficiaries of several new weapons systems and capabilities; these included the introduction of 50mm AT guns into their *Panzerjäger* units, small numbers of 20mm *Vierling Flak*, and 280/320mm rocket launchers (*Stuka zu Fuss*), as well as upgrades to artillery, signal, combat engineer, and supply units.[35]

The reorganization and expansion effort had not always proceeded smoothly, with shortages in motor vehicles creating serious bottlenecks that delayed equipping the divisions and adversely affected their training. To provide even tolerable levels of motorization, the Army was forced to turn to foreign materiel (mostly French) to fully outfit both the panzer and motorized units. Some units received their vehicles so late they barely had time to become acquainted with them before being sent into action in Russia, while the bewildering diversity in types of vehicles posed problems with spare parts and maintenance. The 17 Panzer Division alone was outfitted with some 240 different types of vehicles;[36] moreover, it did not receive its full complement of vehicles until late May 1941, only weeks before Barbarossa began. No matter—by mid-July 1941, 17 PD—"this brave division," as Guderian characterized it—had destroyed 502 Red Army tanks.

While it is difficult to generalize about the 1941 panzer division's order of battle—given the lack of uniformity in numbers of tanks, for example—some basic observations are in order: The personnel strength ranged from roughly 13,000 to 16,000 officers, NCOs, and men; they all wore the pink (*rosa*) piping first worn by their predecessors in the motor trucking battalions (*Kraftfahrtruppen*) of the former *Reichsheer.* The "typical" panzer division possessed less than 300 tracked vehicles (of which just under 200 were tanks), as well as some 3,000 wheeled vehicles; if arrayed in single file on a road, this massive armada would have stretched for 130 kilometers![37] The total firepower of a panzer division encompassed approximately 620 automatic weapons and 260 guns of all calibers (excluding 50mm and 81mm mortars). (In comparison, the German army corps of 1914 was equipped with only 160 77mm and 105 150mm guns.)[38]

The fighting core of the 1941 panzer division's tank forces was represented by the Pz 38(t) and Pz III, which together made up 1,630 of the 3,250 tanks assigned to Operation Barbarossa. Yet, while the order of battle included some 600 more Pz IIIs in comparison to 1940, the number of Pz IV medium tanks allocated for the attack on Russia (444) was barely 150 more than had been available for the campaign in the west. Moreover, more than 50 percent of the German tank force (Pz I, Pz II, Pz 35[t], Pz 38[t]) was outdated and thus ill-suited for the rigors of combat in the east. Even the medium tank models were no match for the Soviet T-34s and KV-1s, which enjoyed a vast qualitative advantage over all types of German tanks. One can readily conclude that, while much was done to augment the firepower of the German tank fleet, in terms of both quantity and quality the results fell far short of what was required to successfully confront an adversary like the Soviet Union.

Ending this section are a few observations about the expansion of the motorized divisions: The motorized infantry had all originally been foot infantry, numbered in the normal sequence and trained and equipped as regular infantry of the line; as such, they wore the traditional white piping of the infantry service. The only difference from the line infantry—albeit a major one—was that the motorized troops were transported to and from the battlefield in trucks or, to a much lesser degree, in armored personnel carriers (APCs). In 1939 there were four motorized divisions (2, 13, 20, and 29),[39] all belonging to the 14 Motorized Corps. Early in 1940, each of these divisions was reduced from three to two regiments, while the elite motorized Greater Germany (*Grossdeutschland*) Regiment was established from the ceremonial *Wachregiment Berlin*.[40]

By the spring of 1941, two motorized divisions—2 ID (mot.) and 13 ID (mot.)—had been converted to panzer divisions, while eight foot infantry divisions—3, 10, 14, 16, 18, 25, 36, and 60—had been reorganized as fully motorized formations, making for a total of ten motorized infantry divisions in the regular German Army. Other motorized units included the *Lehr-Brigade* 900 (Instructional Brigade 900), the Infantry Regiment *Grossdeutschland*, and several Waffen-SS divisions, including the SS-*Leibstandarte* "Adolf Hitler."[41]

With only two regiments of truck-borne troops, the motorized division deployed just six battalions of infantry (versus nine for a typical three-regiment foot infantry division). The artillery was towed by trucks or half-track prime movers, while the reconnaissance units were made mobile with motorcycles and armored cars. In 1942 a battalion of self-propelled guns or tanks would be added to the division's order of battle, and APCs began to appear in greater numbers. However, in 1941, these formations were essentially infantry units with greater mobility.[42]

Following the attack on the Soviet Union, the motorized infantry divisions—despite their diminutive numbers—and the mounted infantry elements of the panzer divisions were immediately recognized for their great value and saw continuous action. In fact, the physical and psychological demands placed on them were "immense." As one soldier complained, "Motorized transport is only there to make certain we poor *Panzergrenadiers* are brought up against the enemy more often than our fellows in the infantry divisions . . . so that we have the dubious advantage of being in action more often."[43]

Notes

DEDICATION

1. Walther K. Nehring served as Guderian's chief of staff during the Polish campaign (1939) and the French campaign (1940). During Operation Barbarossa, he commanded 18 Panzer Division in Guderian's 2 PzG / Second Panzer Army.

FOREWORD

1. Robert Kirchubel is a retired US Army armor branch lieutenant colonel, PhD, and author of many books and articles on the Nazi-Soviet War.

INTRODUCTION

1. The "Craig W. H. Luther Papers," research materials I have collected over several decades—more than sixty-five bankers boxes of diverse holdings (e.g., field post letters, personal diaries and official war diaries, battle reports, questionnaires completed by German World War II veterans, maps, hundreds of photographs, etc.)—are located at the Hoover Institute, Stanford University, Palo Alto, California.

2. In any case, I do address at some length the issue of war crimes on the eastern front (committed by *both* sides) in Luther, *Barbarossa Unleashed*, 420–81.

3. Pöhlmann, *Der Panzer und die Mechanisierung des Krieges*, 492.

4. In his memoir, Guderian insisted that the Commissar Order was never carried out by his panzer group; in fact, he asserted (quite falsely) that he was unaware of it (Guderian, *Panzer Leader*, 152). However, while he most likely did not issue the order directly, German war diaries reveal that the order still managed to reach the troops and was "almost universally followed" (Hart, *Guderian*, 71). Guderian also claimed (again falsely) that he "forbade" implementation of the so-called Decree on Military Justice (*Gerichtsbarkeitserlass*). Drafted by the OKW legal office and released on 13 May 1941, the decree "withdrew crimes committed by enemy civilians in the east from the jurisdiction of military courts, required that partisans be 'brutally eliminated' and ordered that *Wehrmacht* soldiers committing crimes against the civilian population no longer needed to be prosecuted"; in effect, it stripped Soviet citizens of all legal protections and functioned as an amnesty for crimes of German soldiers against Russians in and out of uniform. Wegner, "The Road to Defeat," 108.

5. Pöhlmann, *Der Panzer und die Mechanisierung des Krieges*, 492 (n. 642). Perhaps the worst thing that can be said about Guderian in this context is that, whatever he knew about violations of the laws of war on the eastern front, he simply ignored them—focused as he was on inflicting a fatal military defeat on Soviet Russia in the summer/fall of 1941.

6. The words belong to Alan Clark. As a teenager, I read his book *Barbarossa: The Russian-German Conflict, 1941–45*, and it sparked my lifelong fascination with Hitler's attack on Soviet Russia.

7. The book aggregator/reviewer is Stone & Stone Second World War Books.

8. To be sure, Guderian was not alone among Germany's top generals in accepting large financial gifts from Hitler, the secret funds dispensed by the German dictator's Chancellery Office. These payments were clearly considered bribes by Hitler (and by Guderian as well). Hart, *Guderian*, 82–84.

PROLOGUE

1. Boog et al., *Germany and the Second World War*, Vol. IV, 2; Boog et al., *Das Deutsche Reich und der Zweite Weltkrieg*, Bd. 4, xiv.

2. Reuth (ed.), *Hitler*, 525; Yahil, *The Holocaust*, 244.

3. Below, *At Hitler's Side*, 101–2.

4. At the Reich Chancellery in Berlin (30 March 1941), Hitler, in an address that lasted for more than two hours, for the first time openly revealed to his chief military commanders what war with Russia actually signified for Germany. After the conference Halder jotted in his journal that Barbarossa would be not only a "clash of two ideologies" but a "war of extermination . . . very different from the war in the west. In the east, harshness today means lenience in the future. Commanders must make the sacrifice of overcoming their personal scruples." (For more details, see Halder, *The Halder War Diary*, 345–46.) While Guderian made no reference to this conference in his memoir, he was most certainly a participant. In any case, none of the general officers in attendance that day would openly criticize Hitler's clearly criminal and genocidal intent. Following the war, Hermann Hoth, who commanded a panzer group on the eastern front in 1941, offered at least a partial explanation of why that was so: On 30 April 1948, before the Nuremberg Military Tribunal, he admitted, "In 1941, at the start of the Russian campaign, I still had complete faith [*volles Vertrauen*] in Hitler" (Hürter, *Hitlers Heerführer*, 213).

5. GFM von Bock, *The War Diary*, 220–21. For an in-depth discussion of the concepts of preventive and preemptive war as they pertain to Operation Barbarossa, see Luther, *Barbarossa Unleashed*, 191–97. Simply put, my view is that Hitler's oft-stated conviction that Barbarossa barely preempted an impending Soviet attack on Germany was little more than a cynical fiction.

6. Leningrad was also recognized by both Hitler and his Army General Staff as one of Soviet Russia's primary armament centers. Schramm (ed.), *Kriegstagebuch des OKW*, Bd. I, 208.

7. Guderian, *Panzer Leader*, 150.

8. Ibid., 150.

PART I. FROM THE FRONTIER TO SMOLENSK

1. For a detailed examination of German military planning—including its many shortcomings—for Operation Barbarossa, see Luther, *Barbarossa Unleashed*, 43–49, 57–70, etc.

2. Mawdsley, *Thunder in the East*, 66. With its long and bloody history—a "vital crossroads" fought over by Poles and Lithuanians in the Middle Ages; seized by the Russians in the sev-

enteenth century and used by Peter the Great as a base of operations against Charles XII of Sweden; captured by Napoleon in August 1812—Smolensk was a cherished historical symbol to all Russians.

3. As cited in Macksey, *Guderian*, 142.

CHAPTER 1. PREPARATIONS FOR THE EASTERN CAMPAIGN

1. At just twenty-five, he was the youngest of 168 officers selected to attend the prestigious *Kriegsakademie* in Berlin in October 1913. Macksey, *Guderian*, 7.

2. While posted as an intelligence officer to Fifth Army headquarters on the Verdun front, Guderian helped to prepare operational analyses of the German offensive's failure, concluding that artillery firepower alone was not sufficient to neutralize a well-entrenched enemy and that only maneuver warfare offered a less costly way to success on the battlefield—convictions that would "profoundly shape his subsequent ideas and his career." Hart, *Guderian*, 10–11.

3. Ibid., 3–4. According to Hart, the panzer general was a "good tactician and technician" who "suffered from strategic myopia." He was also "impetuous, liable to react and act instinctively, sometimes without thinking." Moreover, he "led too much from the front, which hampered the smooth functioning of his headquarters." While a "great organizer, an intellect, a theorist, and a technician," in the final analysis "his deficiencies outweighed his strengths and he contributed directly to Germany's defeat." Ibid., 115–17.

4. Guderian, *Panzer Leader*, 142.

5. In May 1941, Guderian "again willingly embraced and disseminated Hitler's official justification for aggression—that Barbarossa was a defensive preemptive strike and a noble undertaking to save Western civilization from being destroyed by the 'Asiatic Bolshevik-Jewish menace.' Guderian's actions thus intimate that by 1941 he had at least outwardly embraced the core tenets of National Socialism—the necessity both of violent German expansion and of the destruction of the supposed Jewish-Bolshevik threat. Moreover, throughout the war Guderian never seems to have given much thought to the profound consequences of the brutal ideological war of annihilation (*Vernichtungskrieg*) that Hitler ordered German forces to wage in the east" (Hart, *Guderian*, 69–70).

6. For the Barbarossa directive, see Trevor-Roper, *Hitler's War Directives*, 48–52. For the original German text of the directive, see Hubatsch (ed.), *Hitlers Weisungen für die Kriegführung*, 84–88.

7. While the *Luftwaffe* collected some good tactical intelligence, it did a poor job of assessing the strength of the Soviet Air Force. For example, it underestimated the number of Soviet aircraft available and "fecklessly disregarded" major technical advances in Soviet aircraft design. The "failure of *Luftwaffe* intelligence to produce a complete assessment of Soviet capabilities was to have dire consequences on both the strategic level in the coming years and on the tactical conduct of the first campaigning season" (Muller, *The German Air War in Russia*, 41).

8. "Aufmarschanweisung Barbarossa," in Halder, *Kriegstagebuch*, Bd. 2, 468 (appendix 2). *Luftwaffe* attacks on Russian industrial sites were only to begin *after* the Army had reached its operational goals.

9. "Auf die Verwendung chemischer Kampfmittel auch aus der Luft durch den Gegner muss die Truppe sich einstellen," OKH Genst. d. H. Op.Abt. (1), Nr. 050/41 g.K., Aufmarschanweisung OKH vom 31.1.1941 "Barbarossa," in Halder, *Kriegstagebuch*, Bd. 2, 465. (Note: Soviet Russia was not a signatory to the Geneva Conventions of 1929. The USSR,

however, had signed the 1925 Geneva protocol prohibiting the use of poison gas and bacteriological warfare. See Bellamy, *Absolute War*, 20.)

10. Gschöpf, *Mein Weg mit der 45. Inf.-Div.*, 197–99.

11. Hart, *Guderian*, 69.

12. For more details on the German force structure for Operation Barbarossa, see the relevant chapters in Luther, *The First Day on the Eastern Front*; see also Boog et al., *Germany and the Second World War*, Vol. IV, 316–19.

13. Note: This figure for artillery excludes infantry fieldpieces and mortars.

14. On 22 June 1941, two of the nineteen panzer divisions (2 PD and 5 PD) were still undergoing maintenance and refurbishment following the Balkan campaign in the spring of 1941; they would not be committed to eastern front until September, when they joined Army Group Center for Operation Typhoon.

15. Luther, *Barbarossa Unleashed*, 144–46.

16. Glantz, *Barbarossa*, 216 (n. 7). (Note: On 22 June 1941, Soviet 13 Army was an HQ only, with no combat units assigned.)

17. Williamson Murray, "May 1940: Contingency and Fragility of the German RMA," in Knox and Murray (eds.), *The Dynamics of Military Revolution*, 166.

18. The training regimen of 241 Infantry Regiment (106 ID) at the troop training grounds in Wahn, Germany, included marches of up to 90 kilometers a day (135 kilometers in two days), along with field exercises and firing practice. These long marches usually ended with a parade—for example, in front of the Opera House in Cologne. Meyer, *Infanterie-Regiment Grenadier-Regiment 241*, 8.

19. Paul, *Panzer-General Walther K. Nehring*, 113.

20. Hart, Hart, and Hughes, *The German Soldier in World War II*, 8.

21. Throughout World War II, in fact, the Germans sometimes trained with live ammunition during periods of rest, refitting, or rebuilding. DiNardo, *Germany's Panzer Arm in WWII*, 62.

22. As cited in Pöhlmann, *Der Panzer und die Mechanisierung des Krieges*, 329.

23. Allmendinger et al., FMS T-34: "Terrain Factors in the Russian Campaign," 25–29; Paul, *Panzer-General Walther K. Nehring*, 113.

24. Kluge fought on the western front during World War I and was seriously wounded at Verdun in 1918. Mitcham, *Hitler's Field Marshals and Their Battles*, 295.

25. Hürter, *Hitlers Heerführer*, 231. Conferencing with the staff of Fourth Army, Brauchitsch said, "The Russian will conduct the war by all possible means [*Krieg mit allen Mitteln*]: Gas, spoiling of stores, and contamination of wells" (Ibid., 231 [n. 139]).

26. Lewis, *Forgotten Legions*, 131–32. Of course, plans for war against Soviet Russia were a closely guarded secret, in the field known only to top commanders, like Kluge, and a small number of staff; thus, while the *Landser* no doubt had their own thoughts and suspicions—and, of course, the wildest rumors abounded, including a potential advance into Iran or India—they would not learn the purpose of their training until just hours before launch of the Barbarossa campaign.

27. Still, it would be false to imply that Germany's political and military leadership actually did their "due diligence" in their preparations for the eastern campaign, for it is now apparent they did not—despite the unprecedented scope of the challenge presented by Operation Barbarossa. It is astounding that Germany's overall armaments production (weapons and ammunition) in the second year of the war hardly increased at all, whereas the Soviet Union and Great Britain almost doubled, and the United States tripled, their armaments production. Moreover, increases in production that *were* achieved were largely due to draconian cutbacks in the output of ammunition—cutbacks that would affect German operations in the east as early

as August 1941 and seriously so in the fall and winter of 1941/42. By the beginning of the eastern campaign, production of major types of ammunition had, in some cases, been reduced to a fraction of what it had been in mid-1940. For example, the monthly output of shells for light field howitzers had averaged 1.1 million in mid-1940; in June 1941, production plunged to just 50,000 shells and, in August 1941, to the pathetic figure of 11,000. Manufacture of 81mm mortar shells, which had averaged 1.6 million a month in mid-1940, fell to just 100,000 in June and 62,000 in August 1941. Müller-Hillebrand, *Das Heer 1933–1945*, Bd. 2, 92.

28. Stahel, *Operation Barbarossa and Germany's Defeat in the East*, 112–13.

29. As cited in Walde, *Guderian*, 115. Paulus had taken part in the exercise as the representative of OKH.

30. Ibid., 116.

31. A *Rollbahn*, or *Panzerstrasse*, was a road designated as a main axis of advance for panzer and motorized formations. Normally, foot (marching) infantry divisions were barred from using these "good" roads, which were vital to the forward progress of the mobile units.

32. As cited in Dinglreiter, *Die Vierziger*, 38.

33. Paul, *Panzer-General Walther K. Nehring*, 115. From Paul's account, which lays out Nehring's briefing in very general terms, it does not appear that Nehring divulged the Barbarossa plan to his staff at this time. As for the panzer general, he had become certain that Russia was the target of the impending campaign since his participation in a map exercise led by Guderian in Berlin on 20/21 March. (*Gewissheit erhielt er bei einer Planübung, die Guderian am 20. und 21. März 1941 in Berlin abhielt.*) Ibid., 103.

34. Hart, *Guderian*, 72.

35. Guderian, *Panzer Leader*, 146.

36. Ibid., 149. Apparently, Guderian had made much the same claim for the campaign in the west in 1940—a claim that German historian Roman Töppel (based on his research into the papers of GFM Erich von Manstein) called a "blunt lie." Email, R. Töppel to C. Luther, 19 August 2024.

37. "Aufmarschanweisung Barbarossa," in Halder, *Kriegstagebuch*, Bd. 2, 466 (appendix 2).

38. Noted Colonel Albert Seaton, "The population [of Belorussia] was mainly rural and, even by the Russian standards of the time, was very poor and almost unbelievably primitive" (Seaton, *The Battle for Moscow*, 41).

39. Guderian, *Panzer Leader*, 147.

40. Ibid., 147.

41. Luther, *The First Day on the Eastern Front*, 153–54.

42. "Kriegsgliederung Barbarossa," Stand 18.6.41, in Mehner (ed.), *Die Geheimen Tagesberichte der deutschen Wehrmachtführung im Zweiten Weltkrieg*, Bd. 3; at https://lexikon-der-wehrmacht.de.

43. Walde, *Guderian*, 119.

44. BA-MA N 910/5, *Tagebuch* Lemelsen, 10.6.41, 15.6.41, 17.6.41.

45. Guderian, *Panzer Leader*, 153.

46. Carell, *Hitler Moves East*, 11–12; Carell, *Unternehmen Barbarossa*, 11.

47. Guderian, *Panzer Leader*, 153.

48. As cited in Stahel, *Hitler's Panzer Generals*, 184.

49. Luttichau, *The Road to Moscow: The Campaign in Russia—1941*, VI: 8.

50. Carell, *Hitler Moves East*, 16–17; Carell, *Unternehmen Barbarossa*, 19.

51. Günther Blumentritt, "Moscow," in Richardson and Freidin (eds.), *The Fatal Decisions*, 46–47.

52. BA-MA N 910/5, *Tagebuch* Lemelsen, 21.6.41.

CHAPTER 2. THE FRONTIER BATTLES

1. Note: The fighting along the frontier lasted for eighteen days—from 22 June to 9 July 1941, when the cauldron battle of Belostok-Minsk came to an end. In Soviet/Russian nomenclature this initial period of the war is called the *pogranichnaia srazheniia* (the border battles). David M. Glantz, "The Border Battles on the Siauliai Axis, 22–26 June 1941," in Glantz (ed.), *The Initial Period of War on the Eastern Front*, 78.

2. Opitz, "Die Stimmung in der Truppe am Vorabend des Überfalls auf die Sowjetunion," 236.

3. Luttichau, *The Road to Moscow: The Campaign in Russia—1941*, VI: 3–4.

4. As cited in Bunke, *Der Osten blieb unser Schicksal*, 208–9.

5. Kirchubel, *Operation Barbarossa 1941 (3). Army Group Center*, 32.

6. GFM von Bock, *The War Diary*, 224; BA-MA H 08-22/9, *Nachlass Generalfeldmarschall Fedor von Bock, Tagebuchnotizen Osten I*, 22.6.41.

7. Kirchubel, *Hitler's Panzer Armies on the Eastern Front*, 63.

8. Kempowski (ed.), *Das Echolot*, 23.

9. Schick, *Die Geschichte der 10. Panzer-Division*, 270–71.

10. Ibid., 271.

11. Detailed sketches of the stages of the firing plan can be found in NARA, T-311, Roll 226, Heeresgruppe Mitte / Stoart, KTB mit Anlagen.

12. Gschöpf, *Mein Weg mit der 45. Inf.-Div.*, 204.

13. Bunke, *Der Osten blieb unser Schicksal*, 218.

14. As cited in Kershaw, *War Without Garlands*, 47.

15. As cited in Aliev, *The Siege of Brest*, 64–65.

16. Higgins, *Guderian*, 25.

17. BA-MA RH 27-18/20, *KTB 18. Pz.-Div.*, 22.6.41.

18. Görlitz, *Strategie der Defensive*, 91.

19. Schäufler (ed.), *Knight's Cross Panzers*, 72.

20. The village of Stradecz was in German hands by 0715 hours. Urbanke and Türk, *Als Sanitätsoffizier im Russlandfeldzug*, 35.

21. BA-MA RH 27-3/14, *KTB Nr. 3, 3. Pz.-Div.*, 22.6.41.

22. Newton, *Hitler's Commander*, 122.

23. All of the tanks in 14 Mechanized Corps were T-26s with the exception of a few also outmoded BT models. Forczyk, *Tank Warfare on the Eastern Front*, 31.

24. Glantz, *Red Army Ground Forces in June 1941*, 21. The 14 Mechanized Corps should have been outfitted with 1,031 tanks.

25. *Geschichte der 3. Panzer-Division Berlin-Brandenburg*, 109–10.

26. BA-MA RH 27-3/14, *KTB Nr. 3, 3. Pz.Div.*, 22.6.41.

27. Luttichau, *The Road to Moscow: The Campaign in Russia—1941*, VI: 9.

28. Carell, *Hitler Moves East*, 23.

29. Garden and Andrew (eds.), *The War Diaries of a Panzer Soldier*, 31.

30. BA-MA RH 27-18/20, *Ia KTB, 18.Pz.Div.*, 22.6.41.

31. Kempowski (ed.), *Das Echolot*, 23.

32. Carell, *Hitler Moves East*, 25.

33. Schulze, *General der Panzertruppe a.D. Walther K. Nehring*.

34. Guderian, *Panzer Leader*, 153.

35. BA-MA N 910/5, *Tagebuch* Lemelsen, 25.6.41.

36. Sandalov, *Perezhitoe* (That Which Has Been Lived Through), 95.

37. Ibid., 108–9.

38. BA-MA RH 27-18/20, *Ia KTB, 18.Pz.Div.*, 22.6.41; BA-MA RH 21-2/927, *KTB Nr. 1, Pz.Gr. 2*, 22.6.41. In the war diary of 18 PD, the figure for the division's tank losses is obscured; its losses, however, were negligible.

39. Axell, *Russia's Heroes*, 23–24; Kershaw, *War Without Garlands*, 29–30; Gschöpf, *Mein Weg mit der 45. Inf.-Div.*, 206–7.

40. BA-MA RH 26-45/20, *KTB 45. Inf.-Div.*, 22.6.41.

41. BA-MA RH 26-45/20, *KTB 45. Inf.-Div.*, 22.6.41; Gschöpf, *Mein Weg mit der 45. Inf.-Div.*, 207.

42. Gschöpf, *Mein Weg mit der 45. Inf.-Div.*, 208.

43. "Die ersten acht Tage," in Oberkommando der Wehrmacht (ed.), *Kampf gegen die Sowjets*, 37–38.

44. Guderian, *Panzer Leader*, 153–54.

45. "Tagesmeldungen der Operations-Abteilung des GenStdH," in Schramm (ed.), *Kriegstagebuch des OKW*, Bd. I, 492.

46. Halder, *The Halder War Diary*, 412–13.

47. Ibid., 412–13.

48. Ibid., 413.

49. Due to poor intelligence, the breakdown in communications, and the general chaos caused by the sudden and staggering German invasion, it was not until 24 June (at the earliest) that Pavlov became aware that the left flank of his Western Front was facing almost the full weight of Guderian's panzer group (specifically, four of his five panzer divisions). Early that morning, following a skirmish between Soviet 155 Rifle Division and advance elements of Guderian's group near the town of Slonim, Soviet troops seized a map left inside a hastily abandoned German staff vehicle. The map, which revealed the dispositions of 24 and 47 Panzer Corps and their routes of advance, laboriously made its way via courier from the headquarters of 155 RD to Pavlov's new headquarters (six to eight kilometers north of Minsk, the location of his original HQ), where it "had the effect of an explosion." While the map and its astonishing contents most likely reached Pavlov by late 24 June, it is not addressed in the evening operational report of front headquarters for that day, finally showing up in its operational report of 1000 hours on 25 June. Yet, regardless of when this information reached Pavlov, it arrived much too late to alter the course of events in his favor. See A. V. Isaev, *Neizvestnyi 1941. Ostanovlennyi Blitskrig* [*Unknown 1941: The Blitzkrieg Halted*] (Moscow: "Yauza" "EKSMO," 2010); TsAMO, f. 208, op. 2511, d. 206, ll. 35–36. (Note: TsAMO is the abbreviation for the Central Archives of the Ministry of Defense [Tsentral'nyi Arkhiv Ministerstva Oborony] of the Russian Federation.) For the operational and intelligence reports of Western Front, see https://docs.historyrussia.org/ru/nodes/218200-sbornik-boevyh-dokumentov-velikoy-otechestvennoy-voyny-vyp-35#mode/grid/page/35/zoom/1. Special thanks to Dr. Mikhail Partala for making this information available to me just as this book went into production, and to Dr. Richard Harrison for once again helping with translations of the key documents from Russian to English.

50. David M. Glantz, "The Border Battles on the Bialystok-Minsk Axis: 22–28 June 1941," in Glantz (ed.), *The Initial Period of War on the Eastern Front*, 202; Paul, *Geschichte der 18. Panzer-Division*, 17.

51. BA-MA RH 27-18/20, *KTB 18. Pz.-Div.*, 23.6.41.

52. BA-MA RH 20-4/1199, *KTB AOK 4*, 23.6.41.

53. Glantz, *Zhukov's Greatest Defeat*, 31. As Glantz opined, "Model was not a philosopher, he was a fighter [who] radiated confidence."

54. A town or village on Panzer Route 1, some 50 kilometers east of Kobrin. In the Thies atlas of Army Group Center, the town is designated as "Kartuska-Bereza." Thies, "Lage am 23.6.1941 abds., Heeresgruppe Mitte," in *Der Zweite Weltkrieg im Kartenbild*, Bd. 5, Teil 1.1.

55. *Geschichte der 3. Panzer-Division Berlin-Brandenburg*, 110–12. For an equally graphic account of the advance of 3 PD on this day, see Röll, *Oberleutnant Albert Blaich*, 45–48, 69–72.

56. *Geschichte der 3. Panzer-Division Berlin-Brandenburg*, 112; Colonel H. Zobel (ret.), "3rd Panzer Division Operations," in Glantz (ed.), *The Initial Period of War on the Eastern Front*, 242. Recalled Zobel, at the time a young platoon leader in 6 Panzer Regiment, "During the first two days of combat, unarmored troops and rear echelons suffered considerable losses inflicted by hostile enemy troops cut off from their main bodies. They hid beside the march routes, opened fire by surprise, and could only be defeated in intense hand-to-hand combat. German troops had not previously experienced this type of war."

57. *Geschichte der 3. Panzer-Division Berlin-Brandenburg*, 112.

58. Ibid., 112–13.

59. BA-MA RH 20-4/1199, *KTB AOK 4*, 23.6.41; Weal, *Jagdgeschwader 51 "Mölders,"* 58.

60. Guderian, *Panzer Leader*, 154, 156; Guderian, *Erinnerungen eines Soldaten*, 141.

61. Guderian, *Panzer Leader*, 156.

62. Glantz, "The Border Battles on the Bialystok-Minsk Axis," 210.

63. *Geschichte der 3. Panzer-Division Berlin-Brandenburg*, 112.

64. Röll, *Oberleutnant Albert Blaich*, 73.

65. Schramm (ed.), *Kriegstagebuch des OKW*, Bd. I, 420; Thies, "Lage am [26–27.]6.1941 abds., Heeresgruppe Mitte," in *Der Zweite Weltkrieg im Kartenbild*, Bd. 5, Teil 1.1; Kirchubel, *Hitler's Panzer Armies on the Eastern Front*, 64; Seaton, *The Russo-German War*, 121.

66. BA-MA RH 21-2/927, *KTB Panzergruppe 2*, 28.6.41.

67. This excellent motorized division would find itself in the path of a series of furious Soviet breakout attempts between 27–30 June near the village of Zelva, west of Slonim. The Russians attacked repeatedly in waves only to be mowed down by the German machine guns. According to one account, "Never before had the troops of the [29 ID (mot.)] witnessed such slaughter. Yet there were no surrenders" (Luttichau, *The Road to Moscow: The Campaign in Russia—1941*, VI: 46). While the Russians did not break out at Zelva, the division paid dearly for its defensive success, its dreadful losses including forty-seven officers KIA or wounded. BA-MA RH 26-29/6, *KTB 29. Inf.-Div. (mot.)*, 1.7.41. For a detailed account of this action, see Luther, *Barbarossa Unleashed*, 290–91.

68. As cited in Macksey, *Guderian*, 136.

69. Seaton, *The Russo-German War*, 121; Hoth, *Panzer-Operationen*, 66; Thies, "Lage am 30.6.41 abds., Heeresgruppe Mitte," in *Der Zweite Weltkrieg im Kartenbild*, Bd. 5, Teil 1.1.

70. As cited in Macksey, *Guderian*, 134, 136.

71. BA-MA 27-3/14, *KTB 3. Pz.-Div.*, 29.6.41.

72. By 30 June 1941, 3 PD was on the move toward the Dnepr; two days later, lead elements were nearing Rogachev. Stein, *Generalfeldmarschall Walter Model*, 238.

73. Pleshakov, *Stalin's Folly*, 144–45.

74. As cited in Stahel, *Hitler's Panzer Generals*, 184.

75. Macksey, *Guderian*, 137.

76. Hart, *Guderian*, 72. On multiple occasions, advance units of the *Einsatzgruppen* were attached to frontline combat formations within Guderian's zone of operations. "In light of [such] evidence," averred Hart, "it is impossible to accept Guderian's postwar claim that he was ignorant both of their [the *Einsatzgruppen*] existence and the nature of their missions" (ibid., 72).

77. As cited in Macksey, *Guderian*, 137.

78. Guderian, *Panzer Leader*, 160.

79. GFM von Bock, *The War Diary*, 234.

80. Stahel, *Operation Barbarossa and Germany's Defeat in the East*, 187–88.

81. Luttichau, *The Road to Moscow: The Campaign in Russia—1941*, VI: 52–53.

82. Nehring, "Die 18. Panzerdivision 1941 im Rahmen der Panzergruppe Guderian," in *Deutscher Soldatenkalender 1961*, 194–96. Nehring's advance detachment for the raid included a tank battalion from 18 Panzer Regiment (II./PzRgt 18), one battalion from 52 Rifle Regiment (I./SR 52), two motorcycle companies, and a battery of 88 Artillery Regiment. BA-MA RH 27-18/20, *KTB 18. Pz.-Div.*, 1.7.41.

83. BA-MA N 910/5, *Tagebuch* Lemelsen, 1.7.41.

84. Stein, *Generalfeldmarschall Walter Model*, 57 (n. 215). Clemens Graf Kageneck, in the summer of 1941 an *Oberleutnant* and company commander in 6 Pz.Rgt. (3 PD), wrote of Model, "[He] was constantly at the front. He was a man who demanded much from us [*viel von uns verlangte*], but who spared himself the least." His bravery was "legendary." Ibid., 57 (n. 215).

85. Thies, "Lage am 2.7.1941 abds., Heeresgruppe Mitte," in *Der Zweite Weltkrieg im Kartenbild*, Bd. 5, Teil 1.1.

86. BA-MA N 910/5, *Tagebuch* Lemelsen, 30.6.1941.

87. Halder, *The Halder War Diary*, 442.

88. Stahel, *Operation Barbarossa and Germany's Defeat in the East*, 191.

89. As cited in Macksey, *Guderian*, 136. Conversely, one could argue that it was Guderian's insubordination that was actually resulting in higher losses, for the more Soviet soldiers escaped from the pocket, the more units the Red Army could reestablish to fight the Germans.

90. Guderian, *Panzer Leader*, 161–62; Stahel, *Operation Barbarossa and Germany's Defeat in the East*, 191, 193. Amusingly, it seems that the "generals' conspiracy" went well beyond Guderian and Hoth. In his memoir Guderian wrote that "the OKH was secretly hoping that the commanders of the panzer groups would continue to go for their original objectives, whether without orders or even against orders." Such was the Byzantine world in which Guderian and Hoth operated in the summer of 1941. Guderian, *Panzer Leader*, 167.

91. In his diary (3 July), Halder noted that the panzer groups "are launching the offensive today. Both armored groups have already started off. Guderian forced the Berezina River this forenoon; Hoth's left wing reached the Dvina northwest of Polotsk by noon" (Halder, *The Halder War Diary*, 445).

92. On this day, however, 17 PD, 29 ID (mot.), IRGD, and MG Battalion 5 were still in place along the Belostok-Minsk cauldron and, thus, not initially available to join Guderian's drive on the Dnepr. Thies, "Lage am 3.7.1941 abds., Heeresgruppe Mitte," in *Der Zweite Weltkrieg im Kartenbild*, Bd. 5, Teil 1.1.

93. Ibid., 3.7.1941.

94. GFM von Bock, *The War Diary*, 239.

95. Glantz, *Barbarossa Derailed*, 1:68; *Geschichte der 3. Panzer-Division Berlin-Brandenburg*, 123–24; Thies, "Lage am 3.7.1941 abds., Heeresgruppe Mitte," in *Der Zweite Weltkrieg im Kartenbild*, Bd. 5, Teil 1.1.

96. *Geschichte der 3. Panzer-Division Berlin-Brandenburg*, 124.

97. Ibid., 125.

98. "After Action Report of Panzer-Regiment 35," in Schäufler (ed.), *Knight's Cross Panzers*, 78–79.

99. Newton, *Hitler's Commander*, 126.

100. Ibid., 126–27.

101. The maps of Operations Branch of the German Army General Staff show that 3 PD occupied two tiny bridgeheads across the Dnepr on 6 July 1941; by evening the next day, both had been abandoned. Thies, "Lage am [6./7.]7.1941 abds., Heeresgruppe Mitte," in *Der Zweite Weltkrieg im Kartenbild*, Bd. 5, Teil 1.1.

102. Newton, *Hitler's Commander*, 128.

103. *Geschichte der 3. Panzer-Division Berlin-Brandenburg*, 126.

104. The reference here is most likely to the Soviet KV-1A tank, which actually weighed about forty-seven tons. The KV-2 weighed just under fifty-two tons, but few of them were built. Winchester, *Tanks and Armored Fighting Vehicles of WWII*, 256, 263.

105. Nehring, "Die 18. Panzerdivision 1941 im Rahmen der Panzergruppe Guderian," in *Deutscher Soldatenkalender 1961*, 197.

106. Wrote a *Leutnant* in Nehring's 18 PD early in the campaign, "The tank scare [among our troops] is still quite great!" (*Die Panzerschreck ist noch immer gross!*). *Tagebuch* Kreuter, 26.6.1941. To calm their fears, Lt. Kreuter made a point of talking to the men in his rifle regiment. Ironically, this tank scare, affecting Kreuter's unit less than a week into the campaign, was most certainly not attributable to T-34s and KVs but perhaps simply the result of the alarming number of Soviet tanks encountered in the first days of Barbarossa. (Note: A typed transcript of Kreuter's diary is among the "Craig W. H. Luther Papers" at the Hoover Institute, Stanford University, Palo Alto, California.)

107. Boltenstern's 29 ID (mot.) had finally been withdrawn from the encirclement ring by 7 July and, by day's end, was approaching Borisov on the Berezina River. Thies, "Lage am 7.7.1941 abds., Heeresgruppe Mitte," in *Der Zweite Weltkrieg im Kartenbild*, Bd. 5, Teil 1.1.

108. BA-MA N 910/5, *Tagebuch* Lemelsen, 6.7.41.

109. On 22 June 1941, 17 PD was commanded by *Generalleutnant* von Arnim; he was wounded at the end of the month and temporarily replaced by *Generalmajor* Johannes Streich. Weber took command of the division on 7 July. At https://lexikon-der-wehrmacht.de.

110. BA-MA N 910/5, *Tagebuch* Lemelsen, 10.7.41.

111. Guderian, *Panzer Leader*, 167.

112. Ibid., 167–68.

113. Guderian, *Panzer Leader*, 169; Guderian, *Erinnerungen eines Soldaten*, 153.

114. Glantz, *Barbarossa Derailed*, 1:129 (n. 4); GFM von Bock, *The War Diary*, 244.

115. Krivosheev (ed.), *Soviet Casualties and Combat Losses in the Twentieth Century*, 111.

116. Ibid., 260.

117. As cited in Kershaw, *War Without Garlands*, 169–70.

CHAPTER 3. THE SMOLENSK CAULDRON BATTLE

1. Hillgruber, *Hitlers Strategie*, 541–43; Andreas Hillgruber, "Die 'Endlösung' und das deutsche Ostimperium als Kernstück des rassenideologischen Programms des Nationalsozialismus," in Funke (ed.), *Hitler, Deutschland und die Mächte*, 102.

2. "Vortragsnotiz über die Besetzung und Sicherung des russischen Raumes und über den Umbau des Heeres nach Abschluss Barbarossa," in Schramm (ed.), *Kriegstagebuch des OKW*, Bd. I, 1022–25.

3. Overmans, *Deutsche militärische Verluste im Zweiten Weltkrieg*, 277.

4. As cited in Mackey, *Guderian*, 142.

5. Glantz, *Barbarossa Derailed*, 1:92.

6. Kirchubel, *Operation Barbarossa 1941 (3). Army Group Center*, 54.

7. Thies, "Lage am 10.7.1941 abds., Heeresgruppe Mitte," in *Der Zweite Weltkrieg im Kartenbild*, Bd. 5, Teil 1.1.

8. According to David Glantz, the Dnepr "ranged in width from 250 to 300 feet at Bychov and was no obstacle, the only problem [Guderian] had to surmount was the swampy meadows and forests on the river's eastern bank" (Glantz, *Barbarossa Derailed*, 1:93).

9. Schäufler (ed.), *Knight's Cross Panzers*, 81.

10. Thies, "Lage am 11.7.1941 abds., Heeresgruppe Mitte," in *Der Zweite Weltkrieg im Kartenbild*, Bd. 5, Teil 1.1.

11. Guderian, *Panzer Leader*, 171.

12. The IRGD was a reinforced infantry regiment. It began the eastern campaign with twenty companies distributed among five battalions; heavy weapons included the 400 Artillery Battalion with three artillery batteries. Spaeter, *Die Geschichte des Panzerkorps "Grossdeutschland,"* 248.

13. Schick, *Die Geschichte der 10. Panzer-Division*, 300–301.

14. The fighting at Hill 215 apparently took place on the evening of 10 July. Ibid., 302.

15. Guderian, *Panzer Leader*, 172; "Tagesmeldungen der Operations-Abteilung des GenStdH," in Schramm (ed.), *Kriegstagebuch des OKW*, Bd. I, 519; Thies, "Lage am 11.7.1941 abds., Heeresgruppe Mitte," in *Der Zweite Weltkrieg im Kartenbild*, Bd. 5, Teil 1.1.; Schick, *Die Geschichte der 10. Panzer-Division*, 302.

16. As cited in Macksey, *Guderian*, 140.

17. As cited in Stahel, *Hitler's Panzer Generals*, 184.

18. Stahel, *Hitler's Panzer Generals*, 184. Continues Stahel, "Such initial optimism, excitement and anticipation go a long way toward explaining Guderian's psychological decline over the course of the year as the campaign transformed from an impending victory to exhaustion, stagnation and ultimately forced retreat in winter" (ibid., 184).

19. Kirchubel, *Hitler's Panzer Armies on the Eastern Front*, 67. At Mogilev, Guderian encircled 13 Army's 61 Rifle and 20 Mechanized Corps.

20. Glantz, *Barbarossa Derailed*, 1:101.

21. "Tagesmeldungen der Operations-Abteilung des GenStdH," in Schramm (ed.), *Kriegstagebuch des OKW*, Bd. I, 521.

22. Kirchubel, *Operation Barbarossa 1941 (3). Army Group Center*, 56.

23. Boog et al., *Germany and the Second World War*, Vol. IV, 770. In mid-July 1941, Chief of the Army General Staff Halder seemed highly satisfied with the results of the *Luftwaffe*'s interdiction campaign against Soviet rail lines, although he overestimated its strategic impact. "[The] *Luftwaffe*," he wrote in his diary on 11 July, "now seems to have succeeded in wrecking Russian railroads also far to the rear of the enemy communications zone. The number of lines with immobilized railroad transport is growing most satisfactorily, and the good work is being continued" (Halder, *The Halder War Diary*, 466).

24. Nehring, "Die 18. Panzerdivision 1941 im Rahmen der Panzergruppe Guderian," in *Deutscher Soldatenkalender 1961*, 197–98. The incident at Dobryn also resulted in a field hospital of 18 Panzer Division being attacked, resulting in serious casualties.

25. "Tagesmeldungen der Operations-Abteilung des GenStdH," in Schramm (ed.), *Kriegstagebuch des OKW*, Bd. I, 524; for a recent account of the Battle of Smolensk, see Töppel, "Sprungbrett nach Moskau," 8–21.

26. Glantz, *Barbarossa Derailed*, 1:159. Even after the Germans captured Smolensk, skirmishing would go on in the city into late July. According to Heinz Magenheimer, the Germans required ten days to clear all the Russians from the city. Magenheimer, *Moskau 1941*, 50.

27. BA-MA 910/5, *Tagebuch* Lemelsen, 16.7.41.

28. Stahel, *Operation Barbarossa and Germany's Defeat in the East*, 268.

29. Hans Joachim Schröder, "Erfahrungen deutscher Mannschaftssoldaten während der ersten Phase des Russlandkrieges," in Wegner (ed.), *Zwei Wege nach Moskau*, 312.

30. *Feldpost*, Heinemann, 17.7.41. (Note: This letter, and others of Werner Heinemann, can be found in the "Craig W. H. Luther Papers" at the Hoover Institute, Stanford University, Palo Alto, California.)

31. "Tagesmeldungen der Operations-Abteilung des GenStdH," in Schramm (ed.), *Kriegstagebuch des OKW*, Bd. I, 539; Thies, "Lage am 15.7.1941 abds., Heeresgruppe Mitte," in *Der Zweite Weltkrieg im Kartenbild*, Bd. 5, Teil 1.1.

32. Piekalkiewicz, *Die Schlacht um Moskau*, 88.

33. Guderian, *Panzer Leader*, 178. Hoth and Richthofen (8 Air Corps) were also awarded the Oak Leaves to the Knight's Cross on this day.

34. Michulec, *4. Panzer-Division on the Eastern Front*, 4.

35. Risse, "Das IR 101 und der 2. Weltkrieg."

36. Stahel, *Operation Barbarossa and Germany's Defeat in the East*, 272–73.

37. Glantz, *Barbarossa Derailed*, 1:249.

38. *KTB Panzergruppe 3*, 15.7.41, as cited in Stahel, *Operation Barbarossa and Germany's Defeat in the East*, 264; see also BA-MA RH 21-3/732, "Gefechtsberichte Russland 1941/42."

39. At https://lexikon-der-wehrmacht.de; Dinglreiter, *Die Vierziger*, 47.

40. BA-MA N 910/5, *Tagebuch* Lemelsen, 20.7.41.

41. "Tagesmeldungen der Operations-Abteilung des GenStdH," in Schramm (ed.), *Kriegstagebuch des OKW*, Bd. I, 528.

42. Kershaw, *War Without Garlands*, 95.

43. GFM von Bock, *The War Diary*, 254.

44. Ibid., 254–55. Apparently, Kluge had not wanted to speak to Bock that morning, initially instructing Blumentritt to tell Bock that he, Kluge, had just driven away and was unavailable. When Kluge finally intervened in the conversation to defend Guderian, he was, no doubt, also defending himself against Bock's rather pointed line of questioning.

45. Stahel, *Operation Barbarossa and Germany's Defeat in the East*, 268–69.

46. Guderian, *Panzer Leader*, 181; Guderian, *Erinnerungen eines Soldaten*, 164.

47. GFM von Bock, *The War Diary*, 256.

48. Ibid., 255.

49. Kesselring, *Soldat bis zum letzten Tag*, 123.

50. "Verlustmeldungen 5.7.1941–25.3.1942," BA-MA RH 21-2/757, Fol. 4, as cited in Stahel, *Operation Barbarossa and Germany's Defeat in the East*, 279 (n. 68, 71). By 25 July 1941, total casualties in Guderian's panzer group had increased to 20,271, making for an average daily loss of almost 600 men. The losses included 1,023 officers (306 dead, 690 wounded, 27 missing). Over the same thirty-four-day period 2 Panzer Group received less than 10,000 replacements. BA-MA RH 21-2/928, *KTB Panzergruppe 2*, 29.7.41.

51. In 4 PD at this time, forty-nine tanks were under short-term repair, and forty more were unable to be repaired due to the lack of replacement parts (above all, engines and transmissions). Total losses amounted to forty-two tanks. Schäufler (ed.), *Knight's Cross Panzers*, 93–94.

52. BA-MA RH 21-2/928, *KTB Panzergruppe 2*, 28.7.41.

53. On this day (21 July), the KTB of 10 PD also noted that, despite all efforts, the division's tanks would be without oil in the coming days. In desperation, 10 PD considered using captured stocks of Russian oil, which turned out to be unsuitable. Schick, *Die Geschichte der 10. Panzer-Division*, 322.

54. Kershaw, *War Without Garlands*, 97.

55. Thies, "Lage am 25.7.1941 abds., Heeresgruppe Mitte," in *Der Zweite Weltkrieg im Kartenbild*, Bd. 5, Teil 1.1.

56. On the evening of 24 July, a nervous and increasingly impatient Hitler telephoned Bock, asking about the "status of the hole in the pocket." The field marshal "briefed him on all the details, which he took in calmly." Hitler responded by offering suggestions of his own on how the cauldron might be closed. The next day (25 July), GFM Keitel, Chief of the OKW, arrived at Bock's CP to continue the dialogue. Hitler, it seems, still had "ideas on the subject," which Keitel was to convey. GFM von Bock, *The War Diary*, 261–62.

57. BA-MA RH 21-2/928, *KTB Panzergruppe 2*, 28.7.41. Without citing a source, the German quasi-official history of World War II states that the "hole" east of Smolensk "was not closed until 24 July" (Boog et al., *Germany and the Second World War*, Vol. IV, 536.) The OKH Operations Branch reported that it was closed two days later, on 26 July. ("Tagesmeldungen der Operations-Abteilung des GenStdH," in Schramm [ed.], *Kriegstagebuch des OKW*, Bd. I, 540–41.) Yet, according to 2 Panzer Group (i.e., the command on the spot), Soviet forces were still escaping across the Dnepr River at Ratchino late on 27 July 1941. BA-MA RH 21-2/928, *KTB Panzergruppe 2*, 27.7.41.

58. Buchbender and Sterz (eds.), *Das andere Gesicht des Krieges*, 75.

59. BA-MA RH 27-18/20, *KTB 18. Pz.-Div.*, 25./26.7.41, as cited in Stahel, *Operation Barbarossa and Germany's Defeat in the East*, 308.

60. BA-MA RH 27-18/26, 27.7.41, as cited in Bartov, *Hitler's Army*, 21.

61. From 21–26 July, *Grossdeutschland* fought off powerful Soviet thrusts about Rudnia, less than 30 kilometers northwest of Roslavl. A wartime publication of IRGD's replacement brigade (*Ersatz-Brigade*), targeted at recruiting German youth, featured a heroic account of the fighting, noting that "the superior Russian forces were frequently only beaten down in close combat" and that "for six long days, two Russian divisions, with their supporting artillery, were beaten back with bloody losses for the enemy." "Der Kampf gegen den Bolschewismus," in *Infanterie Division (mot.) Grossdeutschland ruft die Jugend des Grossdeutschen Reiches*, 22.

62. Mawdsley, *Thunder in the East*, 69.

63. Glantz, *Forgotten Battles of the Soviet-German War*, 1:47–51; Kirchubel, *Hitler's Panzer Armies on the Eastern Front*, 69.

64. Thies, "Lage am 28.7.1941 abds., Heeresgruppe Mitte," in *Der Zweite Weltkrieg im Kartenbild*, Bd. 5, Teil 1.1.

65. Guderian's direct subordination under Army Group Center went into effect at midday, 28 July 1941. BA-MA RH 21-2/928, *KTB Panzergruppe 2*, 28.7.41.

66. BA-MA RH 21-2/928, *KTB Panzergruppe 2*, 29.7.41. The figures, however, do not include 10 PD; as of 25 July 1941, its entire panzer brigade was out of action due to a lack of oil and spare parts.

67. Röll, *Oberleutnant Albert Blaich*, 87–88.

68. The *Luftwaffe* also contributed flak units to the offensive. Kesselring, *Soldat bis zum letzten Tag*, 125; Boog et al., *Germany and the Second World War*, Vol. IV, 773. In its war diary, 2 Panzer Group stated that three flak battalions were loaned to Guderian from Second Army to support the attack. BA-MA RH 21-2/928, *KTB Panzergruppe 2*, 31.7.41.

69. The Il-2 *Sturmovik* had only begun to enter the inventory of the Soviet Air Force (VVS) in the spring of 1941. Hans Schäufler recalled the incident: "A daredevil low-level attack by armored aircraft against the division command post. Our four-barreled flak fired back in truly self-sacrificing fashion. Their hits seemed to have no effect, since the aircraft were armored.

They fired their rockets at us from the side. It was our first experience with this type of aircraft. . . . We had to bury 5 dead and transport 14 wounded to the aid station" (Schäufler [ed.], *Knight's Cross Panzers*, 100–101).

70. GFM von Bock, *The War Diary*, 271.

71. BA-MA RH 21-2/928, *KTB Panzergruppe 2*, 3.8.41.

72. In late July 1941, German movements on the central front were often hampered by sudden downpours and thundershowers. For example, the daily reports of the Operations Branch of OKH recorded bad weather across the front of Army Group Center, or localized weather problems within the army group's area, from 21–26 July. Although less pronounced, occasional rainfall and thundershowers also took place in August 1941. "Tagesmeldungen der Operations-Abteilung des GenStdH," in Schramm (ed.), *Kriegstagebuch des OKW*, Bd. I, 532–41; 550–603.

73. Dollinger (ed.), *Kain, wo ist dein Bruder?*, 92.

74. "Tagesmeldungen der Operations-Abteilung des GenStdH," in Schramm (ed.), *Kriegstagebuch des OKW*, Bd. I, 561; Glantz, *Barbarossa Derailed*, 1:319, 326.

75. Guderian, *Panzer Leader*, 193.

76. Halder, *The Halder War Diary*, 498.

77. Stahel, *Operation Barbarossa and Germany's Defeat in the East*, 330.

78. Ibid., 330–31.

79. As cited in Macksey, *Guderian*, 143–44.

80. Ibid., 144.

81. On 2 August 1941, *Generalmajor* Wolfgang Fischer, hitherto commander of the division's 10 Rifle Brigade, replaced Schaal as commander of 10 PD. At https://lexikon-der-wehrmacht.de.

82. "Tagesmeldungen der Operations-Abteilung des GenStdH," in Schramm (ed.), *Kriegstagebuch des OKW*, Bd. I, 532; Schick, *Die Geschichte der 10. Panzer-Division*, 320–22.

83. Wray, *Standing Fast*, 40.

84. Boog et al., *Germany and the Second World War*, Vol. IV, 1126.

85. Fugate and Dvoretsky, *Thunder on the Dnepr*, 170–71. Many older German officers compared their experiences at El'nia to those at Verdun in 1916.

86. For an in-depth and insightful report on the Germans' initial experiences with Soviet artillery, see BA-MA RH 26-6/16, "Erfahrungsbericht über russische Artillerie," *Artillerie Regiment 78*, 29.8.1941, in *Anlagenband 1 zum KTB Nr. 5 der 6. Inf.-Div., Ia.*

87. Ibid.

88. Geyer, *Das IX*, 98–99.

89. Stahel, *Operation Barbarossa and Germany's Defeat in the East*, 328–29.

90. Unfortunately, in his memoir (*Soldat bis zum letzten Tag*), GFM Kesselring (C-in-C 2 Air Fleet) does not address his support of German forces in the El'nia salient.

91. Günther, *Hot Motors, Cold Feet*, 100–102; Günther, *Heisse Motoren, kalte Füsse*, 123.

92. U.S. military equivalents for Waffen-SS ranks: (1) SS-*Sturmmann* = acting corporal; (2) SS-*Rottenführer* = corporal; (3) SS-*Unterscharführer* = sergeant (NCO).

93. Günther, *Hot Motors, Cold Feet*, 102–3; Günther, *Heisse Motoren, kalte Füsse*, 123–24.

94. Ellipses have been removed from the text of these diary entries to render them more readable. All underscores are in the original text.

95. All diary entries gleaned from BA-MA RH 21-2/928, *KTB Panzergruppe 2*, 22–31.7.41.

96. In late July, Stalin dismissed Zhukov as Chief of the Red Army General Staff. Apparently, Zhukov's outspokenness was his undoing. He had served as chief of staff since January 1941.

97. Glantz, *Barbarossa Derailed*, 1:535.

98. BA-MA RH 21-2/928, *KTB Panzergruppe 2*, 5.8.41.

99. Thies, "Lage am 8.8.1941 abds., Heeresgruppe Mitte," in *Der Zweite Weltkrieg im Kartenbild*, Bd. 5, Teil 1.1.

100. BA-MA N 910/5, *Tagebuch* Lemelsen, 10.8.41.

101. Glantz, *Barbarossa Derailed*, 1:539; Weidinger, *Das Reich III*, 7.

102. On 1 August, 10 PD had occupied a security line (*Sicherungslinie*) southwest of El'nia, a quieter sector that shielded the right flank of the El'nia salient. On orders from 46 Panzer Corps, the division also established an operational reserve (*Einsatzgruppe*) that included a rifle battalion and two tank companies; intended as the corps reserve, the *Einsatzgruppe* was to be ready to intervene at any crisis point along the salient within two hours of being notified. While both actions (security line and reserve force) were unavoidable, they disrupted efforts to refurbish the panzer regiment, whose tanks were still mostly out of action—awaiting oil, spare parts, new engines, and maintenance. Schick, *Die Geschichte der 10. Panzer-Division*, 333–38.

103. Schick, *Die Geschichte der 10. Panzer-Division*, 343–45; Thies, "Lage am 23.8.1941 abds., Heeresgruppe Mitte," in *Der Zweite Weltkrieg im Kartenbild*, Bd. 5, Teil 1.1.

104. GFM von Bock, *The War Diary*, 281. As long as artillery shells remained in such short supply, the Stukas of Kesselring's 2 Air Fleet functioned as flying artillery for both 20 AK and 46 PzK. BA-MA RH 21-2/928, *KTB Panzergruppe 2*, 13.8.41.

105. BA-MA RH 21-2/928, *KTB Panzergruppe 2*, 13.8.41.

106. Stahel, *Operation Barbarossa and Germany's Defeat in the East*, 392.

107. Stahel, *Operation Barbarossa and Germany's Defeat in the East*, 392; BA-MA RH 21-2/928, *KTB Panzergruppe 2*, 14.8.41.

108. GFM von Bock, *The War Diary*, 281–82. According to former *Luftwaffe* General Hermann Plocher, Göring's decision was indeed the proper one: "A concentrated commitment of the 2 Air Corps in the El'nia salient would at best have been able to achieve only a tactical defensive victory on a relatively small sector of the front. . . . In contrast, the concentrated employment of *Luftwaffe* forces in front of the Second Army and the 2 Panzer Group in and east of the Gomel area enabled the right wing of Army Group Center, which was behind the others, to advance and thereby eliminated the deep Soviet wedge between Army Groups South and Center." See Plocher, *The German Air Force versus Russia*, 107–11.

109. This must be a reference to SS *Reich* and 10 PD, neither of which were still inside the salient proper; rather, they were deployed behind its left and right flanks, respectfully. Thies, "Lage am 15.8.1941 abds., Heeresgruppe Mitte," in *Der Zweite Weltkrieg im Kartenbild*, Bd. 5, Teil 1.1.

110. GFM von Bock, *The War Diary*, 283.

111. Ibid., 282. As Bock wrote in his diary, "I received the decision on the El'nia salient in the evening; it contains many 'ifs' and 'buts' and turns responsibility over to me."

112. On 14 August, Halder recorded in his diary, "I warned him [Greiffenberg] against abandoning El'nia. No matter how badly off our troops are, it is worse even for the enemy" (Halder, *The Halder War Diary*, 508).

113. Guderian, *Panzer Leader*, 194–95. While in his memoir Guderian does not make precisely clear when he changed his mind and proposed to OKH and Army Group Center that the El'nia salient be given up, he appears to have come to this decision on or just after 15 August 1941.

114. Both the Barbarossa directive of 18 December 1940 and the OKH deployment directive that followed weeks later underscore Moscow's secondary significance.

115. This must be a reference to El'nia, which the Germans normally spelled *Jelnja*. "Hans-Otto" may have simply been unaware of the proper spelling.

116. *Feldpostbrief*, "Hans-Otto," 15.8.41.

117. German intelligence estimated that fifteen Soviet rifle divisions and six tank divisions were trapped inside the pocket. Thies, "Lage am 2.8.1941 abds., Heeresgruppe Mitte," in *Der Zweite Weltkrieg im Kartenbild*, Bd. 5, Teil 1.1.

118. Glantz, *Barbarossa Derailed*, 1:334; BA-MA RH 21-2/928, *KTB Panzergruppe 2*, 2.8.41.

119. As noted in the diary of Army Group Guderian on the afternoon of 2 August, the efforts of 17 Panzer to reach the bridge just east of Ratchino failed due to marshy and heavily mined terrain. The next day (3 August) a battalion of infantry from Boltenstern's splendid 29 ID (mot.), supported by an artillery battery, managed to make it to within two kilometers of the Ratchino bridge, which they took under fire; they got no farther, however. BA-MA RH 21-2/928, *KTB Panzergruppe 2*, 2–3.8.41.

120. *Tagebuch* (author unknown), as cited in Duesel (ed.), *Gefallen!*, 23–24.

121. Frisch and Jones, *Condemned to Live*, 74.

122. BA-MA N 910/5, *Tagebuch* Lemelsen, 21.7.41.

123. As cited in Macksey, *Guderian*, 141–42.

124. "Tagesmeldungen der Operations-Abteilung des GenStdH," in Schramm (ed.), *Kriegstagebuch des OKW*, Bd. I, 556.

125. BA-MA RH 20-4/337, *Kämpfe der 4. Armee im ersten Kriegsjahr gegen die Sowjet Union (22.6.41–22.6.42).*

126. GFM von Bock, *The War Diary*, 273–74.

127. Glantz, *Barbarossa Derailed*, 1:358–59.

128. Magenheimer, *Moskau 1941*, 52. According to the study by Russian Col.-Gen. G. F. Krivosheev, only 1,348 tanks—less than half the number claimed by Bock and the German High Command—were lost during the Battle of Smolensk (i.e., the fighting along the central axis), which in the Soviet chronology of the war lasted from 10 July to 10 September 1941. Adding to this figure the 4,799 tanks lost by Soviet Western Front during the eighteen-day battle of the frontier would bring total Russian tank losses through 10 September 1941 opposite Army Group Center to 6,147. Krivosheev (ed.), *Soviet Casualties and Combat Losses in the Twentieth Century*, 260.

129. BA-MA RL 2-II/4327, *Tagebuch* Waldau, 14.8.41.

130. As noted by Roman Töppel, the German victory in the Battle of Smolensk was a Pyrrhic victory (*Pyrrhussieg*) for two overarching reasons: (1) the heavy (and irreplaceable) losses incurred by the Germans of both men and materiel, and (2) the fact that the Red Army had, for the first time, brought the German blitzkrieg to a temporary standstill. Recognizing the latter, the Japanese General Staff concluded that Soviet Russia would not collapse even if the *Wehrmacht* succeeded in taking Moscow; hence, Imperial Japan, after months of deliberation, finally reached a decision not to intervene in Operation Barbarossa but to strike out into Southeast Asia and the Pacific to acquire the raw materials it desperately needed to sustain operations of its armed forces. Töppel, "Sprungbrett nach Moskau," 21.

131. As cited in Macksey, *Guderian*, 142.

PART II. INTO THE UKRAINE

1. Förster, *Die Wehrmacht im NS-Staat*, 173–74.
2. BA-MA N 664/3, *Tagebuch* Thilo, 24.8.41.
3. Förster, *Die Wehrmacht im NS-Staat*, 174, 176.
4. GFM von Bock, *The War Diary*, 305.

CHAPTER 4. INDECISION AND DELAY

1. Germany and German-occupied Poland used standard gauge rail lines (1,435mm); the Soviets used wider gauge lines (1,528mm), a legacy of the czarist era. Before 22 June 1941, in order to receive the large quantities of foodstuffs and raw materials Soviet Russia was obligated to deliver to Germany under the 1939 pact, Germany had constructed two special gauge conversion yards on its eastern frontier. These two rail yards also became key rail centers after the start of Operation Barbarossa. "Deutsche Reichsbahn—the German State Railway," Feldgrau, https://www.feldgrau.com/ww2-german-state-railway-deutsche-reichsbahn.

2. Overmans, *Deutsche militärische Verluste im Zweiten Weltkrieg*, 277. Over a similar six-week period in May/June 1940, during the campaign against France and the Low Countries, the Germans had recorded 29,640 fatal casualties (Army and Air Force). Dear (ed.), *The Oxford Companion to World War II*, 326. The Germans also had slightly more than 13,000 missing in France in 1940.

3. On *Barbarossatag*, at OKH headquarters in Zossen, south of Berlin, Paulus briefed GFM von Brauchitsch on the initial reports from the front. The reports were good. Brauchitsch asked Paulus how long he thought the war against Russia would last. Paulus, the consummate general staff officer and normally sober judge of events, predicted the war would last only six to eight weeks. "Ja, Paulus, you are certainly correct," replied the field marshal. "We will need about eight weeks for Russia." (*Ja, Paulus, Sie werden Recht haben, acht Wochen werden wir wohl für Russland brauchen.*) Meyer, *Adolf Heusinger*, 151, 850 (n. 23).

4. Although a precise date is not given, the meeting most likely took place sometime after mid-July, as Smolensk was not reached by the Germans until 15/16 July 1941.

5. Diedrich, *Paulus*, 183.

6. Ibid., 187.

7. Halder, *The Halder War Diary*, 457.

8. Kershaw, *Hitler*, 409.

9. Halder, *The Halder War Diary*, 485.

10. Irving, *Hitler's War*, 286.

11. As cited in Stahel, *Operation Barbarossa and Germany's Defeat in the East*, 253.

12. BA-MA N 664/3, *Tagebuch* Thilo, 25.7.41.

13. Below, *At Hitler's Side*, 109.

14. Reuth (ed.), *Joseph Goebbels Tagebücher*, Bd. IV, 1645.

15. Ibid., 1627.

16. Musial, *Kampfplatz Deutschland*, 458.

17. BA-MA N 813, *Tagebuch* Münchhausen, August 1941.

18. American troops had landed on Iceland on 7 July 1941. Mühleisen (ed.), *Hellmuth Stieff Briefe*, 221 (n. 10).

19. Stieff's reference here is to "Führer Directive" No. 33 ("Continuation of the War in the East") of 19 July 1941.

20. Mühleisen (ed.), *Hellmuth Stieff Briefe*, 113–15. Under Keitel at OKW, a special office, headed by a colonel, was responsible for preparing the daily *Wehrmacht* reports. While Stieff's assertion that Hitler personally prepared the reports is highly doubtful—although Hitler may very well have intervened on occasion in their preparation—his damning critique of the reports is quite accurate. Email, C. Nehring to C. Luther, 30 May 2012.

21. Megargee, *Inside Hitler's High Command*, 133.

22. Ibid., 133.

23. Halder, *The Halder War Diary*, 506.

24. For the details of these directives (33 and 33a), see Trevor-Roper, *Hitler's War Directives*, 85–90; see also Hubatsch (ed.), *Hitlers Weisungen für die Kriegführung*, 140–44.

25. As cited in Shirer, *The Rise and Fall of the Third Reich*, 856.

26. GFM von Bock, *The War Diary*, 261.

27. Trevor-Roper, *Hitler's War Directives*, 91–93.

28. Sweeting, *Hitler's Personal Pilot*, 166.

29. "Besprechung gelegentlich Anwesenheit des Führers und Obersten Befehlshabers der Wehrmacht bei Heeresgruppe Mitte am 4. August 1941," in Schramm (ed.), *Kriegstagebuch des OKW*, Bd. I, 1042–43.

30. The only exception was Guderian, who was to continue his operations (beginning with Roslavl) to stabilize and clear his right flank.

31. "Besprechung gelegentlich Anwesenheit des Führers und Obersten Befehlshabers der Wehrmacht bei Heeresgruppe Mitte am 4. August 1941," in Schramm (ed.), *Kriegstagebuch des OKW*, Bd. I, 1043.

32. Guderian, *Panzer Leader*, 190.

33. "Besprechung gelegentlich Anwesenheit des Führers und Obersten Befehlshabers der Wehrmacht bei Heeresgruppe Mitte am 4. August 1941," in Schramm (ed.), *Kriegstagebuch des OKW*, Bd. I, 1043; Guderian, *Panzer Leader*, 190; Hoth, *Panzer-Operationen*, 117.

34. In his memoir, Guderian (*Panzer Leader*, 190) stated, falsely it seems, that Hitler had promised just 300 new tank engines for the entire eastern front; the actual figure was 400, and they were to go exclusively to Hoth and Guderian. For more details, see chapter 6, discussion on attrition.

35. BA-MA RH 21-2/928, *KTB Panzergruppe 2*, 4.8.1941; Stahel, *Operation Barbarossa and Germany's Defeat in the East*, 341–42.

36. As cited in Irving, *Hitler's War*, 298 (n. 1).

37. Irving, *Hitler's War*, 298; Boog et al., *Germany and the Second World War*, Vol. IV, 584; Heusinger, FMS T-6: "Eastern Campaign, 1941–1942 (Strategic Survey)," 82–83. According to David Irving, when Hitler visited Bock's headquarters on 4 August, he "had not yet made up his mind on how to fight the next phase of the campaign." However, Irving then argued that, by 6 August (visiting Rundstedt at Army Group South), "Hitler's mind was all but made up. He would make his main push southeastward toward the oil fields, while the northern advance on Leningrad from the Luga bridgeheads began. Moscow would be left for last." Irving, *Hitler's War*, 297–98.

38. Boog et al., *Germany and the Second World War*, Vol. IV, 591. As noted in this volume, the OKH memorandum made clear that Halder believed "the decisive moment had arrived to obtain Hitler's final consent" for his (Halder's) Moscow-centric proposals for the next phase of the campaign.

39. Both of Halder's assumptions were highly questionable, given the *Ostheer*'s strained supply situation and rapidly diminishing combat strength. For the memorandum, see "Vorschlag für Fortführung der Operation der Heeresgruppe Mitte im Zusammenhang mit den Operationen der Heeresgruppe Süd und Nord," ObdH, H.Qu. OKH, 18.8.41, in Schramm (ed.), *Kriegstagebuch des OKW*, Bd. I, 1055–59.

40. "Wehrmachts-Führungsstab/L, Nr. 441412/41 g.Kdos. Chef, 21. August 1941," in Schramm (ed.), *Kriegstagebuch des OKW*, Bd. I, 1062–63.

41. Kotze (ed.), *Heeresadjutant bei Hitler*, 110.

42. BA-MA N 813, *Tagebuch* Münchhausen, ca. 22.8.41. In his diary, Münchhausen also stated that the new directive "struck like a bomb."

43. BA-MA N 664/3, *Tagebuch* Thilo, 24.8.41.

44. As Münchhausen exclaimed in his diary with obvious disgust, "The courage of one's convictions [*Zivilcourage*] is precisely what these folks lack!" BA-MA N 813, *Tagebuch* Münchhausen, ca. 22.8.41.

45. Haape, *Moscow Tram Stop*, 61.

46. Guderian, *Panzer Leader*, 195; Guderian, *Erinnerungen eines Soldaten*, 176. Panzer artilleryman Franz Frisch recalled "seeing with amusement several signs raised by *Panzer* tank troops along the roads leading from Smolensk that read, 'To Moscow.'" Frisch and Jones, *Condemned to Live*, 74.

47. Guderian, *Panzer Leader*, 198.

48. Guderian, *Panzer Leader*, 198–99; GFM von Bock, *The War Diary*, 291.

49. Guderian, *Panzer Leader*, 199–200.

50. Ibid., 200. In his biography of Guderian, Kenneth Macksey points out that there may well have been another reason why Guderian refrained from making "an angry scene" in Hitler's presence: the panzer general, it seems, was being considered by a "small and influential caucus of officers"—including Hitler's *Luftwaffe* adjutant *Oberst* von Below—as a possible replacement for GFM von Brauchitsch, the weak and ineffectual C-in-C of the Army, who was increasingly despised by Hitler. According to Macksey, Below asked Guderian "what his reactions would be if he were asked to be C-in-C." Guderian answered that he would "follow the call." In *Panzer Leader*, Guderian "gives no hint of this approach . . . though in his correspondence there is ample evidence of his realization that new horizons were appearing." See Macksey, *Guderian*, 144–49.

51. Guderian, *Panzer Leader*, 202; Guderian, *Erinnerungen eines Soldaten*, 183.

52. Commenting long after the war (May 1967), Geyr von Schweppenburg expressed understanding for Guderian's demand of Hitler that, if against his own wishes he had to push south into the Ukraine, then he be given his entire panzer group with which to do so. As Geyr put it, Guderian's demand was "simply the most obvious demand [*selbstverständlichste Forderung*]" for him to make. Pöhlmann, *Der Panzer und die Mechanisierung des Krieges*, 353 (n. 192).

CHAPTER 5. GUDERIAN CLEARS HIS RIGHT FLANK

1. "Erwägungen und Anordnungen des Führers am 28. Juli 1941," in Schramm (ed.), *Kriegstagebuch des OKW*, Bd. I, 1040–41; Trevor-Roper, *Hitler's War Directives*, 90–93.

2. GFM von Bock, *The War Diary*, 292–93.

3. Halder, *The Halder War Diary*, 493; Boog et al., *Germany and the Second World War*, Vol. IV, 590; "OKW Nr. 441 386/41 g.K. Chefs. WFSt/L (I Op.)," 15.8.41, in Schramm (ed.), *Kriegstagebuch des OKW*, Bd. I, 1045; Thies, "Lage am 15.8.1941 abds., Heeresgruppe Mitte," in *Der Zweite Weltkrieg im Kartenbild*, Bd. 5, Teil 1.1.

4. Guderian, *Panzer Leader*, 193.

5. Ibid., 193–94. Of course, it goes without saying that the German military administration inside occupied Soviet Russia was far from "benevolent" (*die wohlwollende Militärverwaltung*). Guderian, *Erinnerungen eines Soldaten*, 174. The complicity of the *Wehrmacht* in war crimes on the eastern front has been sedulously researched and confirmed by historians for decades. Among the plethora of source materials on this topic, see Jürgen Förster, "Wehrmacht, Krieg und Holocaust," in Rolf-Dieter Müller and Hans-Erich Volkmann (eds.), *Die Wehrmacht. Mythos und Realität* (Munich, 1999); see also Christian Hartmann, "Verbrecherischer Krieg—verbrecherische Wehrmacht?," in *Vierteljahrshefte für Zeitgeschichte* (Sonderdruck aus Heft 1/2004).

6. BA-MA RH 21-2/928, *KTB Panzergruppe 2*, 9–10.8.41; see also Glantz, *Barbarossa Derailed*, 1:387.

7. The 7 Infantry Division had been detached from 7 Army Corps and assigned to 24 Panzer Corps on 31 July 1941. At https://lexikon-der-wehrmacht.de.

8. BA-MA RH 21-2/928, *KTB Panzergruppe 2*, 13.8.41; Thies, "Lage am 13.8.1941 abds., Heeresgruppe Mitte," in *Der Zweite Weltkrieg im Kartenbild*, Bd. 5, Teil 1.1.

9. BA-MA RH 27-4/10, *KTB 4. Pz.-Div.*, 14.8.41, as cited in Stahel, *Operation Barbarossa and Germany's Defeat in the East*, 385–86.

10. Guderian, *Panzer Leader*, 195.

11. Glantz, *Barbarossa Derailed*, 1:387.

12. Stahel, *Operation Barbarossa and Germany's Defeat in the East*, 385.

13. Bollmann and Flörke, *Das Infanterie-Regiment 12*, 101.

14. Glantz, *Barbarossa Derailed*, 1:390; Thies, "Lage am 15.8.1941 abds., Heeresgruppe Mitte," in *Der Zweite Weltkrieg im Kartenbild*, Bd. 5, Teil 1.1.

15. Carell, *Hitler Moves East*, 108.

16. Glantz, *Barbarossa Derailed*, 1:390; Bollmann and Flörke, *Das Infanterie-Regiment 12*, 102.

17. Thies, "Lage am 22.8.1941 abds., Heeresgruppe Mitte," in *Der Zweite Weltkrieg im Kartenbild*, Bd. 5, Teil 1.1.

18. BA-MA N 910/5, *Tagebuch* Lemelsen, 22.8.41.

19. Hürter, *Ein deutscher General an der Ostfront*, 74–75.

20. Ibid., 75.

21. GFM von Bock, *The War Diary*, 286; Thies, "Lage am 19.8.1941 abds., Heeresgruppe Mitte," in *Der Zweite Weltkrieg im Kartenbild*, Bd. 5, Teil 1.1.

22. Glantz, *Barbarossa Derailed*, 1:399–401; BA-MA RH 21-2/928, *KTB Panzergruppe 2*, 19–20.8.41.

23. Mehner (ed.), *Die Geheimen Tagesberichte der deutschen Wehrmachtführung im Zweiten Weltkrieg*, Bd. 3, 288 (21.8.41).

24. GFM von Bock, *The War Diary*, 287.

CHAPTER 6. THE KIEV CAULDRON BATTLE

1. The Soviet defenses of Leningrad included 1,000 kilometers of earthworks, 645 kilometers of anti-tank ditches, 600 kilometers of barbed wire, and some 5,000 pillboxes and fire points. Kershaw, *War Without Garlands*, 124; Erickson, *The Road to Stalingrad*, 192.

2. Luther, *Barbarossa Unleashed*, 636–37.

3. Among the Soviet prisoners were the commanders of 6 and 12 Armies. "Tagesmeldungen der Operations-Abteilung des GenStdH," in Schramm (ed.), *Kriegstagebuch des OKW*, Bd. I, 560. For a detailed account of the Uman cauldron battle, see C. Luther, "German Armoured Operations in the Ukraine, 1941. The Encirclement Battle of Uman," *Army Quarterly and Defence Journal* 108, no. 4 (October 1978): 454–69.

4. "Tagesmeldungen der Operations-Abteilung des GenStdH," in Schramm (ed.), *Kriegstagebuch des OKW*, Bd. I, 589–605; Boog et al., *Germany and the Second World War*, Vol. IV, 597–601.

5. GFM von Bock, *The War Diary*, 276.

6. The latter figure is Halder's. Halder, *The Halder War Diary*, 521.

7. By 31 August 1941, more than 14,000 officers had become casualties. The daily losses of slightly more than 200 officers were equal to almost 40 percent of the 518 officers in the organization table of a typical German infantry division. Kershaw, *War Without Garlands*, 172.

8. The 126,000 figure is derived from the analysis by Rüdiger Overmans. See Overmans, *Deutsche militärische Verluste im Zweiten Weltkrieg*, 277.

9. The march battalions each consisted of about 1,000 soldiers. Army Group Center would receive 154 of these battalions, beginning in mid-August and ending in October 1941, by which time the trained manpower of the Replacement Army had been exhausted. Hofmann and Toppe, FMS P-190: "Verbrauchs- und Verschleißsätze während der Operationen der deutschen Heeresgruppe Mitte vom 22.6.41–31.12.41," 68–69.

10. Overmans, *Deutsche militärische Verluste im Zweiten Weltkrieg*, 277.

11. BA-MA RH 19 II/386, *KTB H.Gr.Mitte*, 22.8.41, as cited in Stahel, *Operation Barbarossa and Germany's Defeat in the East*, 419.

12. "Panzerlage an der Ostfront am 4.9.1941," in Müller-Hillebrand, *Das Heer*, Bd. 3, 205. Figures on tanks under repair and total losses for 2 Panzer Group are not broken out in this source. At the time, 10 Panzer Division (previously assigned to the panzer group's 46 Panzer Corps) had been temporarily subordinated to Kluge's Fourth Army; it boasted 159 operational tanks.

13. Boog et al., *Germany and the Second World War*, Vol. IV, 1127.

14. "Tagesmeldungen der Operations-Abteilung des GenStdH," in Schramm (ed.), *Kriegstagebuch des OKW*, Bd. I, 565–68.

15. Corum, *Wolfram von Richthofen*, 274.

16. Boog et al., *Germany and the Second World War*, Vol. IV, 1126–31; Hofmann and Toppe, FMS P-190: "Verbrauchs- und Verschleißsätze während der Operationen der deutschen Heeresgruppe Mitte vom 22.6.41–31.12.41," 85–87; see also Kirchubel, *Operation Barbarossa 1941 (3). Army Group Center*, 68.

17. Luther, *Barbarossa Unleashed*, 622.

18. Kershaw, *War Without Garlands*, 168; van Creveld, *Supplying War*, 170; Seaton, *The Russo-German War*, 175; Reinhardt, *Moscow*, 62.

19. Kershaw, *War Without Garlands*, 168.

20. Van Creveld, *Supplying War*, 155, 157; Boog et al., *Germany and the Second World War*, Vol. IV, 1130.

21. Haape, *Moscow Tram Stop*, 339.

22. BA-MA RH 19 II/386, *KTB H.Gr.Mitte*, 1.8.41, as cited in Stahel, *Operation Barbarossa and Germany's Defeat in the East*, 332.

23. BA-MA N 813, *Tagebuch* Münchhausen, 12–15.8.41.

24. Windisch, FMS P-201: "Personal Diary Notes of the G-4 of the German 9th Army," 59. By late August 1941, wear and tear on the medium field howitzers was also taking a toll, the army noting an increased incidence of barrels bursting when firing (*Rohrkrepierer*). Ibid., 20.

25. In June 1941, the artillery regiment of a typical German infantry division had thirty-six light (le.FH) and twelve medium (s.FH) howitzers (forty-eight guns in twelve batteries) in its table of organization.

26. Grassmann, FMS D-221: "An Artillery Regiment on the Road to Moscow (22 June to December 1941)," 14–15.

27. Boog et al., *Germany and the Second World War*, Vol. IV, 1126.

28. The maximum production of artillery ammunition in 1941 was reached in February, with outlays of 69.1 million *Reichsmarks*; not until the spring of 1942 would production again reach that level. Donat, *Der Munitionsverbrauch im Zweiten Weltkrieg im operativen und taktischen Rahmen*, 7.

29. GFM von Bock, *The War Diary*, 288.

30. Reinhardt, *Moscow*, 151.

31. Van Creveld, *Supplying War*, 170–71. According to van Creveld, motor oil was also in short supply; in fact, it signified the "bottleneck of the entire transportation system."

32. Hart, *Guderian*, 76.

33. Following incorporation of the Central Front, Eremenko had under his command 3, 13, 21, and 50 Armies. Of these, "only 50 Army was fresh and capable of undertaking sustained offensive action." However, due to mistaken Soviet intelligence, 50 Army was sent off to meet what turned out to be a nonexistent threat on Eremenko's northern (right) wing; thus, it was not available to contest Guderian's advance. "The blunder was greatly to weaken Eremenko's counterattacks, which became an exceptionally tall order for the many battered and understrength divisions of the Briansk Front." Stahel, *Kiev 1941*, 120–21, 180.

34. Guderian, *Panzer Leader*, 204.

35. Ibid., 206.

36. Newton, *Hitler's Commander*, 137–38. For his decisive action, *Leutnant* Störck was awarded the Knight's Cross (*Ritterkreuz*) on 22 September 1941. At https://lexikon-der-wehrmacht.de.

37. Carell, *Hitler Moves East*, 115.

38. Newton, *Hitler's Commander*, 138.

39. Carell, *Hitler Moves East*, 120–21; Carell, *Unternehmen Barbarossa*, 108–9.

40. Stahel, *Kiev 1941*, 162.

41. BA-MA RH 24-47/2, *KTB Nr. 2, 47 PzK*, 31.8.1941, as cited in Stahel, *Kiev 1941*, 162–63.

42. Stahel, *Kiev 1941*, 163. Again, as noted earlier in this text, the reference is most likely to the forty-seven-ton KV-1A.

43. Ibid., 121.

44. Thies, "Lage am 1.9.1941 abds., Heeresgruppe Mitte," in *Der Zweite Weltkrieg im Kartenbild*, Bd. 5, Teil 1.1.

45. As cited in Macksey, *Guderian*, 149, 151; see also Walde, *Guderian*, 134.

46. Stahel, *Kiev 1941*, 124.

47. GFM von Bock, *The War Diary*, 294. In late August 1941, Vietinghoff's 10 PD and IRGD were in reserve south of Smolensk; SS *Reich*, however, while still a component of 46 PzK, was in position east of Smolensk and, since 20 August, at the direct disposal (*zur Verfügung*) of Army Group Center. Thies, "Lage am 27.8.1941 abds., Heeresgruppe Mitte," in *Der Zweite Weltkrieg im Kartenbild*, Bd. 5, Teil 1.1; Weidinger, *Das Reich III*, 7; at https://lexikon-der-wehrmacht.de.

48. GFM von Bock, *The War Diary*, 294–95; Guderian, *Panzer Leader*, 206–7.

49. GFM von Bock, *The War Diary*, 298.

50. Ibid., 298.

51. Halder, *The Halder War Diary*, 521–22.

52. Ibid., 523.

53. Elements of 46 PzK dispatched by Bock to Guderian did not include Fischer's 10 Panzer Division. After helping Kluge's Fourth Army clear up the enemy breakthrough south of El'nia, 10 PD was withdrawn from the front and positioned south of Smolensk as an "intervention reserve" (*Eingreifreserve*), a roll it had also played after being pulled from the El'nia salient at the start of August 1941. However, formal subordination of 10 PD to Vietinghoff's panzer group did not end until 18 September. Schick, *Die Geschichte der 10. Panzer-Division*, 352–54.

54. Thies, "Lage am 3.9.1941 abds., Heeresgruppe Mitte," in *Der Zweite Weltkrieg im Kartenbild*, Bd. 5, Teil 1.1.

55. BA-MA RH 21-2/819, *KTB der O.Qu.-Abt. Pz. A.O.K. 2*, 4.9.1941, as cited in Stahel, *Kiev 1941*, 183, 395 (n. 53).

56. Thies, "Lage am 5.9.1941 abds., Heeresgruppe Mitte," in *Der Zweite Weltkrieg im Kartenbild*, Bd. 5, Teil 1.1.

57. Guderian, *Panzer Leader*, 210.

58. Ibid., 214.

59. Thies, "Lage am 6.9.1941 abds., Heeresgruppe Mitte," in *Der Zweite Weltkrieg im Kartenbild*, Bd. 5, Teil 1.1.

60. Weidinger, *Das Reich III*, 15.

61. Ibid., 18–19; Mattson, *SS-Das Reich*, 94.

62. Weidinger, *Das Reich III*, 19; Lucas, *Das Reich*, 65–69.

63. Weidinger, *Das Reich III*, 19–20.

64. Günther, *Hot Motors, Cold Feet*, 143. For the original German edition, see Günther, *Heisse Motoren, kalte Füsse*, 173–83.

65. Guderian, *Panzer Leader*, 212–13.

66. Walde, *Guderian*, 135.

67. "Tagesmeldungen der Operations-Abteilung des GenStdH," in Schramm (ed.), *Kriegstagebuch des OKW*, Bd. I, 618; Guderian, *Panzer Leader*, 213.

68. GFM von Bock, *The War Diary*, 308.

69. Guderian, *Panzer Leader*, 213.

70. GFM von Bock, *The War Diary*, 310–311.

71. As cited in Kershaw, *War Without Garlands*, 155.

72. Stahel, *Kiev 1941*, 219–22; Carell, *Hitler Moves East*, 123.

73. Newton, *Hitler's Commander*, 143. On or around 14 September, the advance headquarters of Model's corps commander, Geyr von Schweppenburg, was suddenly attacked by a Soviet column trying to break out of the pocket. Only the timely arrival of a company of German panzer troops saved Geyr and his staff from almost certain death.

74. Sources differ on the size of Model's battlegroup. According to Werner Haupt, it consisted of a lone Pz III, a command tank with a radio, and a clutch of all-terrain vehicles—a total of two officers and forty-five men (Haupt, *Kiew. Die grösste Kesselschlacht der Geschichte,* 106; see also Haupt, *Army Group Center*, 74). In contrast, Model biographer Steven Newton maintained that the combat group included the last ten tanks of 3 Panzer Division (Newton, *Hitler's Commander*, 143). Paul Carell, who interviewed hundreds of German veterans for his popular early-1960s work on Operation Barbarossa, also noted a "small combat group," but one consisting of perhaps a company of tanks and some armored scout cars (Carell, *Hitler Moves East*, 124–26). In his memoir, Guderian stated that 3 PD's 6 Pz.Rgt. was down to ten tanks (one Pz IV, three Pz IIIs, six Pz IIs) on 15 September (Guderian, *Panzer Leader*, 219).

75. Haupt, *Army Group South*, 74–75.

76. Carell, *Hitler Moves East*, 126.

77. Stahel, *Kiev 1941*, 229. Tannenberg was the site of the great German victory against Russia in August 1914.

78. Carell, *Hitler Moves East*, 126; Carell, *Unternehmen Barbarossa*, 113; Haupt, *Army Group South*, 75.

79. Stahel, *Kiev 1941*, 229.

80. GFM von Bock, *The War Diary*, 313.

81. Alexander and Kunze (eds.), *Eastern Inferno*, 97.

82. Ibid., 103–6.

83. Vogt (ed.). *Herbst 1941 im "Führerhauptquartier,"* 29.

84. Kesselring, *Soldat bis zum letzten Tag*, 126–27. In his memoir, Kesselring praised 2 Air Corps for its "decisive impact" (*ausschlaggebende Wirkung*) in the Kiev *Kesselschlacht*. He also noted that *II Fliegerkorps* had to fight "under difficult conditions," because the Russians, having

learned from previous battles, had almost completely throttled their daytime traffic to avoid hostile aircraft. Poor weather also affected operations of the air corps.

85. Haupt, *Army Group South*, 75.

86. Luther and Stahel (eds.), *Soldiers of Barbarossa*, 172–73.

87. As cited in Stahel, *Kiev 1941*, 254.

88. Plocher, *The German Air Force versus Russia*, 131–32; Boog et al., *Germany and the Second World War*, Vol. IV, 784. Plocher, who served as Chief of Staff of 5 Air Corps, wrote, "The German isolation of the Kiev pocket was exemplary, with the bombers of the 5 Air Corps (4 Air Fleet) operating from the Kirovograd area in the south and those of the 2 Air Corps (2 Air Fleet) operating from north of Gomel and Orsha in the north" (Plocher, *The German Air Force versus Russia*, 127–28).

89. As cited in Kershaw, *War Without Garlands*, 159. He was unable to tell whether the acrid odor was of men or horses.

90. Ibid., 162.

91. "Tagesmeldungen der Operations-Abteilung des GenStdH," in Schramm (ed.), *Kriegstagebuch des OKW*, Bd. I, 661.

92. Erickson, *The Road to Stalingrad*, 209–10.

93. Stahel, *Kiev 1941*, 255–56.

94. Below, *At Hitler's Side*, 112. As von Below also noted, "When I explained the facts to Hitler at *Wolfsschanze* [the dictator's HQ in East Prussia] he thought about it for some time and said finally that [the] General Staff ought to know: then they might take a different view of the sort of enemy we were fighting against" (ibid., 112).

PART III. OPERATION TYPHOON

1. Macksey, *Guderian*, 154. According to Macksey, Guderian's rapid shift of his panzer group in late September from containment of the Kiev pocket to being ready to begin his assault toward Moscow on 30 September was "as a feat of sheer brilliance . . . almost unparalleled." While I find Macksey's analysis a trifle overwrought, Guderian's achievement was certainly impressive.

2. Forczyk, *Tank Warfare on the Eastern Front*, 141.

3. Thies, "Lage am 6.12.1941 abds., Heeresgruppe Mitte," in *Der Zweite Weltkrieg im Kartenbild*, Bd. 5, Teil 1.1.

CHAPTER 7. OPERATION TYPHOON

1. Kluge's Fourth Army had assumed control of the El'nia sector from Guderian's HQ on 22 August. On 30 August 1941, the Red Army began its final push to capture the salient. Zhukov's Reserve Front once again unleashed Rakutin's 24 Army, recently reinforced by three additional divisions, bringing its total strength to ten divisions (including 102 and 105 Tank and 103 Motorized Divisions). The German defenders were ill prepared for the Soviet onslaught. Because of the chronic shortage of combat infantry, their defenses typically consisted of little more than a single trench line, instead of a multizone, elastic defense in depth, as prescribed by German doctrine. On 2 September, Bock noted that his divisions within the El'nia salient were simply being "bled white," and after several conversations with Kluge, he decided the time had finally come to abandon it. GFM von Bock, *The War Diary*, 302.

2. For having distinguished themselves in the fighting at the town of El'nia, four Soviet rifle divisions (100, 127, 153, and 161 RDs) became the first to be redesignated as "guards" divisions. Mawdsley, *Thunder in the East*, 72.

3. Glantz, *Barbarossa*, 90. From the German perspective, the "operational withdrawal from El'nia was the first imposed on the German Army in World War II" (Wray, *Standing Fast*, 47).

4. According to official Russian figures, between 10 July and 10 September (termed, in the Soviet periodization of the "Great Fatherland War," the "Battle of Smolensk") the four Soviet fronts in action along the central axis (Western, Central, Reserve, Briansk) sustained a total of 759,974 casualties, of which 486,171 were irrecoverable losses (the majority having been taken prisoner in the Smolensk pocket and other pocket battles). Equipment losses of the Soviet fronts amounted to 1,348 tanks, 9,290 guns and mortars, and 903 aircraft. Krivosheev (ed.), *Soviet Casualties and Combat Losses in the Twentieth Century*, 116, 260.

5. On 11 September 1941, the war diary of Ninth Army observed that a "certain relaxation" had set in along the front; on 14 September, it reported that a "conspicuous calm" was continuing in the army's sector. BA-MA RH 20-9/16, *KTB AOK 9*, 11./14.9.41.

6. Trevor-Roper (ed.), *Hitler's War Directives*, 96–97; Hubatsch (ed.), *Hitlers Weisungen für die Kriegführung*, 150–52.

7. Trevor-Roper (ed.), *Hitler's War Directives*, 97; Hubatsch (ed.), *Hitlers Weisungen für die Kriegführung*, 151.

8. Stahel, *Operation Typhoon*, 50. By the end of September 1941, "successes in the north and the south, sealing off Leningrad and capturing Kiev, had reinvigorated enthusiasm and raised expectations that the Soviet state was approaching collapse. Crucial in this regard were Goebbels' string of *Sondermeldungen* (special news bulletins), which openly declared the war was nearing its end. . . . While many men at the front expressed their reservations and longed for an end to the war, Goebbels' victory propaganda was still largely successful, especially in Germany" (ibid., 50).

9. Mühleisen (ed.), *Hellmuth Stieff Briefe*, 128.

10. Kirchubel, *Operation Barbarossa 1941 (3). Army Group Center*, 66.

11. For an excellent treatment of Typhoon—the buildup for and the operation itself—see Glantz, *Barbarossa*, 137–82.

12. Guderian, *Panzer Leader*, 226; Guderian, *Erinnerungen eines Soldaten*, 204.

13. GFM von Bock, *The War Diary*, 314.

14. Boog et al., *Germany and the Second World War*, Vol. IV, 670.

15. GFM von Bock, *The War Diary*, 318.

16. Guderian, *Panzer Leader*, 225.

17. GFM von Bock, *The War Diary*, 317.

18. Reinhardt, *Moscow*, 59.

19. GFM von Bock, *The War Diary*, 319.

20. BA-MA N 664/3, *Tagebuch* Thilo, 27.9.41.

21. BA-MA RH 20-9/16, *KTB AOK 9*, 2.9.41.

22. GFM von Bock, *The War Diary*, 319; BA-MA H 08-22/9, *Nachlass Generalfeldmarschall Fedor von Bock, Tagebuchnotizen Osten I*, 29.9.41.

23. Guderian, *Panzer Leader*, 225.

24. De Beaulieu, *Generaloberst Erich Hoepner*, 192, as cited in Stahel, *Kiev 1941*, 297–98.

25. Thies, "Lage am 29.9.1941 abds., Heeresgruppe Mitte," in *Der Zweite Weltkrieg im Kartenbild*, Bd. 5, Teil 1.1.

26. The total of 400 operational tanks includes 60 belonging to 9 PD, 91 to 3 PD, and 93 to 4 PD. BA-MA RH 21-2/910, *Die Operationen der 2. Pz.Armee in der Doppelschlacht von Bryansk und Wyazma und beim Vorstoss auf Moskau 30.9. bis 5.12.1941*, 6 (Tabelle, 115). In his memoir, Guderian stated that his panzer group had "at last been given 100 tanks as replacements for our

panzer divisions"; however, he went on to note that fifty of these tanks were misdirected to Orsha and "therefore arrived too late" (Guderian, *Panzer Leader*, 227).

27. Kesselring, *Soldat bis zum letzten Tag*, 129.

28. Walde, *Guderian*, 138–40; Thies, "Lage am 29.9.1941 abds., Heeresgruppe Mitte," in *Der Zweite Weltkrieg im Kartenbild*, Bd. 5, Teil 1.1.

29. Kershaw, *War Without Garlands*, 164.

30. According to the Liebenstein study, German logisticans estimated that it would require five "units of consumption" (*Verbrauchssätze*) of fuel, one "initial issue" (*erste Munitionsausstattung*) of ammunition, and ration requirements (*Tagessätze*) for five days for 2 Panzer Group to reach its initial objective—the Orel-Briansk line. A unit of consumption was the amount of fuel required by a division to move 100 kilometers: 25 tons for an infantry division; 150 to 200 tons for a tank division. An initial issue of ammunition amounted to about 500 tons for an infantry division and 600 to 700 tons for a tank division; under normal combat conditions it was expected to last for ten days. Ration requirements for infantry divisions (including oats and roughage for 5,000 horses) amounted to 50 tons per day; for panzer and motorized divisions, just 20 tons per day. The above figures, however, are accurate for 22 June 1941; given the major losses sustained by Guderian's divisions by the start of Typhoon, actual logistical needs of his panzer group on 30 September were likely much less. Whatever Guderian's *actual* requirements, they would not be met due to the ongoing shortages of supply trains and trucks. BA-MA RH 21-2/910, *Die Operationen der 2. Pz.Armee in der Doppelschlacht von Bryansk und Wyazma und beim Vorstoss auf Moskau 30.9. bis 5.12.1941*, 6–7. Supply figures gleaned from Luttichau, *The Road to Moscow: The Campaign in Russia—1941*, IV: 41–42.

31. BA-MA RH 19 II/120, *KTB H.Gr.Mitte*, 2.10.41; Magenheimer, *Moskau 1941*, 120. For Army Group Center's complete order of battle, see Boog et al., *Germany and the Second World War*, Vol. IV, 668–69.

32. One source claims that, of these 1,000 aircraft, only 549 (among them 158 bombers and 172 fighters) were mission capable when Typhoon began. See Bergström, *Barbarossa*, 90. Christer Bergström's claim is indirectly supported by Halder, who, in his diary on 12 September, put the total for operational aircraft on the eastern front (three air fleets) at 1,005 (including 440 bombers, 186 dive-bombers, and 295 fighters). Halder, *The Halder War Diary*, 529.

33. Boog et al., *Germany and the Second World War*, Vol. IV, 671.

34. Glantz, *Barbarossa*, 142.

35. Ibid.

36. Ibid.

37. Meyer, *Infanterie-Regiment Grenadier-Regiment 241*, 14.

38. Luther and Stahel (eds.), *Soldiers of Barbarossa*, 186.

39. Pabst, *The Outermost Frontier*, 26.

CHAPTER 8. THE FINAL DESPERATE PUSH

1. Luttichau, *The Road to Moscow: The Campaign in Russia—1941*, XXX: 1; Gutenkunst, *Geschichte der 3. Kompanie des Infanterie-Regiments 109 im Krieg*, 223.

2. BA-MA RL 8/49, "VIII. Fl.K., Einsatz Russland," 2.10.41.

3. Lierow, *Persönliches Tagebuch*, 2.10.41.

4. *Tagebuch* (author unknown), as cited in Duesel (ed.), *Gefallen!*, 39.

5. Pabst, *The Outermost Frontier*, 27.

6. GFM von Bock, *The War Diary*, 320; BA-MA H 08-22/9, *Nachlass Generalfeldmarschall Fedor von Bock, Tagebuchnotizen Osten I*, 2.10.41.

7. Irving, *Hitler's War*, 319.
8. Ibid., 320.
9. Jacobsen (ed.), *1939–1945*, 38.
10. Weal, *Jagdgeschwader 51 "Mölders,"* 70.
11. Glantz, *Barbarossa*, 144.
12. Guderian, *Panzer Leader*, 228, 230.
13. Ibid., 230.
14. The Soviet aerial assaults were carried out by a stream of mostly one or two bombers at a time with fighter protection. In its war diary, 4 PD complained that, since 2 October, the Russians "still" possessed complete air superiority in its area of operations. T-315, Roll 195, Ia KTB 4 PD, 3.10.1941.
15. Guderian, *Panzer Leader*, 230, 232. Guderian also wrote, "The evacuation of industrial installations [from Orel], carefully prepared by the Russians, could not be carried out. Along the streets leading from the factories to the station lay dismantled machines and crates filled with tools and raw materials."
16. T-315, Roll 195, Ia KTB 4 PD, 3.10.1941; Schäufler (ed.), *Knight's Cross Panzers*, 124–27. While it appears that none of Wollschlaeger's four tanks were lost inside the city on 3 October, earlier that day his company had lost three tanks to enemy action.
17. Stahel, *Operation Typhoon*, 59–60.
18. Glantz, *Barbarossa*, 147.
19. As briefly addressed in chapter 2, VVS losses at the start of Operation Barbarossa were nothing short of spectacular, resulting in the *Luftwaffe* enjoying air superiority (even air supremacy) over most of the eastern front during the initial weeks of the campaign. In the intervening months, however, Soviet air forces would undergo a rapid and (to the Germans at least) bewildering regeneration of their force structure. By later summer and fall, the VVS had even regained air superiority over certain sectors of the eastern front. And this despite losing more than 20,000 aircraft (all types) by the end of 1941. See Mawdsley, *Thunder in the East*, 59.
20. Guderian, *Panzer Leader*, 232–33.
21. Forczyk, *Tank Warfare on the Eastern Front*, 120; Stahel, *Operation Typhoon*, 77.
22. *Generalleutnant* von Arnim had replaced *Generalmajor* von Thoma on 19 September 1941 as division commander. Von Arnim had commanded 17 PD at the beginning of the Russian campaign until wounded in late June. At https://lexikon-der-wehrmacht.de.
23. Stahel, *Operation Typhoon*, 76.
24. BA-MA RH 19 II/120, *KTB H.Gr.Mitte*, 6.10.41; Thies, "Lage am 13.10.1941 abds., Heeresgruppe Mitte," in *Der Zweite Weltkrieg im Kartenbild*, Bd. 5, Teil 1.1. (Note: The Thies atlas jumps from 6 to 13 October 1941; however, the latter date clearly shows the two Soviet pockets.)
25. *Tagebuch* Rupp, 7.10.1941. I have removed many of the ellipses in this diary entry to render it more readable. (Note: A typed transcript of Robert Rupp's diary [in German] is among the "Craig W. H. Luther Papers" at the Hoover Institute, Stanford University, Palo Alto, California.)
26. Halder, *The Halder War Diary*, 546.
27. "Erich Hoepner's Letters to His Wife Irma," BA-MA N 51-9 (6.10.41). Hoepner went on to complain about both Bock and Kluge interfering in his operations. Like Guderian, he seemed to take particular issue with the latter: "Kluge also interferes in my affairs, which always causes trouble. . . . I already experienced that with Kluge in the west, but I won't put up with it." (Note: Many thanks to Dr. Stahel for sharing Hoepner's letters with me.)
28. Glantz, *Barbarossa*, 149.

29. Irving, *Hitler's War*, 321–22.

30. Domarus, *Hitler*, Bd. II, 1767. The euphoria at the Wolf's Lair at this time (8/9 October 1941) was captured in a detailed report prepared by Werner Koeppen, Alfred Rosenberg's personal representative at Hitler's East Prussian headquarters. In July 1941, Hitler had appointed Rosenberg to head the Reich Ministry for the Occupied Eastern Territories. See Vogt (ed.), *Herbst 1941 im "Führerhauptquartier,"* 69–71.

31. BA-MA RH 19 II/120, *KTB H.Gr.Mitte*, 8.10.41.

32. Guderian, *Panzer Leader*, 234–35.

33. Kershaw, *War Without Garlands*, 192.

34. The Mozhaisk Defense Line "stretched for [about 200 kilometers] in an arc from the Moscow reservoir to the north of the city, around the small city of Volokolamsk, across the 1812 battlefield of Borodino just to the west of Mozhaisk itself, and down to the confluence of the Ugra and the Oka rivers" (Braithwaite, *Moscow*, 225–26).

35. Zhukov, *Marshal Zhukov's Greatest Battles*, 34.

36. Roberts, *Stalin's Wars*, 108. Over the course of the battle for Moscow, nearly 100 divisions would be transferred to the central sector of the front; nine of these would come from the Far East, as Stalin had decided that the Japanese were not likely to join Hitler's Russian crusade.

37. Guderian, *Panzer Leader*, 232; Guderian, *Erinnerungen eines Soldaten*, 210.

38. As of 4 October, 4 PD had fifty-nine operational tanks. Neumann, *Die 4. Panzer-Division*, 311.

39. Macksey, *Guderian*, 155.

40. The previous day (5 October) had witnessed a skirmish between a tank company (and some recon troops) of 4 PD and a clutch of Soviet T-34s as the former had attempted to move up the Orel-Tula road. After losing some recon vehicles to the T-34s, the Germans had withdrawn; however, they left behind several wounded soldiers who revealed to the Russians that 4 PD would soon advance up the road toward Mtsensk. Armed with this intelligence, the Soviets pulled their armor (two battalions) back to the Lisiza River and deployed it on high ground overlooking a bridge. It was a "perfect ambush position." Forczyk, *Tank Warfare on the Eastern Front*, 121.

41. Stahel, *Operation Typhoon*, 66.

42. Ibid., 66.

43. As noted by Robert A. Forczyk, who described the tank battle at Mtsensk in some detail, the vanguard of 4 PD on this day also included one battery of medium artillery (10cm s.K18) and one battery of 105mm light field howitzers. In the ensuing action, the Germans lost two 88mm flak guns, two 105mm howitzers, and one 105mm gun. Forczyk, *Tank Warfare on the Eastern Front*, 121–22. (Note: The 10cm s.K18 "standard medium gun" had a caliber of 105mm. U.S. War Department, *Handbook on German Military Forces* [March 1945], 334.)

44. Langermann-Erlencamp's mention of "special ammunition" for tanks is intriguing. In the fall of 1941, the Germans tested the so-called *Rotkopf* (redhead) munition—a hollow-charge artillery shell that could penetrate the armor of a T-34; in fact, "a direct hit with a *Rotkopf* shell could generally be counted on to kill the whole tank crew and any infantry riding on the vehicle." While the Army apparently deployed at least a small number of these new artillery shells to the eastern front, Hitler temporarily recalled them in late November 1941, for it had occurred to him that, should the Soviets learn the secret, the shell would be much more effective against his own less well-armored tanks! Despite the almost daily pleading from his army groups and armies at the front, Hitler did not release the embargo on the shell until 22 December. It seems he had wanted to hold back use of the new hollow-charge shell until 1942, when, he reasoned, its surprise impact (most likely due to increased availability) would

be greater. See Ziemke and Bauer, *Moscow to Stalingrad*, 92, 126; Mühleisen (ed.), *Hellmuth Stieff Briefe*, 139–40; Irving, *Hitler's War*, 356, 363; Woche, *Zwischen Pflicht und Gewissen*, 139.

45. As cited in Jentz (ed.), *Panzer Truppen*, 205, 208.

46. Ibid., 208.

47. Guderian, *Panzer Leader*, 233.

48. Macksey, *Guderian*, 155.

49. Guderian, *Panzer Leader*, 233–34.

50. *Tagebuch* Kreuter, 6.10.41. (Note: A typed transcript of Kreuter's diary is among the "Craig W. H. Luther Papers" at the Hoover Institute, Stanford University, Palo Alto, California.)

51. As cited in Kershaw, *War Without Garlands*, 185–86.

52. Guderian, *Panzer Leader*, 234.

53. BA-MA RH 19 II/120, *KTB H.Gr.Mitte*, 9.10.41.

54. It is perhaps a great irony that, despite the inarguably dramatic impact of the fall weather on German troop and supply movements, the amount of precipitation in October and November 1941 was actually *below* the historical average. Magenheimer, *Moskau 1941*, 158.

55. Luther and Stahel (eds.), *Soldiers of Barbarossa*, 202–3.

56. GFM von Bock, *The War Diary*, 340.

57. BA-MA RH 21-2/910, *Die Operationen der 2. Pz.Armee in der Doppelschlacht von Bryansk und Wyazma und beim Vorstoss auf Moskau 30.9. bis 5.12.1941*, 49 (Tabelle, 114).

58. BA-MA N 910/6, *Tagebuch* Lemelsen, 16.10.41.

59. Luther and Stahel (eds.), *Soldiers of Barbarossa*, 223.

60. Thies, "Lage am 13.10.1941 abds., Heeresgruppe Mitte," in *Der Zweite Weltkrieg im Kartenbild*, Bd. 5, Teil 1.1.

61. Ibid.

62. BA-MA RH 19 II/120, *KTB H.Gr.Mitte*, 14.10.41. On 13, 14, and 15 October, 18 PD, supported by IRGD, along the northern pocket, fought off massed Soviet breakout attempts (*massierte Durchbruchsversuche*); while losses were high on both sides, the Germans managed to capture a large number of Red Army artillery pieces. BA-MA RH 21-2/910, *Die Operationen der 2. Pz.Armee in der Doppelschlacht von Bryansk und Wyazma und beim Vorstoss auf Moskau 30.9. bis 5.12.1941*, 40.

63. Forczyk, *Tank Warfare on the Eastern Front*, 120.

64. As cited in Stahel, *Operation Typhoon*, 160.

65. Luther and Stahel (eds.), *Soldiers of Barbarossa*, 211.

66. BA-MA RH 21-2/910, *Die Operationen der 2. Pz.Armee in der Doppelschlacht von Bryansk und Wyazma und beim Vorstoss auf Moskau 30.9. bis 5.12.1941*, 41.

67. Glantz, *Barbarossa*, 153. Glantz estimated the number of Soviet soldiers who escaped the Viaz'ma cauldron at 85,000.

68. BA-MA RH 19 II/120, *KTB H.Gr.Mitte*, 19.10.41; GFM von Bock, *The War Diary*, 336. In his diary, Bock pegged Soviet losses at eight Russian armies with seventy-three rifle and cavalry divisions, thirteen tank divisions and brigades, and "strong army artillery"; total "booty" he estimated at 673,098 prisoners, 1,277 tanks, 4,378 artillery pieces, 1,009 anti-tank and anti-aircraft guns, and 87 aircraft.

69. Reinhardt, *Moscow*, 110–11(n. 45).

70. *Feldpost*, Heinemann, 27.10.41. (Note: This letter, and others of Werner Heinemann, can be found in the "Craig W. H. Luther Papers" at the Hoover Institute, Stanford University, Palo Alto, California.)

71. Lt. Joachim H. (18 967), *Bibliothek für Zeitgeschichte* [Library of Contemporary History], Stuttgart, Germany.

72. BA-MA RH 27-4/10, *Ia KTB 4. Pz.Div.*, 9.10.41, as cited in Stahel, *Operation Typhoon*, 67.

73. Forczyk, *Tank Warfare on the Eastern Front*, 123.

74. Guderian, *Panzer Leader*, 237

75. In some cases, recalled Eberbach, the men "had not had warm rations since Orel" (Schäufler [ed.], *Knight's Cross Panzers*, 138).

76. Ibid., 138.

77. As cited in Forczyk, *Tank Warfare on the Eastern Front*, 124.

78. Efforts to clear Soviet forces from Mtsensk continued at least through 12 October, German forces also fending off repeated enemy attempts to recapture the town. "Tagesmeldungen der Operations-Abteilung des GenStdH," in Schramm (ed.), *Kriegstagebuch des OKW*, Bd. I, 695.

79. Guderian, *Panzer Leader*, 237.

80. The commission, which included top industry representatives, would arrive at Guderian's HQ on 20 November. After inspecting captured T-34 tanks, it returned to Berlin, and before the end of the month, the *Reichsministerium für Bewaffnung und Munition* (Reich Ministry for Armaments Production and Munitions) had issued a "formal request for proposals for a new 30-ton tank outfitted with 60mm sloped armor—this became the genesis of the Pz.V Panther tank. Both MAN and Daimler-Benz began developing prototypes during the winter of 1941–42." Forczyk, *Tank Warfare on the Eastern Front*, 144; see also Jentz, *Germany's Panther Tank*, 14–15.

81. Stein, "Verteidigung an der OKA: das LIII Armeekorps im Rahmen der 2. Pz. Armee vom Dez. 41 bis Jan. 42," 49–50 (MGFA); Reinhardt, *Moscow*, 115 (n. 100). However, as noted by Reinhardt, this figure of tank strength gives "no indication about the actual 'operational capability' of the panzers, which was much lower."

82. Reinhardt, *Moscow*, 92; BA-MA RH 19 II/123, "Zahl der bei den Panzer-Divisionen vorhandenen Panzer," 16.10.41.

83. According to the situation map of the Army General Staff, 9 Panzer Division was still some 50 kilometers (linear distance) northwest of Kursk on 19 October. Thies, "Lage am 19.10.1941 abds., Heeresgruppe Mitte," in *Der Zweite Weltkrieg im Kartenbild*, Bd. 5, Teil 1.1.

84. Stahel, *Operation Typhoon*, 160–61.

85. Guderian's letters as cited in Stahel, *Hitler's Panzer Generals*, 61, 211.

86. BA-MA RH 21-2/910, *Die Operationen der 2. Pz.Armee in der Doppelschlacht von Bryansk und Wyazma und beim Vorstoss auf Moskau 30.9. bis 5.12.1941*, 58.

87. Guderian, *Panzer Leader*, 242.

88. Forczyk, *Tank Warfare on the Eastern Front*, 140.

89. "Tagesmeldungen der Operations-Abteilung des GenStdH," in Schramm (ed.), *Kriegstagebuch des OKW*, Bd. I, 727. As Guderian noted in his memoir, "On the 27th and 28th of October I accompanied Eberbach in his advance" (Guderian, *Panzer Leader*, 244).

90. "Tagesmeldungen der Operations-Abteilung des GenStdH," in Schramm (ed.), *Kriegstagebuch des OKW*, Bd. I, 731. Fighting, however, with the remnants of Soviet units (*Feindresten*), went on in the wooded area 15 kilometers to the south of Tula. Moreover, because the road from Mtsensk to Chern was still impassable for wheeled vehicles, elements of 3 PD near Tula had to be supplied by the *Luftwaffe*.

91. Forczyk, *Tank Warfare on the Eastern Front*, 141–42.

92. Ibid., 142.

93. As determined by the great Prussian military philosopher and theorist Carl von Clausewitz (1780–1831), the culmination (or culminating) point is reached when the strength and resources of the attacker are suddenly superseded by those of the defender.

94. Guderian, *Panzer Leader*, 244. In his memoir, Guderian praised General Heinrici as "always a practical and sensible man."

95. As cited in Stahel, *Hitler's Panzer Generals*, 212.

96. GFM von Bock, *The War Diary*, 347.

97. "Tagesmeldungen der Operations-Abteilung des GenStdH," in Schramm (ed.), *Kriegstagebuch des OKW*, Bd. I, 737.

98. "Erich Hoepner's letters to his wife Irma," BA-MA N 51-9 (30.10.41).

99. GFM von Bock, *The War Diary*, 347.

100. Guderian, *Panzer Leader*, 246.

101. At a top-level conference at the headquarters of Army Group Center in Orsha (13 November), in weather of −22°C, Halder—as part of orders for the renewed offensive—attempted to assign Guderian's panzer army the objective of capturing Gorki, roughly 400 kilometers east of Moscow, to cut off the Soviet capital from its eastward communications. Opposition to Halder's plans, however, resulted in the decision to limit a renewed offensive to a direct assault on Moscow. "This was pushed through," noted Ian Kershaw, "in full recognition of the insoluble logistical problems and immense dangers of an advance in near-arctic conditions without any possibility of securing supplies" (Kershaw, *Hitler*, 437–38).

102. Hürter, *Hitlers Heerführer*, 302, 307. Surprisingly, Hitler had little to do with the decision making at this time; in fact, during October and November 1941, the dictator hardly intervened at all in the operational decisions of OKH, assuming instead an "astonishingly passive" role. According to Hürter, instead of intervening in the OKH conduct of operations, which was driven by Halder, Hitler had "fatalistically" awaited the outcome of operations in the east. Only after the local reverse suffered by Army Group South at Rostov (30 November 1941), did Hitler begin again to intervene energetically. Ibid., 310, 315.

103. GFM von Bock, *The War Diary*, 357.

104. Stahel, *The Battle for Moscow*, 107.

105. The Liebenstein study gives a figure of 201 combat-capable tanks for 9 November 1941 (BA-MA RH 21-2/910, *Die Operationen der 2. Pz.Armee in der Doppelschlacht von Bryansk und Wyazma und beim Vorstoss auf Moskau 30.9. bis 5.12.1941* [Tabelle, 115]). However, Guderian wrote, "Eberbach's fine brigade had only some 50 tanks left, and that was all we had available. The establishment for the three divisions [3, 4, 17 PD] should have been 600" (Guderian, *Panzer Leader*, 248). Still another source put the number of operational tanks as of 9 November for 4 PD and 18 PD at just twenty and nine, respectively (Stahel, *The Battle for Moscow*, 108).

106. Ziemke and Bauer, *Moscow to Stalingrad*, 51.

107. Guderian, *Panzer Leader*, 248–49; Guderian, *Erinnerungen eines Soldaten*, 225–26. In late November, the 112 ID had an infantry combat strength (*Gefechtsstärke*) of not more than 800 men, about the size of a full-strength battalion. BA-MA RH 21-2/910, *Die Operationen der 2. Pz.Armee in der Doppelschlacht von Bryansk und Wyazma und beim Vorstoss auf Moskau 30.9. bis 5.12.1941*, 67.

108. As of 11 November, Guderian's intelligence officer (Ic) estimated the strength of Soviet forces around Tula (excluding Aleksin) at four divisions. BA-MA RH 21-2/910, *Die Operationen der 2. Pz.Armee in der Doppelschlacht von Bryansk und Wyazma und beim Vorstoss auf Moskau 30.9. bis 5.12.1941*, 78.

109. In mid-November 1941, Model, promoted to *General der Panzertruppe*, took command of 41 Panzer Corps. After five months of "incessant campaigning," wrote biographer Steven H. Newton, he had "justifiably earned a reputation as one of the finest panzer division commanders in the German Army" (Newton, *Hitler's Commander*, 147).

110. According to Forczyk, Guderian had "massed 102 operational tanks from the three panzer divisions [3, 4, 17 PD] into an armored fist and attacked southeast of Tula at 0530 on 18 November" (Forczyk, *Tank Warfare on the Eastern Front*, 142).

111. "Tagesmeldungen der Operations-Abteilung des GenStdH," in Schramm (ed.), *Kriegstagebuch des OKW*, Bd. I, 764.

112. Carell, *Hitler Moves East*, 188.

113. Boog et al., *Germany and the Second World War*, Vol. IV, 696.

114. GFM von Bock, *The War Diary*, 366.

115. This letter of Guderian's was cobbled together from three sources: Guderian, *Panzer Leader*, 251–52; Guderian, *Erinnerungen eines Soldaten*, 228; and Macksey, *Guderian*, 156.

116. Stahel, *The Battle for Moscow*, 191.

117. Garden and Andrew (eds.), *The War Diaries of a Panzer Soldier*, 59.

118. Stahel, *The Battle for Moscow*, 189, 191. The figure of thirty-two tanks does not include 18 Panzer Division, which did not belong to Eberbach's battle group. Nehring's 18 PD (still part of 47 PzK), was defending well to the south at Efremov (approximately 150 kilometers east of Orel) on Guderian's eastern flank.

119. BA-MA RH 21-2/910, *Die Operationen der 2. Pz.Armee in der Doppelschlacht von Bryansk und Wyazma und beim Vorstoss auf Moskau 30.9. bis 5.12.1941* (Tabelle, 115).

120. Glantz, *Barbarossa*, 173.

121. As cited in Reinhardt, *Moscow*, 234–35 (n. 84).

122. Forczyk, *Tank Warfare on the Eastern Front*, 143.

123. "Tagesmeldungen der Operations-Abteilung des GenStdH," in Schramm (ed.), *Kriegstagebuch des OKW*, Bd. I, 776; Thies, "Lage am 25.11.1941 abds., Heeresgruppe Mitte," in *Der Zweite Weltkrieg im Kartenbild*, Bd. 5, Teil 1.1.

124. From late September, 29 ID (mot.) was commanded by *Generalmajor* Max Fremerey. At www.lexicon-der-wehrmacht.de.

125. Lemelsen's 47 PzK was covering Guderian's long eastern flank of about 150 kilometers with weak forces. These forces would become even weaker at beginning of December, when 29 ID (mot.) was transferred to 53 AK, and 25 ID (mot.) was shifted to Venev as panzer army reserve. This left Lemelsen to perform this vital mission with only 18 PD and 10 ID (mot.), both divisions (having lost so many of their vehicles) now assessed as being only "1/3 motorized." BA-MA RH 21-2/910, *Die Operationen der 2. Pz.Armee in der Doppelschlacht von Bryansk und Wyazma und beim Vorstoss auf Moskau 30.9. bis 5.12.1941*, 73–74.

126. Guderian, *Panzer Leader*, 254.

127. GFM von Bock, *The War Diary*, 370. Panzer Brigade Eberbach appears on the *Lage Ost* map of the German Army Operations Branch for 28 November 1941 (designated as "Gr. E." and shown with 17 PD just south of Kashira); however, Eberbach's special reinforced command must have been dissolved shortly thereafter. Unfortunately, the precise date of its dissolution is unclear, as the maps in my possession skip from 28 November to 6 December (with no reference to Eberbach's command on the latter date). Thies, "Lage am 25.11.1941 [and 6.12.1941] abds., Heeresgruppe Mitte," in *Der Zweite Weltkrieg im Kartenbild*, Bd. 5, Teil 1.1.

128. Guderian, *Panzer Leader*, 255.

129. Hürter, *Ein deutscher General an der Ostfront*, 115–16.

130. Hossbach, *Infanterie im Ostfeldzug*, 134.

131. As noted in the Liebenstein study, on 1 December Second Panzer Army possessed 105 operational tanks; hence, the army's tank strength had held steady since 23 November (BA-MA RH 21-2/910, *Die Operationen der 2. Pz.Armee in der Doppelschlacht von Bryansk und Wyazma und beim Vorstoss auf Moskau 30.9. bis 5.12.1941* [Tabelle, 115]). Geyr's panzer corps

had a total of fifty-eight tanks at this time (30 November): 3 PD (twenty-eight), 4 PD (twenty), and 17 PD (ten). Stahel, *The Battle for Moscow*, 237.

132. Hossbach, *Infanterie im Ostfeldzug*, 134.

133. "Tagesmeldungen der Operations-Abteilung des GenStdH," in Schramm (ed.), *Kriegstagebuch des OKW*, Bd. I, 790.

134. Higgins, *Guderian*, 215. Heinrici's army corps, however, was now too weak to close the final distance to meet 4 PD.

135. BA-MA RH 27-3/15, *KTB 3. Pz.Div.*, 4.12.41, as cited in Stahel, *The Battle for Moscow*, 281.

136. Guderian, *Panzer Leader*, 257; Guderian, *Erinnerungen eines Soldaten*, 234.

137. Guderian, *Panzer Leader*, 258.

138. Hossbach, *Infanterie im Ostfeldzug*, 134.

139. The bizarre behavior that could result from hypothermia is illustrated by the following incident, as described by an officer in 20 PD: "A tub arrived with Glysantin, an anti-freeze solution [*Frostschutzmittel*] for the motor vehicles that we had been feverishly waiting on for weeks. We opened the tub and were dumbfounded. The Glysantin was frozen solid; it hadn't counted on 50 below zero. We were overcome by a hysterical gaiety. We laughed and danced around the tub, like it was some kind of morbid joke" (*Tagebuch Oblt.* "K," 15.2.42, as cited in Andres, *Panzersoldaten im Russlandfeldzug*, 114).

140. Higgins, *Guderian*, 214–15.

141. Hürter, *Ein deutscher General an der Ostfront*, 116–17.

142. BA-MA RH 21-2/910, *Die Operationen der 2. Pz.Armee in der Doppelschlacht von Bryansk und Wyazma und beim Vorstoss auf Moskau 30.9. bis 5.12.1941*, 95.

143. Kirchubel, *Hitler's Panzer Armies on the Eastern Front*, 81.

144. The combat strength of 3 PD amounted to some fourteen rifle companies (fifty to sixty men each), twenty Pak, and twenty-two tanks with enough fuel to travel 30 kilometers. BA-MA RH 21-2/910, *Die Operationen der 2. Pz.Armee in der Doppelschlacht von Bryansk und Wyazma und beim Vorstoss auf Moskau 30.9. bis 5.12.1941*, 95.

145. Higgins, *Guderian*, 215.

146. Guderian, *Panzer Leader*, 258–59.

147. *Generalmajor* von Thoma had taken command of 20 PD on 14 October 1941. It will be remembered that he had commanded 17 PD in Guderian's 2 Panzer Group from late July through mid-September. At https://lexikon-der-wehrmacht.de.

148. Stahel, *The Battle for Moscow*, 288–89. Stahel writes, "Contrary to a lot of what has been written about the Fourth Army's role in the battle of Moscow, Kluge was by no means responsible for Army Group Center's failed offensive. . . . The Fourth Army's weak right wing never came close to making the difference between victory and defeat at Moscow, but that has not saved Kluge from becoming a scapegoat for much more important German deficiencies and weaknesses." For more on this topic, see ibid., 287–90.

149. BA-MA RH 21-2/244, *KTB Pz.AOK 2*, 5.12.41.

150. Guderian, *Panzer Leader*, 259.

CHAPTER 9. DEFEAT AND DISMISSAL

1. Hossbach, *Infanterie im Ostfeldzug*, 134.

2. BA-MA RH 21-2/244, *KTB Pz.AOK 2*, 5.12.41; Higgins, *Guderian*, 214; Irving, *Hitler's War*, 350; Dinglreiter, *Die Vierziger*, 78–80.

3. Second Panzer Army had lost 252 tanks in the *Kesselschlacht* of Briansk and in the battles around Mtsensk; dozens more were lost in the battle for Tula and in fighting at Kashira, Stalinogorsk, Efremov, and other towns. BA-MA RH 21-2/910, *Die Operationen der 2. Pz.Armee in der Doppelschlacht von Bryansk und Wyazma und beim Vorstoss auf Moskau 30.9. bis 5.12.1941*, 116.

4. Thies, "Lage am 6.12.1941 abds., Heeresgruppe Mitte," in *Der Zweite Weltkrieg im Kartenbild*, Bd. 5, Teil 1.1.

5. Reinhardt, *Moscow*, 249 (n. 2). Even Chief of the Army General Staff Halder, in a moment of sober reflection, was forced to admit that Germany would never again possess an Army as magnificent as the *Ostheer* of June 1941. Halder, *The Halder War Diary*, 562.

6. Glantz, *Barbarossa*, 182.

7. Stahel, *Hitler's Panzer Generals*, 186.

8. As cited in Stahel, *Hitler's Panzer Generals*, 186. Guderian went on to say, "Our losses, particularly due to sickness and frostbite, were bad. . . . The losses of motor vehicles and guns due to frost damage surpass all our fears [*übersteigen alle Befürchtungen*]." See also Bradley, *Generaloberst Heinz Guderian und die Entstehungsgeschichte des modernen Blitzkrieges*, 232.

9. Stahel, *Hitler's Panzer Generals*, 186.

10. Guderian, *Panzer Leader*, 261.

11. Stahel, *Hitler's Panzer Generals*, 186.

12. The winter of 1941/42, observed the late military historian Russel H. S. Stolfi, was the "coldest winter in the east in possibly a quarter of a millennium" (Stolfi, "Chance in History," 222).

13. Guderian wrote, "In the morning of 14 November, I visited the 167 Infantry Division and talked to a number of officers and men. The supply situation was bad. Snow shirts, boot grease, underclothes and above all woolen trousers were not available. A high proportion of the men were still wearing denim trousers, and the temperature was 8 below zero! At noon I visited the 112 Infantry Division, where I heard the same story. Our troops had got hold of Russian overcoats and fur caps and only the national emblem showed that they were Germans. All the stocks of clothing that the Panzer Army held were immediately sent to the front, but the shortages were so great that these provided a mere drop in the ocean" (Guderian, *Panzer Leader*, 248).

14. Dinglreiter, *Die Vierziger*, 75.

15. Ibid., 78.

16. As cited in Bergström and Mikhailov, *Black Cross Red Star*, 2:45–46.

17. Orenstein (trans.), *Soviet Documents on the Use of War Experience*, 3:15.

18. The Red Army had begun the war with 33,200 artillery pieces and had lost 24,440 of them in six months. Mawdsley, *Thunder in the East*, 194.

19. Army Group Center identified seventy-two new Soviet formations in December 1941: thirty rifle divisions, thirty-three rifle brigades, six tank brigades, and three cavalry divisions. BA-MA RH 20-4/337, *Kämpfe der 4. Armee im ersten Kriegsjahr gegen die Sowjet Union (22.6.41–22.6.42)*.

20. On 12 February, GFM von Kluge submitted his first situation report in weeks in which he had no impending disaster to report. Ziemke and Bauer, *Moscow to Stalingrad*, 171–72.

21. "Weisung für die Kampfführung im Osten nach Abschluss des Winters," in Schramm (ed.), *Kriegstagebuch des OKW*, Bd. I, 1093–96.

22. A. S. Knjaz'kov, "Die sowjetische Strategie im Jahre 1942," in Förster (ed.), *Stalingrad*, 39.

23. As argued by Markus Pöhlmann, Second Panzer Army now found itself in a particularly perilous situation—in badly exposed positions and thus in danger of being encircled. Pöhlmann, *Der Panzer und die Mechanisierung des Krieges*, 356.

24. As cited in Schäufler (ed.), *Knight's Cross Panzers*, 180–81.

25. Forczyk, *Tank Warfare on the Eastern Front*, 157.

26. Guderian, *Panzer Leader*, 259.

27. GFM von Bock, *The War Diary*, 385–86; see also BA-MA H 08-22/9, *Nachlass Generalfeldmarschall Fedor von Bock, Tagebuchnotizen Osten I*, 8.12.41.

28. GFM von Bock, *The War Diary*, 388.

29. As cited in Bradley, *Generaloberst Heinz Guderian und die Entstehungsgeschichte des modernen Blitzkrieges*, 233.

30. As cited in Stahel, *Retreat from Moscow*, 95.

31. GFM von Bock, *The War Diary*, 393.

32. Guderian, *Panzer Leader*, 262.

33. Stahel, *Retreat from Moscow*, 96. In his memoir, Guderian claimed that, by 14 December, the gap between 43 AK and 24 PzK had grown to about 40 kilometers in width. Pushed off toward Kaluga and away from Second Panzer Army, 43 AK was subordinated to Fourth Army on 19 December. Guderian, *Panzer Leader*, 262; see also BA-MA RH 20-4/337, *Kämpfe der 4. Armee im ersten Kriegsjahr gegen die Sowjet Union (22.6.41–22.6.42).*

34. "Erich Hoepner's Letters to His Wife Irma," BA-MA N 51-9 (12.12.41).

35. While the command reorganization had been proposed by Second Army's chief of staff to GFM von Bock on 12 December, Schmidt seems not to have liked the idea. Stahel, *Retreat from Moscow*, 95; BA-MA RH 21-2/244, *KTB Pz.AOK 2*, 12.12.41.

36. Guderian, *Panzer Leader*, 262.

37. Pöhlmann, *Der Panzer und die Mechanisierung des Krieges*, 356. The *Ist-Stärke* embraces operational tanks and those in short-term repair.

38. BA-MA RH 37/6332, *Tagebuch Oblt.* Beck-Broichsitter, 17.12.1941. *Oblt.* Beck was a recipient of the *Ritterkreuz*. His diary was used as a training aide by the *Bundeswehr*. He was a "soldiers' soldier," a man of courage and an exemplary leader of men. Indeed, it was only because of a handful of men like *Oblt.* Beck—low-ranking officers and NCOs—that Army Group Center avoided complete collapse in the winter of 1941/42.

39. Irving, *Hitler's War*, 357.

40. Guderian was not the only one now deeply concerned about whether Hitler was being adequately informed about the situation at the front. Apparently, GFM von Bock had, a few days before, prepared a detailed and gloomy situation report for Hitler that the latter never received. In his journal Bock wrote (16 December), "It is regrettable that it turns out that the Führer was not properly informed of the seriousness of the situation" (GFM von Bock, *The War Diary*, 395).

41. As cited in Stahel, *Hitler's Panzer Generals*, 186–87, and in Bradley, *Generaloberst Heinz Guderian und die Entstehungsgeschichte des modernen Blitzkrieges*, 234.

42. Stahel, *Hitler's Panzer Generals*, 187.

43. Irving, *Hitler's War*, 358.

44. "There is only one thing that ails our front," Hitler assured Brauchitsch and Halder. "The enemy just has more soldiers than us." Hence, the simplest reinforcements—riflemen, provisioned with eight to ten days of canned food, alcohol, and chocolates—were to be rushed by train to the front. Also, 1,000 trucks and 2,000 Waffen-SS from Kraków were to be dispatched to Army Group Center. Ibid., 358.

45. Guderian, *Panzer Leader*, 265.

46. Note: I have quoted at length from this discussion between Hitler and Guderian because it is instructive on many levels—for instance, Hitler's utter intransigence as he refuses to tolerate any withdrawal; Guderian's insights into the sorry state of his two armies and winter conditions in Russia. Of course, the entire account comes from Guderian, who clearly seeks to justify his position. So a certain caution is in order.

47. Guderian, *Panzer Leader*, 264–66; Guderian, *Erinnerungen eines Soldaten*, 240–42.

48. Guderian, *Panzer Leader*, 267–68; Guderian, *Erinnerungen eines Soldaten*, 243.

49. Hitler's halt order "was dictated to Bock over the telephone by Halder at 12:10 p.m." on 16 December 1941. "Hitler made it obvious that he was going to ignore Brauchitsch and deal directly with the army groups in the future" (Irving, *Hitler's War*, 357).

50. Hitler's halt order, however, was somewhat more nuanced than often depicted. Although it directed Kluge's Fourth Army not to take "a single step back," it did give room for 3 and 4 Panzer Groups—should the situation leave them no choice—to fall back gradually (*schrittweise*) to a "chord position" (*Sehnenstellung*) along the general line of the Rusa River–Volokolamsk–Staritsa. While the order made no direct mention of Guderian's Second Panzer Army, it stressed the need to close the gap west of Tula. It also called for Army Group Center to hold the general line Livny (northeast of Kursk)–Dubna–Aleksin (northwest of Tula). "Fernschreiben Chef OKW/WFSt/L," 15.12.41, in Schramm (ed.), *Kriegstagebuch des OKW*, Bd. I, 1083.

51. "Fernschreiben OKH (GenStdH OpAbt [III]) an H.Gr.Mitte," 18.12.41, in Schramm (ed.), *Kriegstagebuch des OKW*, Bd. I, 1084–85. While Army Group Center received no new divisions in December 1941, it did receive some infantry battalions flown in by troop transports. In January 1942, the army group got four new divisions; in February 1942, it got five. During the same period, the Red Army was massively reinforced. Hofmann, "Die Schlacht von Moskau 1941," 181.

52. Hart, *Guderian*, 79–80. In his postwar study of the German tank arm, former panzer general Walther K. Nehring wrote, "Through Hitler's intervention, a panic and disintegration of the Army was most likely avoided" (Nehring, *Die Geschichte der deutschen Panzerwaffe*, 238).

53. For example, some three dozen corps and divisional commanders were dismissed by Hitler during the winter of 1941/42. Keegan, *The Second World War*, 206.

54. On 20 February 1942, Goebbels wrote in his personal diary, "The Führer tells me that he has just put three weeks of the most barbaric work [*drei Wochen barbarischster Arbeit*] behind him. On most days, he has stood in the map room, from early morning to late at night, which has caused his feet to swell up" (Reuth [ed.], *Joseph Goebbels Tagebücher*, Bd. 4, 1735).

55. Stahel, *Retreat from Moscow*, 163–64.

56. Ibid., 166.

57. Guderian, *Panzer Leader*, 269.

58. Ibid., 269–70.

59. Stahel, *Retreat from Moscow*, 196. The dispute between Kluge and Guderian can be followed in the war diaries of Army Group Center and Second Panzer Army; for example, see BA-MA RH 21-2/244, *KTB Pz.AOK 2* (December 1941).

60. In his diary on 25 December Halder wrote, "Without saying a word to army group [*ohne der Heeresgruppe ein Wort zu sagen*] Guderian is moving back to the Oka-Susha line" (Halder, *Kriegstagebuch*, Bd. III, 366).

61. Stahel, *Retreat from Moscow*, 197.

62. Guderian, *Panzer Leader*, 270.

63. Guderian, *Panzer Leader*, 270–71; Guderian, *Erinnerungen eines Soldaten*, 246.

64. As cited in Jones, *The Retreat*, 234.

65. Stahel, *Retreat from Moscow*, 197–98.

EPILOGUE

1. Bauer, *Der Panzerkrieg*, Bd. I, 113. German tank production would increase modestly in the second half of 1941, resulting in an average of 271 units per month for all of 1941.

2. Magenheimer, *Hitler's War*, 67. Magenheimer writes, "Even if in certain sectors the Army was expanded and improved in quality, mainly by utilizing weapons captured so far, it is still true to say that the eastern army in June 1941 was only slightly stronger and larger than the western army had been in the spring of 1940. . . . This leads to the conclusion that the campaign against the Soviet Union did not occupy the central position—neither in overall planning, nor in armaments production—that it merited, given the requirements it demanded of the *Wehrmacht*. The campaign in the east was seen merely as an intermediate, albeit important, step designed to create the conditions for the 'final battle' in the west" (ibid., 67–68).

3. Other reasons for the anemic production figures include habitual shortages of manpower (tank production alone was short more than 6,000 skilled workers in January 1941), raw materials, and specialized machine tools, as well as the hopelessly Byzantine nature of the Nazi regime, with its systemic inefficiencies, lack of coherent planning, corruption, and stifling rivalries. Boog et al., *Germany and the Second World War*, Vol. IV, 210.

4. See Klaus Reinhardt, "Moscow 1941: The Turning Point," in Erickson and Dilks (eds.), *Barbarossa*, 209, 217–19.

5. Johnson, *Modern Times*, 377. As late as 1943, German factories produced 120,000 typewriters, 13,000 duplicating machines, 50,000 address machines, 3,000 accounting machines, 200,000 radios, 150,000 electric bedwarmers, and 3,600 refrigerators. If harmful militarily, this did give Germany a measure of political stability it had not enjoyed in World War I. DiNardo, *Germany's Panzer Arm in World War II*, 6.

6. Reinhardt, *Moscow*, 148, 158 (n. 73); "Beurteilung der Kampfkraft des Ostheeres (ohne die in Finnland eingesetzten Kräfte)," in Schramm (ed.), *Kriegstagebuch des OKW*, Bd. I, 1074–75.

7. Irving, *Hitler's War*, 205. Irving's book unleashed a storm of controversy in the late 1970s for its peculiar (and indefensible) revisionist history addressing Hitler's role in the Holocaust. Still, *Hitler's War*, if used with caution, remains a most useful source on Hitler's conduct of the war.

8. According to German historian Gerhard P. Gross, when Barbarossa began, the Army High Command was actually more optimistic than Hitler about bringing the war to an end in just a few short weeks: At OKH, Brauchitsch, Halder, and Paulus all anticipated a short, decisive campaign of eight to ten weeks, while Hitler, more cautious than his generals, envisaged a campaign lasting up to twenty-one weeks. Gross, *Mythos und Wirklichkeit*, 226; see also Meyer, *Adolf Heusinger*, 151, 850 (n. 23). The reader will recall, however, that at the final pre-Barbarossa conference in Berlin on 14 June 1941, Hitler had stated that the worst of the fighting would be over in about six weeks.

9. As noted by the late Andreas Hillgruber, a towering mid- and late-twentieth-century figure in the historiography of Hitler's Germany, "How little of concrete value the documents were overall, on which German military planning could be based, was shown in a particularly stark way in the 'Handbook' about the 'Wartime Armed Forces of the USSR,' which the FHO [Foreign Armies East] department published on 1 January 1941. Here, it was conceded that practically nothing was known about the Soviet order of battle. Yet it was still maintained that the Red Army '[is] not suited to a modern war nor in a condition to provide decisive resistance to a boldly led fighting force with modern arms'" (Hillgruber, "Das Russland-Bild der führenden deutschen Militärs vor Beginn des Angriffs auf die Sowjetunion," 264–65).

10. For an insightful study of the German generals' *Russland-Bild* on the eve of Barbarossa, see ibid., 256–72.

11. According to the Oxford English Dictionary, the earliest known use of the noun *va banque* was by renowned English historian A. J. P. Taylor in a course on German history in 1946: "Both dynasties desired the defeat of Napoleon; but the Hohenzollerns, having nothing more to lose, were ready to bid *va banque*—the Habsburgs were not." At https://languagehat.com/va-banque.

12. Hart, *Guderian*, 79.

13. Hürter, *A German General on the Eastern Front*, 121.

14. The "OODA loop" concept was invented by late US Air Force fighter pilot and strategist John Boyd. For more details, see Luther, *Barbarossa Unleashed*, 266, 329 (n. 20).

15. Email, R. Töppel to C. Luther, 19 August 2024.

16. Hart, *Guderian*, 75.

17. Foreword by Liddell Hart in Guderian, *Panzer Leader*, 15.

18. Stahel, *Hitler's Panzer Generals*, 221.

19. Mellenthin, *German Generals of World War II as I Saw Them*, 93. Mellenthin's remarks appear to be in reference to the French campaign of 1940, but they are certainly applicable to Guderian in general.

20. Roth also attained the rank of *Brigadegeneral* in Germany's postwar *Bundeswehr* and served as chief of the Military History Research Center (*Militärgeschichtliches Forschungsamt*) from 1985 to 1995. His assessment of Guderian is gleaned from his brief foreword to Georg Meyer's "Generaloberst Guderian zur Erinnerung an seinen 100. Geburtstag," in *Militärgeschichtliches Beiheft zur Europäischen Wehrkunde / Wehrwissenschaftliche Rundschau* 3 (June 1988).

21. From June through December 1941, the Soviet mobilization system turned out some 285 rifle divisions, 88 cavalry divisions, 12 re-formed tank divisions, 174 rifle brigades, and 93 tank brigades. "Whereas prewar German estimates had postulated an enemy of approximately 300 divisions, by December the Soviets had fielded twice that number. This allowed the Red Army to lose more than 4 million soldiers and 200 divisions in battle by 31 December, roughly equivalent to its entire peacetime army, yet still survive to continue the struggle." For more details, see Glantz, *Barbarossa*, 68.

22. Jacobsen (ed.), *Generaloberst Halder Kriegstagebuch*, Bd. III, vii. [Halder, *Kriegstagebuch*].

23. This was the second unconditional surrender document signed by the Germans. The first had been signed by General Alfred Jodl (Chief of the OKW Operations Branch) in Reims, France, early on the morning of 7 May; it stipulated that German forces cease active operations at 2301 hours Central European Time on 8 May. The next day (8 May), Keitel and other OKW representatives traveled to the Berlin district of Karlshorst, where the second act of surrender took place shortly before midnight, which was already 9 May Moscow time.

24. Bradley, *Generaloberst Heinz Guderian und die Entstehungsgeschichte des modernen Blitzkrieges*, 247. How peculiar that, with Germany prostrate and in ruins and all that Dönitz—a faithful follower of Hitler to the end—had striven for shattered beyond repair, his first thoughts were of his colleague, Heinz Guderian, the "creator" (so Dönitz) of the Third Reich's panzer weapon!

POSTSCRIPT

1. Guderian, *Panzer Leader*, 272.

2. Hart, *Guderian*, 82–83. "Guderian had already been receiving special, regular, tax-free monthly payments of 2000 *Reichsmarks*—effectively doubling his gross salary—since August 1940, after he was promoted to [*Generaloberst*] in the aftermath of the successful western campaign. Such 'honorific reimbursements' were specifically designed to bind senior military officers to Hitler and the Nazi state" (ibid., 83).

3. Guderian, *Panzer Leader*, 273–74; Guderian, *Erinnerungen eines Soldaten*, 248, 250.
4. Hart, *Guderian*, 82–83.
5. Blank et al., *Germany and the Second World War*, IX/1:652–53.
6. Hart, *Guderian*, 103.
7. It was, however, not only a sense of duty that compelled Guderian to return to service; likely more important was the fact that senior officers still on duty on 1 May 1945 (the day after Hitler's suicide below the Reich Chancellery in Berlin) received a double bonus! Noted Hart, "It is this double bonus that, perhaps, explains why Guderian bothered to return to a lost post that same day" (ibid., 113).
8. At https://lexikon-der-wehrmacht.de.

APPENDIX A. EQUIVALENT MILITARY RANKS

1. Megargee, *Inside Hitler's High Command*, 238; U.S. War Department, *Handbook on German Military Forces* (March 1945), 5–7; Buchner, *The German Infantry Handbook*, 6. At https://feldgrau.com.

APPENDIX B. 2 PANZER GROUP ORDER OF BATTLE (22.6.1941)

1. Guderian, *Panzer Leader*, 145–46; GHQ units gleaned from "Kriegsgliederung Barbarossa," Stand 18.6.41, in Mehner (ed.), *Die Geheimen Tagesberichte der deutschen Wehrmachtführung im Zweiten Weltkrieg*, Bd. 3.
2. General HQ *Luftwaffe* units assigned to 2 Panzer Group included ten reconnaissance squadrons, eight of which were distributed among the three panzer corps, one to 12 Army Corps, and a long-range (strategic) squadron (3.[F]31) controlled by Guderian's headquarters (*z.V.Pz.Gr.*).
3. The flamethrower tank battalion included twenty-five Pz IIs, forty-two *Flammenwerfer* tanks, and five Pz IIIs; it was assigned to 18 Panzer Division. Jentz (ed.), *Panzer Truppen*, 193.

APPENDIX C. ORDER OF BATTLE OF A (NOTIONAL) GERMAN PANZER DIVISION (JUNE 1941)

1. Note: This order of battle—simplified from Keilig, *Das Deutsche Heer*—portrays a "typical" German panzer division with a tank regiment of two battalions equipped with German tanks only. There were, of course, many variations to this "normal" order of battle (*Normalgliederung*).
2. Nine panzer divisions (3, 6, 7, 8, 12, 17, 18, 19, and 20) had three tank battalions. Keilig, *Das Deutsche Heer*, Bd. II, Abschnitt 103, S. 18.
3. These were armored cars with a 20mm main armament.
4. The actual German term, *Panzerjäger*, literally means "tank hunter."
5. This flak company was not in the order of battle of 3, 15, 19, and 20 Panzer Divisions.
6. No number is given for tanks; however, this company in the Armored Engineer Battalion of 4 PD had a dozen Pz Is and Pz IIs. Michulec, *4. Panzer-Division on the Eastern Front*, 4.
7. SPW = *Schützenpanzerwagen*, or armored personnel carrier. These vehicles (in German nomenclature Sd.Kfz. 250 or 251) offered significantly more protection than the typical troop transports then in service and were highly valued by the *Landser* lucky enough to ride in them. However, in June 1941, most panzer and motorized divisions possessed but a small number

of these SPWs. Not uncommon was the situation of 10 Panzer Division, whose entire rifle brigade had just a single company mounted in SPWs. Schick, *Die Geschichte der 10. Panzer-Division*, 263.

8. Keilig, *Das Deutsche Heer*, Bd. II, Abschnitt 103, S. 18–20.

APPENDIX D. 292 INFANTRY DIVISION

1. Figures for "combat strength" exclude rear-area services, medical personnel, and personnel belonging to the divisional baggage trains.

2. Civilian officials of the armed forces (*Wehrmachtbeamte*) had nominal rank and wore uniforms; they were classified as combatants.

3. NCOs include *Unteroffiziere* and sergeants.

4. Figures for "ration strength" include all *Wehrmacht* personnel (combat, supply, administrative, etc.) and horses provisioned by the division; figures also embrace men/units assigned to, but not organic to, the division.

5. For definitions, please see the list of abbreviations. These data are gleaned directly from the division's war diary. According to Nafziger (*The German Order of Battle: Infantry in World War II*, 279), the division also boasted 2,300 pistols, 800 machine pistols, and 13,541 98K rifles.

APPENDIX E. 2 PANZER GROUP ORDER OF BATTLE (30.9.1941)

1. Boog et al., *Germany and the Second World War*, Vol. IV, 669; Guderian, *Panzer Leader*, 226. In the weeks prior to the start of Typhoon, tank maintenance personnel worked tirelessly to repair damaged vehicles and return them to service, while 2 Panzer Group also received an allotment of eighty-five new tanks (according to Guderian's former chief of staff, *Oberst* von Liebenstein). Yet despite such measures, on 30 September 1941 the panzer group fielded at best 40 percent of its authorized tank strength (some 400 tanks in all). BA-MA RH 21-2/910, *Die Operationen der 2. Pz.Armee in der Doppelschlacht von Bryansk und Wyazma und beim Vorstoss auf Moskau 30.9. bis 5.12.1941*, 6, (Tabelle, 107–8), 115.

2. Commander of I Flak Corps was *Generalmajor* Walther von Axthelm.

APPENDIX F. *PANZERMÄNNER* IN OPERATION BARBAROSSA

1. Excerpt from Luther, *Barbarossa Unleashed*, 350–66. (Note: Portions of this excerpt have been reworked and some new material added. While this excerpt [inevitably] has several passages duplicative of the primary narrative, efforts were made to reduce such duplication.)

2. Hartmann, *Wehrmacht im Ostkrieg*, 257.

3. According to Eddy Bauer's detailed study of German tank operations, the "typical" panzer division of 1941 actually possessed some 3,500 motor vehicles and, single file on a road, would have stretched for about 130 kilometers. Bauer, *Der Panzerkrieg*, Bd. I, 113.

4. Plievier, *Moscow*, 44–46.

5. As noted by David Glantz, "Attacking just east of Raseinai with [2 Tank Division of Soviet 3 Mechanized Corps], two battalions of T-34 and KV tanks crushed the 6 Panzer Division's reconnaissance elements and drove the division to the outskirts of the town. After the Soviets failed to exploit their success, German sappers systematically destroyed the Soviet tanks with explosive charges. Later they learned that the Soviet tanks ran out of fuel and had orders to 'ram' the German tanks, since the T-34s and KVs had not been bore-sighted and thus could

not fire a round. Within 24 hours after the engagement, German forces bypassed, encircled and destroyed the immobile Soviet tank division" (Glantz, *Barbarossa*, 216–17 [n. 24]).

6. Helmut Ritgen, "6th Panzer Division Operations," in Glantz (ed.), *The Initial Period of War on the Eastern Front*, 114. Addressing the incipient "tank panic" affecting some of the men, Ritgen recalled, "One of our reserve officers—today a well-known German author—lost his nerve. Without stopping at the headquarters of his regiment, the division, or the corps he simply rushed to the command post of General Hoepner [C-in-C 4 PzG] to report that 'everything was already lost!'" (ibid., 114).

7. Opined Evan Mawdsley, "A major problem for the Red Army in the early war years had been the lack of effective anti-tank (AT) guns" (Mawdsley, *Thunder in the East*, 194).

8. For a short, yet detailed primer illustrating the tenacity of the Red Army in combat from literally the first hours of the war, see Robert A. Forczyk's account of the initial operations of 4 Panzer Group in *Tank Warfare on the Eastern Front*, 38–44.

9. Guderian, *Panzer Leader*, 174.

10. Kershaw, *War Without Garlands*, 72–74.

11. Garden and Andrew (eds.), *The War Diaries of a Panzer Soldier*, 33–34. (Note: To make Hager's account more readable, I have slightly recast this translation of the original German *Sütterlin* script.)

12. Ibid., 35.

13. BA-MA MSg 1/3268, *Tagebuch* Fritz Fahrnbacher, 22.6.41, as cited in Hartmann, *Wehrmacht im Ostkrieg*, 251.

14. The reference here is to one of the panzer routes used by Hoth's 3 Panzer Group; it is not to be confused with the Panzer Route 1 used by Guderian's group.

15. Hinze, *19. Infanterie- und Panzer-Division*, 133–34. To combat fatigue, the *Wehrmacht* made use of a stimulant called Pervitin. The drug, developed by a Berlin-based pharmaceutical company, had first been introduced in 1938 and quickly became popular among the German civilian population. In the military, the drug was first tested on Army drivers during the invasion of Poland; between April and July 1940, more than 35 million tablets of Pervitin and Isophan (a slightly modified derivative) were shipped to the German Army and *Luftwaffe*. The drug was widely used during the French campaign of 1940, and although Pervitin was classified as a restricted substance on 1 July 1941, 10 million tablets were shipped to the troops in 1941. It is unclear, however, just how widespread use of the stimulant may have been during the Russian campaign. Ulrich, "Hitler's Drugged Soldiers."

16. Hinze, *19. Infanterie- und Panzer-Division*, 133–34.

17. Steiger, *Armour Tactics in the Second World War*, 28.

18. Newton, *Hitler's Commander*, 133.

19. As cited in Woche, *Zwischen Pflicht und Gewissen*, 104.

20. Ibid., 107.

21. Ibid., 107–8.

22. It should be noted that the Soviets, whose anti-tank weapons were of limited efficacy, experienced their own "tank panic" (*tankoboiazn'*) at the beginning of the war; in fact, it was a "major problem in the Red Army." Mawdsley, *Thunder in the East*, 27.

23. As cited in Paul, *Geschichte der 18. Panzer-Division*, 31.

24. As cited in Andres, *Panzersoldaten im Russlandfeldzug*, 24–25.

25. Ibid., 25.

26. Ibid., 22.

27. Guderian, *Panzer Leader*, 233; Guderian, *Erinnerungen eines Soldaten*, 212. For a detailed account of the German debacle at Mtsensk in early October 1941, see chapter 8.

28. Foedrowitz, *Stalin Organs*, 11.

29. The German Army General Staff's *Lage Ost* map for 15 July 1941 indicates that the only German unit in the vicinity of Rudnia at this time was 12 PD. K.–J. Thies, "Lage am 15.7.1941 abds., Heeresgruppe Mitte," in *Der Zweite Weltkrieg im Kartenbild*, Bd. 5, Teil 1.1.

30. As cited in Werth, *Russia at War*, 172.

31. Letter, R. Adler to C. Luther, 24 November 2004.

32. BA-MA N 10/9: *Lebenserinnerungen Smilo Frhr. von Lüttwitz*, Bl. 128, as cited in Hartmann, *Wehrmacht im Ostkrieg*, 255.

33. Paret, "Clausewitz," in Paret (ed.), *Makers of Modern Strategy*, 202.

34. Kershaw, *War Without Garlands*, 238.

35. Andres, *Panzersoldaten im Russlandfeldzug*, n.p.

36. According to the late U.S. Army Colonel David Hackworth, 15 to 20 percent of American fatal casualties during the Vietnam War resulted from "friendly fire." Shay, *Achilles in Vietnam*, 125. The percentage of soldiers on both sides killed by their own forces during World War II was undoubtedly higher, in part because communications between friendly forces were much more primitive.

37. Going into battle in their original gray cotton hats (instead of helmets), and only days before being equipped with the standard German infantry rifle (*Gewehr* 98), which they had not been trained to use, the soldiers of the List Regiment were mistaken by other German units for British soldiers and fired upon with devastating results. For a detailed account of this action, see Weber, *Hitler's First War*, 40–47.

38. Fussell, *Wartime*, 26.

39. *Tagebuch* Kreuter, 23.6.41. It is unclear whether Kreuter was referring to the losses of the division as a whole or simply to those of his regiment. (Note: A typed transcript of Kreuter's diary is among the "Craig W. H. Luther Papers" at the Hoover Institute, Stanford University, Palo Alto, California.)

40. Guderian, *Panzer Leader*, 186. Observed Guderian, "Insufficient training and a lack of combat experience on the part of the young aviators were the cause of this unfortunate occurrence; and this despite clear recognition signals on the part of the troops on the ground and very plain orders to the fliers concerning the roads that we would be using." In this case, the German unit affected by the bombing was 23 Infantry Division.

41. Kenneth Macksey, "The Smolensk Operation, 7 July–7 August 1941," in Glantz (ed.), *The Initial Period of War on the Eastern Front*, 346.

42. H. Zobel, "3rd Panzer Division Battles in the Smolensk Area," in Glantz (ed.), *The Initial Period of War on the Eastern Front*, 435–36.

43. Neumann, *Die 4. Panzer-Division*, 491.

44. Richardson (ed.), *Your Loyal and Loving Son*, 115.

45. Schick, *Die Geschichte der 10. Panzer-Division*, 325.

46. Stahel, *Operation Barbarossa and Germany's Defeat in the East*, 268; Paul, *Panzer-General Walther K. Nehring*, 121; Bartov, *Hitler's Army*, 20; Nehring, "Die 18. Panzerdivision 1941 im Rahmen der Panzergruppe Guderian," 198; Kershaw, *War Without Garlands*, 169.

47. 20. Pz.Div. Abt. Ia, *Zustandsmeldung an 57. Pz. Korps*, 27.7.41, as cited in Steiger, *Armour Tactics in the Second World War*, 30.

48. BA-MA N 910/5, *Tagebuch* Lemelsen, 25.7.41.

49. Ibid., 16.7.41.

50. BA-MA N 813, *Tagebuch* Münchhausen, August 1941.

51. Nehring, "Die 18. Panzerdivision 1941 im Rahmen der Panzergruppe Guderian," in *Deutscher Soldatenkalender 1961*, 198.

52. BA-MA RH 27-18/17, 11.7.41, as cited in Kershaw, *War Without Garlands*, 170.

53. H. Gr. Mitte, Abt. Ia, KTB Nr. 1, 22.8.41, as cited in Steiger, *Armour Tactics in the Second World War*, 126.

54. Richardson (ed.), *Your Loyal and Loving Son*, 117.

APPENDIX G. GERMAN ARMY ORGANIZATION AND WEAPONRY (JUNE 1941)

1. For example, General Nehring's 18 Panzer Division of Guderian's 2 Panzer Group was outfitted with no less than 96 different types of personnel carriers, 111 types of trucks, and 37 types of motorcycles. All told, the eastern armies began the campaign with some 2,000 different types of vehicle in their inventories. Steiger, *Armour Tactics in the Second World War*, 127; Stahel, *Operation Barbarossa and Germany's Defeat in the East*, 131.

2. Boog et al., *Germany and the Second World War*, Vol. IV, 221. Of the twenty infantry divisions in the Fourth and Ninth Armies of Army Group Center, fully eleven had a complement of French anti-tank weapons; of these divisions, four were also partially equipped with French vehicles, while one division had French vehicles (but no French anti-tank weapons). Only five of the twenty divisions—all of the first wave—were equipped exclusively with German weapons, vehicles, and equipment. Ibid., 222–23.

3. Stahel, *Operation Barbarossa and Germany's Defeat in the East*, 131.

4. Repair_Man_Jack, "The Wages of Short-Sighted War Are Rape," *RedState*, 24 March 2011, https://redstate.com/repair_man_jack/2011/03/24/the-wages-of-short-sighted-war-is-rape-n38402.

5. Hart, Hart, and Hughes, *The German Soldier in World War II*, 21.

6. This compares to fifty-seven Army and Waffen-SS panzer and panzer grenadier divisions established during the war. Nafziger, *The German Order of Battle*, 23.

7. A German infantryman was allotted sixty rounds of ammunition as a basic issue. Freitag, *Aufzeichnungen aus Krieg und Gefangenschaft*, 55 (n. 4).

8. U.S. War Department, *Handbook on German Military Forces* (March 1945), 310–15.

9. Scheibert, *Die 6. Panzer-Division*, 76.

10. U.S. War Department, *Handbook on German Military Forces* (March 1945), 326–27.

11. Scheibert, *Die 6. Panzer-Division*, 76.

12. The word can be translated as "recklessness" or "foolhardiness," but a *Draufgänger* was a daredevil mostly admired by other *Landser* for his willingness to risk all for his men.

13. Despite the inability of the Pak 35/36 to handle the heavier and better-armored Russian tanks, the weapon did earn an excellent reputation as an infantry close-support weapon. See, for example, Moeller, *Gratwanderung am Rande des Geschehens*, 241–56. Early in the eastern campaign, a German *Panzerjäger* crew (Pz.Jg.Abt. 31/31 ID), using a 37mm Pak, performed a fire trial on an abandoned (fully intact) Soviet T-28 tank; the trial was successful, their gun easily knocking out the older Soviet tank (the T-28 entered service in early 1930s) at 800 meters. While the medium T-28 had some laudable features (e.g., decent speed and agility), its armor plating was insufficient, and the 37mm gun was able to easily penetrate it, proving that the Pak 35/36 could be effective against older and outmoded Red Army tanks. Bunke, *Der Osten blieb unser Schicksal*, 233–34.

14. Beinhauer, *Artillerie im Osten*, 8.

15. Ibid., 8.

16. The German Army's "long-desired range of 10 kilometers had finally been exceeded!" Engelmann, *German Light Field Artillery*, 13.

17. Hogg, *Twentieth-Century Artillery*, 41, 53. According to Hogg, the s.FH 18 "had the distinction of being the first gun ever to be issued with a rocket-assisted shell, in 1941, which gave it a maximum range of 19,000 meters. However, it was not very accurate and wore out the gun rather rapidly" (ibid., 53). For more technical information on German light and medium field howitzers, see Buchner, *The German Infantry Handbook*, 88–90; also, U.S. War Department, *Handbook on German Military Forces* (March 1945), 332–33.

18. Seaton, *The German Army*, 173; U.S. War Department, *Handbook on German Military Forces* (March 1945), 395–99; Schick, *Die Geschichte der 10. Panzer-Division*, 264.

19. When the campaign against France and the Low Countries began on 10 May 1940, just six assault guns were available to the German Army. Boog et al., *Germany and the Second World War*, Vol. IV, 219.

20. Bauer, *Der Panzerkrieg*, Bd. I, 113; U.S. War Department, *Handbook on German Military Forces* (March 1945), 365. During the second half of 1941, German factories produced an additional 285 StuG IIIs.

21. Lt. J. Hahn, *Feldzug gegen Russland* (collection of unpublished field post letters). In one action on the central front in December 1941, two StuG IIIs assigned to 260 ID would destroy twelve T-34s and two KV-1s that had broken through the division's main battle line. Such successes were hardly uncommon on the eastern front. Kameradenhilfswerk und Traditionsverband der 260. ID (ed.), *Die 260. Infanterie-Division*, 90.

22. All figures gleaned from Boog et al., *Germany and the Second World War*, Vol. IV, 219.

23. Hereafter, the shortened designation of "Pz" will be used for each tank model. For example, "Pz I" in place of "Pz Kpfw I."

24. Jacobsen (ed.), *Generaloberst Halder Kriegstagebuch*, Bd. III, 42. [Halder, *Kriegstagebuch*]

25. Hogg, *Armoured Fighting Vehicles*, 82–83; U.S. War Department, *Handbook on German Military Forces* (March 1945), 384. After production of the Pz II had been discontinued, its modified hull would still be in use late into the war as a self-propelled gun carriage, most notably for the 150mm s.IG 33 and the 105mm le.FH 18.

26. Jentz (ed.), *Panzer Truppen*, 190. As of 13 December 1941, 6 Panzer Division had lost every one of its tanks and had only 350 combat infantry (*Schützen*) remaining. Reinhardt, *Die Wende vor Moskau*, 206.

27. According to Thomas L. Jentz, more than 500 Pz 38(t)s were assigned to *Generaloberst* Hoth's 3 Panzer Group. See Jentz (ed.), *Panzer Truppen*, 190–93.

28. Nehring, *Die Geschichte der deutschen Panzerwaffe*, 118.

29. Hogg, *Armoured Fighting Vehicles*, 84–86; Stahel, *Operation Barbarossa and Germany's Defeat in the East*, 111.

30. Guderian, *Panzer Leader*, 138; Guderian, *Erinnerungen eines Soldaten*, 124.

31. Hogg, *Armoured Fighting Vehicles*, 87.

32. Halder, *The Halder War Diary*, 210.

33. Keilig, *Das Deutsche Heer*, Bd. II, Abschnitt 103, S. 1; Battistelli, *Panzer Divisions*, 10.

34. Müller-Hillebrand, *Das Heer 1933–1945*, Bd. II, 107.

35. For a detailed breakdown of the reorganization and expansion of the panzer divisions, see Keilig, *Das Deutsche Heer*, Bd. II, Abschnitt 103, S. 1–20. For the complete order of battle of 10 Panzer Division (46 PzK/ 2 PzG) on 22 June 1941, see Schick, *Die Geschichte der 10. Panzer-Division*, 254–66.

36. Keilig, *Das Deutsche Heer*, Bd. II, Abschnitt 103, S. 11–12.

37. One of the best equipped was the elite 4 PD. Its inventory of weapons and vehicles in June 1941 included the following: 177 tanks in its 35 Panzer Regiment (105 Pz IIIs, 20 Pz

IVs), 35 armored cars, 43 armored personnel carriers, 185 prime movers, 1,992 trucks, 1,001 cars, and 1,586 motorcycles. In addition to the tanks in the panzer regiment, the division's artillery regiment possessed several Pz II observation tanks (*Beobachtungswagen*), while the combat engineer battalion was outfitted with a dozen Pz I and Pz II tanks. The 4 PD's anti-tank battalion was equipped mainly with 37mm AT guns; however, just prior to the start of *Barbarossa*, it received three batteries of 50mm AT guns (all towed by half-track prime movers). Michulec, *4. Panzer-Division on the Eastern Front*, 4.

38. Bauer, *Der Panzerkrieg*, Bd. I, 113.

39. This figure excludes the four so-called light divisions, which at the time were also classified as motorized divisions; they were soon reorganized as panzer divisions.

40. Seaton, *The German Army*, 264.

41. Seaton, *The German Army*, 264; Keilig, *Das Deutsche Heer*, Bd. II, Abschnitt 100, S. 6–7.

42. Winchester, *Hitler's War on Russia*, 21–22.

43. As cited in Kershaw, *War Without Garlands*, 88.

Select Bibliography

This bibliography lists most of the primary and secondary sources consulted in the preparation of this book; archival materials (for the most part) are not included.

Alexander, Christine, and Mark Kunze, eds. *Eastern Inferno: The Journals of a German Panzerjäger on the Eastern Front, 1941–43* (Philadelphia, 2010).

Aliev, Rostislav. *The Siege of Brest, 1941: The Red Army's Stand against the Germans during Operation Barbarossa* (Mechanicsburg, 2015).

Allmendinger, Karl, et al. *Terrain Factors in the Russian Campaign* (U.S. Army Foreign Military Study T-34, 1950).

Andres, Kurt Werner. *Panzersoldaten im Russlandfeldzug 1941 bis 1945. Tagebuchaufzeichnungen und Erlebnisberichte* (unpublished manuscript).

Axell, Albert. *Russia's Heroes, 1941–45* (New York, 2001).

Barnett, Correlli, ed. *Hitler's Generals* (New York, 1989).

Bartov, Omer. *The Eastern Front, 1941–45: German Troops and the Barbarisation of Warfare* (New York, 1985).

———. *Hitler's Army: Soldiers, Nazis, and War in the Third Reich* (New York, 1991).

Battistelli, Pier Paolo. *Panzer Divisions: The Eastern Front, 1941–43* (Oxford, 2008).

Bauer, Eddy. *Der Panzerkrieg. Die wichtigsten Panzeroperationen des zweiten Weltkrieges in Europa und Afrika*. Bd. I: *Vorstoss und Rückzug der deutschen Panzerverbände* (Bonn, 1965).

Beinhauer, Eugen. *Artillerie im Osten* (Berlin, 1944).

Bellamy, Chris. *Absolute War: Soviet Russia in the Second World War* (New York, 2007).

Below, Nicolaus von. *At Hitler's Side. The Memoirs of Hitler's Luftwaffe Adjutant, 1937–1945* (London, 2001).

Bergström, Christer. *Barbarossa—the Air Battle: July–December 1941* (Hersham, 2007).

Bergström, Christer, and Andrey Mikhailov. *Black Cross Red Star: The Air War over the Eastern Front*. Vol. 1: *Operation Barbarossa, 1941* (Pacifica, 2000).

———. *Black Cross Red Star: The Air War over the Eastern Front*. Vol. 2: *Resurgence, January–June 1942* (Pacifica, 2001).

Blank, Ralf, et al. *Germany and the Second World War*. Vol. IX/1: *German Wartime Society, 1939–1945: Politicization, Disintegration, and the Struggle for Survival* (Oxford, 2008).

Boatner, Mark M. *Biographical Dictionary of World War II* (Novato, 1996).

Bock, Fedor von. *Generalfeldmarschall Fedor von Bock. The War Diary 1939–1945*. Klaus Gerbet (ed.) (Atglen, 1996).

Bollmann, Albert, and Hermann Flörke. *Das Infanterie-Regiment 12 (3. Folge von 1933–1945). Sein Kriegsschicksal im Verbande der 31. (Löwen)–Division* (Göttingen, 1975).

Boog, Horst, et al. *Das Deutsche Reich und der Zweite Weltkrieg*. Bd. 4: *Der Angriff auf die Sowjetunion* (Stuttgart, 1983).

———. *Germany and the Second World War*. Vol. IV: *The Attack on the Soviet Union* (Oxford, 1998).

Bradley, Dermot. *Generaloberst Heinz Guderian und die Entstehungsgeschichte des modernen Blitzkrieges* (Osnabrück, 1986).

Braithwaite, Rodric. *Moscow, 1941: A City and Its People at War* (London, 2006).

Buchbender, Ortwin, and Reinhold Sterz, eds. *Das andere Gesicht des Krieges. Deutsche Feldpostbriefe 1939–1945* (Munich, 1982).

Buchner, Alex. *The German Infantry Handbook, 1939–1945: Organization, Uniforms, Weapons, Equipment, Operations* (Atglen, 1991).

Bunke, Erich. *Der Osten blieb unser Schicksal 1939–1944. Panzerjäger im 2. Weltkrieg* (self-published, 1991; courtesy of author).

Carell, Paul. *Hitler Moves East, 1941–1943* (Boston, 1964).

———. *Unternehmen Barbarossa. Der Marsch nach Russland* (Berlin, 1963).

Clark, Alan. *Barbarossa: The Russian-German Conflict, 1941–45* (New York, 1985).

Corum, James S. *Wolfram von Richthofen: Master of the German Air War* (Lawrence, 2008).

Creveld, Martin van. *The Changing Face of War: Lessons of Combat from the Marne to Iraq* (New York, 2006).

———. *Supplying War: Logistics from Wallenstein to Patton* (Cambridge, 1977).

Cuno, Genlt. Curt. *German Preparations for the Attack against Russia (The German Build-up East of Warsaw)* (U.S. Army Foreign Military Study D-247, 1947).

Dear, I. C. B., ed. *The Oxford Guide to World War II* (Oxford, 1995).

Diedrich, Torsten. *Paulus. Das Trauma von Stalingrad. Eine Biographie* (Paderhorn, 2008).

DiNardo, R. L. *Germany's Panzer Arm in WWII* (Mechanicsburg, 1997).

Dinglreiter, Obstlt. a.D. Joseph. *Die Vierziger. Chronik des Regiments. Kameradschaft Regiment 40* (Augsburg, 1959).

Dollinger, Hans, ed. *Kain, wo ist dein Bruder? Was der Mensch im Zweiten Weltkrieg erleiden musste—dokumentiert in Tagebüchern und Briefen* (Munich, 1983).

Domarus, Max. *Hitler. Reden und Proklamationen 1932–1945*. Bd. 2: *Untergang (1939–1945)* (Würzburg, 1963).

Donat, Gerhard. *Der Munitionsverbrauch im Zweiten Weltkrieg im operativen und taktischen Rahmen* (Osnabrück, 1992).

Duesel, Hans H., ed. *Gefallen! . . . und umsonst—Erlebnisberichte deutscher Soldaten im Russlandkrieg 1941–1945* (self-published, Bad Aibling, 1993).

Dupuy, R. Ernest, and Trevor N. Dupuy. *The Encyclopedia of Military History—from 3500 B.C. to the Present* (New York, 1986).

Ellis, Frank. *Barbarossa, 1941: Reframing Hitler's Invasion of Stalin's Soviet Empire* (Lawrence, 2015).

Engelmann, Joachim. *German Light Field Artillery, 1935–1945* (Atglen, 1995).

Erickson, John. *The Road to Stalingrad: Stalin's War with Germany* (New Haven, 1975).

Erickson, John, and David Dilks, eds., *Barbarossa: The Axis and the Allies* (Edinburgh, 1994).

Foedrowitz, Michael. *Stalin Organs: Russian Rocket Launchers* (Atglen, 1994).

Forczyk, Robert A. *Tank Warfare on the Eastern Front, 1941–42* (New York, 2013).

Förster, Jürgen., ed. *Stalingrad. Ereignis—Wirkung—Symbol* (Munich, 1992).

———. *Die Wehrmacht im NS-Staat. Eine strukturgeschichtliche Analyse* (Munich, 2007).

Freitag, August. *Aufzeichnungen aus Krieg und Gefangenschaft (1941–1949)*. Eingeleitet und annotiert von Karl Sattler (Bochum, 1997).

Frisch, Franz A. P., and Wilbur D. Jones Jr. *Condemned to Live: A Panzer Artilleryman's Five-Front War* (Shippensburg, 2000).

Frontschau Nr. 2, "Russischer Stellungsbau," in *Die Frontschau* (distributed by International Historic Films).

Frontschau Nr. 3, "Vormarsch," in *Die Frontschau* (distributed by International Historic Films).

Fugate, Bryan, and Lev Dvoretsky. *Thunder on the Dnepr: Zhukov-Stalin and the Defeat of Hitler's Blitzkrieg* (Novato, 1997).

Funke, Manfred, ed. *Hitler, Deutschland und die Mächte. Materialien zur Aussenpolitik des Dritten Reiches* (Düsseldorf, 1978).

Garden, David, and Kenneth Andrew, eds. *The War Diaries of a Panzer Soldier: Erich Hager with the 17th Panzer Division on the Russian Front, 1941–1945* (Atglen, 2010).

German Infantry Weapons. Special Series, No. 14 MIS 461, Military Intelligence Service, U.S. War Dept., May 25, 1943.

Geschichte der 3. Panzer-Division Berlin-Brandenburg 1935–1945, edited by Traditionsverband der Division (Berlin, 1967).

Geyer, Hermann. *Das IX. Armeekorps im Ostfeldzug 1941* (Neckargemünd, 1969).

Glantz, David M. *Atlas and Operational Summary: The Border Battles, 22 June–1 July 1941* (self-published, 2003).

———. *Atlas of the Battle of Smolensk, 7 July–10 September 1941* (self-published, 2001).

———. *Barbarossa Derailed: The Battle for Smolensk, 10 July–10 September 1941*. Vol. 1: *The German Advance to Smolensk, the Encirclement Battle, and the First and Second Soviet Counteroffensives, 10 July–24 August 1941* (Solihull, 2010).

———. *Barbarossa Derailed: The Battle for Smolensk, 10 July–10 September 1941*. Vol. 2: *The German Advance on the Flanks and the Third Soviet Counteroffensive, 25 August–10 September 1941* (Solihull, 2012).

———. *Barbarossa: Hitler's Invasion of Russia, 1941* (Charleston, 2001).

———. *Forgotten Battles of the Soviet-German War (1941–1945)*. Vol. 1: *The Summer-Fall Campaign (22 June–4 December 1941)* (self-published, 1999).

———, ed. *The Initial Period of War on the Eastern Front, 22 June–August 1941* (London, 1993).

———. *Red Army Ground Forces in June 1941* (self-published, 1997).

———. *Zhukov's Greatest Defeat: The Red Army's Epic Disaster in Operation Mars, 1942* (Lawrence, KS, 1999).

Goette, Franz, and Herbert Peiler. *Die 29. Falke-Division 1936–1945* (Dörfler Zeitgeschichte, n.d.).

Görlitz, Walter. *Strategie der Defensive. Model* (Munich, 1982).

Grassmann, Genmaj. Gerhard. *An Artillery Regiment on the Road to Moscow (22 June to December 1941)* (U.S. Army Foreign Military Study D-221, 1947).

Greiffenberg, Gen. Hans von, et al. *Battle of Moscow (1941–1942)* (U.S. Army Foreign Military Study T-28, n.d.).

Gross, Gerhard P. *Mythos und Wirklichkeit. Geschichte des operativen Denkens im deutschen Heer von Moltke d.Ä bis Heusinger* (Paderborn, 2012).

Gschöpf, Rudolf. *Mein Weg mit der 45. Inf.-Div.* (Nürnberg, 2002; first published, 1955).

Guderian, Heinz. *Achtung-Panzer! The Development of Armoured Forces, Their Tactics and Operational Potential*. Translated by C. Duffy (London, 1992).

———. *Erinnerungen eines Soldaten* (Heidelberg, 1951).

———. *Panzer Leader* (New York, 1952).

Günther, Helmut. *Heisse Motoren, kalte Füsse. Kradschützen der Waffen-SS vor Moskau* (Coburg, 2003).

———. *Hot Motors, Cold Feet: A Memoir of Service with the Motorcycle Battalion of SS-Division "Reich," 1940–1941* (Winnipeg, 2004).

Gutenkunst, Alfred. *Geschichte der 3. Kompanie des Infanterie-Regiments 109 im Krieg 1939–1945* (self-published, 1985, 1991).

Haape, Heinrich. *Moscow Tram Stop: A Doctor's Experiences with the German Spearhead in Russia*, edited by C. Luther (Guilford, 2020).

Halder, Franz. *The Halder War Diary, 1939–1942.* Edited by Charles B. Burdick and Hans-Adolf Jacobsen (Novato, 1988).

———. *Kriegstagebuch: Tägliche Aufzeichnungen des Chefs des Generalstabes des Heeres 1939–1942.* Bd. 2: *Von der geplanten Landung in England bis zum Beginn des Ostfeldzuges (1.7.1940–21.6.1941).* Edited by Hans-Adolf Jacobsen and Alfred Philippi (Stuttgart, 1963).

———. *Kriegstagebuch: Tägliche Aufzeichnungen des Chefs des Generalstabes des Heeres 1939–1942.* Bd. 3: *Der Russlandfeldzug bis zum Marsch auf Stalingrad (22.6.1941–24.9.1942).* Edited by Hans-Adolf Jacobsen and Alfred Philippi (Stuttgart, 1964).

Handbook on German Military Forces (Baton Rouge, 1990; originally published by U.S. War Department as TM-E 30-451, March 1945).

Hart, Russell A. *Guderian: Panzer Pioneer or Myth Maker?* (Washington, DC, 2006).

Hart, S., R. Hart, and M. Hughes. *The German Soldier in World War II* (Osceola, 2000).

Hartmann, Christian. *Wehrmacht im Ostkrieg: Front und militärisches Hinterland 1941/42* (Munich, 2009).

Haupt, Werner. *Army Group Center: The Wehrmacht in Russia, 1941–1945* (Atglen, 1997).

———. *Army Group South: The Wehrmacht in Russia, 1941–1945* (Atglen, 1998).

———. *Kiev. Die grösste Kesselschlacht der Geschichte* (Dorheim, 1980).

———. *Sturm auf Moskau 1941. Der Angriff—Die Schlacht—Der Rückschlag* (Friedberg, 1990).

Heer, Hannes, and Klaus Naumann. *War of Extermination: The German Military in World War II, 1941–1944* (New York, 2000).

Heusinger, Genlt. Adolf. *Eastern Campaign, 1941–42 (Strategic Survey).* (U.S. Army Foreign Military Study T-6, 1947).

Higgins, David R. *Guderian, 1941: The Barbarossa Campaign* (Philadelphia, 2023).

Hillgruber, Andreas. "Die Bedeutung der Schlacht von Smolensk in der Zweiten Julihälfte 1941 für den Ausgang des Ostkrieges," in *Die Zerstörung Europas. Beiträge zur Weltkriegsepoche 1914 bis 1945*, by Andreas Hillgruber (Frankfurt, 1988).

———. "Das Russland-Bild der führenden deutschen Militärs vor Beginn des Angriffs auf die Sowjetunion," in *Die Zerstörung Europas. Beiträge zur Weltkriegsepoche 1914 bis 1945*, by Andreas Hillgruber (Frankfurt, 1988).

———. *Die Zerstörung Europas. Beiträge zur Weltkriegsepoche 1914 bis 1945* (Frankfurt, 1988).

———. *Hitlers Strategie. Politik und Kriegführung 1940–1941* (Munich, 1982).

Hinze, Rolf. *19. Infanterie- und Panzer-Division. Divisionsgeschichte aus der Sicht eines Artilleristen* (Düsseldorf, 1997).

Hofmann, Rudolf. "Die Schlacht von Moskau 1941," in *Entscheidungsschlachten des zweiten Weltkrieges*, edited by Hans-Adolf Jacobsen and Jürgen Rohwer (Frankfurt, 1960).

Hofmann, Gen. Rudolf, and Genmaj. Alfred Toppe. *Verbrauchs- und Verschleißsätze während der Operationen der deutschen Heeresgruppe Mitte vom 22.6.41–31.12.41* (U.S. Army Foreign Military Study P-190, 1953).

Hogg, Ian V. *Armoured Fighting Vehicles* (2000).
———. *Twentieth-Century Artillery* (New York, 2000).
Hossbach, Friedrich. *Infanterie im Ostfeldzug 1941/42* (Osterode, 1951).
Hoth, Hermann. *Panzer-Operationen. Die Panzergruppe 3 und der operative Gedanke der deutschen Führung Sommer 1941* (Heidelberg, 1956).
Hubatsch, Walther, ed. *Hitlers Weisungen für die Kriegführung 1939–1945* (Frankfurt, 1962).
Hürter, Johannes. *Ein deutscher General an der Ostfront. Die Briefe und Tagebücher des Gotthard Heinrici 1941/42* (Erfurt, 2001).
———. *Hitlers Heerführer. Die deutschen Oberbefehlshaber im Krieg gegen die Sowjetunion 1941/42* (Munich, 2006).
———. *A German General on the Eastern Front: The Letters and Diaries of Gotthard Heinrici, 1941–1942* (Barnsley, 2021).
Irving, David. *Hitler's War* (New York, 1977).
Jacobsen, Hans Adolf, ed. *1939–1945. Der Zweite Weltkrieg in Chronik und Dokumenten* (Darmstadt, 1959).
Jentz, Thomas L., ed. *Panzer Truppen: The Complete Guide to the Creation and Combat Employment of Germany's Tank Force, 1933–1942* (Atglen, 1996).
Johnson, Paul. *Modern Times: The World from the Twenties to the Nineties* (rev. ed., New York, 1991).
Jones, Michael. *The Retreat: Hitler's First Defeat* (New York, 2009).
Keegan, John. *The Second World War* (New York, 1989).
Keilig, Wolf. *Das Deutsche Heer 1939–1945. Gliederung, Einsatz, Stellenbesetzung* (Bad Nauheim, 1956).
Kempowski, Walter. *Das Echolot. Barbarossa '41. Ein kollektives Tagebuch* (Munich, 2002).
Kershaw, Ian. *Hitler, 1936–1945: Nemesis* (New York, 2000).
Kershaw, Robert J. *War Without Garlands: Operation Barbarossa, 1941/42* (New York, 2000).
Kesselring, Albert. *The Memoirs of Field-Marshal Kesselring* (Novato, 1989).
———. *Soldat bis zum letzten Tag* (Bonn, 1953).
Kirchubel, Robert. *Hitler's Panzer Armies on the Eastern Front* (Great Britain, 2009).
———. *Operation Barbarossa, 1941 (3). Army Group Center* (New York, 2007).
Kleindienst, Jürgen, ed. *Sei tausendmal gegrüsst. Briefwechsel Irene und Ernst Guicking 1937–1945* (Berlin, 2001).
Knox, MacGregor, and Williamson Murray, eds. *The Dynamics of Military Revolution, 1300–2050* (Cambridge, 2001).
Kotze, Hildegard von, ed. *Heeresadjutant bei Hitler 1938–1943. Aufzeichnungen des Majors Engel* (Stuttgart, 1974).
Krivosheev, Col.-Gen. G. F., ed. *Soviet Casualties and Combat Losses in the Twentieth Century* (London, 1997).
Lewis, S. J. *Forgotten Legions: German Army Infantry Policy. 1918–1941* (New York, 1985).
Lexikon-der-Wehrmacht. At www.lexicon-der-wehrmacht.de.
Lierow, Hans. *Persönliches Tagebuch* (unpublished diary; courtesy of his son, Dr. Konrad Lierow-Mueller).
Lucas, James. *Das Reich: The Military Role of the 2nd SS Division* (London, 1991).
Luther, Craig W. H. *Barbarossa Unleashed: The German Blitzkrieg through Central Russia to the Gates of Moscow, June–December 1941* (Atglen, 2014).
———. *The First Day on the Eastern Front: Germany Invades the Soviet Union, June 22, 1941* (Guilford, 2018).

Luther, Craig W. H., and David Stahel, eds. *Soldiers of Barbarossa: Combat, Genocide, and Everyday Experiences on the Eastern Front, June–December 1941* (Guilford, 2020).

Luther, Craig W. H., and Hugh Page Taylor, eds. *For Germany: The Otto Skorzeny Memoirs* (San Jose, 2005).

Luttichau, Charles v. P. *The Road to Moscow: The Campaign in Russia, 1941* (unpublished manuscript; many thanks to David Glantz for making this document available to me).

Macksey, Kenneth. *Guderian: Panzer General* (London, 1975).

Magenheimer, Heinz. *Hitler's War: Germany's Key Strategic Decisions, 1940–1945* (New York, 2003).

———. *Moskau 1941. Entscheidungsschlacht im Osten* (Selent, 2009).

Mark, Jason D. *Guderian's Foxes: Aufklärungs-Abteilung 29 in Photos from Barbarossa to Typhoon* (Sydney, 2021).

Mattson, Gregory L. *SS-Das Reich: The History of the Second SS Division, 1941–45* (St. Paul, 2002).

Mawdsley, Evan. *Thunder in the East: The Nazi-Soviet War, 1941–1945* (London, 2005).

Megargee, Geoffrey P. *Inside Hitler's High Command* (Lawrence, 2000).

———. *War of Annihilation: Combat and Genocide on the Eastern Front, 1941* (Oxford, 2006).

Mehner, Kurt, ed. *Die Geheimen Tagesberichte der deutschen Wehrmachtführung im Zweiten Weltkrieg 1939–1945*. Bd. 3: *1. März 1941–31. Oktober 1941* (Osnabrück, 1992).

Mellenthin, F. W. von. *German Generals of World War II* (Norman, 1977).

Meyer, August. *Infanterie-Regiment Grenadier-Regiment 241. 1940–1944* (Bonn-Beuel, 1999).

Meyer, Georg. *Adolf Heusinger. Dienst eines deutschen Soldaten 1915 bis 1964* (Hamburg, 2001).

Michulec, Robert. *4. Panzer-Division on the Eastern Front (1) 1941–1943* (Hong Kong, 1999).

Mitcham, Samuel W., Jr. *Hitler's Field Marshals and Their Battles* (New York, 2001).

———. *The Men of Barbarossa: Commanders of the German Invasion of Russia, 1941* (Philadelphia, 2009).

Mueller, Rolf-Dieter, and Gerd R. Ueberschaer. *Hitler's War in the East: A Critical Assessment* (New York, 2002).

Mühleisen, Horst, ed. *Hellmuth Stieff Briefe* (Berlin, 1991).

Muller, Richard. *The German Air War in Russia* (Baltimore, 1992).

Müller-Hillebrand, Burkhart. *Das Heer 1933–1945*. Bd. 2: *Die Blitzfeldzüge 1939–1941. Das Heer im Kriege bis zum Beginn des Feldzuges gegen die Sowjetunion im Juni 1941* (Frankfurt, 1956).

———. *Das Heer 1933–1945*. Bd. 3: *Der Zweifrontenkrieg. Das Heer vom Beginn des Feldzuges gegen die Sowjetunion bis zum Kriegsende* (Frankfurt, 1969).

Murray, Williamson. *Strategy for Defeat: The Luftwaffe, 1933–1945* (Maxwell Air Force Base, 1983).

Musial, Bogdan. *Kampfplatz Deutschland. Stalins Kriegspläne gegen den Westen* (Berlin, 2008).

Nafziger, George F. *The German Order of Battle: Infantry in World War II* (London, 2000).

———. *The German Order of Battle: Panzers and Artillery in World War II* (London, 1995).

Nehring, Walther K. "Die 18. Panzerdivision 1941 im Rahmen der Panzergruppe Guderian," in *Deutscher Soldatenkalender 1961* (Munich-Lochhausen).

———. *Die Geschichte der deutschen Panzerwaffe 1916–1945* (Stuttgart, 2000).

Neumann, Joachim. *Die 4. Panzer-Division 1938–1943. Bericht und Betrachtung zu zwei Blitzfeldzügen und zwei Jahren Krieg in Russland* (Bonn, 1985).

Newton, Steven H. *Hitler's Commander: Field Marshal Walther Model—Hitler's Favorite General* (2006).

Oberkommando der Wehrmacht, ed. *Kampf gegen die Sowjets. Berichte und Bilder vom Beginn des Ostfeldzuges bis zum Frühjahr 1942* (Berlin, 1943).

Opitz, Alfred. "Die Stimmung in der Truppe am Vorabend des Überfalls auf die Sowjetunion," in *Der Krieg des kleinen Mannes. Eine Militärgeschichte von unten*, edited by Wolfram Wette (Munich, 1992).

Orenstein, Harold S. (trans.). *Soviet Documents on the Use of War Experience*. Vol. 3: *Military Operations, 1941 and 1942* (London, 1993).

Overmans, Rüdiger. *Deutsche militärische Verluste im Zweiten Weltkrieg* (Munich, 2004).

Pabst, Helmut. *The Outermost Frontier* (London, 1958).

Paret, Peter. "*Clausewitz*." In *Makers of Modern Strategy. From Machiavelli to the Nuclear Age*. edited by Peter Paret (Princeton, 1986).

Paul, Wolfgang. *Geschichte der 18. Panzer-Division 1940–1943. Streiflichter aus 4 Kriegsjahren* (ca. 1975).

———. *Panzer-General Walther K. Nehring. Eine Biographie* (Stuttgart, 2002).

Philippi, Alfred, and Ferdinand Heim. *Der Feldzug gegen Sowjetrussland 1941 bis 1945. Ein operativer Überblick* (Stuttgart, 1962).

Piekalkiewicz, Janusz. *Die Schlacht um Moskau. Die erfrorene Offensive* (Augsburg, 1998).

Pleshakov, Constantine. *Stalin's Folly: The Tragic First Ten Days of World War II on the Eastern Front* (Boston, 2005).

Plievier, Theodor. *Moscow* (New York, 1953).

Plocher, Genlt. Hermann. *The German Air Force versus Russia, 1941* (USAF Historical Studies No. 153, July 1965).

Pöhlmann, Markus. *Der Panzer und die Mechanisierung des Krieges. Eine deutsche Geschichte 1890 bis 1945* (Paderborn, 2016).

Prien, Jochen, et al. *Die Jagdfliegerverbaende der Deutschen Luftwaffe 1934 bis 1945*. Teil 6/1: *Unternehmen "Barbarossa," Einsatz im Osten 22.6. bis 5.12.1941* (2003).

Reinhardt, Klaus. *Moscow—the Turning Point: The Failure of Hitler's Strategy in the Winter of 1941–42* (Oxford, 1992).

———. *Die Wende vor Moskau. Das Scheitern der Strategie Hitlers im Winter 1941/42* (Stuttgart, 1972).

Remak, Joachim, ed. *War, Revolution and Peace: Essays in Honor of Charles B. Burdick* (New York, 1987).

Reuth, Ralf Georg, ed. *Hitler. Eine politische Biographie* (Munich, 2003).

———. *Joseph Goebbels. Tagebücher 1924–1945*. Bd. 4: *1940–1942* (Munich, 1992).

Richardson, Horst Fuchs, ed. and trans. *Your Loyal and Loving Son: The Letters of Tank Gunner Karl Fuchs, 1937–41* (Washington, DC, 1987).

Richardson, William, and Seymour Freidin, eds. *The Fatal Decisions* (London, 1956).

Risse, S. "Das IR 101 und der 2. Weltkrieg" (unpublished report; courtesy of Klaus Schumann).

Roberts, Geoffrey. *Stalin's Wars: From World War to Cold War, 1939–1953* (New Haven, 2006).

Röll, Hans-Joachim. *Oberleutnant Albert Blaich. Als Panzerkommandant in Ost und West* (Würzburg, 2009).

Sandalov, L. M. *Perezhitoe* (That Which Has Been Lived Through) (Moscow, 1966).

Schäufler, Hans, ed. *Knight's Cross Panzers: The German 35th Panzer Regiment in WWII* (Mechanicsburg, 2010).

Scheibert, Horst. *Die 6. Panzer-Division 1937–1945. Bewaffnung, Einsätze, Männer* (n.d.)

———. *Das war Guderian. Ein Lebensbericht in Bildern* (Friedberg, 1989).

Schick, Albert. *Die Geschichte der 10. Panzer-Division 1939–1943* (Cologne, 1993).

Schneider, Wolfgang. *Panzer Tactics: German Small-Unit Armor Tactics in World War II* (Mechanicsburg, 2000).

Schramm, Percy E., ed. *Kriegstagebuch des Oberkommandos der Wehrmacht (Wehrmachtführungsstab) 1940–1945.* Bd. 1: *1. August 1940–31. December 1941*, zusammengestellt und erläutert von Hans-Adolf Jacobsen (Frankfurt, 1965).

Schulze, Günter A. *General der Panzertruppe a.D. Walther K. Nehring. Der persönliche Ordonnanzoffizier berichtet von der Vormarschzeit in Russland 1941–1942* (unpublished manuscript).

Seaton, Albert. *The Battle for Moscow, 1941–1942* (New York, 1971).

———. *The German Army, 1933–45* (New York, 1982).

———. *The Russo-German War, 1941–1945* (London, 1971).

Shay, Jonathan. *Achilles in Vietnam: Combat Trauma and the Undoing of Character* (New York, 1994).

Shirer, William L. *The Rise and Fall of the Third Reich. A History of Nazi Germany* (New York, 1960).

Showalter, Dennis. *Hitler's Panzers: The Lightning Attacks That Revolutionized Warfare* (New York, 2009).

Spaeter, Helmuth. *Die Geschichte des Panzerkorps Grossdeutschland.* Bd. 1 (Duisburg-Ruhrort, 1958).

Stahel, David. *The Battle for Moscow* (Cambridge, 2015).

———. *Hitler's Panzer Generals: Guderian, Hoepner, Reinhardt and Schmidt Unguarded* (Cambridge, 2023).

———. *Kiev 1941: Hitler's Battle for Supremacy in the East* (Cambridge, 2012).

———. *Operation Barbarossa and Germany's Defeat in the East* (Cambridge, 2009).

———. *Operation Typhoon: Hitler's March on Moscow, October 1941* (Cambridge, 2013).

———. *Retreat from Moscow: A New History of Germany's Winter Campaign, 1941–1942* (Cambridge, 2019).

Steiger, Rudolf. *Armour Tactics in the Second World War: Panzer Army Campaigns of 1939–41 in German War Diaries* (New York, 1990).

Stein, Marcel. *Generalfeldmarschall Walter Model. Legende und Wirklichkeit* (Bissendorf, 2001).

Stein, Oberstlt. H. P. "Verteidigung an der OKA: das LIII Armeekorps im Rahmen der 2. Pz. Armee vom Dez. 41 bis Jan. 42." (Militärgeschichtliches Forschungsamt, Freiburg).

Stolfi, R. H. S. "Chance in History: The Russian Winter of 1941–1942." *History* 65, no. 214 (1980).

———. *German Panzers on the Offensive: Russian Front, North Africa, 1941–1942* (Atglen, 2003).

Sweeting, C. G. *Hitler's Personal Pilot: The Life and Times of Hans Baur* (Washington, DC, 2000).

Thies, Klaus-Jürgen. *Der Zweite Weltkrieg im Kartenbild.* Bd. 5, Teil 1.1: *Der Ostfeldzug Heeresgruppe Mitte 21.6.1941–6.12.1941. Ein Lageatlas der Operationsabteilung des Generalstabs des Heeres* (Bissendorf, 2001).

Töppel, Roman. "Sprungbrett nach Moskau: Kesselschlacht von Smolensk, 1941." *Militär & Geschichte* 23, no. 5 (2024).

Trevor-Roper, H. R. *Hitler's War Directives, 1939–1945* (London, 1964).

True to Type: A Selection from Letters and Diaries of German Soldiers and Civilians Collected on the Soviet-German Front (London, n.d.).

Turney, Alfred W. *Disaster at Moscow: Von Bock's Campaigns, 1941–1942* (1970).

Ulrich, Andreas. "Hitler's Drugged Soldiers" (*Spiegel Online*, May 05).

Urbanke, Axel, and Dr. Hermann Türk. *Als Sanitätsoffizier im Russlandfeldzug: Mit der 3. Panzer-Division bis vor Moskaus Tore* (Bad Zwischenahn, 2016).

Vogt, Martin, ed. *Herbst 1941 im "Führerhauptquartier." Berichte Werner Koeppens an seinen Minister Alfred Rosenberg* (Koblenz, 2002).

Walde, Karl J. *Guderian* (Frankfurt, 1976).

Weal, John. *Jagdgeschwader 51 "Mölders"* (Oxford, 2006).

Weber, Thomas. *Hitler's First War: Adolf Hitler, the Men of the List Regiment, and the First World War* (Oxford, 2010).

Wegner, Bernd. "The Road to Defeat: The German Campaigns in Russia, 1941–43," *Journal of Strategic Studies* 13, no. 1 (March 1990).

———., ed. *Zwei Wege nach Moskau. Vom Hitler-Stalin-Pakt zum "Unternehmen Barbarossa"* (Munich, 1991).

Weidinger, Otto. *Das Reich III 1941–1943* (Winnipeg, 2002).

Werth, Alexander. *Russia at War, 1941–1945* (New York, 1964).

Wette, Wolfram, ed. *Der Krieg des kleinen Mannes. Eine Militärgeschichte von unten* (Munich, 1992).

Wetzig, Sonja. *Die Stalin-Linie 1941. Bollwerk aus Beton und Stahl* (Dörfler Zeitgeschichte, n.d.).

Winchester, Charles D. *Hitler's War on Russia* (New York, 2007).

Winchester, Jim. *Tanks and Armored Fighting Vehicles of WWII: The World's Greatest Military Vehicles, 1939–1945* (Edison, 2003).

Windisch, Genmaj. Josef. *Personal Diary Notes of the G-4 of the German Ninth Army, 1 Aug 1941 to 31 Jan 1942* (U.S. Army Foreign Military Study P-201, 1953).

Woche, Klaus-R. *Zwischen Pflicht und Gewissen. Generaloberst Rudolf Schmidt 1886–1957* (Berlin-Potsdam, 2002).

Wray, Major Timothy A. *Standing Fast: German Defensive Doctrine on the Russian Front during World War II: Prewar to March 1943* (Fort Leavenworth, 1986).

Yahil, Leni. *The Holocaust: The Fate of European Jewry, 1932–1945* (Oxford, 1990).

Zabecki, David T., ed. *World War II in Europe: An Encyclopedia* (New York, 1999).

Zhukov, Georgi K. *Marshal Zhukov's Greatest Battles*, edited by Harrison E. Salisbury (New York, 2002).

Ziemke, Earl F., and Magna E. Bauer. *Moscow to Stalingrad: Decision in the East* (New York, 1988).

Index